Java Servlets by Example

Java Servlets by Example

ALAN R. WILLIAMSON

MANNING

Greenwich
(74° w. long.)

For electronic browsing and ordering of this and other Manning books,
visit http://www.manning.com. The publisher offers discounts on this book
when ordered in quantity. For more information, please contact:

Special Sales Department
Manning Publications Co.
32 Lafayette Place   Fax: (203) 661-9018
Greenwich, CT 06830   email: orders@manning.com

Library of Congress Cataloging-in-Publication Data
Williamson, Alan   (Alan R.)
          Java servlets by example / Alan Williamson.
              p.   cm.
          ISBN 1-884777-66-X   (alk. paper)
              1.   Java (Computer program language)   I. Title.
          QA76.73.J38W552   1999
          005.2'762--dc21   99-20762
                                                                    CIP

Manning Publications Co.   Copyeditor: Kristen Black
32 Lafayette Place   Typesetter: Jimmie Young
Greenwich, CT 06830   Cover designer: Leslie Haimes

Printed in the United States of America
1 2 3 4 5 6 7 8 9 10 – CR – 01 00 99 98

contents

preface

Servlets … servlets … servlets. That's all you hear—well, in this book, at any rate. I hope this book will give you a good grounding, and that after reading it, you'll get a feel for where servlets can best be used. By no means does this book cover all the uses of servlets; such a book could never exist. Servlets are a lightweight/heavyweight solution to the problem of server-side processing.

Java has proven to be a serious contender in the field of commercial software. It has delivered on nearly all of its highly over-hyped claims, failing on only a few bothersome issues that have been cleared up as the Java Development Kit (JDK) version numbers creep on.

Look at what Java has done for the browser. No other plug-in or extension has grown as quickly. If a Java applet could do this for the client, just think what the servlet can do for the server.

It's up to you now as our frontline troops in the server wars. You are now in possession of a technology that allows you to get on with what you know best and leave all the administrative hassles of server dependency behind.

Servlets give you the power to develop a sophisticated, platform-independent solution. This is the most scalable software you could ever build. With the Java servlet combination, you can easily upgrade any of your components without redeveloping any classes.

With the new generation of servlet Application Program Interfaces (API), server farms are no longer a problem. As far as your servlet is concerned, it is running on a single server with all the resources at hand. But in reality, the picture could be different. Your server could be part of a larger server pool, sharing resources and load balancing between all the machines.

But you as the servlet developer need not worry about such things. If you stick to the API, you shouldn't have any problems in the future as the success of your creation grows.

Servlets are the solution the server has been looking for for a very long time.

acknowledgments

This is the part of the book where I get the chance to stand up and thank everyone. But I've been told to keep it below ten pages, so I had better do the shortened version! First of all, let me thank the team behind me at Manning. My publisher, Marjan Bace, has been one of the best publishers I could have asked for. Considering I may have overrun on a couple of deadlines by a teeny-weeny bit, he was very understanding. So thank you, Marjan, for sticking by me; it is much appreciated.

This has been my first time writing for Manning, and thanks to everyone on both sides of the Atlantic it has been both an enjoyable and a rewarding experience. Thanks to Mary Piergies for her support and excellent production management skills. I would also like to thank Ted Kennedy for organizing all the reviewers and keeping me up to date with the latest feedback. Speaking of feedback, thanks to all the reviewers who took the time to read the manuscript.

I have to give the majority of my thanks and gratitude to the best friend a man could ever wish for: Ceri Moran. This woman has been a tower of strength, and has kept everything I should've been doing ticking along quite nicely—so much so, I am no longer needed! Such is the price of being an author. Ceri has kept both the home and company running very smoothly and when things were getting a little down, she would pick me up and tell me it was all worth it, which would give me the boost I was looking for. Behind every great man, there is an even greater woman. Well, Ceri is mine. I thank you.

Another man who has continually kept my morale high with his refreshing outlook on life and his great glossary of sayings is Mike "the accountant" Edhouse. One of the phrases he quotes is "Luck is what happens when preparation meets opportunity." Many an hour has been spent debating whether luck actually exists, and I suspect the debate will continue for quite some time yet. It's not all Java, you know!

Writing this book has taken me to working even later at night than I normally do. I wouldn't have thought I'd use the phone that much at 2 or 3 in the morning, but with Frode Hegland, time holds no authority. Frode and I have debated long and hard the chapters that should be in the book and what subjects should be covered. Each time I would say "I am doing this," he would say, "Cool, but can it do this?" So, Frode, now I have the time to do all the extras you wanted.

I would also like to thank Beth Barratt for compiling that dossier on our lives. Thanks to my parents for trying to understand what I do for a living, but I suspect it will always remain a mystery to you. Thanks to Herman Verkade for helping me see the path through the corporate minefield.

Thank you all, and I hope we get the chance to work together again soon!

how to use this book

This is one of those things that has always amused me—a section on how to read a book. But here I find myself inserting such a section into my own book. Of course, opening this book and reading from page one right through to the final page would be the desirable approach. But for those of you who will use this book as a reference guide, take a moment and read this small section that will serve as a roadmap through the pages of this book.

Each chapter is presented as a complete learning experience. Each servlet example is built up bit by bit, allowing you to see how the servlet is made up. You are never presented with a massive block of Java code and expected to know it. This way, when you do get to the "massive" block of code at the end of the example, you'll understand every line.

This book is split into four separate sections.

Chapters 1 through 6 form the first section: a background on servlets. Chapter 1 introduces you to the wonderful world of servlets and sets the background that will allow you to use the rest of the book. Chapter 2 covers the servlet API itself. This chapter details the basic makeup of the servlet and lets you taste some of the facilities and features that the API affords you. Chapters 3 and 4 cover the Java Web Server and two popular servlet engines. With these chapters, you should find at least one servlet environment in which you will be able to set up. Chapter 5 is a general Java chapter about helping you debug and optimise your servlets. To round off this section, chapter 6 looks at the history of CGI, which is the technology that servlets will be replacing (I hope).

Chapters 7 through 24 form the second section, which is the bulk of the book. They walk you through real-life examples of servlet usage, with each chapter introducing a new aspect or custom use of a servlet. Chapters 7 and 9 look at ways of treating HyperText Markup Language (HTML) forms, while chapter 7 looks at some of the more utility-type servlets (such as the file upload servlet). Chapter 10 looks at implementing a guest book for your web site (a guest book is where visitors to a site can leave comments for others to see).

Chapter 11 implements a web-based forum which allows users to post and answer questions. Chapters 12 and 13 look at giving a visitor to your web site a different page every time he or she views the site, through randomized links and HTML.

Chapter 14 shows you how to generate server-side images using servlets, and chapter 15 shows you how to build a servlet that will strip out certain keywords before sending it to the browser.

Chapters 16, 17, and 18 look at how servlets can help you maintain and manage your web site. A search engine and link checker is present here, including a servlet that automatically inserts HTML.

Chapter 19 discusses how servlets can manage client data through cookies and session management. Chapter 20 introduces servlets to the wonderful world of entertainment through two HTML-based games. Chapter 21 implements a banner rotation servlet that allows you to have an advertising section on your web site.

Chapter 22 presents an implementation of an email fortune cookie. This feature allows you to maintain a mailing list; it also demonstrates how email can be generated from a servlet.

Chapter 23 looks at the total implementation of an online shop, complete with a shopping basket and a virtual checkout. Chapter 24 implements a chat system that can be used with an applet and/or HTML. This chapter also looks at applet-to-servlet communication.

The third section covers the advanced uses of servlets. Chapter 25 looks at integrating databases with servlets through the use of Java Database Connectivity (JDBC). It also presents a sophisticated database pooling class. Chapter 26 tackles the exciting area of Remote Method Invocation (RMI), which is the ability to use methods from another virtual machine. This chapter shows how a servlet can act as an RMI server. Rounding out this section is chapter 27, which looks at interservlet communication. This chapter uses the latest methods from the 2.1 API, which allows servlets to forward requests to other servlets for processing or to add their content to the output of others.

The final section is the appendices. Appendix A is a complete reference to the servlet 2.1 API. This is not just a blind reprint of the reference material—every method is accompanied by an example use of code. Appendix B lists all the old CGI variables and the servlet counterparts. And finally, appendix C is a list of Java resources from around the world.

The book has been thoroughly researched to give you the best scope of examples possible. Of course, not every single use of servlets is presented here, but these examples should give you a good background with which you can tackle any new areas.

author online

Purchase of *Java Servlets by Example* includes free access to a private Internet forum where you can make comments about the book, ask technical questions, and receive help from the author and other users. To access the forum, point your web browser to http://www.manning.com/Williamson. There you will be able to subscribe to the forum. This site also provides information on how to access the forum once you are registered, what kind of help is available, and rules of conduct on the forum.

All source code for the examples presented in *Java Servlets by Example* is available to purchasers from the Manning web site. The book's web page includes a link to the source code files.

about the cover illustration

The cover illustration of this book is from the 1805 edition of Sylvain Maréchal's four-volume compendium of regional dress customs. This book was first published in Paris in 1788, one year before the French Revolution. Its title alone required no fewer than 30 words.

> *Costumes Civils actuels de tous les peuples connus dessinés d'après nature gravés et coloriés, accompagnés d'une notice historique sur leurs coutumes, moeurs, religions, etc., etc., redigés par M. Sylvain Maréchal*

The four volumes include an annotation on the illustrations: "gravé à la manière noire par Mixelle d'après Desrais et colorié." Clearly, the engraver and illustrator deserved no more than to be listed by their last names—after all they were mere technicians. The workers who colored each illustration by hand remain nameless.

The colorful variety of this collection reminds us vividly of how culturally apart the world's towns and regions were just 200 years ago. Dress codes have changed everywhere and the diversity by region, so rich at the time, has faded away. It is now hard to tell the inhabitant of one continent from another. Perhaps we have traded cultural diversity for a more varied personal life—certainly a more varied and exciting technological environment.

At a time when it is hard to tell one computer book from another, Manning celebrates the inventiveness and initiative of the computer business with book covers based on the rich diversity of regional life of two centuries ago, brought back to life by Maréchal's pictures. Just think, Maréchal's was a world so different from ours people would take the time to read a book title 30 words long.

CHAPTER 1

Introduction

- Understand the need for server-side processing in today's world wide web environment.

- Get a quick overview of the Java language that forms the basis of all the solutions presented within this book.

- Discover the Java servlet API and the role it plays in delivering the next generation of server-side processing.

The Internet, with particular respect to the world wide web, is growing at a tremendous rate. With over one million new pages going live every day, each one vying for our attention, greater emphasis is being placed on the servers delivering this information. The Internet is no longer a colorful brochure, where the user merely flicks from page to page. It has become a fully interactive experience, complete with inline video and stereo sound. However, not everyone can enjoy the rich bandwidth that is required to enjoy streamed video.

Because of the bandwidth issue, the popularity of Common Gateway Interface (CGI) and other server-side technologies quickly grew, filling the gap for the user in providing an interactive session. Although it is very powerful, CGI quickly outgrew its use, for in the world of openness and platform independence, CGI simply cannot compete. The time has come for a new kid on the block to pick up the gauntlet and complete the journey.

1.1   The world wide web

J. Robert Oppenheimer, an American nuclear physicist, is reported to have said the following after the first atomic bomb test was complete:

"We knew the world would not be the same."

There was never a truer statement. However, maybe Tim Berners-Lee and his colleagues at CERN (the European Particle Physics Laboratory) should have muttered somewhat the same sentiment when they unleashed the HyperText Transfer Protocol (HTTP) and HTML protocols to the world, forming what we know now regard as "the web." Out of this discovery, a whole new industry was born. To compare the web with, say, the discovery of the combustion engine, may seem a little adventurous, since we don't think of the engine as revolutionary. But at the time it was invented, it was very revolutionary. Not everyone had seen its true potential; there were even a few who claimed there would be no future in it. But as Father Time marched on, the engine was used in more and more application areas, until it got to the stage where people couldn't remember life without it. Even simple grass-cutting chores have been replaced with by a lawn mower powered with a two-stroke combustion engine.

Sound familiar? I am not advocating that a browser should be developed for a lawn mower, but the web is going through the same Darwinian changes the engine did in its early days. The web, introduced in the early '90s, is still an infant stumbling around, looking to find its feet in the world. How the web will look when it's entering its teen years is anyone's guess, and everyone is making a guess. Whatever application areas come along, the need to implement or realize them will still be a requirement.

This book is intended to be to the developer what guides are for new parents. With the web changing so rapidly, the person making all these dreams come true has to be armed with enough knowledge and tools to be able to cope with an ever-changing environment.

Java has evolved to meet all current and future demands. Current computer languages aren't up to the task of providing solutions for such demanding surroundings. The idea behind the original web was to easily share and distribute information, without respect to the computer platform the user may be surfing from. If more companies would remember that prime objective, instead of concentrating on their own agendas, competition for Java would simply not exist. Deciding on the development language would be as logical as choosing HTML for web pages.

Historically, Java has been employed at the client side for providing user applets, which extend the functionality of the client browser. However, the trend is changing from the client to the server. With the combination of Java applets and browser plug-ins, the web is shaping up to look like the thick client scenario in figure 1.1, where the majority of the processing is performed at the client side.

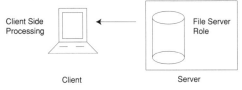

Figure 1.1 Thick client

For example, consider an applet whose main role is to guide the user through a virtual 3D world. Processing the data to create this world would be done in real time by the processor running the browser, which in this case is the client computer. The web server in this instance is merely posing as a file server, passing data to the client applet.

Although nothing is wrong with this model, the web is moving toward the thin client model. This model, as you may have guessed, sits halfway between the client/server model and the thick client model. The thin client in figure 1.2 is where the majority of processing is performed at the server, with some execution occurring at the client. The client/server model is where all processing is performed at the server end, with the client acting as a dumb terminal. This places an enormous amount of stress on the server, and in the busy environment of the web, the client/server model is not really applicable.

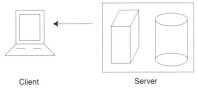

Figure 1.2 Thin client

The web is moving toward the thin model, with less emphasis on the client side and more on the server side. By moving the majority of processing to the server, a variety of new applications can be developed. Historically, any web processing that was required at the server side was implemented as a CGI script.

CGI defines a standard for communication between the web server and a separate program running on the same machine. CGI doesn't define anything else, and as a consequence, CGI scripts may be implemented in any language the platform will run.

> ***Note*** One of the misconceptions of CGI is the terminology. CGI is not, as many people
> are led to believe, a programming language. It is merely a standard. So when something is
> referred to as being a CGI script or program, that merely tells us the program conforms to
> the CGI interface. CGI is explored in greater depth in chapter 6, CGI overview.

This lack of standardization at the server has meant CGI scripts implemented for one server platform have had to be redeveloped when required to run on another web server, on another platform. This issue has not been a major consideration for many organizations in the past, and to a certain degree, it still isn't. But for software vendors producing custom server-side solutions, it has been a headache.

Another problem area within CGI-based solutions is their overall efficiency. Every client request that requires processing by a CGI script spawns a separate program instance. This takes time. The operating system has to load the program, allocate memory for the program, and then deallocate and unload the program from memory. While the operating system is performing the housekeeping, nothing else can run. This is known as a heavyweight context switch.

This is the reason CGI scripts are not suitable for applications that receive many client requests. As you will see in later chapters, certain applications require various state information to be saved between client requests. For example, a CGI script that counts the number of visits to a web page needs the value of the count to be kept between each client request. With CGI programs being loaded and unloaded between each client request, storing the count value in memory is not possible. Parameter storing between CGI programs is performed using files. When the CGI program has completed its main task, a file is opened and a value is written. Conversely, when the CGI script is first loaded, the file is opened and the value is read.

Opening and closing files can be notoriously slow at the best of times, due to the fact that the process relies on system calls to complete. This leads into another problem area where CGI scripts fail miserably: process synchronizing. With the very nature of the web, it is not uncommon for multiple client requests to be serviced at once, thus rendering multiple program instances of the same CGI program running. Suppose this CGI program has to open the file storing the state information; not all the instances are going to succeed. Only one will be successful, and the others will fail.

Because of this reliance on the operating system to synchronize processes, CGI-based solutions are not suitable for applications that require simultaneous access to resources, as the programs have to rely on the operating system to lock and unlock resources.

Java doesn't suffer from any of these hurdles, and for this reason, it is the best choice for server-side processing. Sun, then under JavaSoft, developed an API to replace CGI programs and to provide a much better and richer framework for server-side processes to exist. These programs are known as servlets, and they run in response to client requests. Unlike CGI programs, as you will discover in the chapter detailing the servlet API, servlets load and run in a completely different manner. When they are first called upon, the servlets are loaded into memory. However, the difference in operation becomes apparent when they finish executing. They are not removed; instead, they remain in memory, and subsequent requests simply result in a method call to the servlet class in question. This can be considered a lightweight context switch.

With Java, every program is a class, and this thinking is carried through to servlets. Implementing servlets as classes that conform to a specific interface allows them to easily remain in memory, and to be efficiently called upon time and time again.

Servlets are to the server what applets are to the client. They extend the functionality of the web server in much the same way an applet extends the browser. To demonstrate the power of servlets, Sun developed the Java Web Server using the Java Server API. This is a complete web server, supporting both servlets and CGI, written entirely in Java. Implementing the web server in Java allows the web server to run on any platform with a Java Virtual Machine (JVM).

Note The Java Web Server is not the only web server to be implemented in Java; another example is the Jigsaw Web Server. Jigsaw comes from the World Wide Web Consortium, and at the time of this writing, it is freely available for anyone to use. Jigsaw also supports the notion of servlets, although servlets written for the Java Web Server are not completely compatible with Jigsaw.

From here on in this book, wherever the Java Web Server is mentioned, the Java Web Server will be assumed.

This is a significant step forward. The Java Web Server, formally referred to as Jeeves, is a fully featured, commercial web server, whose installation and administration is detailed in later chapters.

The server API, designed by Sun, allows the creation of complete server-side applications in Java. For example, the list includes mail servers, ftp servers, and the best example: web servers. The servlet API forms part of the server API, where servlets extend the functionality of servers.

The Java Web Server is not the only web server to support servlets from Sun. At the time of this writing, Apache, Netscape, and Microsoft had released versions of their web server that supported the servlet API. Nearly every commercial web server available today is looking to include support for the servlet API.

The most flexible and useful API of the family is the servlet API. It is this API that this book primarily concentrates on, as the majority of the web servers available today support this interface. Unlike CGI, the Java servlet API defines both the interface and the language, thus making it extremely transportable.

This book is intended for users with all levels of expertise. It serves as both a reference and guide to the servlet API. For seasoned CGI programmers, the book serves as a "cookbook," illustrating well-known CGI implementations in Java. Web designers and developers already conversant with the wonders of Java applets will be able to implement server-side applications by following the examples in the chapters that follow.

1.2 Current applications

The web is finding new application areas on a daily basis. Not a day goes by that the trade journals don't report on some new area or way the web is being employed. With more and more Java applets coming online, adding all this extra functionality to the browser, you may be excused for thinking the web is becoming saturated, with all the good ideas already taken. Fortunately, it's not as bad as all that. Nearly all new technology is being applied at the client side. Now it's the server's turn to do some processing.

It is all well and good to develop at the client side, but with some of the physical constraints imposed on the Internet today, such as bandwidth, cost, and speed of response, users are becoming impatient waiting for the client-side software to download or to compute. The surfer's computer environment may not be powerful enough to execute the applet or plug-in. Are we to build web sites where the user must be running at least a Pentium Pro with 32 MB of memory just to be able to use some of the plug-ins or applets?

As bizarre as this may sound, the web is closer to this than you may think. For example, try going to all your favorite haunts on the web with an Apple Newton or some other hand-held device. You'll see a completely different picture, so to speak. It is easy to dismiss such devices as not being serious viewing mediums, but with Windows CE becoming more commonplace, the web is going mobile.

For this reason, relying on the client side to do the processing is inappropriate. If the solution is run on the server, then the developer can at least rely on a certain level of processing power. Much of today's web processing is increasingly moving toward the server. However, with most of it being performed by CGI scripts, the server has suffered badly, especially when accessed by multiple clients at once. But by employing servlets, the server can now happily process all the clients' requests much more efficiently and, most significantly, much faster.

Areas in which conventional-based CGI processing can be replaced include the following:

- HTML form processing

  HTML form processing is just what it sounds like—the processing of web-based forms, whether it's storing the data to a file or packaging it up and emailing it to an administrator. These functions have conventionally been performed by CGI scripts. For example, one of the most common CGI scripts in use for this very task is the `form2email.cgi` program.

- HTML page counters

  Page counters are very popular additions to many web pages. They can track the number of times a user has accessed a given page by incrementing a counter file somewhere on the server. Although they're popular, they tend to place a significant overhead on the server when implemented using CGI scripts.

- Newsgroups

  A newsgroup is a mechanism that allows users to exchange data by leaving messages for everyone to read; these messages can be replied to, if necessary. Threads of conversions take place, in which people reply to replies. This is a web-based version of the Usenet groups that are found on the Internet.

- Guest books

  A guest book is, as the name suggests, intended as a place for guests to a web site to leave their comments or suggestions for the webmaster. This process differs from merely sending them an email, as other visitors can see the previous comments which have been posted.

- Search engines

  A site search engine allows the user to find information quickly and easily from within the site, without the user having to root around for it. Although CGI-based search engines do exist, it has been left to the built-in capabilities of the web server to provide such functionality.

- Banner advertising

  Online advertising is becoming increasingly popular with the more highly accessed sites selling banner space to potential advertisers. A banner allows the advertiser to display a small image that, when clicked, will take the user to an alternative site. This ability to steal surfers has made online advertising something that will stay for a long time yet on the web.

- Quote generators

  A quote generator is a small program that, when run, generates a new line of text. For example, UNIX fortune cookies run every time a user logs into the system, presenting the user with a new pearl of wisdom. Web-based generators operate on somewhat the same lines, inserting a new line of text into the web page every time it is accessed.

- Random links

  It is both common and courteous to have a place on a web site that offers a list of additional places that the user may wish to visit. These lists can sometimes get very long. Instead of having the user wade through lists, you can have them click on one link that will take them to a new link, randomly chosen from the list of possible links.

- Chat programs

  Chat programs allow users to talk to each other in real time on the Internet. IRC, or Internet Relay Chat, is one of the most common protocols for conversing on the net. A separate program, out with the web environment, is required to use IRC. However, CGI was one of the tools used to bring an HTML version of chat to the user.

As an illustration of the power and ease of servlet coding, this book presents case studies which outline many of these server processes in detail.

1.3 Future applications

When server-side processes are implemented using Java, a whole new world of applications can be realized. Applications that previously required a sophisticated language solution can now be easily implemented for a multiplatform environment in Java servlets. These are:

- Advanced database access

  Providing access to databases via CGI scripts was never much of a problem; however, controlling the number of sessions and security issues sometimes was.

- Virtual shopping baskets

  The web is an ideal place to allow users to purchase goods online. Virtual shopping baskets allow users to browse a site, adding items to be purchased to a list as they go. Once they've finished shopping, they then visit the virtual checkout for payment and delivery details. All this happens without the users having to log in beforehand.

- Online quizzes

  In web-based quizzes, users answer multiple-choice questions as they race against a clock. The server must keep track of the answers as it also keeps an accurate record of the time. Again, all this happens without users having to log in to the game beforehand.

- Dynamic images

  Dynamic images are generated by drawing on a virtual canvas in the server's memory; everything on the canvas is then converted to an image. The image can then be transmitted to the client browser via a .gif or .jpg image file.

- Advanced HTML filters

  Before a web page is delivered to a client, it can be preprocessed, removing any references to words that may be deemed unsuitable by the web or site administrator. This process can also be extended to replace terms, as opposed to search-and-destroy-type applications.

- Advanced HTML form processing

  Users have the ability to send files or data in a secure format to the server from a web-based form.

- Email transmitting servers

  More sophisticated email distribution list applications are available. Users can sign up to receive email such as a new joke every day, or a different passage from a book.

- Site analysis

  In addition to providing weekly and daily statistical information regarding the number of visitors to a web site, up-to-the-second information can be made available to site administrators. They then have the ability to see who is viewing the pages at any one point in time.

- News feeds

  Broadcast systems are systems in which the user is informed of an event the second it happens, as opposed to the user having to look for the information. With news feeds, the information finds the user.

It would be unfair to say the implementation of the items listed above would not be possible using CGI scripts. They are. Nevertheless, the scripts could become very difficult, as the majority of these situations require information to be held between client requests; and since many of the CGI implementations rely on files for this processing, it can make such solutions very inefficient.

As a demonstration of the available power of a Java servlet solution, each of the areas listed above will be carefully detailed and implemented in the following chapters.

1.4 Java language

This section of the chapter is intended to help those of you who are new to Java and who are wondering what all the fuss is about. Those of you familiar with Java may skip this section and move on to the next, without fear of missing an integral part of the book. If you are new to Java, and would like to learn a little more about the language that provides the key to servlets, read on.

1.4.1 In the beginning...

It is hard to believe a world without Java. It's true! There was a time in the history of the web when you could quite happily surf without encountering the gray rectangle that symbolized the loading of a Java applet. But like many great things in history, Java almost didn't come to be.

Java, or as it was known in its humble beginnings, Oak, was never intended to be used for the web, let alone the Internet. Its original purpose was to fulfill what the industry thought was a rather tall order: construct a language that could run consumer electronics, such as televisions, videos, and toasters; be platform independent; and be free of bugs.

It had to be platform independent because the processor differed from device to device. It had to be bug free, which is fair enough to ask; you don't want to have to reboot your toaster when the operating system controlling the burn setting has locked up and all toast is coming out black, for example.

Sun Microsystems, a leading supplier of the servers that powered most of the web sites, assigned three men to the task of building a hand-held remote control using a new language. James Gosling, Patrick Naughton, and Mike Sheridan headed up Project Oak.

Note The name Oak, it is said, came from the need for a name. As legend now states, James Gosling looked out of his office window, and his eyes fell upon a big old oak tree in the garden. The name stuck.

The computer industry is littered with languages, and each has its own traits and application areas. But none could be found to satisfy the original need. However, many languages had features that could simply not be ignored; Smalltalk offered object-orientation, C/C++ offered flexible syntax, Ada offered multithreading, and Eiffel offered platform independence. By taking all the best bits from all these languages and removing all the bad bits, Oak was designed, and it didn't suffer from any of the constraints found in the other languages.

Oak was designed, built, and packaged as a proper development language. A specific company, FirstPerson Inc., was formed to promote and sell this solution to the very industry that drove its creation. You might have thought it would have been a relatively simple sale—after all, they did ask for it. But convincing the industry proved too difficult, and the company soon disbanded.

While this process was happening, the world wide web was rapidly growing in popularity. With the introduction of Mosaic and then the Netscape browsers, web sites were coming online daily, at a tremendous rate. Sun had a man who had a vision: Bill Joy. Being personal friends of both Gosling and Naughton, Joy knew of Project Oak, and he could see the potential such a language could have on the web. He quickly rescued the project, bringing Oak back under the Sun umbrella.

Considering Sun's primary focus was hardware, going into the software business was a bold move for them. But it was a move that has since proved to be wise and prosperous. The first thing Sun changed was the name. Oak was already taken by another language, and it could not be used. So Java was chosen, and it stuck.

However, the team, and now Sun, had to demonstrate this new language to the world in such a way that would ensure its future. With Java now being pitched at the web, creating the first web browser entirely written in Java seemed a logical step. Thus Hot Java was born. With its release in the summer of 1995, Java caught the attention of the Internet community. When Netscape released the next update of its browser, which was Java-enabled, Java's place in the history of the web was made sure.

1.4.2 How it works

Java is platform independent, meaning the same code doesn't require modification or recompilation if it is run on another machine or operating system. This flexibility is achieved by designing Java to run not on any one specific processor, but to run on a virtual processor. The virtual processor, or JVM as it is more commonly called, resembles a normal processor in every detail: it has registers, op-codes, and a program counter, among other things, except it is implemented in pure software.

A Java program is compiled to produce a format known as byte codes, which is ready to run on any JVM. When a Java program runs, it is interpreted and run on the JVM. Fortunately, as Java developers, you do not need to worry about the Java interpreter or how it operates. You can rest secure in the knowledge that the program you are developing will run successfully on a JVM no matter the underlying processor or operating system.

At the time of this writing, Java interpreters are available for the majority of operating systems in use today: Solaris, Windows95, Windows NT, Linux, UNIX, Novell, AIX, and Mac OS, to name a few. This list doesn't include all the Java-enabled browsers that exist on a variety of platforms to run applets. The technical difference between an applet and an application or servlet is how they are run. An applet is run on the JVM provided by the browser, whereas for an application, the JVM is provided by a specific program or the operating system itself. However, this definition no longer holds up in the ever-changing world of Java. When an applet is run on a Java Station, it is the operating system that is providing the virtual machine, not the browser, which in this instance is the Hot Java browser.

1.4.3 Strengths

One of the better ways to demonstrate a language strength is to contrast it with another comparable language. The best, and probably the closest, language to Java for this task is C++. With most of Java's features based on C++, it is very easy to see why people are choosing Java over C++.

- Java makes bug-free code possible

  Maybe this statement would be a lot less controversial if it were reworded. Let's say, instead, that Java produces syntactically bug-free code. It is a well-known fact that for every fifty lines of C/C++ code, at least one new bug is introduced into the system. The majority of these bugs are due to memory overruns and the developers' lack of understanding about memory pointers. A Java program does not have pointers, thus rendering direct memory access impossible.

- Garbage collection

  The term garbage collection was first commonly used for the Eiffel language in the late '70s. As stated in the previous section, pointers were a major contributor to the number of bugs in a program. A pointer in C/C++ is, in reality, a memory address pointing to an area of memory. For example, say the memory for a particular object was freed in C/C++, and then in another dark corner of the program, another pointer tried to access it. The program would most certainly crash. Java has eliminated this scenario, and many like it, by not providing any mechanism to manually free an object. Instead, the Java interpreter keeps track of all the objects still in scope and frees each only when the object is no longer referenced anywhere. The garbage collector only runs when the interpreter is not busy, or when memory is running low. Since Java treats all objects this way, it is no longer possible to create static objects, such as an object instance at compile time.

- References, not pointers

  Although pointers have been eliminated and replaced with references, references can still be thought of as pointers to allow the creation of standard data structures such as linked lists. Since pointers are no longer available, this has the effect of eliminating all memory leaks and overruns. Arrays are no longer accessible via pointer arithmetic; instead, they must be accessed using the [...] notion. Accessing raw memory is no longer possible by simply casting an integer to a pointer.

- Multiple inheritance

  Java does not implement multiple inheritance, which is the ability to inherit from more than one base class. As powerful a mechanism as it is, it has always been a housekeeping nightmare to keep under control. Through the use of interfaces, Java provides a much easier way for developers intent on using multiple inheritance.

- Global data types

  One of the major problems with porting C/C++ programs was that you could not guarantee the size of data types. For example, one processor may implement integers as 16-bit numbers while another processor may implement the same integer as 32-bit numbers. This lack of standardization has led to many hard-to-find bugs. Java has eliminated this problem by insisting on a virtual machine, where all the data types are continually a consistent size.

- Easier project management

  Java has eliminated the need for header files to describe classes to the outside world. Instead, if a class is declared as public, then it must reside in its own file of the same name. Thus, dependencies are no longer a complicated issue in Java; in C/C++ the use of conditional #if statements played a major part when attempting the build of a large project.

- Multithreading

  Instead of relying on a third-party library or the underlying operating system, Java has multithreading built in to the standard structure from the start. Building multithreading applications is now a very trivial task using Java.

- Communications

  With Java initially targeted at the Internet, it was important that the ability to communicate was built in as part of the standard library. Java offers both socket-level communication and URL communication, thus allowing it to communicate with a wide range of applications and machines on the Internet.

- Security

  Security was a word that previous languages did not have in their vocabulary, and as a consequence, they have been open to many malicious attacks. Java designed a very tight security model into the interpreter. This model is called the security manager, and it determines which programs get access to which resources. For example, it is the security manager that stops an applet from reading and writing files on the client machine it is running. In addition to the security manager, the ability to add digital signatures and use secure sockets are all built in to the system.

- Portability

    Although the ANSI board has ratified C++, this does not necessarily mean it is an industry standard. It just means a certain flavor of C++ will guarantee to compile on a compiler conforming to this standard. Porting between different flavors can be time consuming, and very frustrating. Java does not suffer from this due to its virtual processor model.

The features listed above only touch on the broad issues; many other features are left to be discovered. Building these functions into the standard library has meant a whole new generation of developers would emerge who never had the joy of working with raw pointers and working out the intricacies of ** !

Note Those of you unfamiliar with C/C++ will not recognize the ** notion. This is used to denote a "pointer to a pointer," which can become very complicated very quickly, especially if you're trying to follow someone else's code.

1.4.4 Performance

With Java running on a virtual machine, each byte code that is run must be translated, or interpreted, to an equivalent set of instructions on the target processor. This can be a time-consuming process. It's no surprise that this has been touted as the major reason for not employing Java in time-critical applications. However, it is a concern that has been grossly exaggerated. When a Java program is compared to the equivalent natively compiled C program, of course the C program will run faster—it has no level of interpretation. But this is not a fair comparison, as Java brings a great deal more functionality and security with it than its C counterpart.

In a bid to improve performance of the executed program, a technique developed for Smalltalk by L. Peter Deutsch was employed for Java interpreters. This technique is known as the just-in-time compiler, or JIT.

A JIT-enabled interpreter interprets a block of code into native code and performs an optional optimization on it. This code is logged and then run. The real magic of JIT comes when this block of code is called on to execute again. Instead of reinterpreting the byte code, the interpreter simply runs the stored native, optimized code, thus eliminating the overhead of translation. Sun Microsystems has published results of this technique, showing how speed increases up to ten times faster than non-JIT interpreters, with programs running comparably with C and C++ programs.

> **Note** Many of the browsers available today have enabled JIT interpreters as part of their Java environment. With Microsoft's Internet Explorer, the JIT part of the interpreter can be turned off by simply selecting the appropriate check box. Experiment with it, and see if you notice a difference in applet speed when it's turned on or off. You should notice a difference in applets that are computationally intensive.

Since servlets rely on the underlying Java run time for its interpretation, replacing the interpreter for a JIT-enabled version will allow your servlets to benefit in the speed gain also.

1.5 Java server API

The foundation of the Server Toolkit is the Java Server API. This API allows the building of complete server-side applications. A servlet merely extends the functionality of a server, and using this API, the server may be built. The best example of a server built using this API is the Java Web Server from Sun.

Although it is a very powerful and feature-rich API, it is not expected to be useful for everyone; instead, many developers will be more interested in the servlet API.

1.6 Java servlet API

The servlet API allows the development of servlets. A servlet is designed to extend the functionality of the server it is running under. The servlet API comes as a set of classes that are used to form the base class for any user servlets. Any server supporting the servlet API will run any servlets developed using the servlet toolkit.

This API is detailed in a later chapter, with a reference to the complete API and all its methods found in the appendix.

1.7 The future of Java and servlets

All right, it's crystal ball time:

Ode to Java

Oh, mystic ball of time,

Clear your water's droplets,

To see what you have in mind

For the wonderful world of servlets!

The problem with the future is that as soon as it's predicted, you have to start the prediction cycle all over again. However, the function the web is playing is changing. Until now, the web has been very much a showpiece for many companies; merely having "a presence" was good enough for many companies. But now that so many people have a web site, they're starting to ask questions like "What now?" "What can it do?" and probably the most important question, "Can it make us money?"

In order for a web site to be successful, not only does it have to provide a valued service, but it must entertain at the same time. But providing such services takes processing power and bandwidth. The Java applet, though very powerful, takes time to download, and while it's downloading, the user must sit and look at a wonderfully interactive, gray rectangle. Not a very exciting pastime, I must say—frustrating for the developer, and boring for the user.

Many of the applets on the web today are doing fancy animations that eat up valuable bandwidth. Applets are employed to add an extra level of interactivity to the session, to make the visit to a site more enjoyable. However, this can be achieved without the overhead of the applet.

When the developer places the processing at the server side, users can have a perceived instant response to their session, without the additional overhead of an applet having to load and run. Not that the future of the applet is in doubt—it's just that with the limitations on bandwidth, more processing will have to be performed at the server side, with the result being sent to the client.

This book arms you with the necessary tools and knowledge to take the processing to the server.

1.8 Who should read this book?

Well, if I had my way, everyone in the world should read this book! If truth be known, however, there may not be a need for it in the more far-flung corners of the globe, such as the Scottish Highlands. There is only so much help a servlet can give when herding sheep.

The aim of this book is to provide an illustrated tour of the Java servlet API, and to show how it is used in real-life situations, with real-life examples. Along with detailed case studies, this book covers the majority of the applications currently found running as CGI scripts on web servers. Existing CGI developers will see Java implementations of their favorite scripts, while existing Java developers will be able to see how easy it is to provide server-side solutions.

Web designers who dabble with Java applets will also see the simplicity of the servlet architecture, and they may look to add functionality to their web site.

Whoever ends up reading this book will see for himself the power this relatively simple set of classes holds. It is my hope that you never look at an alternative again.

C H A P T E R   2

Java Servlets API

- Learn what the servlet 2.1 API is, what it includes, and what makes a servlet different from other server programs.

- Starting and stopping a servlet is different from conventional programs. Learn what these differences are.

- Understand what a servlet can and can't do, and look at its security restrictions.

- Take a detailed look at the core classes that form the basis of the Java servlet model.

- With servlets being employed mainly on the web, a number of specific classes have been developed to speed up user development. Discover what these helper classes are.

A servlet is a small program that runs in response to a client connection to a server. Regardless of the type of server (web server, mail server, or any other server), a servlet is intended to extend a server's functionality. Think of a servlet as a server-side applet. In much the same way an applet extends the functionality of a browser, a servlet extends a server.

For this reason, servlets have found many application areas in which they can be made useful, especially in the web arena where conventional technologies such as CGI provide additional dynamic processing for web servers. Where a CGI script is inefficient and nonportable, a Java servlet is both efficient and 100% portable across all platforms supporting the Java run time interface. This chapter will show you what a servlet actually looks like, and it will explain the core class structure that makes up the servlet API. This chapter only uses the classic "Hello World" examples, since the whole book from this point on will give many well-defined, real-world examples.

In appendix A: Java servlet API, you will find a complete, detailed API overview that may be used as reference.

2.1   Servlet introduction

There are many definitions for a servlet; each one is perfectly correct in its own right, but they are all different from each other. Not to be outdone, I will present another servlet definition—one I think best describes a servlet, regardless of where the term is used in this book:

Servlet: A small program that extends the functionality of a server.

Some people may argue with this definition, saying, "Okay, but what's your definition of a server in that context?" Frankly, it doesn't matter what the server is. A server is something that serves connections; whether it is a mail server processing requests for a mail account or an File Transport Protocol (FTP) server processing requests for file transfers, the principle is the same. When a connection from a client is made, something has to process that connection. It is at this point in the process that the servlet solution comes to life. This concept is illustrated with a simple server example, as shown in figure 2.1.

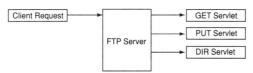

Figure 2.1 FTP

Assume an FTP server was implemented with support for Java servlets. The FTP system operates by sending requests, or commands, to the server, which result in certain actions being executed. For example, the command

```
GET C:\TEMP.TXT
```

asks the server to send the file `TEMP.TXT` to the client. Instead of the server servicing this request itself, it could pass the request on to the servlet specifically designed for sending files, thus freeing up the server to service additional or subsequent requests. Following this model, the server can be extended to support additional commands by simply implementing new servlets to handle the new commands.

An additional benefit is the ease of upgrading. You can replace the servlet that handles the GET requests without having to restart the whole server.

The server sets up the connection, and once it is successfully connected, the servlet can then be employed to service the client request. When the servlet is run, the connection has already been made. The servlet makes no attempt to process any part of the connection process with the client.

A servlet runs in a separate thread of execution that remains alive for the duration of the client connection, with many thread instances of the same servlet servicing multiple clients at any one point. How a servlet differs from a conventional program depends on the way in which it is constructed. For the sake of discussion, a servlet is sometimes referred to as a separate program from the server; however, depending on the server architecture, the servlet may be an integral part of the server.

A servlet is simply a Java class—once it is loaded, one of its class methods is called to service the request. Normal programs would, at this point, remove themselves from memory after the client had been serviced, but not the servlet. A servlet may remain in memory for subsequent client requests; the method is merely accessed once more, without the overhead of reloading and initializing the servlet again. This significantly improves the efficiency of the server.

Another advantage of a servlet-based solution is the ability for servlets to communicate easily with one another. Since all the servlets are implemented in Java, the standard Java communication mechanisms may be employed. In other words, a servlet can get a reference to another servlet and make a call to any of its public methods. Another form of communicating is sometimes referred to as chaining, which is when one servlet passes the client request to another servlet for processing.

The Java Web Server was built using the server API, which is not to be confused with the servlet API. The server API is a set of classes that allows for the easy building of server-side applications in Java. Part of the server API is the ability to support servlets.

The Java Web Server is the best example of how servlets can be used in today's environment; it's the best example of how they directly replace the need for CGI alternatives. However, as this book will illustrate, this is only one side of the coin, because by using Java servlets to process client requests, more sophisticated server-side applications can be developed without increasing the stress on either the server or the developer.

Note The Java Web Server is not the only server that runs servlets. Any server supporting the servlet API will support any servlet developed in conformance to the API and Java. At the time of this writing, all the major web servers are supporting the servlet API, with servlet engines providing the servlet processing until they do.

The servlet API is a set of classes and interfaces that are used to build servlets. The servlet API facilitates the building of two types of servlets: basic and web-based servlets.

The basic servlet is what all servlets are derived from. These servlets provide the basic functionality required for dealing with a client request. Web-based servlets are servlets that have been specifically designed for use with the HTTP protocol. Since web-based servlets derive their functionality from the basic servlets, they demonstrate the ease of extending the servlet classes to provide additional functionality.

The remaining sections in this chapter will detail what a servlet looks like and how it interacts with the rest of the system.

2.2   A day in the life of a servlet

Since servlets come in the form of Java objects, there are many different variations on not only how they are loaded but also how they are unloaded again, if at all. When the server decides a particular servlet is to be loaded, it uses the standard Java class loading mechanisms to create the class instance. Using this technique, servlets can be loaded from anywhere on the network, and if the server is connected to the Internet, from anywhere in the world.

```
Class c = Class.forName( "http://<server>/testclass");
```

Once this method has returned, the class can be accessed as normal. Asuming the URL doesn't upset the security of the system, classes can be located anywhere on the network.

Note   Loading classes from within a Java servlet, applet, or any Java program is achieved through the `java.lang.Class` class. This class method returns the class object associated with the full URL that was passed in.

Forgetting about the potential security implications this may have (these are addressed in the next section on servlet security) this provides a great advantage to distribution and resource sharing. Unlike the applet-loading model, where every client running the applet loads the applet from the same origin, the servlet has the ability to load from multiple hosts. For example, as shown in figure 2.2, one server can run the servlet code that originated from another.

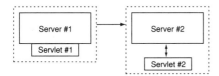

Figure 2.2 Locating servlets

The actual loading and execution of the servlet is straightforward enough—when a client connection is accepted and the servlet is not in memory, it is loaded. However, a servlet can be loaded if it has not yet been addressed. A servlet can be loaded either at server startup or dynamically when it is accessed.

The Java Web Server has an administration section that allows the administrator to specify which servlets are loaded at startup. This allows the servlet to be ready in memory forthe first client request to come in. Generally, only servlets that are expected to be heavily usedare loaded at server startup. Loading the servlet at startup ensures the response time for all requests is kept to a minimum, as opposed to waiting for the servlet to be loaded.

Alternatively, the servlet can be loaded when it is first accessed. No matter how it is loaded, all servlets follow the same cycle as shown in figure 2.3.

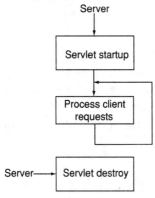

Figure 2.3 Servlet cycle

When the servlet is first loaded, a single method is called that can be used to initialize any startup data. For example, if the servlet is to be used for accessing a database, then the database connection could be opened from this method. Since the database connection need be opened only once, this is the perfect place for it.

Once the servlet class object has been initialized, it is ready to serve client requests. Servicing a client request is performed by the server (or another servlet, if they are in a chain) calling a predefined method for servicing requests. Since the servlet will be used in a multithreaded environment, the method servicing the request has to be made thread-safe, assuming shared variables are being accessed. For example, assume the servlet begins to service one client request, and halfway through it, another request comes in. If the first instance of the servlet had set any global variables, then it is possible for the second instance to change them. The first one will then read the wrong values.

Servlets are generally unloaded and removed from memory only when the server shuts down. However, there are situations when a servlet is unloaded immediately after completing a client request; some server-side includes servlets are good examples. This will be detailed in the server-side includes section at the end of this chapter.

2.3 Servlet security

Servlets are implemented in Java, so consequently, they benefit from all of the security features offered by Java. Java servlets come in two different modes: trusted and untrusted. A trusted program, such as a Java application, has the same access to the system as any other program, including the following:

- Read/write files on the local machine

- Open connection to any host on the network

- Execution of other programs

Security features are controlled through the `SecurityManager` class of the run time environment. This determines whether a class has sufficient access rights to use a particular file, device, or program.

Note   Java, unlike conventional programming languages, has a great deal of security built into the language itself, even before `SecurityManager` is called upon for its services. A Java program, whether it be an applet, servlet, or any other code variation, cannot access memory directly. Casting an integer to a memory pointer and accessing it simply cannot be done. By disallowing this action, the Java code cannot eavesdrop on other programs or corrupt areas of memory. The benefit of this is if for some reason a Java program crashes, no other program in the system is affected.

All of these security features are not unique to Java servlets only, but to all Java programs. As handy as these features are, they can severely hamper functionality in some instances. Imagine a servlet that was designed to process HTML forms by storing them in a file. If the `SecurityManager` did not permit writes to occur, then it would be impossible to create the file. But before you start reaching for the CGI book, know that help is at hand.

To understand why Java has such tight security when compared to other alternative technologies such as CGI and ActiveX, you have to look at the context in which the applications will be running. One of the goals of Java is to build a completely open, distributed-computing model which will allow users to download and run code on demand, as opposed to installing the code beforehand. On the face of it, this is not a bad idea, but do you really want to download and execute a program that has the potential of reading your personal files, or, even worse, reformatting your hard disk?

In order to gain the trust of users, the makers of Java had to build in very tight security features that could not be compromised. The reason for this need-to-know type of protection is that the user cannot be sure of a developer's intentions. Maybe they are a trustworthy organization and won't mess up a user's hard disk, but on the other hand, they may be a consortium of hackers masquerading behind a legitimate company, out to steal information. The user has no way of knowing.

For this reason, all Java programs coming from an outside resource, such as the Internet, are considered untrusted. Can Java programs become trusted? The short answer is yes.

A trusted program is one the user feels won't do anything it shouldn't do. For example, servlets definitely need to have the ability to read and write files if they are to serve any useful function in the areas of HTML processing. A servlet can be trusted by the server if it is or has one of the following:

- Built-in servlets
- Digital signatures

Servlets that are built-in are those which have been verified by the administrator and allow the server to load them with full permission. Generally, this is achieved by giving the server a list of servlets that are considered built-in or trusted; this list is checked every time a servlet is requested. If a request is made for a servlet that doesn't appear as part of this list, the servlet's access rights are severely restricted to the status of an applet running in the client browser.

The other method for creating a trusted servlet is to digitally sign each servlet. Before running the code, the server can check to see if the signature is from a known, trusted source before granting full access to it.

Note Simply adding a digital signature doesn't prevent attacks. For example, a servlet developer with a known, trusted signature may wake up one morning, think, "What the heck?" and then develop a rogue piece of software that completely erases the system directory.

Some technologies, ActiveX for example, completely rely on this type of security. One of the most famous examples of bad security is the Internet Exploder, which was an ActiveX plug in. Once it was loaded, it shut down the client's machine without warning. The signature, or certificate as it is known in the ActiveX world, was attained legitimately. When the developer was challenged, the reply was that a new Internet-based utility had been developed to allow users to turn off their machines.

By implementing the previously discussed security systems, administrators can sleep a little easier at night, safe in the knowledge that their servers aren't being taken over by rogue servlets.

2.4 Java Servlet Development Kit installation

Installing the Java Servlet Development Kit (JSDK) is a simple matter of retrieving the servlet files, which you can find in a variety of archive formats at the Java home site (http://java.sun.com). Before installing the servlet toolkit, be sure you have at least version 1.1 of the Java Development Kit. Again, you can find this at the Java web site. Once the downloaded file is extracted, the directory structure shown in figure 2.4 is constructed.

The ./bin directory contains the test servlet runner you can use to test servlets. (More details about this can be found at the end of this chapter in the section titled "Testing web-based servlets.") The ./doc directory contains all of the class and interface documentation, which can be viewed using any web browser. The ./lib directory contains the ./lib/jsdk.jar file, which the compiler uses to compile the servlet API. The ./examples directory contains some examples of servlets which you are free to edit. Finally, the ./src directory contains the source code for the servlet API, which you may look at but not modify.

Figure 2.4 JSDK directory structure

Before compiling any servlets, you have to add the file name jsdk.jar to the CLASS-PATH environment variable. An example of the resulting CLASSPATH may look something like this:

```
SET CLASSPATH=.;C:\JAVA\LIB\CLASSES.ZIP;C:\JSDK\LIB\jsdk.jar;
```

Setting this variable allows the compiler to find the servlet classes and successfully produce the .class file. Testing the servlet depends on the intended server.

Because the majority of servlets developed will be for use in web servers, a test server comes with the toolkit that allows the testing of web-based servlets without the need to disrupt the target web server. Details on how this operates are given later in this chapter in the section titled "Testing web-based servlets."

2.5 Servlet structure

Up till now, you have seen what a servlet is, where it is run, how it is run, and why it needs to be run. Now it is time to look at the actual servlet classes and interfaces that make up the servlet API. This section details the JSDK. This is the stand-alone API that facilitates the creation of servlets, regardless of the target platform. All servlet classes and interfaces that form the API are found in the javax.servlet package.

2.5.1 Servlet interface

All servlets, no matter what type of server they are destined to be used with, implement the javax.servlet.Servlet interface. This interface defines the basic functionality that a servlet must possess, as shown in example 2.1.

```
public interface Servlet {
  public void init(ServletConfig config) throws ServletException;
  public void service(ServletRequest req, ServletResponse res) throws
ServletException, IOException;
  public void destroy();
  public ServletConfig getServletConfig();
  public String getServletInfo();
}
```

Example 2.1   javax.servlet.Servlet

As stated previously, a servlet has three main stages in its life: startup, servicing requests, and close down. The interface definition in example 2.1 shows the methods for these three states.

The first method, `init(…)`, is called once by the system. It is the first method to be called. Execution will be finished before any client requests are serviced.

Each client request that comes in is processed using the `service(…)` class method. For the sake of discussion, think of this method as having an input stream and output stream to the client via the parameters passed in to the method. We will look into this method in more detail later in this chapter.

Finally, at the end of the servlet's life cycle when it is to be removed from memory, the `destroy()` method is called. Just as `init(…)` was the first method to be called, this is the last call the servlet will get. This method is designed to allow the servlet to do any final saving to disk of configuration or run time data.

The method `getServletConfig()` is used to return an instance to the `ServletConfig` instance that was passed in to the `init(…)` method. More information on this will be presented later on in this chapter.

The method `getServletInfo()` is the servlet's equivalent of the `java.lang. Object`'s `toString()` method. This returns information about the servlet that the author has deemed useful.

ServletConfig   When the servlet first starts up, the system can pass specific initialization information to the servlet for possible processing via the `init(…)` method. A servlet, just like a Java applet, can have parameters passed to it at startup, and the servlet must have some way to retrieve these. Example 2.2 shows the class definition for `ServletConfig`.

```
public interface ServletConfig {
  public ServletContext getServletContext();
  public String getInitParameter(String name);
  public Enumeration getInitParameterNames();
}
```
Example 2.2   javax.servlet.ServletConfig

Parameters are passed in using a key/value pairing, and two methods are provided to access this data: `getInitParameter(…)` and `getInitParameterName()`.

Another piece of useful information that is available regards the environment in which the servlet is running. This information is passed using the `ServletContext` class as returned by the `getServletContext()` method.

ServletContext   This interface, shown in example 2.3, allows the servlet to interrogate the server about various pieces of environmental data. If a servlet is running within a virtual host, the `ServletContext` will be different for each virtual host.

```
public interface ServletContext {

  public ServletContext getContext(String uripath);
```

```
public int getMajorVersion();
public int getMinorVersion();

public String getMimeType(String file);

public URL getResource(String path) throws MalformedURLException;
public InputStream getResourceAsStream(String path);

public RequestDispatcher getRequestDispatcher(String urlpath);
public void log(String msg);
public void log(Exception exception, String msg);

public void log(String message, Throwable throwable);
public String getRealPath(String path);

public String getServerInfo();

public Object getAttribute(String name);
public Enumeration getAttributeNames();
public void setAttribute(String name, Object object);
public void removeAttribute(String name);
}
```
Example 2.3   Javax.servlet.ServletContext

Many servers, particularly web servers, refer to files and resources as virtual files. However, this makes opening up files difficult, as the virtual file or alias needs to be mapped onto a real file. The `ServletContext` interface, for example, provides a method to convert an alias and real path file names. This method is `getRealPath(…)`; examples of it can be found throughout this book.

Many methods in this class allow you to interrogate the other resources that may be present in the system. All of these methods will be explained in depth in the methods appendix at the end of this book.

2.5.2 GenericServlet

The base class on which the majority of servlets are based is the `GenericServlet` class. This base class, shown in example 2.4, brings together the common methods from the servlet interface and presents a rich method list from which to override methods for custom processing.

```
public abstract class GenericServlet implements Servlet, ServletConfig,
                        java.io.Serializable{

  private transient ServletConfig config;
  public GenericServlet();
  public void destroy();

  public String getInitParameter(String name);
  public Enumeration getInitParameterNames();

  public ServletConfig getServletConfig();
```

```
public ServletContext getServletContext();
public String getServletInfo();

public void init(ServletConfig config) throws ServletException;
public void init() throws ServletException;

public void log(String msg);
public void log(String message, Throwable t);

public abstract void service(ServletRequest req, ServletResponse res)
                       throws ServletException, IOException;
}
```
Example 2.4   javax.servlet.GenericServlet

In addition to the methods that handle the three states the servlet finds itself in, there are supporting methods that can be called to receive information about aspects of the server and the servlet.

Some of the more useful functions provided by the `GenericServlet` class are the `log(...)` methods. A servlet can write to the standard output stream using the `System.out.println(...)` method. However, this information is lost as soon as it is printed. If, on the other hand, your servlet needs to ensure that certain error messages (or other types of messages) get stored, using one of the `log(...)` methods allows you to write lines of text directly into the server log file.

Initialization   When the system loads the servlet, the `init(...)` method is called automatically. Developers wishing to perform any initialization (such as setting up any data variables) can override this method, as shown in example 2.5.

```
public void init(ServletConfig _config) throws ServletException {
  super.init(_config );
  String strCount = _config.getInitParameter("init_count");
  count = Integer.parseInt(strCount);
}
```
Example 2.5   Overriding the init(...) method

If the `init(...)` method is overridden, it is important that the base method is called. This is achieved through the `super.init(...)` call.

In this example, the servlet is expecting a parameter named `init_count` at startup. This parameter will contain a starting value for the count variable that will be kept for some reason, specific to the servlet being implemented.

Although both methods are provided, use the `init()` method if you don't want to worry about calling the base method. The `GenericServlet` class will make sure the `init(...)` is called and the necessary information is stored in the `ServletConfig`.

Client request servicing   The `service(...)` method is called for every single client request that comes in. Since the `service(...)` method is marked as abstract, it must be implemented. This method is the most important method found in any servlet. It is from the service(…) method that the servlet processes each client request. As shown in figure 2.5, the servlet has input from the client and output back to the client.

Figure 2.5 Servlet input/output

ServletRequest   The `ServletRequest` class, shown in example 2.6, is used to facilitate the input connection to the client. From this class, you can retrieve data from the client through a variety of different interfaces. For example, if the data is coming via the HTTP protocol, the data is generally paired in key/value sequences. The input data can easily be retrieved using the `getParameter(…)` methods.

Other methods associated with the HTTP protocol include `getContentLength()`, which returns the length of the data sent, and `getContentType()`, which returns the Multi-purpose Internet Mail Extensions (MIME) type of the data sent.

```
public interface ServletRequest {

  public Object getAttribute(String name);

  public void setAttribute(String key, Object o);
  public Enumeration getAttributeNames();

  public ServletInputStream getInputStream() throws IOException;
  public BufferedReader getReader () throws IOException;

  public String getParameter(String name);
  public Enumeration getParameterNames();
  public String[] getParameterValues(String name);

  public String getCharacterEncoding ();
  public int getContentLength();
  public String getContentType();
  public String getProtocol();
  public String getScheme();
  public String getServerName();
  public int     getServerPort();
  public String getRemoteAddr();
  public String getRemoteHost();

  public String getRealPath(String path);
}
```
Example 2.6   javax.servlet.ServletRequest

If, on the other hand, data is coming from a non-HTTP client, then the data may be coming in as a stream. The `ServletInputStream` can be used to read this stream. Additional information about the client that may be useful is the home network address from which it is sending. This information can be made available through the getRe-moteAddr() and getRemoteHost() methods.

The ServletInputStream is derived from the standard Java java.io. Input-Stream class. All the methods from this class can be used to read data from the client in exactly the same way you would read data from a file. To make the creation process more simple, ServletRequest has a method to return a BufferedReader instance that can be used directly.

ServletResponse   The ServletResponse class, shown in example 2.7, deals with the other side of the equation, which is sending data back to the client. The most important method of this interface is the getOutputStream() method. This returns the Serv-letOutputStream, which can be used to provide any other preferred output stream class from the java.io package.

```
public interface ServletResponse {

  public String getCharacterEncoding ();

  public ServletOutputStream getOutputStream() throws IOException;
  public PrintWriter getWriter() throws IOException;

  public void setContentLength(int len);
  public void setContentType(String type);
}
```
Example 2.7   javax.servlet.ServletResponse

To make things easier, this method provides access to the PrintWriter object. This is a much cleaner way of outputting lines of text to the client.

GenericServlet example   Having now examined the classes and interfaces that make up the GenericServlet class, let's now look at a very simple example that illustrates some of the more common method calls. This servlet will simply print the message
        "Hello World: You are number x to use this servlet."
to the client. As an illustration of how data is maintained between client requests, a simple counter of the number of people visiting the servlet will be kept (this is represented by count in the message). Example 2.8 shows this simple example.

```
import javax.servlet.*;
import java.io.*;

public class simple extends GenericServlet {
  private int count = 0;

  public void init(ServletConfig _config) throws ServletException  {
    super.init(_config);
    String strCount = getInitParameter("init_count");
    count = Integer.parseInt(strCount);
  }
```

```
    public void service(ServletRequest _req, ServletResponse _res)
                        throws ServletException, IOException {
        count++;
        _res.setContentType("text/plain");
        PrintWriter Out = _res.getWriter();
        Out.println("Hello World: You are number " + count + "to use this
                        servlet.");
        Out.flush();
    }
}
```
Example 2.8 "Hello World"

As you may have guessed, when the servlet is first initialized, the counter variable must be set. The `init(…)` method is used to do this. From here, the `init_count` parameter passed to the servlet is read and converted to an integer, which then is used as the starting value for the counter.

For every client request that comes in, the `service(…)` method is called. Each time this occurs, the counter is incremented by one to show another usage for the servlet. Next, the output is prepared by first setting the content type of the output to plain text.

An instance of the `PrintWriter` class is fetched using the call to `getWriter()`. This allows you to easily print lines to the client using the `PrintWriter.println(…)` method.

Although this is a very basic and relatively useless servlet, it shows how easy it is to construct a server-side extension. A more in-depth example of the classic counter problem will be seen later in this book.

2.6 Web-based servlets

The developers at Java recognized the fact that the majority of servlets would be employed in the field of the Internet, with particular emphasis on the world wide web. The servlet API offers you a direct alternative to using CGI and Microsoft's Active Server Pages (ASP) to implement server-side solutions. To make coding servlets for the web relatively easy, a special `HttpServlet` class was developed. This provided methods to access the more common header fields found in the HTTP protocol.

2.7 HttpServlet

The `HttpServlet`, based on the `GenericServlet` class, is shown in example 2.9. It provides an improved interface for dealing with HTTP-specific client requests. In addition to the `service(…)` method that is used to deal with all requests, seven additional methods exist for processing requests; `doGet(…)`, `doPost(…)`, `doHead(…)`, `doPut(…)`, `doTrace(…)`, `doOptions(…)`, and `doDelete(…)`.

When a client makes a request to the server, the request can be one of seven types: GET, POST, HEAD, PUT, TRACE, OPTIONS, and DELETE. These methods provide a way of processing each type without having to explicitly check the type using the `service(…)` method.

```
public abstract class HttpServlet extends GenericServlet implements
                           java.io.Serializable {
   protected void service (HttpServletRequest req,
                           HttpServletResponse resp)
                           throws ServletException, IOException;
   protected void doGet (HttpServletRequest req, HttpServletResponse resp)
                           throws ServletException, IOException;
   protected void doPost (HttpServletRequest req,
                           HttpServletResponse resp)
                           throws ServletException, IOException;
   protected void doHead (HttpServletRequest req,
                           HttpServletResponse resp)
                           throws ServletException, IOException;
   protected void doTrace (HttpServletRequest req,
                           HttpServletResponse resp)
                           throws ServletException, IOException;
   protected void doPut (HttpServletRequest req, HttpServletResponse resp)
                           throws ServletException, IOException;
   protected void doOptions (HttpServletRequest req,
                           HttpServletResponse resp)
                           throws ServletException, IOException;
   protected void doDelete (HttpServletRequest req,
                           HttpServletResponse resp)
                           throws ServletException, IOException;
}
```

Example 2.9   javax.servlet.http.HttpServlet

HttpServletRequest   As shown in the previous section, the alternative service(...)
for client requests uses two different input and output classes: HttpServletRequest
(shown in example 2.10) and HttpServletResponse (shown in example 2.11). Both of
these classes are derived from their respective input and output classes shown in the
GenericServlet section earlier in this chapter.

HTTP is the protocol used by the web for transferring different kinds of data. For
this flexibility, a lot of administration information is transferred in the header of the protocol for each transfer. Some examples of this administrative information include the
resource being accessed, the date the request was sent, and the data transfer type.

```
public interface HttpServletRequest extends ServletRequest {
   public String getAuthType();
   public Cookie[] getCookies();

   public long getDateHeader(String name);
   public String getHeader(String name);
   public Enumeration getHeaderNames();
   public int getIntHeader(String name);

   public String getMethod();
   public String getPathInfo();
   public String getPathTranslated();
   public String getQueryString();
   public String getRemoteUser();
```

```
  public String getRequestedSessionId ();
  public String getRequestURI();
  public String getServletPath();

  public HttpSession getSession (boolean create);
  public HttpSession getSession();
  public boolean isRequestedSessionIdValid ();
  public boolean isRequestedSessionIdFromCookie ();
  public boolean isRequestedSessionIdFromURL();
  public boolean isRequestedSessionIdFromUrl ();
}
```
Example 2.10   javax.servlet.http.HttpServletRequest

Instead of having the user decode the fields manually, the HttpServletRequest class presents a detailed set of methods to easily access all HTTP-specific data. See appendix A: Java servlet API, for a complete description of the data returned by these methods.

HttpServletResponse   The output from the HttpServlet is much the same as the output from the GenericServlet, except that all the fields in the HTTP protocol that could be read by HttpServletRequest must be set before sending. The HTTPServletResponse class, shown in example 2.11, provides a rich method set for performing any HTTP header changes that may be required.

```
public interface HttpServletResponse extends ServletResponse {

  public void addCookie(Cookie cookie);

  public boolean containsHeader(String name);

  public String encodeURL (String url);
  public String encodeRedirectURL (String url);
  public String encodeUrl(String url);
  public String encodeRedirectUrl(String url);

  public void sendError(int sc, String msg) throws IOException;
  public void sendError(int sc) throws IOException;
  public void setStatus(int sc);
  public void setStatus(int sc, String sm);

  public void sendRedirect(String location) throws IOException;

  public void setDateHeader(String name, long date);
  public void setHeader(String name, String value);
  public void setIntHeader(String name, int value);

  public static final int SC_CONTINUE = 100;
  public static final int SC_SWITCHING_PROTOCOLS = 101;
  public static final int SC_OK = 200;
  public static final int SC_CREATED = 201;
  public static final int SC_ACCEPTED = 202;
  public static final int SC_NON_AUTHORITATIVE_INFORMATION = 203;
  public static final int SC_NO_CONTENT = 204;
```

```
public static final int SC_RESET_CONTENT = 205;
public static final int SC_PARTIAL_CONTENT = 206;
public static final int SC_MULTIPLE_CHOICES = 300;
public static final int SC_MOVED_PERMANENTLY = 301;
public static final int SC_MOVED_TEMPORARILY = 302;
public static final int SC_SEE_OTHER = 303;
public static final int SC_NOT_MODIFIED = 304;
public static final int SC_USE_PROXY = 305;
public static final int SC_BAD_REQUEST = 400;
public static final int SC_UNAUTHORIZED = 401;
public static final int SC_PAYMENT_REQUIRED = 402;
public static final int SC_FORBIDDEN = 403;
public static final int SC_NOT_FOUND = 404;
public static final int SC_METHOD_NOT_ALLOWED = 405;
public static final int SC_NOT_ACCEPTABLE = 406;
public static final int SC_PROXY_AUTHENTICATION_REQUIRED = 407;
public static final int SC_REQUEST_TIMEOUT = 408;
public static final int SC_CONFLICT = 409;
public static final int SC_GONE = 410;
public static final int SC_LENGTH_REQUIRED = 411;
public static final int SC_PRECONDITION_FAILED = 412;
public static final int SC_REQUEST_ENTITY_TOO_LARGE = 413;
public static final int SC_REQUEST_URI_TOO_LONG = 414;
public static final int SC_UNSUPPORTED_MEDIA_TYPE = 415;
public static final int SC_INTERNAL_SERVER_ERROR = 500;
public static final int SC_NOT_IMPLEMENTED = 501;
public static final int SC_BAD_GATEWAY = 502;
public static final int SC_SERVICE_UNAVAILABLE = 503;
public static final int SC_GATEWAY_TIMEOUT = 504;
public static final int SC_HTTP_VERSION_NOT_SUPPORTED = 505;
}
```

Example 2.11   javax.servlet.http.HttpServletResponse

Example use of HttpServlet   To illustrate `HttpServlet` in action, the example presented in the `GenericServlet` section will be rewritten using the `HttpServlet` as its base class. As before, the class overrides the initialization section of the servlet, so it may set the counter value as specified with the input parameter `init_count`. An example servlet using the `HttpServlet` as the base class is shown in example 2.12.

```
import javax.servlet.*;
import java.io.*;

public class simple extends HttpServlet {
  private int count = 0;

  public void init(ServletConfig _config) throws ServletException  {
    super.init(_config);
    String strCount = getInitParameter("init_count");
    count = Integer.parseInt(strCount);
  }

  public void service(ServletRequest _req, ServletResponse _res)
                           throws ServletException, IOException {
```

```
      count++;
      _res.setContentType("text/html");
      _res.setStatus( HttpServletResponse.SC_OK );
      PrintWriter Out = _res.getWriter();

      Out.println("<HTML><TITLE>Test Servlet</TITLE><BODY>");
      Out.println("Hello World: You are number <B>" + count +
                              " </B> to use this servlet.");
      Out.println("</BODY></HTML>");
      Out.flush();
   }
}
```
Example 2.12   Example of HttpServlet

Instead of sending back a line of text, the servlet generates a very simple web page for the client to display. As before, the counter variable is incremented to indicate another request has been made. Next, the content type of the data is set to the MIME type `text/html`, indicating an HTML page is being sent.

The status field for this transfer is set to SC_OK, with the HTML code being sent out using the `PrintWriter` class again. Setting the status in the header of the HTTP packet will allow the client browser to correctly decode the data coming from the output of the `PrintWriter` class.

Note   Creating web pages dynamically is a simple matter of sending the HTML tags to the client and setting the content type to `text/html` beforehand. If the content type is not set, then plain text is assumed; the client browser will display it as text and not encode the HTML tags.

2.7.1 Accessing web-based servlets

At this point, we have examined the basics of the servlet API and you have seen how to build and compile simple servlets. Now the servlets must be activated, or executed. Since how the servlets are called from the client depends upon the server to which they are attached, this section will assume that the servlets are running on a web server.

URL-based access   Assume the servlets' class file has been placed in the server's servlets directory. The servlet can be called by including /servlet/ before the servlet name in the URL. For example, if you set the class name of the sample servlet to `TestServlet`, then it could be accessed using http://<hostname>/servlet/TestServlet

This would load the servlet and execute its `service(…)` method. Subsequent visits would not reload the servlet again. If the servlet is part of a package, then include the complete class name in the URL http://<hostname>/servlet/com.nary.http.servlet.TestServlet

An alternative to this is to set up a complete alias for the servlet from the web server's administration section. This allows the servlet to masquerade as any name on your system, fooling the user into thinking the site is completely servlet- or CGI-free.

Server-side includes   One of the best uses of servlets is a feature known as server-side includes (SSI). References to servlets are embedded in HTML files. When they are referenced, they are invoked, with the output of the servlet being fed to the client at the point in the HTML file where the servlet was. After the servlet has completed, the HTML is processed and sent as normal. This allows the server to insert text straight into the output stream of HTML files, creating a completely dynamic page on the client side.

SSI HTML files are usually denoted with the SHTML file extension, which informs the web server that this file must be preprocessed before sending it out to the client. To reference a servlet from within an HTML file, the syntax shown in example 2.13 is used.

```
SERVLET name=ServletName code=ServletCode.class iParam1=iArg1
                            iParam2=iArg2 >
<param name="param1" value="val1">
<param name="param2" value="val2">
<param name="param3" value="val3">
.
.
<param name="paramX" value="valX">
</SERVLET>
```
Example 2.13   Server-side include syntax

Notice how similar the syntax is to the HTML <APPLET> tag. The similarity is not just coincidence; they both behave and look the same. When it encounters the <SERVLET> tag, the server performs the following procedure:

1 The servlet with the ServletName is located. If found, the server jumps to step 3.

2 The servlet class is loaded and assigned the ServletName, using the startup parameters iParam1 … iParamX, which can be picked up in the init(…) method.

3 The service(…) method is called with the param1 … paramX parameters accessible.

4 If the name parameter has been supplied, the server jumps to step 6.

5 The servlet is removed from memory.

6 The server continues processing the HTML file.

Notice how the servlet can be removed from memory again, if a logical name hasn't been given. This has the advantage of allowing servlets to be loaded and then removed from the server once they are completed, thereby freeing up server memory and resources if the servlet is not intended to be called often.

Note   This technique of loading and unloading on demand has reduced the servlet to that of the CGI model, as discussed in chapter 6, CGI overview. This is not recommended for servlets that will be used on a daily basis, as time will be lost loading and unloading servlets.

As a way to illustrate the different loading and unloading mechanisms, two different HTML files will be created: one where the servlet is logically named and another where it is not. We will use the SSI mechanism for loading the servlet, as shown in example 2.14.

```
<HTML><HEAD><TITLE>Hello World</TITLE></HEAD>
<BODY>
<H1>This servlet has been logically named:</H1>
<SERVLET NAME=TESTSERVLET INIT_COUNT=10>
</SERVLET>
</BODY></HTML>
```
Example 2.14   An HTML file where the servlet is logically named

Both HTML files are using the same servlet class, but see what happens when they are accessed one after another. Example 2.15 shows the servlet that isn't given a logical name.

```
<HTML><HEAD><TITLE>Hello World</TITLE></HEAD>
<BODY>
<H1>This servlet has not been logically named:</H1>
<SERVLET NAME=sample.class INIT_COUNT=10>
</SERVLET>
</BODY></HTML>
```
Example 2.15   An HTML file where the servlet is not logically named

When the HTML file that logically named the servlet is accessed, the output to the client is produced with an output value of 11, as shown in example 2.16. But when the HTML file that doesn't name the servlet is loaded, the output in example 2.17 is produced, showing an output of 100.

```
<HTML><HEAD><TITLE>Hello World</TITLE></HEAD>
<BODY>
<H1>This servlet has no name:</H1>
Hello World: You are number 11 to use this servlet
</BODY></HTML>
```
Example 2.16   The output from a logically named servlet

```
<HTML><HEAD><TITLE>Hello World</TITLE></HEAD>
<BODY>
<H1>This servlet has no name:</H1>
Hello World: You are number 100 to use this servlet
</BODY></HTML>
```
Example 2.17   The output from a nonnamed servlet

These different outputs occur because when the second HTML file is accessed, the logical name of the servlet has been given; therefore, it cannot be found running on the server, so the server loads a new instance and runs the servlet.

This demonstrates a very powerful, and sometimes annoying, feature of servlets. Powerful, because servlets can be loaded and unloaded on demand. Annoying, because it may take a long time for you to figure out why your SSI are not working on repeated visits.

Testing web-based servlets Included for development purposes as part of the servlet toolkit is a small web server on which servlets can be tested. This program, `servletrunner`, is found on both UNIX and NT platforms. To run it, you must have the JDK1.1 installed on the system.

The `servletrunner` program can take in a variety of command-line arguments as part of its startup. These are detailed in table 2.1.

Unlike the Java web server, aliases cannot be set up for servlets running under this environment. Instead, they must be accessed using the URL method detailed earlier in the section "URL-based access."

The `servletrunner` does not attempt to serve static HTML pages; therefore, it can become frustrating when you're attempting to test an overall system. The `servletrunner` is shipped purely for convenience and if any testing needs to be performed, look to one of the servlet engines that will be detailed in the following chapters.Servletrunner flags

Table 2.1 Servletrunner flags

Flag	Description
`-p <port>`	The port number to which the server will bind.
`-b <backlog>`	The backlog parameter for connecting new clients.
`-m <max>`	The maximum number of connection handlers.
`-t <timeout>`	The time out value for connections, in milliseconds.
`-d <directory>`	The directory in which all the servlet .class files are located.
`-r <directory>`	The directory in which all the HTML files are located.
`-s <filename>`	The file that holds all the servlet startup properties.
`-v`	The command to turn verbose output on.

Unlike the Java web server, aliases cannot be set up for servlets running under this environment. Instead, they must be accessed using the URL method detailed earlier in the section "URL-based access."

The `servletrunner` does not attempt to serve static HTML pages; therefore, it can become frustrating when you're attempting to test an overall system. The `servletrunner` is shipped purely for convenience and if any testing needs to be performed, look to one of the servlet engines that will be detailed in the following chapters.

2.8 From here

Now you've seen the nuts and bolts of the servlet API and how it operates. The remaining chapters will take a close look at how servlets can be used in real-world web-based applications.

This chapter, along with appendix A: Java servlet API, can be used as a reference for the forthcoming examples.

C H A P T E R   3

Java web server

- Learn the ins and outs of the Java Web Server from Sun Microsystems. Emphasis will be placed on the installation and setup procedures.

This book is all about Java servlets. As you know by now, a Java servlet is a small Java class that runs in response to a client request, and it is typically used within the web environment. Back in the early days of the Java servlet's history, a web server was built to prove the technology. In much the same way HotJava was developed to demonstrate the power of Java applets, the Java Web Server (JWS) was developed to show the world the power of Java at the server side through the use of servlets.

Since the JWS is technically the first web server ever to support servlets, it deserves a little honor. This chapter will look at its installation and administration. When I began writing this book, the Java Web Server was freely available as a download. But when the book went to print, it was no longer available as a free download. However, it is available as a thirty-day try-before-you-buy version. So you can use this chapter to preview the JWS, and then you can determine whether it is right for you.

3.1 Installation

The JWS comes in two flavors: Windows NT and Solaris. Each one uses the exact same class files, since the Java Web Server was built using only Java. The Windows version has a complete installation wizard with it, which creates all the necessary directories and offers the ability to set up the server as an NT service.

Figure 3.1 shows the resulting directory structure after the installation is complete. As you can see, the majority of the directories are self-explanatory.

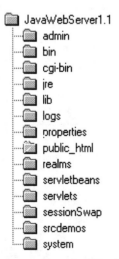

Figure 3.1 The Java Web Server directory structure

The scripts for starting the server are located in ./bin/httpd; this is a small executable that sets up the necessary environment variables and passes the correct class for execution to the Java Virtual Machine. It will then spawn an MS-DOS box and run quite happily in the background. Pressing CTRL-C will stop the server. Do not close the MS-DOS box down before stopping the server. Although it will stop the server, it isn't the cleanest way of shutting it down.

By default, the JWS ships with a virtual machine already installed. The scripts all use this one (again, by default), but you can change the virtual machine the web server uses by changing the scripts and using the ./bin/jserv program instead.

All the user-defined servlets are located in the ./servlets directory. If you are using the Java Web Server examples in this book, then copy the compiled class files to this directory. Doing so will allow you to access them using the URL http://<your server>/servlet/<yourServlet>

The default document root for all your html files is located in ./public_html. As you will see later in this chapter, this directory can be changed to specify another location. All the log files will be created in the ./logs directory, with the /sessionSwap holding all the session management sessions.

The web server starts up on port 8080 by default, and once it is started, it serves pages from the ./public_html directory. The ./lib directory is where the Java libraries reside, including the jws.jar file. The configuration information for all the web services that have been installed is held in the ./properties and ./realms directories.

The next section will describe the administration process of JWS.

3.2 Administration

The administration of this web server is performed through an applet, which can be accessed at the URL http://<yourserver>:9090/index.html

This URL will display an applet; the applet will ask you to supply a username and password. If this is the first time you've accessed the site, use the username/password pair admin/admin to log in.

You will then be shown a list of all the servers that are currently running. The Java Web Server ships with a proxy server, and depending on which version you purchase, it may come with a secure web server.

Note At some point, you may forget your password and be locked out of the administration applet. If this occurs, then don't fret. Help is at hand. Go to the file realms/data/adminRealm/keyfile in the server root directory, and open it in a text editor. Find the line admin::xxxxx= and replace it with admin::YWRt aW4=. Then save the file again. This procedure will reset the password and username back to admin/admin.

The remaining sections of this chapter will look at all the different options that can be configured. You're probably wondering why you should go into such detail with a web server that is not freely available. The reason is simple. The Java Web Server was the first server to support servlets. Consequently, the majority of web servers and servlet engines that were produced afterwards very closely mirror the options available here. Knowing how to configure the JWS will enable you to understand any other alternative servlet platform without too much difficulty.

3.2.1 Setup: network

Clicking the Setup button and selecting the Network option in the left-hand frame displays the panel shown in figure 3.2. If JWS is the only web server that will be running on the machine, the standard port for HTTP (which is 80) may be employed. However, you can choose any number between 1 and 65,535, after you make sure the number won't clash with any other Transmission Control Protocol (TCP) service running on the same machine. For this reason, I recommend you choose a port number greater than 1023. That way, possible conflicts with standard services such as File Transfer Protocol (FTP) can be avoided. All the standard TCP services (FTP, POP, NNTP) have port numbers below 1023 allocated to them.

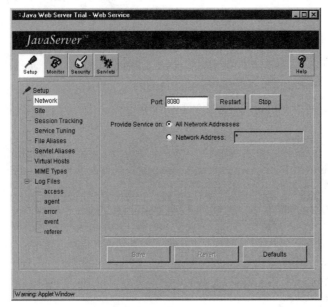

Figure 3.2 JWS: network options

JWS can run on a multihomed machine that listens on more than one Internet Protocol (IP) address. If you wish to force JWS to listen for requests on only one of the IP addresses, you can specify it by clicking the Network Address radio button and supplying the desired IP address.

From here, you can also restart or shutdown the server. This is necessary if you change particular server parameters, such as the port number. Not all changes require the web server to be restarted.

3.2.2 Setup: site

The Site option allows you to control the behavior of the web server as it serves documents to the client. Within this panel are four separate tabs: Contents (figure 3.3), Languages, Character Sets, and Options.

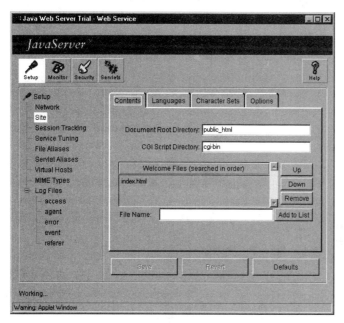

Figure 3.3 JWS: site setup

The manner in which JWS serves HTML files is determined within the Contents section. The first parameter that can be changed is the Document Root directory. This is the pathname for the location where all the HTML files will be stored. It can be relative to the installation directory, or, if it's a full system pathname, it can map on to any directory available to the machine. The CGI Script directory option follows the same format and describes the location of the CGI scripts. Of course this directory will be *very* empty, since this is a book on servlets and I don't want to unnecessarily promote CGI!

When the user enters a URL without explicitly naming a file, the web server must determine which file to serve the user. Most web servers only allow one default file to be specified, but JWS allows multiple types to be defined. It will search for the files in the order they appear in the list until one of the criteria is satisfied. If none are found, then the directory listing will be displayed (assuming the administrator hasn't disabled the feature in another section).

Use the Languages and Character Sets tabs to define the different languages and character sets the web server can serve, and in what order it serves them.

The Options tab allows you to toggle a number of options on and off. Using one of the options, you can instruct JWS to perform security checks, where each request is checked against all the known Access Control Lists (ACLs) that have been set up in the Security section (this will be discussed later in this chapter). Another option will determine whether JWS displays the directory listing if the user doesn't supply a filename with the URL, and the file isn't one of the welcome-html files as described earlier.

You can also disable and enable servlet chaining, which is where the output of one servlet feeds the input of another.

3.2.3 Setup: session tracking

The Session Tracking option controls how the web server will handle the session management implementation. You can optionally turn session tracking on or off, and you can decide whether it should use URL rewriting or cookies as a means of storing session mappings.

3.2.4 Setup: service tuning

Within the Service Tuning option, you have control over the performance of JWS. Three sets of parameters can be set: General, Handler Threads (figure 3.4), and Connection Persistence.

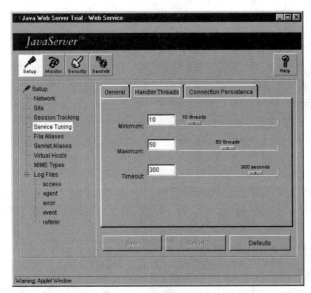

Figure 3.4 JWS: service tuning options

Under the General tab, you can specify the maximum number of client connections the server will attempt to service. It is set at the default of 50, but it can go up to 100. If your web server is particularly servlet-intensive (meaning that each servlet takes a significant amount of time to service), I suggest that you lower this figure so the web server has more processing cycles to devote to each client request (and so it might possibly complete the service in less time). In this section, you can also set the amount of memory the server will use as a cache.

In the Handler Threads tab, you control how the server uses the thread pool it reserves for handling incoming requests. You can set the minimum and maximum number of threads that the pool will contain. If the expiration time passes, then threads are removed until at least the minimum number remains in the pool.

In the Connection Persistence tab, you can control the connection between the server and the client. The HTTP protocol is a stateless communication medium. The client opens up a socket connection to the server and makes a request for a resource. The server then services that request. If the client makes another request, then another connection is opened. It is possible to keep too many connections from being open and reuse the existing connection for a number of requests. In the Connection Persistence tab, you can set the number of requests the server can service in the one socket connection. The timeout before the socket is closed is also set. Be careful not to set this too high, or the server will be hanging on to socket connections too long.

3.2.5 Setup: file aliases

The File Aliases option allows you to create file mappings. This is a very powerful mechanism for providing shortcuts to long pathnames that result in very long URL addresses. For example, assume you have a directory that is packed full of valuable information, but it is ten levels deep. You could create an alias for the directory that allows the user to access it without typing in the full pathname. For example:

```
Real Path: /dictionary/a/2/anteater/african/north
File Alias: /anteater
```

When the user entered the pathname "anteater," he would be accessing the files found in the real path.

As soon as the file alias is accepted, it is active. There is no need to restart the server when adding or removing such mappings. All settings are relative to the document root, not the server root. You can, of course, put in the complete pathname of the directory.

If the web server is to act for multiple users' home pages, they can be set up using the standard ~ notion, where the URL would become http://<yourdomain>/~username

On the server, each user would have a directory named exactly the same as their username.

3.2.6 Setup: servlet aliases

The Servlet Aliases option (figure 3.5) allows you to set up mappings between logical URLs and servlets. Doing so allows users to access a servlet as if it were a normal HTML file. For example, let's say the default mapping .shtml is mapped onto the ssinclude servlet. This means that all files requested with a sthml extension will be passed to the ssinclude file for processing.

The servlet is referenced by a logical name, which is set up in the Servlets section described later in this chapter.

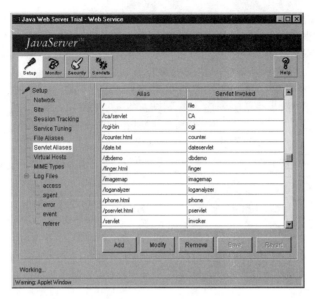

Figure 3.5 JWS: servlet aliases

In a servlet chain, the output of one servlet is fed into the input of another servlet, and then the output of the last servlet in the chain is fed to the client making the original request. Creating an alias and then specifying the servlets as a comma-separated list with no spaces can set up a chain. For example, to set up a chain where the `ghostfile` servlet gets called before the `file` servlet, the alias would be:

```
Alias: /
Servlet Invoked: ghostfile,file
```

The first servlet in the chain is the first servlet listed in the Servlet Invoked column. Be aware that this isn't the only way to set up a servlet chain—you can also associate a MIME type with a servlet. This will be detailed later in the MIME Types section.

3.2.7 Setup: virtual hosts

There are two main ways in which a virtual host can be used with the JWS. The first is where each virtual host has a separate IP address associated with it; the second is where one IP address is used for all virtual hosts.

The first method is the most common. It assumes the machine on which the JWS is running is set up to receive packets for more than one IP address. Setting this up is specific to the operating system running the JWS (and therefore it won't be covered in this book). One of the most popular web servers available is the free UNIX-based Apache server. This server is especially popular due to the easy way it handles multiple virtual hosts without the need for complicated configuration files. This server uses the one-IP-per-virtual-host mechanism. Although it's very functional, the Internet community is facing a serious IP shortage problem—the Internet is running out of addresses. Therefore, using virtual hosts you can host multiple servers on one IP address.

To overcome this problem, an extension built into the next version of the HTTP protocol allows many web servers running on the same machine to share the same IP address. The new version of HTTP (1.1) specifies the domain name of the destined packet inside the header of each packet. The new version operates by having the domain name servers return the same IP address for all the virtual hosts running on one machine. Before the packet is sent out, the HTTP protocol specifies the IP and domain address of the server it is attempting to connect to. Therefore, IP addresses are not used unnecessarily. The majority of the mainstream client browsers in use today support this new addition to the HTTP protocol, and they can safely connect and transfer documents from a virtual host that's sharing an IP address.

In the Virtual Hosts option, you can also set the hostname and the document route where all the files for this host will be located. The hostname would be the fully qualified domain name, such as www.another.web.server.atmydomain.com. The document root is relative to the server root directory; it can be a full pathname to a location outside of this directory.

All servlet and file aliases, servlet names, and log files are shared among the virtual web servers.

This process will work for the majority of modern-day browsers, but the ones that do not support the HTTP 1.0 protocol will not be able to use this feature. They will be served from the default document root.

3.2.8 Setup: MIME types

The MIME Types option is used to add, modify, or delete MIME types that JWS uses to transfer files to the client.

A MIME type is described as `type/subtype`, and it is associated with a particular file format. For example, a standard HTML document has a MIME type of `text/html` for extensions of .html and .htm. This allows the server to correctly deal with any incoming client requests and send the data back properly formatted. If a particular file extension is not found, then the `text/plain` MIME type is assumed.

To add a new MIME type or a new extension, click the Add button and fill in the extension and MIME type.

Servlets can be chained using MIME types, and at the time of this writing, the support for this chaining through the administration applet was nonexistent. A servlet can be associated with a unique, user-defined MIME type. When another servlet generates output of this type, the servlet associated with the MIME is invoked, with the output of the previous servlet forming the input of the recently invoked servlet. The file

`/properties/process/javawebserver/webpageservice/mimeservlets.properties` which is located in the server root, contains a list of servlet MIME mappings. To create a mapping, add a new line to the file in the form `MIME=<servlet>`. For example, the mapping

```
alan/db-output=parseHtmlForm
```

would invoke the `parseHtmlForm` servlet if another servlet used the MIME type `alan/db-output`. A servlet sets the MIME type of its outgoing data using the `setContentType(...)` method.

3.2.9 Setup: log files

The Log Files option, shown in figure 3.6, controls the logging facilities of the log files that are produced by the server's services. The setup of each log file is exactly the same. Five different log files can be produced: access, agent, error, event, and referer.

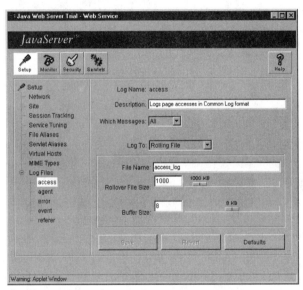

Figure 3.6 JWS: log files options

The access log file logs all incoming client requests, such as the date, client, and resource request. This log is used to produce many of the statistics about how the site is running. The agent log stores information about the browser types being used to connect to the site. The error log, as the name suggests, logs all errors encountered by the server. This log captures all logging from user servlets. The event log is used to log when the server was started and closed down. Finally, the referer log stores information regarding the file the client was accessing.

The Description field contains a single line of text that describes the operation of the log file. This may be changed, if you want, but it serves no real purpose. The Which Messages field lets you control the amount of data the server writes to the log file. The log type will determine what options are available. For example, the error log allows you to log only the major problems and leave the rest.

Note The more information the server has to write, the more time it takes to do so, and the more disk space it uses. If the log files are never intended to be used, I recommend that you turn them off. By default, only the access, error, and event logs are used.

The Log To field determines the type of log output that will be produced. A number of options are available.

- Rolling file
  A rolling file is continually written to until the size specified in Rollover File Size is reached. A file is then created. The previous file is named whatever is listed in the File Name field, plus a .X file extension. As more files are written, the older files are renamed to .X+1 until 9 is reached; after that point, they are deleted. Historical data can therefore be kept without the fear of deleting anything important. The Buffer Size field specifies the amount of data the server should buffer before writing the log file. The maximum size a rolling log file can become is 10 MB, with up to nine files before deletion occurs. A maximum of 100 MB of log data (including the active file) of log files is allowed.

- Single file
  The single file option writes to the same file. The directory is allocated a specific disk space through the operating system, and if the limit is reached, then the server starts writing at the start of the file again.

- Standard output
  Instead of logging to a file, the terminal window the JWS is running from will be used to display data. If the JWS is run under Windows 95 or WindowsNT, this will be the MS-DOS console window.

- Error output
  The log entries will be written to whatever the server is using as the standard error output.

Separate log files are kept for each type of service that is running on the system, making it easy to determine which event was for which service.

3.2.10 *Monitor: log output*

This section of the administration applet allows you to view in real-time what is happening to the service. Each service has its own Monitor section that will operate on its own set of log files.

Clicking the Monitor button at the top of the JWS window and selecting the Log Output option from the left-hand frame will display the panel shown in figure 3.7. This panel is used to view the output to any of the active log files as and when an update occurs.

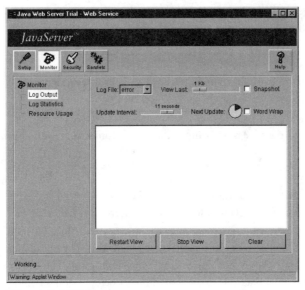

Figure 3.7 JWS: log output

Using this facility is analogous to using the UNIX tail command, which is used to view the end of files and is updated when the file is updated. The Log File drop-down list allows you to select which log file will be examined. Only the server log files that have been activated as described in the previous section will be available for viewing.

The View Last field determines the amount of data that will be displayed in the output window, which is equal to the amount of data that will be viewed from the log file. The Snapshot checkbox controls how the data is fed. If the box is unchecked, then the data is displayed as the data is written out to the log file. If the box is checked, the data is read back from the end of the file up to the size of the value in the View Last field. Clicking the Restart View button sets all this in motion.

The Update Interval option sets the number of seconds between updates of the output window. The range is one to fifteen seconds. The Word Wrap checkbox controls how the data is displayed in the output window. If the checkbox is checked, then the text is wrapped; otherwise, a horizontal scroll bar is required to view the data.

Clicking the Restart View and Stop View buttons respectively starts and stops the viewing of the output logs. Take note that these actions have no effect on what is written out to the log file as specified in the Log File field.

3.2.11   *Monitor: log statistics*

The Log Statistics option provides a simple log file analysis of the access log file, which is the log file that records the client request. This function can be run while the server is running (and logging) in the background.

Data can be sorted two different ways: by domain or by time. Sorting by domain name means the data is arranged in alphabetical order (.com, .co.uk, etc.) Sorting the data by time means the data is arranged in increasing time increments, which is how it is written to the log file.

Once you choose the sorting method, you can choose the reporting period. Data can be charted for the current day, month, or week, or since the log file was started.

Finally, select the data format: pie chart, bar chart, or simple table list.

3.2.12   Monitor: resource usage

The last of the real-time reporting facilities is the Resource Usage option shown in figure 3.8. This is used to take a peek at what is happening inside the server for the given service. As with the log file, each resource usage section is independent of the log files and of the other services.

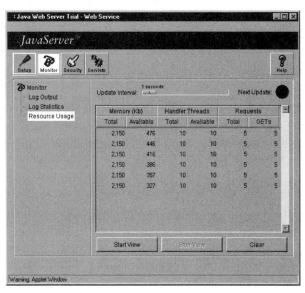

Figure 3.8 JWS: resource usage

The Next Update option sets the time interval between each update. With every update, a new entry is appended to the end of the table shown in the panel.

The Memory column shows the amount of data available to the system (the Available column) and the amount of data being used by the particular service (the Total column). This allows you to adjust the memory setting as described in the earlier section on server settings to a more efficient size, depending on the environment the service is running under.

The Handler Threads column details the total number of available threads that the service has for servicing client requests, as well as the number of threads that are currently available to service new client requests. The busier the service is, the smaller the number of available threads should be. Increasing the total number of threads, as described earlier, may increase the performance of your service.

The Requests column lists the total number of requests that have been handled by the service, along with the number of GETs. A GET request is the most common request type; it is used whenever the user asks for any document or file.

3.2.13 Security: users

The administrator can maintain the security of the web server within the Security section of the JWS administration. Click the Security button at the top of the JWS screen to display the options. JWS can restrict access to both files and servlets for specific users or groups of users. This section will explain how you, as the administrator, can protect a resource.

The lowest common denominator in setting up a security system is the user list, which is the list of users that will be associated with particular groups and resources, and who will be denied or granted access. Each user is associated with a realm, which is the collective name for a list of users, groups, or ACLs.

JWS has three default realms when it is first installed: defaultRealm, certificate-Realm, and servletMgrRealm. If the JWS is running under UNIX, then an additional realm, Unix, exists. If JWS is running under NT, then the NT realm is listed. The default-Realm is used to control access to the entire example servlets area and resources, and it may be used for general document security. The servletMgrRealm is used to control access to signed servlets, and it is control by the software vendors of the particular servlets and classes. The certificateRealm is used to authenticate users making requests on the HTTPS protocol.

To add a new user to any given realm, select the relevant realm and click the Add button. A small dialog box will be displayed; enter a username and password here. Click OK, and that user will be created as part of that realm.

Note If the JWS is running under UNIX or NT, then users cannot be added to the Unix or NT realms through the administration applet.

If a user has been added to a particular realm, he is not automatically part of any other realm. Even if the usernames are identical, users that are in one or more realms are considered distinct from each other.

3.2.14 Security: groups

Groups are, as the name suggests, groups of users that have the same security rights. Assigning a group of users to a resource is much more efficient than individually assigning users to each resource, and it's a lot easier for the administrator. For example, imagine a resource being controlled by a list of users. When a new user is added to the list the user must also be added to all the resources the administrator deems fit for his access. If more than one resource is involved, this can quickly become an administrative nightmare. Using the Groups option, a group can be assigned to a resource, and any new users who are added to the group are automatically given access to all the resources the group has.

A group is considered as part of a realm, and as with the users, groups in different realms (even if they have the same name) are considered distinct from each other. For this reason, before any operations can be performed on a group, the correct realm has to be chosen, using the Realm drop-down list at the top of the panel shown in figure 3.9.

To create a group that is to be associated with the realm selected in the Realm drop-down list, click the Add Group button. A small dialog box will prompt you for the name of the new group. Type the name and click OK. In the bottom half of the panel, you'll see two list boxes. The Members list shows users who are members of the group, and the Non-Members list shows all the remaining users that exist in that particular realm. Users can be added and removed using the Add and Remove buttons between the lists; these buttons move users from one list to the other.

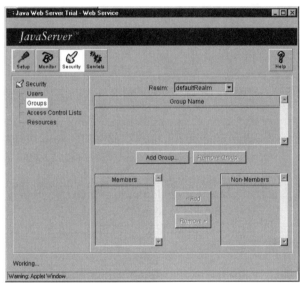

Figure 3.9 JWS: groups of users

3.2.15 *Security: Access Control Lists*

An ACL, a list that is associated with a particular resource, determines what actions may be performed on a resource and which groups or users may access it.

An ACL is associated with a particular realm. Using the panel shown in figure 3.10, ACL lists can be created. Clicking the Add button displays a small dialog box which prompts you for a new ACL name. Once an ACL is created, it may be assigned permissions and groups of users.

To add a permission set for files and directories, fill in the dialog box shown in figure 3.11. Click the Add Permission button to open this dialog box.

Using the Add Permisson dialog box, you can deny or allow access to certain operations for any user, group, or computer. Selecting the user, group, or computer is done by

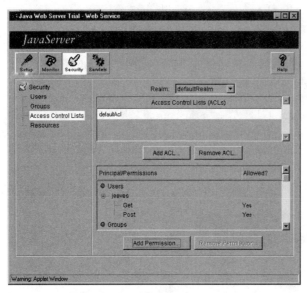

Figure 3.10 JWS: viewing ACLs

checking the correct radio button and then selecting the name from the Principal Name list. Three different operations can be either denied or allowed when you're dealing with files and folders: GET, POST, or PUT. These are the basic HTTP operations. For example, if the ACL were to be used to deny access to a specific directory, then selecting GET and checking the Denied radio button would ensure that no documents or directory listings would be sent to the client, unless they had permission to access them.

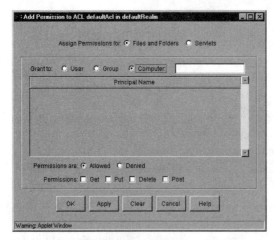

Figure 3.11 JWS: adding permissions

Since servlets are an intricate part of the JWS, they may be secured in the same way files and folders are. Security for a servlet can be set up by clicking the Servlets radio button at the top of the Add Permission window; the panel will change to the one shown in figure 3.12.

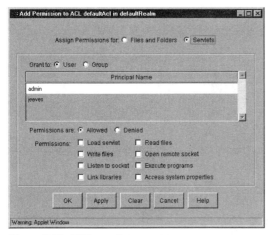

Figure 3.12 JWS: servlet security

Setting the permissions is performed in much the same way as it is for files and folders, except there are eight different operations that can be either denied or allowed.

Clicking the Apply button will make the changes active, but keep the dialog window open in case you want to modify additional parameters.

3.2.16 Security: resources

The Resources option, shown in figure 3.13, is where specific resources are assigned to specific ACLs. Three pieces of information are required for each type of resource: the type of resource, the authentication scheme, and the ACL assigned to the resource.

Click the Add button to set up a new resource to be protected. The dialog box shown in figure 3.14 will be displayed. The first thing that has to be set is the authentication method the JWS will use to retrieve the username and password from the client. The difference between the two mechanisms is the way the password is sent from the client to the server.

Select the ACL list that will be assumed for this resource from the ACL drop-down list. Now that you've set up the "way" and the "how," the final parameter is the "what." The actual resource that is to be protected can be a file, a folder, or a servlet.

The file or directory that is entered in the Pathname field is relative to the document root. If a folder is protected, all the files and subfolders underneath this resource are also protected.

To protect a servlet, click the Servlet radio button and choose the servlet that is to be protected from the drop-down list.

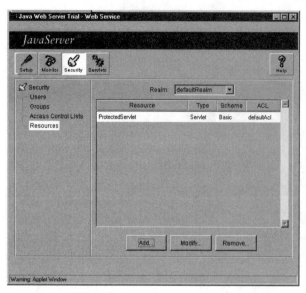

Figure 3.13 JWS: protecting resources

Note If any security measure is added, modified, or deleted, you don't need to restart the server in order for the changes to take effect.

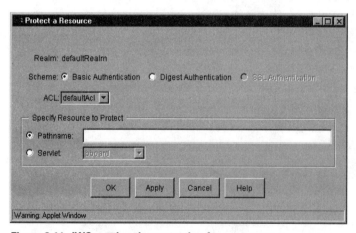

Figure 3.14 JWS: setting the protection for a resource

The file or directory that is entered in the Pathname field is relative to the document root. If a folder is protected, all the files and subfolders underneath this resource are also protected.

Table 3.1 Security Operations

Operation	Description
Load servlet	Controls whether a named servlet can be loaded.
Write files	Controls whether the servlet is allowed to write files on the local system. If the servlet is a user-defined servlet, which has not been verified, it is wise to disallow files from being written.
Listen to socket	Controls the access to the network operations that control sockets.
Link libraries	Allows the servlet to link to any other library or servlet.
Read files	Controls whether the servlet may be allowed to read any file on the local file system. If the servlet has not been verified, allowing this operation could be potentially fatal.
Open remote socket	Controls whether the servlet can open a connection to any machine on the network.
Execute programs	Controls the ability for the servlet to run local programs.
Access system properties	Determines whether the servlet is allowed to look at the system properties of the server.

To protect a servlet, click the Servlet radio button and choose the servlet that is to be protected from the drop-down list.

> **Note** If any security measure is added, modified, or deleted, you don't need to restart the server in order for the changes to take effect.

3.2.17 Servlets

Use the Servlet section to add, modify, and remove servlets from the service (click the Servlet button at the top of the screen to display the options). If a servlet is to be called using a URL, invoked remotely, or even started automatically at server startup, then it must be added to the list of known servlets.

To add a servlet, first select the Add option to display the panel shown in figure 3.15. The Servlet Name is a unique name by which the servlet will be known. It can be an alphanumeric string with no spaces. Type the class name that represents the servlet in the Servlet Class text box. Be aware that the class extension should not be entered. If no package information is specified as part of the servlet class, then it is assumed that it resides in the /servlets directory from the server root. If the servlet you are adding is a ServletBean, click the Yes button next to Bean Servlet and type the filename in the Jar File text box.

After you've added a new servlet, you can configure additional parameters as shown in figure 3.16.

The Name field displays the unique name that has been assigned to the servlet, and the Description field gives a quick overview of the servlet. It is very common for the description to be left blank.

The Class Name field shows the name of the servlet class file, minus the .class extension. Use the Load at Startup radio button to determine whether the servlet should be

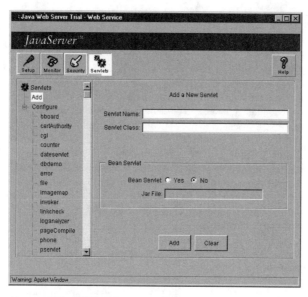

Figure 3.15 JWS: adding a servlet

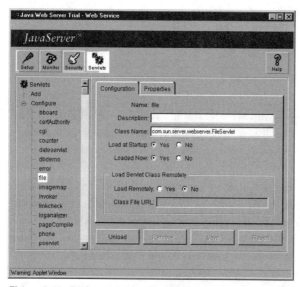

Figure 3.16 JWS: servlet configuration

loaded at the server startup, and use the Loaded Now radio button to indicate whether the servlet is currently in memory.

Servlets do not necessarily have to reside on the local system to be loaded—they may be located on any server connected to the network. If the server is on the Internet, then any machine may source a servlet. If the servlet is remote, then check the Load Remotely Yes radio button and type the URL of the servlet in the Class File URL field. This field should only contain enough information to describe the location of the servlet, and it must not include the servlet class name. For example, if the ghostfile servlet is located in the main document root directory on the www.n-ary.com server, then the Class File URL field should contain: http://www.n-ary.com/

When the servlet is first called, it will be loaded from the remote location and executed using the resources on the local machine. The servlet does not use any of the remote location resources when executing. The remote location merely acts as a file server.

Using the Properties tab (figure 3.17), you can enter in key/value pairs that will be passed to the servlet when it first loads up. You can retrieve the parameters using the `get-InitParameter(…)` method call.

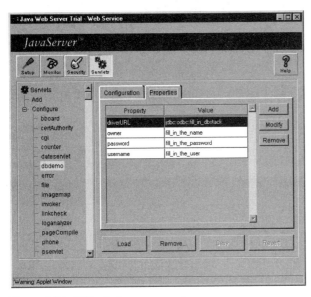

Figure 3.17 JWS: startup arguments

3.3 Proxy server

This service, shown in figure 3.18, allows for the fine-tuning of the proxy run time parameters.

The caching attributes of the proxy server are set within the Disk Cache tab. If caching is enabled (select the On radio button to enable it), then the directory where all the cache files will be stored has to be specified. This is relative to the server root. The Max. Cache Size field sets the maximum number of bytes the cache directory will hold. The largest cachc is 10 MB.

The proxy server can be part of a proxy chain, meaning the proxy service has to request documents from another proxy before it can service the client request. If this is the

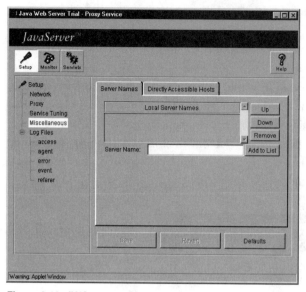

Figure 3.18 JWS: proxy settings

case, then the Host and Port tab allows you to change the port number the proxy server will use.

The proxy can be configured to not act as a proxy for certain hosts. This is particularly useful for machines located within the same network.

3.4 Secure web server

JWS comes with a secure web server that allows it to service HTTPS requests. The settings for this server are identical to those described in the Web Server section in this chapter.

3.5 Core servlets

This chapter introduces you to the JWS which is completely written in Java using the JDK1.1 library; it can run on any platform supporting this run time environment.

The JWS is based on the Java server API. The JWS is one of the best examples of where servlets can be used to extend the functionality of a server, as the majority of the web server's functionality is written entirely with servlets.

The JWS uses servlets to extend the functionality of the basic web server. These are:

- File servlet
  The file servlet is the most important servlet of the JWS, since it serves all the documents to the client, and as part of its functionality, it offers a caching feature to improve document retrieval.

- Invoker servlet
  The invoker servlet is used to launch other servlets in the server.

- Server-side include servlet
  The SSI servlet is used to provide the necessary redirection and execution of servlets when used with HTML documents. An SSI takes the output of the servlet and places it in the output stream of the HTML document.

- CGI servlet
  The CGI servlet is used to launch and control CGI scripts.

- Imagemap servlet
  The imagemap servlet is used to provide server-side image map processing.

When you look at the administration section, you will notice that these servlets are already loaded, because they provide the core functionality of JWS. It is important to know they exist, especially when you're writing custom servlets to take over the responsibility of other servlets, or when you're deploying a servlet in a chaining configuration.

C H A P T E R   4

Servlet engines

- Take a quick look at the two most popular servlet engines available commercially: JRun and ServletExec.

- Examine the installation and maintenance procedures for each of these servlet engines.

In the last chapter we looked at the JWS from Sun. The reason we studied this server is simple: chances are, the majority of developers will have exposure to it at some point in their servlet-development career. It is one of the easiest ways to have a development environment with a fully functional web server. But what happens when you want to deploy your servlet applications to another server platform? What if that server platform has no support for servlet execution? What are you to do?

Well, help is at hand. You can request the services of a third-party piece of software that will run your servlets for you. This software, known as a servlet engine, or runner, is available from a variety of well-known Java companies who support all the major web servers.

4.1 Test environment

This chapter is not meant to be used as a sales tool. It is not intended to recommend products or make criticisms on the products listed. That's your job as systems integrator. We will merely look at each product in a little detail. Understanding these products will prepare you better if you decide you need the services of a servlet engine.

For the sake of fairness, I took a standard PII-300 PC machine, cleaned it, and installed a fresh copy of Microsoft NT 4.0 Server (Service Pack 4) on it. For the web server, I installed one of the most popular servers, Netscape Enterprise Server 3.0, as an NT service.

Each of the servlet runners/engines in this chapter supports many different web servers. Although I have chosen to demonstrate only one, the others are just as easy to install.

Each section will look at the installation and the administration of one servlet runner.

4.2 ServletExec

ServletExec is produced by New Atlanta Communications, which is based in Atlanta, GA. Vince Bonfanti, the CEO of New Atlanta, is one the main driving forces behind this web-based application server. Bonfanti leads a team of dedicated developers who, as a group, have produced a whole range of server-based products. Only a small number of companies have been at the forefront of servlet development from the beginning. New Atlanta is one of them. ServletExec is available from New Atlanta's web site: http://www.newatlanta.com/

After you download a 1.6 MB file, a module that will make Netscape Enterprise servlet-enabled is ready to install. The next sections will take you through the complete installation and configuration of ServletExec.

4.3 Installation

The file you download is a limited demo version. It is limited in the fact that it will only serve 100 requests before it must be registered. After 100 requests, ServletExec switches to Lite mode, in which the majority of the advanced features are disabled. However, you can restart the web server and gain all features back again, so ServletExec is developer friendly—developers testing their servlet applications can freely use it. Registering the software is a simple matter of purchasing a serial key from the New Atlanta web site. No further download is required.

Double-clicking on the downloaded file launches the installation wizard, which will guide you through the installation process. This installation wizard is smart enough to find Netscape for itself and discover the multiple virtual hosts that Netscape is hosting. You have to run the installation program again for each virtual host, but when the process is this easy, it's not a problem to go through the process again.

After you've run the installation, restart the Netscape server, and it is ready to serve servlets. Here's one thing you should know, however: ServletExec does not ship with a Java Virtual Machine. It assumes a JVM has already been installed somewhere on the machine. If it has, ServletExec will find it; otherwise, you will not be able to service servlets.

Figure 4.1 shows the directory structure that is created from the install. This directory is installed underneath the main Netscape Enterprise directory within the plug ins directory. For each virtual host that Netscape is hosting, separate log and servlet directories exist within this directory structure.

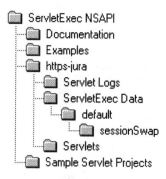

Figure 4.1 ServletExec directory structure

All your developed servlets are installed in the /ServletExec NSAPI/https-????/Servlets directory. After installation, only a few test servlets exist in this directory. You can test the validity of the installation by visiting the URL: http://<your host>/servlet/TestServlet

This servlet displays an HTML page which contains a variety of parameters about the HTML request that has just been serviced. If you do not see this page, or if the browser refuses to find the resource, restart your server and see if the problem still exists. If anything serious went wrong, the installation program will have found it and flagged the warning. Finally, make sure you're accessing the correct virtual host. The installation is now complete and you're ready to look at the administration issues.

4.3.1 Administration

Now that ServletExec is up and running, you will want to change some of its operational parameters, such as how it deals with preloaded servers.

New Atlanta hasn't felt the need to completely Java-itize the administration system. As a result, instead of a Java applet gathering the administrators' requests, very clean, well-laid-out HTML is presented (figure 4.2). This gives you more speed, which is a big advantage. Changing a parameter quickly is very easy, which is important when you're administrating the system and you want to see the results of your changes quickly.

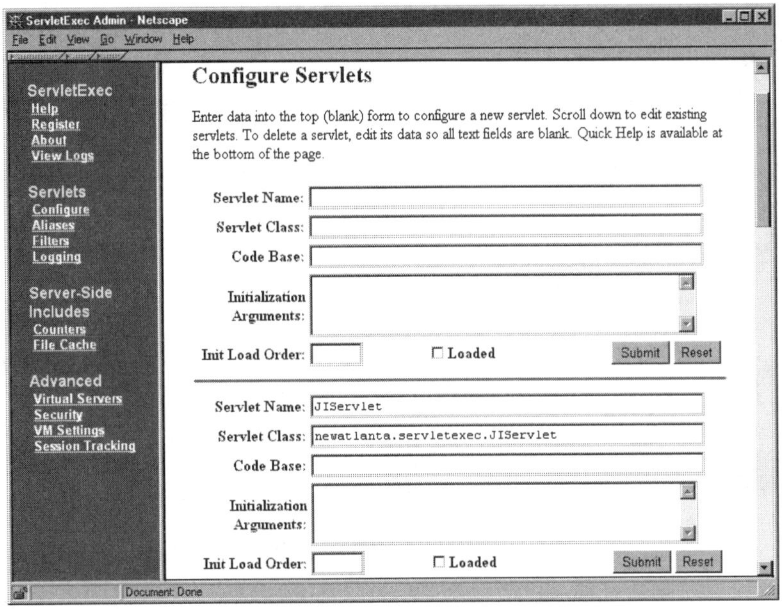

Figure 4.2 ServletExec servlets

The layout of the administration tool consists of two frames: menu and active frame. You can choose which of the many features you wish to access from a list of possible items.

The demo version does not protect the administration page behind a username/password combination. You need to purchase the full version to gain this functionality.

The overall administration facility closely mirrors the options that are available to the Java Web Server, as discussed in the previous chapter.

Servlets   You specify the servlets you wish to register with the engine in the Servlet section in the left-hand frame. This enables you to refer to them through a logical name, maintain more than one instance of the servlet, source the servlet class files from a remote machine, or specify to start the servlet running at startup.

Figure 4.3 shows the HTML page that is used to set up this information. As you can see, the top half of the page contains fields in which you provide information about your servlet. The bottom half of the page shows existing servlets; you can edit these as you want. One of the nice features of ServletExec is the ability to select the order in which the servlets are loaded (notice the Init Lead Order field at the bottom of each section). In some instances this can be a very desirable feature, such as when you need to specify the order in which a system is booted.

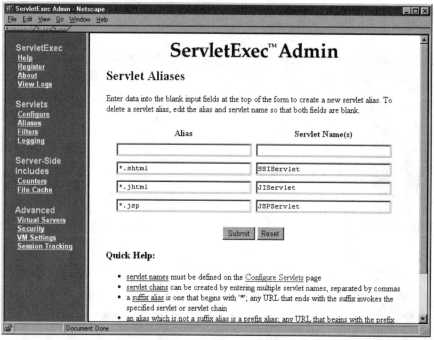

Figure 4.3 ServletExec servlet aliases

Using the "Code Base" field you can load servlets from another location. However, since they are untrusted they are limited in their functionality. ServletExec does not allow untrusted servlets to access the following:

- The Java networking classes
- External (native) processes
- Dynamic (native) libraries
- File operations that require permission

After you register a servlet with the engine, you can set up aliases and chains. Using the HTML page, from the left-hand frame shown in figure 4.4, you can easily set up an alias to the servlet named in the previous setup phrase.

To create a servlet chain, use a comma-delimited list to specify the servlets that should be included. Servlet execution is done in a left-to-right order.

Under the Filters option, you can set up servlet-to-MIME mappings. This allows you to have your servlet respond to a specific MIME type it is asked to serve. For example, you could set up a MIME filter to check all HTML pages being served for bad spelling.

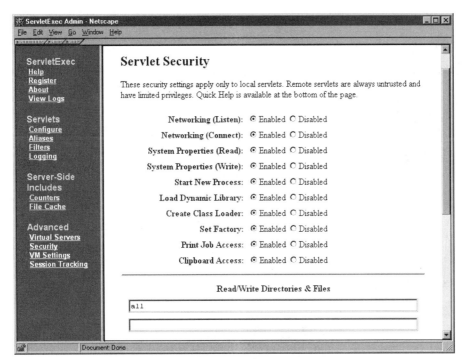

Figure 4.4 ServletExec security

This makes for a processor-intensive operation, but it allows you to develop your own MIME types and create the necessary processing for them.

The Logging option allows you to control the log settings for your servlets. The log file will receive all the data from calls to the `log(...)` method from the main servlet API. You can control how big this file becomes and whether it is enabled.

Server-side includes ServletExec contains very powerful control over server-side includes. SSI are where the servlet is triggered by servlet tags, and the output of the servlet is replaced inside those tags before the HTML file is sent out to the client.

ServletExec manages an internal counter for each SSI. Using the Counters option, you can view the latest statistics for the number of times that each servlet has been hit.

The File Cache option controls, shown in figure 4.5, allow you to set whether ServletExec should cache all the HTML documents that include SSI. The file cache is a significant improvement over performance; from here, you can specify the amount of memory you wish to devote to this cache.

Advanced features You'll find many of the more sophisticated features under the Advanced section. For example, ServletExec can provide servlet processing for servers that are hosting multiple virtual servers on one machine. Each individual virtual server can have its own particular servlet requirements and it can be kept separate from other virtual servers.

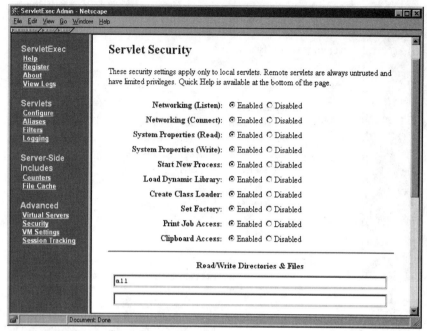

Figure 4.5 ServletExec security

This is particularly useful in ISP environments where the need to keep clients separate from one another is paramount. Use the Virtual Servers option in the Advanced section if you want this functionality.

Figure 4.6 illustrates the HTML page that is used to create and edit virtual hosts. On this page, you can set the servlets directory from which ServletExec will load the servlets. This is especially useful when you want to give outside clients the ability to upload new servlets for execution.

In the registered version of the program, you can specify a username/password combination that can be used to restrict access to that particular virtual host.

Be aware that it is not necessary to set up a different virtual servlet engine for each virtual host. You can set up only one that can serve all the virtual hosts running on the server.

In an ISP environment, it is important to have control over the operation of each virtual servlet engine. The ability to restrict access to various privileges can be controlled using the Security option in the "Advanced" section, as shown in figure 4.7.

Using this option, you can specify which directories the servlet can read and/or write. You can also control whether the servlet can open up server sockets or connect to other servers. Figure 4.7 shows the list of restrictions that the servlet virtual machine can have.

The VM Settings option lets you control the options of the virtual machine, such as the ability to allocate more memory.

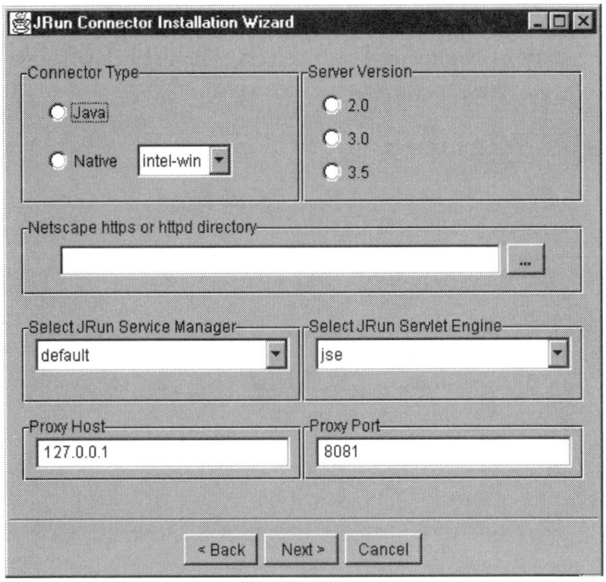

Figure 4.6 JRun installation, part one

The Session Tracking option gives you access to all the options associated with the session tracking API of the servlet API. These options were discussed in the previous chapter about the Java Web Server.

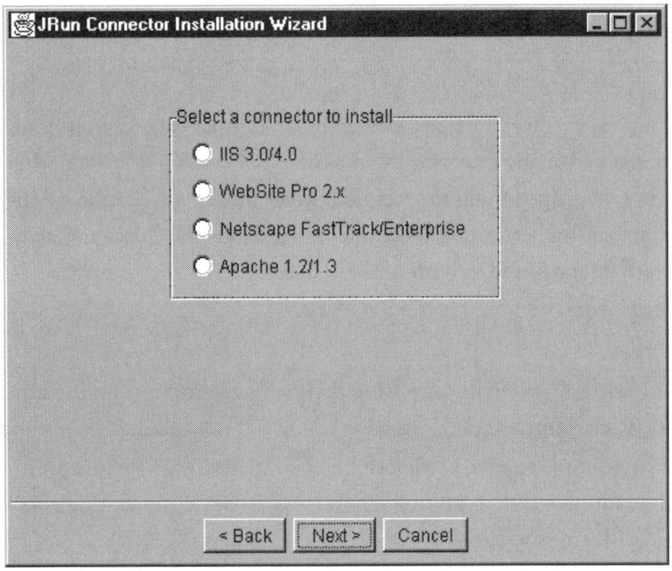

Figure 4.7 JRun installation, part one

4.3.2 Feature summary

ServletExec supports a whole tapestry of commercial web servers. The list below shows what was supported at the time this book was published.

- Netscape FastTrack + Enterprise 3.0/3.5.1
- Windows NT
- Solaris
- HP-UX
- Microsoft IIS 3.0/4.0, PWS
- Windows NT/95/98
- Apache 1.3.x
- Linux
- Mac OS Web Server
- WebSTAR 2.0/2.1/3.0
- Quid Pro Quo 2.0/2.1
- AppleShareIP 5.0.2
- WebTen 1.1.1/2.0

Each of the listed operating platforms requires a separate installation of the Java Virtual Machine to be installed and operational beforehand.

4.4 JRun

JRun is designed and produced by Live Software, located in California. Paul Colton heads up Live Software, and he has personally designed the majority of JRun. Colton is another early adopter of Java servlets; he helped mold the technology we are using today. Live Software produces a whole range of servlet-related tools, including debugging tools and standard libraries. Live Software can be found at both of these sites:

http://www.livesoftware.com/

http://www.jrun.com/

You can download a variety of different tools from their web site, and the online support for all their products is very impressive.

Downloading JRun is a simple matter of choosing which platform you wish to run, filling out the simple online form, and then waiting for an email to be delivered. The email will contain the URL for the JRun software.

Downloading JRun results in a 7 MB Zip file. Once it's decompressed, it is a full installation routine. This section, much like the previous section detailing ServletExec, will take you through the complete installation and administration of JRun.

4.4.1 Installation

JRun comes in two flavors: the professional version and the normal version. The free download is the normal version, and this product is not restricted in any way. If, however, you are going to use it for commercial use you must purchase a license for it. The professional version adds a whole host of features, including a more comprehensive security model for ISP hosting.

We will set up JRun for use with Netscape Enterprise, but as part of the download, Microsoft IIS, Apache, and WebSite Pro are all supported. Double-clicking on the setup.exe file launches the installation wizard; simply follow the instructions from that point.

JRun is much more than a servlet engine—it is a complete application server. To this end, a web server comes as part of the installation. JRun calls the interface to the third-party web server's connectors. A connector can be thought of as a plug in or module that makes the necessary connections between the web server and the servlet engine.

During the installation process, you are asked which connector you wish to install. Figure 4.8 shows the options available if you run the Windows NT installation. Don't worry too much about not configuring all your web servers at once; the option to revisit this section is available.

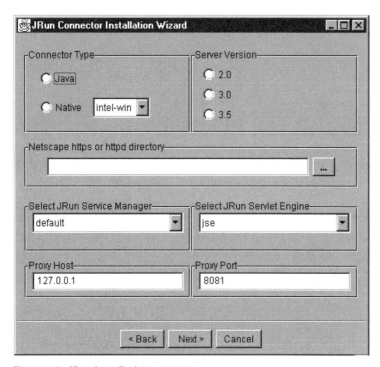

Figure 4.8 JRun installation, part two

In our example, we are installing the connector for Netscape, so choose the Netscape FastTrack/Enterprise option. This displays a window of parameters (see figure 4.9) associated with the connector for Netscape.

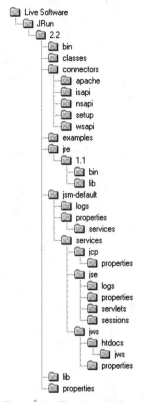

Figure 4.9 JRun installation tree

There are two ways in which the JRun servlet engine can communicate with Netscape. One is through the Netscape Java interface, and the other is through the Netscape Server API (NSAPI) interface. The NSAPI is the more efficient and faster of the two options, but if for some reason you cannot get the native NSAPI to function properly, use the Java interface. Note that in order for the Java interface to operate correctly, you must enable Java from within the Administration section of the Netscape web server. Without this option on, JRun will not be able to communicate with Netscape.

You need to select both the version number of the Netscape server and the directory where the https-???? is located. You can leave the remaining options at their default settings for the moment.

After the installation is complete, you have the option to install JRun as an NT service. I recommended that you take this route if the installation is to be permanent, as this will take the headache out of remembering to start JRun every time the server starts. If it is installed as an NT service, you will notice a small JRun logo in the task bar; this indicates the servlet engine is running successfully. It doesn't necessarily mean the servlet engine can communicate with any web servers, but it does mean the engine itself is up and running.

JRun installs itself into its own directory, away from the main web server as shown in figure 4.10. The default location for your servlets is the ./jsm-default/services/jse/servlets directory. This is where you can place your servlets.

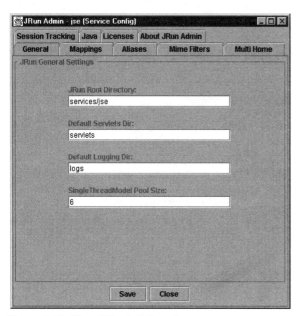

Figure 4.10 JRun JSE administration

Assuming everything installed correctly, start JRun, restart the Netscape server, and visit the following URL to make sure your installation is successful: http://<your host>/servlet/SnoopServlet

The servlet located at this URL runs the standard SnoopServlet that ships with the Java Web Server. SnoopServlet is becoming very famous; it is to the servlet world what dir was to MS-DOS. It's the first thing you should try to ensure everything is working properly.

If nothing is displayed, check to make sure JRun is running. If you are using the Java interface to connect to Netscape, also make sure you have enabled Java from within the Netscape administration tool.

4.4.2 Administration

In the version we downloaded, administration is performed through a number of Java applets. These applets must be run from the local machine—they cannot be accessed remotely. (The professional version of JRun offers this remote functionality.) As part of the installation, a folder is placed on the desktop with icon shortcuts to the administration tools of JRun, as well as shortcuts to the programs that stop and start JRun.

This section will give you an overview of the JRun Servlet Engine (JSE) configuration. You'll notice that many of the parameters will be familiar to you if you have read the previous chapter and section.

The look and feel of the administration section closely models the one seen in the JWS. This makes for an easy transition for people migrating to a JRun environment from a JWS platform. Starting up the administration tool will first display a splash screen. You'll then be presented with a list of services that can be configured. Choose the JSE option. The window shown in figure 4.11 will then be displayed.

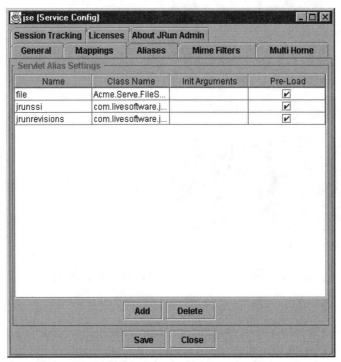

Figure 4.11 JRun JSE servlet aliases

From here, you can change the location of the Servlets and Logs directory. You also have the ability to change the size of the pool that is used to control the `SingleThread-Model` interface.

The applet for the administration of JSE is a very clean and well-laid-out tool. Access to all the different areas is controlled through tabs, which are displayed at the top of the window. Clicking on a particular tab will change the bottom panel to reflect the new area. This administration applet is a very good example of the advancements made in the Java applet arena with the swing API.

Figure 4.12 shows the screen for registering a servlet alias with the JSE. The normal version of JRun does not permit remote servlets to be loaded—only local trusted ones. You supply a servlet alias, the full class pathname of the servlet, any initial arguments, and whether it should be loaded automatically at server startup.

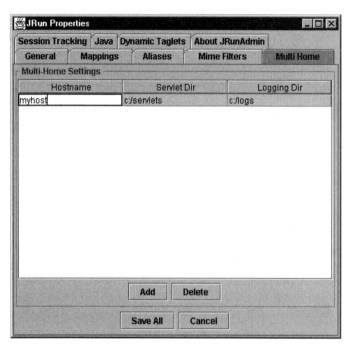

Figure 4.12 JRun JSE session management

You can then use this alias to set up any servlet mappings you want. This is performed in much the same way as the Java Web Server.

Figure 4.13 shows the configuration panel for setting up multihome hosts. This is where JSE can be used to serve more than one virtual host, each with its own servlets directory. You'll find this particularly useful in ISP environments. Please note that the JRun professional version gives you much finer control over this area.

As with ServletExec, JRun supports the session management section of the servlet API. From the panel shown in figure 4.14, you can configure many aspects of the session management. If you decide to use cookies, as opposed to URL rewriting, this panel allows you to control the attributes associated with the cookie.

JRun Professional is designed with the ISP in mind. It has many additional features that complement the normal version. It offers the ability to have multiple virtual machines, finer granularity over the security of the servlets, the ability to remotely administer the servlet engine, and some useful servlets.

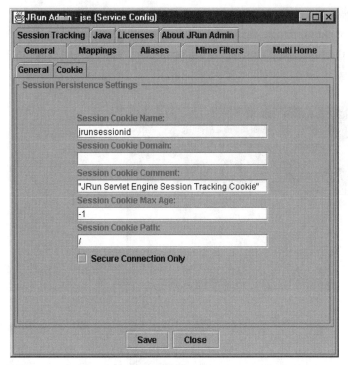

Figure 4.13 JRun JSE multiHome

4.4.3 Feature summary

JRun supports nearly all of the commercially available web servers in the market.

- Netscape FastTrack + Enterprise 3.0/3.5.1
- Windows NT
- Solaris
- AIX
- IRIX
- HP-UX
- Microsoft IIS 3.0/4.0, PWS
- Windows NT/95/98
- Apache 1.3.x
- Unix
- WebSite Pro
- Windows NT
- WebSTAR
- Macintosh

JRun, unlike ServletExec, comes bundled with the JVM, which makes installing it on remote servers a single-step process, as opposed to the prerequisite of having to install the Java Virtual Machine.

4.5 Other servlet engines

ServletExec and JRun are not the only products that are available. Many of the core web servers are beginning to introduce native support for Java servlets as part of their core product. In addition to this, the trend toward application servers has seen the servlet API being implemented by Oracle and IBM in their core products.

C H A P T E R   5

Debugging and optimization techniques

- Understand the basics of debugging the code you develop, and learn some techniques to make it easier for you.

- Follow the creation of a debugging utility class that simplifies the debugging process.

- Learn how to optimize your programs for size and for speed.

Java is a programming language that runs programs known as class files. A class file is a sequence of instructions that performs some logical task. Sometimes these instructions run as expected…and sometimes they do not.

With most Integrated Developer Environments (IDEs), some form of debugger is available for use in developing applications or applets. However, due to the very nature of servlets, setting up a debugging environment isn't always easy.

This chapter will present a simple general debugging class that will aid you in quickly locating and fixing problems.

Just because Java makes coding easy doesn't mean that all standard coding practices go out the window. This chapter will look at a number of simple steps that can be used to speed up your class objects.

5.1 Debugging

Debugging programs is one of those annoying tasks that the majority of us have to perform at some point in our developer lives. As soon as we write a piece of code, be it a class or a method, we like to think it is perfect. "That won't need testing," we say to ourselves. However, nine out of ten times, it does require testing, and sometimes it requires some intensive detective work as well.

Many people dislike the debugging process. Fixing problems—yech! It is even worse if you have to try to fix somebody else's code. Many developers view this as a necessary evil that simply has to be done.

But it's all a state of mind. Think of it as a big game. Imagine the thrill of the chase. Somewhere in there, lurking under lines and lines of code, is a small bug that is causing the whole system to come crashing down. It becomes a game to try to flush it out into the open. When you think of it this way, suddenly that horribly small bug you've been putting off becomes much more attractive.

Many techniques are available to aid you in the debugging process. Most techniques rely on the tools provided by their development environment. Generally these tools allow for the inspection of variables, stepping into code, freezing output, and modification, to name but a few of the features available. Some rely on the old-fashioned method of debugging: print statements.

The print statement method is coming back in vogue; it has never been so popular. Thanks to Java, the developer has the ability to print information that used to be available only to the debugger and the compiler.

One of the most common types of bugs is the one that is the most obvious when it's found. For example, a wrong variable name or an incorrect assignment can leave you kicking yourself for putting it in there in the first place. A debugger, which is a very handy tool, will generally tell you which line the program crashed in by highlighting it when it crashes.

Java, with the combination of `Exception` and `Throwable`, has given you the power to trace statements yourself. By identifying the line that is causing a problem, the problem as a whole becomes much clearer.

Java uses the `System.out.println(…)` method to display messages on the console. Every object can be printed as a string. Since every object in Java is classed from `java.lang.Object,` this allows the `toString()` method to be overridden and provides useful information regarding the status of the class.

However, the console window isn't much use with servlets. When you're doing the actual programming, you can monitor the console, but more often than not, a bug comes to light through heavy use of the program or after some time has passed—at any rate, the console is usually not being monitored when it happens.

The servlet API defines a class method that allows you to output textual information to the main log file used by the web server. This gives you a certain level of control, but it still doesn't give you instant access to the information that may be critical in catching a bug.

The class presented here gives all the functionality required to fully utilize the print statement method. This class has these features:

- Easy access throughout the virtual machine
- File logging
- Socket logging
- Exception logging

The main advantage of this class, as you will discover, is that it is not restricted for use in the servlet environment. Any Java environment can utilize the features of the following debugging class.

5.1.1 Debugging class

One of the most important features of any debugging class is its simplicity. The class is not to impact on the overall execution performance of the final application. A class that takes up too much processing time can't be utilized as a debugging tool.

This performance issue is the developers' equivalent of the age-old problem facing engineers who build measurement tools. How do you build a tool that will accurately measure a given flow, substance, mixture, temperature, for example, without interfering with the original environment where the measurement will be taken? A system that measures the rate of water flow will unintentionally slow the flow down a small amount by its very presence. A rod that measures temperature will either heat or cool the particles or atoms around about it. The smaller the impact the better the tool; the problem is in finding the right tool.

Debugging is no different. If you want to find a bug during development, then the tool you use isn't considered a major problem. The tool is allowed to impact the environment if necessary. However, if the debugging tool is to ship with a production version in order to catch any of those long-term bugs, then it has to have minimum impact.

The class presented here serves both the debugging and the production phases.

Class structure   Let's assume that the class will be used throughout the virtual machine. Let's further assume that you don't want to keep a specific object instant to the class; you simply want to use it. You can achieve this by making the methods `static`, which means you don't ever have to manually instantiate the class.

Since objects provide a `toString(…)` method, which returns a string representation of the object, you only need to support the ability to print strings. The calling method can then control the output by conditionally calling the `toString()` method. You can outline the class as shown in example 5.1.

```
public final class Debug extends Object {
  private Debug(){}

  public static void println( String _line ){
    //-- Do some processing
  }
}
```
Example 5.1   Debug.java definition

Notice the constructor. You declared it `private` to safeguard against anyone creating an instance of it. This ensures only one instance of the class will exist in the virtual machine. Coupling that with the fact that you have made your class `final` means that no one can extend it using it as a base class for another.

Simple console output   One of the most primitive things you should control is whether the output is sent to the console. You can control this through a simple `boolean` value, `bSystemOut`; when it is set to `true`, it will display all output on the console. You can write your core output function with this ability, as shown in example 5.2.

```
static boolean bOn = true;
static boolean bSystemOut = true;
static SimpleDateFormat DateFormat = null;

public synchronized static void println( String Line ){
  if ( !bOn )
    return;

  if ( DateFormat == null )
    DateFormat = new SimpleDateFormat( "dd/MMM HH:mm.ss: " );

  String D = DateFormat.format(new java.util.Date()) + Line + "\r\n";

  if ( bSystemOut )
    System.out.println( D );
}
```
Example 5.2   Modification of the core output routine

Notice the provision of an extra variable, bOn. This gives you control to all debugging processes through the use of one variable. The debugging output can be turned off with a single method call.

Regardless of the output method, the string will not be changed. This will be the original string from you with the current date inserted at the beginning. Having the date included in the output is very handy as you can see a historical execution map build up, especially when it comes to debugging threads.

Example 5.3 shows the methods that are available to you for controlling the output of the debugging class.

```
public static void On(){
  bOn=true;
}

public static void Off(){
  bOn=false;
}

public static void SystemOn(){
  bSystemOut=true;
}

public static void SystemOff(){
  bSystemOut=false;
}
```
Example 5.3   Controlling the output

File output   Having output sent to the console is useful, but it can sometimes be impractical. For example, someone would have to constantly watch the console for any messages, as they are lost once they scroll by. Of course, this assumes you don't redirect the console window to a file, but this is generally operating-system specific.

As was mentioned earlier, sending the output to a file is a much more convenient way for you to trace what has been printed out. You can easily build this functionality into your debugging class.

One of things you have to ask of the file feature is to not overwrite any existing debug information. This is a fairly important concept, as subsequent runs of the servlet or application may overwrite valuable debug information.

Many of the standard file handling classes that come as part of the Java libraries do not handle writing to the end of a file. However, the RandomFileAccess class does. It allows you to open a file and append data to it.

To make the class more efficient, open the debugging output file only once and leave it open for subsequent writes. This requires you to hold a reference to it throughout the life cycle of the debugging class. By initializing this file reference variable with the value of null, you can easily detect if the file is already available. If it is not available, open it and move the file pointer to the end of the file so all output will be appended. Example 5.4 illustrates this process.

```
if ( bFile ){
  try{
    if ( OutFile == null ){
      OutFile = new RandomAccessFile( filename, "rw" );
      OutFile.seek( OutFile.length() );
      OutFile.writeBytes( "\r\n------Logging Restarted------
                                n-ary limited v1.3 ---------\r\n" );
    }
    OutFile.writeBytes( D );
    }catch(Exception E){}
  }
}
```

Example 5.4   Creating the file instance

Notice again how you control the use of the file through a variable called bFile. This particular piece of code will be placed inside the core print routine after the call to display the information on the console window.

This class assumes it will be opening up the same file each time. Therefore, the name of the file can be fixed in the class. For this example, all file output will go to a file called "debug.txt." This file will be created in the current directory of the running application.

Socket output   So far, you have the ability to send output to the console and to a file. Wouldn't it be nice if you could log on to a port from anywhere and view the output when it happened?

With Java, answering this sort of question has become very trivial. Adding such networking capabilities to a class is no big task. You need the ability to connect to a known port and view all the output through a standard TELNET session.

You need two things to handle this—first, a thread that will listen for incoming client connections, and second, a class that will handle the communications for each client.

You first need to define the method for setting up a listening socket. You want to be able to handle many client connections at once, so create a simple loop that will listen for a connection; once it's connected, it will create a class to handle that connection, then return to listen for more connections.

Since you already have a class (your debugging one), there is no point in creating another one. Extend this class to use the Thread class, and define a run() method that will be used to listen for client connections (see example 5.5).

```
public final class Debug extends Thread {
  static Vector clients = null;
  static int SOCKET_PORT = 2000;

  public void run(){
    Socket sIN;
    ServerSocket sSERVER;

    try{
      sSERVER = new ServerSocket( SOCKET_PORT );
    }catch(Exception E){
```

```
        return;
    }

    for(;;){
      try{
        sIN = sSERVER.accept();
        clients.addElement( new clientDebug( sIN ) );
      }catch(Exception E){}
    }
  }
}
```
Example 5.5   Listening for client connections

In order for you to send out all messages to all the clients, you need to keep a reference to each client. This is done through the `Vector` class, which keeps a reference to the `clientDebug` class. This is the class you are going to use to handle each client, as shown in example 5.6.

When this class is created, the first thing it does is attempt to create an instance of `DataOutputStream`, which gives you a means to easily send strings to the socket. Since this is purely an output class, there is no need to get an input stream to the socket. If creating this stream fails, then an exception will be thrown and the class reference will be set to null.

```
class clientDebug {
  private Socket sIn;
  private DataOutputStream out;

  public clientDebug(Socket _sIn){
    sIn = _sIn;
    try{
      out = new DataOutputStream( sIn.getOutputStream() );
      out.writeBytes( "------Logging Restarted-------
                       n-ary limited v1.3 ---------\r\n" );

      out.writeBytes( "[os.name]     = [" + System.getProperty
                       ("os.name") + "]\r\n" );
      out.writeBytes( "[os.arch]     = [" + System.getProperty
                       ("os.arch") + "]\r\n" );
      out.writeBytes( "[os.version]  = [" + System.getProperty
                       ("os.version") + "]\r\n" );

      out.writeBytes( "[java.version] = [" + System.getProperty
                       ("java.version") + "]\r\n" );
      out.writeBytes( "[java.vendor]  = [" + System.getProperty
                       ("java.vendor") + "]\r\n" );

      Runtime RT = Runtime.getRuntime();
      out.writeBytes( "[total memory] = [" + RT.totalMemory() +
                       " bytes]\r\n" );
      out.writeBytes( "[free memory]  = [" + RT.freeMemory() +
                       " bytes]\r\n" );
      out.writeBytes( "----------------\r\n" );
```

```
      }catch(Exception E){
        out = null;
      }
    }

  public boolean println( String _D ){
    try{
      out.writeBytes( _D );
      return true;
    }catch(Exception E){
      return false;
    }
  }
}
```
Example 5.6   Handling the client connection

If the stream opens successfully, then some information regarding the current operating system and available memory is printed. This is an informative read, and it also confirms to the client that a good connection has indeed been made.

The debugging class will print to socket by calling the `println(…)` method. If the client is no longer available or has disconnected, then an exception will be thrown. This will cause the method to return a false result, so the debugging class will know to remove the client from the list of available clients.

The method shown in example 5.7 details the output to the client connections. The method sets up an `Enumeration` to the `Vector`, which will allow it to run through the list easily. If the method returns `false`, then it is removed from the list.

```
private static void printToClients( String D ){
  Enumeration E = clients.elements();
  clientDebug CD;
  while (E.hasMoreElements()){
    CD = (clientDebug)E.nextElement();
    if ( CD.println( D ) == false )
      clients.removeElement( CD );
  }
}
```
Example 5.7   Sending output to the clients

Example 5.8 shows the code to control the socket connections. At the core print routine, if the Vector that holds the client's connection is `null`, then it is assumed the server hasn't been started. The server is then started by creating an instance of the debugging class and calling the `start()` method. This will invoke the thread and call the `run()` method.

```
if ( bSocket ){
  if ( clients == null ){
    new Debug().start();
    clients = new Vector();
  }
```

```
   if ( clients.size() > 0 )
     printToClients( D );
}
```
Example 5.8   Creating the new server

After the new server has been created, it calls the method in example 5.7.

Exception handling   Generally, you most often need a debugging class when things start going wrong, which usually happens when a lot of exceptions are thrown. The ability to properly handle these exceptions would increase the usefulness of a debugging class.

One of really nice features of Java is the ability to display a complete stack trace, where each method that was called leading up to the problem is displayed, complete with the line number (if it's available). This alone can save many hours of debugging time.

When an exception is thrown, the stack trace is available using a method call from the `printStackTrace()` method. The output from this method is sent to the standard error stream, so you need to redirect it in order to get a copy of this invaluable data.

```
public static void printStackTrace( Exception E ){
  ByteArrayOutputStream OS = new ByteArrayOutputStream();
  PrintStream ps = new PrintStream( OS );
  System.setErr( ps );
  E.printStackTrace();
  System.setErr( System.err );
  println( OS.toString() );
}
```
Example 5.9   Redirecting the standard error

Example 5.9 illustrates this redirection. Instead of sending the output straight to an output stream, store it in a string and then send it on through the normal print routine. This way, you will still control the output flow.

Sending a stream to a string is simply a matter of creating an instance of a `ByteArrayOutputStream`, which will hold all the data. Once the data is collected, simply call the `toString()` method to get the contents of this buffer returned as a string.

5.1.2 Using the class
Now that you have the class built, let's look at how you can use it. As you can see in example 5.10, the code will most definitely throw an exception since the variable `Temp` is `null`.

```
try{
  String Temp = null;
  Temp = Temp.toLowerCase();
catch(Exception E){
  Debug.println( "This will throw an exception" );
  Debug.println( E );
  Debug.printStackTrace( E );
}
```
Example 5.10   Using the debugging class

When this exception occurs, a number of methods of the Debug class are called. In the default state, this series of calls would mirror all the print statements to the console and file, and any client connections that may exist.

5.1.3 Complete source

Example 5.11 shows the complete code for the debugging class.

```
public final class Debug extends Thread {

    static RandomAccessFile OutFile = null;
    static SimpleDateFormat DateFormat = null;
    static boolean bOn = true;
    static boolean bSystemOut= true;
    static boolean bSocket = true;
    static boolean bFile = true;
    static String filename = "./debug.txt";
    static Vector clients = null;
    static int SOCKET_PORT = 2000;

    private Debug(){}

    public static void setPort(int _nPort){
        SOCKET_PORT = _nPort;
    }

    public static void On(){
     bOn=true;
    }

    public static void Off(){
     bOn=false;
    }

    public static void SystemOn(){
        bSystemOut=true;
    }

    public static void SystemOff(){
     bSystemOut=false;
    }

    public static void SocketOn(){
        bSocket = true;
    }

    public static void SocketOff(){
        bSocket = false;
    }

    public static void FileOn(){
        bFile = true;
    }
    public static void FileOff(){
```

```
      bFile = false;
  }

  public static void println( boolean t, String Line ){
    bSystemOut = true;
    println( Line );
    bSystemOut = false;
  }

  public static void println( boolean t, Exception E ){
    bSystemOut = true;
    println( E );
    bSystemOut = false;
  }

  public static void println( Exception E ){
    println( E.toString() );
  }

  public static void printStackTrace( Exception E ){
    ByteArrayOutputStream OS = new ByteArrayOutputStream();
    PrintStream ps = new PrintStream( OS );
    System.setErr( ps );
    E.printStackTrace();
    System.setErr( System.err );
    println( OS.toString() );
  }

  public synchronized static void println( String Line ){
    if ( !bOn )
      return;

    if ( DateFormat == null )
      DateFormat = new SimpleDateFormat( "dd/MMM HH:mm.ss: " );

    String D = DateFormat.format(new java.util.Date()) + Line + "\r\n";

     if ( bSystemOut )
       System.out.println( D );

    if ( bFile ){
      try{
        if ( OutFile == null ){
          OutFile = new RandomAccessFile( filename, "rw" );
          OutFile.seek( OutFile.length() );
          OutFile.writeBytes( "\r\n------Logging Restarted-------
                               n-ary limited v1.3 ------\r\n" );
        }
        OutFile.writeBytes( D );
      }catch(Exception E){}
    }
    if ( bSocket ){
      if ( clients == null ){
        new Debug().start();
```

```
        clients = new Vector();
      }

      if ( clients.size() > 0 )
        printToClients( D );
  }
}

private static void printToClients( String D ){
  Enumeration E = clients.elements();
  clientDebug CD;
  while (E.hasMoreElements()){
    CD = (clientDebug)E.nextElement();
    if ( CD.println( D ) == false )
      clients.removeElement( CD );
  }
}

public void run(){
  Socket sIN;
  ServerSocket sSERVER;

  try{
    sSERVER = new ServerSocket( SOCKET_PORT );
  }catch(Exception E){
    return;
  }

  for(;;){
    try{
      sIN = sSERVER.accept();
      clients.addElement( new clientDebug( sIN ) );
    }catch(Exception E){}
  }
}
}
```

Example 5.11   The complete debugging class

5.1.4 Future extensions

This chapter presented a simple class implementation of a very powerful debugging tool. A number of improvements could be made to the class to make it more flexible.

1   Give the client the ability to send commands to the debugging class. For example, add a command to restart the virtual machine or to perform a garbage collection.

2   Buffer the last ten items that were printed. If you do this, a client could request a historical output.

3   Add a method to change the name of the destination file where all file output is saved.

Keep in mind that any features that are added must not take over the complete resources and processing cycles of the virtual machine.

5.2 Optimization

There are many sides to developing. First, you have to create the logical program flow. Second, you have to develop the code. Third, you need to debug and test the program. Finally, you need to optimize the code to run more efficiently.

Many developers forget the last step. This is a shame, because software size seems to be ever increasing. If the code doesn't run fast enough, then developers simply require that the application is run on a faster processor. But with some care and diligence, software can be written to utilize less memory and consume fewer processor cycles.

The optimizations that are presented in this section are grouped into two sections: optimizing for size and optimizing for speed.

5.2.1 Optimizing for size

We can split this section into two further subsections: common sense optimization techniques, and not-so-obvious techniques.

Let's begin with the common sense ways to reduce the size of a class. One technique involves using smaller names to name variables and methods. Java has given you the ability to use really long method names. While this is handy, the names have to be stored in the class file. Reducing their size can significantly decrease the size of the class file.

The Java library includes a rich tapestry of classes. They do many tasks, and with over 1500 classes to chose from, there is a wide scope for deployment. So don't rewrite any functionality that may already exist. This seems obvious, but you will be surprised at the number of developers who have redeveloped standard classes that were unknown to them at the time. Not only will this reduce your code complexity, but chances are, the class you are using may be a native class (and therefore it will run much faster).

Another tip is to reuse methods. If you have developed many different methods that don't really need an object instance to operate, place them in a class of their own and declare them as static methods. This will reduce the need to repeat them in classes that need them.

Now, on to the not-so-obvious optimization tricks.

The "+" operator is commonly used in code to add strings together. This is convenient, but it's very slow. The compiler will generally replace each operator with an instance of `StringBuffer(...)`. To reduce file size, replace the operators with one instance of `StringBuffer` and use the `append(...)` method to add strings together.

Another technique involves dates. Storing dates can be a pain, especially if you're moving between databases. Instead of storing a date, store the millisecond equivalent in a `long (java.util.Date.getTime())`. This not only saves space in the database table and the virtual machine, but it makes querying on the dates very efficient—you're simply comparing two numbers, as opposed to two dates.

Finally, remember to compile with optimizations turned on. This will automatically attempt to reduce the code size by eliminating dead code and converting some methods into inline calls.

5.2.2 Optimizing for speed

Optimizing for speed follows the same principles illustrated in the previous section. But remember to time your code's execution before and after performing any optimizations. This way you can confidently convince yourself that your work has actually made an improvement—sometimes execution time has been known to increase, instead.

One of the most expensive operations (in terms of processor cycles) you can do is exception handling. Try to replace exception blocks with logical tests, if possible, and reduce the number of lines contained within a block.

The `synchronized` method used for ensuring thread-safe execution is also a large speed increase factor. Minimize the use of this, where possible.

Creating objects in Java is a breeze, but they cost time and resources. Try to reuse objects instead of creating new ones. Every time you create an object, memory has to be allocated until the garbage collector can clean up all unused objects. This is common in loops.

If you're doing a lot of division, think of reworking your logic so you can divide by 2. Dividing is a very expensive operation, but if you're dividing by 2, it can be replaced with shift operations. Many computer game developers optimize their code to take into account the remainder or overflow from the calculation that may be lost.

5.2.3 Warning

Before you start modifying all your code, remember it is important to get it working first. Optimizing as you develop is never a good idea; more often than not, it distorts the logic, which makes it harder to find unwanted features or bugs. Many of the optimizations mentioned in this chapter will make a difference, but use them wisely. There is no need to completely redo every class you wrote just to save a few bytes.

C H A P T E R   6

CGI overview

CHAPTER CONCEPTS

- Learn exactly what CGI is. The term is used quite often, but you may not have a complete understanding of this technology.

- CGI does not operate like conventional programs; learn how it differs from others.

- Discover what CGI can and can't do as you understand its strengths and weaknesses.

- Learn how to implement CGI.

When dealing with a new technology, particularly one that is either replacing or presenting a serious alternative to a current one, it is always best to know as much as possible about the technology it will replace. Not only it is good to understand how they did it in the "good old days," but you'll also be prepared to support your move to the new technology (for example, if a manager challenges your decision to ditch the traditional CGI program for a cleaner Java-based solution).

This chapter does not bash CGI. Contrasting the strengths of servlets while highlighting CGI's weaknesses would be very easy. Instead, once you've read this chapter, I'll let you draw your own conclusions about CGI.

6.1   What Is CGI?

The Common Gateway Interface defines a standard for the way web servers communicate with back-end processes or programs. CGI is merely a specification that facilitates the creation of web solutions in a variety of different languages.

The HTTP protocol is responsible for ensuring that data is sent correctly between the client and the web server, whereas CGI ensures that data communication is not broken when the server interfaces with programs and processes external to the web server. Figure 6.1 shows how CGI fits into the web environment.

Figure 6.1 CGI in the overall client/server equation connection process

One could say that if it weren't for CGI, the Java servlet API may not have come along when it did. CGI's evolution brought life to a well-established world of static HTML pages. CGI was designed to allow various programs to generate dynamic HTML pages on the fly. Examples of such dynamic HTML pages include formatted results from a database or up-to-date statistics on the number of people visiting a web site.

CGI, like servlets, is completely transparent to the client; the client simply makes a request for a resource on the network. It doesn't matter whether that resource represents a static HTML page or one that is generated dynamically by a separate program. As long as the data is transferred in the same manner, the client will still use the data no matter when it was generated.

Another important aspect of the CGI specification is that the complete connection is stateless. This means that neither end has any historical information regarding previous transfers or connections. Therefore, every time the client requests an HTML page, the browser connects to the server, transfers the page, and then disconnects. When an HTML page is retrieved, each resource within that is encountered (such as a page or an image) would also have to be retrieved from the server, thus incurring another connect-transfer-disconnect procedure. Fortunately, many of today's browsers have a caching mechanism that keeps a local copy of the resource and serves the local version instead of continually asking the server for the same files.

Note When data is passed from the server to the client, it has to be recognized. In other words, a GIF data stream must not be mistaken for an HTML page and vice versa. To make the data easily identifiable, the server sends a special header before each data block. Within this data block is a sequence of characters that describes the forthcoming data. This is known as the MIME header. You may have seen long lists of MIME types in your client browser. They allow the browser to determine what to do with the data once it's received. For example, the text/html MIME type is nearly always displayed in the browser, whereas an application/x-Zip-compressed MIME type tells the browser that the incoming data is a Zip file, which is generally not shown but is saved to disk.

If you're bored one day, go into your browser and change some of the MIME types in the Options or Preferences section. See what a JPEG image looks like when its data stream is interpreted as ASCII text. This may not be that practical, but it's a fun experiment. But before you do this, remember to make a backup of the previous settings— each browser stores this information in different ways, and it's not always easy to restore it.

However, this caching stage can be counterproductive when accessing CGI-based pages. The idea behind a CGI-produced page is that it is dynamic and generated fresh on each visit. When the browser has cached a number of resources, it could possibly serve the client with an out-of-date version of the resource. Since a cached copy of the resource is used, the connection to the server is not even made, rendering the CGI program dormant during the request. Although this situation is a problem, CGI is not alone; servlets can suffer from the same caching fate.

6.2 CGI in operation

Now that you have learned what CGI is, we can take a look at how it is implemented and what is involved in running an actual CGI program. A CGI program starts under the control of the web server, typically in response to a client request for a given resource.

A CGI program is also commonly known as a script. When you hear the word script, you might generally think of interpreted languages, but in this instance a script applies equally to both interpreted and compiled programs. The reason for this confusion is more historical than malicious. With the Internet sprouting from the UNIX world, the first CGI programs were actually shell scripts, written to be interpreted by using the sh, bash, ksh, or csh logon shells. Thus, when you hear CGI script, it's equivalent to the CGI program.

To understand how a CGI program operates, we will go through the steps required to process a client request to a CGI program.

1 The client connects to the server specified in the URL.

2 The server accepts the connection and receives the path and name to the resource in question.

3 The server translates the URL resource into a real path and name that can be read by the local program.

4 The server, because of its list of MIME types, discovers that the resource should be executed and not just read back to the client.

5 The server prepares to execute the resource by setting up environment variables to describe the state of the connection and the client.

6 The server launches the resource, passing all remaining data to the resource.

7 The server redirects the output of the resource to the client.

8 The resource executes, and all output goes to the client.

9 The resource completes, and the server closes the connection to the client.

The preceding steps are important for two reasons. First, the steps necessary to successfully execute a CGI program are listed. Second, seeing these steps clearly shows where the CGI model is at a disadvantage to the servlet model. I'll explain this in detail in the next section.

6.2.1 CGI and server communication

Step 5 in the previous mentions setting up environment variables, but what is an environment variable? Every process that runs has its own environment or address space. Within this environment, certain characteristics are set, such as the IP address of the client making the request. These characteristics allow the program that is running to make an informed decision about its running state. Environment variables are very common in the UNIX world. Table 6.1 shows some of the more familiar environment variables.

Table 6.1 Sample environment variables

Environment variable	Description
TERM=vt100	Sets the terminal type to vt100.
SHELL=/bin/csh	Sets the shell to use the C shell.
HOME=/home/al	Sets the home directory to /home/al.

Before launching the CGI program, the server sets a standard set of variables that allows the program to assess the state of the current connection. Table 6.2 details the environment variables that are set by the server before any CGI program is executed.

Environment variables convey very important information regarding the client session. The more common variables are accessible through method calls from the servlet API; the remaining variables are accessible through a standard call that retrieves individual variables. As you read through this chapter, you will see examples where each type of variable is used.

Table 6.2 CGI environment variables

CGI variable	Description
AUTH_TYPE	The authentication type of the server.
CONTENT_LENGTH	If the data is sent via a POST, this is the length of the data.
CONTENT_TYPE	The MIME type of the data.
GATEWAY_INTERFACE	The version number of the CGI interface that is employed.
HTTP_ACCEPT	A list of MIME types the client can accept.
HTTP_USER_AGENT	The name and possible version number of the client's browser.
PATH_INFO	Extra path information passed to the script.
PATH_TRANSLATED	The translated path from the virtual path.
QUERY_STRING	Any extra information supplied as parameters to the script. Data from a GET is generally supplied via this variable.
REMOTE_ADDR	The IP address of the client.
REMOTE_HOST	The resolved host name.
REMOTE_USER	If the authentication method has been set, this variable contains the username.
REQUEST_METHOD	The type of posting to the script, either POST or GET.
SCRIPT_NAME	The name of the script.
SERVER_NAME	The IP, host, or alias of the server.
SERVER_PORT	The TCP port on which the server is running.
SERVER_PROTOCOL	The name and version of the protocol the server uses to communicate with the client.
SERVER_SOFTWARE	The name and version of the server.

6.2.2 Launching CGI programs

By their very nature, CGI programs are separate programs running on the processor. They require loading, memory allocation, and resource allocation, and once they have finished executing, they require unloading and resource deallocation. The CGI program must run separately from the web server since the web server cannot wait for the program to finish. If the program were to pause the web server execution, the web server could not continue to service requests from other clients.

Note This spawning of new programs is a well-known downside of using CGI programs. In a bid to address this, the CGI community came up with a variation to the specification called FastCGI. FastCGI is a means of eliminating or significantly reducing the startup overhead of loading and initializing programs. This is achieved by caching commonly used programs and allowing the web server to run the cached version, as opposed to loading a new instance from disk. Communication between FastCGI programs is still a major problem area.

FastCGI is generally implemented in C or C++ to eliminate the interpretation overhead of scripted solutions, such as Perl or shell scripts.

From that viewpoint, running the script as a separate process is the ideal way of sidestepping the problem of not being able to service multiple clients at once. It doesn't take long on a popular server for the CGI scripts to consume all the resources of the operating system. This results in either a denied CGI request or very slow processing of a request as the underlying operating system is stressed and potentially thrashes (meaning it is spending more time context switching between CGI processes than actually doing

6.2.3 CGI communication

Since a CGI program or script can be thought of as a standalone process, it must have a convenient and easy way of communicating with the web server and the client. This is achieved through the standard programming interfaces STDIN and STDOUT, as illustrated in figure 6.2.

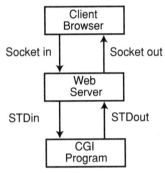

Figure 6.2 Communication between a CGI program and the client

STDIN and STDOUT (Standard In and Standard Out) are simply file streams that the program can read and write to. STDIN is for reading input to the program—for example, in a command-line environment, this could be the parameters passed in to the program. This is a read-only handle. On the other side of the fence is STDOUT. This is a write-only handle that allows programs to output ASCII text. The best examples of programs that use STDOUT as its output are the ls or grep UNIX commands.

Note Not all operating system environments readily support STDIN and STDOUT. For example, what is STDOUT for a program running Windows NT? In short, STDOUT and STDIN are only available to nongraphical processes. However, this still presents a hurdle. To get around this limitation, wrapper programs exist that put an extra level around the process to make CGI possible under such environments. However, wrappers are notoriously inefficient. They operate by taking the STDOUT from the web server and writing it to a file. The file is then opened by the process, and its output is written to another file. The wrapper comes along, opens up the file, and copies it to the STDIN of the web server.

With all the file operations, along with the delay introduced by waiting for the process to start and terminate, wrappers should be used only when other solutions are not at all possible.

When the web server launches a CGI program, it connects its STDOUT to the CGI's STDIN. Data from a POST or a GET, including all headers, is sent over this connection. The STDOUT from the CGI program is redirected back to the client. In reality, it goes straight back to the web server, which then passes it on to the client. But from the CGI developer's viewpoint, it's as if the program is connected directly to the client. This technique makes implementing CGI programs very easy from the developer's point of view.

6.3 General limitations

The biggest problem with CGI is that it only defines an interface. Some may argue this is one of its strengths. CGI doesn't impose any language constraints, which makes porting CGI programs a simple matter of copying files.

CGI has no standard or built-in library functions. Instead, CGI relies on third-party software to complete most of its tasks. Take, for instance, a CGI program that is written in Perl and running on a UNIX box, using the sendmail program to forward any outbound email. It would not operate on a Windows NT machine unless the sendmail program existed somewhere on the system. Thus, when a CGI program is to be ported, porting of the actual script is only half of the equation. All supporting programs that aid in the execution must have equivalents somewhere on the system.

Note   In this example, we are assuming the Perl interpreter is actually installed on the system. Without this, the script cannot even begin to run. Fortunately, many Perl interpreters exist for Windows NT, so it's not all doom and gloom.

Some CGI implementations cannot be ported readily. Scripts that have been compiled to run in a UNIX environment will need to be recompiled for another operating system; conversely, a script designed to run under Windows NT will probably need to be rewritten for UNIX.

The point may be argued that having a script that is portable over several web servers is not an issue. But in today's ever-changing computing world, why limit yourself to just one platform? If your company decides today that it wants to support Sun instead of Microsoft, you don't want to spend months porting all your well-established scripts to a system whose structure you know very little about.

Here's another question that causes some developers to stop and think: What happens to the program when more than one person accesses or tries to access it at the same time? Many languages do not provide adequate protection against this scenario. Process synchronization is inherently difficult to control if no help from the operating system or underlying libraries is present. A good example is when two instances of the same script attempt to open a common file. One will fail, assuming that the operating system locks the file properly in the first place, and one will succeed. What happens to the one that fails? Does it report back to the user with some error message asking for the user to resubmit the query?

A better solution is for the failed script to wait until the other has finished, and then attempt its update. But many CGI implementations do not allow this, since it can be very difficult to implement. This is why most web servers will return an "Internal Server" error.

Note Developers generally become politicians and quickly sidestep the issue of what happens when multiple clients attack the script at once. But with Java under your belt, you can now stand firm when such a question of multiple requests is fired at you.

6.4   CGI implementation

To round off our look at CGI, the following sections take a quick look at each of the different languages for implementing CGI programs. The purpose is twofold:

1   You can appreciate the number of different implementation methods that exist.

2   You can spot and make sense of a CGI program in preparation for the day when you are called to port it to Java.

The various languages listed in this section can be used to implement the CGI specification. Each language has its own strengths and weaknesses, depending on the environment and the application area in which it will be employed.

6.4.1   Perl

Type: Interpreted
Platform: UNIX / Windows NT / VMS / Apple Macintosh / OS/2

The Practical Extraction and Report Language (Perl) was originally developed by Larry Wall to handle large data sets and to create reports. With its roots in data processing, Perl's file handling is superb and it makes manipulating large files a trivial task. Perl is an interpreted language, making the actual script files pure ASCII. To run a Perl script, a Perl interpreter must be used; it's generally a simple matter of passing the script file as a parameter to the interpreter. A sample Perl script can be seen in example 6.1.

```
sub get_num {
   open(COUNT,"$count_file")
|| die "Can't Open Count Data File: $!\n";
   $count = <COUNT>;
   close(COUNT);
   if ($count =~ /\n$/) {
      chop($count);
   }
   $count++;
   open(COUNT,">$count_file") || die
"Can't Open Count Data File For Writing: $!\n";
   print COUNT "$count";
   close(COUNT);
}
```
Example 6.1   Sample Perl program which maintains a web counter using files

6.4.2 Shell scripts

Type: Interpreted
Platform: UNIX

Because the Internet grew from the UNIX world, the popularity of using shell scripts to create CGI programs is not really surprising. The downside is that only servers running UNIX can use this technique. A shell script is to UNIX what the batch file is to MS-DOS—it merely describes a sequence of programs that are run one after another. CGI programs written as shell scripts are very easy and quick to develop.

For example, a shell script program that can be used very easily within the CGI environment is the `cal` command. This command prints out the current month's calendar in a formatted text format. However, the major downside of using shell scripts is the security. If, for some reason, the account from which the script is running is the root, the script has the potential to do untold damages, ranging from deletion and reformatting to integrating user passwords.

6.4.3 C

Type: Compiled
Platform: UNIX / Windows NT / VMS / Apple Macintosh / OS/2

C is one of the most popular and well-known languages in use today. UNIX and C go hand in hand, considering C was developed to write UNIX in the first place. Hence, seeing CGI programs written in C is not surprising. C has many disadvantages and advantages associated with it. One of its strengths is its speed of execution because the program is compiled on the target platform. However, this is also one of its major disadvantages. Because each program needs to be ported, copying CGI programs from one server to another can actually turn out to be a major headache if you're going between servers of different hardware or software platforms.

Since much of CGI processing involves string manipulation, either decoding user strings or building new response pages, a strong string library would be advantageous. Alas, C falls short in this area. Since string manipulation in C is handled through memory pointers, getting it wrong can be very unforgiving to sloppy development. Stray CGI-C programs are known to take down complete web servers. An example of a C program can be seen in example 6.2.

```
#include <stdio.h>
main (int argc, char** argv, char** env)
{
  printf ("Content-type: text/html\n\n"); /* yes, two \n */
  printf ("<html><head><title>hello</title></head><body>\n");
  printf ("Hello, World!\n");
  printf ("<p>%s", env[0]);
  printf ("<p></body></html>\n");
}
```

Example 6.2   Sample C program which prints the famous "Hello, World!"

6.4.4 C++

Type: Compiled
Platform: UNIX / Windows NT / VMS / Apple Macintosh / OS/2

One of the most well-known object-oriented languages in use is C++ (next to Java, that is). This language from Bjarne Stroustrup is based on all the strengths of C and Small-Talk (another popular object-oriented language), and it removes all their weaknesses. Although it is based on C, C++ is an entirely different language. C++ is the foundation of Java; it is in itself a very strong language, especially in the way it handles object orientation. Building larger applications with C++ is much easier when using classes; they allow you to build sophisticated applications using previously developed blocks of code. However, porting and string manipulation is still a problem with C++. Example 6.3 shows a sample C++ program.

```
void main()
{
  //- Variable Initialization

  ifstream count_in;
  ofstream count_out;

  // Print Content-type header for browser
  cout << "Content-type: text/html\n\n";

  // Get the page location from the DOCUMENT_URI or QUERY_STRING
  // environment variables.
  if (!getenv("DOCUMENT_URI") && !getenv("QUERY_STRING"))
    error("no_uri","X");
}
```
Example 6.3 Sample C++ program which prints the content header of a request

6.4.5 TCL

Type: Interpreted
Platform: UNIX / Windows NT / VMS

Another popular interpreted language from the UNIX stable is the Tool Command Language (TCL, or "tickle" to its friends). TCL is simply a library of C routines that allows quicker responses than conventional script-based solutions. The problem with TCL is that porting between different UNIX platforms can be a headache; although the TCL script needs minimal adjustments, the TCL libraries need to be ported. Example 6.4 shows a simple "Hello, World!" example written in TCL.

```
#!/export/home/libes/bin/tclsh

package require cgi

cgi_eval {
```

```
source example.tcl
cgi_input

cgi_title "TCL example"

proc script {name} {
    global target
    cgi_url "$name.cgi" [cgi_cgi $name] $target
}

cgi_body bgcolor=#d0a0a0 text=#000000 {
    p "Hello World"
  cgi_li "Hello World!"
  }
}
```
Example 6.4 Sample TCL script which prints "Hello World!"

6.4.6 AppleScript

Type: Interpreted

Platform: Apple Macintosh (System 7 and later)

As you may have already guessed, AppleScript is specifically designed for the Macintosh platforms, and there is no move to port it to any other operating system. If the web server is running on an Apple and you need CGI scripting, then AppleScript is a very easy and quick language to learn for implementing CGI programs. Again, this language is interpreted and not at all portable.

6.4.7 Visual Basic

Type: Compiled

Platform: Windows NT

Visual Basic is a language that is ever growing in popularity. Born from the Microsoft stable, this language was originally developed to allow quick-and-easy Windows-based applications to be built. Visual Basic is finding new application areas in new fields. Although Visual Basic is only suitable for Windows-based platforms, the connectivity offered for communicating with other Windows applications makes this a very viable solution for Windows-based web servers.

Note Visual Basic is rapidly dominating the CGI arena with many ports from Perl to the new solution. More and more web administrators are switching from their tried-and-trusted UNIX platforms to Windows NT machines, thus pushing out Perl as the natural selection for CGI programs.

6.5 Future of CGI

Since this book focuses on the Java servlet API, this section is intentionally short—unlike CGI's future. In my opinion, it will take some time for CGI to completely die out, and it won't go without a fight, if the battle between Visual Basic and C++ for Windows is anything to go by. The Achilles' heel of CGI is that it is not readily portable to other operating systems. Although this is not a major issue for some developers, it is a serious concern for others. Another drawback is its speed. Although certain implementations have addressed this, CGI-based solutions are not as fast as Java-based servlets.

6.6 From here

This chapter presented a quick tour of CGI and highlighted alternatives to the Java servlet when embarking on server-side processing. Two of the main drawbacks to CGI are its poor handling of concurrent client requests and its inefficiency when first accessed.

The remaining chapters of this book take you through various server-side problems and show how servlets can be employed to solve them. As you review the examples, notice how Java handles the deficiencies inherent in CGI.

HTML page counters

CHAPTER CONCEPTS

- Discover counters, which provide analysis for page visits.

- Learn how to implement a simple hit counter. As the most basic form of a counter, it has little functionality.

- Learn how to use the same simple hit counter for multiple users, instead of having a new program instance for each counter.

- Understand remote counter administration, including the ability to edit counter attributes without resetting the counter.

Fashions come and go—in the '70s, flared trousers were all the rage; in the '80s, corduroy took over. Now, in the '90s, we're all wearing jeans. These fashion trends have evolved over three decades. Who knows what we will all be wearing after the turn of the century?

The world wide web has gone through its own "fashion" phases when you look at how HTML is used. It used to be very trendy to have a hit counter on your home page to show the number of visitors to your site. However, counters appear to have died away. It's a bit like having money—the more you have of it, the more you want to tell people about it; and the less you have, the less you want to tell people about it. In order for a hit counter to look impressive, it really needs to be of a significant value to show how popular the site is. But you need the traffic to legitimately increase the counter. Herein lies the Catch-22.

This chapter introduces the basic servlet API and implements a relatively powerful page or hit counter.

7.1 What is a hit counter?

"I counted them all out and I counted them all back."
  - Brian Hanrahan (BBC Journalist, 1982)

A hit counter is a simple program that counts the number of times a particular resource has been accessed. This is the most rudimentary form of analysis a web page can have, and for the majority of users this is all the information they really need. From this simple figure, they can gauge the popularity of their site, and they can publish this figure if they deem it significant enough.

One of the many misconceptions about a hit counter is that it represents the number of users that have accessed the site. This is not the case. It merely shows the number of times a page has been loaded. For example, a user pressing his browser reload button continuously will keep incrementing the counter. You would not consider this to be accurate statistics, as it's only one person artificially inflating the count. As you'll see later in this chapter, there are simple techniques for safeguarding against such underhanded tactics.

The reason some people have argued hit counters are redundant is that the log files show this figure anyway. To a certain extent, this is the case. However, a log file count will not distinguish between repeated hits from the same user, nor is it very accessible to the outside world. For example, placing the number of hits live on your home page may lead to running continual analysis on the log file. This is definitely not desirable.

The hit counter example presented in this chapter does not require access to any of the server logs, nor does it need to be running on the same server as the pages it is counting. This allows you to offer the services of your servlet to count page hits on friends' and colleagues' web sites.

7.1.1 How do you use a hit counter?

Before you get too concerned about how the counter actually operates, some consideration has to be given to how the counter will be used. A counter can be triggered in two main ways. We will look at each in turn.

- Server-side include
- Browser requesting a URL

Server-side include   An SSI is a special file which gets processed before it is sent out in response to each client request. The server parses the file, and inserts additional data at known tags.

SSI is the simplest and most flexible way of returning the counter information. For example, the counter could be referenced in an HTML file as shown in example 7.1.

```
<HTML><BODY>
<P>You are number <B>
<SERVLET NAME="ncount" CODE="ncount"></SERVLET>
</B> to have accessed this page
</BODY></HTML>
```
Example 7.1   Sample SSI with a page counter

When the user accesses this page, the server reads the HTML file and begins sending the file to the user. When it encounters the `<SERVLET>`...`</SERVLET>` tags, the servlet is run and the output from the servlet is sent to the client. Once the servlet is finished, the remaining HTML is sent. The resulting HTML file that appears in the user's browser is shown in example 7.2.

```
<HTML><BODY>
<P>You are number <B>
17654
</B> to have accessed this page
</BODY></HTML>
```
Example 7.2   The resulting HTML output from the server

The main advantage of this method is that it allows the HTML designer to format the text as he sees fit and not how the servlet developer perceives it should be. For example, since the output from the counter servlet is text, the HTML designer is free to place heading or font tags around the text to make it fit with the overall design of the page. An advantage to using this implementation is that the HTML that is produced gives no clue as to how the counter is operating.

Inline images   The second method of using a hit counter is to have the servlet create a GIF or JPEG representation of the value the counter is representing. Figure 7.1 shows one such possible output, in the form of a GIF image.

12874

Figure 7.1 The counter output as a simple image

One of the easiest ways to produce an image of this type is to make it up as a series of single images, where each image represents a single digit. For example, the image shown in figure 7.1 would be made up of five such images. To reference this new image from HTML, you would use the <IMG> tag, as shown in example 7.3.

```
<P>You are number
<IMG SRC="/ncount">
to have accessed this page
```
Example 7.3   The HTML code for the counter image

This method, though very simple, produces the most load on a server, in terms of both processor load and bandwidth stress. When this servlet is accessed, it not only has to increment the counter, but it also has to produce a separate GIF or JPG file and pass it to the client.

Note   Although an implementation of this method will be detailed later in this chapter, I don't recommend it, especially for sites with high traffic. The extra overhead the servlet has to perform to create the images costs time, and the extra data being sent to the client costs bandwidth. For this reason, many home pages that contained counters simply stalled at the place where the counter was supposed to be.

Maybe this is the reason they went out of fashion—sheer frustration on the part of the users!

7.2   Simple counters

Before we head on into the world of Java code, let's stop for a minute to define the exact problem we are trying to solve.

We need a counter that

- Increments a counter every time it is called.
- Offers a level of protection against false or bogus hits.
- Returns the value of the counter as ASCII text.

The first requirement should be straightforward enough. The second requirement needs a little thought. The simplest way to safeguard against bogus hits is to keep a record of the IP addresses accessing the servlet. The client's IP address is available in the header of the request. If you keep the IP address of the last person to increment the counter, you can run a simple check before adjusting the count. If the IP address of the calling client is different from the last IP to increment the counter, then allow the counter to increase. This stops users from continually hitting the reload or refresh button on the browser to cause the counter value to grow artificially.

It's important to note that this method will fail for users coming from behind firewalls and proxies. For example, a large company may direct all its Internet access through one proxy server. Therefore if multiple users from the same company visit your web page, each user request will have the same IP address—that of the proxy server.

7.2.1 ncount (version 1)

Before we actually define the servlet framework we intend to use, let's define the information we need to hold for any given counter. A counter has many attributes associated with it, as shown in table 7.1.

Table 7.1 Counter attributes

Member	Description
hitCount	Place to hold the number of hits.
lastIP	Last IP address to increment the counter.
lastDate	Date/time of the last increment.

The lastDate is a useful piece of information to hold. It essentially gives the counter a timestamp (which you'll learn how to use later in the chapter). For the moment, it can be set and then ignored.

The lastIP is the IP address of the last client to increment the counter. This is useful if the counter is to safeguard against bogus counts. Another advantage of holding this information is that it allows the counter to act as an alerting mechanism. For example, you might want to be alerted when users from a certain domain view your site. You'll learn more about this later.

For the first version of the counter, we will package this information into a separate class called cCountObject, as shown in example 7.4.

```
class cCountObject {
   private int hitcount;
   private String lastIP;
   private String lastDate;

   public cCountObject(){
     hitcount = 0;
     lastIP   = null;
   }

   public void increment(String _IP){
      if ( lastIP != null && lastIP.compareTo( _IP ) != 0 )
        hitcount++;

      lastIP = _IP;
      lastDate= new Date().toString();
   }

   public void increment(){
      hitcount++;
      lastDate= new Date().toString();
   }
```

```
public intgetHit(){
   return hitcount;
}
```
}

Example 7.4   The class to hold the counter information

Notice the two implementations of the overloaded method `increment(...)`. One simply increments the counter without worrying about the last IP address that incremented the count, and the other makes sure the IP address is different from the last. Both timestamp the last increment with the current time, because the variable `lastDate` represents the last time the counter was accessed (from where and by whom is immaterial).

Now let's move on to developing the actual servlet to handle this counter. The class we will base the counter servlet on will be the `GenericServlet` class from the `javax.servlet` package. This is the simplest form of servlet, and it will serve adequately as the base class for our counter.

Note   Although in this example we have used the class `GenericServlet`, there's nothing really stopping us from using an alternative base class such as `HttpServlet`.

We will override two methods of the `GenericServlet` class: `init(...)` and `service(...)`. The `init(...)` method is called only once when the servlet is first loaded. In this method we will instantiate our `cCountObject` class. Example 7.5 shows the initializing method for the code in our servlet.

```
public void init(ServletConfig _config) throws ServletException {
   super.init();
   Counter= new cCountObject();
   DateStarted= new Date().toString();
}
```
Example 7.5   The initializing method

For pure novelty value, we will keep the time the servlet was started (it can be used for later analysis). The `service(...)` method is a little more complicated. It has two functions: to increment the counter, and to format and send an output back to the client.

```
public void service( ServletRequest _req, ServletResponse _res)
                         throws ServletException, IOException {
   //- Increment the counter
   Counter.Increment( _req.getRemoteAddr() );

   //- Format the output
   _res.setContentType("text/plain");
   PrintWriter Out = _res.getWriter();
   Out.println( Counter.getHit() );
```

```
Out.flush();
}
```
Example 7.6   The service method for a simple counter

As you can see in example 7.6, the incrementing of the counter simplifies to one method call from the `cCountObject` class. However, note the additional call to the method `getRemoteAddr()` from the `ServletRequest` class. This is used to determine the host name of the client that made the request, and it will return the IP address of the client. Another method that is available in the `ServletRequest` class is the `getRemote-Host()` method, which returns the fully qualified name of the client.

Note `getRemoteAddr()` returns the same information as the CGI variable `REMOTE_HOST`.

This version of the counter outputs the result as plain ASCII text, which the HTML designer can then format as he wants. The complete code for the counter can be seen in example 7.7.

```java
import java.io.*;
import javax.servlet.*;

public class ncount1 extends GenericServlet {
   private cCountObject Counter;
   private String  DateStarted;

   public void init(ServletConfig _config) throws ServletException {
     super.init();
     Counter= new cCountObject();
     DateStarted= new Date().toString();
   }

   public void service( ServletRequest _req, ServletResponse _res )
                            throws ServletException, IOException {
     //- Increment the counter
     Counter.Increment( _req.getRemoteAddr() );

     //- Format the output
     _res.setContentType("text/plain");
      PrintWriter Out = _res.getWriter();
     Out.println( Counter.getHit() );
     Out.flush();
   }

   public String getServletInfo(){
     return "nCount Hit Servlet v1";
   }
}
```
Example 7.7   The complete source code for the first counter (ncount1.java)

Once this servlet has been added to the web server's sandbox, it can be called using the following HTML tags:

```
<SERVLET NAME="ncount1" CODE="ncount1"></SERVLET>
```

That's all that is required. Although it's very functional, this implementation of the counter has many drawbacks. First, it's not very flexible. For example, if the site needed more than one counter, then a separate instance would need to be created for each new counter. This, therefore, would be no more efficient than some CGI implementations that require separate program instances for each counter.

Second, the counter would be reset if the server were shut down; no mechanism is provided to store the state between server power cycles.

Another major flaw with this method is the fact that it could very easily produce invalid results if many users call it at the same time. The `Counter` object is not thread-safe. It is very possible for the servlet to be accessed by more than one instance at a time, thus rendering the count invalid.

The remainder of this chapter focuses on a much cleaner and safer solution.

7.3 Advanced counters

The previous section looked at a very simple implementation of a basic web counter and introduced the framework required to build a servlet. This section builds upon the previous version to include:

- The ability to handle multiple counters
- Thread-safe handling
- A variety of user options
- Various output options
- The ability to store a counter's states

7.3.1 Multiple counters

Extending `ncount` to handle multiple counters is not a complicated procedure. The first thing to recognize is that this can be easily accomplished by keeping a list of `cCountObject` objects where each one is identified by a unique key.

This key is then used in the servlet's HTML tags to ensure the correct counter is incremented. This counter implementation has been made as hassle-free as possible; if a user passes in a key that is not recognized, then a counter will be created and incremented. The main advantage of this method is that it keeps server-side administration to a minimum—there is no need for an administrator to manually add or install new counters.

Java has many different data storage classes available to you as a developer. For this implementation, we will use the hash table, which is found in the `java.util` package.

Note A hash table is a very powerful data storage mechanism which uses a key to look up its data members. Unlike a linked list, where every member has to be visited in turn and checked, the hash table performs a mathematical translation on the key to produce a value that can be used as a direct reference to the element. In general, this results in a much faster retrieval system than the conventional search-and-compare data structures. The main advantage of the hash table is that the retrieval performance is not affected by the number of elements in the table; thus, it's not uncommon to see hash tables used in a hybrid solution for database indexes.

Declaring the hash table is very easy, as you can see in example 7.8.

```
private Hashtable Counters;
Counters = new Hashtable( 10 );
```
Example 7.8   Declaring a list of counters

This example declares a hash table with an initial capacity of ten elements. When this limit is reached, the hash table automatically resizes itself to accommodate the extra element. Inspecting and inserting elements from the hash table is a straightforward process, and it is illustrated in example 7.9.

```
cCountObject CountObject;

String CounterID = _req.getParameter( "countid" );
CountObject      = (cCountObject)(Counters.get( CounterID ));

if ( CountObject == null ) {
   CountObject = new cCountObject( CounterID );
   Counters.put( CounterID, CountObject );
}
```
Example 7.9   Using the hash table

The ID of the counter is retrieved using the getParameter(…) method. This method attempts to retrieve the value of the given field from the query string. Since we are using the hash table data structure, we don't need to impose any rules on the ID chosen by the user. The ID can be a number or a text string. Using the ID, we now need to try to retrieve the element from the hash table that represents the object. If an element does not exist, then the get() method of Hashtable returns null. If this is the case, then we need to create a cCountObject and place it into the hash table using the key passed in by the user.

From this point on, we have a cCountObject which can be used, irrespective of whether it was recently created or came from the list.

7.3.2 IP protection

In the previous version of ncount, we assumed the user wanted to check for repeated IP counts. In other words, he didn't mind another user repeatedly reloading or revisiting a page. To ensure such assumptions aren't made again, we'll make this feature optional via the use of parameter tags. These tags may or may not be passed in with the call to the servlet.

```
String ipcheck= _req.getParameter( "lastip" );
if ( ipcheck.compareTo( "1" ) == 0 )
  CountObject.Increment( _req.getRemoteAddr(), 1 );
else
  CountObject.Increment( _req.getRemoteAddr(), 0 );
```
Example 7.10   IP protection

This extra functionality is easily given by simply checking the value of the parameter lastip, and then by calling the corresponding method from the cCountObject class. Example 7.10   illustrates the code to handle this optional facility.

7.3.3 Counter reset

Resetting the counter value back to zero is useful, and it's very easy to do. Again, this powerful feature can be easily integrated into the functionality of the counter through the use of query fields passed into the servlet.

```
String sReset= _req.getParameter( "reset" );
if ( sReset.compareTo( "1" ) == 0 )
  CountObject.reset();
```
Example 7.11   Counter reset shows the procedure for this feature

7.3.4 Counter output

There are many different ways for the servlet to output results to the end user. The servlet should:

- Be able to register the count, but output nothing.
- Output only the current count value.
- Output the current count and the last IP address.
- Output the current count, the last IP address, and the date of the last update.
- Output all the counters and their associated data.

These features can be controlled using the parameter tags, which are passed to the servlet using the query string.

```
String silent = _req.getParameter( "silent" );
if ( silent.compareTo( "1" ) == 0 )
  return;

_res.setContentType("text/plain");
PrintWriter Out = _res.getWriter();

Stringdall= _req.getParameter( "dall" );
if ( dall.compareTo( "1" ) == 0 ) {
  EnumerationiE= Counters.elements();
  while ( iE.hasMoreElements() ){
    CountObject = (cCountObject)iE.nextElement();
    Out.println( CountObject.getID() + "  -  " +
                 CountObject.getHit() + " - " +
                 CountObject.getIP() + " - " +
                 CountObject.getTime() );
  }
  return;
}

Stringdcount= _req.getParameter( "dcount" );
if ( silent.compareTo( "1" ) == 0 )
  Out.println( CountObject.getHit() );

Stringdip= _req.getParameter( "dip" );
if ( dip.compareTo( "1" ) == 0 )
  Out.println( " " + CountObject.getHit() );

Stringdtimestamp= _req.getParameter( "dtimestamp" );
if ( dtimestamp.compareTo( "1" ) == 0 )
  Out.println( " " + CountObject.getTime() );

Out.flush();
```
Example 7.12   Controlling output from the servlet

As shown in example 7.12, the output is controlled by determining the value in each parameter tag. Notice the `while(...)` loop. This is used to cycle through all the elements contained in the hash table. Having cycled through the list, there is no point in continuing with the remaining parameter checks (which is why the `return` is executed once the loop has finished).

7.3.5 Counter storage

In a perfect world, the server would run forever without error. Then there would be no need to write routines to store the state of the counter. But alas, this is not a perfect world, and servers have a tendency to be restarted every so often—if not on their own accord, then by the hands of an administrator. Therefore, the requirement to store the counter information is quite important.

However, the time it takes to write data out to a file is very costly in computing terms. Because of this, instead of writing the log file every time a counter changes, we will write it once every ten changes. Of course, this value should be increased or decreased accordingly, depending on the expected traffic.

Note   This method of looping through the hash table,

```
Enumeration iE = Counters.elements();
while ( iE.hasMoreElements() )
   CountObject = (cCountObject)iE.nextElement();
```

can be used with the majority of the data structures in Java's standard library. This has the advantage of allowing you to change the data storage method without worrying about the retrieval routines. However, some care has to be taken for data insertion, as some data structures require additional information when adding data objects.

Write log file   The method for writing the counter information is shown in example 7.13. This involves opening up an output stream to a file, then running through the list of counters and saving the necessary information, such as the number of hits and the last IP address.

```
private void writeFile( String _filename ){
  try{
   RandomAccessFile fileOut = new RandomAccessFile( _filename, "rw" );
  cCountObject CountObject;
  EnumerationiE = Counters.elements();
  while ( iE.hasMoreElements() ){
    CountObject= (cCountObject)iE.nextElement();
    fileOut.writeBytes( CountObject.getID()+"," );
    fileOut.writeBytes( CountObject.getHit()+"," );
    fileOut.writeBytes( CountObject.getIP()+"," );
    fileOut.writeBytes( CountObject.getTime()+"\n" );
  }
  }catch ( Exception E ){
    System.out.println( "FILEERROR: " + E );
  }
}
```
Example 7.13   Writing counter information

The file is written as a comma-delimited file. Here's an example of this file:

```
Counter#1,132,193.164.187.3,Sat Mar 22 16:36:03 PST 1997
Counter#2,11,193.164.187.3,Sat Mar 22 16:39:01 PST 1997
```

Note   The RandomAccessFile is a convenient class for reading and writing files. Although we simply open a file and rewrite the contents in this example, this class could easily be used for appending data. It allows for reading and writing anywhere in the file, using a file pointer that points to the current offset into the file. This class is extremely useful for files of fixed record sizes. Records may be updated without needing to rewrite the complete file again. This class is found in the java.io package.

Read log file   The method for reading the log file is shown in example 7.14. It is called once, at startup, from the `init()` method.

```
private void readFile( String _filename ){
  try
  {
    BufferedReader filein = new BufferedReader(
                           new InputStreamReader(
                           new FileInputStream( _filename ) ) );

    String LineIn;
    while( (LineIn = filein.readLine()) != null ){
      StringTokenizer st = new StringTokenizer( LineIn, "," );
      cCountObject count = new cCountObject(  st.nextToken(),
                                              st.nextToken(),
                                              st.nextToken(),
                                              st.nextToken() );
      Counters.put( count.getID(), count );
    }
  }catch ( Exception E ){
    System.out.println( "FILEERROR: " + E );
  }
}
```
Example 7.14   Reading the log file

As you can see, the file is read line by line, and then it is passed into the `StringTokenizer` class, which gives us an easy method of getting the tokens, or values, between the commas.

The method illustrated in this section wrote out simple ASCII text files. As you will see later in the book, to simply this procedure, we will use Object Serialization instead.

7.3.6 *Thread-safe execution*

Although this servlet doesn't explicitly use threads, it is itself a threaded application. For this reason, you cannot assume you're the only thread of execution running through it.

Due to the global hash table class `Counters`, we have to ensure that only one thread at a time modifies this structure. We can achieve this in two ways.

Note   Instead of using the `RandomAccessFile` class for reading, we have used a different method for reading, due to the fact that the `RandomAccessFile` does not provide us with a mechanism for reading lines one at a time. Besides, change is good.

`BufferedReader` is a new class found in JDK1.1. Coupled with `InputStream-Reader` and `FileInputStream`, it provides us with the ability to read line by line. This may seem like a long-winded way of getting to the necessary methods, and in a way it is. However, it is a very flexible and efficient way of handling streams.

The simpler way is to enclose the `service(...)` body inside a `synchronized` block. For example, example 7.15 shows one possible use of the `synchronized` keyword.

```
synchronized( Counters )
{
   //-- Place body of service(…) here
}
```
Example 7.15   Safeguarding from multiple access

This example shows how to control thread access to the variable `Counters` using the standard mechanisms provided in Java. The method shown here still allows multiple threads to execute, but when they come to the `synchronized` block, they are queued and executed in turn.

Note Although it's thread-safe, this is not the most efficient method. A more efficient technique would be to only synchronize the code accessing the `Counters` data structure. For example, we could do all accessing and modifying in the first part of the method, and have all the output in another section. This would allow us to synchronize the first part only.

Therefore, if two threads arrived at the `service(…)` method at once, then one thread would get to execute part one, while the other waited. Once the thread was finished with the first part, it would then allow the second thread to enter the first part, while the other thread formatted the output. This technique allows requests to be processed much more quickly, as the waiting time for thread collisions is kept to a minimum.

The servlet API provides an alternative to the normal Java thread protection through an interface from the `javax.servlet` package known as the `SingleThreadModel`. If it's implemented, this interface ensures that the servlet will be thread-safe, guaranteeing that no two instances will be executing the `service(…)` method at once. To utilize this feature, simply implement the interface as shown in example 7.16.

```
public class ncount extends GenericServlet implements SingleThreadModel
{
   //-- Place body of servlet here
}
```
Example 7.16   Using the javax.servlet.SingleThreadModel

7.3.7 The complete example
Example 7.17   shows the complete code for the counter servlet.

```
import java.io.*;
import java.util.*;
import javax.servlet.*;

public class ncount extends GenericServlet
{
   private HashtableCounters;
   private StringDateStarted;
   private intsaveFile;
```

```
public void init(ServletConfig _Config) throws ServletException{
   super.init();
   Counters= new Hashtable( 10 );
   DateStarted= new Date().toString();

   //- Read any previous information
   saveFile= 0;
   readFile( "./ncount.ini" );
}

public void service( ServletRequest _req, ServletResponse _res)
                             throws ServletException, IOException{
   synchronized( Counters )
   {
      cCountObjectCountObject;

      String CounterID= _req.getParameter( "countid" );
      CountObject= (cCountObject)(Counters.get( CounterID));

      if ( CountObject == null )
      {
         CountObject = new cCountObject( CounterID );
         Counters.put( CounterID, CountObject );
      }

      //- Increment the counter
      String ipcheck= _req.getParameter( "lastip" );
      if ( ipcheck.compareTo( "1" ) == 0 )
         CountObject.increment( _req.getRemoteAddr(), 1 );
      else
         CountObject.increment( _req.getRemoteAddr(), 0 );

      //- Save the file, if necessary
      saveFile+= 1;
      if ( saveFile > 10 )
      {
         writeFile( "./ncount.ini" );
         saveFile = 0;
      }

      String silent= _req.getParameter( "silent" );
      if ( silent.compareTo( "1" ) == 0 )
         return;

      _res.setContentType("text/plain");
      PrintWriter Out = _res.getWriter();

      Stringdall= _req.getParameter( "dall" );
      if ( dall.compareTo( "1" ) == 0 )
      {
         EnumerationiE= Counters.elements();
         while ( iE.hasMoreElements() )
         {
            CountObject=(cCountObject)iE.nextElement();
```

```
            Out.println(CountObject.getID() + ": <B>" +
                    CountObject.getHit() +
                    "</B><BR>Last IP: <B>" +
                    CountObject.getIP() +
                    "</B><BR>Last Update: <B>" +
                    CountObject.getTime() +
                    "</B><BR><BR>" );
        }
        Out.flush();
        return;
    }

    String dcount= _req.getParameter( "dcount" );
    if ( silent.compareTo( "1" ) == 0 )
        Out.println( CountObject.getHit() );

    String dip= _req.getParameter( "dip" );
    if ( dip.compareTo( "1" ) == 0 )
        Out.println( " " + CountObject.getHit() );

    String dtimestamp= _req.getParameter( "dtimestamp" );
    if ( dtimestamp.compareTo( "1" ) == 0 )
        Out.println( " " + CountObject.getTime() );

    Out.flush();
    }
}

private voidwriteFile( String _filename ){
    try{
        RandomAccessFile fileOut = new RandomAccessFile( _filename,
                            "rw" );

        cCountObjectCountObject;
        EnumerationiE= Counters.elements();
        while ( iE.hasMoreElements() )
        {
            CountObject= (cCountObject)iE.nextElement();
            fileOut.writeBytes( CountObject.getID()+"," );
            fileOut.writeBytes( CountObject.getHit()+"," );
            fileOut.writeBytes( CountObject.getIP()+"," );
            fileOut.writeBytes( CountObject.getTime()+"\n" );
        }
    }
    catch ( Exception E ){
        System.out.println( "FILEERROR: " + E );
    }
}

private voidreadFile( String _filename ){
    try{
        BufferedReader filein = new BufferedReader(
                            new InputStreamReader(
                            new FileInputStream( _filename ) ));
```

```
        String LineIn;
        while( (LineIn = filein.readLine()) != null )
        {
            StringTokenizer st = new StringTokenizer( LineIn, "," );
            cCountObjectcount = new cCountObject( st.nextToken(),
st.nextToken(),
                            st.nextToken(), st.nextToken() );

            Counters.put( count.getID(), count );
        }
    }catch ( Exception E ){
        System.out.println( "FILEERROR: " + E );
    }
}

public String getServletInfo(){
    return "Page Hit Servlet";
}
}
```

Example 7.17   The complete counter servlet code

7.3.8 Using the counter servlet

This section demonstrates how to use the counter servlet within HTML pages. Including a counter in an HTML page is very easy. Simply add the lines shown in example 7.18 anywhere in the page. Since this combination of parameters doesn't provide any output, it will not show up on the page when it is displayed, but the count will still have taken place.

```
<servlet name="ncount" code="ncount">
<param name="countid" value="N-ARY Homepage">
<param name="lastip" value="0">
<param name="dip" value="0">
<param name="silent" value="1">
<param name="dcount" value="0">
<param name="dtimestamp" value="0">
<param name="dall" value="0">
</servlet>
```

Example 7.18   Example HTML servlet reference

If the parameter `dall` is set to 1, then the output shown in figure 7.2 is generated. This triggers the servlet to print out all the counter values on one page.

7.4 Further development

Although the servlet we've created in this chapter is very usable and feature rich, there are many enhancements that could be added to it:

- The ability to reset the counter to zero via parameter tags.
- A much tighter thread control mechanism.
- An administration FORM to make the creation and administration of counters much easier.

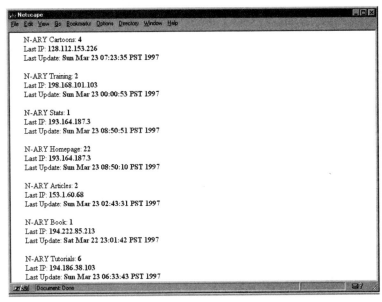

Figure 7.2 Example output from the servlet

- Optional graphical output (the chapter on ASCII to GIF conversion will illustrate this method).

In its current state, this servlet is a very efficient means of counting the number of the hits to an HTML page. Once the servlet is installed, it never needs any maintenance, and it can be left to run quietly in the background.

Who knows? Maybe now that counters have become much faster and more efficient, they will come back into vogue and once again grace many a home page, just as so many of our fashion trends have come back. But as so many of the fads have disappeared forever, maybe the fate of counters has already been sealed.

C H A P T E R   8

General HTML utilities

- Forms are not only for gathering data—see how they can be used to provide a very powerful and clean navigational tool.

- Some browsers, namely Netscape, support the file upload HTML form tag. Learn how to create a servlet that handles the data returned from the client.

- Use a servlet to deliver files to the client from a Zip/gzip file and save space on the server.

- Discover a utility class that uses HTML templates, complete with a simple cache system.

Servlets can be used in many different application areas—this book is a testament to that. Not only are they useful in the bigger areas, but a number of smaller areas benefit as well. This chapter presents a few small but very functional servlets.

The first set of servlets is based on HTML forms. HTML forms are very powerful mechanisms; they were one of the first ways a web user could communicate back to a server. In the last chapter, we saw how servlets can be used to process forms with the intent to either store the results on the server or package up the data and email it to an administrator. As you go through the rest of this book, you will see HTML forms being employed in a variety of applications, each passing valuable data back to the server for processing. In addition to the form-based utilities, you'll see a servlet that can be used in sites that have limited disk space available to them, such as the free disk space found with dialup accounts.

8.1   Navigational forms

When a user is presented with an HTML page, there are a number of ways he can move off that original page. The most obvious way is to offer the user a clickable link to another page, using a phrase, word, or image. Although links are very flexible, they sometimes don't quite provide the interface the web designer is looking for. An alternative to a link is an HTML form button; when it's clicked, it will take the user to any resource available on the network.

Processing this button can be done either at the client side or the server side. At the client side, a Javascript script could be defined in the HTML file, and instead of the form invoking a server-side process, it would process the Javascript. This solution has the downfall of requiring the user's browsers to support Javascript. Although the majority of the mainstream browsers do support Javascript, there is quite a compatibility problem between Netscape and Microsoft.

Note   Javascript is the brainchild of Netscape Communications and it is intended to be a halfway house between Java and HTML. Javascript is a scripting language that runs at the client side, and it looks very similar to Java. But that's where the similarity ends. Javascript's name alone begs confusion. It is not truly compatible across all the client browsers, with Microsoft's implementation slightly different from the original Netscape standard. This can be annoying to visitors who can't run the client program, especially if the site relies heavily on it. This is why a lot of design companies don't use Javascript anywhere on their sites.

The second method is to use some sort of server-side solution (and since this book is about servlets, it would seem a shame to use anything else!). To make this a server-side solution, there needs to be a form on the HTML page for the user to fill out. When the user returns the form to the server, the servlet is invoked. This is shown in example 8.1. A button is displayed on the page, and when the user clicks on it, a single parameter is sent to the servlet. The parameter details the URL the client should be taken to.

```
<HTML><BODY>
<FORM ACTION="/servlet/nav_form" METHOD="GET">
<INPUT TYPE="HIDDEN" NAME="GOTO" VALUE="http://www.n-ary.com">
<INPUT TYPE="SUBMIT" NAME="ACTION" VALUE="Jump to somewhere">
</FORM>
</BODY></HTML>
```
Example 8.1   HTML navigational code

When the servlet receives the request from the client, it simply extracts the parameter and sends the client to the new location. Sending the client to another URL is a simple method call from the `HttpServletResponse` class: `sendRedirect(…)`. This method uses the functionality found in the HTTP protocol to accomplish the task. For example, the code

```
_res.sendRedirect( "http//www.liquid.org");
```
would open the URL and at display the page for the user. Any further client data from the current request would be ignored. This client redirection is used in many different applications, and as you'll see in other chapters, there are a number of ways to redirect the user to another URL. This method, however, is by far the cleanest.

With the servlet processing an HTML form, navigational tools can be built from the majority of the controls found in the HTML arsenal, as shown in figure 8.1.

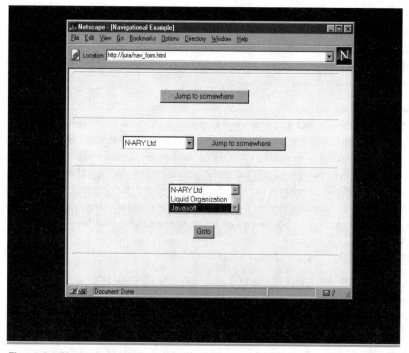

Figure 8.1 Navigational forms

8.1.1 Complete servlet source code

Example 8.2 shows the complete servlet class for implementing the redirection. The servlet is based on `HttpServlet`, since we need to be able to use the methods from the `Http ServletResponse` class. If for some reason the parameter `GOTO` is not present, then the servlet returns a No Content flag in the HTTP protocol.

```
import java.io.*;
import javax.servlet.*;
import javax.servlet.http.*;

public class nav_form extends HttpServlet {
  public void doGet( HttpServletRequest _req, HttpServletResponse _res)
                             throws ServletException, IOException {
    String strGoto = _req.getParameter( "GOTO" );
    if (  strGoto != null && strGoto.length() != 0 )
      _res.sendRedirect( strGoto );
    else
      _res.setStatus( HttpServletResponse.SC_NO_CONTENT );
  }
}
```
Example 8.2 Navigational servlet

For this implementation, we overrode the `doGet(…)` method, as opposed to the `service(…)` method. Since our HTML form specified a GET method, this method will be executed every time the user presses the button. However, if the HTML is changed to a POST method, then the servlet would not be executed. To respond to a POST, the `doPost(…)` method needs to be overridden.

8.2 File uploading

An HTML form allows many different application areas to come alive on the world wide web, as this book demonstrates. Giving the user a mechanism to pass data back to the server via the browser gave CGI and servlets a purpose. However, many applications only require simple data, such as user details like name and address. Netscape Communications recognized the need to give users the flexibility to send more than simple textual information to the server. They added a new input control to the HTML form list; this control enables users to send files from their client machines to the server.

This new HTML tag, FILE, can be used inside the HTML <FORM> tags, which render a new field for the form. You can see the FILE tag in use in example 8.3. The first thing you will notice is the inclusion of the ENCTYPE in the form definition tag. This tells the browser how to package the data coming from the form; in this instance, the MIME type of the data will be a `multipart` form. This MIME type allows different MIME types to be transmitted together as one single MIME transfer. Another example of this `multipart` MIME type can be seen in chapter 14.

```
<FORM ENCTYPE="multipart/form-data" ACTION="/servlet/upload"
METHOD="POST">
```

```
Upload file: <INPUT TYPE="FILE" NAME="USERFILE">
<INPUT TYPE="SUBMIT" VALUE="Upload">
</FORM>
```
Example 8.3   HTML file upload

When the page is rendered, it creates two controls: a text input field and a button marked Browse. When the button is clicked, the user is presented with his standard file selection box, from which he can choose any file on his local machine. Once a file is selected, the full path of the file is printed in the text box on the HTML page. Sending the file (including any additional form data) to the server is then a matter of clicking the Upload button.

At the server side, decoding this data takes a bit of care and some knowledge on how it is transmitted. When this book was published, the servlet API had no support for multipart MIME types, so this section presents a small utility class that can be used to decode such input streams.

The data read from the chosen local file is packaged up at the client side in a particular MIME format, depending on the file type. For example a JPEG image would be encoded as an `image/jpeg` type. Decoding the incoming file data at the server side must be performed manually, since no API calls exist to aid this process. The idea of the multipart MIME type is to be able to transmit, in a block or session, multiple data types. Each data type is packaged with a small header that describes its content. The different blocks are then appended to each other, with a unique delimiter/separator string. Once the format of the blocks is known, decoding it is academic.

As an example, the test form we are using will send another field in the data stream. This additional field is a simply a normal text field named GOTO. The extra field will show how the client packages the data.

The data received by the servlet when the user clicks the Submit button can be seen in the postmortem dump shown in example 8.4. This output was obtained by temporarily inserting a print statement (`System.out.println(…)`) into the servlet and printing each line as it came in. To make things easier to read, we will send a pure text file so we can easily identify the boundaries between each data block.

```
---------------------------294591272419378
Content-Disposition: form-data; name="GOTO"

http://www.n-ary.com
---------------------------294591272419378
Content-Disposition: form-data; name="userfile"; file-
name="C:\temp\quiz.txt"
Content-Type: text/plain

<EMBED SRC="http://jura/baywatch.mid" AUTOSTART=TRUE CONTROLS=true><BR>
Is it…
Baywatch ?
Dallas ?
Batman ?
```

```
1
<EMBED SRC="http://jura/x_files.mid" AUTOSTART=TRUE CONTROLS=true><BR>
Is it…
Star Trek: Voyager ?
Twin Peaks ?
The X-Files ?
3
<EMBED SRC="http://jura/friends.mid" AUTOSTART=TRUE CONTROLS=true><BR>
Is it…
I Love Lucy ?
Friends ?
The Flintstones ?
2
----------------------------294591272419378--
```

Example 8.4   The output resulting from a multiform post

Is you look closely at the data, the way each MIME or data field is separated should become readily apparent. The first thing the originator sends out is the delimiting string. This is a unique string that is calculated to be distinct every time a transmission occurs. This string is then used to section off each field, with the final line being the delimiter plus two dashes. This signals the end of the stream. Using this information we can easily determine the start and finish of any incoming files.

The line immediately preceding the delimiter describes the makeup of the data block (known as the Content-Disposition field). This generally describes the MIME type of the whole block of data, complete with the field name for the block. The field name is described in the name parameter on the same line. If the block represents a file sent by the user, then an additional field parameter is found which details the complete pathname of the file transmitted in the filename parameter. This information is important, since it allows the server to accurately save the file using the same name it was given at the client.

Optionally, the next line may contain the Content-Type field. This describes the MIME type of the data block. If the Content-Type field is unknown, then this line is omitted. Two hard returns separate the header from the data. Data is then everything that appears between the second of the two hard returns and a hard return followed immediately by the delimiter. By counting the number of hard returns, the header and data fields can be easily distinguished.

Since the order of these fields can never be guaranteed, we will develop a general utility class to handle this incoming data stream.

When you're building such a class, a number of issues have to be considered. First, given the nature of the data that will be posted, it is unwise to give the developer the ability to pick out data as often as he wishes—for example, to retrieve the last data field and then ask for the first data field. The fields must be retrieved in the order they are posted. For example, consider a file that is many megabytes in size. It would be silly to try to buffer this in memory, on the off-chance the user may want it. Since the class will be decoding a live input stream, each parameter will be presented to the user when it arrives. Because of the enumerationlike interface to the class, the user will be presented with the name of the field that is about to be received; it's then up to him to call the correct function to return the data.

Note When a post of this kind comes to the server, many of the supporting functions that provide assistance for the decoding process return invalid or null values; therefore, they must not be relied on. For example, making a call to the HttpRequest class to return the content-length will produce an invalid figure. This happens because nine out of ten times the content-length is unknown, and the this method will return the size of the last block size it received. As a domino effect, some of the underlying InputStream methods will not operate correctly since the size of the stream will be invalid. For example, calls to determine how much is left to read will also return misleading values.

When file data comes in, the best way to handle it is to have it passed out to an output stream, such as a FileOutputStream instance. This saves the servlet from having to buffer the complete file, which may be in the megabyte range, before finally writing out to disk. The interface to the utility class will consist of the methods described in table 8.1.

Table 8.1 The parseMultiForm **interface**

Method	Description
parseMultiForm(ServletRequest)	Creates an instance of the class based on the ServletRequest class.
String getNextParameter()	Returns the field name of the next parameter in the stream.
String getFilename()	If the next data block is a file, then this returns the filename of the data; otherwise, it returns null.
boolean getParameter(OutputStream)	Writes the data out to the OutputStream, returning true or false depending on its success.
String getParameter()	Returns the data as a string.

8.2.1 *Initializing the class*

Example 8.4 gave us a postmortem dump of the data the browser physically sent to the server. By retrieving an object instance to the input stream from the client, a class could be built that would dissect the data block line by line. However, this isn't the most efficient way to handle this particular MIME type.

The ServletRequest class has a number of methods associated with it that allow you to easily extract various pieces of information without having to parse the complete block. This sounds good, but know that a significant amount of parsing still needs to be performed.

The key to parsing the incoming data stream is knowing the delimiter—the boundary string. This is the string that marks the beginning and end of each MIME type that is transferred. Example 8.5 shows the procedure for extracting the boundary information from a given client connection.

```
delimitor    = _req.getContentType();
if ( delimitor.indexOf("boundary=") != -1 ){
  delimitor = delimitor.substring( delimitor.indexOf("boundary=")+9,
                                   delimitor.length() );
  delimitor = "--" + delimitor;
}
```
Example 8.5   Delimiter extraction

The method `getContentType()` from the `ServletRequest` class essentially returns the first line sent by the browser. This contains the MIME type of the complete block (in this instance, `multipart/form`) and the boundary string, if present.

By performing a basic parse of the string, we can easily extract the bounding string. You'll notice the addition of a few extra hyphens; the actual delimiter used inside the block always begins with "—" followed by the actual boundary string itself.

The `getNextParameter()` method of our new class will be used to read the header section of each data block and to position the input pointer at the start of the data. Since we will be reading this data one line at a time, a number of options are open to us. We could create an instance of `BufferedReader` and use the `readLine()` method to read each line. Although this is perfectly legal, we may as well use the methods provided as part of the servlet API. The `ServletInputStream` has an optimized `readLine(…)` method for this very task.

Before we can use this method, we need to do a little conversion. The method, in its raw format, only reads into a byte array—ultimately, we need it in a `String` format, which will allow for easy parsing.

Example 8.6 shows the private method of our new class, which will read the next line from the client using the `readLine(…)` from the `ServletInputStream`. In our private class variables, we have declared a `byte` buffer of 4K, which will be useful throughout the execution life of the class.

```
private String readLine(){
  try{
    int noData = In.readLine( buffer, 0, buffer.length );
    if ( noData != -1 )
      return new String( buffer, 0, noData, "ISO-8859-1");
    }catch(Exception E){}
    return null;
}
```
Example 8.6   Reading a line from the stream

Reading each block is a two-step process. The first step is to retrieve the meta-data, and the second step is to set the stream pointer to the start of the data, as shown in example 8.7.

Once the Content-Disposition line has been found in the incoming stream, the parameter name of the field is extracted using a combination of the `indexOf(…)` and `substring(…)` methods from the `String` class. If the data block represents a file, then the additional `File` field will exist in the same line.

```
while ( (LineIn=readLine()) != null ){
  if ( LineIn.indexOf( "name=" ) != -1 ){
    int c1 = LineIn.indexOf( "name=" );
    int c2 = LineIn.indexOf( "\"", c1+6 );
    paramName = LineIn.substring( c1+6, c2 );

    if ( LineIn.indexOf( "filename=") != -1 ){
      c1 = LineIn.indexOf( "filename=" );
      c2 = LineIn.indexOf( "\"", c1+10 );
      filename = LineIn.substring( c1+10, c2 );
      if ( filename.lastIndexOf( "\\" ) != -1 )
        filename = filename.substring( filename.lastIndexOf( "\\" )+1 );

      if ( filename.length() == 0 )
        filename - null;
    }

    //- Move the pointer to the start of the data
    LineIn = readLine();
    if ( LineIn.indexOf( "Content-Type" ) != -1 )
      LineIn = readLine();

    return paramName;
  }
}
```

Example 8.7   Reading the block header

Checking for the presence of the File tag is performed using the indexOf(...) method again. If the field is present, then it will contain the complete pathname of the file, which is too much information for the servlet. It merely requires the filename only. Extracting this filename is a case of removing all the data before and including the last "\" symbol in the field value. If no filename is present in this data block, then the variable filename is set to null, and this block is deemed a normal HTML variable.

Before this method returns the call, it positions the stream pointer to the start of the data; this is done with a single readLine() call.

8.2.2 Reading the file data

If the data for the block is a nonfile (in other words, an actual HTML form field), then retrieving the data for it is simply an additional readLine() call. Things get a little trickier for file data.

Once we have read the header information for the block, we can assume the stream pointer is at the start of the data. Therefore, all the data from here and up to the next pointer can be considered file data, and be saved accordingly.

Example 8.8 illustrates the code that will save the data to an output stream. We read a new line into the buffer, and if the buffer starts with a hyphen, then it could possibly be a delimiter. We check this by converting the buffer into a string and then comparing it against the delimiter. If it is a delimiter, then we break out of the loop and flush out the data in the output stream.

```
int noData;
while ( (noData=In.readLine(buffer,0,buffer.length)) != -1 ){
  if ( buffer[0] == '-' ){
    if ( new String( buffer, 0, noData, "ISO-8859-1").indexOf(delimitor)
                          == 0 )
      break;
  }else
    _Out.write( buffer, 0, noData );
}
_Out.flush();
```
Example 8.8 Reading the file data

By using the readLine(...) method, we have reduced the complexity of reading files down to a matter of six lines.

8.2.3 parseMultiForm class
Packaging the functionality described above into a single class makes the parsing of such data a trivial matter when receiving such posts in future, as shown in example 8.9.

```
class parseMultiForm extends java.lang.Object {
  private ServletInputStream In;
  private byte buffer[] = new byte[4096];
  private String delimitor = null;
  private String filename=null;

  public parseMultiForm( ServletRequest _req ) throws IOException{
    In  = _req.getInputStream();
    delimitor  = _req.getContentType();
    if ( delimitor.indexOf("boundary=") != -1 ){
      delimitor = delimitor.substring( delimitor.indexOf("boundary=")+9,
                            delimitor.length() );
      delimitor = "--" + delimitor;
    }
  }

  private String readLine(){
    try{
      int noData = In.readLine( buffer, 0, buffer.length );
      if ( noData != -1 )
        return new String( buffer, 0, noData, "ISO-8859-1");
    }catch(Exception E){}
    return null;
  }

  void test() throws IOException{
    String LineIn;
    while( (LineIn=readLine()) != null )
      System.out.println( LineIn  );
  }

  public String getFilename(){
    return filename;
  }
```

```java
public String getParameter(){
    return readLine();
}

public String getNextParameter() {
    try{
        String LineIn=null, paramName=null;

        while ( (LineIn=readLine()) != null ){
            if ( LineIn.indexOf( "name=" ) != -1 ){
                int c1 = LineIn.indexOf( "name=" );
                int c2 = LineIn.indexOf( "\"", c1+6 );
                paramName = LineIn.substring( c1+6, c2 );

                if ( LineIn.indexOf( "filename=") != -1 ){
                    c1 = LineIn.indexOf( "filename=" );
                    c2 = LineIn.indexOf( "\"", c1+10 );
                    filename = LineIn.substring( c1+10, c2 );
                    if ( filename.lastIndexOf( "\\" ) != -1 )
                        filename = filename.substring( filename.lastIndexOf( "\\"
                                        )+1 );

                    if ( filename.length() == 0 )
                        filename = null;
                }

                //- Move the pointer to the start of the data
                LineIn = readLine();
                if ( LineIn.indexOf( "Content-Type" ) != -1 )
                    LineIn = readLine();

                return paramName;
            }
        }
    }
    catch( Exception E ){}
    return null;
}

public boolean getParameter( OutputStream _Out ){
    try{
        int noData;
        while ( (noData=In.readLine(buffer,0,buffer.length)) != -1 ){
            if ( buffer[0] == '-' ){
                if ( new String( buffer, 0, noData,
                                "ISO-8859-1").indexOf(delimitor) == 0 )
                    break;
            }else
                _Out.write( buffer, 0, noData );
        }

        _Out.flush();
        return true;
    }
```

```
  catch( Exception E ){
    System.out.println( E  );
  }

  return false;
  }
}
```
Example 8.9   The complete source code for `parseMultiForm`

8.2.4 Using the class

Example 8.10 shows a sample use of the utility class developed for parsing multiform data. Multiform data is posted to the server in a series of header and data fields, which must be decoded accurately to ensure that no data is lost.

We can use the `getNextParameter()` method to determine which form data is next, then we use the corresponding method to correctly retrieve the data.

Since we know the amount of data being posted by the client will be greater than the maximum limited imposed by the GET method, the form will be using POST. Therefore, we can override the `doPost(...)` method.

```
import java.io.*;
import javax.servlet.*;
import javax.servlet.http.*;

public class upload extends HttpServlet {

  public void doPost( HttpServletRequest _req, HttpServletResponse _res )
                          throws ServletException, IOException{

    parseMultiForm pMF = new parseMultiForm( _req );

    String param;
    while ( (param = pMF.getNextParameter()) != null ){
      if ( param.equalsIgnoreCase("USERFILE") ){
        FileOutputStream OutFile = new FileOutputStream(
                            pMF.getFilename() );
        pMF.getParameter( OutFile );
        OutFile.close();
      }else{
        System.out.println( "Key   : " + param );
        System.out.println( "Value: " + pMF.getParameter() );
      }
    }
    _res.setStatus( HttpServletResponse.SC_NO_CONTENT );
  }
}
```
Example 8.10   The code for the `upload.java` **method**

8.3 Zip archive retrieval

One of the nicer additions to the JDK1.1 API is the Zip package. This package gives an easy-to-use Java interface to files that have been archived using the Zip or gzip compression format. This feature has opened up a number of possibilities that were previously quite messy to implement. Sites that use many static text files and find themselves running short of disk space may benefit from zipping up the lesser-used files, uncompressing them only when they are accessed. This technique of compressing files is greatly encouraged on sites where traffic is low and disk space is scarce. CGI programs do a wonderful job here in running a shell script and redirecting the output back out to the client, but the Zip package is much more convenient.

The servlet presented in this section will take two parameters from the client, open up the archive, and then send the resulting uncompressed file back to the client. The first parameter specifies the archive or Zip file. Using this parameter, an instance of the `Zip-File` class is created.

```
ZipFile zF = new ZipFile( _strArchive );
```

This class opens a reference to the archive file using the `RandomAccessFile` class. Why is this level of detail important? It determines how the file should be translated from its logical path to real path information. Any filename specified must first be translated to a real pathname; this is done through a call to the `getRealPath(...)` method from the `Serv-letRequest` class.

Each Zip file may contain more than one file, thus allowing complete directory structures to be compressed. Fortunately the Zip API has taken care of this structure. Each file that appears in the archive is described using the `ZipEntry` class. This class gives you access to a whole host of information about the file and its compressed state. But the most important aspect of this class is its ability to retrieve an input stream to the file in the archive.

```
ZipEntry zE = zF.getEntry( _file );
DataInputStream In = new DataInputStream(zF.getInputStream(zE));
```

This input stream represents the uncompressed version of the file in the archive. From here, we can simply read a line from the input stream and send it straight out to the client.

Note The Zip package supports both the creation and the reading of compression files using either the Zip format or the UNIX compression standard gzip. Since each format can have more than one file associated with it, extracting all the file entries is done by getting an `Enumeration` instance to it.

```
      Enumeration E = zF.getEntries();
      while ( E.hasMoreElements() )
          System.out.println( E.nextElement() );
```

This code fragment prints out all the filenames that are present in the archive file.

8.3.1 Complete servlet source

Example 8.11 shows the complete source code for the unzip servlet. This servlet can be invoked just as any other URL is:

```
<A HREF="http://www.n-ary.com/servlet/
unzip?archive=file.html&file=1.htm">Display</A>
```

The archive parameter defines the archive file from which the file specified in the file parameter will be extracted. The servlet is based on the HttpServlet class, with the implementation being thread-safe from other client requests to the same servlet.

```
import java.io.*;
import javax.servlet.*;
import javax.servlet.http.*;
import java.util.*;
import java.util.zip.*;

public class unzip extends HttpServlet
{
  public void service( HttpServletRequest _req, HttpServletResponse _res)
                              throws ServletException, IOException
  {
    String strArchive = _req.getParameter( "archive" );
    String strFile = _req.getParameter( "file" );
    if ( strArchive != null && strArchive.length() != 0 &&
      strFile != null && strFile.length() != 0 ){
      unzipFile( _req.getRealPath(strArchive), strFile, _res );
    }
    else
      _res.setStatus( HttpServletResponse.SC_NO_CONTENT );
  }

  private void unzipFile( String _strArchive, String _file,
                          HttpServletResponse _res ) throws IOException
  {
    ZipFile zF = new ZipFile( _strArchive );
    ZipEntry zE = zF.getEntry( _file.toUpperCase() );

    _res.setContentType( "text/html" );
    PrintStream    Out = new PrintStream( _res.getOutputStream() );
    DataInputStream In = new DataInputStream( zF.getInputStream( zE ) );
    String LineIn;
    while ( (LineIn=In.readLine()) != null )
      Out.println( LineIn );
```

```
      zF.close();
      Out.flush();
   }
}
```
Example 8.11   The complete unzip servlet class

8.4 HTML template class

This book will use many servlets that need to produce dynamic HTML code. As always, we have at least two options available to complete this—we can hardcode all the HTML into the servlets and have complete control, or we can develop a template system that will allow us to easily pour data into predefined HTML pages. The advantage of the latter is that it allows a professional HTML designer to concentrate on the look and feel of the document, and leave the servlet developer the worry of having to recompile the code all the time.

This section will present a solution that is based on HTML comment tags. In addition, another set of classes will be shown that will allow you to efficiently work with many of these templates using a fairly sophisticated caching system.

8.4.1 htmlTemplate class

We want to build a system that will give maximum control to the HTML designer, while also giving flexibility and ease of use to the servlet developer. The system that will be shown will operate from HTML comment tags, and the servlet will replace the tags with good data. Therefore, these tags will operate as placeholders. The sample HTML file shown in example 8.12 illustrates one such example.

```
<HTML><BODY>
This is a small test. Today's date is <!--date-->.
</BODY></HTML>
```
Example 8.12   The HTML template

As you can see, the HTML comment tag `<!--date-->` is one such placeholder; when it's used by a given servlet, it will be replaced with the current date.

Let's define the loading of the HTML file. To make it as flexible as possible, we will provide the facility to either source the file from the local system or from a remote machine using a URL. Doing so allows templates to be shared all over the world.

```
private void readInFile( String _filename ) throws IOException {
   //- Reads in the template file
   fileName = new Vector( 30, 5 );
   RandomAccessFile fptr = new RandomAccessFile( _filename, "rw" );
String line;
   while ( (line = fptr.readLine()) != null ){

     try{
       line = line.substring( 0, line.length() );
       if ( line.indexOf( "\r" ) != -1 )
         line = line.substring( 0, line.length()-1 );
```

```
        }catch(Exception E){}
        fileName.addElement( line );
    }
    fptr.close();
}


private void readInURL( String _filename ) throws IOException {
    //- Reads in the template file
    URL    Host;
    Host   = new URL( _filename );
    BufferedReader InFile = new BufferedReader( new InputStreamReader
                            (Host.openStream()) );
    fileName = new Vector( 30, 5 );

    String line;
    while ( (line = InFile.readLine()) != null ){
        try{
            line = line.substring( 0, line.length() );
            if ( line.indexOf( "\r" ) != -1 )
                line = line.substring( 0, line.length()-1 );

        }catch(Exception E){}
        fileName.addElement( line );
    }
    InFile.close();
}
```

Example 8.13   Reading in the templates

Example 8.13 shows the two very similar methods for reading from both a file and a URL. The file is stored in a `Vector` data structure, with each element representing a single line.

We could implement the data output mechanism in many different ways. One is to write straight out to the client; another would be to write to a file and then have the file sent out.

To make the class as versatile as possible, we will output to a `Writer` stream, and use a pair of `string` arrays to determine which placeholders are to be replaced. Generating the new HTML file will then be a trivial task.

Each line is read one at a time, and it is searched for any placeholders you have specified. If one such string is found, then it is replaced with the new data. Once the line has been parsed, it is sent out to the `Writer` stream.

```
public synchronized void print( PrintWriter _Out, String _keys[],
                                String _data[] )
                                throws IOException {
    if ( fileName == null ) return;

    Enumeration E = fileName.elements();
    String LineIn;
```

```
     int x,c1=0;
     while ( E.hasMoreElements() ){
       LineIn = (String)E.nextElement();
       for (x=0;x < _keys.length; x++ ){
         c1 = LineIn.indexOf(_keys[x]);
         while ( c1 != -1 ){
           try{
             LineIn  = LineIn.substring( 0, c1 ) + _data[x] +
                       LineIn.substring( c1+_keys[x].length(),
                                LineIn.length() );
             c1 = LineIn.indexOf(_keys[x],c1+1);
           }catch(Exception E1){}
         }
       }
       _Out.println( LineIn );
     }
     _Out.flush();
   }
```

Example 8.14   Producing the output

Example 8.14 shows the `print(...)` method of the `htmlTemplate` class. This method takes two string arrays which represent the placeholders and the respective data to be inserted. For example, `_key[2]` will be replaced with the string in `_data[2]`, and so on. In addition to the arrays, one of the more convenient `Writer` classes is passed in—the `PrintWriter`. We use this one to allow us access to the `println(...)` method.

As you can see, this method loops through each line using an `Enumeration` declared to the `Vector` class holding the complete file. For each line, the `_key[]` array is checked against each element, using the `indexOf(...)` method from the `String` class. Notice how this is performed within a `while` loop to allow multiple placeholders to appear on a single line.

Using the class is a simple matter of declaring an instance, then using the `print(...)` method, as shown in example 8.15.

```
htmlTemplate Tmp = new htmlTemplate( "hello_template.html" );
String key[]     = new String[1];
String dat[]     = new String[1];
key[0]           = "<!--date-->";
dat[0]           = new Date().toString();
PrintWriter Out  = _res.getWriter();
_res.setContentType("text/html");
Tmp.print( Out, key, dat );
Out.flush();
```
Example 8.15   Using `htmlTemplate`

If for some reason the template file can't be found, then an `IOException` will be thrown. The above example doesn't show this exception being caught.

8.4.2 Cache system

The class developed in the previous section comes in very handy in a heavy traffic environment where the performance of the server would be impaired due to the continual loading of the HTML template files. A much cleaner system would be to implement a caching mechanism that would return an already loaded copy of the template, and if one didn't exist, it would load it.

The cache manager can also check the date of the file on disk before it loads and returns a reference. If the date of the file is newer than the date stored in memory, then the file can be reloaded with the new version of the template. This has the advantage of not having to restart the server every time an update has been made to the file.

Example 8.16 shows the complete source code for implementing such a cache class. The class is created with a maximum limit on the number of files it will hold in memory at any one time.

Each template is held in the adapter class dbFileCacheHolder. This stores not only the reference to the htmlTemplate instance, but also information such as the time the file was created and when the file was last loaded.

```
public class dbTemplateCache extends java.lang.Object{

  private static Hashtable loadedFiles;
  private static int maxFiles=1;

  public dbTemplateCache(){}

  public dbTemplateCache(int _maxFiles){
    maxFiles    = _maxFiles;
    loadedFiles = new Hashtable();
  }

  public synchronized htmlTemplate getFile( String _filename,
                      HttpServletRequest _req ){

    //- Check to see if the file already exists
    if ( loadedFiles.containsKey(_filename) ){
      dbFileCacheHolder FC =
                      (dbFileCacheHolder)loadedFiles.get(_filename);
      if ( FC.creation == new File(FC.file.nameOfFile).lastModified() )
        return FC.file;
      else
        loadedFiles.remove(_filename);
    }

    //- Need to load the file from disk
    dbFileCacheHolder FC = new dbFileCacheHolder();
    try{
      FC.file     = new htmlTemplate(_req.getRealPath(_filename));
      FC.age      = System.currentTimeMillis();
      FC.creation = new File(FC.file.nameOfFile).lastModified();
    }catch(Exception E){
```

```
                return null;
        }


        //- Check to see if the maximum number of files has been reached
        if ( loadedFiles.size() > maxFiles )
            deleteFile();
        loadedFiles.put( _filename, FC );
        return FC.file;
    }


    private void deleteFile(){
        //- Runs through the list and removes the oldest file
        Enumeration E = loadedFiles.keys();
        dbFileCacheHolder FC;
        String key, togoKey=null;
        long min = System.currentTimeMillis();

        while ( E.hasMoreElements()){
            key = (String)E.nextElement();
            FC = (dbFileCacheHolder)loadedFiles.get(key);
            if (FC.age <= min){
                togoKey = key;
                min    = FC.age;
            }
        }

        if ( togoKey != null )
            loadedFiles.remove(togoKey);
    }


    class dbFileCacheHolder extends java.lang.Object{
        public long        age;
        public long        creation;
        public htmlTemplate file;
    }
}
```

Example 8.16   The complete source code for the cache system class

The whole class operates from the getFile(...) method. This method determines if
the file is in cache, and if it is, the method returns a reference back to it. If the file isn't
available from immediate cache, then it is loaded, and assuming a slot is available, it is
stored for future use. However, if no space is free, then the oldest file in the cache is dis-
carded. The oldest file is the one that was accessed the longest time ago.

This cache class is a system that can be easily converted to store any type of object,
not necessarily the class that was hardcoded in the example above.

By using the cache instead of manually loading the file each time, performance speed increases almost 400%. This can be easily verified; for example, time the system with the cache set at 1 and then 100. The maximum size of the cache depends on a lot of factors, the most important one being the average size of the file compared with the amount of available memory. Sadly, determining the maximum size of the cache is a trial-and-error process.

8.5 *Other application areas*

This chapter took a quick look at where servlets can be used to provide fast and simple custom services. The servlets are small and quickly developed, and they utilize the majority of features found in other areas of the JDK to provide a richer server environment. The servlets in the remaining chapters of this book are more application-orientated.

C H A P T E R   9

HTML form processing

- Learn what the different types of HTML forms are.

- There are a number of ways in which a form may be posted to a server—discover the subtle differences between them.

- Once a form has been submitted to your server, learn how to retrieve all the user information supplied within it.

- Create an email from the information inside the form and send it straight to an administrator.

- Learn how to save data to files from a servlet.

- See how easy it is to provide the user with a confirmation page before he finally submits the information.

Forms are quickly becoming a major part of the world wide web. Many sites now use this technique to gather information from site visitors. Whether the forms ask for email addresses, usernames, or simply comments from visitors, web designers are using them in many places. This means that more and more processing has to be allocated to forms. This collating of responses is probably one of the most popular areas in which conventional CGI programs are currently used.

Writing servlets to process forms is rather easy. However, as this chapter will illustrate, there are one or two things that you must consider in order to have a smoothly running form processor.

9.1 Form introduction

"Still glides the Stream, and shall for ever glide;
The Form remains, the Function never dies."

The River Duddon, 1820

A form is one of the most basic and rudimentary methods available to site administrators and HTML designers for gathering user information from the web. A form is just a means of packaging data to send to the server. Data can be passed to the server in one of two basic ways: through a GET command or a POST command.

When you set up your HTML form, you specify in the tag what type of data transfer will take place. This merely determines how the data will be packaged and delivered to the server. For example, the HTML code in example 9.1 shows how to set the form up to use a GET request.

```
<FORM ACTION="/servlet/formServlet" POST="GET">
:
:
</FORM>
```
Example 9.1   HTML FORM tags

Fortunately, in the world of Java servlets, there is no need to worry about the two different methods. The interface for gathering the information is the same. This is not the case for conventional CGI-based implementations, where a different data extraction routine has to be written for each type to accommodate the different posting methods.

As you've already read, there are two main methods for sending data to the server. The first is GET, which is a request for data. This is the standard method the browser uses for retrieving HTML pages. This method sends all parameters as part of the URL string. For example, http://www.n-ary.com/form?name=ceri& age=21 is an example of an HTTP GET. The parameter name has the value ceri associated with it. Each parameter pair is separated by an ampersand (&), and the parameter list begins with a question mark (?).

Due to the restrictions placed on the maximum length of a URL (1024 characters), this method is not recommended for large data transfers. Also, note that every GET is logged in the server logs. If the site generates a lot of user responses, then the log file will grow enormously in a very short time.

The second method for sending data to the server is the POST method. When you use this method, the data is not transferred via the URL. Instead, the data is sent in exactly the same way the web server sends out pages to the client. Because the URL address is not being used, the amount of data transferred has no upper limit. This is the recommended way to send form data.

Note The servlet API provides separate methods to override depending on the posting type: doGet(…) and doPost(…). However, it is better to use the service(…) method, since it does not differentiate between the two methods. That way, you can be assured the data will get through to the servlet no matter which posting method the HTML developer decides to use. You'll see examples of these methods throughout this book.

Figure 9.1 shows a simple form that requests basic information from the user, such as name, phone number, and job title. The HTML code for this form is displayed in example 9.2. Notice how the form is embedded inside a table to improve the general look of the form. Using the properties of the HTML table, you can easily line up all the input fields in one vertical line.

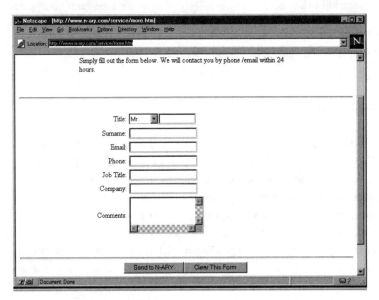

Figure 9.1 A very simple HTML form

```
<FORM METHOD="POST" ACTION="/servlet/formServlet">
<CENTER>
```

```
<TABLE BORDER=0 CELLPADDING=0 WIDTH=80%>
<TR>
<TD ALIGN=RIGHT>Title:</TD>
<TD><SELECT NAME="title">
<OPTION>Mr.</OPTION>
<OPTION>Ms.</OPTION>
<OPTION>Mrs.</OPTION>
<OPTION>Miss</OPTION>
<OPTION>Dr.</OPTION>
<OPTION>Other:</OPTION>
</SELECT>
<INPUT TYPE="text"NAME="other_title" VALUE="" SIZE=10></TD>
</TR>
<TR>
<TD ALIGN=RIGHT>Surname:</TD>
<TD><INPUT TYPE="text" NAME="Surname" VALUE="" SIZE=20></TD>
</TR>
<TR>
<TD ALIGN=RIGHT>Email:</TD>
<TD><INPUT TYPE="text" NAME="Email" VALUE="" SIZE=20></TD>
</TR>
<TR>
<TD ALIGN=RIGHT>Phone:</TD>
<TD><INPUT TYPE="text" NAME="Phone" VALUE="" SIZE=20></TD>
</TR>
<TR>
<TD ALIGN=RIGHT>Job Title:</TD>
<TD><INPUT TYPE="text" NAME="Job_Title" VALUE="" SIZE=20></TD>
</TR>
<TR>
<TD ALIGN=RIGHT>Company:</TD>
<TD><INPUT TYPE="text" NAME="Company_Name" VALUE="" SIZE=20></TD>
</TR>
<TR>
<TD ALIGN=RIGHT>Comments:</TD>
<TD><TEXTAREA NAME="Comments" VALUE="" ROWS=3 COLS=18></TEXTAREA></TD>
</TR>
</TABLE>
</CENTER>

<BR><HR>
<CENTER>
<INPUT TYPE="submit" NAME="name" VALUE="Send to N-ARY">
<INPUT TYPE="reset" VALUE="Clear This Form">
</CENTER>
</FORM>
```

Example 9.2 The code for the HTML form shown in figure 9.1

That's about all the HTML form code you will find in this chapter, since this is a book about Java, not HTML. The remaining sections in this chapter focus on processing this information using a servlet.

9.2 Basic form processing

Once the HTML page has been designed to include the form, the data gathered from the form has to go somewhere. Sure, it will be sent to the servlet, the servlet then will take the parameters, and…and then what? Fortunately, there are a number of options open to you. Here's what you can do:

- Package up the HTML form data and post it as an email.
- Append the data to a file.
- Insert the data into a database.
- Do nothing with it!

Granted, the last option isn't really much use, but it is an option. Depending on the environment and the nature of the form, you may want to format the data and pass it on to a database for possible inclusion. Formatting the data and inserting it in a database will be covered later in the chapter on database access. This chapter will illustrate the first two options: emailing the data and storing it in a file.

Note After compiling this servlet, you can set up a servlet alias to it, so it may be referenced like an ordinary HTML page. Otherwise, the URL that would activate the servlet would be `/servlet/<classname>`. It won't make a single bit of difference to the servlet how it was accessed.

Before you worry about sending the data on, you first need to receive the data. The class you will use as your base class will be the `HttpServlet` class from the `javax.servlet` package. There is no real need to use this class; you could easily use the `GenericServlet` class instead. However, later in this chapter, you'll be using some of the information contained in the HTTP header, so you may as well use `HttpServlet` from the start.

```
public class formServlet extends HttpServlet {
  public void service(HttpServletRequest _req, HttpServletResponse _res)
                            throws IOException{
    //- service body in here
  }
}
```

Example 9.3 The definition for the form servlet based on the `HttpServlet` **class**

The `HttpServlet` class provides an additional method, `init(…)`, which is used to initialize any startup procedures. But in this instance we have no startup procedures—the servlet can still function properly without any special processing at startup. There are three distinct steps in form processing, as shown in figure 9.2.

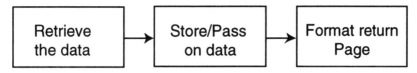

Figure 9.2 HTML form processing steps

9.2.1 Retrieving the data

You first need to retrieve the data from the posted data. This is done using the getParameter(…) method from the HttpServletRequest class. An example use of this method is shown in example 9.4; the name of the HTML form field is passed in to the method, and the data is returned as a String.

```
String stitle        = _req.getParameter( "title" );
String sother_title   = _req.getParameter( "other_title" );
String sSurname       = _req.getParameter( "Surname" );
String sEmail         = _req.getParameter( "Email" );
String sPhone         = _req.getParameter( "Phone" );
String sJob_Title     = _req.getParameter( "Job_Title" );
String sCompany_Name  = _req.getParameter( "Company_Name" );
String sComments      = _req.getParameter( "Comments" );
```
Example 9.4   Getting the data from the form

If, for some reason, the parameter doesn't exist or is blank, then the resulting value returned is null.

It is possible, and completely legal, for an HTML form to be posted with fields that have identical names. For example, an Address field commonly has more than one value associated with it (as some addresses take more than the usual three lines).

But how do you get the second value posted to the servlet? The getParameter(…) method will only return one value for every parameter. Early incarnations of the method would bring back the values as a comma-separated list, but this was useless if the data itself contained a comma. So another method was introduced.

Note   You may or may not have noticed that the space character is not allowed in a URL. For example, http://www.n-ary.com/about us.html, would not yield a proper result, as there is a space between the "about" and "us." So how on earth do you post data with a GET operation that might have spaces in it? Can you? Should users be restricted to a continuous stream of nonspaced text?

Fortunately, it isn't as fatal as it sounds. Defined in the HTTP/1.0 specification is an encoding mechanism that gets around this dilemma. In this mechanism, special characters are inserted into the data. For example, all characters whose ASCII value is less than 0x21 and greater than 0x7f, are escaped, meaning they are replaced with %xx, where xx is the hexadecimal value of the character being escaped. The space character is replaced with a +.

However, you need not concern yourself with this, as the client and server perform this task for you. By the time the parameters get to your servlet, they have already been decoded.

But don't forget about this problem. If you are coding applets to communicate with servlets or with CGI programs (if you're still using such old technology!), you will need to encode the GET and POST yourself, manually.

The getParameterValues(...) method handles multiple values by returning an array of strings. Example 9.5 shows how to use this method. It is used in much the same way as when you're retrieving single values—it returns either an array of strings, or null if no values are present.

```
String saddress[]    = _req.getParameterValues( "ADDRESS" );
```
Example 9.5 Getting multiple data values

9.2.2 Store/pass on data

Now that you've retrieved the data the user provided and it's in a format you can use, you must decide what to do with it. We will look at two possible routes you can take.

Appending the form to a file   The easiest and quickest method, from the developer's point of view, would be to write the data straight out to a file. Not only does this remove the responsibility of processing the data from the servlet, but it also serves to keep a record of the form submission.

To write the data to a file, create a function that takes in the parameters to be written and then appends the data to a file. This is shown in example 9.6.

```
private void writeToFile( String stitle, String sother_title,

                          string sSurname,
                          String sEmail,String  sPhone,String sJob_Title,
                          String sCompany_Name, String Comments ){
  try
  {
    RandomAccessFile fileOut = new RandomAccessFile("form.log","rw");

    //- Set the pointer to the end of file
    fileOut.seek( fileOut.length() );
    fileOut.writeBytes( "---------------------------\n" );
    fileOut.writeBytes( "Date: " + (new Date()).toString() +"\n");
    fileOut.writeBytes( "Title: " + stitle + "\n" );
    fileOut.writeBytes( "Title (other): "+sother_title+"\n" );
    fileOut.writeBytes( "Surname: " + sSurname + "\n" );
    fileOut.writeBytes( "Email: " + sEmail + "\n" );
    fileOut.writeBytes( "Phone: " + sPhone + "\n" );
    fileOut.writeBytes( "Job Title: " + sJob_Title + "\n" );
    fileOut.writeBytes( "Company: " + sCompany_Name + "\n" );
    fileOut.writeBytes( "Comments: " + Comments + "\n" );
  }
```

```
    catch( Exception E ){}
}
```
Example 9.6   Writing the form data to a file

This results in a file that maintains a record of each form transmitted. Each record is separated from the next by a line of dashes, so parsing the file in the future is much easier.

Note   If you use this method of storing forms, you need to make the file-thread-safe, meaning if more than one thread tries to open the file for writing, then one will fail and the other will succeed. One form of submission will be lost in the process. Making the thread-safe can be achieved by wrapping the call to this function with the synchronized keyword:

```
    synchronized( this ){
      //- Call to the: writeToFile([el])
    }
```

Sending the form as an email   Although appending the data to a file is handy, it's not the best solution for dealing with form data, particularly for web designers who don't have access to the server. For example, a service provider that is hosting many web sites on one machine would not want its clients to generate potentially huge files on their server. The alternative solution is to take each form submission, package it up, and email it to some mailbox on the Internet.

This is a very easy feature to add. Mailing text is just a matter of opening up a connection to an SMTP mail host and sending the message body to it. SMTP usually resides on TCP port 25, and you can use the majority of mail hosts on the Internet.

Note   A relatively unknown fact about mail gateways is that you can use any publicly available gateway to send your email. For example, you could be in New York and use the smtp.mail.n-ary.com server in Britain to send all of your outgoing mail.

The way Internet mail works is not all that distant from how the postal service works. After you write a letter and stick a stamp on it, you look for the closest available mailbox in which to deposit your letter. Once it's in the system, the letter will be eventually delivered to its intended destination. It doesn't really matter what mailbox you place the letter in—it will still get to its destination. Internet mail is exactly the same; you are merely calling upon the services of this or that machine to pass your email on to its intended destination.

Because of this wonderful flexibility, it is sometimes better to find a relatively quiet mail host to handle all of your outgoing mail. That way your mail will go quickly and safely, instead of getting bounced back because the mail server is too busy.

Opening up a connection to a port is performed through sockets, and the Java API supports this operation very adequately. However, this can get a little messy, especially if you don't really know how to format the text so the mailer can interpret it correctly. But fear not; help is at hand.

In forthcoming chapters you will develop your own email class for sending email, but in this one we will look at an alternative.

A relatively unknown and undocumented Java package is the sun.net.smtp package from the Java Web Server library. It is not available as part of the standard servlet API. Using the SmtpClient class from the servlet makes the whole process of sending an email a very trivial task.

Constructing an email is a matter of creating the header and the message body. Creating the message header is done by calling a set of methods that set up the to, from, and subject fields.

```
SmtpClient sendmail;
sendmail = new SmtpClient("smtp.n-ary.com");
sendmail.from( sEmail );
sendmail.to( "info@n-ary.com" );
```
Example 9.7   Constructing the email header

As shown in example 9.7, the SmtpClient constructor takes in the IP or domain address of the outgoing mail host to which this email will be sent. From there, you simply call the from and to methods to set the email addresses of the originator and the recipient.

To construct the message body, the SmtpClient class has a method to return an output stream in the form of a PrintStream class.

```
PrintStream OutMail = sendmail.startMessage();
```

Once the message body has been created, the message is closed down and sent as shown in example 9.8.

```
OutMail.flush();
OutMail.close();
sendmail.closeServer();
```
Example 9.8   Sending the completed email body

Example 9.9 shows the complete method for constructing and sending an email.

```
privatevoid writeToEmail( String stitle,String sother_title,
                          String sSurname, String sEmail,
                          String sPhone, String sJob_Title,String
                          sCompany_Name,String Comments){
  PrintStream OutMail;
  SmtpClient  sendmail;

  try
  {
    sendmail = new SmtpClient("mail.yourdomain.com");
    sendmail.from( sEmail );
    sendmail.to( "info@n-ary.com");
    OutMail = sendmail.startMessage();
```

```
    OutMail.println("From: " + sSurname);
    OutMail.println("To: FormMaster");
    OutMail.println("Subject:Online Form" );
    OutMail.println( "--------------------------" );
    OutMail.println( "Date:" + (new Date()).toString());
    OutMail.println( "Title: " + stitle );
    OutMail.println( "Title( other): " + sother_title);
    OutMail.println( "Surname:    " + sSurname);
    OutMail.println( "Email:      " + sEmail);
    OutMail.println( "Phone:        " + sPhone);
    OutMail.println( "Job Title: " + sJob_Title);
    OutMail.println( "Company:    " + sCompany_Name );
    OutMail.println( "Comments:   " + Comments );
    OutMail.println( "--------------------------" );

    OutMail.flush();
    OutMail.close();
    sendmail.closeServer();
  }
  catch ( IOException E ){}
}
```

Example 9.9   The complete method for constructing and sending an email

9.2.3 Formatting a return page

Now that you've retrieved the form information from either a POST or a GET, you now have to format a response page to send back to the user. Although this is not mandatory, it is polite to do so. It lets the user know that the form data actually made it to the server and that it has been processed. Example 9.10 shows how the servlet can be used to create a suitable response page.

```
_res.setContentType("text/html");
PrintWriter Out = _res.getWriter();

Out.println( "<HTML><BODY>" );
Out.println( "<B><I><FONT COLOR=#0000FF SIZE=+2>Thank you, " );
Out.println( sTitle + " " + sSurname + "</FONT></I></B>" );
Out.println( "<BR><BR><B><FONT COLOR=#0000FF SIZE=+1>…for taking");
Out.println( " the time to fill out this form.</FONT></B>" );
Out.println( "<BR><BR><BR><BR><BR><BR><B><FONT COLOR=#0000FF>");
Out.println( "A response has been sent.</FONT></B>" );
Out.println( "</BODY></HTML>" );
Out.flush();
```

Example 9.10   Formatting a response to send back to the user upon completion of the form

An alternative to generating a page is to use the sendRedirect(…) method, which instructs the client to ignore the last request and get an alternative resource. For example, you could redirect the user to an already prepared thank-you page:

```
_res.sendRedirect("http://www.n-ary.com/thankyou.html");
```

Note that in order for this method to be successful across all platforms, you need to include the full URL of the resource you are redirecting to.

9.2.4 The complete service(...) method

If you bring together all the methods detailed earlier in this chapter, you'll come to the completed service(...) implementation shown in example 9.11. This method is called whenever the user presses the Submit button on the form page; the button triggers an email to be sent and it writes the data received to a file.

```
public void service( HttpServletRequest _req,HttpServletResponse _res )
                     throws IOException
{
  //- Get Parameters
  String stitle       = _req.getParameter( "title" );
  String sother_title = _req.getParameter( "other_title" );
  String sSurname     = _req.getParameter( "Surname" );
  String sEmail       = _req.getParameter( "Email" );
  String sPhone       = _req.getParameter( "Phone" );
  String sJob_Title   = _req.getParameter( "Job_Title");
  String sCompany_Name = _req.getParameter( "Company_Name" );
  String sComments    = _req.getParameter( "Comments" );

  //- Write to file and send email
  synchronize( this ){
    writeToFile( stitle,sother_title,sSurname,sEmail,
                      sphone,sJob_Title,sCompany_Name,sComments );
    writeToEmail( stitle,sother_title,sSurname,sEmail,
                      sPhone,sJob_Title,sCompany_Name,sComments );
  }

  //- Format Response
  _res.setContentType("text/html");
  PrintWriter Out = _res.getWriter();
  Out.println( "<HTML>" );
  Out.println( "<B><I><FONT COLOR=#0000FF SIZE=+2>Thank you, " );
  Out.println( sTitle + " " + sSurname + "</FONT></I></B>" );
  Out.println( "<BR><BR><B><FONT COLOR=#0000FF SIZE=+1>");
  Out.println( "…for taking the time to fill out this form.</FONT></B>");
  Out.println( "<BR><BR><BR><BR><BR><BR><B><FONT COLOR=#0000FF>");
  Out.println( "A response has been sent.</FONT></B>" );
  Out.println( "</BODY></HTML>" );
  Out.flush();
}
```

Example 9.11   The complete service(...) **method**

Did you notice the synchronize block? This is to safeguard the calls to both the file and email routines from being corrupted by simultaneous accesses from multiple clients. Notice also how we didn't synchronize the whole method. This was to keep the potential waiting time for queued clients to a minimum, since the only critical part of the method is the writing to file. That way, other clients can be processed when the previous client request is preparing the output.

Although this is a very complete and functional implementation of the form servlet, the servlet we have created is not very flexible. For this implementation, the field names from the form must be known in advance. A service provider would not want to write different versions of what is essentially the same servlet for each different customer. Not only is this an administrative nightmare, but also it increases the load on the server. Instead of just one servlet running, it would result in many different form-processing servlets running at the same time, taking up server resources and performing a task that is essentially the same as any other form processor.

A much better and more flexible solution is presented in the next section.

9.3   Generic form2email

The major problem with the previous solution was the fact that if the web designer decided to add or remove a field to the form, the servlet would have to be modified to take this change into account.

A much cleaner and more efficient solution is to have the servlet not know anything specific about each form; it would therefore treat each one in exactly the same way. Fortunately, there are mechanisms to do just this.

9.3.1   Retrieving form parameters

The first problem that is very apparent is the field name. How do you get the name of the field in the form?

The ServletRequest class has a method that allows you to cycle through the field names sent from the client, picking each one out separately. This task is performed through the standard Java enumeration mechanism, as shown in example 9.12.

```
Enumeration keys;
String key;
String value;

keys = _req.getParameterNames();
while ( keys.hasMoreElements() ){
  key = (String) keys.nextElement();
  value = _req.getParameter(key);

  //- Do something with value
}
```
Example 9.12   Running through the parameters

You have already seen the method getParameter(…) in action, where it simply returns the value associated with a form field. The Enumeration interface feeds that method with a field name using the while loop.

By replacing the body of the writeToEmail(…) method with this new means of retrieving HTML parameters, you have a much smaller and more efficient means to process forms, while keeping the service method relatively untouched. This results in the new writeToEmail(…) method shown in example 9.13.

Note The `java.util.Enumeration` defines a very simple interface that, when implemented, delivers sequenced objects to the method. For example, the majority of the data structures, such as `Vector` and `HashTable`, all implement the `Enumeration` interface.

This is a very powerful and common way of accessing values from a structure. It allows you to change the storage method without fearing the domino effect from such a decision that may lead to extreme code or logic code changes.

```
public interface java.util.Enumeration

{

  public abstract boolean hasMoreElements();

  public abstract Object nextElement();

}
```

The enumeration interface defines these two methods, which can be used to transverse most data structures. The first method is called first to determine whether an item is available for reading, and if it is, then a call to the second method, `nextElement()`, will retrieve it.

```
private void writeToEmail( HttpServletRequest _req ){
  PrintStream OutMail;
  SmtpClient  sendmail;

  try
  {
    sendmail = new SmtpClient("mail.yourdomain.com");
    sendmail.from( "webmaster@n-ary.com" );
    sendmail.to( "info@n-ary.com" );

    OutMail = sendmail.startMessage();
    OutMail.println("From: webmaster@n-ary.com" );
    OutMail.println("To: info@n-ary.com" );
    OutMail.println("Subject: Online Form" );

    Enumeration keys;
    String key;
    String value;

    keys = _req.getParameterNames();
    while ( keys.hasMoreElements() ){
      key = (String) keys.nextElement();
      value = _req.getParameter(key);
      OutMail.println( key + " = " + value + "\n" );
    }

    OutMail.print("\r\n");
    OutMail.println( "** This email was prepared @ N-ARY Limited(
                      http://www.n-ary.com ) **" );
    OutMail.flush();
```

```
        OutMail.close();
        sendmail.closeServer();
    }
    catch ( IOException E ){}
}
```
Example 9.13 The new `writeToEmail(…)` method

9.3.2 Making it generic

The next stage in making this a truly generic servlet is to control who receives the resulting email. This means you can allow the web designer to decide who should receive the email rather than the servlet developer, as this doesn't require any recompilation. This can be done using a set of secret, or hidden, fields.

For example, the HTML code shown in example 9.14 will not be displayed in the HTML page produced by the browser.

```
<INPUT TYPE="hidden" NAME="TO" VALUE="alan@n-ary.com">
<INPUT TYPE="hidden" NAME="FROM" VALUE="info@n-ary.com" >
<INPUT TYPE="hidden" NAME="SUBJECT" VALUE="Online Registration">
```
Example 9.14 Hidden fields

Using this technique, you can use the form fields themselves to pass data back to the servlet. In this example, you would modify the section of code within the `writeToEmail(…)` method to use the email address from the HTML form field FROM (see example 9.15).

```
sendmail.from( _req.getParameter( "FROM" ) );
sendmail.to(_req.getParameter( "TO" ));

OutMail.println("From: " + _req.getParameter( "FROM" )  );
OutMail.println("To: " + _req.getParameter( "TO" ) );
OutMail.println("Subject: " + _req.getParameter( "SUBJECT" ) );
```
Example 9.15 Sending the email to a custom mailbox

9.4 Confirmation forms

The final section in this chapter will look at giving the generic form2email servlet a final professional look. At this moment, the form2email servlet has the ability to send email to anyone the web designer has designated.

Although it's useful, the page generated by the servlet to thank the user for taking the time to fill out the form is not very friendly, navigationally speaking. The user has to use his browser's Back button twice to get to the same point he was before he submitted the form (once to get back to the form, and the second time to get to the page before the form).

This section will show you how to implement a much better navigational screen. It will also show you an optional confirmation screen that allows the user to confirm the details before he actually submits the form. This saves the recipient from getting invalid or duplicated information from users who have made a mistake in one or more of the fields.

The confirmation screen is implemented using hidden fields to pass information between servlet calls. The order in which this will operate is as follows:

1 The user fills in the form with data and clicks the Submit button. The form is sent to the servlet.

2 The servlet reads the CONFIRM field. If the field is set to 1, the servlet formats an HTML page that displays the user's options. The servlet then inserts the hidden field CONFIRM in the HTML page and sets it to 0.

3 The user decides whether the information he supplied is correct. If it is, he clicks the Confirm button, which sends the form back to the servlet.

4 The servlet reads the CONFIRM field. If the field shows a value of 0 or null, the servlet presents the thank-you HTML page to the user.

By using the extra hidden fields, the servlet can determine which action to take next, if any is needed.

9.4.1 The service(...) method

The main purpose of the service method is to determine which page to send back to the client. It either sends the confirmation page or a thank-you screen and an email, as shown in example 9.16.

```
public void service( HttpServletRequest _req, HttpServletResponse _res)
                            throws IOException{
  String sCONFIRM = _req.getParameter( "CONFIRM" );
  if ( sCONFIRM != null && sCONFIRM.compareTo( "1" ) == 0 )
    sendConfirmScreen( _req, _res );
  else
    sendConfirmation( _req, _res );
}
```
Example 9.16 Servicing the client request, depending on the form data

By checking for the presence of the HTML form field CONFIRM, the correct method call can be made.

9.4.2 Preparing the confirmation page

The confirmation page allows the user to check the data he previously filled in. He can make any changes to the data on the confirmation page, and then when he's satisfied the data is correct, he can submit the data to be processed. The same servlet is used to perform the validation and confirmation tasks, except that the confirmation screen is created by the servlet, not the web designer. The code to create this confirmation page is shown in example 9.17.

The confirmation page will be displayed with the HTML fields formatted in a table; each field will take a hidden field value inside a form object.

```
private void sendConfirmScreen(HttpServletRequest _req,
                    HttpServletResponse _res){
```

```
Enumeration keys;
String key;
String value;
PrintWriter Out;

try{
  _res.setContentType("text/html");
  Out = _res.getWriter();
} catch (IOException E){
  return;
}

Out.println( "<HTML><BODY>" );
Out.println( "<BR> Please confirm the following information" );
Out.println( "<FORM METHOD=POST ACTION=/form2email" );
Out.println("<CENTER><TABLE BORDER=0 CELLPADDING=0 WIDTH=80%>");

keys = _req.getParameterNames();
while (keys.hasMoreElements()) {
  key = (String) keys.nextElement();
  value = _req.getParameter(key);

  //- Check for CONFIRM
  if ( key.compareTo( "CONFIRM" ) == 0 ){
    Out.println( "<INPUT TYPE=\"HIDDEN\" NAME=\"" + key );
    Out.println( "\" VALUE=\"" + 0 + "\">" );
  }
  else if ( key.compareTo( "SUBJECT" ) == 0 ||
            key.compareTo( "BACKURL" ) == 0 ||
            key.compareTo( "TOEMAIL" ) == 0 ||
            key.compareTo( "FROMEMAIL" ) == 0 ){
    Out.println( "<INPUT TYPE=\"HIDDEN\" NAME=\"" + key );
    Out.println( "\" VALUE=\"" + value + "\">" );
  }else{
    Out.println( "<TR>" );
    Out.println( "<INPUT TYPE=\"HIDDEN\" NAME=\"" + key );
    Out.println( "\" VALUE=\"" + value + "\">" );
    Out.println( "<TD ALIGN=RIGHT>" + key + "</TD>" );
    Out.println( "<TD ALIGN=LEFT>" + value + "</TD>" );
    Out.println( "</TR>" );
  }
}
Out.println( "</TABLE></CENTER><BR><HR><CENTER>" );
Out.println( "<INPUT TYPE=submit NAME=name VALUE=\"Confirm\"" );
Out.println( "</CENTER></FORM></BODY></HTML>" );
Out.flush();
}
```

Example 9.17   Formatting the confirmation page

As you can see, the code to put this file together is not very complicated. The majority of the work is in building and constructing the HTML code. Notice how you screen the fields SUBJECT, BACKURL, TOEMAIL, and FROMEMAIL–these parameters are hidden and really shouldn't show up in the confirmation table.

You also need to look for the CONFIRM field. Not only should this field not show up in the visible part of the table, but you need to change the value of the CONFIRM field from 1 to 0 so that the next time the servlet is run, it will not display this page and go straight to the thank you page.

9.4.3 Complete source code

We're now ready to take all of the modifications detailed above and put them together. The result is the form2email servlet shown in example 9.18. This servlet can be used as a solution for sites that need to process forms with unknown field names.

```java
import java.io.*;
import java.util.*;
import java.net.InetAddress;
import javax.servlet.*;
import javax.servlet.http.*;
import sun.net.smtp.SmtpClient;

public class form2email extends HttpServlet
{
  public void service(HttpServletRequest _req, HttpServletResponse _res)
                          throws IOException{
    String  sCONFIRM  = _req.getParameter( "CONFIRM" );
    if ( sCONFIRM != null && sCONFIRM.compareTo( "1" ) == 0 )
      sendConfirmScreen( _req, _res );
    else
      sendConfirmation( _req, _res );
  }

  public String getServletInfo(){
    return "N-ARY: Form 2 Email";
  }

  private void sendConfirmScreen(HttpServletRequest _req,
                          HttpServletResponse _res){
    Enumeration keys;
    String key;
    String value;
    PrintWriter Out;

    try{
      _res.setContentType("text/html");
      Out = _res.getWriter();
    }
    catch (IOException E){
      return;
    }

    Out.println( "<HTML><BODY>" );
    Out.println( "<BR> Please confirm the following information" );
    Out.println( "<FORM METHOD=POST ACTION=/form2email" );
    Out.println( "<CENTER><TABLE BORDER=0 CELLPADDING=0 WIDTH=80%>" );
```

```java
    keys = _req.getParameterNames();
    while (keys.hasMoreElements()){
      key = (String) keys.nextElement();
      value = _req.getParameter(key);

      //- Check for CONFIRM
      if ( key.compareTo( "CONFIRM" ) == 0 ){
        Out.println( "<INPUT TYPE=\"HIDDEN\" NAME=\"" + key );
        Out.println( "\" VALUE=\"" + 0 + "\">" );
      }
      else if ( key.compareTo( "SUBJECT" ) == 0 ||
                key.compareTo( "BACKURL" ) == 0||
                key.compareTo( "TOEMAIL" ) == 0 ||
                key.compareTo( "FROMEMAIL" ) == 0 ){
        Out.println( "<INPUT TYPE=\"HIDDEN\" NAME=\"" + key );
        Out.println( "\" VALUE=\"" + value + "\">" );
      }else{
        Out.println( "<TR>" );
        Out.println( "<INPUT TYPE=\"HIDDEN\" NAME=\"" + key );
        Out.println( "\" VALUE=\"" + value + "\">" );
        Out.println( "<TD ALIGN=RIGHT>" + key + "</TD>" );
        Out.println( "<TD ALIGN=LEFT>" + value + "</TD>" );
        Out.println( "</TR>" );
      }
    }

    Out.println( "</TABLE></CENTER><BR><HR><CENTER>" );
    Out.println( "<INPUT TYPE=submit NAME=name VALUE=\"Send to N-ARY\"");
    Out.println( "<INPUT TYPE=reset VALUE=\"Clear This Form\" " );

    Out.println( "</CENTER></FORM></BODY></HTML>" );
    Out.flush();
  }

  private void sendConfirmation(HttpServletRequest _req,
                               HttpServletResponse _res) {
    //- Write to file and send email
    writeToEmail( _req );

    //- Format response
    try{
      _res.setContentType("text/html");
      PrintWriter Out = new PrintWriter( _res.getOutputStream() );

      Out.println( "<HTML><BODY>" );
      Out.println( "<B><I><FONT COLOR=#0000FF SIZE=+2>");
      Out.println( "Thank you</FONT></I></B>" );
      Out.println( sTitle + " " + sSurname + "</FONT></I></B>" );
      Out.println( "<BR><BR><B><FONT COLOR=#0000FF SIZE=+1>…for taking");
      Out.println( " the time to fill out this form</FONT></B>" );
      Out.println( "<BR><BR><BR><BR><BR><BR><B><FONT COLOR=#0000FF>");
      Out.println( "A response has been sent.</B>" );
      Out.println( "<BR><BR><BR><A HREF=" + _req.getParameter(
                          "BACK_TO_HTTP" ) );
```

```
      Out.println( ">Go Back.</A></FONT>" );
      Out.println( "</BODY></HTML>" );
      Out.flush();
    }
  catch ( IOException E ){}
}


private void  writeToFile( HttpServletRequest _req ){
  try{
    RandomAccessFile fileOut = new RandomAccessFile("form.log","rw");

    //- Set the pointer to the end of file
    fileOut.seek( fileOut.length() );

    fileOut.writeBytes( "---------------------------\n" );

    Enumeration keys;
    String key;
    String value;

    keys = _req.getParameterNames();
    while (keys.hasMoreElements()){
      key = (String) keys.nextElement();
      value = _req.getParameter(key);
      fileOut.writeBytes( key + " = " + value + "\n" );
    }

    fileOut.writeBytes( "---------------------------\n" );
  }
  catch( Exception E ){}
}


private void  writeToEmail( HttpServletRequest _req ){
  PrintStream OutMail;
  SmtpClient  sendmail;

  try
  {
    sendmail = new SmtpClient("mail.yourdomain.com");
    sendmail.from( "webmaster@n-ary.com" );
    sendmail.to( "info@n-ary.com" );

    OutMail = sendmail.startMessage();

    OutMail.println("From: webmaster@n-ary.com" );
    OutMail.println("To: info@n-ary.com" );
    OutMail.println("Subject: More Information" );

    Enumeration keys;
    String key;
    String value;

    keys = _req.getParameterNames();
    while (keys.hasMoreElements()){
```

```
          key = (String) keys.nextElement();
          value = _req.getParameter(key);
          OutMail.println( key + " = " + value);
        }

      OutMail.print("\r\n");
      OutMail.println( "** This email was prepared @ N-ARY Limited
                              ( http://www.n-ary.com ) **" );

      OutMail.flush();
      OutMail.close();
      sendmail.closeServer();
    }
    catch ( IOException E ){}
  }
}
```

Example 9.18 The complete `form2email` source code

9.5 Future extensions

This chapter presented the basics of processing HTML forms from the client. An overview
of the posting methods was presented, along with the recommended API methods that are
suited to this task. A servlet was presented at the end of the chapter; this servlet provides
complete generic servlet processing, thus allowing it to be used in environments where the
form fields are unknown.

Here are two possible extensions to the servlet:

- Template guides
  Right now, the servlet produces a standard Thank you page for the client when a form
  is submitted. A much better solution would be to allow the web designer to specify a
  template for this response that would allow the page to fit in with the look and feel of
  the site. This way, one servlet could be used on any site without breaking the site
  design.

- Email confirmations
  The servlet could send an email confirmation to the client that filled in the form. This
  would serve as a peace-of-mind exercise for the client so he would know his form
  arrived safely.

CHAPTER 10

Guest books

- Learn what a web-based guest book can add to your web site.

- Discover how a servlet can be used to implement a very simple guest book with a little functionality.

- Using servlets as the basis of the guest book, learn how to extend the functionality without increasing the complexity of the servlet.

- Learn how to send email as a custom class using SMTP.

After a pleasant weekend break in a country hotel, it is often customary to pay your compliments to the management. They will then usually invite you to sign the visitors' book or guest book. This is a nice way of collecting the guests' comments in one place. Not only does it provide excellent feedback for the hotel, but it also allows potential guests to see what other people think of the place before they stay. But why limit such a great idea to the hotel industry?

10.1 What is a guest book?

"When I make a feast, I would my guests should praise it…"
                - Sir John Harington (English writer, 1561)

Let's continue with the hotel analogy. The guest book (or comments page, as it's also known), allows a visitor to leave comments regarding the establishment. These comments or snippets of information are generally placed where all other visitors can see them. Assuming that the majority of the comments are positive and complimentary, the guest book is often touted in advertising and marketing campaigns.

Guest book or comment pages also exist on the Internet. Many sites invite comments or suggestions and allow users to actively display their views on the site. An example of one such guest book is seen in figure 10.1. This page is implemented in CGI and it runs on the majority of current platforms without too many hassles.

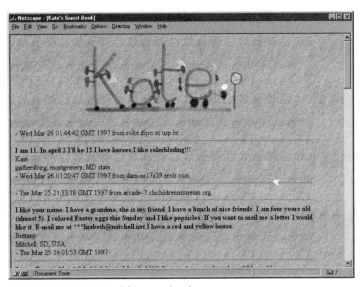

Figure 10.1 A sample CGI guest book

Katie's page is implemented using a Perl script from the Matt Wright CGI archive (www.cgi-resource.com). As you can see in figure 10.2, users are invited to fill out and submit a small form. The Perl script can either create the entry instantly or email the new submission to the site administrator for authorization.

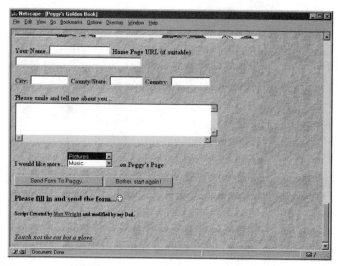

Figure 10.2 Submitting a new guest entry to the CGI form

You might think that the number of available guest book features is endless. The list is not infinite, but there are many options that allow web designers great flexibility when designing guest books for their sites.

As this chapter will illustrate, the Java code that makes up the guest book servlet is not that complicated. It builds on the knowledge you've gleaned from the previous chapters in this book. Once it's compiled and installed, the guest book servlet may service many guest book sites at once, while maintaining minimal server overhead.

10.2   A simple guest book servlet

We will develop a simple guest book containing a minimum number of features in this section. The features of this first version will include a user-defined comment field, a hyperlinked email address, and web site fields.

Before we head into the wonderful world of Java code, it's wise to first define exactly what a guest book is, technically speaking, and determine a way to implement it.

In its simplest form, a guest book is just an ordinary HTML page that is displayed every time a user accesses the page. The page is made up of two components: a section in which the user enters his comments, and a section where the previous comments are displayed.

On the simplest level, it's an HTML form. When it's submitted, the information from the form will be inserted into the same file that contains the form. This may sound complicated, but using the `htmlTemplate` utility class we developed in chapter 8, we can easily accomplish this with very little code.

Let's look at the HTML page that will be used as the basis for the guest book. Figure 10.3 shows the output from the HTML page we will use as our working example. Notice the form at the bottom of the page. The user fills in the fields with personal information and the comments he wishes to leave regarding the web site.

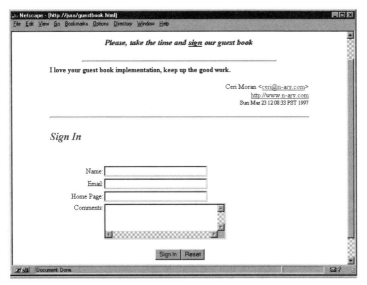

Figure 10.3 An HTML guest book

In addition to these fields, we need some extra information passed to us in order to allow the servlet to correctly process the outgoing file. Since the servlet will be writing a new version of this page out to disk when the servlet is run, we need the actual physical pathname of the guest book page so the servlet can open the file for reading and writing. We also need to know where the web designer wants the user to be taken after the entry has been submitted. This can be controlled through a hidden field indicating the URL to which the user should be redirected.

Note   Those of you who are more astute may wonder why we are passing in the full pathname of the file when we can have the servlet determine it from the referring page sent by the browser. Although that is perfectly acceptable, it would tie the web designer into having the form for submitting comments in the exact same page that displays previous comments. Sometimes, though, it's helpful to have the comments separated from the submission process.

The layout of the actual HTML page can be left to someone who knows what he is doing with HTML—namely the web designer. Fortunately, we're building a solution that doesn't rely on our knowing the format up front. The design can change without bothering the servlet developer.

We will inform the web designer what the fields we require, as illustrated in table 10.1. We'll also ask him to insert a special tag, <!--newentry-->, which will mark the area of the file where new user entries will be placed. The servlet will look for the tag to know how to treat the file.

Table 10.1 HTML parameters for the guest book form

HTML Parameter	Description
NAME	The user's name.
EMAIL	The user's email address.
HOMEPAGE	The user's home page.
COMMENTS	The user's comments.
GUESTPAGE	The full pathname of the file where the entry will be inserted.
GOODURL	The full URL of the file where the user will be redirected after an entry has been submitted.

10.2.1 Processing the request

After the user has filled out his comments, he will press the Submit button. This will invoke the servlet, which will then insert the information into the guest book HTML file. Using the htmlTemplate class we developed earlier, this turns out to be a rather trivial task as you can see in example 10.1.

```
public void service( HttpServletRequest _req, HttpServletResponse _res )
                            throws ServletException, IOException{

  String outFile = _req.getParameter("GUESTPAGE");
  htmlTemplate guestPage = new htmlTemplate(outFile);

  PrintWriter Out = new PrintWriter( new FileWriter(outFile) );
  String key[] = new String[1];
  String dat[] = new String[1];

  key[0] = "<!--newentry-->";
  dat[0] = buildEntry( _req );

  guestPage.print( Out, key, dat );
  Out.close();

  _res.sendRedirect( _req.getParameter("GOODURL") );
}
```
Example 10.1   The service(...) method

The first thing we must do is retrieve the full pathname of the file that is to be used as the guest book. This is found in the parameter GUESTPAGE; we can use the parameter to create an instance of htmlTemplate, and then create an output stream to the file, so we may write the new file back out.

We then simply create a couple of `String` arrays, insert our key and data pair, then call the `print(...)` method of the `htmlTemplate` class. Notice how we are using the `htmlTemplate` class. Remember how it was developed for use in creating dynamic HTML pages, where the output stream was generally accepted to be the output to the client? In this instance, we are using it to create a file. This is the result of a good design and Java. True class reuse is possible when careful thought is given to the initial design of a class.

After we call the `print(...)` method, we close down the `Writer` class to make sure the file doesn't become locked so the web server can no longer serve it. Finally, we make a call to `sendRedirect(...)`, which directs the user to a new URL.

An alternative to this redirect would be to reuse the `htmlTemplate` instance and send out the file dynamically, instead of having the client access it again. The reason this is not implemented is that the web designer may not always want the user to go back to that page. He may want the user to visit another part of the site.

10.2.2 Building a new entry

As part of the service method shown in the previous section, you may have noticed an unknown method call to `buildEntry(...)`. This method constructs our new user entry, making it ready for insertion into the file.

```
private String buildEntry( HttpServletRequest _req ){
  StringBuffer buffer = new StringBuffer(100);
  String content = _req.getParameter("COMMENTS");

  buffer.append("<!--newentry-->");
  buffer.append("<P><HR WIDTH=\"75%\"><B>" + content + "</B></P>");
  buffer.append( "<DIV ALIGN=right><P>" + _req.getParameter("NAME") );

  String temp = _req.getParameter("EMAIL");
  buffer.append("&lt;<A HREF=\"MAILTO:"+temp+"\">"+temp+"</A>&gt<BR>");

  temp = _req.getParameter( "HOMEPAGE" );
  buffer.append( "<A HREF=\""+temp+"\">" + temp + "</A><BR>");
  buffer.append( "<FONT SIZE=-1>"+new Date().toString()+"</FONT></
                          P></DIV>" );
  return buffer.toString();
}
```
Example 10.2 Constructing a new entry

Example 10.2 shows a new entry being built using a `StringBuffer` to construct the HTML code. The `StringBuffer` is more efficient than simply adding `String`s together. We end the call by returning a `String` representation of the buffer, which is done by calling the `toString()` method.

10.2.3 Complete source code

Example 10.3 shows the complete source code for this implementation of a guest book. You can see there's really very little code for such a powerful solution.

```java
import javax.servlet.*;
import javax.servlet.http.*;
import java.io.*;
import java.util.*;

public class guestBook extends HttpServlet implements SingleThreadModel {

  public void service(HttpServletRequest _req, HttpServletResponse _res )
                            throws ServletException, IOException{

    String outFile = _req.getParameter("GUESTPAGE");
    htmlTemplate guestPage = new htmlTemplate(outFile);

    PrintWriter Out = new PrintWriter( new FileWriter(outFile) );
    String key[] = new String[1];
    String dat[] = new String[1];

    key[0] = "<!--newentry-->";
    dat[0] = buildEntry( _req );

    guestPage.print( Out, key, dat );
    Out.close();

    _res.sendRedirect( _req.getParameter("GOODURL") );
  }

  private String buildEntry( HttpServletRequest _req ){
    StringBuffer buffer = new StringBuffer(100);
    String content = _req.getParameter("COMMENTS");

    buffer.append("<!--newentry-->");
    buffer.append("<P><HR WIDTH=\"75%\"><B>" + content + "</B></P>");
    buffer.append( "<DIV ALIGN=right><P>" + _req.getParameter("NAME") );

    String temp = _req.getParameter("EMAIL");
    buffer.append("&lt;<A HREF=\"MAILTO:"+temp+"\">"+temp+
                            "</A>&gt;<BR>");

    temp = _req.getParameter( "HOMEPAGE" );
    buffer.append( "<A HREF=\""+temp+"\">"+temp+"</A><BR>");
    buffer.append( "<FONT SIZE=-1>"+new Date().toString()+"</FONT>
                            </P></DIV>" );
    return buffer.toString();
  }
}
```

Example 10.3   The complete source code

This class, though powerful, could potentially suffer from a major problem. What would happen if more than one person attempted to add a comment at the same time? The underlying guest book file has a very high chance of becoming corrupt. We need to make sure that only one client request is processed at any one time.

To keep track of the client requests, we could make the service(...) method synchronized, which would mean all client requests would be queued up, each one waiting for the one before it to finish. This method of keeping track of requests is perfectly legal, but the servlet API provides a much cleaner solution in the form of the javax.servlet.SingleThreadModel interface. When this interface is implemented, the servlet is guaranteed to be accessed by only one client request at a time. Building this functionality in is as simple as declaring it in the class definition and doing nothing more.

This is one of the joys of working with Java. Just when a potential show-stopping problem presents itself, Java pops up with a perfectly legal, clean solution. Can you imagine implementing such a locking system as easily with CGI?

10.3 Email class

The ability to email a thank-you message to the user when he successfully submits a new entry would make your guest book come alive. In a previous chapter we looked at a very crude way to send email; in this chapter, we will present a complete custom class that will be used time and time again throughout the remaining chapters.

One of the most popular and widely used protocols for sending email over TCP/IP is the Simple Message Transport Protocol (SMTP). You may have noticed this field in your email software where it asks for the outgoing host. SMTP hosts come as part of the standard operating system on the majority of UNIX systems. For this reason, it has gained widespread acceptance.

10.3.1   SMTP communication

Communicating with an SMTP server is not unlike communicating with the majority of other TCP servers. Like other TCP servers (such as NEWS, FTP, and POP), SMTP uses command strings formatted as ASCII lines and terminating with the carriage return/new line (\r\n) sequence. Depending on the command, the server responds with a status code that indicates the success of the previous operation. This status code is formatted as a three-digit number followed by an optional message.

Sending email via an SMTP server can be broken down into three distinct stages:

1 Establishing a connection to the server.

2 Sending emails.

3 Disconnecting from the server.

10.3.2   Creating a connection

Creating a connection to an SMTP host involves opening up the network connection and communicating to the host that our server exists. It is at this point that most people new to Java and programming start shaking. Traditionally, network programming has never been easy—anyone who has tried to code an application for Windows using Winsock will testify to that. Java has made network programming child's play.

Connecting to any TCP server can be done using the `Socket` class from the `java.netpackage`. Once a class instance has been created, an input stream and an output stream is retrieved, and communication can begin. For example, take a look at example 10.4.

```
Socket smtpHost;
BufferedReader In;
DataOutputStream Out;

smtpHost = new Socket( "mail2.n-ary.com", 25 );
Out      = new DataOutputStream( smtpHost.getOutputStream() );
In       = new BufferedReader( new InputStreamReader
                                  ( smtpHost.getInputStream() ));
```
Example 10.4   Opening up a connection with the SMTP host

Notice how easy it is to create a connection to the host. If, for some reason, the connection can't be created, then the `Socket` class throws an exception. Now that the connection has been created, we create two streams, `BufferedReader` and `DataOutputStream`, to handle all the communication.

All communication is formatted as ASCII text. Therefore, the class `BufferedReader` (from JDK1.1) gives us a clean function for reading lines back from the server using the `readLine()` method. Conversely, sending lines out can be easily done through the `DataOutputStream` class using the `writeBytes(...)` method.

With the connection created, the first thing we will expect from the SMTP server is a line that identifies itself. Here's an example:

```
220 mail.n-ary.com ESMTP Sendmail 8.7.5/8.7.3; Sun, 21 Sep 1997
12:42:00 GMT
```

The first three digits signify the status code. If we receive a 220 response, we can assume the server is ready and waiting for us. Example 10.5 shows how we sit and listen for this status code. We use the `indexOf(...)` method from the `String` class, which returns an integer index of the position of the string specified. If the string doesn't exist, then `-1` is returned.

```
String LineIn = In.readLine();
if ( LineIn.indexOf("220") == -1 ) throw new Exception("Bad Server");
```
Example 10.5   Reading a response from the server

Once we receive this response we can send the `HELO` command which tells the server which domain we are calling from. Again, successful execution of this command will result in a 250 status code being sent back from the server.

Now we are ready to format and send emails.

10.3.3 Sending an email

An email has a number of properties but for this example, we will use four of them: sender, recipient, subject, and body. This information is sent to the server in a series of short messages.

Sending the sender and recipient of the email is performed using the MAIL_FROM and RCPT TO: commands. They are formatted with the email address appearing on the same line inside angular brackets (<>). Example 10.6 shows sending the server these two commands and waiting for the respective status codes.

```
//- Set the FROM field
Out.writeBytes( "MAIL FROM:<" + _from + ">\r\n" );
LineIn = In.readLine();
if ( LineIn.indexOf("250")==-1 ) throw new Exception("Bad MAIL FROM:");

//- Set the TO field
Out.writeBytes( "RCPT TO:<" + _to + ">\r\n" );
LineIn = In.readLine();
if ( LineIn.indexOf("250")==-1 ) throw new Exception("Bad RCPT TO:");
```
Example 10.6   Sending the TO and FROM fields

Incidentally, although we have not given the functionality here, you can send the same email to multiple users by sending the server repeated RCPT TO: commands. This is particularly useful if you are operating with mailing lists and you don't need to send the email body to the server a certain number of times.

Sending the email body to the server is very easy. First, send a DATA command. When the server responds with a 354 status code, you can send the body to the server as a series of lines ending in a single dot (.) on a single line. Example 10.7 illustrates this process.

```
//- Set the DATA field
Out.writeBytes( "DATA\r\n" );
LineIn = In.readLine();
if ( LineIn.indexOf("354")==-1 ) throw new Exception("Bad DATA");
Out.writeBytes( "From: " +_to + "\r\n" );
Out.writeBytes( "Subject: " + _subject + "\r\n");

Out.writeBytes( _body );
Out.writeBytes( "\r\n.\r\n" );
```
Example 10.7   Sending the email header and body

Notice anything? Before sending the email body, we resent the email sender and sent the subject line of the email inside the body. This information is optional and doesn't need to be present for successful delivery. Document RFC822, the blueprints of the Internet, details the exact format the body text can take. For example, another field that can be added is the data's MIME type. Using this, you can send attachments and even email formatted as HTML text (which is becoming commonplace in most email clients).

10.3.4 Closing a connection

After the emails are sent, the connection to the server must be terminated. This is a two-step process. We first need to send the QUIT command to the server, then we need to close the socket connection. No status code is sent from the server, so as soon as we have sent the QUIT command we can safely close the socket using the close() method.

10.3.5 Complete source code

Example 10.8 illustrates the complete class that will be used throughout this book for sending email.

```java
import java.net.*;
import java.io.*;

class sendEmail extends java.lang.Object{
    private Socket smtpHost;
    private BufferedReader In;
    private DataOutputStream Out;

    public sendEmail(String _Host){
        try{
            smtpHost = new Socket( _Host, 25 );
            Out = new DataOutputStream( smtpHost.getOutputStream() );
            In  = new BufferedReader( new InputStreamReader
                            (smtpHost.getInputStream()) );

            //- Read Welcome message from server
            String LineIn = In.readLine();
            if ( LineIn.indexOf("220")==-1 )
                            throw new Exception("Bad Server");

            //- Introduce ourselves to the server
            Out.writeBytes( "HELO n-ary.com\r\n" );
            LineIn = In.readLine();
            if ( LineIn.indexOf("250")==-1 )
                            throw new Exception();
        }
        catch( Exception E ){
            smtpHost = null;
        }
    }

    public boolean send( String _to, String _from, String _subject,
                            String _body ){
        //- Send one email
        if ( smtpHost == null ) return false;

        try{
            String LineIn;

            //- Set the FROM field
            Out.writeBytes( "MAIL FROM:<" + _from + ">\r\n" );
            LineIn = In.readLine();
```

```
            if ( LineIn.indexOf("250")==-1 ) throw new Exception
                            ("Bad MAIL FROM:");

            //- Set the TO field
            Out.writeBytes( "RCPT TO:<" + _to + ">\r\n" );
            LineIn = In.readLine();
            if ( LineIn.indexOf("250")==-1 ) throw new Exception
                            ("Bad RCPT TO:");
            //- Set the DATA field
            Out.writeBytes( "DATA\r\n" );
            LineIn = In.readLine();
            if ( LineIn.indexOf("354")==-1 ) throw new Exception
                            ("Bad DATA");
            Out.writeBytes( "From: " +_to + "\r\n" );
            Out.writeBytes( "Subject: " + _subject + "\r\n");

            Out.writeBytes( _body );
            Out.writeBytes( "\r\n.\r\n" );

            LineIn = In.readLine();
            if ( LineIn.indexOf("250")==-1 ) throw new Exception
                            ("Bad End of Data");

        }catch(Exception E){
            System.out.println( "send: " + E );
            return false;
        }

        return true;
    }

    public void close(){
        try{
            if ( smtpHost != null ) smtpHost.close();
        }catch( Exception E ){}
    }

    protected void finalize() throws Throwable{
        close();
    }
}
```

Example 10.8   The complete email class source code

10.3.6   Using the email class

To use the class we developed in the previous section, you simply need to create a function that will take an email address as a parameter and then send it out (see example 10.9).

```
private void sendThankyouMail(String _email){
    sendMail Out = new sendMail("mail.n-ary.com");
    Out.send( _email, "info@n-ary.com", "Thank you",
                          "Thank you for visiting" );
    Out.close();
}
```

Example 10.9   Sending a thank-you email

10.4 HTML removal

Allowing users the ability to use free-form text in their comments opens the doors to untold horrors. For example, the way the servlet is currently implemented, the user could enter HTML tags in the Comments field, and the tags would get correctly interpreted as HTML when displayed by the browser. This would allow users to place a graphic or even a Java applet in the Comments field.

Of course, the final decision on whether this should be allowed should rest with the web designer. It certainly makes for a more interesting site, but, like many things on the web, it is open to abuse. Instead of letting your servlet make the choice, why not leave it up to the designer to decide the fate of the guest book?

Letting the designer make the decision can be controlled through the use of a hidden field, removetags. If this field is present, the tags will be removed or rendered useless. Then, when the servlet formats the Comments field for insertion into the file, the string would be run through an optional HTML tag removal method as demonstrated in example 10.10. This piece of code would be part of the buildEntry(...) method shown in example 10.2.

```
if ( _req.getParameter( "removetags" ) != null )
  temp = removeHtmlTags( _req.getParameter("comments") );
else
  temp = _req.getParameter("comments");

buffer.append( "<P><HR WIDTH=\"75%\"><B>" + temp + "</B></P>" );
```
Example 10.10   Checking the removetags variable

Removing the HTML tags is not complicated. A quick and easy solution that has been implemented for this example is to replace all the "<" characters with spaces, thus rendering the HTML text useless. This is illustrated in example 10.11.

```
private String removeHtmlTags( String _line ){
  int x;
  while (( x=_line.indexOf("<")) != -1 )
    _line=_line.substring(0,x-1).concat(" ").concat
                         (_line.substring(x+1,_line.length()));

  return _line;
}
```
Example 10.11   Removing the HTML tags

Although the code looks busy, it is actually a very quick way of scanning the line of text while looking for the "<" character. The indexOf (...) method returns the index value of "<" in the string (if one exists), and using this value, a new string is constructed by concatenating either side of the "<" character.

10.5 Other application areas

While we've coded this implementation of the guest book, we always assumed it would be employed as a guest book. But that doesn't have to be the case. Without any changes, the same servlet can be used on pages where you are inviting feedback.

For example, the Liquid Information Organisation site (http://www.liquid.org) uses this technique extensively for its article section. This gives a user the chance to comment on a particular page and see what other visitors thought of it.

This servlet could also be used to provide a very basic rating system for the site. The user could choose the rating he would give the site from a drop-down menu. This rating would then be added to the list of other visitors' ratings to see how they compare.

10.6 From here

This chapter introduced the idea of having some pages being created by the users instead of them just looking at flat HTML files. An extension of this idea can be seen in the next chapter, which takes the guest book idea a step further to implement a discussion forum, or newsgroup.

C H A P T E R   1 1

Newsgroups

- Learn how a web-based newsgroup solution differs slightly from the conventional newsgroup implementation.

- Using a servlet, an efficient and very flexible newsgroup can be easily implemented.

- Discover how to cleverly link HTML files together to seamlessly provide newsgroup functionality.

One of the strengths of the Internet is its ability to share information among users. Information is not always that easy to find on the Internet, as it is strewn over a variety of applications and sources: the web, newsgroups, IRC, and FTP, to name but a few of the mainstream data sources. One of the richest sources of information is the newsgroup area. A newsgroup can be thought of as an electronic bulletin board. Someone pins, or posts, a question or statement to the board, and that message can be read by anyone viewing the board. The person viewing the board has the option of responding to the post or creating a completely new post. This is how the newsgroups function.

Special programs, such as Free Agent from Forte or Netscape's News, interface to the main world wide newsgroup network. However, these are not web-based programs, and they require a special piece of software to be able to access them. For this reason, many of the new users coming onto the web today do not even know the newsgroups exist.

There are over 45,000 different groups that cover a wide variety of subjects, but creating a new group is not that easy, and it can be quite a lengthy chore. One alternative is to use a web-based newsgroup that can be fully administered and integrated into an existing web site so that everyone can fully access it.

11.1   What is a newsgroup?

As I explained in the introduction, a newsgroup is a place where users exchange information. This has historically been done through the Usenet groups—at the time this book was published, over 45,000 different Usenet groups were in existence. These groups cover diverse topics ranging from computers to knitting to parenting to stock trading—you're sure to find a Usenet group that covers anything you're interested in. In order to view or post news items, you need a Usenet client program. This is simply a program that interfaces with a Usenet server and retrieves and posts messages. One of the most popular programs is Free Agent from Forte, as seen in figure 11.1.

Once the user has downloaded and installed the client program, navigating through the newsgroups is a relatively trivial task that depends very much on the client he is using. However, the basics of each program are usually the same: choose the newsgroup, view the topics that have already been posted, reply to some if you want, or create a new thread. It's as simple as that.

Note   A thread, in newsgroup jargon, is a sequence of replies to a single question. For example, if two or more people were to reply to a single statement or question posed by someone else, this would be considered a thread of conversation.

A newsgroup can be thought of as a series of structured emails, but instead of a single person reading them, anyone with access to the group can read them, without your having to individually distribute them.

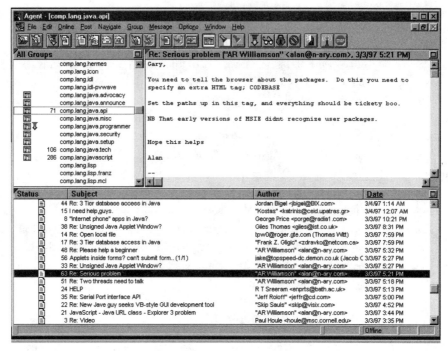

Figure 11.1 The Free Agent usenet client

11.1.1 Web-based newsgroups

For the majority of applications, the Usenet groups serve as an adequate service, as they exchange information on a worldwide scale. However, it is for this same reason that this type of information exchange is not always suitable for all applications.

Companies often like to provide some sort of technical support forum for their products or services. They may only want the group to be accessible to registered users. This would render the Usenet mechanism useless, since it gives the world access to the posts. A Usenet group wouldn't be very helpful if you wanted to use this method to announce a new product line to wholesalers before the general public got to hear about it.

One way to keep your newsgroups small and controlled is to manage a private Usenet group that is not accessible to the outside world. Although this is a very effective solution, it can still be a messy way to do what you want, as it places an extra overhead on the user—he has to have another package to view the information, and he has to remember usernames and passwords.

A much cleaner solution is to manage a newsgroup via the web. This would allow the user to view all messages via his web browser without having to drop into another application. From the web designer's point of view, it keeps everything in one place—not only is the administration easier, but the look and feel of the messages can have the same style as the surrounding pages to make them look like an integrated part of the web site and not an afterthought.

This is just one example where a web-based solution serves as a much better newsgroup solution than the Usenet alternative. The advantages of a web-based solution include:

- Easier access to the information—no need to rely on a third-party piece of software.
- Greater control over the look and feel of the messages.
- Increased security, as it is easier to restrict unwanted users.
- Increased web traffic, if people are using the newsgroup regularly.
- Easier to announce information to a targeted audience, including new products, shows, or general advertisements.

Web-based newsgroups are not a new concept. There are many implementations in CGI/PERL occupying web pages all over the world. However, as you may be beginning to appreciate, if the newsgroup is heavily used, an enormous amount of strain is placed on the server.

If the newsgroup engine is written as a servlet, the server is no longer under the same strain, as the same servlet can support many different newsgroups at the same time. With the CGI alternative, a new program instance is loaded and started with each new posting.

11.2 Implementing a newsgroup

Now that you've seen the differences between a web-based solution and the actual Usenet groups, it's time to learn exactly what the web-based solution entails.

11.2.1 The problem with newsgroups

Although one of our most important criteria for a newsgroup service is that the solution needs to be web based, we haven't determined what the final web solution will be. There are two possibilities:

1 Java applet running on the client feeding data from the server.
2 Pure HTML solution, with a servlet feeding the data.

Java applet solution   As shown in figure 11.2, this Java applet involves a three-tier solution to the newsgroup facility problem. The client side uses a Java applet to perform all the front-end tasks, such as user navigation and posting messages.

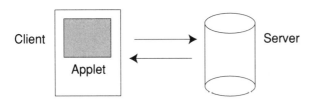

Figure 11.2 A Java applet solution

Advantages of the Java applet system include greater control over the user front end and reduced overhead on server. However, this solution is also flawed. The disadvantages:

- Increased download time as the applet classes are loaded.
- Further load is placed on the client side.
- The client side must be Java enabled.
- Difficult for the client to print and save messages.

Note   You may have noticed the point that seems to dismiss Java at the client side. This is not the case; however, at the time of this writing, Java at the client side is not always possible. For example, at the moment, my Apple Newton's installed web browser is not Java enabled. Be aware of an increasing number of hand-held machines that have limited memory and bandwidth. Providing a Java solution at the client side is not always the best route to take.

Pure HTML solution   An alternative to the applet solution is to have everything performed through HTML and the browser, as illustrated in figure 11.3.

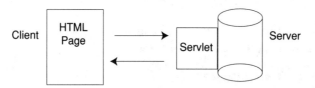

Figure 11.3 An HTML solution

The servlet creates all the HTML files that the web server will deliver. A precise explanation of the HTML files required in order for the system to correctly function will be detailed in the following section. These are the advantages of an HTML solution:

- Reduced bandwidth usage.
- Much faster loading.
- No need to rely on Java-enabled browsers.
- Users can print and save pages of information with great ease.

Among the disadvantages you'll find reduced user functionality and an increased load on the server.

11.2.2   Overall solution specification

Taking all the advantages and disadvantages outlined in the previous section into consideration, we will implement the HTML solution. Since this is a book on servlets, it would be shame to implement a complete applet.

The final system will use HTML pages that are first created by the servlet, then fed statically by the web server. A single newsgroup is made up of a list of topics, each represented in its own HTML page.

The list of topics can appear in a single HTML page, with the topic titles being hyperlinked into the series of HTML pages that represent replies to the threads. This page will be known as the index page (index.html), and it will simply list all the topic titles, with an HTML form at the bottom for new message submissions.

From this page the user can browse the list of topics that have been posted to the newsgroup, and the number of responses to each thread. Figure 11.4 shows one possible representation of the presentation of this page, with a form appended to the bottom to allow the user to post new messages.

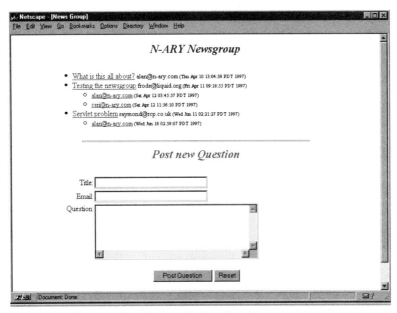

Figure 11.4 The page that displays the list of topics

Not only does this make the thread harder to read, but it also cluters up the screen with unnecessary information.

For this reason, I've decided to take all the good bits from the Usenet for my examples and leave all the bad bits!

If the user decides to look at a particular topic or thread of conversation, he simply clicks one of the hyperlinks. A separate page will be displayed, as illustrated in figure 11.5.

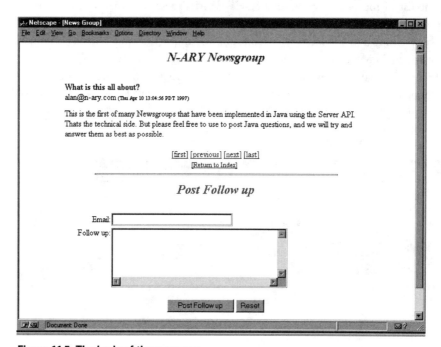

Figure 11.5 The body of the message

This page shows the title of the thread, complete with the message and the email address of each person who responded to the thread. In addition to the message body, a set of navigational tags is given to allow the user to move easily around the thread.

Figure 11.6 shows which message each link will take the user to. This feature makes the HTML user group very easy to navigate and use. Without this facility, the navigation would not only be awkward, as users would have to page back to the index file each time they wanted to move to another topic, but it would deter users from using it often.

The solution that is to be implemented must therefore satisfy the following criteria:

- Completely HTML-based.

- Be able to process HTML forms.

- Create all HTML links.

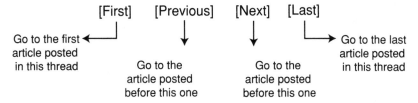

Figure 11.6 Thread navigational tags

11.2.3 Servlet overview

To increase the overall efficiency of the system, all HTML files will be created as and when the user posts a new message. This way the files are delivered in the normal way through the web server, and they will not increase the load placed on the server by running a servlet each time a user views the newsgroup. Therefore all the servlet execution is performed only when the user posts a new message.

Since the servlet will be activated when the user posts a new message from the HTML form, the class best suited for this is the `HttpServlet` class. The servlet has to deal with two types of postings: new messages and updated messages.

Instead of using two separate servlets, one servlet can be used, and using a special control tag we can handle both new messages and updates to current topics.

```
public void service(HttpServletRequest _req, HttpServletResponse _res)
                             throws IOException {
  if ( bCheckParameters( _req ) == false )
    return;

  String posttype = _req.getParameter( "SYS_POSTTYPE" );
  if ( posttype.compareTo( "NEW" ) == 0 )
    serviceNew( _req, _res );
  else if ( posttype.compareTo( "UPDATE" ) == 0 )
    serviceUpdate( _req, _res );
  else
    _res.setContentType( HttpServlet.SC_NO_CONTENT );
}
```
Example 11.1 The `service(...)` method

As shown in example 11.1, the `SYS_POSTTYPE` parameter is checked. The method that gets called depends on its value. Regardless of the control, notice the call to the `bCheckParameters(...)` method. Since this servlet will only ever be called for creating a new post or updating an existing one, both scenarios share the same need—the correct data must be posted. This condition makes sure that all the parameters are present and correct before the servlet execution continues. This method will be detailed later on in this chapter.

11.2.4 Creating a message

When a user posts a completely new message, a number of steps must be completed so the message can be added to the newsgroup thread.

1 Create a message body file.

2 Create links to the first and last files for the thread.

3 Insert a new title and a link to the index.html page.

Creating a message body file When a new message is posted, three files are created: the head, the tail, and the message body file. Why three, you ask? Well, the main reason is that it will make things easier for us in the future. The most complicated part of the whole system is linking all the files together so that the navigational bar can take the user up and down the topic list. On the face of it, it doesn't sound that difficult, but upon closer inspection, you'll find that this area can become a potential minefield if it's not treated carefully.

Naming conventions Throughout this book, you'll see several uses of the `System.currentTimeMillis()` method. It returns the amount of milliseconds that have elapsed since the epoch, which in this instance is January 1, 1972, 00:00:00. This is a reliable means of generating a unique number. We will name all our files with some derivation of the value returned from this method.

To make the navigational bar much easier to maintain, we'll also use a known convention to name the head and tail files in each topic thread. All head files will be prefaced by the letter "f," and all tail files will be prefaced by the letter "l."

When a thread is created, it is assigned a unique thread number. This number will be used to control the messages that are posted, and it guarantees that the updates are placed in the correct place. The head and tail files will be named `f<threadno>.html` and `l<threadno>.html`, respectively, where `<threadno>` is the value returned from the method `System.currentTimeMillis()`.

HTML template The servlet must create each message file from scratch. In this instance, the servlet needs to have a detailed knowledge of the overall look and feel of the final page that will be produced. This solution is not very flexible. If the web designer wants to change the color of the heading text, a complete recompile and reloading of the servlet would be required.

A much cleaner and flexible approach is to have a template file for the message body file, and to use this file every time a file is created.

```
<HTML>
<HEAD>
<META HTTP-EQUIV=Expires CONTENT="Sat, 09 Dec 1972 06:00:00 GMT">
<TITLE>newsgroup</TITLE>
</HEAD>
<BODY BGCOLOR="White">
```

```
<P><B><CENTER><FONT SIZE=+2>N-ARY newsgroup</FONT></CENTER></B>

<TABLE WIDTH="80%" ALIGN="CENTER">
<TR>
   <TD><B><FONT COLOR="#0000FF"><!--SYS_SUBJECT--></FONT></B><BR>
   <FONT SIZE=-1><!--SYS_EMAIL--></FONT> <FONT SIZE=-2>
                            <!--SYS_DATE--></FONT>
   <P>
   <!--SYS_BODY-->
   <P>
   <CENTER>
   [<A HREF="<!--SYS_FIRST-->">first</A>] [<A HREF="<!--SYS_PREVIOUS--
                            >">previous</A>]
   [<A HREF="<!--SYS_NEXT-->">next</A>]
                            [<A HREF="<!--SYS_LAST-->">last</A>]<BR>
   <FONT SIZE=-1>[<A HREF="index.html">return to index</A>]</FONT>
   </CENTER>
   <HR SIZE="1" WIDTH="80%">
   </TD>
</TR>
</TABLE>

<CENTER><B><FONT SIZE=+2>Post Follow Up</FONT></B><BR></CENTER>

<FORM METHOD="POST" ACTION="/servlet/newsgroup">
<INPUT TYPE="hidden" NAME="SYS_POSTTYPE" VALUE="UPDATE">
<INPUT TYPE="hidden" NAME="SYS_PATH" VALUE="/newsgroup">
<INPUT TYPE="hidden" NAME="SYS_MOTHERURL" VALUE="/newsgroup/index.html">
<INPUT TYPE="hidden" NAME="SYS_TEMPLATE"
                            VALUE="/newsgroup/template.html">
<INPUT TYPE="hidden" NAME="SYS_THREADNO" VALUE="<!--SYS_THREADNO-->">
<INPUT TYPE="hidden" NAME="SYS_SUBJECT" VALUE="<!--SYS_SUBJECT-->">
<INPUT TYPE="hidden" NAME="SYS_NEXT" VALUE="<!--SYS_NEXT-->">
<INPUT TYPE="hidden" NAME="SYS_FIRST" VALUE="<!--SYS_FIRST-->">
<INPUT TYPE="hidden" NAME="SYS_PREVIOUS" VALUE="<!--SYS_PREVIOUS-->">
<INPUT TYPE="hidden" NAME="SYS_LAST" VALUE="<!--SYS_LAST-->">

<TABLE WIDTH="80" BORDER="0" CELLPADDING="0" ALIGN="CENTER">
<TR>
     <TD ALIGN=RIGHT>Email:</TD>
     <TD><INPUT TYPE="text" NAME="SYS_EMAIL" VALUE="" SIZE=32></TD>
</TR>
<TR>
   <TD ALIGN=RIGHT VALIGN=TOP>Follow up:</TD>
   <TD><TEXTAREA NAME="SYS_BODY" VALUE="" ROWS=5 COLS=40></TEXTAREA></TD>
</TR>
</TABLE>

<CENTER>
<BR><INPUT TYPE="submit" VALUE="Post Follow up"> <INPUT TYPE="reset"
VALUE="Reset">
</CENTER>
</FORM>

<CENTER>
<P><I><FONT SIZE=-2>Newsgroup Servlet by A.R. Williamson</FONT></I>
```

```
</CENTER>
</BODY>
</HTML>
```
Example 11.2 The HTML template file used to create the message body

Example 11.2 shows the HTML template file used in creating the message body. Notice how the file is constructed. The HTML comment tags, `<!--SYS_XXXX-->`, are used as placeholders for various pieces of information that will be filled in when the actual file creation takes place. Table 11.1 shows a list of placeholders and their descriptions.

Table 11.1 The HTML tags used to create a message

Tag	Description
SYS_SUBJECT	The subject of the message.
SYS_EMAIL	The email address of the person who posted the message.
SYS_DATE	The date the message was created.
SYS_FIRST	The HTML file that represents the head file.
SYS_PREVIOUS	The HTML file that represents the previous file.
SYS_NEXT	The HTML file that represents the next file.
SYS_LAST	The HTML file that represents the last file.
SYS_THREADNO	The thread number of this message thread.

Notice the use of the HTML code:

```
<META HTTP-EQUIV=Expires CONTENT="Sat, 09 Dec 1972 06:00:00 GMT">
```

This is a fix (or hack!) to fool the browser into reloading the document each time it is accessed—otherwise the browser may deliver the file from cache which may be outdated. A problem occurs when a new message is posted and the user attempts to navigate through the thread using the next and previous links. Instead of the browser loading the new copy from the server, it uses instead a previously cached version, which is incorrect. The META tag variation forces the document to go out of date; therefore, the next time it is referenced from the client side, the browser recognizes that the document is old and therefore requests a new version from the server. This technique is used quite often in writing server-side applications that create static HTML pages.

Loading the template file   Having the template file load each time a user posts a new message is very inefficient. It would be better to load the template file into memory and access it when it's called upon. Think of it as a very basic form of caching. The htmlTemplate class developed in a previous chapter will be used for this task, so we will have a very easy mechanism for searching out and replacing text.

We can declare a static reference to the class instance and create it the first the time the service(...) method is called. Each subsequent request to the servlet will simply use the template file and not load it again. Example 11.3 shows the modified service(...) method.

```
static htmlTemplate HT = null;
public synchronized void service(HttpServletRequest _req,
                                 HttpServlet Response _res) throws
ServletException {
  if ( HT == null )
    HT = new htmlTemplate( _req.getRealPath(_req.getParameter
                           ("SYS_TEMPLATE")) );

  //- As normal…
}
```
Example 11.3   Loading the template file

Parameter passing   The servlet, for all intents and purposes, must not hold too much state information. It's not that it shouldn't or can't, but the addition of such information can be a headache to manage and it can introduce more of an unnecessary load on the server. In order to make the servlet small, efficient, and generic, certain state information (such as message title and message number) has to be stored elsewhere.

When the user first posts a message for a brand new topic, he supplies a title and the servlet produces a unique number for this topic thread. This is the title that is placed in all subsequent updates, so the users don't have to enter it again. One solution would be that each message has its own configuration file so the servlet can write this state information every time a new message is posted. Consequently, when a new update for this message is created, the servlet can open this configuration file, retrieve the filename and index number, and continue the update procedure.

Although this is a very valid method, it is not the best way to do what we need. It requires the extra overhead of opening and closing files, and a technique must be maintained for the naming convention the configuration files will take. It also makes the servlet installation much more problematic, as the administrator has to worry about configuration files.

If we take a step back and look at the problem as part of the whole servlet, a much cleaner solution soon presents itself. Each message has its own set of HTML pages which allows the user to navigate around the topic with relative ease. The servlet is only activated when the user decides to create or update a posting and this is through an HTML POST. But what is a POST?

A POST is simply a set of key/value data that has been sent or passed to the servlet. Since each thread has its own set of HTML pages, we can use this feature to store and pass state information. Using the HIDDEN field feature of HTML forms, we can have the HTML files themselves store the necessary data for future use.

```
<INPUT TYPE="hidden" NAME="SYS_THREADNO" VALUE="<!--SYS_THREADNO-->">
```
Example 11.4   The HIDDEN field example

Using this hidden field, we can pick up information for message updates in exactly the same way as new messages are posted, thus reducing the complexity of the servlet solution.

To make this solution tie in with our template, we can use the `<!-SYS_XXXX-->` HTML comment tags to identify where we should place these fields in the file. The web designer would then have the flexibility to move the form around on the page without having to modify the servlet code.

Note This technique of using HTML files to hold information between posts is very powerful and very useful. It frees the servlet from having to worry about holding information that may never be used again. If you carefully design the servlet from the beginning, you'll save yourself many hours of headache.

Writing a new file At this point, it would be good to review what we've done. When a new message is posted to a newsgroup, a template is used to create this HTML file. You've learned techniques for constructing this template file, and you've learned how to make the job of reading and writing the new file much easier through the use of the `htmlTemplate` class.

A certain number of parameters are required to guarantee the safe creation of a new message file. They are shown in table 11.2.

Table 11.2 The parameters needed to create a file

Parameter	Definition
_threadno	The thread number of the message thread.
_filename	The name of the file for the message.
_first	The name of the HTML file that a logical link will be created to.
_prev	The name of the HTML file that a logical link will be created to.
_next	The name of the HTML file that a logical link will be created to.
_tail	The name of the HTML file that a logical link will be created to.

By encapsulating the file creation into one method, we can pass these parameters into a function method. This function method will use the template file and this information to create a file.

When creating the file, the method simply writes out the template file, replacing or inserting the information as per the comment tags.

```
private void writeNewPage(HttpServletRequest _req, long _threadNo, String
_file, String _first, String _next, String _prev, String _last )
                              throws ServletException, IOException {
  //- Creates a new page
  String key[] = {"<!--SYS_BODY-->","<!--SYS_SUBJECT-->",
                  "<!--SYS_EMAIL-->","<!--SYS_DATE-->",
                  "<!--SYS_LAST-->","<!--SYS_FIRST-->",
                  "<!--SYS_NEXT-->","<!--SYS_PREVIOUS-->",
                  "<!--SYS_THREADNO-->"};
  String dat[] = new String[9];
  dat[0]  = _req.getParameter("SYS_BODY");
```

```
dat[1]   = _req.getParameter("SYS_SUBJECT");
dat[2]   = _req.getParameter("SYS_EMAIL");
dat[3]   = getDate();
dat[4]   = _last + ".html";
dat[5]   = _first + ".html";
dat[6]   = _next + ".html";
dat[7]   = _prev + ".html";
dat[8]   = _threadNo + "";

FileWriter fOut  = new FileWriter( _req.getRealPath(
                           _req.getParameter("SYS_PATH")+"/")+_file );
PrintWriter Out  = new PrintWriter( fOut );
HT.print( Out, key, dat );
Out.flush();
fOut.close();
}
```
Example 11.5   Creating a file

As example 11.5 shows, the main bulk of the method is simply setting up the String array that will be used to replace the tags. The static String array key is used to store the names of the tags that will eventually be replaced. Since this text will not change between requests, it is kept static to make the servlet much more memory efficient.

Creating links to the first and last files for the thread   Now that we have developed routines to create files from a template, we must coordinate how the routines operate. To keep the number of files that have to be modified when a new posting occurs to a minimum, a certain number of files have to be created at the start.

As you've learned, the three basic files are the head file, the tail file, and the message file. Each of these files is exactly the same, except for the links in the navigational bar (figure 11.7).

By creating the head and tail file in the topic list, we can then make all the links to the head and tail files very easily. Then when a new file is to be inserted, only the minimal amount of files will have to be modified.

The key to the system is the way the files are named (figurre 11.8). Since we've written a function that writes to all the files, it is a simple matter of setting up all the filenames and calling the function three times to insert the new message.

```
private void serviceNew(HttpServletRequest _req,
                         HttpServletResponse _res)
                         throws ServletException, IOException {
  //- Read in the variables
  long newThreadNo = System.currentTimeMillis();

  //- Write the index file
  updateMotherPage(_req, true, newThreadNo, newThreadNo );

  //- Write the HEAD file
```

```
        writeNewPage( _req, newThreadNo, "f"+ newThreadNo +".html", "f"+
                                 newThreadNo+"", newThreadNo+"",
                                 newThreadNo+"", "l"+newThreadNo+"" );
        //- Write the LAST file
        writeNewPage( _req, newThreadNo, "l"+ newThreadNo +".html", "f"+
                                 newThreadNo+"", newThreadNo+"",
                                 newThreadNo+"", "l"+newThreadNo+"" );

        //- Write the normal file
        writeNewPage( _req, newThreadNo, newThreadNo+".html", "f"+
                                 newThreadNo+"", newThreadNo+"",
                                 newThreadNo+"", "l" +newThreadNo+"" );

        _res.sendRedirect( _req.getParameter("SYS_MOTHERURL") );
}
```
Example 11.6   Writing the files

Example 11.6 details the file creation process, which is a series of calls to the `write-NewPage(…)` method. Since this is a new thread, the thread number is created using a call to `System.currentTimeMillis()`. This number is then used to create the file links for the navigation bar.

Note   You may have noticed a small pattern forming in the general layout of the HTML files. With talk of head and tail files, the overall structure of the files resembles the link list data structure. As you will see in the following sections on updating an already posted message, the link list metaphor continues throughout the servlet.

Inserting a new title and a link to the index.html   Now that we've created all the supporting HTML files, it is now time to update the main index page with a link to this newly created posting. By employing the same technique of using templates, we can construct an index.html file, and strategically placing HTML comment tags makes adding message titles to the file very straightforward.

```
<HTML>
<HEAD>
<META HTTP-EQUIV=Expires CONTENT="Sat, 09 Dec 1972 06:00:00 GMT">
<TITLE>newsgroup</TITLE>
</HEAD>

<BODY BGCOLOR="White">
<P>
<B><CENTER>
<FONT SIZE=+2>N-ARY newsgroup</FONT>
</CENTER></B>
<BR><BR>
<TABLE WIDTH="80%" BORDER="0" ALIGN="CENTER">
<TR><TD>
<UL>
```

```
<!--SYS_ITEM_0-->
</UL>
<HR SIZE="1" WIDTH="50%">
</TD></TR>
</TABLE>
<BR><BR>
<CENTER>
<B><I><FONT SIZE=+2>Post New Question</FONT></I></B>
</CENTER>
<P>
<FORM METHOD="POST" ACTION="/servlet/newsgroup">
<INPUT TYPE="hidden" NAME="SYS_POSTTYPE" VALUE="NEW">
<INPUT TYPE="hidden" NAME="SYS_PATH" VALUE="/newsgroup">
<INPUT TYPE="hidden" NAME="SYS_MOTHERURL" VALUE="/newsgroup/index.html">
<INPUT TYPE="hidden" NAME="SYS_TEMPLATE"
                         VALUE="/newsgroup/template.html">

<TABLE WIDTH="80" BORDER="0" CELLPADDING="0" ALIGN="CENTER">
<TR>
   <TD ALIGN=RIGHT>Title:</TD>
   <TD><INPUT TYPE="text" NAME="SYS_SUBJECT" VALUE="" SIZE=32></TD>
</TR>
<TR>
   <TD ALIGN=RIGHT>Email:</TD>
   <TD><INPUT TYPE="text" NAME="SYS_EMAIL" VALUE="" SIZE=32></TD>
</TR>
<TR>
   <TD ALIGN=RIGHT VALIGN=TOP>Question:</TD>
   <TD><TEXTAREA NAME="SYS_BODY" ROWS=5 COLS=40></TEXTAREA></TD>
</TR>
</TABLE>
<CENTER>
<BR><INPUT TYPE="submit" VALUE="Post Question"> <INPUT TYPE="reset"
VALUE="Reset">

<P><I><FONT SIZE=-1>newsgroup Servlet by A.R. Williamson</FONT></I>
</CENTER>
</FORM>
</BODY>
</HTML>
```

Example 11.7   The template for the index.html page

The HTML file found in example 11.7 shows the index page before any postings have been made. In the original specification, we stated that each thread of discussion should have its own unique identifier. By combining this identifier with carefully placed special HTML comment tags, individual threads can be found within the file.

To arrange the message titles, we will place them inside an HTML bulleted list. This list is constructed using the <UL></UL> tags, with each item denoted by the <LI> tag. To make the parsing method easier to write, each bullet or list item will have a comment tag with its unique number beside it. For example, <!--SYS_ITEM_4--> means this is thread number 4.

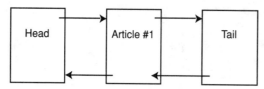

Figure 11.7 The minimum file set

We will use the `<!--SYS_ITEM_0-->` tag to denote an empty or vacant slot. The parsing program can then run through the file and look for this string. Once it's found, it can be replaced with a new item list. After the new item list has been appended, `<!--SYS_ITEM_0-->` is written afterwards, so the next new thread can be placed.

```
private void updateMotherPage(HttpServletRequest _req, boolean _bNew,
                              long _threadNo, long _link )
                              throws ServletException, IOException {
  //- Updates the mother page
  String key[] = new String[1];
  String dat[] = new String[1];

  String title      = _req.getParameter("SYS_SUBJECT");
  String email      = _req.getParameter("SYS_EMAIL").toLowerCase();
  String indexPage  = _req.getRealPath(_req.getParameter
                         ("SYS_MOTHERURL"));

  if ( _bNew ){
    key[0]  = "<!--SYS_ITEM_0-->";
    dat[0]  = key[0];
    dat[0] += "\n<LI><A HREF=\"f" + _threadNo + ".html\">" + title +
                       "</A><FONT SIZE=-2> ";
    dat[0] += email + " (" + getDate() + ")</FONT><UL>";
    dat[0] += "<!--SYS_ITEM_" + _link + "_0--></UL>\n";
  }else{
    key[0]  = "<!--SYS_ITEM_" + _threadNo + "_0-->";
    dat[0] = "\n<LI><FONT SIZE=-2><A HREF=\"" + _link + ".html\">" +
                       email + "</A> (";
    dat[0] += getDate() + ")</FONT>";
    dat[0] += key[0];
  }

  htmlTemplate HT = new htmlTemplate( indexPage );
  FileWriter fOut = new FileWriter( indexPage );
  PrintWriter Out = new PrintWriter( fOut );
  HT.print( Out, key, dat );
  Out.flush();
  fOut.close();
}
```

Example 11.8   Updating the index.html page

The `updateMotherPage(...)` method illustrated in example 11.8 takes in as parameters all the information required to open up the main index file and update it with the new message data. The easiest way of doing this is to read the file into memory, reconstruct it again using the `htmlTemplate` class, and then take the output of this class and redirect it back out to the file representing the index file.

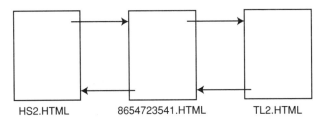

HS2.HTML   8654723541.HTML   TL2.HTML

Figure 11.8 Filenames

Depending on the modification (whether it's a new message or an update to an existing thread), the method will look for one of the two tags that represent the messages. The resulting HTML code produced for this list item is shown in example 11.9.

```
<!--SYS_ITEM_0-->
<LI><A HREF="f123456789.html">This is a test post</A>
<FONT SIZE=-2>alan@n-ary.com (6 June 1999 18:12.21)</FONT><UL>
<!--SYS_ITEM_123456789_0--></UL>
```
Example 11.9   A new list item

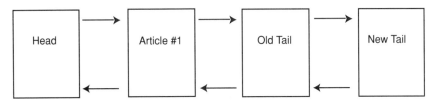

Head   Article #1   Old Tail   New Tail

Figure 11.9 Inserting a new message into a thread

Notice how the list item has a new HTML tag, `<!--SYS_ITEM_123456789_0-->`, which is inserted at the end of the block. This is done so we can post a new follow-up message with the same ease as the new thread. When we are updating the thread with another message, we can simply look for the `<!--SYS_ITEM_123456789_0-->` tag and then replace the new update with this tag. Look at example 11.10 to see how this new HTML code is updated.

```
<!--SYS_ITEM_123456789_0-->
<LI><A HREF="123456799.html"><FONT SIZE=-2>alan@n-ary.com
                    (6 June 1998 18:12.21)</FONT>
```
Example 11.10   The update thread

11.2.5 Posting a follow-up message

At this point, the user can view messages that have been posted, read messages, and add new message threads. However, the functionality to post a follow-up message has not yet been implemented. A follow-up message is created using the HTML form at the bottom of an message page. This procedure would then include the new message in the current thread and not post it as a new thread. There are two steps to insert a new message:

1 Insert the file into the current thread.

2 Update the index.html page.

Inserting the file into the current thread When a new update has been posted, it is inserted at the end of the file list, in the current thread. The first thing we need to do is create all the filenames and real pathnames. This is performed in much the same way as it was done in the previous sections. Once we have a filename for the new thread, we have to update the next link in the old tail to point to the new message file.

Before we update the file, we need to know the name of it so we can open it for reading and writing. The name is found by opening up the tail file and reading the filename its previous link points to. Since the tail file follows a known naming convention, we can recalculate the filename very easily.

```
private String getPrevFile(String _file) throws Exception{
  BufferedReader In = new BufferedReader( new FileReader(_file) );
  String LineIn;
  while ( (LineIn=In.readLine()) != null ){
    if ( LineIn.indexOf("SYS_NEXT") != -1 ){
      int c1 = LineIn.indexOf("VALUE=");
      int c2 = LineIn.indexOf(".html", c1+1 );
      return LineIn.substring( c1+7, c2 );
    }
  }
  return "";
}
```
Example 11.11   Retrieving the previous filename

Example 11.11 shows the code that is used to open up the tail file and find the name of the file of the previous message. The filename is buried in the hidden HTML tag

```
<INPUT TYPE="hidden" NAME="SYS_NEXT" VALUE="123456789.html">
```

Once the tag is found, the filename is extracted.

Now that we have the filename for the last file in the list (other than the tail file), it must be opened, and its next pointer must be changed to point to the new filename.

```
private void updatePreviousFile(HttpServletRequest _req,
                    String prevFile, long newFile )
                    throws Exception{
```

```
String fileName = _req.getRealPath(_req.getParameter("SYS_PATH")+"/
        "+prevFile+".html");
htmlTemplate HT = new htmlTemplate( fileName );
FileWriter fOut = new FileWriter( _req.getRealPath(
        _req.getParameter("SYS_PATH") +"/"+prevFile+".html")  );
PrintWriter Out = new PrintWriter( fOut );

String key[] = new String[1];
String dat[] = new String[1];

key[0]  = "[<A HREF=\"" + prevFile + ".html\">next";
dat[0]  = "[<A HREF=\"" + newFile + ".html\">next";

HT.print( Out, key, dat );
Out.flush();
fOut.close();
}
```
Example 11.12   Updating the previous file

Changing the link in the previous file can be done through a clever use of the htm-lTemplate class. The first step is to create an instance of the htmlTemplate class using the previous file as the basis. Since we also know what the previous link was, we can search for it and replace it with the new link. This is shown in example 11.12.

```
private void serviceUpdate(HttpServletRequest
        _req, HttpServletResponse _res)
        throws ServletException, Exception {
long newThreadNo = Long.parseLong( _req.getParameter("SYS_THREADNO") );
long newFile  = System.currentTimeMillis();

//- Update the home page
updateMotherPage(_req, false, newThreadNo, newFile );

String prevFile  = getPrevFile( _req.getRealPath
        (_req.getParameter("SYS_PATH") +"/l"+newThreadNo+".html") );

//- Write the actual file
writeNewPage( _req, newThreadNo, newFile +".html",
        "f"+newThreadNo+"", newFile+"", prevFile, "l"+newThreadNo );

//- Write the last file
writeNewPage( _req, newThreadNo, "l"+ newThreadNo +".html",
        "f"+ newThreadNo, newFile +"", prevFile, "l"+newThreadNo );

//- Update the previous file
updatePreviousFile( _req, prevFile, newFile );
_res.sendRedirect( _req.getParameter("SYS_MOTHERURL") );
}
```
Example 11.13   Creating the update files

Example 11.13 shows the method used to update the current thread that is being posted to. This, as you can see, is very similar to the method that was used to create the new thread, except the navigational tags are slightly different.

11.3 Complete source code

Here is the complete source code for the newsgroup servlet we have created.

```
import javax.servlet.*;
import javax.servlet.http.*;
import java.util.*;
import java.io.*;
import java.net.*;
import java.text.*;

public class newsgroup extends HttpServlet{
  static htmlTemplate HT = null;
  public synchronized void service(HttpServletRequest _req,
                                   HttpServletResponse _res)
                           throws ServletException, IOException {
    try{
    if ( HT == null )
      HT = new htmlTemplate( _req.getRealPath(_req.getParameter
                             ("SYS_TEMPLATE")) );

    if ( bCheckParameters( _req ) == false )
      return;

    String posttype = _req.getParameter( "SYS_POSTTYPE" );
    if ( posttype.compareTo( "NEW" ) == 0 )
      serviceNew( _req, _res );
    else if ( posttype.compareTo( "UPDATE" ) == 0 )
      serviceUpdate( _req, _res );
    else
      _res.setStatus( HttpServletResponse.SC_NO_CONTENT );

    }catch(Exception E){
      System.out.println(E);
      E.printStackTrace();
    }
  }

  private boolean bCheckParameters( HttpServletRequest _req ){
    String email = _req.getParameter("SYS_EMAIL");
    if ( email.indexOf("@") == -1 || email.indexOf(".") == -1 )
      return false;

    String title = _req.getParameter("SYS_SUBJECT");
    if ( title.length() < 2 )
      return false;
    String body = _req.getParameter("SYS_BODY");
    if ( body.length() < 5 )
      return false;
```

```
        return true;
    }

    private void serviceNew(HttpServletRequest _req,
                            HttpServletResponse _res)
                            throws ServletException, IOException {
        //- Read in the variables
        long newThreadNo = System.currentTimeMillis();

        //- Write the index file
        updateMotherPage(_req, true, newThreadNo, newThreadNo );

        //- Write the HEAD file
        writeNewPage( _req, newThreadNo, "f"+ newThreadNo +".html",
                            "f"+ newThreadNo+"", newThreadNo+"",
                            newThreadNo+"", "l"+newThreadNo+"" );

        //- Write the LAST file
        writeNewPage( _req, newThreadNo, "l"+ newThreadNo +".html",
                            "f"+ newThreadNo+"", newThreadNo+"",
                            newThreadNo+"", "l"+newThreadNo+"" );

        //- Write the normal file
        writeNewPage( _req, newThreadNo, newThreadNo+".html",
                            "f"+ newThreadNo+"", newThreadNo+"",
                            newThreadNo+"", "l"+newThreadNo+"" );

        _res.sendRedirect( _req.getParameter("SYS_MOTHERURL") );
    }

    private void writeNewPage(HttpServletRequest _req, long _threadNo,
                            String _file, String _first, String _next,
                            String _prev, String _last )
                            throws ServletException, IOException {
        //- Creates a new page

        String key[] = {"<!--SYS_BODY-->","<!--SYS_SUBJECT-->",
                            "<!--SYS_EMAIL-->","<!--SYS_DATE-->",
                        "<!--SYS_LAST-->","<!--SYS_FIRST-->",
                            "<!--SYS_NEXT-->","<!--SYS_PREVIOUS-->",
                        "<!--SYS_THREADNO-->"};
        String dat[] = new String[9];

        dat[0]  = _req.getParameter("SYS_BODY");
        dat[1]  = _req.getParameter("SYS_SUBJECT");
        dat[2]  = _req.getParameter("SYS_EMAIL");
        dat[3]  = getDate();
        dat[4]  = _last + ".html";
        dat[5]  = _first + ".html";
        dat[6]  = _next + ".html";
        dat[7]  = _prev + ".html";
        dat[8]  = _threadNo + "";
```

```java
        FileWriter fOut  = new FileWriter( _req.getRealPath(
                           _req.getParameter("SYS_PATH")+"/")+_file );
        PrintWriter Out  = new PrintWriter( fOut );
        HT.print( Out, key, dat );
        Out.flush();
        fOut.close();
    }

    private void updateMotherPage(HttpServletRequest _req, boolean _bNew,
                           long _threadNo, long _link )
                           throws ServletException, IOException {
        //- Updates the mother page
        String key[] = new String[1];
        String dat[] = new String[1];

        String title      = _req.getParameter("SYS_SUBJECT");
        String email      = _req.getParameter("SYS_EMAIL").toLowerCase();
        String indexPage   = _req.getRealPath(_req.getParameter
                           ("SYS_MOTHERURL"));

        if ( _bNew ){
            key[0]  = "<!--SYS_ITEM_0-->";
            dat[0]  = key[0];
            dat[0] += "\n<LI><A HREF=\"f" + _threadNo + ".html\">" + title +
                           "</A><FONT SIZE=-2> " + email + "
                           (" + getDate() + ")</FONT><UL>";
            dat[0] += "<!--SYS_ITEM_" + _link + "_0--></UL>\n";
        }else{
            key[0]  = "<!--SYS_ITEM_" + _threadNo + "_0-->";
            dat[0]  = "\n<LI><FONT SIZE=-2><A HREF=\"" + _link + ".html\">" +
                           email + "</A> (" + getDate() + ")</FONT>";
            dat[0] += key[0];
        }

        htmlTemplate HT = new htmlTemplate( indexPage );
        FileWriter fOut = new FileWriter( indexPage );
        PrintWriter Out = new PrintWriter( fOut );
        HT.print( Out, key, dat );
        Out.flush();
        fOut.close();
    }

    public static String getDate(){
        SimpleDateFormat formatter  = new SimpleDateFormat(
                           "HH:mm:ss dd/MM/yy" );
        formatter.setTimeZone( TimeZone.getDefault() );
        return formatter.format( new java.util.Date() );
    }

    private void serviceUpdate(HttpServletRequest _req,
                           HttpServletResponse _res)
                           throws ServletException, Exception {
        long newThreadNo = Long.parseLong( _req.getParameter
                           ("SYS_THREADNO") );
        long newFile  = System.currentTimeMillis();
```

```
//- Update the home page
    updateMotherPage(_req, false, newThreadNo, newFile );

    String prevFile  = getPrevFile( _req.getRealPath
            (_req.getParameter("SYS_PATH")+"/l"+newThreadNo+".html") );
    System.out.println( prevFile );

    //- Write the actual file
  writeNewPage( _req, newThreadNo, newFile +".html","f"+newThreadNo+"",
            newFile+"", prevFile, "l"+newThreadNo );

    //- Write the last file
    writeNewPage( _req, newThreadNo, "l"+ newThreadNo +".html", "f"+
            newThreadNo, newFile +"", prevFile, "l"+newThreadNo );

    //- Update the previous file
    updatePreviousFile( _req, prevFile, newFile );

    _res.sendRedirect( _req.getParameter("SYS_MOTHERURL") );
  }
  private String getPrevFile(String _file) throws Exception{
    BufferedReader In = new BufferedReader( new FileReader(_file) );
    String LineIn;
    while ( (LineIn=In.readLine()) != null ){
      if ( LineIn.indexOf("SYS_NEXT") != -1 ){
        int c1 = LineIn.indexOf("VALUE=");
        int c2 = LineIn.indexOf(".html", c1+1 );
        return LineIn.substring( c1+7, c2 );
      }
    }
    return "";
  }

  private void updatePreviousFile(HttpServletRequest _req,
            String prevFile, long newFile ) throws Exception{
    htmlTemplate HT = new htmlTemplate( _req.getRealPath
            (_req.getParameter("SYS_PATH")+"/"+prevFile+".html") );
    FileWriter fOut = new FileWriter( _req.getRealPath
            (_req.getParameter("SYS_PATH")+"/"+prevFile+".html")  );
    PrintWriter Out = new PrintWriter( fOut );

    String key[] = new String[1];
    String dat[] = new String[1];

    key[0]  = "[<A HREF=\"" + prevFile + ".html\">next";
    dat[0]  = "[<A HREF=\"" + newFile + ".html\">next";

    HT.print( Out, key, dat );
    Out.flush();
    fOut.close();
  }
}
```

Example 11.14   The complete source code for the newsgroup servlet

11.4 Future extensions

This chapter presented a very functional servlet that implements a web-based discussion forum, or newsgroup. It operates purely from HTML files, and requires no special installation or setup on the server.

Although it's very functional as is, this servlet can be used as the basis for a much more complicated and complete system. Additions may include:

- Newsgroup hierarchy.
- The original post as part of the new reply when posting a follow-up.
- A link into the main Usenet groups.

CHAPTER 12

Quote generator

- Build a simple quote generator, and understand the basics of a generic quote generator servlet.

- Modify the servlet to provide a level of randomness for the information it serves.

- The more data the servlet has to choose from, the greater the chances of each user seeing something new. Discover how to handle large volumes using a database.

- Learn how the basic quote servlet can be modified to provide new pages to the user.

199

When web users come back to a site, it's always nice to have something different for them, something new to make their next visit worthwhile. I'm not talking about a complete site redesign for each subsequent visit—that would be an enormous amount of work for very little gain. There is an easier way to provide an ever-changing environment.

If you are familiar with the UNIX environment, then you'll know that when you log on to most systems, they provide you with a small pearl of wisdom known as a fortune cookie. Most fortune cookies are generally very amusing, and they make the whole UNIX experience a more enjoyable one.

In this chapter, you'll see how you can add this functionality to any HTML page using server-side includes. Using the exact same servlet, you can provide a variety of different look and feel home pages.

12.1   Simple quote generator

The first thing we need to do is create the servlet framework. For this servlet, we will use the `GenericServlet` class, which will adequately perform the task of inserting text into an HTML page. Since we won't need any specific HTTP functionality, we don't need to use `HttpServlet` as the base class.

Before we begin, let's define what constitutes a quote. A quote is a piece of text that will be selected and displayed. This doesn't necessarily have to be an actual quote from someone famous—it can simply be a short piece of text.

We will store our list of quotes in a simple flat ASCII text file, with each line representing one single quote. Example 12.1 shows a quote file.

```
Nothing increases your golf score like witnesses.
Nobody can be just like me. Even I have trouble.
If others have sinned you need not mention it.
Life is like an analogy.
If at first you don't succeed, destroy all evidence that you tried.
Hard work never killed anyone, but why take a chance?
We will cross that bridge when we come back to it later.
Shin: A piece of equipment for finding furniture in the dark.
```
Example 12.1   An example of a quote file

Note   There is no need to worry about where to get such witticisms, because the Internet is full of them. Infoseek has an excellent list of links to sites that hold many of these one-liners; go to:

http://www.infoseek.com/Arts_and_Entertainment/Humor_and_fun/
Humorous_quotes.

Every time the servlet is called, it will select a new quote from the file and return it to the client. As you can imagine, this process can be implemented in many ways, depending on the size of the text file holding the quotes. For the moment, assume that the total number of quotes is relatively small and that they all can be loaded into memory at once. At the end of this chapter, the section *Handling much larger data sets* shows you how to cope with larger data sets.

12.1.1 Loading a quote file

For this implementation, we will assume that the total number of quotes is small, so we will attempt to load them all into memory as shown in example 12.2. We will use the Vector class as our data storage structure.

```
private void loadQuotes( String _filename ){
  //- Initialize the storage area
  URL Host;
  URLConnection  Uc;
  BufferedReader Ds;

  Quotes = new Vector( 25, 1 );
  Quotes.addElement( new String("Java is for life…not just Christmas"));

  try{
    Host  = new URL( _filename );
    Uc = Host.openConnection();
    Ds = new BufferedReader( new InputStreamReader
                            (Uc.getInputStream()) );

    String LineIn;
    while( (LineIn = Ds.readLine()) != null )
      Quotes.addElement( LineIn );
  }
  catch (Exception E ){}

  CurrentQuote  = 0;
}
```

Example 12.2 Loading in the quotes

Notice how the file is opened as a URL. This allows you to use any text file on the Internet as your quote database. Since this is a trusted servlet, it has the security rights to connect to any host on the Internet. A trusted servlet is one that has no security restrictions placed on it, unlike a Java applet running within a client's browser.

With Java, you can open a URL and read it like an ordinary file, line by line. This can be done with most URLs that are text-based. The URLConnection class gives you an input stream for the URL that can then be passed into any of the normal buffered reading classes, giving you line-by-line functionality.

Just in case the URL doesn't exist or an error occurs with it, you can initialize the list of quotes with at least one hard-coded value. This is a small fix so the servlet can produce at least some output, as opposed to none at all. This loading process should ideally be performed only once, at startup, from the init(…) method.

Note The `Vector` is another data storage class that is found in the Java package `java.util`. It is simply an array of objects that can be referenced using a numbered index. The advantage of using the `Vector` class, rather than simply an array, is that if the end of an array is reached when a new element is inserted, the `Vector` automatically grows to accommodate the extra member. Although the `Vector` class gives an array-type interface to its data members, it does not necessarily mean that the objects are stored in an array. The `Vector` class could be using some other method to store the data, which may prove more efficient. This is the beauty of classes: they abstract the details of the implementation away from the user.

12.1.2 Displaying a quote

Displaying the quote is a rather trivial task. We will display the quotes in order, with every hit advancing the pointer into the data storage as shown in example 12.3.

```
public void service( ServletRequest _req, ServletResponse _res)
                              throws ServletException, IOException {
  _res.setContentType("text/plain");
  PrintWriter Out = _res.getWriter();
  Out.println( (String)Quotes.elementAt( CurrentQuote ) );
  Out.flush();

  synchronized (this){
    CurrentQuote  += 1;
    if ( CurrentQuote >=  Quotes.size() )
      CurrentQuote  = 0;
  }
}
```
Example 12.3   Displaying the quote

Accessing the actual quote is very easy, thanks to the choice of data storage. Think how complicated this would be if you had chosen a hash table, for example.

Notice in example 12.4 how we have made the `service(...)` method thread-safe.

```
synchronized (this){
  //- Sensitive code
}
```
Example 12.4   Making a block of code thread-safe

We have made it thread-safe because the variable `CurrentQuote` is global to the class, and if two threads were to reach it at the same time, it could inadvertently increment the value past the end of the `Vector` class. This would then result in an `ArrayIndexOutOf BoundsException` being thrown the next time you were to call `Quotes.elementAt(CurrentQuote)`.

12.1.3   Complete source code

Example 12.5 shows the complete source code for the simple quote generator servlet. Since this servlet will be used in another page on a web site as part of a server-side include, it need only output the text of the quote.

```java
import java.io.*;
import java.net.*;
import java.util.*;
import javax.servlet.*;

public class quote1 extends GenericServlet {
  private Vector   Quotes;
  private int      CurrentQuote;
  private String   filename="http://www.n-ary.com/quotes.txt";

  public void init( ServletConfig _config ) throws ServletException  {
    super.init( _config );
    loadQuotes( filename );
  }

  public void service( ServletRequest _req, ServletResponse _res)
                                throws ServletException, IOException{
    _res.setContentType("text/plain");
    PrintWriter Out = new PrintWriter( _res.getOutputStream() );
    Out.println( (String)Quotes.elementAt( CurrentQuote ) );
    Out.flush();

    synchronized (this){
      CurrentQuote  += 1;
      if ( CurrentQuote >=  Quotes.size() )
        CurrentQuote  = 0;
    }
  }

  public String getServletInfo(){
    return "Quote Servlet";
  }

  private void loadQuotes( String _filename ){
    //- Initialize the storage area
    URL Host;
    URLConnection  Uc;
    BufferedReader Ds;

    Quotes  = new Vector( 25, 1 );
    Quotes.addElement(new String("Java is for life...not just Christmas"));

    try{
      Host = new URL( _filename );
      Uc = Host.openConnection();
      Ds = new BufferedReader(new InputStreamReader
                      (Uc.getInputStream()));
```

```
String LineIn;
    while( (LineIn = Ds.readLine()) != null ){
      Quotes.addElement( LineIn );
    }
  }
  catch (Exception E ){}

  CurrentQuote  = 0;
  }
}
```
Example 12.5   The complete source code for the simple quote generator

12.2 Advanced quote generator

You may have noticed in the previous section that the name of the quote file was hard coded, and the quotes were taken in order, as opposed to randomly. A generic and more usable solution would be to have the quote file passed in as a parameter, and to have the quotes delivered in a random order. Adding this extra functionality to your servlet is not difficult.

12.2.1   Dynamically loading the quote file

First, to allow the quote file to be dynamically specified, you can pass it to a servlet in the form of a startup parameter or a run time parameter. To utilize the quote file at startup, modify the init(…) method to that is shown in example 12.6.

```
public void init(ServletConfig _config) throws ServletException{
  super.init(_config);
  String newfile = getInitParameter("quotefile");

  if ( newfile != null )
    filename = newfile;

  loadQuotes( filename );
}
```
Example 12.6   The enhanced init(…) method

Getting a parameter passed in at servlet startup is similar to getting a run time parameter, except you use the method getInitParameter(…) instead of getParameter(…). To give the ability to reset and reload the file at run time, as opposed to doing so at startup, we can check for parameters to the service request. Example 12.7 shows the process of checking for two such parameters and acting upon them, if they're found.

```
String  newfile = _req.getParameter("newfile");
if ( newfile != null )
  filename  = newfile;
```

```
String  input = _req.getParameter("reload");
if ( input != null && input.compareTo("1")==0 )
  loadQuotes( newfile );
```
Example 12.7   Reloading the quote file

12.3 Random quote generator

From a user's point of view, the quote generation may look random, but we know it's not. The quotes are delivered to the client in a predetermined order, one after another. A user who visits your site a number of times may notice, after a while, that there's a pattern to the quote generation. To make it more interesting for repeat users, you do have the ability to make the quote delivery truly random. You can accomplish this by replacing the `service(...)` method with the one in example 12.8.

```
public void service( ServletRequest _req, ServletResponse _res)
                             throws ServletException, IOException {
  String  newfile = _req.getParameter( "newfile" );
  if ( newfile != null )
    filename  = newfile;

  String  input = _req.getParameter("reload");
  if ( input != null && input.compareTo("1")==0 )
    loadQuotes( newfile );

  int rand;
  for (;;){
    rand  = (int)(Math.random() * randfactor);
    if ( rand >= 0 && rand < Quotes.size() )
      break;
  }

  _res.setContentType("text/plain");
  PrintWriter Out = new PrintWriter( _res.getOutputStream() );
  Out.println( (String)Quotes.elementAt( rand ) );
  Out.flush();
}
```
Example 12.8   A random quote `service(...)` method

Notice how we are calculating the random number. First, the `random()` method generates a double value between 0.0 and 1.0. This isn't much use in its present form; what you ideally need is a value between 0 and the number of quotes. Generating the random value is done using the `for(;;)` loop.

Before we can calculate the random quote, we must calculate a `randfactor`. This is a factor by which the return value of `random()` is applied. For example, suppose you need a number between 0 and 10. Our `randfactor` would be 10. Table 12.1 shows a set of possible outputs from `random()`. To calculate the `randfactor`, look at the weight of the maximum figure you want to make random. For example, you can apply the following formula to determine the `randfactor`: 1 x 10 x number of digits of upper range.

Table 12.1 The `random()` output results

random()	random()*10
0.6754345321	6
0.8532465234	8
0.7432565424	7
0.4212542342	4

As you can see, the `randfactor` is simply a technique for moving the decimal point down *x* number of places, as shown in example 12.9. The number of places to move is calculated by determining the number of elements in the `Vector` class.

```
//- Choosing the randfactor. This affect the decimal place.
if ( Quotes.size() < 10 )
  randfactor = 10;
else if ( Quotes.size() < 100 )
  randfactor = 100;
else
  randfactor = 1000;
```
Example 12.9   Calculating the `randfactor`

12.4   Handling much larger data sets

So what happens when you want to handle much larger volumes of quotes? For example, suppose you have a file with 10,000 quotes in it, which will pretty much guarantee that no one user will see the same quote twice. This information should ideally be held in a database and referenced using the JDBC API, but in this section I'll show you two separate alternatives. Although the database solution is the tidiest, it's not always practical to set up a database. Besides, setting up a database would further complicate the installation of this servlet.

The two solutions use a technique known as a look-ahead buffer. Essentially, instead of reading the complete file into memory, the servlet reads only a portion into memory, such as ten records at a time. Then, with each subsequent client request, a quote is served from the memory buffer. For both methods, you can define some common ground.

Assume that the buffer will be of length 10 and it will use the `Vector` class. Each client request reads out of the buffer until the end is reached, at which time the buffer needs to be topped off. This is illustrated by the block of code in example 12.10.

```
Out.println( (String)Quotes.elementAt( CurrentQuote ) );
CurrentQuote++;

if ( CurrentQuote >= Quotes.size() ) {
  refillQuoteBuffer();
  CurrentQuote = 0;
}
```
Example 12.10   Buffer extraction

The two techniques differ in the method they use for refilling the buffer with quotes. The next two sections will outline each technique.

12.4.1 Technique #1: line-by-line

Reading the file line by line, as shown in figure 12.1, is the easier of the two techniques, but it relies on keeping a connection to the file open. Depending on the server, this method may not be the most efficient way of reading new quotes.

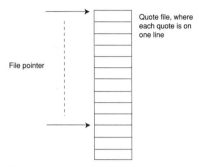

Figure 12.1 Line-by-line reading

Every time the `refillBuffer()` function is called, it reads the next ten lines from the file, filling up the buffer accordingly. If the end of the file is reached before the buffer is filled, the function reopens the file and begins reading from the beginning again. The file then has the characteristics of a cyclical buffer. Example 12.11 shows the code for filling up the buffer.

```
private void refillBuffer(){
  //- Reset Buffer
  Quotes  = new Vector( 10 );
  int x=0;

  try{
    for ( x=0; x < 10; x++ )
      Quotes.addElement( Ds.readLine() );
  }
  catch (Exception E ){
    try{
      Host  = new URL( filename );
      Uc    = Host.openConnection();
      Ds = new BufferedReader(new InputStreamReader
                         (Uc.getInputStream()));

      //- Fill up the buffer from the start of the file
      for ( int y=0; y < 10-x; y++ )
        Quotes.addElement( Ds.readLine() );
    }
    catch(Exception E2){}
  }
}
```
Example 12.11 `refillBuffer()` **version 1**

Notice how we are checking to see if the end of the file has been reached. This isn't the best way of doing it, but it is the simplest. We have nested a `try...catch` exception block inside the catch of the first. We are assuming that if the end of the file is reached, an exception is thrown by the `readline()` method. If the exception was an end-of-file, then we should be able to reopen the file again without too much difficulty. If, on the other hand, the error was something a little more serious, such as a loss of connection, then an exception is thrown when you attempt to reopen the file. At that point, we give up.

Although this is a very practical solution, it's not the best one, since a connection to the file must be maintained throughout the servlet's life. The second technique eliminates this requirement.

12.4.2 Technique #2: record-by-record

This method is much more efficient than the first one, as it doesn't require a connection to the quote file to be open all the time. However, a small modification to the quote file is required for this method to function properly.

Instead of using lines of arbitrary length, you have to fix the length of the lines to a known size. This way you can use the `RandomAccessFile` class to accurately jump to the correct record in the file. To do this, calculate an offset into the file by multiplying the line size by the record number, as shown in figure 12.2.

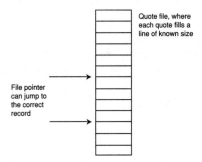

Figure 12.2 Using fixed record sizes

The specification shown in figure 12.2 can be implemented using the code in example 12.12

```
private void refillBuffer(){
  //- Reset Buffer
  Quotes  = new Vector( 10 );
  byte[]  buffer  = new byte[ linesize ];
  int Ret = 0;
  String LineIn, quote;
  StringTokenizer st;

  try{
    RandomAccessFile  fileIn  = new RandomAccessFile( filename, "r" );
```

```
      //- Set the pointer
      fileIn.seek( currentFileRecord*linesize );

      for (int x=0; x < 10; x++ ){
        Ret = fileIn.read( buffer, 0, linesize );
        if ( Ret == 0 )
        {
          LineIn  = new String( buffer, 0, 0, linesize );
          st      = new StringTokenizer( LineIn, "|" );
          Quotes.addElement( st.nextToken() );
        }
        else{
          //- End of file
          fileIn.seek( 0 );
        }
      }
    }
  catch( Exception E ){}
}
```

Example 12.12 `refillBuffer()` **version 2: fixed record size**

When we open the file, we position the file pointer in the file depending on the number of records already read. Next, we loop. With each full iteration, we read ten records at a time, incrementing the `currentFileRecord` with each iteration, so that we may return to this point in the file.

Notice how the line is formatted before it's inserted into the buffer. Although each record is a fixed size, each quote will not fill up the entire buffer. So to mark the end of the quote inside the record, the pipe symbol ("|") will be used. Use the `StringTokenizer` class to copy all of the text before the pipe into the buffer.

This second technique of reading the quotes is the more efficient of the two, because it doesn't require a continual connection to the file. However, the quote file does require a bit of preprocessing to ensure that all of the quotes are of a fixed length. We can write a simple Java program to convert the quotes into fixed-length records. Note that this method to convert all quotes to a fixed length has to use the sequential method of displaying quotes, where each quote is read in the order it appears in the file, as opposed to the random method, where the quote is chosen at random.

Note This technique of look-ahead buffers can be used in a variety of places, such as word processors which handle large files. A more elaborate solution would be to spawn another thread and have it continually checking for the end of the buffer and filling it up, hopefully before the end is reached.

For this application, if you expect the number of quotes to be high, then you would have to seriously consider the database solution. For more details on this, see the chapter detailing database access with JDBC.

TECHNIQUE #2: RECORD-BY-RECORD

12.5 Possible alternative uses for the quote generator

Once this servlet is up and running, there is no reason why it can't be used to feed users random HTML pages when they visit a particular page. For example, assume that we set the servlet up as an alias to the file, which is the default page the server uses when no file is specified.

Every time a user visits the page, the quote generator servlet is called. The quote generator is a server-side include servlet, meaning it inserts text into the file. Instead of inserting a text message, each quote could be a set of HTML tags that describe a frame set; once they're run on the client side, they load one or more HTML files.

If this is used on the home page of a site, users can discover a completely different page every time they visit. Although this means more work for the web designers who must design more than one home page, it doesn't take that many different combinations to provide a very exciting site.

The main advantage of this over a client-side solution, such as a Javascript program, is that users can be guaranteed a new page regardless of whether their browser supports Javascript.

12.6 From here

This chapter discussed how a simple quote generator servlet could be adapted to provide a complete new look and feel to a site for each user who visits it. In order to further enhance each different page or style, the following chapters will look at some exciting servlets that can add a whole new level of interaction without much effort on your part.

Random Links

- Learn how to provide a link that takes a user to a completely new site every time he clicks it.

- Provide a simple administration system that allows a web designer to change links without manually editing any configuration files or HTML files.

Virtually every web site contains link sections, whether they are other pages or lists of links to other interesting sites. These lists are often organized by related topics. Sometimes the links are not even related to the page you're on—they might just be listed for fun.

This chapter will take a look at the time-honored tradition of link pages and it will present an alternative to them that may renew the excitement of surfing the web and discovering the unknown.

13.1 What is a random link?

What is a random link? First of all, what is a link? A link is a piece of text or an image. Clicking a link takes you to a predetermined web page. This is commonly seen in HTML. Here's an example:

```
<A HREF="newpage.html">Take me to a new page</A>
```

To set up such a link, the web designer has to manually code all the links, determine where each one goes, and make sure they're all still valid. Figure 13.1 shows a typical page full of links. If you've ever set up a link page, you can appreciate the time it takes to create one.

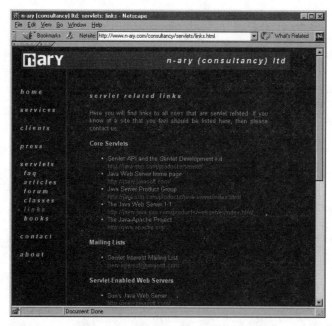

Figure 13.1 A typical link page

Forgetting the ethics of encouraging people to leave your site, a page of links can prove to be both productive and counterproductive. As you can see in figure 13.1, it doesn't take long before a list of links can grow out of control. It's not very professional or productive to ask users to scroll down the list as they look for things that may interest them. Long lists of links quickly lose their impact when important references get lost in a sea of links and descriptions. A page of links has to be short, or users will not bother reading through them. They may as well not exist.

13.1.1 Link page alternative

Links to pages outside of the current web site can be classified into two broad areas:

- Further reading, or reference sites
- Recreational sites

A user may visit a link page on a site in the hope of finding a link to a site related to the subject he has just been reading about. On the other hand, the user may visit the link section just to see what exciting or interesting sites you've found.

Note The definitions of "user" and "surfer" are very close, yet very different. A user is someone who has a narrow goal during a web-browsing session—he is researching or looking for a particular topic. A surfer, on the other hand, may start out looking for something, but is easily redirected by unrelated, irrelevant links that will take him into completely different areas. He is riding the surf, letting the links take him anywhere. The servlet presented in this chapter caters to the surfer, allowing him to be transported a completely new, unrelated site.

An awful lot of link pages are constructed as a goodwill gesture. In other words, two parties will have an agreement: "We'll place a link to your site on ours if you place a link to our site on yours." The main purpose of this agreement is to generate more traffic for both sites. Although this may seem a good idea, it is not always the best way to increase your company's or site's name recognition.

Consider this: suppose you maintain a page of links to all the sites that have your site listed on them. You're returning the favor. But what are the chances of somebody looking at your page of links and choosing a link that isn't near the top of the list—especially if the page requires several scrolling operations to read it all?

An alternative to having a long list is to have just one link; when it's clicked, it picks a link at random and delivers the user to the new site. This has many advantages:

- The probability of links being visited increases, because it doesn't matter where a link appears on the list.

- The popularity of your link page increases. It becomes a real surfing session, with the user being taken for a ride to somewhere new every time he visits.

- The traffic to your site increases. People may start using your site as a stepping stone into a completely new world every time they visit.

13.1.2 Implementation

One of the easiest ways of implementing this random link functionality is to use server-side includes. Although it's very appropriate, the server-side include solution also has some disadvantages:

- The page in question must be set to be preprocessed.

- Once it is created, the link that will be used is clearly visible in the HTML source.

- Random links can only be run on the site where the servlet is to run. In other words, no one else could use the same link page, unless their page was located on the same web server.

A much better implementation is to have the servlet produce the HTML link when the user clicks it. The HTML reference in the page would look like this:

```
<A HREF="/randompage.html">Take me to a random page</A>
```

This reference assumes that an alias to the servlet has been set up in the web server. This way, the user has no idea where the link will take them. On the other hand, if setting up an alias proves difficult, simply use this reference:

```
<A HREF="/servlet/randompage">Take me to a random page</A>
```

Another advantage to this implementation is link sharing. Instead of giving a link space to users, you can give them access to the random engine, and they can use the same servlet as you by referencing the full URL to it. For example, if the servlet were located on the n-ary server, the full URL would be

```
<A HREF="http://www.n-ary.com/randompage.html">Take me to a random
page< A>
```

When it is accessed, the servlet will choose from a list of links and transport the user to a random link. Loading the list of links at servlet startup can be done in the `init(…)` method, as shown in example 13.1.

```
private Vector PageList;

public void init(ServletConfig _config) throws ServletException{
    super.init(_config);
    PageList = new Vector(10);
    readFile("./randomlinks.ini");
}
```
Example 13.1   Loading the links

Before the servlet is accessed, it must load all the links it will choose from. For example, the code in example 13.1 shows the `init(…)` method. This method opens up a configuration file that contains a new link on every line. Loading this into the `Vector` class gives you an easy interface to the data.

Now that you've loaded all the links into memory, the next problem is to determine how to serve the page to the client. You have two options. First, you can take the complete URL, manually open the file, and send the file to the client. However, when you use this method, you'll encounter a major problem (see figure 13.2). The grayed-out rectangle represents an HTML page that is being delivered to the client.

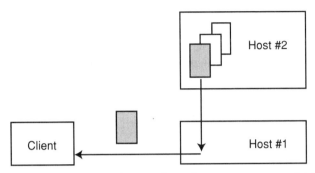

Figure 13.2 Fetching the page from the remote server and delivering it to the client

Although the client will correctly receive the HTML file, it will be from the wrong host. So when the client processes the file that contains links to images, it will try to load them from Host #1 instead of Host #2, where the actual file originates. The document base for the HTML file will be incorrect. This isn't too much of a problem if all the links are within the same host. To make the client correctly process the document, the document has to come from the correct host and not an intermediary.

Fortunately, you can do this by sending a small HTML page to the client. Once the page is loaded, it tells the client to go find another document. This may seem a little laborious, but it ensures that the document base for the page is from the correct host. Figure 13.3 shows the client receiving the small HTML page from the servlet, then retrieving the page in question from the server in which it resides.

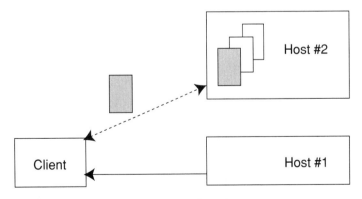

Figure 13.3 Sending the client to retrieve the page

The HTML page, which is generated on-the-fly, can be seen in example 13.2.

```
<HTML>
<HEAD>
<META HTTP-EQUIV="Refresh" CONTENT="0;URL=http://www.liquid.org">
</HEAD>
</HTML>
```
Example 13.2   The HTML page

This example uses the META REFRESH tag, which says, "Wait 0 seconds, then load the page at the given URL." You may think that doing this introduces quite a delay, and it does, in computer terms. However, the user won't even notice the delay; he won't be aware of the second page request. To the user, it looks like a seamless page load.

Serving the page is therefore a matter of constructing the HTML code in example 13.2 and inserting a random link string into the output stream at the URL point. Choosing a random link is a simple matter of choosing a number between 0 and the number of links in the Vector class, and using this number as an index into the Vector data structure. Rendering the page posting method is shown in example 13.3.

```
private void sendRandomLink(HttpServletResponse _res)
                        throws IOException {
  _res.setContentType("text/html");
  PrintWriter Out = _res.getWriter();
  Out.println( "<HTML><HEAD><META HTTP-EQUIV=\"Refresh\" CONTENT=
                        \"0;URL="
               + (String)PageList.elementAt(pickNumber())
                        +"\"></HEAD></HTML>" );
  Out.flush();
}
```
Example 13.3   Posting a new page

This is one way to have the client reload a document. The other method is part of the servlet API; the method sendRedirect(…) accomplishes the same technique. As you can see, there are many ways to accomplish the same goal.

13.2   Random link administration

In its current implementation, the servlet feeds random pages from an initial configuration file. Therefore, to add another link, the configuration file would need to be modified and the servlet would need to be restarted so it can reread the file. This is quite an administrative hassle. Of course, you could build in the functionality for the servlet to reread the configuration on a periodic basis, but again, this still leaves the manual editing of the file. A much cleaner solution is to provide an administration form, shown in figure 13.4, that allows the servlet to be updated live. From the form, the web designer should be able to add and delete links from the current choice.

To make everything simple, have the servlet itself produce the administration page. To produce the administration page, the web designer can pass in a parameter that signifies the servlet should return the administration page instead of the random link page.

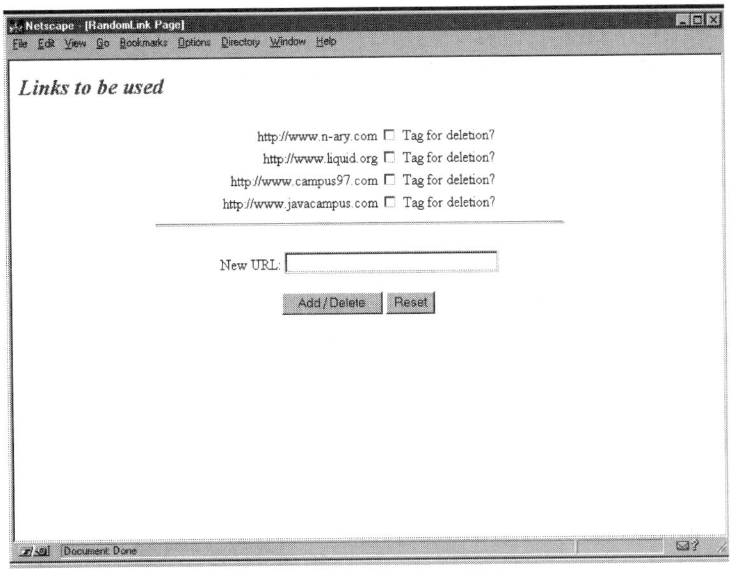

Figure 13.4 The administration form for updating the links

The administration page is essentially an HTML form, so the same servlet must be able to handle three different requests: random page, administration page, and administrative posting. The `service(...)` method is shown in example 13.4.

```
public void service(HttpServletRequest _req, HttpServletResponse _res)
                           throws IOException {
  if (_req.getParameter("admin")!=null)
    sendOutAdminForm( _res );
  else if (_req.getParameter("form")!=null)
    processAdminForm( _req, _res );
  else
    sendRandomLink( _res );
}
```
Example 13.4 The `service(...)` method

13.2.1   Creating the administration form

The administration form allows the user to delete or add new URLs to be included in the random pickings. As you saw in figure 13.4, each URL is displayed with a checkbox; when the checkbox is clicked, it will mark the URL for deletion. Building this list is very straightforward, as it only involves giving each URL in the `Vector` class a unique number. The unique number isn't that unique, actually. It's the index number of the URL in the list. The code for building this list is shown in example 13.5.

```
Enumeration E = PageList.elements();
String Line;
int    index = 0;
while ( E.hasMoreElements() ){
```

```
Line = (String)E.nextElement();
Out.println("<TR><TD ALIGN=RIGHT>" + Line);
Out.println("</TD><TD ALIGN=LEFT><INPUT TYPE=CHECKBOX NAME=\"");
Out.println(index + "\"> Tag for deletion?</TD></TR>");
index++;
}
```
Example 13.5   Creating the administration form

13.2.2   Processing the administration form

When the form has been posted to the servlet, the first thing you must code the servlet to do is delete the marked URLs. This is done by checking each list item to see if all parameters on the page are set to "on." When you remove an item from the list, the index of the remaining items is incorrect. To track these changes, an offset variable is kept, and every time an item is removed, this offset variable readjusts the index value. Example 13.6 shows the code for deleting the marked items.

```
int NoElements = PageList.size();
int offset     = 0;

for ( int x=0; x < NoElements; x++ ){
  if ( _req.getParameter( x + "" ) != null &&
       _req.getParameter( x + "" ).compareTo( "on" ) == 0 ){
    PageList.removeElementAt( x - offset );
    offset++;
  }
}

//- Add new URL if present
if ( _req.getParameter( "newurl" ) != null && _req.getParameter(
                         "newurl" ).length() != 0 )
  PageList.addElement( (String)_req.getParameter( "newurl" ) );

writeFile( "./randomlinks.ini" );
```
Example 13.6   Processing the administration form

After the marked items are deleted, the new URL is added to the list (assuming the user has entered a new URL). After the URL is added, the configuration file is updated with the new information; now when the servlet is restarted, all changes will be remembered.

Note   By combining the administration duties with the servlet execution, the system is presented as a complete package. This is a very easy way of taking the web administrator out of the loop; whenever a user wishes to make any changes to the links, the servlet doesn't need to be restarted.

When you are designing servlets, this sort of functionality should be kept in mind. It makes the servlets not only easy to design, but easier to maintain.

13.3 Complete source code

Example 13.7 shows the completed source code for the servlet we've created. This servlet will be used to provide both a random link function and an administration function for the list of links.

```java
import java.io.*;
import java.util.*;
import javax.servlet.*;
import javax.servlet.http.*;

public class randomlink extends HttpServlet {
  private Vector PageList;

  public void init(ServletConfig _config) throws ServletException {
    super.init(_config);
    PageList = new Vector( 10 );
    readFile( "./randomlinks.ini" );
  }

  public void service(HttpServletRequest _req, HttpServletResponse _res)
                            throws IOException{
    if ( _req.getParameter( "admin" ) != null)
      sendOutAdminForm( _res );
    else if ( _req.getParameter( "form" ) != null)
      processAdminForm( _req, _res );
    else
      sendRandomLink( _res );
  }

  private void sendOutAdminForm( HttpServletResponse _res )
                            throws IOException {
    _res.setContentType("text/html");
    PrintWriter Out = _res.getWriter();

    Out.println( "<HTML><HEAD><META HTTP-EQUIV=Expires CONTENT=\"" );
    Out.println( "Sat, 09 Dec 1972 06:00:00 GMT\">");
    Out.println( "<TITLE>RandomLink Page</TITLE></HEAD>" );
    Out.println( "<BODY TEXT=#000000 BGCOLOR=#FFFFFF LINK=#0000EE" );
    Out.println( "VLINK=#551A8B ALINK=#FF0000>" );
    Out.println( "<P><B><I><FONT COLOR=#0000FF SIZE=+2>");
    Out.println( "Links to be used</FONT></I></B></P>" );
    Out.println( "<FORM METHOD=POST ACTION=/randompage.html>");
    Out.println( "<CENTER><TABLE BORDER=0>" );
    Out.println( "<INPUT TYPE=hidden NAME=form VALUE=1>" );

    Enumeration E = PageList.elements();
    String    Line;
    int       index=0;
    while ( E.hasMoreElements() ){
```

```
      Line = (String)E.nextElement();
      Out.println( "<TR><TD ALIGN=RIGHT>" + Line + "</TD>");
      Out.println( "<TD ALIGN=LEFT><INPUT TYPE=CHECKBOX NAME=\"" );
      Out.println( index + "\"> Tag for deletion?</TD></TR>" );
      index++;
    }

    Out.println( "</TABLE><HR ALIGN=CENTER WIDTH=60%></P>");
    Out.println( "New URL:  <INPUT TYPE=text NAME=newurl ");
    Out.println( "VALUE=\"\" SIZE=32><BR><BR>");
    Out.println( "<INPUT TYPE=\"submit\" VALUE=\"Add / Delete\">" );
    Out.println( "<INPUT TYPE=reset VALUE=Reset>");
    Out.println( "</CENTER></FORM><P></BODY></HTML>" );
    Out.flush();
  }

  private void processAdminForm( HttpServletRequest _req,
                       HttpServletResponse _res) throws IOException {
    _res.setContentType("text/html");
    PrintWriter Out = _res.getWriter();

    //- Run through the list and delete the parameters that are not on
    int NoElements = PageList.size();
    int offset     = 0;

    for ( int x=0; x < NoElements; x++ ){
      if ( _req.getParameter( x + "" ) != null &&
                     _req.getParameter(x+"").compareTo("on")==0){
        PageList.removeElementAt( x - offset );
        offset++;
      }
    }

    //- Add new URL if present
    if ( _req.getParameter( "newurl" ) != null &&
                     _req.getParameter( "newurl" ).length() != 0   )
      PageList.addElement((String)_req.getParameter("newurl"));

    writeFile( "./randomlinks.ini" );
    Out.println( "<HTML><HEAD><TITLE>RandomLink Page</TITLE></HEAD>" );
    Out.println( "<BODY TEXT=#000000 LINK=#0000EE ");
    Out.println( "VLINK=#551A8B ALINK=#FF0000>");
    Out.println( "<FONT COLOR=#0000FF SIZE=+2>Thank you</FONT>" );
    Out.println( "</BODY></HTML>" );
    Out.flush();
  }

  private void sendRandomLink( HttpServletResponse _res)
                       throws IOException {
    _res.setContentType("text/html");
    PrintWriter Out = new PrintWriter(_res.getOutputStream());
    Out.println( "<HTML><HEAD><META HTTP-EQUIV=\"Refresh\"
```

```
                 CONTENT=\"0;URL=" + (String)PageList.elementAt
                        (pickNumber()) + "\"></HEAD></HTML>" );
  Out.flush();
}

private void readFile( String _filename ){
  FileIntputStream    FS = new FileInputStream(_filename);
  ObjectOutputStream  IS = new ObjectInputStream(FS);
  PageList = (Vector)IS.readObject();
}

private void writeFile( String _filename ){
  FileOutputStream    FS = new FileOutputStream(_filename);
  ObjectOutputStream  OS = new ObjectOutputStream(FS);
  OS.writeObject( PageList );
}

private int pickNumber(){
  int rand, randfactor    = 10;

  if ( PageList.size() < 10 )
    randfactor  = 10;
  else if ( PageList.size() < 100 )
    randfactor  = 100;
  else
    randfactor  = 1000;

  for (;;){
    rand  = (int)(Math.random() * randfactor);
    if ( rand >= 0 && rand < PageList.size() )
      break;
  }
  return rand;
}
}
```

Example 13.7   The complete source code for the random link servlet

13.4 Future extensions

The purpose of this chapter was to show you an alternative to the long-standing tradition of providing pages full of links to other sites. Although the method shown in this chapter is a very exciting way of presenting the information, it does not need to be implemented as an alternative to the traditional page full of links. A hybrid of the two is possible; you could have the existing list of links underneath the random link section, and you could tell the user that instead of scrolling through the list, he can receive a random link from the list by clicking on the Random Link link.

Another possible addition to the system would be to modify the servlet to handle groups of links. That way one servlet could handle many different lists, saving on both resources and management.

13.5 From here

This chapter showed how a boring links page could be improved to provide the user with a more entertaining link choice. This idea could also be extended using cookies.

C H A P T E R 1 4

Dynamic images

- Learn how to accept a character and serve the corresponding image.
- Learn how to serve dynamic images to the client in response to an HTML <IMG> tag.
- Discover how to create completely dynamic images for the client.
- Learn how to push images to the client using animation and video techniques.

223

Every so often, web designers may want to use dynamic images (also called server-side images) to give their pages a fresh look every time someone visits the site. For example, instead of displaying just an ASCII text string, the designer could replace the characters with something a bit more visually pleasing, such as GIF images. This is done using HTML <IMG> tags instead of SSIs. As you will see in this chapter, SSIs are not at all suitable for displaying an image instead of characters. The technique presented in this chapter can be applied in many ways, such as creating dynamic real-time graphs for plotting data that is changing rapidly.

14.1 Serving images

Serving images to the client is probably one of the easiest things a servlet can do. To the client, there's no difference between receiving an image from the core web server and receiving an image from a servlet. The file in question is opened and transmitted to the client. No encoding or special preprocessing is required; the client has requested an image and is expecting an image in return. No content type or special headers need to be sent.

So what is the point in writing a servlet that performs one of the tasks already performed by the web server? (The "just to see" argument only goes so far.) This servlet will accept as a parameter the character that is to be represented by a GIF, and the servlet will choose the corresponding GIF file and send it. Granted, this is not exactly rocket science, but the following technique will be extended for the forthcoming sections on dynamic images and server-side push.

One of the first things you must do before serving any image to the client is to get an output stream to the client. This is collected through the getOutputStream() method from the ServletResponse class. To be most efficient, use this method to construct a BufferedOutputStream instance, as the following code line demonstrates:

```
BufferedOutputStream OS = new
                BufferedOutputStream(_res.getOutputStream());
```

Now that you've created an output stream to which the image will be sent, you now need to create an input stream from which the image, or GIF file, will be read.

```
BufferedInputStream IS = new BufferedInputStream(
    new FileInputStream(_req.getParameter("letter")+".gif"));
```

Assuming that you have a set of prepared images sitting in a directory somewhere on the web server, one for each letter of the alphabet (A.gif, B.gif, C.gif, and so on), you can construct the file name from the passed-in parameter by appending the .gif extension.

Since the servlet isn't producing any HTML code or directly interfacing with the HTTP protocol, the GenericServlet class can be used to subclass the new servlet. The code shown in example 14.1 shows the complete code for the servlet that will serve individual images to the client depending on the input parameter.

```
import java.io.*;
import java.util.*;
import javax.servlet.*;

public class ascii2gif extends GenericServlet {
  public void service( ServletRequest _req, ServletResponse _res)
              throws IOException {
    BufferedOutputStream OS = new BufferedOutputStream
              (_res.getOutputStream());
    BufferedInputStream IS = new BufferedInputStream(
              new FileInputStream(_req.getParameter("letter")+".gif"));
    byte  buffer[]= new byte[1024];
    int   noRead  = 0;

    noRead  = IS.read( buffer, 0, 1023 );
    while ( noRead != -1 ){
      OS.write( buffer, 0, noRead );
      noRead  = IS.read( buffer, 0, 1023 );
    }
    OS.flush();
  }
}
```

Example 14.1   Serving GIF images to the client

Now that a reference to both streams has been established, all that remains is to read from one stream and write to the other. Example 14.1 illustrates this with the while loop in the service(...) method. The file is read in blocks of 1K and written out to the client in blocks of 512 bytes, which is the default block size employed by the BufferedOutputStream class when no block size is specified while creating the class instance. Calling or activating the servlet is done using the HTML <IMG> tag.

```
<IMG SRC="/ascii2gif.gif?letter=A">
```

To make the servlet easier for the web designer to understand, an alias can be created for it; this results in Ascii2gif.gif for the line of code above. Creating the alias isn't compulsory—the URL below would have resulted in the same output:

```
<IMG SRC="/servlet/ascii2gif?letterA">
```

All servlets placed in the servlet directory are thought to be trusted and can be accessed directly without the need to register them with the web server.

14.1.1 Creating dynamic images

Although the previous section demonstrated how to send the client a GIF file, it didn't really serve as a real usable servlet. You wouldn't use the preceding servlet in a real-life environment because it doesn't offer any extra functionality than the standard web server already offers. This section will demonstrate one of the powerful advantages the servlet has over conventional CGI/Perl solutions: the ability to create dynamic GIF or JPEG images.

Those of you familiar with Java's AWT package will understand the power this library has and its flexibility in the world of independent graphics. This is the library that is used to create completely dynamic server-side images.

To draw anything at the basic level, a Graphics context is required. A Graphics context allows for drawing onto components or inline memory images. Components are objects that are used as base classes for objects that have a visual presence. But servlets are faceless objects; they don't have the references or objects to create or access a visual component.

Note A Graphics context can be thought of like a paint brush. Before you can paint a picture, a wall, or even a house, you need to first have a brush or roller. Java requires the same of a developer. Before he can paint or draw any graphics, the developer has to retrieve a brush, or context, for the type of graphic operation that is to be performed.

To be able to use all the graphics routines, you need either a visual component or a memory image. A visual component isn't really much use in this situation; however, an image in memory is exactly what is required. To make a memory image, you need a reference to some sort of visual component.

It's a Catch-22. You can't make a visual component because you are running on the server, but to make a memory image, you first need a visual component to set the memory up. Fortunately, the situation is not as bad as it may seem. What you can do is fool the classes into thinking there is a visual component by creating a window that will never be displayed. Using this window, a memory image can be created. The code shown in example 14.2 implements an extension to the servlet presented previously. This servlet will accept a text string as a parameter, and then draw a series of images that will be sent out to the client, representing the text string.

```
Frame dummyframe = new Frame();
dummyframe.addNotify();
Image offscreenImg = dummyframe.createImage(50,50);
Graphics offscreen = offscreenImg.getGraphics();
```
Example 14.2   Creating a faceless visual object

Example 14.2 illustrates the procedure to create an inline memory image and retrieve the `Graphics` context for it. You use the `Frame` class because when the Frame is created, it is invisible and gives you all the functionality required to make an `Image` instance.

Any drawing or writing routines are now performed on the image in memory, with no attempt to create or draw on any visible `Frame`. The code shown in example 14.3 implements an extension to the servlet presented earlier in the chapter. This new servlet accepts a text string as a parameter, then it draws an image that will be sent out to the client. This image represents the text string.

Note   This technique of creating a `Frame` instance will not work on all servers. Failure or success will depend on whether a graphics card has been installed on the system. Some sort of graphics card exists on most systems; however, some UNIX machines have had all graphics removed so they are purely character based.

```
import java.io.*;
import java.util.*;
import javax.servlet.*;
import java.awt.*;

public class ascii2gif extends GenericServlet{
  private int charHeight=24, charWidth=24;

  public void service( ServletRequest _req, ServletResponse _res)
          throws IOException{
    if ( _req.getParameter("name")  == null ||
        _req.getParameter("name").length() == 0 )
      return;

    //- Encode the image into a GIF and send it out
    BufferedOutputStream OS = new BufferedOutputStream
          (_res.getOutputStream());

    //- Setup the dummy graphics
    Frame dummyframe = new Frame();
    dummyframe.addNotify();
    Image offscreenImg = dummyframe.createImage(
          charWidth*_req.getParameter("name").length(), charHeight );
    Graphics offscreen = offscreenImg.getGraphics();

    _res.setContentType("image/gif");
    byte SplitBytes[] = new byte[SplitLine.length()];
    offscreen.setColor(Color.white );
```

```
offscreen.fillRect(0,0, charWidth*_req.getParameter
                        ("name").length()-1,charHeight-1 );
offscreen.setColor(Color.red);
offscreen.drawString(_req.getParameter("name"),15,17);
GifEncoder  g = new GifEncoder(offscreenImg,OS);
g.encode();
OS.flush();

dummyframe.dispose();
   }
}
```
Example 14.3   The complete source code, including the extension

Now that you've created the `Image` object, you need to convert the information into either a GIF or JPEG format that can be written out to the client. Use the `GifEncoder` class to do this. This class takes an `Image` and an `OutputStream`, codes the `Image` into a GIF, and sends it out on the stream.

The `GifEncoder` class is not part of the standard Java libraries, but it is lent to us by the kind permission of Jef Poskanzer (`jef@acme.com`). Along with many other excellent utilities, it can be found at his web site at http://www.acme.com. The `GifEncoder` is freely available for use, and can be employed elsewhere.

14.2 Server-side push

In a server-side push, the connection to the server is not closed and data is continually sent to the client to constantly refresh the browser window. This is particularly useful for producing animation techniques. But unlike GIF animation or client-side pull techniques, the data in a server-side push originates from the server. This means that instead of using static images, the data could originate from a video camera or some other real-time device.

Server-side push relies on a variation of the MIME type `multipart/mixed`, commonly named `multipart/x-mixed-replace`. This works by allowing different types of data to be sent to the same connected stream. With conventional mixed types, the browser will interpret the data in each MIME block and attempt to display each file in the same page or window. Using the replace MIME variation, each subsequent MIME block will replace the previous block. For example, in the previous section, a servlet was used to produce a simple server-side animation. The server sent out a series of different images in the `multipart/x-mixed-replace` format. Every time the client receives a new image, it is displayed over the top of the previous image, creating a flicker-book-type animation.

Note   Although server-side push is a nice way to have real-time video without any third-party plug in or software, it has the disadvantage of not working with all browser types.

Implementing server-side push is a simple matter of correctly formatting the data stream from the servlet. When the client receives the header that contains the MIME type of `multipart/x-mixed-replace`, it knows to watch for blocks of data and replace the old block with the new block. Each block is separated from the others by a delimiting string, which is defined as part of the original header. Figure 14.1 shows a possible data stream.

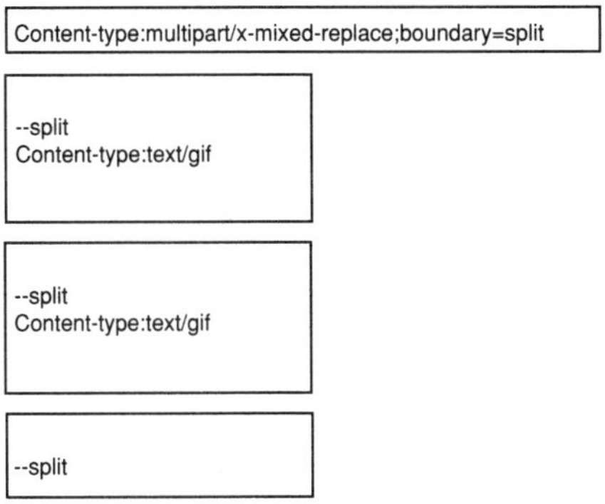

```
Content-type:multipart/x-mixed-replace;boundary=split
```

```
--split
Content-type:text/gif
```

```
--split
Content-type:text/gif
```

```
--split
```

Figure 14.1 A block representation of data being sent to the client

As you can see in figure 14.1, each block of data has a Content-Type associated with it; this Content-Type identifies the type of data in the block. Each block is separated using a text string, `--split`, as specified in the original Content-Type header. For this example, use the servlet from the previous one; instead of repeating one GIF image, create a series of images, with the text string slowly moving across the image area.

The first step is to set the Content-Type and send out the first boundary line. The boundary line will be used by the client to distinguish between the different images. Example 14.4 shows how to set up the Content-Type.

```
_res.setContentType("multipart/x-mixed-replace;boundary=split");
String SplitLine ="\n--split\nContent-type: text/gif\n\n";
byte SplitBytes[] = new byte[ SplitLine.length() ];
SplitLine.getBytes( 0, SplitLine.length(), SplitBytes, 0 );
```
Example 14.4   Setting the content type

Example 14.4 shows how to set the output type using the `setContentType()` method of the `ServletResponse` class. Next, set up the string that is to be used as the boundary text. Since you declared a `BufferedOutputStream` as your output stream, you have to convert the `String` into an array of bytes.

Note   Notice the placement of the carriage returns when formatting the blocks. This is a very important feature—if it's not included, it exposes the data to the possibility of being misinterpreted.

Looping around and sending out chunks or blocks of data is a simple matter of placing the original code inside a `for` loop and adjusting the position of the text with each iteration. With each new iteration, a new image is created and sent to the client, giving the flicker-book animation effect. This technique is shown in example 14.5.

```
for ( int x=0; x < 30; x++ ){
  OS.write( SplitBytes, 0, SplitLine.length() );
  offscreen.setColor( Color.white );
  offscreen.fillRect( 0, 0, charWidth*_req.getParameter
                              ("name").length()-1, charHeight-1 );
  offscreen.setColor( Color.red );
  offscreen.drawString( _req.getParameter("name"), 15 + x, 17 );
  GifEncoder  g = new GifEncoder( offscreenImg, OS );
  g.encode();
  OS.flush();
}

SplitLine ="\n--split\n\n";
SplitBytes  = new byte[ SplitLine.length() ];
SplitLine.getBytes( 0, SplitLine.length(), SplitBytes, 0 );
OS.write( SplitBytes, 0, SplitLine.length() );
dummyframe.dispose();
```
Example 14.5   Sending out each new image to the client

The code in example 14.5 loops thirty times before sending the termination string, which instructs the browser or client to close the connection.

The preceding example illustrates the functionality of server-side push by creating an image for each frame of animation. This is a highly inefficient way of performing animation because each `Image` class has to be encoded into a GIF before any data is transmitted.

If this method is to be used at all, it is best suited for applications that provide real-time video feeds from a web camera, which is a small video camera that is used to broadcast images to the Internet.

14.3   Future extensions

This chapter illustrates the power servlets have in creating true server-side images. These imaging techniques can be used to implement various applications such as the following:

- Dynamic "spot the ball" or scratch-card games.
- Real-time web statistics.
- Current date and time.
- Real-time climate readers.
- Stock market ticker tapes.

C H A P T E R   1 5

HTML filters

- Learn how to use a servlet to serve all requests coming into a web server. In this chapter, you'll learn how to filter out words you don't want on your site.

- Learn how to process all HTML files within a site before the client receives them.

- Learn how to build and maintain glossary tables to match specific words against all outgoing HTML files.

- Construct a search and replace tool.

With the Internet growing at a rate of approximately one million new pages a day, it is impossible to scan each and every one for possible offensive material. Not that you should have to, but in this age of freedom of speech, it's sometimes necessary. But if you're an ISP providing web space to users or an administrator looking after the web pages of school users, it's not always the best policy to allow users to create whatever they desire. For example, the use of swear words on a local church's web site would not sit well with the community. But for the web administrator to go through each page every time a user makes a change would take an awful long time—assuming, of course, the administrator could spot the offensive word or phrase.

One simple way around this is to filter the information coming from the web site using an HTML filtering servlet. This servlet would look through the pages requested and remove offensive words before sending the page out to the client. An extension to this solution is to have the words in question replaced with alternative words. As a simple example which avoids offensive words altogether, you could change every occurrence of "James Gosling" to "Sir James Gosling."

As you go through this chapter, bear in mind that this servlet has many other uses as well. You can use it to replace any words, not just offensive ones.

15.1   HTML filters

Filtering files before they are sent out from your site is a relatively easy task using servlets. Before you send an HTML file to a client, you must first look through it for any words that have been deemed unsuitable. If such a word or phrase is found, it should be either removed or replaced before the page is passed on to the client. The first part of this chapter looks at the implementation for simply removing any inappropriate phrases; the second section deals with the substitution of the phrases in question.

In order for the servlet to be used for every HTML file, the servlet must be set up to parse all HTML files. The servlet must satisfy the following criteria:

- Parse all HTML files.
- Be completely unobtrusive in its execution.

Setting the servlet up to parse all HTML files is a simple matter of setting up an alias in the administration section of the web server, so the servlet is called every time an HTML file is accessed.

For example, in the default setup of the Java Web Server, all files are handled by the "file" system servlet. This servlet processes all requests and prepares the output to the client. In an ideal world, you would simply replace this file servlet with your new filtering servlet, and have it deal with all requests. But this presents more problems. The default JWS file servlet does more than simply deliver HTML files. It also deals with GIF, JPEG, and all other MIME types, as defined in the server setup.

In order for the filtering servlet to successfully replace the file servlet it would need to do the following things, in addition to performing its filtering duties:

- Perform translation for nonspecific HTML files (such as www.n-ary.com).

- Process non-HTML files, such as GIF and JPEG files.

- Prepare error pages when files are not available or do not exist.

Although these are not difficult requests, why reinvent the wheel when the file servlet does the job more than adequately? For the filtering servlet to work its magic, it need only concern itself with HTML files, and possible text files as well, depending on how strictly we wish to police the site.

In order for the browser to load the requested text file as an HTML file and not as a normal file, the file extension has to be either .HTML or .HTM. Setting up the servlet to scan only these types of files is a simple matter of setting an alias so that requests for this type of file are sent for servicing by another servlet. Figure 15.1 shows the administration applet for the Java Web Server and the aliases set up for the filtering servlet.

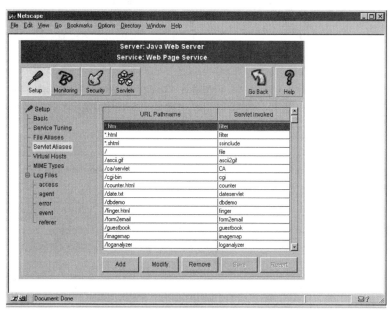

Figure 15.1 Java Web Server: Alias setup

Note This technique describes setting up an alias for all HTML files under the Java Web Server. Not all web servers may support servlets. This is one of the areas in which a CGI-based solution is not at all suitable, due to its large overhead in processing requests.

15.2 Search and destroy

Now that the criteria for the filtering servlet has been defined, we need to remove the questionable words or phrases from the output stream. A number of discrete steps are required:

1 Read the HTML file.

2 Build the glossary of terms and phrases that should be removed.

3 Send the file out to the client, filtering it where necessary.

15.2.1   Reading an HTML file

The servlet will be invoked every time the user accesses an HTML file. The servlet is set up using the alias section in the web administration. This means that all different types of URLs will invoke the servlet.

```
http://www.n-ary.com/index.html
http://www.n-ary.com/docs/homepage.html
http://www.n-ary.com/~user1/insurance/car/quick/quote.htm
```

Example 15.1   Different URLs the servlet must take care of

Notice how all the URLs in example 15.1 do not reference the servlet directly. Assuming the alias has been set up correctly to handle both .HTML and .HTM files, the servlet will be invoked. But how does the servlet know which file to open? Surely the servlet doesn't need prior knowledge of the web site and its directory structure?

Fortunately, it doesn't. This information is available to the servlet through method calls to the HttpServletRequest. One of the methods is to determine the complete translated path of the file being requested, which can be used to open up the file for reading using one of the IO classes.

Note   As you may have figured out by now, many of the available environment variables give the servlet much more power to control its functionality.

```
public void service( HttpServletRequest _req, HttpServletResponse _res)
                          throws ServletException, IOException {
  _res.setContentType( "text/html" );
  PrintWriter out = _res.getWriter();

  RandomAccessFile fptr = new RandomAccessFile(
                          _req.getPathTranslated(), "r");

  //- Remaining
}
```

Example 15.2   The first part of the service(...) **method**

Since this filtering servlet handles only HTML files, it is safe to set the output content type to text/html without too much fear, as shown in example 15.2. The method get-PathTranslated() from the HttpServletRequest class is used to return the complete pathname of the file that is being requested. For example, assuming the standard installation path for the Java Web Server is on Windows NT, the URL

```
http://www.n-ary.com/index.html
```

would return, as its full qualified path:

```
c:\Program Files\JavaServer\public_html\index.html
```

15.2.2   Glossary engine

The glossary is a list of words the servlet will check the file against every time it is accessed. With the servlet being accessed almost continually (as it would be with a popular site), shutting it down and restarting it just to add a new word to the glossary would be very inefficient. Updating the servlet "live" would be the best way to add the new words.

Performing this live update—adding and deleting words—can be done using an administration form.

Note   The administration form to update the state of the servlet uses the same technique as discussed in the chapter on random links.

Administrating a glossary   The easiest way to administer this servlet is to provide the administrator with a web-based tool to allow him to add or delete words to the online glossary. Before we look at how to update the glossary, we need to figure out to implement the glossary or dictionary of terms.

As you are now well aware, Java has a rich library of data storage classes, each with its own qualities and specific uses. For this task, we need a data structure that can handle words very easily and can retrieve words without the need for handling complex indexes or keys. The data structure that best suits this role is the Hashtable class, which allows items to be stored with a key. In this instance, the key would be the word itself, which makes retrieval a very easy task.

```
privateHashtable Glossary;

public void init(ServletConfig _config) throws ServletException {
   super.init(_config);
   Glossary= new Hashtable( 10 );
   readFile( "./glossary.ini" );
}
```
Example 15.3   The `init(...)` **method**

The `init(...)` method of the servlet, shown in example 15.3, sets up the hash table data structure, which allocates enough space for ten items initially. To make the servlet friendlier to the administrator, and save him from reentering the glossary every time the server is restarted, the glossary is saved to a file every time a new item is added. Before it starts, the servlet has to reload any previous items. This is done using the `readFile(...)` and `writeFile(...)` methods.

```
private void readFile( String _filename ){
  FileIntputStream    FS = new FileInputStream(_filename);
  ObjectOutputStream  IS = new ObjectInputStream(FS);
  Glossary = (Hashtable)IS.readObject();
}

private void writeFile( String _filename ){
  FileOutputStream    FS = new FileOutputStream(_filename);
  ObjectOutputStream  OS = new ObjectOutputStream(FS);
  OS.writeObject( Glossary );
}
```
Example 15.4   Reading and writing the glossary

Notice how in example 15.4, when you're inserting new items into the hash table, you use the data as both the key and field value. This is not an uncommon practice, but note that although you are actually storing a value, you could store a simple single character to save space. The Hashtable class does not permit data items to be null.

Now that you've established data storage for the glossary, you need some way to update it. This can be done using an HTML form, which can be accessed by supplying an inline parameter.

```
public void service( HttpServletRequest _req, HttpServletResponse _res)
                      throws ServletException, IOException {
  if (_req.getParameter( "admin" ) != null )
    sendOutAdminForm( _res );
  else if (_req.getParameter( "form" ) != null )
    processAdminForm( _req, _res );
  else{
    //- Load and filter the file
  }
}
```
Example 15.5   The service(…) method

Since the servlet is invoked every time an HTML file is accessed, you simply have to look for a special parameter. For example, the URL http://www.n-ary.com/test.html?admin=0 would invoke the administration section of the servlet. Example 15.5 shows how the service(…) method determines which section to activate. If the admin parameter is detected, regardless of the value, the administration form is created and sent to the client, as illustrated in example 15.6.

```
private void sendOutAdminForm( HttpServletResponse _res)
                          throws IOException {
  _res.setContentType("text/html");
  PrintWriter Out = _res.getWriter();

  Out.println( "<HTML><HEAD><META HTTP-EQUIV=Expires
              CONTENT=\"Sat, 09 Dec 1972 06:00:00 GMT\"><TITLE>Filter
              Administration</TITLE></HEAD>" );
  Out.println( "<BODY TEXT=\"#000000\" BGCOLOR=\"#FFFFFF\"
              LINK=\"#0000EE\" VLINK=\"#551A8B\" ALINK=\"#FF0000\">" );
```

```
Out.println( "<P><B><I><FONT COLOR=\"#0000FF\"><FONT
            SIZE=+2>Dictionary of terms</FONT></FONT></I></B></P>" );
Out.println( "<FORM METHOD=\"POST\"
            ACTION=\"/servlet/filter\"><CENTER><TABLE BORDER=0>" );
Out.println( "<INPUT TYPE=\"hidden\" NAME=\"form\" VALUE=\"1\">" );

Enumeration E = Glossary.elements();
String Line;
while ( E.hasMoreElements() ){
   Line= (String)E.nextElement();
   Out.println( "<TR><TD ALIGN=RIGHT>" + Line + "</TD><TD
            ALIGN=LEFT><INPUT TYPE=CHECKBOX NAME=\"" + Line + "\">
               Tag for deletion?</TD></TR>" );
}

Out.println( "</TABLE><HR ALIGN=CENTER WIDTH=\"60%\"></P>");
Out.println( "New Word:  <INPUT TYPE=\"text\" NAME=\"newword\"
            VALUE=\"\" SIZE=32><BR><BR>");
Out.println( "<INPUT TYPE=\"submit\" VALUE=\"Add / Delete\">
            <INPUT TYPE=\"reset\" VALUE=\"Reset\">");
Out.println( "</CENTER></FORM><P></BODY></HTML>" );
Out.flush();
}
```

Example 15.6 The sendOutAdminForm(...) method

Creating the form is a simple matter of displaying the items of the hash table in a list so the user has a chance to remove them. When you place each item on the HTML page, name the field the same name as the key to the hash table. This allows you to update the hash table very easily when the user submits the form.

```
private void processAdminForm( HttpServletRequest _req,
 HttpServletResponse _res)
throws IOException
{
   _res.setContentType("text/html");
   PrintWriter Out = _res.getWriter();

   //- Run through the list deleting items
   Enumeration E = Glossary.elements();
   String word;
   while ( E.hasMoreElements() ){
      word= (String)E.nextElement();
      if ( _req.getParameter( word ) != null && _req.getParameter( word
               ).compareTo( "on" ) == 0 )
         Glossary.remove( word );
   }

   //- Add new URL if present
   if ( _req.getParameter( "newword" ) != null &&
      _req.getParameter( "newword" ).length() != 0)
      Glossary.put(
               (String)_req.getParameter( "newword" ).toLowerCase(),
```

```
                    (String)_req.getParameter( "newword" ).toLowerCase());

    writeFile( "./glossary.ini" );

    Out.println( "<HTML><HEAD><TITLE>Filter Dictionary</TITLE>
                              </HEAD><BODY>" );
    Out.println( "<FONT COLOR=\"#0000FF\"><FONT SIZE=+2>Thank you.
                              </FONT></FONT>" );
    Out.println( "</BODY></HTML>" );
    Out.flush();
}
```
Example 15.7 Processing the administration form

Example 15.7 shows the method for processing the form once it is submitted by the administrator (figure 15.2). The method performs two roles—it deletes any flagged items and adds items to the glossary. Deleting the items is a simple matter of checking the hash table contents to see whether the flag has been set for deletion. If it has been set, the element is removed from the glossary. Adding an item to the list simply involves checking the newword field; if it's not empty, then add the contents of the field to the list.

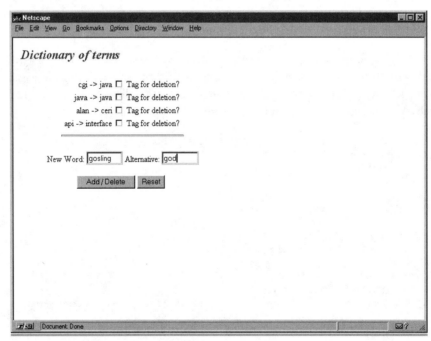

Figure 15.2 The search and replace form

> **Note** Notice how the case of the item is changed to lowercase before it's inserted into the hash table. This makes it easier to see which words need to be replaced. As you'll see in the *Performing search* section, all words can be checked, regardless of their case.

15.2.3 *Performing the search*

So far, in developing this servlet, we've only dealt with the glossary maintenance and data structure. Now you need to put it into operation, scanning each word before sending the file out to the client. Since an HTML file is text-based, you can confidently read and process it line by line, as shown in example 15.8.

```
_res.setContentType( "text/html" );
PrintWriter out = _res.getWriter();

RandomAccessFile fptr = new RandomAccessFile
                            (_req.getPathTranslated(), "rw");

while ( fptr.getFilePointer() < fptr.length() )
  out.println( filterLine( fptr.readLine() ) );

out.flush();
```
Example 15.8 Reading the HTML file line by line

The actual filtering has been reduced to just one method, which takes a line of text and returns a new, clean line that will be sent to the client.

```
private StringfilterLine( String _line ){
   StringTokenizer st = new StringTokenizer( _line, " " );
   StringBuffer newline = new StringBuffer( _line.length() );
   String token;

   while( st.hasMoreTokens() ){
     token= st.nextToken();
     if ( Glossary.get( token.toLowerCase() ) == null )
       newline.append( token + " " );
   }

   return newline.toString();
}
```
Example 15.9 Filtering the line

The filter procedure is to deconstruct the line, parsing it into individual words which can be checked, then rebuilding the line so it's clean of all offensive words. This is simple enough using the `StringTokenizer` and `StringBuffer` classes from the `java.util` package.

The `StringTokenizer` conveniently parses the line into individual words, using the space character as the separator. By looking up each word in the hash table structure, we can determine if the word should be replaced. If the return value is `null`, then the word is clean, and it can be appended to the new line. Notice that when a word is appended to the new line, a space is inserted before the new word.

Note: Please beware of the performance degradation. Parsing each line into individual words takes a finite amount of time, but when this is done on a fast server, the user is unaware of any delay. Extensive tests show that parsing the line into words takes, on average, approximately 5-10% longer than sending it out as normal, depending on the size of the file.

15.3   Search and replace

The filter servlet simply removes any occurrences of words that are present in the glossary. But what if you want to replace those words with alternatives, instead of removing them completely? For example, you might want to change all occurrences of the word "CGI" to "servlets" (which would make a more interesting read, I might add!). Modifying the filter servlet to replace instead of merely deleting doesn't require much extra coding. Here are the only sections that require modification:

1   The processing of the administration form.

2   The `filterLine(...)` method.

The rest of the servlet can remain untouched.

15.3.1   Administrating the search/replace glossary

As you may have already guessed, the administration form needs to be modified to accept alternatives to the words in question. This means you need to add a new field to the form generated by the servlet so that it will accept alternatives from the administrator. In addition, you need to modify the deletion list to display the deleted word and its replacement.

Fortunately, choosing the hash table as your data structure has meant no extra work. Remember how in the simple search and destroy servlet, you used key and data fields to store the exact same information, making most of the functionality of the hash table obsolete by only using the keys? Now you can use the data field as the place to store the new alternative to the questionable word, as shown in figure 15.3.

Example 15.10 illustrates the new modified `sendOutAdminForm(...)` method. This method remains, on the whole, very similar to the previous version, but it does differ in two places. First, instead of enumerating around the data elements, you get an `Enumeration` instance to the hash table's keys. Use each key to retrieve the data, which now contains the alternative word that is to be used. This data is then placed into the deletion list, with the key value being used as the field value.

```
private void sendOutAdminForm( HttpServletResponse _res)
                            throws IOException {
_res.setContentType("text/html");
```

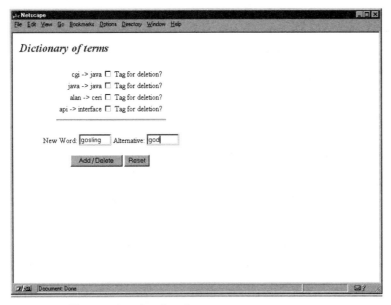

Figure 15.3 The search and replace form

```
PrintWriter Out = new PrintWriter( _res.getOutputStream() );

Out.println( "<HTML><HEAD><META HTTP-EQUIV=Expires
             CONTENT=\"Sat, 09 Dec 1972 06:00:00 GMT\"><TITLE>Filter
              Administration</TITLE></HEAD>" );
Out.println( "<BODY>" );
Out.println( "<P><B><I><FONT COLOR=\"#0000FF\"><FONT SIZE=+2>
                   Dictionary of terms</FONT></FONT></I></B></P>" );
Out.println( "<FORM METHOD=\"POST\" ACTION=\"/servlet/replace\">
                   <CENTER><TABLE BORDER=0>" );
Out.println( "<INPUT TYPE=\"hidden\" NAME=\"form\" VALUE=\"1\">" );

EnumerationE= Glossary.keys();
StringKey, Data;
while ( E.hasMoreElements() ){
  Key= (String)E.nextElement();
  Data= (String)Glossary.get( Key );
  Out.println( "<TR><TD ALIGN=RIGHT>" + Key + " -> " + Data +
              "</TD><TD ALIGN=LEFT><INPUT TYPE=CHECKBOX NAME=\""
                 + Key + "\"> Tag for deletion?</TD></TR>" );
}
Out.println( "</TABLE><HR ALIGN=CENTER WIDTH=\"60%\"></P>");
Out.println( "New Word:  <INPUT TYPE=\"text\" NAME=\"newword\"
             VALUE=\"\" SIZE=8> Alternative:
                   <INPUT TYPE=\"text\" NAME=\"newalternative\"
             VALUE=\"\" SIZE=8><BR><BR>");
Out.println( "<INPUT TYPE=\"submit\" VALUE=\"Add / Delete\">
             <INPUT TYPE=\"reset\" VALUE=\"Reset\">");
```

```
Out.println( "</CENTER></FORM><P></BODY></HTML>" );
Out.flush();
}
```
Example 15.10   Generating the new form

Example 15.11 shows the new `processAdminForm(...)` method for processing the form generated by the `sendOutAdminForm(...)`. Again, with this method, only slight modifications have been made, primarily when deleting—the enumeration retrieved is the one describing the keys, not the data elements. Also, when a new element is added to the glossary, the data value is different from the key.

Note   Notice how the choice of data structure from the beginning made things significantly easier when you wanted to add new features. Some data structures don't allow for any potential growth. When choosing your data structures, you should always make sure that they will allow you to change or modify your design at a later date without your having to redo everything.

```
private void processAdminForm( HttpServletRequest _req,
                       HttpServletResponse _res) throws IOException {
_res.setContentType("text/html");
PrintWriter Out = new PrintWriter( _res.getOutputStream() );

//- Run through the list deleting
EnumerationE= Glossary.keys();
Stringkey;
while ( E.hasMoreElements() ){
  key= (String)E.nextElement();
  if ( _req.getParameter( key ) != null && _req.getParameter(
                   key ).compareTo( "on" ) == 0  )
      Glossary.remove( key );
}

//- Add new URL if present
if ( _req.getParameter( "newword" ) != null &&
  _req.getParameter( "newword" ).length() != 0)
  Glossary.put( (String)_req.getParameter( "newword" ).toLowerCase(),
      (String)_req.getParameter( "newalternative" ).toLowerCase());

writeFile( "./glossary.ini" );

Out.println( "<HTML><HEAD><TITLE>Filter Dictionary</TITLE></HEAD>" );
Out.println( "<BODY>" );
Out.println( "<FONT COLOR=\"#0000FF\"><FONT SIZE=+2>Thank you.
                   </FONT></FONT>" );
Out.println( "</BODY></HTML>" );
Out.flush();
}
```
Example 15.11   Processing the replace form

15.3.2   Performing the replace

Now that the hash table is storing the correct pair information, you need to scan through each line and replace words where necessary. Performing this operation is a simple matter of adding the `filterLine(…)` method to the new version as shown in example 15.12.

```
private StringfilterLine( String _line ){
   StringTokenizerst = new StringTokenizer( _line, " " );
   StringBuffernewline = new StringBuffer( _line.length() );
   Stringtoken, data;

   while( st.hasMoreTokens() ){
      token = st.nextToken();
      data = (String)Glossary.get( token.toLowerCase() );
      if ( data == null )
         newline.append( token + " " );
      else
         newline.append( data + " " );
   }

   return newline.toString();
}
```
Example 15.12   Search and replace

As the line is parsed, each word is treated as a key to the hash table. If the key exists, a data string is returned; otherwise, `null` is returned. By checking the status of the return value, you can decide which data to place into the new line: the value read or the new data value from the hash table.

15.4   Future extensions

This servlet has many potential application areas, such as the fields of censorship and entertainment. As you've learned, you can apply this as a censorship application by using the servlet to filter all user pages to make sure no nasty or potentially offensive words get through to the client. Bear in mind, though, that if any offensive words are placed inside an image such as a GIF or JPEG, the servlet won't be able to detect them.

Modification to include complete phrases instead of just single words is one potential future upgrade. At this point, the servlet is checking for single words that can be replaced by complete phrases, but detecting a sequence of words is not implemented.

C H A P T E R   1 6

Autolinks

CHAPTER CONCEPTS

- Learn how to create a glossary of keywords and learn where they should and shouldn't be used.

- Learn how to maintain the list of keywords through a web-based interface.

- Understand the process behind automatically setting up links, including selecting a directory for parsing and searching for applicable HTML files.

- Discover how easy it is to create autolinks without compromising file format.

Users will generally visit a web site for one of two reasons: entertainment or information. Sometimes they come for both, but there's almost always a goal to their visit. Whether they're looking for information about a particular company or a service, users need to have a certain level of base knowledge. As a very basic example, a site that displays many images of automobiles doesn't expect to have to explain what an automobile is. It is assumed that all visitors to the site know what a car is. But there's nothing to stop web designers from giving such basic information to users.

In the majority of cases, it's not writing the text that's the problem—it's where to put it. When the user comes across a word he is unfamiliar with in a web document, it would be handy if he could click the word in question to display a definition for it. Providing this functionality seems straightforward enough—simply add hyperlinks to the special keywords in each HTML file. But maintaining the HTML file can become very difficult and time-consuming, and it can introduce errors to the file.

This chapter presents a complete servlet-based solution for adding hyperlinks to a site. The servlet will maintain a glossary of keywords, along with their respective hyperlinks. When the servlet is run, it will automatically link all the keywords in the entire site.

16.1 Glossary definition

The official Oxford English Dictionary definition of glossary reads: "list of special or technical words with definitions."

Glossaries are usually placed at the end of a document or publication, and they serve as miniature technical dictionaries. Users refer to them every time they come across a word they may be unfamiliar with or may simply want clarification on. It's an unwritten rule with technical publications that a glossary is generally found at the end of the book. However, anyone who has ever read a book that is introducing many new terms at once might feel the glossary would serve much better as a pull-out section, so he wouldn't have to keep flicking back and forth through the book.

Imagine the same publication online, formatted as an HTML page. How could a glossary be implemented so that it would be both worth doing and easy to use? What options should the reader have if he comes across a word he doesn't understand?

The first option would be for the user to reread the document in the hopes of catching a definition embedded in the text that he might have missed the first time. This is assuming, of course, such a definition even exists in the document.

The second option is for the user to use the site's search engine, assuming such a utility exists. The user could perform a site search to obtain a list of documents containing the word, including the page he has just came from. The user would have to go through each document to seek out a suitable definition, with no guarantee of success.

The third option is to leave the user completely bewildered and confused, and to have him ignore the word in question and carry on. Obviously, this is not really acceptable, especially if you are expecting repeat visits from him.

These are all possible options, but they're not very good. A much tidier and clearer solution would be to give each keyword that you have deemed technical a hyperlink to a definition. This is easier for the user, but harder on the developer. You would have to search each page on the server for keywords and make each one link to a known definition page. This would be a time-consuming task at the best of times.

But you're in luck. The servlet presented in this chapter is designed to do just such a task. The servlet will maintain a list of keywords, each with its own link. When the servlet is called upon, it will look for all the keywords in the glossary and create each link when it finds the word in a document.

16.2 System overview

The system has two main areas: glossary maintenance and HTML file hyperlinks. The servlet will maintain a glossary list that an administrator (you, in this chapter) will be able to update via your web browser. Once the glossary is updated, you will be able to run the new keyword list through the HTML files in a given directory, updating the old links and adding any new links that may exist.

When the servlet is run, the method will have to open up each HTML page, find each keyword, and either update the link or add a new link.

Note This servlet will implement a fairly sophisticated parsing algorithm that may be found in the more mainstream HTML editors. However, implementing it as a servlet gives you the ability to update the keyword list remotely. Whether this is a major concern is arguable. As you will discover, implementing the parser in Java gives the program the functionality to run on any platform. It serves as an excellent example of the power Java can lend to such a task.

As with all servlets, you have to process a client request, and you can choose among the main three methods: doPost(…), doGet(…), and service(…). For this servlet, override the service(…) method, since it's not clear how the data will be posted to us (either in a POST or a GET). For this example, you'll use the same servlet for all aspects of the glossary system, and you can control the operation using HTML parameters. As shown in the following list, the servlet has three options:

1 Generate and display the list of keywords and links.
2 Process the keyword HTML form.
3 Run the autolink servlet through a specific directory containing HTML files.

Each option is controlled through parameters that are passed in with each call to the servlet. For example, the URL used to call the servlet, which generates the keyword form, may be

        http://www.n-ary.com/servlet/autolink?ADMIN=0

assuming the servlet class is named autolink. These three options are demonstrated in example 16.1.

```
public void service( HttpServletRequest _req, HttpServletResponse _res )
                        throws ServletException, IOException{
  if ( _req.getParameter( "ADMIN" ) != null )
    sendOutAdminForm( _res );
  else if ( _req.getParameter( "KEYFORM" ))
    processAdminForm( _req, _res );
```

```
  else if ( _req.getParameter( "RUNINDEX" ) != null)
    runIndex( _req, _res );
  else
    _res.setStatus( HttpServletResponse.SC_NO_CONTENT );
}
```
Example 16.1 The main `service(…)` method

You are essentially looking for the presence of the variable, and if it's found, you need to take the appropriate action. This technique of switching control depending on the input parameter will be used time and time again throughout this book.

16.2.1 Maintaining the glossary

This servlet relies heavily on the glossary list. A URL (or relative link) will be associated with each keyword. Storing these two pieces of information (the keyword and the URL) can be done using the hash table data structure, without the need for any extra wrapping classes. The keyword can act as the key to the hash table, and the URL as the data. Choosing the keyword as the key to the hash table will make finding the technical words much easier when parsing an HTML file.

Note The hash table is one of the most flexible data structures available from the Java library. This data structure differs from the conventional list-based structures in the fact that elements are stored in the hash table much the same way as they are in a database. Each element has a unique index or key value associated with it. This index or key can then be used to retrieve the element back from the structure. The Java implementation of the hash table allows any type of object to be used as the key for the data structure.

Before the servlet can successfully complete the parsing, the hash table must be populated with data. Since this is a servlet-based solution, the easiest interface to the glossary is an HTML form, as shown in figure 16.1.

Since this form represents the current state of the glossary list, it can't be static. It has to be generated dynamically by the servlet. The method in example 16.2 generates the form shown in the previous figure. The function sends out an HTML header, complete with the form definition. Sending out the glossary is a matter of retrieving an enumeration to the hash table and creating a set of controls for every element to administer it.

```
private void sendOutAdminForm( HttpServletResponse _res )
                        throws IOException {
  _res.setContentType("text/html");
  PrintWriter Out = new PrintWriter(_res.getOutputStream());

  Out.println( "<HTML><HEAD><TITLE>Keyword Admin</TITLE></HEAD>" );
  Out.println( "<BODY>"<P><B><I><FONT COLOR=#0000FF SIZE=+2>" );
  Out.println( "Add/Del Keyword form</FONT></FONT></I></B></P>" );
  Out.println( "<FORM METHOD=POST ACTION=/servlet/autolink><CENTER>" );
  Out.println( "<TABLE BORDER=0>" );
  Out.println( "<INPUT TYPE=HIDDEN NAME=KEYFORM VALUE=1>" );
```

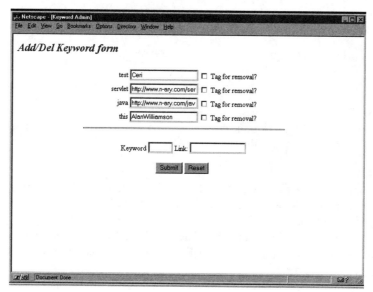

Figure 16.1 Administrating the main glossary of terms

```
Enumeration E = Keywords.keys();
String keyword, jump;
while( E.hasMoreElements() ){
  keyword = (String)E.nextElement();
  jump    = (String)Keywords.get(keyword);

  Out.println( "<TR><TD ALIGN=RIGHT>" + keyword + "</TD>" );
  Out.println( "<TD ALIGN=LEFT><INPUT TYPE=TEXT NAME=" );
  Out.println( keyword+"_E VALUE=\""+jump+"\">" );
  Out.println( "<INPUT TYPE=CHECKBOX NAME=" + keyword );
  Out.println( "_C> Tag for removal?</TD></TR>" );
}

Out.println( "</TABLE><HR ALIGN=CENTER WIDTH=60%></P> " );
Out.println( "Keyword <INPUT TYPE=TEXT NAME=KEYWORD SIZE=6> Link: " );
Out.println( "<INPUT TYPE=TEXT NAME=LINK SIZE=16><BR><BR>" );
Out.println( "<INPUT TYPE=SUBMIT VALUE=Submit>" );
Out.println( "<INPUT TYPE=RESET VALUE=Reset>" );
Out.println( "</CENTER></FORM><P></BODY></HTML>" );
Out.flush();
}
```

Example 16.2   Generating the administration form

From the administration form, you should be able to amend or delete an existing keyword. In order for the controls to be processed again, they are labeled as the keyword plus a known suffix. In this instance the edit control for the "java" keyword will be labeled with an "_E" suffix, resulting in the label name of "java_E." The checkbox label for flagging the keyword for deletion is suffixed with "_C." As you will see, this makes finding the form fields very easy.

When the user posts the form back to the servlet, each keyword field must be looked at and modified, if needed. The first thing that has to be checked is the status of the Tag for deletion checkboxes, to see which keywords have been flagged for deletion. This process is shown in example 16.3.

```
Enumeration E = Keywords.keys();
String keyword;
while ( E.hasMoreElements() ){
  keyword = (String)E.nextElement();

  if ( _req.getParameter(keyword+"_C") != null &&
       _req.getParameter(keyword+"_C").equals("on"))
    Keywords.remove( keyword );
  else if ( _req.getParameter(keyword+"_E").length() != 0 ){
    Keywords.remove(keyword);
    Keywords.put( keyword, _req.getParameter(keyword+"_E"));
  }
}
```
Example 16.3   Updating existing keywords

One of the methods from the `Hashtable` data structure class is the functionality to return an `Enumeration` instance to the key values in the data storage. By going through each key value in the list and creating the corresponding field value, each form field can be checked. If the checkbox is checked, then the element is removed. The link can be edited in the administration form. If the new link is not `null`, the new value is added and the old value is removed.

When you are adding a completely new keyword and link to the glossary page, you have to check it before you add it to the list of existing keywords. The checks include making sure that the keyword and the link are not `null` and that the keyword doesn't already exist (see example 16.4).

```
String newKey  = _req.getParameter("KEYWORD");
String newLink = _req.getParameter("LINK");
if ( newKey  != null && newKey.length()!=0 &&
     newLink != null && newLink.length()!= 0 &&
     Keywords.containsKey(newKey)==false){
  Keywords.put( newKey, newLink );
}
```
Example 16.4   Adding a new keyword

16.3   Linking the keywords

Once you've created or updated the keyword list, all of the HTML files that are to receive the new links have to be processed. You describe the directory from which the search begins (where the files are kept), and every file that is found in that directory and its subdirectories is opened, checked, and rewritten.

16.3.1   Finding the files

Before the HTML files can be processed, they must first be found. This involves listing all the HTML files in the directory you specified. To make the servlet even more functional, all of the subdirectories also will be searched. This section will demonstrate the power Java gives you to accomplish this task, especially when you consider that it operates cross-platform.

The `File` class from the `java.io` package does everything you need. This class is designed to represent a file or directory in the format of the local host, automatically taking care of the different styling conventions that can exist between the various operating systems.

When you want to run the keywords through the directory structure of the HTML files, fill in the top-level directory from which the autolink servlet is to run. Using the form shown in figure 16.2, specify a directory, which is then submitted to the servlet.

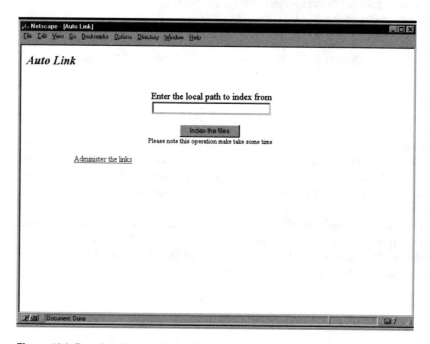

Figure 16.2 Running the autolink servlet

When the servlet receives the form post, it first must determine whether the directory you submitted is valid, as shown in example 16.5.

```
File RootDir = new File( startPoint );
if ( RootDir.isDirectory() == false ){
  System.out.println( "Invalid directory submitted" );
  _res.setStatus( HttpServletResponse.SC_NO_CONTENT );
  return;
}
```
Example 16.5   Determining the directory

This validity is achieved by creating a instance of `File` and then immediately calling the `isDirectory()` method. This method returns `true` or `false`, depending on the validity of the pathname represented by the `File` object. If the `File` represents a filename, a call to this method would result in a `false` also.

Note Under certain circumstances, a call to the `File.isDirectory()` method may result in a `SecurityException` being thrown. If the program instance doesn't have sufficient access rights to read the directory, the exception is thrown. This will occur if the `File` method is called from an applet running in a browser or an untrusted servlet.

Directory listings With the directory now validated, the method must search out all of the HTML files and subdirectories. As with many things in Java, there is more than one way to accomplish this task. The `File` class provides two versions of the same method `list(…)`. The first version, when called, will return a list of all the files and directories (excluding the . and .. directories) found in the directory represented by the `File` object. The list comes back in the form of an array of Strings. For example, the code fragment in example 16.6 shows the servlet running through the list of files that are returned back from the call to the `list(…)` method. Notice how the end of the list is found; this is another wonder of Java—the ability to know the size of arrays without their having to carry a separate counter around with them.

```
String tList[] = RootDir.list();

for (int x=0;x<tList.length;x++){
    System.out.println( tList[x] );
}
```
Example 16.6   Calling the first version of the `list(…)` method

When printing out, you'll notice the filenames are not expressed in their full path; instead, they're relative to their parent directory. Checking for the existence of HTML files is then a simple matter of extracting the file extension from each name and passing it on to the method that links all the keywords. Although this process is very functional, the `File` class offers a much tidier solution for finding specific files, by allowing a custom filter to be applied to the `list(…)` method.

The second version of the `list(…)` method takes as its parameter a class that implements the `FilenameFilter` interface. This allows you to design your own custom filter, such as the class shown in example 16.7. The `FilenameFilter` interface defines the `accept(…)` method. For every file the `list(…)` finds, it calls this method once, with the directory the file is found in and the name of the file.

```
class htmlFilter implements FilenameFilter {
  public boolean accept(File dir, String name){
    File tF = new File( dir, name );

    if ( tF.isDirectory() )
      return true;
int indx = name.lastIndexOf( "." );
    if ( indx == -1 )
```

```
        return false;

    String Ext = name.substring( indx+1, name.length() ).toLowerCase();

    if (  Ext.equals("html")||Ext.equals("htm")
        ||Ext.equals("shtml")||Ext.equals("shtm"))
      return true;

    return false;
  }
}
```
Example 16.7   The custom filter for the `list(…)` **method**

Example 16.7 shows the implementation of one such filter that will find all of the HTML files and directories. Discovering whether or not the file is a directory is a simple matter of creating an instance of `File`, then calling the `isDirectory()` method.

To determine whether the file is an HTML file, check the file extension. If the filename is to be included in the final list, then the method must return `true`; if not, then the method must return `false`. To use this filter, create an instance of it and pass it into the `list(…)` method.

```
String tList[] = RootDir.list(new htmlFilter());
```

A list of filenames of all the HTML files and directories in the directory the `File` object represents will be returned. If the algorithm were just to modify the files in the current directory, then processing the files would be academic. However, the servlet is going to search all of the subdirectories as well.

Set up this searching mechanism by keeping a list of all the directories that have to be searched. When a new directory is found, add it to the list of directories. Each directory is processed one after another.

Each directory to be checked is retrieved from the list of directories, and the `list(…)` method is called on it. However, a complication will arise. Before each directory can be checked, it must be created relative to its parent directory. Therefore, the parent directory has to be stored along with the directory listing. This allows you to continue checking the top-level directories without the fear of losing the pointer. A special class is created to wrap the two pieces of the data, as shown in example 16.8.

```
class cDirInfo{
  public File rootDir;
  public String[] dirList;

  public cDirInfo( File _r, String[] _d ){
    rootDir = _r;
    dirList = _d;
  }
}
```
Example 16.8   The wrapper class

When a new directory is found, a new instance of this class is created, with the list of files of the new directory and the parent directory stored in the new object. Example 16.9

shows the loop for traversing the directory structure. A new `File` object is created for each file. If the resulting `File` object turns out to be another directory not already found, it is added to the main list of directories to be checked.

The `Vector` data structure is used to store a list of these directory objects. This structure is the best method for maintaining this list, as it allows for easy insertion and removal of directories without the need to worry about keys or indices.

```
Vector toBeDone = new Vector(10);

String dir[] = RootDir.list(new htmlFilter());
cDirInfo tX = new cDirInfo(RootDir,dir);

toBeDone.addElement(tX);
while (toBeDone.isEmpty()==false){
  tX = (cDirInfo)toBeDone.firstElement();

  try{
    for (x=0;x<tX.dirList.length;x++){
      File newFile = new File( tX.rootDir, tX.dirList[x]);
      if ( newFile.isDirectory() ){
        File t = new File( tX.rootDir, tX.dirList[x] );
        String a[] = newFile.list( new htmlFilter() );

        toBeDone.addElement( new cDirInfo( t, a ) );
      }
      else
        linkFile( newFile );

    }
    toBeDone.removeElementAt(0);
    dir = null;
}
```

Example 16.9   Processing the directories

Using the preceding algorithm, all files on any system may be found, assuming the starting directory is the root. The `linkFile(...)` method is the method that is called when an HTML file is found. This is described in the following section.

16.3.2   Indexing the files

Once you have found the correct file, it must be opened, read, parsed, and written back out. Opening the file and reading it line by line doesn't present too much of a problem. You have two options for writing the file out: read the complete file into memory and then write it back out to the file as it is parsed, or read the file in line by line, construct the new file in memory, and write it back out in one operation.

Example 16.10 shows the skeleton for parsing the HTML file, with the new file being stored in the `Vector` data structure. Writing the file out is done in the `writeNewFile(...)` method, which merely resets the file pointer to the beginning of the file and then writes out all the lines from the `Vector` structure, which represents the new file.

```
RandomAccessFile fptr = new RandomAccessFile(_filename,"rw");
Vector newFile = new Vector(50,10);
```

```
String LineIn;

while ( fptr.getFilePointer() < fptr.length() ){
  LineIn = fptr.readLine();

  //- Process line
  newFile.addElement( LineIn );
}


writeNewFile( newFile, _filename, fptr );
fptr.close();
```
Example 16.10   Reading the HTML file

Building a parser for the autolink servlet can become very complicated very quickly if you don't take care. Every word in the glossary that appears in the HTML file needs to be surrounded by the linking tags. This may seem not to be too difficult—separate each line with the StringTokenizer, and then match each token against the glossary. If the glossary were a simple text file, this would not present a problem. However, it is not.

Note   The StringTokenizer is one of the utility classes provided as part of the Java library to parse strings. An instance of this class is created with the string that is to be parsed, along with the delimiter. Then, through a series of calls to methods from the class, all the tokens can be easily retrieved.

Example 16.11 implements one such HTML parser. A new instance is created for each line. The nextToken() method is called repeatedly until an empty string is returned.

```
class cLineParse extends Object {
  String L;

  public cLineParse( String _s ){
    L = _s;
  }

  public String nextToken(){
    String ns="";
    boolean bStart = false;

    for ( int x=0; x < L.length(); x++ ){
      if ( L.charAt(x) == '<' && ns.length() != 0 ){
        L = L.substring( x, L.length() );
        return ns;
      }
      else if ( L.charAt(x) == '<' ){
        ns = ns + L.charAt( x );
        bStart = true;
      }
      else if ( L.charAt(x) == '>' || L.charAt(x) == '\r' ||
              ( L.charAt(x) == ' ' && bStart == false ) ){
        ns      = ns + L.charAt( x );
```

```
          L = L.substring( x+1, L.length() );
          return ns;
       }
       else
          ns = ns + L.charAt( x );
    }

    L = "";
    return ns;
  }
}
```
Example 16.11   The class to parse a line of HTML text

The nextToken() method goes through the line character by character, checking to see if a token has been found. A token is either a complete HTML tag (<xxx>) or a word that is separated with tags or spaces. For example, the line

```
<B>This</B> is a small test<BR>
```

would return the tokens "<B>," "This," "</B>," "is," "a," "small," "test," and "
." Since this class provides the same functionality as the StringTokenizer, the calling method can then perform some top-level processing.

We know the glossary is not to be applied between particular HTML tags. For example, the text contained within the <HEAD> and </HEAD> tags will not get the linking treatment. Many of these blocking tags should not be modified. Here are some examples:

```
<HEAD> ... </HEAD>
<APPLET> ... </APPLET>
<SERVLET> ... </SERVLET>
<A> ... </A>
<TEXTINPUT> ... </TEXTINPUT>
```

In addition, when a word is found that can be linked, it has to be checked to see if it's in the glossary and a link must be created for it. To simplify this process, every link word that is found is passed into the createLink(…) method, as shown in example 16.12.

```
private String createLink( String _keyword ){
  if ( Keywords.containsKey( _keyword.toLowerCase() ) ){
    String nL = "<!--KW:" + _keyword + "><A HREF=\"";
    nL = nL+Keywords.get(_keyword.toLowerCase())+"\">"+_keyword+"</A>";
    return nL;
  }
  else
    return _keyword;
}
```
Example 16.12   Creating a link

To see if a word is in the glossary, use it as a key to index into the hash table. If the key is valid, a link is created. In addition to creating the <A> and </A> link tags, an additional HTML tag is placed at the front of the link to let the servlet know that this is a glossary keyword to be linked, not an already-linked word.

```
<!--KW:java><A HREF="http://www.n-ary.com/java.html>java</A>
```

One of the functions of the servlet will be the ability to modify existing keyword links. Using the comment HTML tag before the main link, the main parsing algorithm can find the comment tags and easily tell which type each link is.

Constructing the intelligence around the token parsing can be done by keeping one state variable, which will determine whether any further tokens should be parsed for keywords. Example 16.13 shows this algorithm.

```
while ( fptr.getFilePointer() < fptr.length() ){
  LineIn  = fptr.readLine();
  lp = new cLineParse( LineIn );
  newLine = "";

  while ( (token=lp.nextToken()) != "" ){
    if ( token.toUpperCase().indexOf( "<A" ) != -1 ||
         token.toUpperCase().indexOf( "<HEAD" ) != -1 ||
         token.toUpperCase().indexOf( "<APPLET" ) != -1 ||
         token.toUpperCase().indexOf( "<SERVLET" ) != -1 ||
         token.toUpperCase().indexOf( "<TEXTINPUT" ) != -1 ){
      bValid  = false;
      newLine = newLine + token;
    }
    else if (token.toUpperCase().indexOf( "</A" ) != -1 ||
             token.toUpperCase().indexOf( "</HEAD" ) != -1 ||
             token.toUpperCase().indexOf( "</APPLET" ) != -1 ||
             token.toUpperCase().indexOf( "</SERVLET" ) != -1 ||
             token.toUpperCase().indexOf( "</TEXTINPUT" ) != -1){
      bValid  = true;
      newLine = newLine + token;
    }
    else if ( token.indexOf( "<!--KW:" ) != -1 ){
      String kw = token.substring( 7, token.length()-1 );
      lp.nextToken(); lp.nextToken(); lp.nextToken();
      newLine = newLine + createLink( kw );
    }
    else if ( bValid ){
      if ( token.charAt( token.length()-1 ) == ' ' )
        newLine = newLine + createLink(
              token.substring(0,token.length()-1))+" ";
      else
        newLine = newLine + createLink( token );
    }
    else
      newLine = newLine + token;
  }
  newFile.addElement( newLine );
}
```

Example 16.13   Parsing each token

Each token is tested to see if it is the start of one of the special blocking HTML tags mentioned earlier; if it is, then the state flag is set to `false`. This means that checking for keywords stops until the servlet finds the end of a blocking HTML tag. Conversely, the end-blocking HTML tag is searched for; if it's found, the flag is set back to `true` again. By holding a status flag, special blocking tags can span multiple lines, without affecting the operation of the servlet.

If the `<!--KW:xxxx>` HTML tag is found, this implies that the file has previously been parsed, and the following link is a keyword. In case the link has been modified or removed, the three HTML tokens that follow are ignored and a link is created. You can safely do this, as the algorithm always places the four HTML tags one after the other in the same line when creating a link.

After the new line has been constructed, it is inserted into the `Vector` data structure, which is written out at a later time.

16.4 Complete source code

Example 16.14 shows the complete source code for the autolink servlet.

```java
import java.io.*;
import java.util.*;
import javax.servlet.*;
import javax.servlet.http.*;

public class autolink extends HttpServlet {
  Hashtable Keywords;

  public void init(ServletConfig _config) throws ServletException{
    super.init(_config);
    Keywords = new Hashtable( 10 );
    readFile( "./autolink.ini" );
  }

  public void service( HttpServletRequest _req,
                       HttpServletResponse _res )
                       throws ServletException, IOException{
    if (_req.getParameter( "admin" ).length()!=0)
      sendOutAdminForm( _res );
    else if (_req.getParameter( "KEYFORM" ).length()!=0)
      processAdminForm( _req, _res );
    else if (_req.getParameter( "RUNINDEX" ).length() != 0)
      runIndex( _req, _res );
    else
      _res.setStatus( HttpServletResponse.SC_NO_CONTENT );
  }

  private void runIndex( HttpServletRequest _req,
                         HttpServletResponse _res ) throws IOException{
    String startPoint = _req.getParameter( "START" );
    if ( startPoint == null || startPoint.length() == 0 ){
      _res.setStatus( HttpServletResponse.SC_NO_CONTENT );
      return;
    }

    //- Start running the indexing program
    File RootDir = new File( startPoint );
    if ( RootDir.isDirectory() == false ){
      _res.setStatus( HttpServletResponse.SC_NO_CONTENT );
      return;
    }

    //- Run through list
    Vector toBeDone = new Vector( 10 );
```

```
      String dir[] = RootDir.list( new htmlFilter() );
      cDirInfo tX = new cDirInfo( RootDir, dir );

      toBeDone.addElement( tX );
      while ( toBeDone.isEmpty() == false ){
        tX = (cDirInfo)toBeDone.firstElement();

        for (int x=0; x<tX.dirList.length;x++){
          File newFile = new File( tX.rootDir,tX.dirList[x]);
          if ( newFile.isDirectory() ) {
            File t = new File(tX.rootDir, tX.dirList[x] );
            String a[] = newFile.list( new htmlFilter() );
            toBeDone.addElement( new cDirInfo( t, a ) );
          }
          else
            linkFile( newFile );
        }
        toBeDone.removeElementAt(0);
        dir     = null;
      }
    }

    private void linkFile( File _filename ){
      //- Links the file
      try{
        RandomAccessFile fptr= new RandomAccessFile( _filename, "rw");
        Vector newFile = new Vector( 50, 10 );
        String LineIn, token, newLine="";
        String tag="";
        StringTokenizer st;
        boolean bValid = true;
        cLineParse lp;
        while ( fptr.getFilePointer() < fptr.length() ){
          LineIn = fptr.readLine();
          lp = new cLineParse( LineIn );
          newLine     = "";

          while ( (token=lp.nextToken()) != "" ){
            if (  token.toUpperCase().indexOf( "<A" ) != -1 ||
                  token.toUpperCase().indexOf("<HEAD")!= -1 ||
                  token.toUpperCase().indexOf( "<APPLET" )!=-1||
                  token.toUpperCase().indexOf("<SERVLET")!=-1||
                  token.toUpperCase().indexOf("<TEXTINPUT")!=-1) {
              bValid = false;
              newLine = newLine + token;
            }
            else if ( token.toUpperCase().indexOf("</A")!=-1||
                  token.toUpperCase().indexOf("</HEAD")!= -1||
                  token.toUpperCase().indexOf("</APPLET")!=-1||
                  token.toUpperCase().indexOf("</SERVLET")!=-1||
                  token.toUpperCase().indexOf("</TEXTINPUT")!=-1){
              bValid = true;
              newLine = newLine + token;
            }
```

```java
        else if ( token.indexOf( "<!--KW:" ) != -1 ) {
          String kw = token.substring(7,token.length()-1);
          lp.nextToken(); lp.nextToken(); lp.nextToken();
          newLine = newLine + createLink( kw );
        }
        else if ( bValid ){
          if ( token.charAt( token.length()-1 ) == ' ' )
            newLine = newLine + createLink(token.substring(0,
                          token.length()-1 )) + " ";
          else
            newLine = newLine + createLink( token );
        }
        else
          newLine = newLine + token;
      }
      newFile.addElement( newLine );
    }
    writeNewFile( newFile, _filename, fptr );
    fptr.close();
  }
  catch( IOException E ){}
}

private String createLink( String _keyword ){
  if ( Keywords.containsKey( _keyword.toLowerCase() ) ){
    String nL = "<!--KW:" + _keyword + "><A HREF=\"";
    nL = nL + Keywords.get(_keyword.toLowerCase())+"\">"
                    +_keyword+"</A>";
    return nL;
  }
  else
    return _keyword;
}

private void writeNewFile( Vector newFile, RandomAccessFile fptr )
                        throws IOException  {
  fptr.seek( 0 );
  Enumeration E = newFile.elements();
  while( E.hasMoreElements() )
    fptr.writeBytes( (String)E.nextElement() + "\n" );
}

private void processAdminForm( HttpServletRequest _req,
                        HttpServletResponse _res )
                        throws IOException {
  //- Delete the forms
  Enumeration E = Keywords.keys();
  String      keyword;
  while ( E.hasMoreElements() )
  {
    keyword    = (String)E.nextElement();
    if ( _req.getParameter( keyword+"_C" ) != null &&
        _req.getParameter( keyword+"_C").equals( "on" ) )
      Keywords.remove( keyword );
```

```java
      else if ( _req.getParameter( keyword+"_E" ).length() != 0 ){
        Keywords.remove( keyword );
        Keywords.put(keyword, _req.getParameter( keyword+"_E" ) );
      }
    }

    //- Add in a new keyword to the hashtable
    String newKey  = _req.getParameter( "KEYWORD" );
    String newLink = _req.getParameter( "LINK" );
    if (newKey != null && newKey.length() != 0 &&
        newLink != null && newLink.length() != 0 &&
        Keywords.containsKey( newKey ) == false )
      Keywords.put( newKey.toLowerCase(), newLink );

    _res.setContentType("text/html");
    PrintWriter Out = new PrintWriter( _res.getOutputStream() );
    Out.println( "<HTML><BODY><CENTER>" );
    Out.println( "<B><I><FONT COLOR=#0000FF SIZE=+2>");
    Out.println( "Thank you</FONT></I></B>" );
    Out.println( "</CENTER></BODY></HTML>" );
    Out.flush();

    writeFile( "./autolink.ini" );
  }

  private void sendOutAdminForm( HttpServletResponse _res )
                         throws IOException{
    _res.setContentType("text/html");
    PrintWriter Out = new PrintWriter( _res.getOutputStream() );
    Out.println( "<HTML><HEAD><TITLE>Keyword Admin</TITLE></HEAD>" );
    Out.println( "<BODY>" );
    Out.println( "<P><B><I><FONT COLOR=#0000FF SIZE=+2>");
    Out.println( "Add/Del Keywordform</FONT></FONT></I></B></P>" );
    Out.println( "<FORM METHOD=POST ACTION=/autolink.html>");
    Out.println( "<CENTER><TABLE BORDER=0>" );
    Out.println( "<INPUT TYPE=HIDDEN NAME=KEYFORM VALUE=1>" );
    Enumeration    E    = Keywords.keys();
    String keyword, jump;
    while( E.hasMoreElements() ){
      keyword = (String)E.nextElement();
      jump    = (String)Keywords.get( keyword );

      Out.println( "<TR><TD ALIGN=RIGHT>" + keyword );
      Out.println( "</TD><TD ALIGN=LEFT><INPUT TYPE=TEXT NAME=");
      Out.println( keyword+"_E VALUE=\""+jump + "\">" );
      Out.println( "<INPUT TYPE=CHECKBOX NAME=" + keyword );
      Out.println( "_C>Tag for removal?</TD></TR>" );
    }

    Out.println( "</TABLE><HR ALIGN=CENTER WIDTH=60%></P>");
    Out.println( "Keyword <INPUT TYPE=TEXT NAME=KEYWORD SIZE=6>");
    Out.println( "Link: <INPUT TYPE=TEXT NAME=LINK SIZE=16><BR><BR>");
    Out.println( "<INPUT TYPE=SUBMIT VALUE=Submit> ");
    Out.println( "<INPUT TYPE=RESET VALUE=Reset>");
```

```
    Out.println( "</CENTER></FORM><P></BODY></HTML>" );
    Out.flush();
  }

  private void readFile( String _filename ){
    FileIntputStream    FS = new FileInputStream(_filename);
    ObjectOutputStream  IS = new ObjectInputStream(FS);
    Keywords = (Hashtable)IS.readObject();
  }

  private void writeFile( String _filename ){
    FileOutputStream    FS = new FileOutputStream(_filename);
    ObjectOutputStream  OS = new ObjectOutputStream(FS);
    OS.writeObject( Keywords );
  }
}
```

Example 16.14   The complete source code for the autolink servlet

16.5   Future extensions

This chapter presented a servlet that produces automatic hyperlinks for certain keywords. This allows you to easily maintain text-intensive pages without compromising the readability of each page. In addition, the servlet could remove the links again, if the overall design of the site were to change. The servlet demonstrated two very powerful features that can be applied to many other roles in both other servlets and other Java applications.

1 Finding files and directories.

2 Parsing HTML files.

You can modify this servlet to provide greater flexibility and feedback:

- Improved reporting
  As the servlet is processing each file, the name of the file, along with the number of modifications, could be built into an HTML page and sent back to the client. In addition, a log file could be maintained to log the changes that were made to each file.

- Single-directory searching
  Sometimes the servlet doesn't need to search all of the subdirectories—it just needs to operate in the top-level directory. This feature could be added to the HTML page so the servlet doesn't need to search every file.

- Multiple keywords
  Although keywords cover the majority of queries, sometimes it can be advantageous to allow complete phrases to be linked. This would involve modifying the tag parser.

- Single files
  At the moment, the servlet operates on all the HTML files in a directory. The servlet could accept a single file and process it on its own.

16.6 From here

This chapter introduced the basic concept of opening up HTML files and parsing them. The next chapter takes this parsing algorithm a step further. It checks each link to see whether it is still valid.

CHAPTER 17

Link validation

CHAPTER CONCEPTS

- Discover what a web crawler actually is and how it relates to link validation.

- Learn how Java has turned the nightmarish task of checking links into a relatively simple one.

- Learn the implications of running a link-testing servlet in terms of how it affects both the server running the servlet and the web site the servlet is testing.

If you've had any experience with link validation, you know it can be a real pain if you do it manually. You'll also know that if you don't check your links, many users will get frustrated because they come across dead or obsolete links. Fortunately many of today's HTML editors provide this checking process automatically, but they fall short when checking external links. If your site has many links from it to other sites scattered around the world, it is important to know that none of these links are dead. But again, checking these usually means taking the time to visit each of the links to see if they are active or not. What you need is a program that will visit each link on a site and report whether the link is valid or not.

Such programs are commonly known as web crawlers. They exist all over the Internet, and many of them are implemented in CGI. This chapter presents a servlet implementation of a link validation crawler. If you combine Java and the servlet API, it will be very easy to construct such a program.

17.1 Introduction to web crawlers

The name web crawler is actually pretty descriptive when you look at what it does—it crawls the web. If we were to use the term web worm, then maybe we would have a better idea of what such a program does. Given any starting page, a web crawler checks every link to other pages and then visits those pages. This is done until every possible link has been checked and visited. So to go back to the definition, the web crawler program worms (or digs) its way down into the web pages, visiting every link it comes across.

As shown in figure 17.1, this can result in quite a maze of pages and links. You may have already guessed that by carefully choosing the root page, it is conceivable that every single linked web page on the Internet would be visited, and that is a serious amount of data. Web crawlers can very quickly get out of control if they're not constrained in some manner. They could possibly crawl forever, filling your hard drive with data as they go.

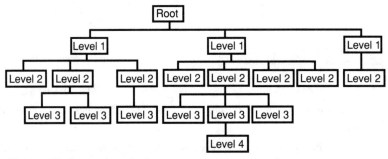

Figure 17.1 A generic web site map

Here are some of the reasons why you'd want to run a web crawler:

- Search engines
  When you submit your URL to a search engine such as InfoSeek (http://www.info-seek.com) or HotBot (http://www.hotbot.com), you are triggering the execution of a worm that will be run on your site. This worm goes through your whole site, storing all text and keywords for inclusion in the engine's database. Then when users perform

a search using the engines you've submitted your site to, they may see your site in their results, if it pertains to their search.

- Link testing

  Having a worm run on your site can be a useful way of validating links within your site. Link-testing programs usually have constraints on them so they can't crawl into domains other than the domain they start from.

- Because you can!

  Not everything is done for a logical reason. Although I don't like the word "hackers," these users will do anything technology will allow simply because they can. There is nothing wrong with this, as long as it doesn't infringe on the rights of the sites they are hacking into.

The search engine application, as you can imagine, could yield serious amounts of data if let loose on the world at large. For more information on search engines and how they operate, see the next chapter.

This chapter will take an in-depth look at a link-testing servlet. This servlet can also be used in many other Internet applications when certain calls and methods are modified.

Once the servlet has been implemented and tested, you'll need to take into account a number of performance issues involved with running such a rodent.

Note: The term "rodent" refers to the mole-like characteristics of the servlet. Just as a real mole digs and burrows into the ground, a servlet mole digs deeply into a site.

17.1.1 Link-testing servlet

The link-testing servlet has one primary task to perform: given a starting page, it must check all of the page's links for their validity, and visit only those links that are within the originating page's domain. This means that if the servlet starts checking from http://www.n-ary.com/ and it comes across a link to http://www.sun.com/, it is not allowed to process that link. It can only check for its valid existence.

But why limit the servlet to just HTML pages? Images are often referenced within documents as well. How many times have you come across a site that has a bad reference to an inline image? Images can also exist outside the domain from which they are displayed and therefore they have a tendency to lose their links.

Essentially anything that can be addressed with a URL can be tested. If the URL is an HTML page, then it is explored further. Determining whether a link is an HTML page is a simple matter of checking the link's content-type field.

These are the steps the servlet will follow:

1 Open up the root URL.

2 Pick out and test all URL references.

3 Store all HTML pages in a list. These will be checked further in section 17.2.

4 Remove the first file in the list of HTML pages and repeat step 2.

Looking at the structure of the servlet, you can see the need for at least one data storage area that will hold a list of the URLs still to be checked. When the file is opened, it is parsed and all the URLs within it are extracted. The file then is closed, and the next HTML file is checked. Seasoned developers will probably scream "What about recursion?" Recursion is when the link is checked and parsed as soon as it is encountered, and it results in too many resources being open at once. It is much more efficient to have only one resource open at a time, for reasons that will be detailed in the *Performance issues* section at the end of this chapter.

However, you must be careful not to have the servlet visit a link more than once; this could result in a continuous loop. If a page is referenced and it finds a link back to itself or a link to the page's parent file, the page would be checked again and again.

For this reason, another list must be maintained. This list will contain all the URLs that have been recognized. It doesn't matter whether they are valid. If an invalid URL is referenced many times in the site, then there is no point in checking it over and over. Therefore, before a URL is added to the to-be-checked list, it is first compared to the list of those that have been found to see if it has been spotted before. If it has, then it is ignored (well, not quite ignored, but more on that later in this section).

Without going too much further, we can identify the two list structures that are needed:

1 `Vector toBeChecked = new Vector( 10, 5 )` This vector will hold all the new URLs that still have to be checked. New elements can be added to the end of the list. When an item is to be checked, it is removed from the list.

2 `Hashtable foundURLS = new Hashtable( 50 )` This data structure will hold all of the URLs that have been found by the link-testing servlet. From this structure, you can determine a variety of statistics, as well as check for duplicate URLs. The hash table is the easiest structure for holding the list and searching on it, as you can use the URL itself as the key and quickly determine the URL's uniqueness.

Using the hash table structure does eliminate the problem of checking repeat URLs; however, it does not stop the servlet from wandering off into the depths of the site. Some mechanism must exist to limit the number of levels the servlet will traverse. The servlet keeps a depth figure with each URL; this is the number of hops it is away from the main root URL. It's relatively easy to track the depth number, as you will see later in this section.

Note One of the standard servlets shipped with JavaSoft's Java Web Server is a servlet called LinkChecker. This servlet performs exactly the same function as the servlet in this chapter, but when you read through its source code, it looks very complicated. The servlet in this chapter is loosely based on the LinkChecker servlet, but it has a number of performance enhancements. I say loosely, because if you compare both servlets, you will see that a significant number of structural differences exist. Take note that the LinkChecker servlet does not check frames, but this servlet implementation does.

17.1.2 Representing a URL

The servlet being developed in this chapter relies heavily on the URL of the resource. This is the URL that is sought from the HTML files being parsed, and it is the one that is checked for accuracy. As part of the standard libraries, Java has a URL class which is used to represent a URL. However, its functionality falls a little short with regard to validating a resource. To compensate for it, we will define a new URL class that will encapsulate the standard URL class along with a host of other flags and data structures. The class outline for this class can be seen in example 17.1.

```
class cURL extends Object {
  public  URL      url;
  public  boolean  bValidURL;
  public  boolean  bGood;
  public  boolean  bExternal;
  public  boolean  bHTMLPage;
  public  Vector   BadLinks;
  public  int      depth;

  //- Other methods to go here
}
```
Example 17.1 The class definition for cURL

The first data type is the URL class. This will hold the URL of the resource to which this class will relate. The URL can be either valid or invalid. This has nothing to do with whether it connects to a valid resource. This boolean value merely indicates if it is syntactically correct. The boolean flag bValidURL holds the boolean value for the URL (either true or false). If the URL is valid, the bGood boolean flag indicates whether it points to a valid or good resource. If the URL is in itself an HTML page, then this makes it eligible for further parsing, in which case the bHTMLPage boolean flag will be true.

As part of the reporting process, it is useful to know which of the other URLs this URL references are invalid. Each URL can therefore have a list of URLs associated with it; these are stored in the BadLinks Vector structure.

The final data element associated with the class is the depth figure. This value is the number of hops this URL is away from the root document.

Having this cURL class means a lot of the processing associated with the URL can placed inside this class and abstracted away. Consequently, two constructors are used to create an instance of this cURL class.

Constructor #1   This constructor (see example 17.2) is used to create an instance of cURL from two strings. The first string represents the new proposed URL, and the second string contains the string version of the root host.

```
public cURL( String _newURL, String _rootHost ){
  try{
    if ( _newURL.endsWith("/") )
      _newURL = _newURL.substring(0,_newURL.length()-1);

    url      = new URL( _newURL );
    bGood    = false;
```

```
      bValidURL = true;
      bHTMLPage = false;
      depth     = 0;

      if (url.getHost().equalsIgnoreCase(_rootHost))
        bExternal    = true;
      else
        bExternal    = false;

      BadLinks = null;
    }
    catch(MalformedURLException E ){
      bValidURL = false;
    }
  }
}
```

Example 17.2   Constructor #1

The convention you will use when creating URLs is to have no trailing "/" characters, as these characters make it a little more complicated to validate URLs. Therefore, the
first thing you need to do is remove any / characters from the front of the proposed URL.

Next, an instance of the URL is created. If the string doesn't represent a true URL,
then an exception is thrown. If an exception is thrown, then it is caught, and the bValidURL flag is set to false. Otherwise, the instance is created with the bExternal flag
being set, regardless of whether the new URL host equals the old host.

Note   The URL class from the standard Java library is rich in functionality only from
the point of view of parsing the URL string. The getHost() method returns the host
part of the URL, which is used extensively in this servlet. For example:

```
String host = new URL("http://www.n-ary.com/index.html" ).getH-
ost();
```

would make the host equal to www.n-ary.com.

Constructor #2   This constructor (see example 17.3) is used by the parsing algorithm
to create an instance of cURL. A URL resource can take many forms, and one of the main
tasks of this constructor is to format the URL into a common format. As with the previous
constructor, the / character is removed from the end of the string.

The first thing this constructor checks is the absolute URL. If the address is prefixed
with an "http://" sequence, then very little preprocessing is required. Once the URL has
been created, it is checked against the host of the root document. If they are different from
each other, then this cURL is marked as external.

```
public cURL(cURL _root, String _link){
  try{
    //- Look at what the _link starts with
    if (_link.endsWith("/"))
      link = _link.substring(0,_link.length()-1);
bValidURL      = true;
```

```
bExternal       = false;
BadLinks        - null;

if ( _link.toLowerCase().indexOf( "http://" ) != -1 ){
  url  = new URL( _link );

  if  (url.getHost().equalsIgnoreCase(_root.url.getHost())==false)
    bExternal = true;
}
else if ( _link.indexOf( "(" ) != -1 || _link.toLowerCase().indexOf
                      ( "mailto" ) != -1 )
  bValidURL = false;
else{
  String  lastURL = _root.url.toString();
  String  newURL;

  if (_link.startsWith("/"))
    newURL = "http://" + _root.url.getHost().concat( _link );
  else
    newURL= lastURL.substring(0,lastURL.lastIndexOf("/")
                      +1).concat(_link);

  url  = new URL( newURL );
  depth = _root.depth + 1;
  }
}
catch( MalformedURLException E ){
    bValidURL = false;
}
}
```

Example 17.3   Constructor #2

A number of extensions to the standard references can be made from within an HTML file. These include references to JavaScript methods and calls to throw mailto: tags to the user. Visiting such links would show most as invalid. Filtering out the JavaScript calls is easy. They include a set of parentheses, (), which is not allowed in a proper URL address. Similarly, to find the mail directives, look for the mailto: tag. Finding either one will cause the bValidURL flag to be set to false.

At this stage, the URL needs the host string, which is inserted at the start of the string representing the link. If the proposed URL string starts with the / character, the path is relative to the root of web site the link tester is working for. For example, if the new URL was /pics/test.jpg, it would translate to http://www.n-ary.com/pics/test.jpg, assuming the root URL was www.n-ary.com.

If the link doesn't start with the / character, then the resource is relative to the path of the current URL. For example, if the URL the reference was found in was http://www.n-ary.com/pics/all.html and the new URL was test.jpg, then the resulting URL would be http://www.n-ary.com/pics/test.jpg. This is determined by appending the new URL after the last / character in the old URL. This is performed through the substring(…) and lastIndexOf(…) methods from the String class.

Finally, the depth figure is calculated from the depth figure of the previous URL plus 1, indicating the new URL is one level below the previous file.

Validating the URL   Checking the validity of a URL is, alas, not a straightforward method call from the URL class. Here are the reasons you have to provide an alternative checking routine:

- You need the content-type of the URL to see if it is another HTML file.
- The URL class doesn't necessarily mean the site exists.

To illustrate the second point, that of the URL class being misleading, consider the code fragment shown in example 17.4, which we would use to open up a connection to a URL resource.

```
try{
  URL url = new URL("http://www.n-ary.com/badpage.html");
  URLConnection Uc = url.openConnection();
  //- Do something
}
catch ( Exception E ){
  //- The connection failed
}
```
Example 17.4   Opening up a URL connection

Assume that we know for a fact that the URL is a nonexistent page. Technically, you would think an exception would be thrown and caught. However, no exception is thrown. The call executes perfectly. Why? The easiest way to show why is to actually enter in the URL and see what the browser displays. This should look something like figure 17.2.

This page is still a valid HTML page, so the call is rendered successfully. This is why we cannot use the URLConnection method to validate a URL, because even if the URL is invalid, the call is still valid.

The information we need is in the HTTP header that is sent back from the server; for every response from the server, an HTTP header is sent detailing information about the request. For example, example 17.5 shows the HTTP header that is sent to the web server and the first part of the HTTP header that is returned.

```
Header Out:      HEAD badpage.html HTTP/1.0
                 From: info@n-ary.com
                 User-Agent: LinkTest/1.0

Header In:       HTTP/1.0 400 Bad Request
                 Server: JavaWebServer/1.1
                 Content-Type: text/html
                 Date: Tue, 27 May 1998 22:12:13 GMT
```
Example 17.5   HTTP headers

The first line of the response from the server has the status code. This code is an indication of the success of the last request. Many status codes exist, but the three important ones that indicate a bad request are 400, 404, and 500. Notice anything else with the header? The MIME type of the file is also included: "Content-Type: text/html." By look-

Figure 17.2 An HTML page returned by the server when a URL doesn't exist

ing for this field, we can determine whether the URL is an HTML file. But how do we get at this information? It's simple. Send the HTTP header to the web server by opening up a socket connection to the web server, as shown in example 17.6.

```
Socket s;
if (url.getPort()==-1)
  s = new Socket(url.getHost(),80);
else
  s = new Socket(url.getHost(),url.getPort());

PrintStream    Out = new PrintStream(s.getOutputStream());
DataInputStream In = new DataInputStream(s.getInputStream());
```
Example 17.6 Opening up the connection to the web server

Notice the two different calls for creating the socket connection. The reason for this is that a URL can specify a custom port number over and above the standard web server port 80. The getPort() method from the URL class returns the port number if one has been specified in the URL. Once the socket connection has opened, input and output streams are created to the connection.

Sending out the header is a simple matter of doing a println(…) to the socket's output stream, as shown in example 17.7.

```
Out.println("HEAD "+url.getFile()+" HTTP/1.0");
Out.println("From: info@"+url.getHost());
Out.println("User-Agent: LinkTest/1.0");
```

```
Out.println();
```
Example 17.7 ending out the HTTP header

Using the two methods from the URL class, constructing the HTTP header is very easy. Once the header is sent out, the server returns a new header. The first line of the response from the server is the HTTP field, which contains the status value. We can check to see if this string has one of the error status codes using the indexOf(…) method from the String class, as shown in example 17.8.

```
String LineIn = In.readLine();
if ( LineIn.indexOf("500")!=-1||LineIn.indexOf("404"
                            )!=-1||LineIn.indexOf("400")!=-1){
  bGood          = false;
  bHTMLPage      = false;
  s.close();
  return;
}

bGood = true;
while ( (LineIn=In.readLine()) != null ){
  if ( LineIn.toLowerCase().indexOf("content-type")!=-1){
    if (LineIn.toLowerCase().indexOf("text/html")==-1)
      bHTMLPage = false;
    else
      bHTMLPage = true;
    break;
  }
}
```
Example 17.8 Reading the HTTP header from the server

The status of the last request is determined by looking at the return code from the server. If the request was successful, the remaining lines are read from the server until the content-type of the file is read. Once the content-type field is found, the second part of the field is checked to see if it contains "text/html." If this text is found, then the bHTM-LPage flag is set to true, to indicate this is a link to an HTML page.

Once the content-type field is read, the connection can be closed and the method can be returned. Although this method for checking a URL seems like a lot of work, it is the most reliable and safest method; since the heart of the servlet is the checking routine, it is important to get it right.

Complete cURL source code Example 17.9 shows the complete source code for the cURL class. In addition to the two constructors and the method for checking the link, there are two other methods. One is for adding new links to the list of bad references, and the other is for printing a list of bad links for reporting purposes. This class is very important to the overall operation of the servlet, as it forms the nucleus of information from which the servlet runs.

```
class cURL extends Object {
  public  URL     url;
  public  boolean bValidURL;
```

```java
public  boolean bGood;
public  boolean bExternal;
public  boolean bHTMLPage;
public  Vector  BadLinks;
public  int     depth;

public  cURL( String _newURL, String _rootHost ){
  try{
    if  ( _newURL.endsWith("/") )
      _newURL = _newURL.substring(0,_newURL.length()-1);

    url       = new URL(  _newURL );
    bGood     = false;
    bValidURL = true;
    bHTMLPage = false;
    depth     = 0;

    if  ( url.getHost().equalsIgnoreCase( _rootHost ) )
      bExternal     = true;
    else
      bExternal     = false;

    BadLinks  = null;
  }
  catch( MalformedURLException E ){
    bValidURL = false;
  }
}

public  cURL( cURL _root, String _link ){
  try{
    //- Look at what the _link starts with
    if  (_link.endsWith("/"))
      _link = _link.substring( 0, _link.length()-1 );

    bValidURL = true;
    bExternal = false;
    BadLinks  = null;

    if  (_link.toLowerCase().indexOf("http://")!=-1){
      url = new URL(_link);

      if  ( url.getHost().equalsIgnoreCase(_root.url.getHost())==false)
        bExternal = true;
    }
    else  if  ( _link.indexOf( "(" ) != -1
                   ||_link.toLowerCase().indexOf( "mailto" )!=-1)
      bValidURL = false;
    else{
      String lastURL = _root.url.toString();
      String newURL;

      if  ( _link.startsWith( "/" ) )
        newURL  = "http://"+_root.url.getHost().concat(_link);
```

```
              else
                 newURL   = lastURL.substring(0,lastURL.lastIndexOf("/")
                                    +1).concat(_link);

              url    = new URL(newURL);
              depth  = _root.depth+1;
           }
        }
      catch( MalformedURLException E ){
        bValidURL = false;
      }
   }

   public  void checkLink(){
     try{
        Socket  s;
        if  ( url.getPort() == -1 )
           s = new Socket( url.getHost(), 80 );
        else
           s = new Socket( url.getHost(), url.getPort() );

        PrintStream Out    = new PrintStream( s.getOutputStream() );
        DataInputStream In  = new DataInputStream( s.getInputStream() );

        Out.println(  "HEAD " + url.getFile() + " HTTP/1.0" );
        Out.println(  "From: info@" + url.getHost() );
        Out.println(  "User-Agent: LinkTest/1.0" );
        Out.println();

        String  LineIn = In.readLine();

        if (LineIn.indexOf("500")!=-1||LineIn.indexOf("404")
                          !=-1||LineIn.indexOf("400")!=-1){
           bGood     = false;
           bHTMLPage = false;
           s.close();
           return;
        }

        bGood = true;
        while ( (LineIn=In.readLine())   != null ) {
           if ( LineIn.toLowerCase().indexOf("content-type")!=-1){
              if  (LineIn.toLowerCase().indexOf( "text/html" )==-1)
                 bHTMLPage = false;
              else
                 bHTMLPage = true;

              break;
           }
        }

        s.close();
        }
      catch( Exception E ) {
```

```
      bGood     = false;
      bHTMLPage = false;
   }
}

public  void addBadLink( cURL badlink ){
  if ( bExternal )
    return;

  if ( BadLinks == null )
    BadLinks  = new Vector( 5 );

  BadLinks.addElement( badlink );
}

public  void printBadLinks( PrintStream Out ){
  if ( bExternal || bHTMLPage == false )
    return;
  if ( BadLinks == null )
    Out.println(  "<UL><LI>No Bad Links</UL>" );
  else{
    Out.println(  "<UL>" );
    Enumeration E = BadLinks.elements();
    while ( E.hasMoreElements() )
      Out.println( "<LI>" + ((cURL)E.nextElement()).url );

    Out.println(  "</UL>" );
  }
}
}
```

Example 17.9   The complete cURL source code

17.1.3   Link-testing servlet

The link-testing servlet we're creating is based on the HttpServlet class, since the output will be an HTML page. Invoking the servlet will be performed through the HTML form shown in figure 17.3. This form asks for the root URL from which the servlet will check and the depth to which the servlet will burrow.

Note: This is a servlet and not an applet—this may seem obvious, but because of this difference, the security restrictions are not as tight. For example, an applet is not allowed to connect to a host outside of the one from which it was downloaded. If the same were true of the servlet, then only the host the servlet was running on could be checked, which wouldn't make the servlet very flexible.

The service(…) method of the servlet has one main job, and that is to run through the list of URLs that still need to be checked. After the user's input URL has been verified and checked, the looping begins, as shown in example 17.10.

```
toBeChecked.insertElementAt(topURL,0);
foundURLS.put(topURL.url,topURL);
```

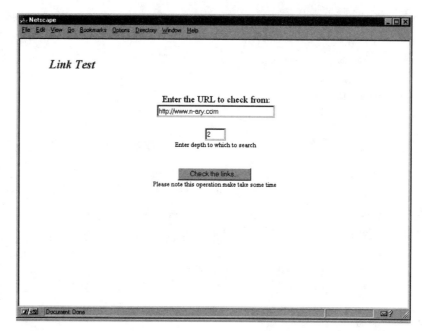

Figure 17.3 Starting the servlet off to check a web site

```
cURL nextURL;

while ( toBeChecked.isEmpty() == false ){
  nextURL = (cURL)toBeChecked.elementAt( 0 );
  if (nextURL.bGood&&nextURL.bHTMLPage && nextURL.bExternal==false)
    lookInsideURL(nextURL,toBeChecked,foundURLS,depth);

  toBeChecked.removeElementAt(0);
}
```

Example 17.10   Looping around the list of links to be checked

The `toBeChecked` variable holds a reference to a `Vector` data structure. When this list is empty, no more items are left to be checked, and the servlet may complete. Running through the list is a simple matter of setting up a `while` loop that checks the `isEmpty()` method to see if any more items exist. Items are removed from the front of the list, and assuming they are good links, HTML files, and in the current domain, they are parsed. Once they are parsed, or if they have failed the preceding checks, they are removed from the list. This ensures they are not repeatedly checked. Upon completion of the loop, all items will have been checked.

Parsing the HTML file   Now that we've identified an HTML page to be searched, we must open the file and check all the links and references within it. We can do this by opening the file and reading it line by line. At this stage you know it is an HTML file, as this was part of the checking process when the `cURL` class was first created. Therefore, we can use the `DataInputStream` class to read the file one line at a time. Getting an input stream from the URL is a simple matter of calling the `openStream()` method from the URL class and then reading every line of the HTML file until a `null` is returned, as shown in example 17.11.

```
DataInputStream In = new DataInputStream(nextURL.url.openStream());
String Line, oldLine;

while ((oldLine = In.readLine())!=null){
  //- Do something with every line of the file
}
```
Example 17.11   Reading the HTML file

For every line that is read, a number of tags have to be searched for:

Tag	Description
HREF=?????? or href=??????	Links to other HTML pages, CGI, or servlets.
SRC=?????? or src=??????	Links to images, or if found in a frame set, links to other HTML pages.
BACKGROUND=?????? or background=??????	Links to the image that is used as the background image for the page.

From these tags we can trace all references to all other resources. Every line must be scanned for an occurrence of these tags. We can scan for a particular string using the `indexOf(...)` method. But a tag could appear more than once on a line, so the `indexOf(...)` method needs to run continually until all of the tags have been found. By packaging the call to the `indexOf(...)` method into a `while` loop, as shown in example 17.12, all the tags in a line can be checked.

```
index = -1;
Line = oldLine;
while((index=Line.toLowerCase().indexOf("href=",index+1))!=-1)
  lookAtHREF(Line,index,5,nextURL,toBeChecked,foundURLS,depth);
```
Example 17.12   Checking for the HREF HTML tag in a line of text

Once a tag has been found, the line is then passed to the `lookAtHREF(...)` method for further parsing. There are three tags to be found: `href`, `src`, and `background`. Repeating the preceding statement for each tag is the easiest and quickest way of parsing the line.

Note   The `indexOf(...)` method from the `String` class is one of those invaluable methods that you'll find yourself using over and over again. This method returns the index of the first occurrence of the string passed in. Subsequent calls may be made by passing in a starting index.

Parsing the HTML tag   Once the HTML tag has been found, the cURL class must be created. The character index of an occurrence of the tag is available in the index variable. We can use this to make the first part of the URL. When a resource is referenced in an HTML document, it can optionally be enclosed in quotation marks.

```
HREF="badpage.html"
HREF=badpage.html
```

If the resource link is enclosed in quotation marks, it should be removed. The code fragment in example 17.13 shows the extraction of the link from the line.

```
int s=0, e;
if ( tLine.charAt(0)=='\"'){
  e = tLine.indexOf("\"",1);
  s = 1;
}
else
  e = tLine.indexOf(" ",1);

tLine = tLine.substring(s,e);

cURL newURL = new cURL(nextURL,tLine);
```
Example 17.13   Extracting the link from the line

This extraction is done by calculating the starting and ending index of the link and then creating a link using the `substring(...)` method. If the link is enclosed in quotation marks, then the starting index is 1 and the ending index is the position where the next quotation mark occurs. On the other hand, if the link is not enclosed in quotation marks, then the next space marks the end of the link. Once the link has been extracted, it is used to create an instance of cURL.

Updating the lists   Once we have created the cURL class, we must add it to the list of elements that still need to be checked. However, only insert tobeChecked using the cURL instance if it is a valid URL or if it hasn't already been checked. The foundURLS hash table keeps a list of all the URLs that have been parsed, so checking to see if a URL is new is a matter of checking the hash table to see if the URL exists using the `containsKey(...)` method. If this returns false and the URL is valid, assuming as well that the depth of the URL is not greater than the depth specified by the user, the link is checked. Example 17.14 shows this procedure.

```
String tLine = Line.substring(index+offset,Line.length());
if ( newURL.bValidURL == true && foundURLS.containsKey(
                              newURL.url ) == false
     && newURL.depth <= depth ){
  newURL.checkLink();
  if ( newURL.bGood ) {
    if (newURL.bHTMLPage&&newURL.bExternal==false)
      toBeChecked.addElement( newURL );
    foundURLS.put( newURL.url, newURL );
  }
  else            //- Add to bad links
```

```
        nextURL.addBadLink( newURL );
}
```
Example 17.14   Adding a new URL to the checking lists

After the link has been checked, a number of parameters are set. If the cURL object is a valid link to a resource, then it is added to the hash table containing all of the URLs. If the URL turns out to be a link to another HTML page, and the page is not external to the domain being checked, it is added to the list of cURLs to be checked. If the new URL is not good, it is added to the list of bad links for the page from which it was referenced.

Outputting the results   Once the servlet has finished checking all the links, the results must be outputted to the user, as illustrated in figure 17.4. There's not much point in running the servlet if you can't see the results. After the servlet has finished checking the links, the toBeChecked structure is empty, as you would expect, but the foundURLS hash table is full of all the URLs found by the servlet, whether good or bad.

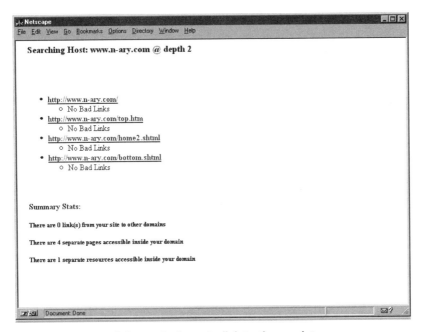

Figure 17.4 Output of the results from the link-testing servlet

From this list of links a number of different lists could be produced. For this application, only the nonexternal HTML pages will be listed, complete with a list of the bad links associated with each page.

Producing this list is a matter of checking the hash table items to see if they satisfy the output criteria, and, if they do, printing them. The code in example 17.15 illustrates this looping procedure.

```
Out.println( "<BR><BR><UL>" );
int extLinks=0, intLinks=0, intPages=0;
```

```
Enumeration E = foundURLS.elements();
while (E.hasMoreElements() ){
  nextURL = (cURL)E.nextElement();

  if ( nextURL.bExternal == false && nextURL.bHTMLPage){
    Out.println("<LI>");
    Out.println("<B><A HREF=" + nextURL.url + ">");
    Out.println(nextURL.url + "</A></B>");
    nextURL.printBadLinks( Out );
    intPages++;
  }
  else if (nextURL.bExternal==true)
    extLinks++;
  else
    intLinks++;
}
```

Example 17.15   Generating the statistical analysis

The servlet execution can take a relatively long time, thus leaving the user at the client side waiting for the servlet to complete before any output is displayed. You might be tempted to display information as the servlet is executing. Though this is possible in principle, in reality it doesn't quite work. Since the data is cached, the user ends up receiving the data in one lump anyway.

17.1.4 Complete servlet source code

Example 17.16 shows the complete source code for the link-testing servlet. The servlet needs no special aliases, and it can be called from any form. Only the URL and DEPTH parameters are required.

If you look at the servlet, you will notice that all the data structures are initialized in the body of the service(...) method. This allows the servlet to be "hit" several times at once, without the fear of overwriting data if two or more servlet calls happen simultaneously.

```
import java.util.*;
import java.io.*;
import javax.servlet.*;
import javax.servlet.http.*;
import java.io.*;
import java.net.*;

public class link_test extends HttpServlet {
  public  void service( HttpServletRequest _req,
                        HttpServletResponse _res)
                        throws ServletException,IOException{
    _res.setContentType( "text/html" );
    PrintStream Out = new PrintStream( _res.getOutputStream(), true );

    Vector toBeChecked = new Vector( 10, 5 );
    Hashtable foundURLS = new Hashtable( 50 );
    cURL topURL = new cURL(_req.getParameter("URL"),"");
    int depth;
```

```
try{
  depth = Integer.parseInt( _req.getParameter("DEPTH" ) );
}
catch( Exception E ){
  depth = 9999;
}

if ( topURL.bValidURL == false ){
  Out.println(topURL.url+": was invalid.Re-enter  a valid URL");
  return;
}

Out.println( "<HTML><BODY>" );
topURL.checkLink();

if ( topURL.bGood ){
  toBeChecked.insertElementAt(  topURL, 0 );
  foundURLS.put(  topURL.url, topURL );
}

cURL nextURL;
String rootHost = topURL.url.getHost();

Out.println( "<H3>Searching Host: " + rootHost + " @ depth " );
Out.println( depth  + "</H3><BR>" );

while ( toBeChecked.isEmpty() == false ){
  nextURL = (cURL)toBeChecked.elementAt(0);

  if (nextURL.bGood&&nextURL.bHTMLPage&&nextURL.bExternal==false)
    lookInsideURL( nextURL, toBeChecked, foundURLS, depth );

  toBeChecked.removeElementAt(  0 );
}

//- Print summary information
Out.println( "<BR><BR><UL>" );
int     extLinks=0, intLinks=0, intPages=0;

Enumeration E = foundURLS.elements();
while (E.hasMoreElements() ){
  nextURL = (cURL)E.nextElement();

  if (nextURL.bExternal==false&&nextURL.bHTMLPage){
    Out.println( "<LI>" );
    Out.println( "<B><A HREF=" + nextURL.url + ">" );
    Out.println( nextURL.url  + "</A></B>" );
    nextURL.printBadLinks( Out );
    intPages++;
  }
  else  if ( nextURL.bExternal == true )
    extLinks++;
  else
    intLinks++;
```

```
        }
        Out.println( "</UL><BR><BR><H4>Summary Stats:</H4>" );
        Out.println( "<H5>There are " + extLinks + " link(s) from your " );
        Out.println( "site to other domains</H5>" );
        Out.println( "<H5>There are " + intPages + " separate pages " );
        Out.println( "accessible inside your  domain</H5>" );
        Out.println( "<H5>There are " + intLinks + " separate resources " );
        Out.println( "accessible inside your domain</H5>" );
        Out.println( "</BODY></HTML>" );
        Out.flush();

        foundURLS.clear();
    }

    private void lookInsideURL(cURL nextURL,Vector
                         toBeChecked,Hashtable foundURLS,int depth ){
        //- Looks for URLs, adding them to the list if necessary
        try {
            DataInputStream In  = new DataInputStream
                              (nextURL.url.openStream());
            String  Line, oldLine;
            int index;

            while ( (oldLine  = In.readLine()) != null ){
                index = -1;
                Line = oldLine;
                while((index=Line.toLowerCase().indexOf("href=",index+1))!=-1)
                    lookAtHREF(Line,index,5,nextURL,toBeChecked,foundURLS,depth);

                index = -1;
                Line = oldLine;
                while((index=Line.toLowerCase().indexOf("src=",index+1))!=-1)
                    lookAtHREF(Line,index,4,nextURL,toBeChecked,foundURLS,depth);

                index = -1;
                Line = oldLine;
                while((index=Line.toLowerCase().indexOf
                              ("background=",index+1))!=-1)
                    lookAtHREF(Line,index,11,nextURL,toBeChecked,foundURLS,depth);
            }
        }
        catch( Exception E ){}
    }

    private void lookAtHREF(String Line,int index,int offset,
          cURL nextURL,Vector toBeChecked,Hashtable  foundURLS,int depth){
        try{
            String  tLine = Line.substring(index+offset,Line.length());
            int s=0,e;

            if (tLine.charAt(0)=='\"'){
                e = tLine.indexOf( "\"", 1 );
                s = 1;
```

```
      }
      else
        e = tLine.indexOf( " ", 1 );

      tLine = tLine.substring(s,e);
      cURL newURL = new cURL(nextURL,tLine);

      if (newURL.bValidURL==true&&foundURLS.containsKey
                          (newURL.url)==false&&newURL.depth<=depth)
      {
        newURL.checkLink();

        if (newURL.bGood){
          if (newURL.bHTMLPage&&newURL.bExternal==false)
            toBeChecked.addElement( newURL );

          foundURLS.put(  newURL.url, newURL );
        }
      }
    }
    catch(Exception E ){}
  }
}
```
Example 17.16   The complete servlet source code

17.2   Performance issues

Running the link-checking servlet can have serious implications on both the server it is running on and the web server it is checking. The web server the servlet is checking will get a series of successive hits, which may impede its response to valid surfers. For this reason, it is best to run the servlet in off-peak hours. That way you can be sure of a fast response from the servlet, and you won't run the risk of upsetting the web administrator.

For large sites, the number of found URLs can become very large; subsequently, they will require a lot of memory to store. To reduce the amount of memory that is consumed, the site can be checked in stages using the depth parameter, which limits the number of levels the servlet will search.

17.3   Future extensions

This chapter gave an overview of a web crawler and link-testing program, and it showed the subtle differences between the two. A web crawler visits every single link, whereas a link tester limits the links it tests to the root host from which it started. The link-testing servlet implemented in this chapter not only gives you a very useful administration tool, but it also demonstrates the power Java has to offer to such applications.

As you learned, testing links involves a lot of string manipulation, gathering the data into a proper, accessible URL. Implementing this process in C or C++ would open up the server to potential crashes, as string manipulation in these languages means accessing raw memory. Array overruns are the most common causes of crashes for C/C++ programs. In comparison, if the array overruns in Java, it doesn't result in the server crashing.

You learned that storing the results wasn't a problem either. Using the standard data structures found inherent in the Java language made this aspect of the servlet child's play.

Although this servlet offers a very flexible solution for validating links, the servlet could benefit from a number of additional features:

- Multiple line processing
  At the moment, if a URL is split across a line break, then the servlet will report it as a dead link. This is a perfectly legal option in HTML, but it is not checked for in this version.

- Improved reporting
  Every valid link and reference is stored in the hash table data structure. This information could be presented to the user in a format that could report more than just faulty or broken links—it could report things like missing images.

- Anchor validation
  Anchors allow references to be made to specific parts of files by appending the # and the name of the anchor after the URL. At the moment, the servlet will not check the anchors.

C H A P T E R   1 8

Search engine

CHAPTER CONCEPTS

- Discover what makes a search engine, and how it may be implemented on a web site.

- Searching through documents can be done in many different ways. Find out the strengths and weaknesses of several different searches.

- Learn about the implementation of a search engine, where users are invited to submit URLs of their own choice, from which a search will run.

- Follow the implementation of a site search engine using servlets.

No matter how structured a web site is, there will always be someone who can't find exactly the information he is after. Some sites, such as those that offer high educational or informational content, attract users that are after a specific piece of data about a certain subject. These people don't want to navigate through hierarchical menus to find information. They want it fast and they want it without having to click through many levels of pages to find it. Another important issue is the addition of information to the site. It must be instantly available to the readers, without their having to find it using navigational links. Too much search effort not only slows down the access time for the users, but it can also mislead them—for example, once they've found a particular topic, there may be additional information lurking in another page, unbeknownst to them.

To greatly improve the usability of even the most basic sites, provide a search facility which allows users to enter specific search criteria, then view a list of all the pages that hold the information satisfying the search parameters. A search page allows users to quickly locate all relevant documents and view them in a list, so they can visit the documents they want one after another.

Search engines come in many different forms, and they can be implemented in many different ways. This chapter will present a servlet search engine that may be used to increase a site's functionality.

18.1 Search engines overview

Search engines are used in a variety of different applications, but they can be generally broken down into two classes:

1 Search engines that operate within a single site

2 Search engines that operate over multiple sites

A search engine that is provided as part of a site usually returns results from the list of HTML files on that site only. Conversely, a site that offers a search engine as its main site content, one such as InfoSeek or Yahoo, will return results from a database of millions of pages found all over the Internet.

18.1.1 Single-site searches

A search engine that is designed to operate within the confines of a single site will be of a different design and operation than one that is designed to return a variety of sites that match a search criteria. The single-site search facility will generally yield a much tighter and more accurate list of matches than the search engine that operates over multiple sites.

There are a number of different ways a search can take place. The first, and most simple, way is to transverse each file on the site each time a new query is submitted. For large sites, or for sites that expect the site search engine to be used many times, this is not very efficient. However, it does offer the advantage of being able to offer the most up-to-date results.

For larger sites, the data from the HTML pages can be indexed into a proper database, which is then processed by a database engine. This method significantly increases the response time of the search, but it has the disadvantage of having the database occupy as much space as the original HTML file it is covering for.

An implementation of this type of search engine will be presented later on in the chapter—the example will look through each file in turn every time a new query is submitted.

18.1.2 Multiple-site searches

Many commercial sites exist that do nothing but catalogue other sites. These sites are then used to perform searches over a wide range of web sites, instead of just one. The bigger search engine sites, such as Yahoo and InfoSeek, offer a lifeline to the smaller sites that wouldn't have as much exposure if they had to rely on their own marketing. Sites that offer this type of service are known as the telephone directory of the Internet, as they offer a very easy and simple interface for finding information.

Multiple-site search engines rely on the webmasters of each individual site to register their sites with the search database. The design of the search engine determines what happens next. Some engines will start with the root URL of the site in question, then automatically visit every link in the site, cataloguing every single word and sentence. This process can take huge amounts of space to store all this information, but it does provide a very thorough search for the user.

Other sites will take an absolute URL of a page and look only at the header section of the HTML file, cataloguing the KEYWORD section and storing the description of the site. This process serves both the search engine and the user with a much-improved service. From the search engine's point of view, the amount of data being stored about each site is significantly reduced, and from the user's point of view, the chances of the same site being returned multiple times, as a result of a query, is also significantly reduced.

```
<HTML>
<HEAD>
<TITLE>This is the definitive Java site</TITLE>
<META NAME="Keywords" CONTENT="java,servlets,applets,beans">
<META NAME="Description" CONTENT="Site all about Java">
</HEAD>
This is a test home page for the Java servlet.
</HTML>
```
Example 18.1   A sample HTML file with header information

This version of the search engine, using only the keywords, will be implemented as a servlet. Remember, the servlet presented in this chapter will not employ an external database to store each new site. The servlet will demonstrate the basic functionality such a search engine would possess. Creating the link to an external database is not that difficult, as you'll see in chapter 24.

18.2 Search logistics

Once a particular file or body of text is found, it has to be compared with the search criteria that was presented by the user. There are many different techniques for searching for particular text strings or phrases, and each search engine employs a different combination of them.

When you combine the different types of searching with different data sets, you can be sure that not all commercial search engines would return the exact same results. It's hard to determine whether this is a good thing or a bad thing. One of the main criticisms of the Internet right now is being able to find relevant information. Filtering out the valuable data from the sea of noise that exists with every page is a task that many developers and web designers are trying to take on.

18.2.1 Exact search

The first and most simple search is to check for exact matches. In an exact match search, each word in the query string is matched against each word found in the database. The results that are returned will contain the relevant documents, but a problem will arise in the documents that will be omitted from the search results. The keywords used in the query string will determine the richness of the resulting search. For example, if the user were searching for the word "monitor," then only sites containing the word "monitor" would be returned; sites containing words such as "monitors" would not. In certain instances this may be a good thing, and in others it may not. Regardless of the issues, this searching method is one of the fastest methods a search engine can employ.

18.2.2 Substring search

The substring search method offers a much-improved result set when it's used to circumvent the problems encountered using the exact-match search technique. Instead of the system rejecting words that don't fit exactly, the query word is matched against all the words in the database. To illustrate, let's return to the example in which the user is searching for information about monitors. In this example, the user enters the word "monitor" but the page that has lots of data about certain "monitors" doesn't actually contain the word "monitor." Instead, it contains the word "monitors." Since the query word "monitor" is part of "monitors," then this page would be returned as part of the result set. However, conversely, if the user entered the word "monitors," then pages that contained only the word "monitor" would not be returned.

18.2.3 Precedence search

One of the problems with searching a particularly busy web site is the number of the results that can be returned. Not only might this result set be daunting to the user, but it has the potential of hiding the more important documents among the documents that merely mention the query word or phrase in passing. There needs to be some way of prioritizing the search results, bringing the more relevant documents to the top of the list and putting the least relevant ones at the bottom. Prioritizing a set of results can be a very difficult process, and there has been quite a lot of debate over how it should be done. Each search engine uses a different technique, and no search engine will agree with another on what constitutes a definitive solution. Some of the ways to prioritize the results include the following:

- Give documents where the keywords appear as titles a higher priority.
- Give documents in which the keyword appears the most a higher priority.
- Give documents where the keyword appears in both the HTML header and the body text a higher priority.

18.2.4   Thesaurus

One of the more sophisticated methods a search engine might employ is to preempt a user's query. For example, say a user was searching for information regarding "monitors." He could also try searching for the terms "screen" or "VDU;" these may return a completely different list of results. By maintaining a thesaurus, the search engine can take the original keyword, look up equivalent phrases, and then perform the search with a greater scope of relevance. Although this method greatly improves the search results, the developer has the additional headache of maintaining the thesaurus and keeping it up to date. Because of this, many sites use this technique only on a limited set of technical words.

18.2.5   Stemming

Stemming works bitlike substring searches, but in reverse. Stemming involves stripping the query word back to its root. To illustrate, in our previous example where the user wishes to search for "monitors," the root word is "monitor." This root word is then used as the keyword in the search. This is a very trivial example; a more in-depth example would be if the user did a search on "snowball." Stripping the word back would reveal the root word of "snow." If the search engine searches on "snow," it could possibly return results ranging from "snowball," "snowboard," "snowdrift," "snowman," "snowshoe," and "snowflake," right through to "snowbound." Such a search may take the user somewhat off his original search track. The complication with stemming is knowing when to trim and when not to trim; each search algorithm is different.

18.2.6   AI search

Artificial intelligence (AI) is becoming more commonplace in our day-to-day work. One of the areas in which AI has made an impact is aiding search engines in performing greater power searches. For example, assume a user is searching for all available data about space travel. Many documents about this topic exist, but very few actually have the words "space" or "travel" in them. An AI engine would read the document stored with the search engine and determine whether not or it was about space travel. As you can imagine, this would take an enormous amount of processing power and time as well as a greater knowledge of the documents held (instead of simply thinking of them as mere clumps of text).

Sadly, search engines that provide this level of query do not yet exist. However, smaller versions that operate within specific boundaries do; many of them are still in their experimental phases.

18.2.7 Building search queries

One of the great features of a search engine is the ability to provide users with logical operators that form part of the query string (for example, AND and OR). Placing AND in the middle of two keywords will narrow a search down so that it only returns documents which contain both words. Conversely, the OR operator will return documents that contain either the first keyword or the second. Many search engines allow a user to have many keywords in one single query—each word is separated by a space. Depending on the default searching criteria employed by the search engine, some engines will default to AND, and some to OR.

18.2.8 Large result sets

Try running a search for the keyword "Java" on one of the commercial search engines—you'll be amazed at the number of results returned. They'll total well into the millions—way too many to be displayed in one HTML page. Instead, the first ten or twenty are returned, and you're presented with links to the next and previous block of results. When this feature was first implemented, it took many different forms, but the majority of all search engines rely on the same basic technique.

Back when the web wasn't as busy (or as big) as it is now, search engines would create, based on the search criteria, a complete set of HTML files that would represent the complete result set of the search. Periodically these files would be deleted. However, as things got bigger and busier this method was very quickly consuming too much of the engine's disk space.

A tidier solution was found when developers realized that search engines are built for extremely fast searches. So when the user clicks the link for the next ten documents, the search is actually performed again, but the first ten documents found are ignored. This technique doesn't require any temporary files, and each result document is created dynamically as and when it is required.

18.3   Global search servlet

A site that provides a global search engine not only increases the usability of the site, but the potential traffic increases as well. This section will present a completely servlet-based version of a search engine which does not employ the services of a database. The servlet is split in two sections:

1 Collating web site data

2 Searching mechanism

A global search engine operates purely on submitted web sites, so the bigger the database, the better the search results will be for the user. In order to make this servlet much faster, and so the resources on the server aren't drained, this version will only catalogue keywords and a site description for each web site submitted, as opposed to trawling the whole HTML file looking for text.

18.3.1 Collating data

The searching algorithm can only be as good as the data it operates on, no matter how good the algorithm is. Therefore, it's advantageous to encourage users to register as many web sites as possible with the database. Many of the commercial web search engines ask a lot of information about the sites submitted to them. The information ranges from the site description to the keywords that should be included. This can be counterproductive, since the more information the search engine requires, the more reluctant the webmaster is about typing it in time after time.

Note Never missing an opportunity to make money, many organizations (such as the one at http://www.businessweb.com.au) were set up to provide professional search engine submission services. For a fixed price, they will register your web site with many different search engines at once, so you don't have to repeat the same information over and over again.

Many of the newer web pages include all the necessary information within META tags in the <HEAD> section of the HTML file, as shown earlier in example 18.1. Using this information, the servlet need only ask the webmaster to submit the URL for inclusion in the database.

Figure 18.1 shows a sample HTML form that may be used to submit a new URL to the database. The main field is the URL field, in which the user fills in the web site he wants to include. Two additional fields are included for the webmaster's use, in case he needs to contact the site's web administrator.

Since this servlet will not be using an external database to store the site records, a special class will be created to store each site. This class can be extended to perform certain operations on the site. Example 18.2 shows the class definition for the site, with variables to hold various pieces of information regarding the site, including the site URL, description, heading, and keyword list.

```
class cSiteInfo extends Object {
    public URL      cHost;
    public String[] KeywordList;
    public int      KeywordNo;
    public String Description;
    public String hostName;
    public String adminName;
    public String adminEmail;
    public Date   lastChecked;
```

```
    //- Class methods ..
}
```
Example 18.2   Site class definition

When the user submits the form for processing, the servlet must perform two steps:

1 Create an instance of `cSiteInfo`.

2 Visit the site and extract the title, description, and keyword list from the `<HEAD>` field.

The site information will be stored in a list using the `Vector` data structure. Since each site record is to be searched, there's no point in storing the site records in any other data structure.

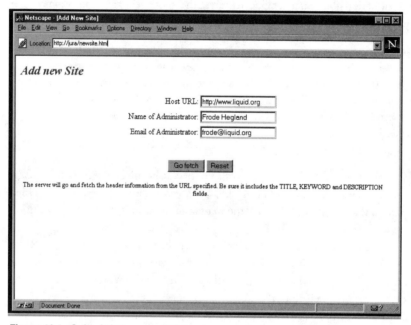

Figure 18.1   Submitting a new URL

Creating a site record   Creating the site record is only a matter of extracting the parameters from the posted form and then calling the class constructor shown in example 18.3. The constructor takes the incoming parameters and initializes all the class variables.

```
public cSiteInfo(String _host, String _name, String _email){
  try{
    cHost = new URL( _host );
  }catch( MalformedURLException E ){
    cHost = null;
    return;
  }
```

```
adminName    = _name;
adminEmail   = _email;
lastChecked  = new Date();
KeywordList  = null;
KeywordNo    = 0;
hostName     = "";
Description  = "";

//- Extract the header information
checkSite();
}
```
Example 18.3   The class constructor for `cSiteInfo`

One of the first validation hurdles is to ensure the supplied URL is syntactically correct. This can be easily checked by creating an instance of the URL class; if it's invalid, it will throw an exception. If the exception is thrown, the URL variable is set to `null`, and the class constructor returns. The calling method can check for this special case and make an informed decision on it. If the URL is created without any exceptions being thrown, then the class variables are initialized and the URL interrogation begins with the call to `check-Site()`.

Extracting header information   The header information of the HTML file at the given URL contains all the data that is necessary to complete the site record. The information is retrieved by going to the URL, opening up the source file, and reading the header information from the incoming data stream from the web server (assuming such information even exists in the first place). The process of opening up a connection to the URL so it may be read line by line has been demonstrated many times throughout this book. When reading the file, only the text between the <HEAD> and </HEAD> tags is required; all the rest can be ignored. Extracting this data is not difficult, with only a small spanner thrown in the works: the header information may stretch over multiple lines.

The necessary data may be extracted in two stages. The first stage is to ignore all text until the <HEAD> string is found. The second stage is to then parse the header section that was retrieved in the first stage. Once the <HEAD> string is found, all subsequent data is copied into a separate string until the </HEAD> string is found. This is demonstrated in example 18.4.

```
DataInputStream In = new DataInputStream(cHost.openStream());
String Line;
StringBuffer headTag = new StringBuffer( 50 );
int index;
boolean bStartFound = false;

while ((Line = In.readLine()) != null){
   if ( bStartFound == false ){
      index = Line.toUpperCase().indexOf( "<HEAD>" );
      if ( index != -1 ){
         bStartFound = true;
         if (Line.toUpperCase().indexOf("</HEAD>") != -1){
```

```
                    headTag.append( Line.substring( index,
                    Line.toUpperCase().indexOf( "</HEAD>")));
            break;
        }
        else
            headTag.append( Line.substring( index, Line.length()));
    }
}
else{
    index = Line.toUpperCase().indexOf( "</HEAD>" );
    if (index == -1)
        headTag.append( Line );
    else{
        headTag.append( Line.substring( 0, index+7) );
        break;
    }
}
}
```

Example 18.4   Extracting the <HEAD> tag

As you can see, a boolean variable holds the information about whether the starting
tag has been found. If it is found, then the data from the tag to the end of the line is copied
into a separate string instance. However, it also checks to see whether the end tag is also
present on the same line. This ensures only the data between the two tags is copied, and
nothing else. The method indexOf(…) from the String class is used to determine the
location of each tag.

Note: The StringBuffer class is designed to be used when building strings of
unknown lengths. For example, it is very inefficient to keep appending to the String
class, since an instance of String has to be created for each addition. The String-
Buffer class allocates a buffer of characters; when it's filled, it is automatically resized to
take the new data into account. After the string has been created, the StringBuffer can
be converted into a String instance.

Once the end header tag is found, the header information is contained inside one
String variable, which makes subsequent parsing much easier since the extra complication
of looking for line feeds is eliminated. Assuming a separate method is created for parsing
the head string, and the string is passed in through the _hd variable, then extraction of the
page title is a simple matter of using the indexOf(…) methods again. The title is declared
using the <TITLE> and </TITLE> tags and if such a tag exists, then it is extracted as
shown in example 18.5.

```
int idx = _hd.toUpperCase().indexOf("<TITLE>" );
if ( idx != -1 )
hostName = _hd.substring( idx+7,_hd.toUpperCase().indexOf("</TITLE>") );
```
Example 18.5   Extracting the title information

CHAPTER 18   SEARCH ENGINE

Extracting the title is relatively easy, when compared to determining the keywords or description. The keywords are formatted as a list of comma-separated values which are embedded inside a META tag. The META tag is a special tag that describes attributes about the document as a whole and performs no formatting changes to the file. It is in the following format:

```
<META NAME="name" CONTENT="xxx">
```

In the case of describing HTML documents, two special META names exist: keywords and description. If the keywords section exists, then the call to find it using `indexOf(…)` will yield a nonnegative result. From here, all the keywords that have been listed in the META tag are taken from the CONTENT field and placed in a separate string instance. This string is then used to create an instance of `StringTokenizer` that will allow easy extraction of the delimited keyword list.

```
idx = _hd.toUpperCase().indexOf( "<META NAME=\"KEYWORDS" );

if ( idx != -1 ){
  idx = _hd.toUpperCase().indexOf( "CONTENT=\"", idx+1 );
  String keylist = _hd.substring(idx+9,_hd.indexOf("\"",idx+10));
  StringTokenizer st = new StringTokenizer( keylist, "," );
  KeywordNo           = st.countTokens();
  KeywordList         = new String[ KeywordNo ];
  int x = 0;
  while( st.hasMoreTokens() ){
    KeywordList[x] = st.nextToken().toLowerCase().trim();
    x++;
  }
}
```

Example 18.6   Extracting the keyword list

The keyword list is stored in an array of `Strings` that has to be allocated for a certain size. One of the best features of the `StringTokenizer` class is the ability to determine the number of tokens before parsing commences. This enables the array to be created to be the exact size for the number of tokens it has to store. Once they are created, each token is extracted one at a time and placed into the array of keywords, as shown in example 18.6.

Extracting the page description is a simple matter of copying all of the CONTENT section from the DESCRIPTION tag. This is demonstrated in example 18.7.

```
idx = _hd.toUpperCase().indexOf( "<META NAME=\"DESCRIPTION" );

if ( idx != -1 ){
  idx = _hd.toUpperCase().indexOf( "CONTENT=\"", idx+1 );
  Description = _hd.substring(idx+9,_hd.indexOf("\"", idx+10));
}
```

Example 18.7   Extracting the description

The extraction of all the details discussed above demonstrates the excellent string-handling functions offered as part of the standard Java library.

18.3.2 Searching the data

With a number of site records stored in the list, the user can be given access to search the list using a very simple two-field HTML form, as shown in figure 18.2. Using this query form, the user will be able to specify single and multiple keyword searches. Multiple keywords are separated using the plus ("+") symbol. Using the plus symbol to separate words (as opposed to using a space), the user can search for complete phrases instead of single words.

Figure 18.2 Searching the site records

Once it is submitted to the servlet, the query string must be transformed into a form that can be readily used and searched for. Since a number of keywords can be presented at once, they are split up and placed into the Vector data structure. This is accomplished by creating an instance of StringTokenizer using the "+" symbol as the separator, and trimming the leading and trailing spaces from each token, as shown in example 18.8.

```
Vector kList = new Vector( 3 );
StringTokenizer st = new StringTokenizer( _kw, "+" );
while ( st.hasMoreTokens() )
  kList.addElement( st.nextToken().trim() );
```
Example 18.8 Preparing the query parameters

Each site record is held in a list using the `Vector` data structure. Since each site record is represented as a class, a method can be provided that will accept the data structure of keywords as a parameter and return the number of hits that are found. If this function is provided, then parsing through the list of site records is a simple matter of setting up an `Enumeration` class that will call the `find(...)` method from each site record, as shown in example 18.9.

```
Enumeration E = siteList.elements();
Vector foundList = new Vector( 4 );
cSiteInfo sInfo;
int freq;
while( E.hasMoreElements() ){
  sInfo = (cSiteInfo)E.nextElement();
  freq  = sInfo.find( kList );

  if ( freq != 0 )
    foundList.addElement( new cFoundSite( sInfo, freq ) );
}
```
Example 18.9   Running the query

A number of parameters are stored for each site record that exists; these parameters include the URL, description, title, and keyword list. Users can search using any of these parameters. The `find(...)` method is implemented as part of the `cSiteInfo` class and is shown in example 18.10.

Each keyword the user has specified in his search query has to be checked against the URL, the title, the description, and the keyword list. This implementation of the search will assume multiple keywords have been specified by the user; it will then perform an exclusive AND—meaning only the sites containing all the keywords will be considered a successful match.

Each keyword in the user list is checked one at a time. Checking for the presence of a keyword can be done using the now infamous `indexOf(...)` method, and by comparing the value returned.

```
public int find( Vector _keys ){
  int freq=0;
  Enumeration E = _keys.elements();
  String key;
  boolean foundSingle=false;

  while ( E.hasMoreElements() ){
    key = ((String)E.nextElement()).toLowerCase();
    foundSingle = false;

    //- Check the URL
    if (cHost.toString().toLowerCase().indexOf( key )!=-1){
      freq++;
      foundSingle = true;
    }
```

```
    //- Check the Title
    if ( hostName.toLowerCase().indexOf( key ) != -1 ){
      freq++;
      foundSingle = true;
    }

    //- Check the Description
    if ( Description.toLowerCase().indexOf( key ) != -1){
      freq++;
      foundSingle = true;
    }

    //- Check the keywords
    for( int x=0; x<KeywordNo; x++ ){
      if ( KeywordList[x].indexOf( key ) != -1 ){
        freq++;
        foundSingle = true;
      }
    }

    if ( foundSingle == false ){
      freq = 0;
      break;
    }
  }

  return freq;
}
```
Example 18.10 Performing the search

For each iteration of each user keyword, a `boolean` flag is set. If the keyword is found in the URL, title, description, or keyword list, then the flag is set to `true`. If the keyword is found, then the next user keyword is processed; otherwise, the search ends and a value of `0` is returned. For each keyword that is found, a value is incremented, and that value is then returned to the calling method for later processing.

Displaying results   Traversing the list and searching out the site records that satisfy the user's query will yield a data set that the user will want to print out. For each record that produces a hit count greater than one, the reference to the file will be stored in a separate list. This list will be used to produce the output for the user. In order to give the set of results some sort of priority, the number of hits found is stored with the site record. One of the best ways of doing this would be to have each site record hold an additional variable that stores the last hit count. This would not work if the servlet were to be accessed by several users at once—each user will have a different set of query words, and when one search is run, all previous hit counts will be overwritten.

```
class cFoundSite extends Object{
  public cSiteInfo cSite;
  public intfreq;
public cFoundSite( cSiteInfo _s, int _f ){
    cSite= _s;
    freq= _f;
  }
}
```
Example 18.11   The wrapper class for the result set

To get around this problem, a wrapper class is created to store the site record reference along with the number of hits it received. This class is shown in example 18.11. The resulting `Vector` list produced after the search is then passed to the output method, which is responsible for displaying the results to the client.

```
Out.println( "Keywords:<B> " );
Enumeration E = _kList.elements();
while ( E.hasMoreElements() )
  Out.println( (String)E.nextElement() + " : " );

Out.println( "</B><BR><BR><CENTER><HR WIDTH=50%></CENTER><BR>" );
E = _fList.elements();
cSiteInfo sInfo;
cFoundSite sFd;
while ( E.hasMoreElements() ){
  sFd = (cFoundSite)E.nextElement();
  sInfo = sFd.cSite;
  Out.println( "<FONT SIZE=-1>(" + sFd.freq + ")</FONT>" );
  Out.println( "<FONT SIZE=+1><A HREF="+sInfo.cHost+">
                            "+sInfo.hostName+"</A></FONT>" );
  Out.println( "<I><FONT SIZE=-1>"+sInfo.cHost+"</FONT></I><BR>" );
  Out.println( sInfo.Description + "<BR><BR>" );
}
```
Example 18.12   Displaying the results

As with the majority of the commercial sites, each site that has been included in the result set is printed out along with the site title and the description. This gives the user a small overview of the sites so he won't have to visit each one. Example 18.12 shows the formatting of the HTML tags that produces the output illustrated in figure 18.3.

18.3.3   Complete servlet source

Example 18.13 shows the complete source code for the global search engine servlet. The `service(...)` makes a program control switch depending on which form it is processing. If the form is an addition to the list, then the `processForm(...)` is called; otherwise, the `performSearch(...)` is executed.

Since the servlet is producing an HTML page to give feedback to the client, the servlet is based on the `HttpServlet` class. When the servlet is performing a search, the number of milliseconds since the epoc is recorded before it begins, as is the number recorded after

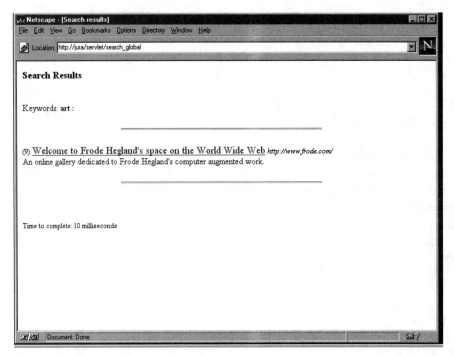

Figure 18.3 Output of the search results

the search has completed. This gives the user some feedback regarding the time taken to complete the search.

```java
import java.io.*;
import java.util.*;
import java.net.*;
import javax.servlet.*;
import javax.servlet.http.*;

public class search_global extends HttpServlet{
  private Vector siteList;

  public void init(ServletConfig _config) throws ServletException{
    super.init(_config);
    siteList = new Vector( 10 );
  }

  public void service(HttpServletRequest _req, HttpServletResponse _res )
                          throws ServletException, IOException {
    if ( _req.getParameter( "add" ) != null )
      processForm( _req, _res );
    else
      performSearch( _req.getParameter( "keyword" ), _res );
  }
```

```
    private void performSearch( String _kw, HttpServletResponse _res )
                              throws IOException {
      long startTime = System.currentTimeMillis();

      Vector kList = new Vector( 3 );
      StringTokenizer st = new StringTokenizer( _kw, "+" );
      while ( st.hasMoreTokens() )
        kList.addElement( st.nextToken().trim() );

      Enumeration E = siteList.elements();
      Vector foundList = new Vector( 4 );
      cSiteInfosInfo;
      intfreq;
      while( E.hasMoreElements() ){
        sInfo = (cSiteInfo)E.nextElement();
        freq  = sInfo.find( kList );

        if ( freq != 0 )
          foundList.addElement( new cFoundSite( sInfo, freq ) );
      }

      long totalTime = System.currentTimeMillis()- startTime;
      formatResults( foundList, kList, totalTime, _res );
    }

    private void formatResults( Vector _fList, Vector _kList,
                               long time, HttpServletResponse _res )
                               throws IOException{
      _res.setContentType("text/html");
      PrintWriter Out = _res.getWriter();

      Out.println( "<HTML><HEAD><TITLE>Search results</TITLE></HEAD>" );
      Out.println( "<BODY><H3>Search Results</H3><BR>" );
      Out.println( "Keywords:<B> " );
      Enumeration E = _kList.elements();
      while ( E.hasMoreElements() )
        Out.println( (String)E.nextElement() + " : " );

      Out.println( "</B><BR><BR><CENTER><HR WIDTH=50%></CENTER><BR>" );
      E = _fList.elements();
      cSiteInfo sInfo;
      cFoundSite sFd;
      while ( E.hasMoreElements() ){
        sFd = (cFoundSite)E.nextElement();
        sInfo = sFd.cSite;
        Out.println( "<FONT SIZE=-1>(" + sFd.freq + ")</FONT>" );
        Out.println( "<FONT SIZE=+1><A HREF=" + sInfo.cHost + ">"
                              + sInfo.hostName + "</A></FONT>" );
        Out.println( "<I><FONT SIZE=-1>" + sInfo.cHost
                              + "</FONT></I><BR>" );
        Out.println( sInfo.Description + "<BR><BR>" );
      }
if ( _fList.size() == 0 )
        Out.println( "<I><B>No sites found!</I></B><BR><BR>");
```

```
Out.println( "<CENTER><HR WIDTH=50%></CENTER>" );
    Out.println( "<BR><BR><BR><FONT SIZE=-1>Time to complete: "
                + time + " milliseconds</FONT>" );
    Out.println( "</BODY></HTML>" );
    Out.flush();
}


private void processForm( HttpServletRequest _req,
                HttpServletResponse _res ) throws IOException{
    //- Processes the form to add new site information
    cSiteInfo sInfo = new cSiteInfo( _req.getParameter( "url" ),
                            _req.getParameter( "name" ),
                            _req.getParameter( "email" ) );
    _res.setContentType("text/html");
    PrintWriter Out = _res.getWriter();

    Out.println( "<HTML><HEAD><TITLE>Submission results</TITLE>
                </HEAD>" );
    Out.println( "<BODY><CENTER><TABLE BORDER=0>" );
    Out.println( "<TR><TD ALIGN=RIGHT><FONT COLOR=#0000FF SIZE=+1>
                URL:</FONT></TD><TD ALIGN=LEFT>" + sInfo.cHost +
                "</TD></TR>" );
    Out.println( "<TR><TD ALIGN=RIGHT><FONT COLOR=#0000FF SIZE=+1> Title:
                </FONT></TD><TD ALIGN=LEFT>" + sInfo.hostName +
                "</TD></TR>" );
    Out.println( "<TR><TD ALIGN=RIGHT><FONT COLOR=#0000FF SIZE=+1>
                Description:</FONT></TD><TD ALIGN=LEFT>" +
                sInfo.Description + "</TD></TR>" );
    Out.println( "<TR><TD ALIGN=RIGHT><FONT COLOR=#0000FF SIZE=+1>
                Admin: </FONT></TD><TD
                ALIGN=LEFT>" + sInfo.adminName +
                "</TD></TR>" );
    Out.println( "<TR><TD ALIGN=RIGHT><FONT COLOR=#0000FF SIZE=+1>
                Adim Email:</FONT></TD><TD ALIGN=LEFT>" + sInfo.admin
                Email + "</TD></TR>" );
    Out.println( "<TR><TD ALIGN=RIGHT><FONT COLOR=#0000FF SIZE=+1>
                Keywords:</FONT></TD><TD ALIGN=LEFT>" );

    for ( int x=0; x < sInfo.KeywordNo; x++ )
      Out.println( sInfo.KeywordList[x] + "," );

    Out.println( "</TD></TR>" );
    Out.println( "<TR><TD ALIGN=RIGHT><FONT COLOR=#0000FF
                SIZE=+1>Checked: </FONT></TD><TD ALIGN=LEFT>"
                + sInfo.lastChecked.toGMTString() +
                "</TD></TR>" );

    Out.println( "</TD></TR></TABLE></CENTER></BODY></HTML>" );
    Out.flush();
```

```
    if ( sInfo.cHost != null )
      siteList.addElement( sInfo );
  }
}
```

Example 18.13   The complete code for the servlet

18.4   Local search servlet

One of the more useful facilities a site can offer to its visitors is a search engine that operates within the confines of the site. This can be an invaluable service, especially for sites
that offer a high content value and have frequently updated HTML pages. Providing a
simple search mechanism for the site allows the reader to quickly locate the information he
is after. This section offers a very simple search engine that can be used to provide this service on any web site supporting servlets.

There are many ways to implement such a search engine, and each has its own advantages and disadvantages. One method would be to catalogue all the data from all the pages
on the site and place the results into a separate database that could be used to perform efficient data searches. This is one of the best options for large sites, but it is sometimes
impractical for smaller sites. The issue of regularly updating the database also rears its ugly
head. If the site is changing often, then the database needs to be reindexed every time. For
these reasons, a separate database will not be used in this example.

This then leads to another decision that must be made—how to transverse the files.
This can be achieved in two ways. The first method starts with the root URL, then visits
each link within the root URL and checks its source file, until all the links have been
checked. The advantage of this method is that only the pages that can be accessed through
clickable links will be checked. However, the disadvantage is also the fact that only the
pages that can be accessed through clickable links will be checked. The other method is to
open up the directory the root file is contained within and to check all the HTML files.

In this servlet example, the directory where all the HTML files are stored will be
opened, and for each one, a search for the user's keywords will be made. This has the
advantage, or disadvantage, depending on how you look at it, of picking up all HTML
files, even the ones that have not been hyperlinked to any other page.

18.4.1   Searching through the files

Running through all the HTML files contained within the root document directory has
already been detailed in chapter 16, which covers autolinks. The same directory example
engine is being used in this servlet, with a few minor changes. Example 18.17 shows the
complete servlet code, with the directory searching occurring in the main `service(…)`
method. Only this time, when a file is found for processing, its keywords are searched, as
opposed to their being linked against a glossary file.

Earlier, in the `autolink` servlet, the user specified the top-level directory from which
the example began. However, in this servlet, the root directory has to be manually entered
or hardcoded into the servlet. Hardcoding any value into a program is considered sacrilege

by some, and in order to help those that feel this way to sleep a little easier, a much cleaner solution will be provided.

```
File RootDir = new File( _req.getRealPath( "/" ) );
if ( RootDir.isDirectory() == false ){
  System.out.println( "Invalid directory" );
  _res.setStatus( HttpServletResponse.SC_NO_CONTENT );
  return;
}
```
Example 18.14   Determining the root document directory

All documents that the web server displays reside under one directory, which is known as the document root directory. Files outside of this directory are not generally accessible to the server. Whenever a user makes a request for a page, it is relative to this document root. One of the class methods for mapping virtual directories to real directories is the `HttpServletRequest` class `getRealPath(…)` method. This takes a virtual path and translates it to an absolute path on the local system. So, by passing in the virtual root directory of "/," the absolute path of the document root directory will be returned. From here the search engine will transverse through the directory structure.

18.4.2   Searching the data

The search engine presented earlier in this chapter that was implemented for the global sites used an exclusive AND policy on the keyword list that the user entered. This version of the search engine will use the exclusive OR policy, meaning an HTML file need only contain at least one of the keywords to be considered a successful match.

Every file that is found is opened and read line by line. As before, this procedure is closely based on the `autolink` servlet that was demonstrated earlier in this book, with a few minor adjustments. The first change is in the class used to read the contents of the file. With this servlet, the file is to be read only and not modified, therefore rendering most of the functionality of the `RandomAccessFile` class redundant. The `FileInputStream` class is used instead.

As before, certain HTML tags have to be ignored, and for this reason the services of the `cLineParse` class, developed in conjunction with the `autolink` servlet, will be called upon again. This class takes in a line of text and parses the line into tokens. It is a more advanced version of the `StringTokenizer` class, as it is intended to extract both words and HTML tags.

```
DataInputStream In = new DataInputStream( new FileInputStream(
                             filename ) );
String LineIn, token;
boolean bValid = true;
Enumeration E;
cLineParse lp;

while ( (LineIn = In.readLine()) != null ){
  lp = new cLineParse( LineIn.toUpperCase() );
```

```
      while ( (token=lp.nextToken()) != "" ){
        if ( token.indexOf( "<" ) != -1 && (
              token.indexOf( "<A" ) != -1 ||
              token.indexOf( "<APP" ) != -1 ||
              token.indexOf( "<SER" ) != -1 ))
          bValid = false;
        else if (token.indexOf( "<" ) != -1 && (
                  token.indexOf( "</A" ) != -1 ||
                  token.indexOf( "</APP" ) != -1 ||
                  token.indexOf( "</SER" ) != -1 ))
          bValid = true;
        else if ( bValid ){
          E = _klist.elements();
          String key;
          while ( E.hasMoreElements() ){
            key = ((String)E.nextElement()).toUpperCase();
            if ( token.indexOf( key ) != -1 )
              frequency++;
        }
      }
    }
  }
In.close();
```
Example 18.15   Searching the file

The method shown in example 18.15 shows the parsing of the file. When a valid
token is found, it is checked against the list of keywords that the user supplied to the servlet. As before, the keywords are packaged into a `Vector` data structure that allows many
keywords to be easily searched for. Each time a keyword is found, a counter is incremented; this counter is returned to the calling procedure at the end of the file.

The calling method of this class looks at the return value. If it is nonzero, then it can
assume that the file did indeed contain a keyword from the user's search criteria. The full
path of this file is then stored in a `Vector` class.

```
class cPage extends Object{
  public int  freq;
  public File cFile;

  public cPage( int _freq, File _cFile ){
    freq = _freq;
    cFile = _cFile;
  }
}
```
Example 18.16   The wrapper class for the results

Displaying results   Once all the files have been opened and checked, the next step is
to report the findings back to the user, as shown in figure 18.4.

Earlier, we had additional information available (such as the page's title and description) but the local search does not have the luxury of such data. It can only display the file
name and the number of times the keywords appeared in the file. One of the main reasons

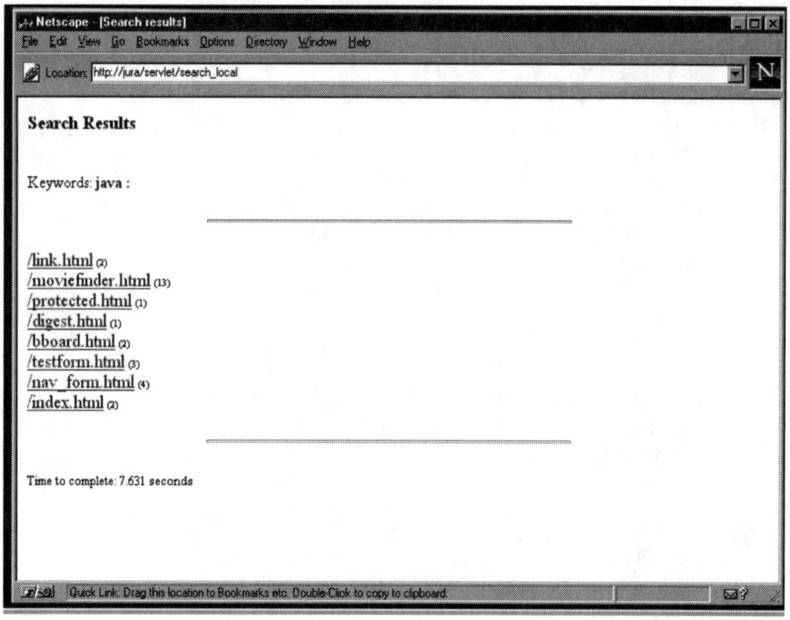

Figure 18.4 Search result

to use a search engine such as this one is to quickly locate files. This is achieved by allowing the user to click on any one of the search results to display that page. Providing such a feature is a simple matter of making the file a hyperlink.

The file name that is stored is an absolute file name, and it is not of any use to any browser outside of the machine it is run on.

```
C:\JavaWebServer1.1\public_html\history\index.html
```

This pathname needs to be converted back into the virtual path that can be accessed through any client browser. Unfortunately, the servlet API doesn't provide any methods for converting back from real to virtual. But doing so isn't difficult.

We know that the file in question is definitely under the document root, in a directory that is accessible, assuming there aren't any security restrictions. By removing the real path of the document root from the file name, and replacing it with the "/" symbol, the file will be accessible. For example, the "index.html" illustrated above would become:

```
/history/index.html
```

The browser would then correctly parse and collect the correct document. This removal can be done using

```
link = "/" + link.substring( link.indexOf( _root ) + _root.length(),
link.length() );
```

assuming the variable link contained the absolute pathname of the file in the first place. By applying this to every file name that is displayed in the search results, the user can easily navigate himself to the corresponding page.

18.4.3 Complete servlet source

Example 18.17 shows the complete servlet source code for the local search engine. The `service(…)` method is where the form is processed and the search is run from. Keeping all the variables inside this method ensures that when the servlet is accessed by many users at once, each thread of execution is kept safe from the others.

```
import java.io.*;
import java.util.*;
import javax.servlet.*;
import javax.servlet.http.*;

public class search_local extends HttpServlet{
  public void service( HttpServletRequest _req, HttpServletResponse
                                 _res )
                               throws ServletException, IOException {
    long startTime = System.currentTimeMillis();

    File RootDir = new File( _req.getRealPath( "/" ) );
    if ( RootDir.isDirectory() == false ){
      System.out.println( "Invalid directory" );
      _res.setStatus( HttpServletResponse.SC_NO_CONTENT );
      return;
    }
Vector kList = new Vector( 3 );
    StringTokenizer st = new StringTokenizer( _req.getParameter(
                                 "keyword" ), "+" );
    while ( st.hasMoreTokens() )
      kList.addElement( st.nextToken().trim() );

    //- Run through list
    Vector toBeDone= new Vector( 10 );
    Vector found= new Vector( 10 );

    String dir[] = RootDir.list( new htmlFilter() );
    cDirInfo tX = new cDirInfo( RootDir, dir );

    toBeDone.addElement( tX );
    while ( toBeDone.isEmpty() == false ){
      tX = (cDirInfo)toBeDone.firstElement();

      for ( int x=0; x<tX.dirList.length();x++){
        File newFile = new File(tX.rootDir,tX.dirList[x]);
        if ( newFile.isDirectory() ){
          File t = new File( tX.rootDir,tX.dirList[x] );
          String a[] = newFile.list( new htmlFilter() );
          toBeDone.addElement( new cDirInfo( t, a ) );
        }else{
          int freq = searchFile( kList, newFile );
```

```
              if ( freq != 0 )
                 found.addElement( new cPage( freq, newFile ) );
           }
        }
        toBeDone.removeElementAt(0);
        dir = null;
     }
     long totalTime = System.currentTimeMillis() - startTime;
     formatResults(found,kList,totalTime,_req.getRealPath( "/" ), _res );
  }

  private void formatResults( Vector _fList, Vector _kList,
                              long time, String _root,
                              HttpServletResponse _res )
                              throws IOException{
    _res.setContentType("text/html");
    PrintWriter Out = _res.getWriter();

    Out.println( "<HTML><HEAD><TITLE>Search results</TITLE></HEAD>" );
    Out.println( "<BODY><H3>Search Results</H3><BR>" );

    Out.println( "Keywords:<B> " );
    Enumeration E = _kList.elements();
    while ( E.hasMoreElements() )
      Out.println( (String)E.nextElement() + " : " );

    Out.println( "</B><BR><BR><CENTER><HR WIDTH=50%></CENTER><BR>" );
    E = _fList.elements();
    cPage sPage;
    String link;
    while ( E.hasMoreElements() ){
      sPage = (cPage)E.nextElement();
      link  = sPage.cFile.toString();
      link  = "/" + link.substring( link.indexOf( _root )
                          +_root.length(), link.length() );
      Out.println( "<FONT SIZE=+1><A HREF=" + link + ">" + link +
                          "</A></FONT>" );
      Out.println( "<FONT SIZE=-2>(" + sPage.freq + ")</FONT><BR>" );
    }

    if ( _fList.size() == 0 )
      Out.println( "<I><B>No sites found!</I></B><BR>");

    Out.println( "<BR><CENTER><HR WIDTH=50%></CENTER>" );
    Out.println( "<BR><FONT SIZE=-1>Time to complete: " +
                          ((double)time/1000) + " seconds</FONT>" );
    Out.println( "</BODY></HTML>" );
    Out.flush();
  }

  private int searchFile( Vector _klist, File _filename ){
    //- Links the file
    intfrequency=0;
    try{
```

```
      DataInputStream In = new DataInputStream(
                          new FileInputStream( _filename ) );
      String LineIn, token;
      boolean bValid = true;
      Enumeration E;
      cLineParse lp;

      while ( (LineIn = In.readLine()) != null ){
        lp = new cLineParse( LineIn.toUpperCase() );

        while ( (token=lp.nextToken()) != "" ){
          if (   token.indexOf( "<" ) != -1 && (
                 token.indexOf( "<A" ) != -1 ||
                 token.indexOf( "<HE" ) != -1 ||
                 token.indexOf( "<APP" ) != -1 ||
                 token.indexOf( "<SER" ) != -1 ||
                 token.indexOf( "<TEX" ) != -1  ))
            bValid  = false;
          else if ( token.indexOf( "<" ) != -1 && (
                 token.indexOf( "</A" ) != -1 ||
                 token.indexOf( "</HE" ) != -1 ||
                 token.indexOf( "</APP" ) != -1 ||
                 token.indexOf( "</SER" ) != -1 ||
                 token.indexOf( "</TEX" ) != -1  ))
            bValid  = true;
          else if ( bValid ){
            E = _klist.elements();
            String key;
            while ( E.hasMoreElements() ){
              key = ((String)E.nextElement()).toUpperCase();
              if ( token.indexOf( key ) != -1 )
                frequency++;
            }
          }
        }
      }
      In.close();
    }
    catch( IOException E ){}
    return frequency;
  }
}
```

Example 18.17   The complete servlet source code

18.5   Summary and possible enhancements

This chapter introduced the concept of search engines and showed the two broad categories a search engine can fit into: global and local. Along with the different search algorithms, the searching methods employed by many sites were also addressed, and the advantages and disadvantages of each were discussed.

The search engine provided for a global search was presented; it had a very rich function set, compared to the size of the servlet. A number of enhancements could be added to make the engine more user-friendly:

- Improved submission form
  At the moment, the user can only enter the site URL and hope the servlet will find all the necessary information in the header field. However, if no data is found, then the facility for the user to reenter the title, description, and keyword list must exist.

- Ordered result list
  Currently, the result list is printed out in the same order in which the sites are found; it is not ordered by the number of hits each site yielded. Sorting the list before the output routine is run would rectify this.

- Data storage
  The servlet stores all the site information in memory, and as the number of sites increases, so do the memory requirements. A much better way would be to employ a structured database engine that the servlet could access via the JDBC API; this would improve both general maintenance and search speed.

- Update mechanism
  There is nothing worse than a search engine that produces URLs that are no longer valid. A date field is given in the site record class to determine the last time a site was visited. A facility could be given to allow the site administrator to periodically visit all the sites, updating the records as necessary. This would ensure the integrity of the information held.

In addition to the global search engine, a version that operates within the confines of one site was implemented. This version opened up each file and ran through the token list, searching out the keyword list. As with the global engine, the local engine could benefit from additional features:

- Database
  Every time a search is run, each file is opened up, read, and closed again. This is very time-consuming, especially for larger sites with many thousands of HTML files. It would be much better to collate all this information inside a structured database and have the database engine perform the actual search.

- Phrase search
  At the moment, the search engine will only search for single keywords. Modification to include complete phrases would mean only slightly changing the algorithm for reading the tokens.

- Improved output
  When a search has been completed, only the file names are printed in a list. It would be much better if, along with the file name, a small snippet of the file was printed alongside the name, to give the user the context in which the keyword was found.

For small sites which have fewer than thirty HTML files, this local search servlet is a very simple addition to a web site, and it makes the information presented more accessible.

C H A P T E R   1 9

Client-side data

CHAPTER CONCEPTS

- CGI programs have long relied on cookies to remember client session information. Discover what a cookie is and how it can be used with servlets.

- Learn about server-side cookies, which are similar to client cookies, except all the manipulation and storage is performed on the server.

- Understand the mechanics of session management, which is another method of storing client information. Session tracking is built right into the API.

It's human nature to want to be a part of something, whether it's a club, a gang, or a relationship. It's comforting to go somewhere where everyone knows your name. People want to belong.

For this reason, many online communities are beginning to emerge all over the world. In an online community, a user first submits basic details about himself; sometimes he also has to pay a fee. He is then granted access to many online facilities where he will be guaranteed the presence of a particular service or person. But as more and more people join the available communities, a problem has surfaced: how do you keep the bad guys out and the good guys in?

Communities or restricted areas are usually controlled via a username and password combination; the user has to enter a username and/or password before gaining access to a particular area of the site. The restricted area may contain many things, including online picture galleries and user chat areas.

A restricted area can be protected in one of two ways: using HTTP cookies, or using access control lists. This chapter will discuss the cookies method, with a look at the session management introduced to the servlet API.

19.1 Cookies

The HTTP protocol, as you know by now, is stateless, meaning each request for data is completely independent and has no influence or memory of past or future requests. From the server's point of view, this makes things rather easy, as there's no need to store information between each request. However, there are instances where this isn't always the desired behavior. Early CGI programs found it extremely difficult to store state information, due to the very nature of the script languages many server-side programs were written in.

One technique that was used to store session data was to hide variables in outgoing HTML forms, which would then be sent back to the server when the user posted the form. (This technique has been demonstrated in many examples throughout this book.) This was sufficient when dealing with forms.

The server program could place important information inside the form. It would then be posted back to the server with the client request, without the need to store the data at the server side. As an example, the task of filling in long forms can be split into a series of smaller steps, with the answers from the previous stages hidden in fields in the current form. This way, the script could be written to process the complete form at the end, with all the information being presented in one posting. But more often than not, state information was required to be stored outside of the HTML form world. This method, therefore, quickly had its limits.

Netscape came to the same conclusion, and in response, it proposed an addition to the HTTP protocol. This addition was the cookie field. Fortunately, the HTTP protocol was flexible enough to allow for user-defined fields, without the need to rewrite every server in the world. Only the browsers needed to be modified to recognize this new HTTP header field.

A cookie operates on the same principle as the hidden fields inside an HTML form. The server sends out a cookie, which represents a particular piece of textual data totaling no more than 4096 bytes in size. This data is accepted by the client and is stored locally on the client's machine. Then, with every request the client makes to the server for resources, the cookie is sent back to the server inside the HTTP header, allowing for any CGI or servlet program to read the data inside and act accordingly.

Therefore, cookies operate just like the hidden fields found in HTML forms, except cookies are sent for every request and not just in response to a form posting. The cookie is a small snippet of information the server asks the client to store on its behalf (such as the username or the last time the user visited the site).

Note The accepting of cookies isn't mandatory. Both Netscape and Microsoft have options within their browsers to disable the acceptance of cookies. All this means is that the client is refusing to store any data for the server, and that for every request that occurs no data is sent to the server in the HTTP cookie field.

On the face of it, cookies sound like an enormous security risk since they allow textual data to be stored on a client machine. In reality, it's quite the opposite: cookies present no risk at all to the client's machine or data. A cookie cannot read any data, nor can it transmit a virus. The cookie is merely a small chunk of data—the browser never attempts to execute it, and it is only passed from one location to another. For the same reason, the cookie has no way to write or access any other resource on the client machine. It is unlike a Java applet or ActiveX control; these technologies run code on the client machine, while a cookie is merely a data depository.

Cookies are commonplace in many of the mainstream web sites. They are used in a variety of different application areas, ranging from providing user registration services to online shopping baskets. The online shopping basket is one of the best examples where cookies can be employed to ease the burden on the server. Without cookies, the server would have to maintain all the shopping baskets on the server. This could amount to a very large volume of user data that may or may not be used. As a user is browsing a shopping site, he can choose various items and place them in his virtual shopping basket by simply clicking on them. The items are then sent to the server.

Instead of the server storing the user's selection, a cookie is created with the current selection, and it is sent back to the client to be stored. A single cookie maintains the list of items the shopper has chosen, with the server removing or adding items accordingly. When the user has finished shopping, he can go to the checkout, where the cookie will be presented back to the server with the complete list of items. The items are then processed and paid for. Advantages are found on both sides of the transaction. The client has the ability to take his time while choosing items, without the fear of the server emptying the shopping cart, even if the network connection is lost. The server has the advantage of not having to store all the redundant shopping baskets which may never make it to the checkout. Managing the shopping carts comes down to a simple cookie management program that will create, modify, and delete cookies.

Note The servlet-based online shopping example can be seen in a later chapter. It does not use cookies; instead, it stores the information on the server. The reason cookies are not used is to give you the chance to see the two different methods and for you to make up your own mind.

Cookies can be used in limitless application areas. In this chapter, the cookie technique will be used to validate a user before he can gain access to an online community. But before we get into the implementation of the servlet, let's take a closer look at what a cookie actually is, and what properties it holds.

19.1.1 Inside a cookie

A cookie takes the form of a single text string inside the HTTP header. The cookie has a number of properties associated with it. When a cookie is sent to the client for storage, you can set a number of options to control the cookie's life—these include the length of time the cookie is valid for and the domain to which the cookie should be sent. A cookie being sent out from the server to the client takes the following format:

```
Set-Cookie: name=value; expires=DATE; path=PATH; domain=DOMAIN; secure
```

Each cookie being set can only support one name/value pairing, as per the cookie specification. For additional data to be set, a new cookie has to be set. The maximum number of cookies that can be set in any one session is twenty, but the specification does not recommend going anywhere near this limit, in case other services are using the HTTP protocol.

Data The information the server wishes to store in the cookie is placed in the cookie's data space. The name of the data can be any nonreserved word as long as it doesn't contain any spaces. The data may not have any spaces associated with it. The maximum amount of data that may be stored is 4096 bytes. But as with the limit for cookies, it is advised that you not use up all of the allocated space. If you need more than 4096 bytes, then you should use server-side cookies, as described in the next section. An example of this data format would be using it to store some information about a user:

```
username=kristen;
email=kristen@n-ary.com;
```

Expiry date One of the nicest features of cookies is the expiry date. It specifies how long a cookie has to live. When the cookie does expire, the browser deletes the cookie so it is no longer sent out. The date is expressed as a text string synchronized to GMT (Greenwich Mean Time). If this field is left out when the cookie is written, or if the date in the field has already expired, then the cookie will be valid only for the length of the user's session. As soon as he shuts down his browser, the cookie is removed. The code that follows will make a cookie expire on Tuesday, December 9, 1998, at 6:20 a.m.

```
expires=Tuesday, 9-Dec-98 06:20:00 GMT;
```

Path   Not only can you specify how long a cookie will live for, you can also control when it will be sent. The path attribute specifies the paths for which the cookie will be sent out when the user accesses any URL from that path downward. For example, assume the following path is set in a cookie:

```
path=/training/course;
```

Whenever the user accesses a resource from the path

```
http://www.n-ary.com/training/course/index.html
```

the cookie will be sent. All subdirectories under this path will also trigger the transmission of the cookie. If the path field is left out, all requests to that host will trigger the cookie's being sent to the server.

Domain   The domain attribute controls the domains the cookie will be sent to. For example, a value of

```
domain=.n-ary.com;
```

would control the cookie from being sent to all servers within the n-ary.com domain, which includes servers such as www.n-ary.com and campus.n-ary.com. If, on the other hand, the domain was specified as

```
domain=www.n-ary.com;
```

then the cookie would only be sent to this server, and no other. The domain field must have at least two periods. This stops the cookie from being sent to all .com or .co.uk domains, for example, which would present a potential security risk.

Secure   When transmitted, the cookie is present in the HTTP header and is in its raw text format, thus allowing potential eavesdroppers to listen in and steal the data. Setting the secure attribute ensures the cookie is only sent when the client is talking with a secure server.

19.1.2   *Cookies: untold dangers*

Before we look at how cookies can be sent and received inside servlets, here's a list of some of the operational differences that are present when using cookies.

- When modifying a cookie, the name, domain, and path must match exactly, including case; otherwise, another cookie will be created.

- There's a small bug in Netscape's 1.1 browser: if the path is not set at all, the cookie will not get created.

- The browser will generally only hold a maximum of 300 cookies.

- Only twenty cookies can be set for the same domain and path.

- Microsoft's Internet Explorer requires that the domain be in lower case. Netscape doesn't care about case.

- Some web servers cannot redirect and set a cookie from one header.

These are some of the reasons many sites have opted not to use cookies and look to alternatives. Used wisely, cookies can save you a large amount of time while removing a lot of dependency from the server.

19.1.3 Cookie class

As you may have expected, cookies can be easily used within servlets. There are two different ways a cookie can be used:

1 Manually encode and decode the HTTP header for each cookie that is to be set.

2 Use the `javax.servlet.http.Cookie` class.

Granted, the second method is going to be a lot less error-prone than the first. The `Cookie` class, as you would expect, provides methods for setting the cookie parameters detailed in the previous section. This section will provide a quick overview of the `Cookie` class. The next section will illustrate a complete servlet example that creates and receives cookies.

Methods for storage and retrieval of the standard parameters include the following:

- `Cookie( String _name, String _value )`

  A cookie is created using the constructor which initially sets the cookie to the given name and value.

- `getName()`

  This method returns the name of the data associated with this cookie. Once the cookie is created, the name of the cookie cannot be changed.

- `setValue(String _value) & getValue()`

  These methods are used to set and retrieve the data associated with the cookie. Certain character strings are not allowed in the data field. This class does not encode any of the data, so the validity of the data is your responsibility.

- `setMaxAge(int _sec) & getMaxAge()`

  These methods are used to set and retrieve the expiration date for the cookie. This date is expressed in seconds. A nonzero value will set the expiration date for the cookie the specified number of seconds in the future. A negative value will delete the cookie as soon as the client browser is shut down. A value of zero will delete the cookie as soon as the browser receives the cookie.

- `setPath(String _path) & getPath()`

  These methods are used to set and retrieve the path on the server where the cookie will be sent.

- `setDomain(String _domain) & getDomain()`

  These methods are used to set and retrieve the domain name to which the cookie will be sent.

- `setSecure(boolean _on) & getSecure()`

  This method sets whether the cookie will be used only when communicating with a secure server.

Now that the `Cookie` class has been created and all the necessary parameters are sent, the cookie must then be sent to the client. Cookies can be saved one at a time using the `HttpServletResponse.addCookie` method, which inserts the cookie into the outward-bound HTTP header.

When a cookie has been sent to the server, the servlet can pick it up using the static method `HttpServletRequest.getCookies`. This method will return an array of `Cookie` objects. From this point, all the cookies sent to the servlet can be accessed.

A cookie is deleted from the client by sending the cookie with an expiration value of `0`.

Note It is possible for multiple cookies to be sent with the same name, but with differing data values. If this occurs, then each cookie can be distinguished from the others using the path and domain attributes.

The following section will detail a small servlet that uses the `Cookie` class described above to send and receive cookies.

19.1.4 Building a cookie servlet

This servlet will provide the front-end to a potential web-based user community. In this example, on the first visit, users enter in user names for the community. On subsequent visits they will be taken straight in, without having to enter their names again.

When a user visits the site, the servlet will look for the presence of two cookies: one for the name of the user and one that stores the date he was last at the site. Searching for cookies from the client can be done by calling the `getCookies(...)` method from the `HttpServletRequest` class. This will return an array of `Cookie` objects. If the client hasn't sent any cookies, this method will return a null value.

```
Cookie InCookieList[] = _req.getCookies();
```

Assuming the method doesn't return a null value, the actual cookie values can be retrieved by running through the list of cookies and looking for the cookies that are relevant to this servlet, as shown in example 19.1. Remember, it is not safe to assume that all the cookies are meant for you. You may be running on a shared server and the client may be handling many different cookies for various parts of the system.

```
//- Retrieve the username or send out the form
for (int x = 0; x < InCookieList.length; x++){
  if ( InCookieList[x].getName().equals("username") )
    name = InCookieList[x].getValue();
  else if ( InCookieList[x].getName().equals("timelastvisit") )
    timeOfLastVisit = Long.parseLong(InCookieList[x].getValue());
}
```
Example 19.1   Retrieving the cookie

As you can see, we are looking for two particular cookies: username and timelastvisit. By running through each Cookie object and looking at the name of the value field, we can easily pick out the two relevant data elements. If the user has not been to the site before, then neither cookie will be present, and the user must then enter a new user name. This task can be accomplished by checking to see if the values were set, and if they weren't, by sending out the HTML form for him to specify a user name.

Using the code in example 19.2, both tasks (sending out and processing the form) can be done in one step.

```
if ( name == null || timeOfLastVisit == 0 ){
  name = _req.getParameter( "username" );
  if ( name == null || name.length() == 0 ){
    sendOutLogin( _res );
    return;
  }
}
```
Example 19.2   Determining a new entry

If the data in the cookie was not found, and this servlet isn't processing a response from an HTML form post, then the login page is sent out to the client.

When the user has been to the site before, a new cookie has to be set to reflect the last time he visited. The easiest way to do this is to recreate both cookies again. This is done by creating an instance of the Cookie class, setting the parameters, and then calling the addCookie(...) method from the HttpServletResponse class.

```
outCookie1 = new Cookie( "username", name );
outCookie1.setPath( "/" );
outCookie1.setDomain( ".n-ary.com" );
outCookie1.setMaxAge( 31 * 24 * 60 * 60 );
_res.addCookie( outCookie );
```
Example 19.3   Setting up the cookie

The code in example 19.3 creates a cookie, with a named value of "username." The domain is set to cover all the servers in this domain, with the path set up to ensure the cookie is sent with each client request. The time to live for this cookie is set for one month, which is assumed to be from today's date.

That's it. Using cookies is as simple as that. Once the user has logged in, or revisits the site before the cookie has had a chance to expire, the HTML page in figure 19.1 is generated by the servlet. From here, the user could move on to the restricted part of the community.

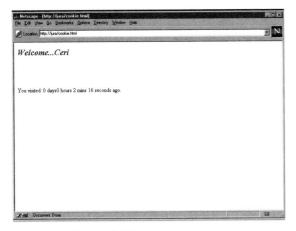

Figure 19.1 Successful login

Complete servlet code   Example 19.4 shows the complete source code for the servlet that uses cookies to validate users. The servlet is based on the `HttpServlet` class; since cookies form part of the HTTP protocol, this class is the best to use.

```
import java.io.*;
import java.util.*;
import javax.servlet.*;
import javax.servlet.http.*;
public class userCookie extends HttpServlet {
  public void service(HttpServletRequest _req, HttpServletResponse _res)
                          throws IOException{
    //- Check to see if the user has registered before
    Cookie InCookieList[], outCookie1 = null, outCookie2 = null;
    String name=null;
    long timeOfLastVisit=0;
    boolean bCookieFound = false;

    InCookieList = _req.getCookies();

    if ( InCookieList != null ){
      //- Retrieve the username or send out the form
      for (int x = 0; x < InCookieList.length; x++){
        if ( InCookieList[x].getName().equals("username") )
          name = InCookieList[x].getValue();
        else if ( InCookieList[x].getName().equals("timelastvisit") )
          timeOfLastVisit = Long.parseLong(InCookieList[x].getValue());
      }
    }
```

```
      if ( name == null || timeOfLastVisit == 0 ){
        name = _req.getParameter( "username" );
        if ( name == null || name.length() == 0 ){
          sendOutLogin( _res );
          return;
        }
      }

      //- Set new cookies value
      outCookie1 = new Cookie( "username", name );
      outCookie1.setPath( "/" );
      outCookie1.setDomain( ".n-ary.com" );
      outCookie1.setMaxAge( 31000 * 24 * 60 * 60 );
     _res.addCookie( outCookie1 );

      outCookie2 = new Cookie( "timelastvisit",
                              System.currentTimeMillis()+"" );
      outCookie2.setPath( "/" );
      outCookie2.setDomain( ".n-ary.com" );
      outCookie2.setMaxAge( 31000 * 24 * 60 * 60 );
     _res.addCookie( outCookie2 );

      //- Display the welcome screen
      LoggedIn( _res, name, timeOfLastVisit );
  }

  private void LoggedIn( HttpServletResponse _res, String _name,
                              long _time ) throws IOException{
    _res.setContentType("text/html");
    PrintWriter Out = _res.getWriter();
    Out.println( "<HTML>" );
    Out.println( "<BODY TEXT=#000000 BGCOLOR=#FFFFFF>" );
    Out.println( "<B><I><FONT COLOR=#0000FF SIZE=+2>Welcome…" + _name );
    Out.println( "<BR></FONT></I></B><BR><BR><BR>" );

    long total = (System.currentTimeMillis()-_time);
    int days  = (int)(total / (1000*60*60*24));
    total     = total - (1000*60*60*24*days);
    int hours = (int)(total / (1000*60*60));
    total     = total - (1000*60*60*hours);
    int mins = (int)(total / (1000*60));
    total     = total - (1000*60*mins);
    int secs  = (int)(total / (1000));
    total     = total - (1000*secs);

    Out.println( "You visited: " + days + " days " + hours + " hours "
                + mins + " mins " + secs + " seconds ago." );
    Out.println( "</BODY></HTML>" );
    Out.flush();
  }

  private void sendOutLogin( HttpServletResponse _res )
                              throws IOException{
    _res.setContentType("text/html");
```

```
    PrintWriter Out = _res.getWriter();
    Out.println( "<HTML>" );
    Out.println( "<BODY TEXT=#000000 BGCOLOR=#FFFFFF>" );
    Out.println( "<B><I><FONT COLOR=#0000FF SIZE=+2
                        Please enter you name</FONT></I></B>" );
    Out.println( "<FORM METHOD=GET ACTION=/cookie.html>" );
    Out.println( "<BR><CENTER>Username:<INPUT NAME=username
                        VALUE=\"\" SIZE=16><BR>");
    Out.println( "<BR><BR><INPUT TYPE=submit VALUE=Login></CENTER>" );
    Out.println( "</FORM></BODY></HTML>" );
    Out.flush();
  }
}
```

Example 19.4   Complete cookie source code

19.1.5   Session management

Due to the nature of the HTTP protocol, there is no inherent means of saving state information from one request to another. The previous section looked at one possible method for storing data between sessions. That method used cookies, which store small amounts of textual information at the client side. Although they are extremely useful, cookies do not lend themselves to storing binary or class information.

However, using the cookie mechanism as a base, a sophisticated method could be built that would allow for the storing and retrieval of class objects using a unique key. The server could store the class between each client request, with the servlet indexing the class using a unique number; this number would be passed back to the server from the client using a cookie.

The server could then save the classes to disk at given intervals, which ensures that no data is lost between server restarts. If the solution were to be of real use, then the server would clean out all data that hadn't been accessed in a given time.

This type of system would be an ideal solution to the restrictions imposed by using cookies, and if it were designed properly, it could be used throughout the virtual machine to allow all servlets to share the data.

Fortunately, we don't need to worry about how to implement this, as the servlet API has such a system built into it. This system is called session tracking.

Session tracking began its existence in the Java Web Server. It has since moved over to form part of the core JDK 1.2 library. The system was designed to give developers the ability to store information between requests without getting bogged down with details.

Session tracking operates in much the same way the cookie system did in the previous section. You have a data-wrapper class that is associated with a particular client. The session management layer stores this class in much the same way a cookie is stored for a client. Retrieving the class back again in a subsequent request is a simple matter of calling a method from the session management class, using the name for the class that is to be retrieved.

To illustrate this, we will take the same problem used in the first section and redevelop it to utilize session tracking.

19.1.6   HttpSession

The session management is used to store class information. So before we begin, let's define a simple class to store all the necessary information about a user. We are primarily interested in the user name, with the time he last logged in as a piece of secondary information (this is for pure interest value only). The code shown in example 19.5 will be sufficient to hold the necessary data.

```
public class cUserInfo implements java.io.Serializable {
  public String userName;
  public long timeLastVisit;
}
```
Example 19.5   Creating a user class to store information

You may have noticed we have implemented the `java.io.Serializable` interface, which allows the object to be written easily out to streams using the Object Serialization API of the JDK. It is the technique the session management uses to store objects, if it has to be paged out.

Note: Here are the guidelines for when objects are written to disk. A fixed amount of memory is allocated to store all session data. When that limit is reached, the oldest objects are written to disk using the serialization techniques. For example, the Java Web Server will create a subdirectory under the server root, and it will store all the session data in there. Objects that do not implement the `java.io.Serializable` will not be written to disk. Therefore, if it is important that data is maintained between sessions and server restarts, then make sure the class supports the necessary base class.

Accessing session data is performed through the `javax.servlet.http.HttpSession` class. This class provides all the necessary functionality to store and retrieve session data. This class is not directly created, but it is retrieved from the `HttpServletRequest` class for all incoming client requests.

```
HttpSession clientSession = _req.getSession( true );
```

The statement above will return an instance of the class `HttpSession` for the current session. Notice the `boolean` value being passed in. If the session for this particular client does not already exist, then one is created. If a value of `false` is passed in, and the session does not exist, then `null` is returned.

For our example, we want a session to be created, so we pass in a value of `true`. From here we can retrieve an instance to our user data, assuming one exists.

```
cUserInfo User = (cUserInfo)clientSession.getValue("user.data");
```

We use the method `HttpSession.getValue(…)` to retrieve the class. This method takes a name of the object, as with the cookie, and returns the class's instance. If no value has been stored, or in other words it's a new or expired session, `null` is returned.

Note The naming convention for the data is much the same as the convention used for cookies. However, here's a tip from Sun about naming. Use the name of the servlet and then a unique name. Since all session data is global throughout the server, this eliminates the possibility of two servlets accidentally using the same name for separate data instances.

We need to catch this `null`, and if it is found we can assume the user has not yet logged in and we must send them to the login page. Otherwise, it's business as usual. Example 19.6 illustrates this.

```
cUserInfo User = (cUserInfo)clientSession.getValue("user.data");
if (User==null){
  sendOutLogin( _res );
  return;
}

User.timeLastVisit = System.currentTimeMillis();
ClientSession.putValue("user.data", User);
LoggedIn( _res, name, timeOfLastVisit );
```
Example 19.6   Acting on the session

Setting the data again is a matter of calling the `putValue(…)` method from the session instance. This will ensure the session manager will store the data when the result is sent back out to the client. If this method is not called, then data will not be updated and subsequent requests may yield incorrect results.

With this new way of operating, we can rewrite the `service(…)` method from the previous example, with the result shown in example 19.7.

```
public void service(HttpServletRequest _req, HttpServletResponse _res)
                         throws IOException{
  //- Check to see if the user has registered before
  HttpSession clientSession = _req.getSession( true );
  cUserInfo User = (cUserInfo)clientSession.getValue("user.data");
  if (User==null){
    sendOutLogin( _res );
    return;
  }

  User.timeLastVisit = System.currentTimeMillis();
  ClientSession.putValue("user.data", User);
  LoggedIn( _res, name, timeOfLastVisit );
}
```
Example 19.7   Updated `service(…)` method

Session maintenance   We have seen how to store and retrieve objects from the session manager. There are a number of additional support methods the HttpSession class affords us. Removing session data can be achieved by making a call to the removeValue(...) method.

```
clientSession.removeValue("user.data");
```

This will cause any notifications to be sent to the class if the class implements the necessary interfaces. This is detailed in the next section.

There are a number of time-related functions associated with each session data. For example, we can determine when the data was first created

```
long createTime = clientSession.getCreationTime("user.data");
```

and when it was last accessed

```
long lastAccessedTime = clientSession.getLastAccessedTime("user.data");
```

Session notification   To allow you to know when a piece of data is being stored or removed from a session manager, a help interface exists: HttpSessionBindingListener. By implementing this class, you have two additional methods you may override: value-Bound(...) and valueUnbound(...), as shown in example 19.8.

```
public class mydata implements HttpSessionBindingListener{
   String someData;

public void valueBound(HttpSessionBindingEvent event){
    System.out.println("I am being stored in a session");
    System.out.println( event.getName() );
  }

public void valueUnbound(HttpSessionBindingEvent event){
    System.out.println("I am being removed from a session");
    System.out.println( event.getName() );
  }
}
```

Example 19.8   Listening for changes in data state

19.2   Future extensions

This chapter presented the fundamentals of cookies and session management. The following chapters will use each of these in real-life scenarios.

C H A P T E R   2 0

Online games

- Learn how to provide a flexible, rich content format for hosting online games.
- Learn the basics of creating two online games using HTML: a slot machine and a roulette wheel.
- Discover the power a servlet solution can add to server-side processing for online games.

One of the great things that CGI allows web designers to do is to provide the user with an interactive web site. With interactivity, users feel like they're in control of how they maneuver through a site, instead of being pushed through it. This level of interaction comes in many forms, as this book clearly testifies. One of the best ways of providing the user with an entertaining online session, without the fear of hogging loads of bandwidth, is through online games.

Online games come in many different formats, ranging from multiple-choice questions to casino-type games, to name but two of the genre. In this chapter, you'll learn how to use servlets to provide a simple slot machine game and a more complex online roulette game.

20.1   Slot machine

One of the most common games found in casinos is the slot machine (sometimes called the one-arm bandit). This modern-day wonder is well over 100 years old; Charles August (1862-1944) is credited with manufacturing the first slot machine in California. The concept is simple. You first insert a coin and pull the lever to spin the wheels. If three matching symbols come up, then you win a prize, generally money or tokens. The Liberty Bell, as it was known then, became the forerunner for the modern-day slot machine, which has now found its way onto the Internet.

In this section we will build a servlet that will offer a simple three-wheeled slot machine. Our slot machine will not ask for money, nor will it pay out any prizes.

Note   Many web sites on the Internet offer the complete Las Vegas gambling experience. Give your credit card details, choose your game, then play. Any prizes that are won are credited back to your credit card. If you visit any of these sites, notice how many of them rely on a CGI program. Think how more efficient they could be if they were implemented with a servlet.

To play this game online, the player first needs to press a button that will reload the web page with three different, random symbols. If all the symbols match, then the player wins. An example of this simple slot machine can be seen in figure 20.1; here, the following servlet is running on the main n-ary web site at http://www.n-ary.com/.

20.1.1   Game format

The concept of the whole game is very simple. Display a sequence of random images; if they match, a win situation is declared. This makes for a very simple implementation.

To begin with, the servlet needs to parse an HTML file and insert the new randomized images. So what information does the servlet require in order to do this?

First of all, it needs the number of slots it will be choosing. In our example, there will be three. Next, it needs to know the number of combinations, or different images, that are

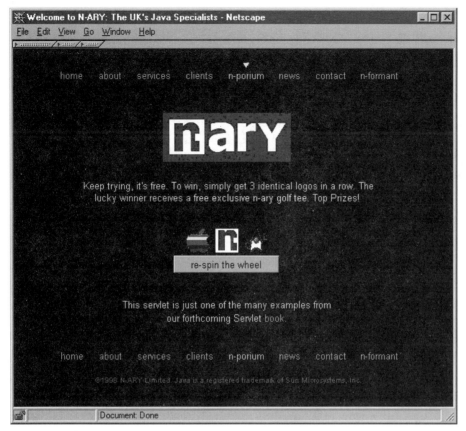

Figure 20.1   The virtual slot machine

being used. Our example will use seven different images. Finally, the servlet needs to know the URL the player will be taken to if a win situation occurs.

Instead of hardcoding this information to the class, pass it all in as HTML parameters. Doing so allows the servlet to act as a server to many different variations of the game. Example 20.1 shows the HTML code for the images.

```
<FORM ACTION="/servlet/com.nary.http.game.oneArmBandit" METHOD="POST">
<INPUT TYPE="Hidden" NAME="SYS_NOSLOTS" VALUE="3">
<INPUT TYPE="Hidden" NAME="SYS_NOIMGS" VALUE="7">
<INPUT TYPE="Hidden" NAME="SYS_RETRYURL" VALUE="/onearmbandit.html">
<INPUT TYPE="Hidden" NAME="SYS_WINURL" VALUE="/onearmbandit_win.html">
<!--HIDDEN-->
<IMG SRC="/n-porium/slot<!--SLOT1-->.gif" WIDTH=32 HEIGHT=32 BORDER=0
                        ALT="">  
<IMG SRC="/n-porium/slot<!--SLOT2-->.gif" WIDTH=32 HEIGHT=32 BORDER=0
                        ALT="">  
<IMG SRC="/n-porium/slot<!--SLOT3-->.gif" WIDTH=32 HEIGHT=32 BORDER=0
                        ALT="">
```

```
<BR><!--SUMBIT-->
</FORM>
```
Example 20.1   The HTML code for the images

Notice how the control information is passed to the servlet via hidden fields. This allows the servlet to remain completely stateless. A number of special tags have been inserted into the HTML code: `<!--SLOT1-->` and `<!--SUBMIT-->`, for example.

With each spin of the wheel, a sequence of images will be displayed. To make the implementation easier, assume that each of these images will be named with a number that will differentiate it from the others. This, therefore, reduces the servlet to a fancy random number generator.

Using the special tag `<!--SLOTx-->`, you can have the servlet replace the tag with a single number. This gives you full control over the type and location of each image. In our example, the image files reside in the /n-porium/ directory, and they are a series of GIF images, numbered from 1 to 7.

The Submit button is produced by the servlet; the servlet can produce different labels on the button depending on the win state.

20.2   Spinning the wheels

Now that the servlet has been reduced to a simple random number generator, the core processing is in determining the numbers and replacing the corresponding `<!--SLOTx-->` tags with the name of the image file. Example 20.2 shows the main `for(...)` loop that is used to replace the tags.

```
int oldNo=-1,newNo;
boolean bWin=true;

for ( int x=0; x < noSlots; x++ ){
  key[x+2]  = "<!--SLOT" + (x+1) + "-->";
  newNo  = getRandomNumber( noImages );
  if ( oldNo == -1 )
    oldNo = newNo;
  else if ( oldNo != newNo )
    bWin = false;

  dat[x+2]  = newNo + "";
}
```
Example 20.2   Creating the images

The number of slots is determined by looking at the HTML variable SYS_NOSLOTS, which is passed in with the request. By looping around this a number of times and generating a new random number, the slots can be quickly determined.

A simple tracking mechanism is used to determine if all the symbols are equal. If the symbols are different, a win is not possible. The procedure starts out assuming a win has occurred, and it is up to the algorithm to prove it hasn't.

20.2.1 Finding a winner

The previous section determined if a win was generated. If it is, before the HTML page with the matching symbols is displayed to the player, a special field is inserted into the HTML page. This field, SYS_WIN, flags that the next time the player presses the Submit button (which he will do when he sees that the symbols match), he will be taken to a URL that will allow him to collect his prize, if one is to be awarded.

Every time the servlet processes a request, it checks for the existence of the SYS_WIN parameter. If it is null (meaning the parameter is not present), then the servlet will generate a new set of images. If the parameter is present, then this is a winning row and the servlet must move the player to the URL that was specified in the SYS_WINURL. This is done using the method in example 20.3.

```
public void win(HttpServletRequest _req, HttpServletResponse _res)
                          throws ServletException, IOException {
  String key[]  = new String[1];
  String dat[]  = new String[1];

  key[0]        = "<!--HIDDEN-->";
  dat[0]        = new SimpleDateFormat( "K:mm aaa  d MMMMM yyyy" ).format(
                     new java.util.Date( Long.parseLong
                        (_req.getParameter( "SYS_WIN" ) ) ) );

  htmlTemplate  winFile = new htmlTemplate( true,
                             _req.getParameter("SYS_WINURL") );
  PrintWriter Out = new PrintWriter( _res.getOutputStream() );
  _res.setContentType( "text/html" );
  winFile.print( Out, key, dat );
  Out.flush();
}
```
Example 20.3   Notifying the winner

As a simple check, the winning date will be inserted into the new HTML file that is generated by the servlet. This is a very basic check to make sure players are not cheating by directly accessing the page.

To keep things simple, the servlet running on the n-ary web site redirects the player to an HTML page with a form on it. The form asks the player for his name and address so a prize can be sent to him. However, if the check date is not found, then we assume the win was invalid and a prize is not sent.

Granted, this isn't exactly the most sophisticated means of stopping bogus wins, but then again, the prize that n-ary gives out is only a golf tee!

20.2.2 Complete source code

That's it. The servlet is complete. Example 20.4 shows the complete servlet to implement the slot machine. Notice how it uses the htmlTemplate class that was developed earlier in this chapter.

```
import javax.servlet.*;
```

```java
import javax.servlet.http.*;
import java.io.*;
import java.util.*;
import java.net.*;
import java.text.*;
import com.nary.html.*;

public class oneArmBandit extends HttpServlet {
  private static htmlTemplate outFile = null;

  public void doPost(HttpServletRequest _req, HttpServletResponse _res)
                          throws ServletException, IOException {

    if ( _req.getParameter( "SYS_WINWIN" ) != null ){
      win( _req, _res );
      return;
    }

    int noSlots   = Integer.parseInt( _req.getParameter("SYS_NOSLOTS") );
    int noImages  = Integer.parseInt( _req.getParameter("SYS_NOIMGS") );

    String key[]  = new String[ 2 + noSlots ];
    String dat[]  = new String[ 2 + noSlots ];

    key[0]        = "<!--HIDDEN-->";
    key[1]        = "<!--SUMBIT-->";
    int oldNo=-1,newNo;
    boolean bWin=true;

    for ( int x=0; x < noSlots; x++ ){
      key[x+2]  = "<!--SLOT" + (x+1) + "-->";
      newNo = getRandomNumber( noImages );

      if ( oldNo == -1 )
        oldNo = newNo;
      else if ( oldNo != newNo )
        bWin = false;

      dat[x+2]  = newNo + "";
    }

    if ( bWin ){
      dat[0] = "<INPUT TYPE=Hidden NAME=SYS_WIN VALUE=" +
                          System.currentTimeMillis() + ">";
      dat[1] = "<INPUT TYPE=submit NAME=SYS_WINWIN VALUE=
                          \"collect prize\">";
    }else{
      dat[0] = "";
      dat[1] = "<INPUT TYPE=submit VALUE=\"re-spin the wheel\">";
    }

    if ( outFile == null )
```

330 CHAPTER 20 ONLINE GAMES

```
        outFile = new htmlTemplate( true, _req.getParameter
                                 ("SYS_RETRYURL") );

     _res.setContentType( "text/html" );
     PrintWriter Out = new PrintWriter( _res.getOutputStream() );
     outFile.print( Out, key, dat );
     Out.flush();
   }

   public void win(HttpServletRequest _req, HttpServletResponse _res)
                               throws ServletException, IOException {
     String key[]  = new String[1];
     String dat[]  = new String[1];

     key[0] = "<!--HIDDEN-->";
     dat[0] = new SimpleDateFormat( "K:mm aaa  d MMMMM yyyy" ).format(
             new java.util.Date( Long.parseLong
                             (_req.getParameter( "SYS_WIN" ) ) ) );

     htmlTemplate  winFile = new htmlTemplate(
                             true, _req.getParameter("SYS_WINURL") );
     PrintWriter Out = new PrintWriter( _res.getOutputStream() );
     _res.setContentType( "text/html" );
     winFile.print( Out, key, dat );
     Out.flush();
   }

   private int getRandomNumber( int _Max ){
     int rand, randfactor= 10;
     if (_Max < 10 )
       randfactor = 10;
     else if ( _Max < 100 )
       randfactor = 100;
     else
       randfactor = 1000;

     for (;;){
       rand = (int)(Math.random() * randfactor);
       if ( rand > 0 && rand < _Max+1 )
         break;
     }
     return rand;
   }
}
```

Example 20.4   The complete source code for the slot machine servlet

20.3 Roulette

If the slot machine is the most common gambling machine around, then the roulette table must run a close second. This is probably one of the least complicated games in a casino. It takes no time at all to figure out the rules: you choose a number and a color, and if the ball lands on that slot in the wheel, you win. It's as simple as that.

This section will implement a roulette game that can be placed on your web site. Although the player's rules are simple, developing such a game takes a bit of care and attention of your part. This section will detail the construction of a servlet to host the roulette game shown in figure 20.2.

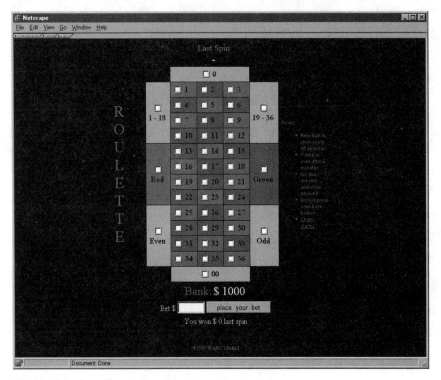

Figure 20.2   An online roulette game

There are many online casinos on the web, but only a very few host an HTML version of their game. HTML holds many advantages over a Java applet or plug in, the main one being download speed. As you'll see, the game our servlet runs is fast to play, and it provides all the necessary safeguards against players attempting to cheat.

20.3.1   Overall structure

The game will be played through standard HTML. Figure 20.2 shows the HTML page we will use. It represents a standard roulette table, except in our version we won't allow players to select rows or groups of numbers—the HTML required to do that would make the table too cluttered, so we'll omit that feature.

To play, the player selects which numbers he wants to bet on, fills in the amount of the bet he wants to place on each number, and presses the Submit button.

The browser sends the data to the servlet for processing; the servlet will generate a random number and calculate any winnings.

This servlet will be special, as it will use a number of safeguards to keep potential cheaters from winning artificially. One of the things we have to do is to make sure a player doesn't simply press the Back button and place his bet again, thinking he knows what the next ball will be. You'll learn how to do this in the following sections.

In addition to providing an enjoyable game of roulette, this servlet can be used to manage the High Score table, which is a list of the top ten winners. This reduces the complexity of the servlet, as all the processing is kept local in one class file.

20.3.2 Starting a new game

Starting a new roulette game won't require any complicated login or signup procedures. The player will simply enter his email address and press a button to begin playing. Easing players into a game will ensure more will play, since many people don't want to bother with lengthy questionnaires.

To ensure everyone gets an even and fair game, the servlet will generate the same ball for everyone on a 15-second interval. This means everyone who is playing the game at the same time will be betting on the same ball. When a player submits a new bet, he will be placed in a queue with the other players until a new ball is generated and the winnings are calculated.

Let's assume a player placed a large bet, but he lost. We have to stop him from paging back on his browser to the point before he placed the bet and continuing on as if nothing had been lost. We can stop this by using a combination of a cookie and an incremental ID that is stored in the HTML page.

At the start of the game, set an HTML form value ID with a value of 0. At the same time, place a cookie with a value of 0 on the client's machine. Every time he places a bet, the cookie and the ID will be sent to the servlet. If the player plays legally, then the value of the ID will be the same as the value in the cookie. After an initial bid, both the ID and the cookie are incremented by 1. If the player pages back, then a previous ID value will be sent the next time he bids, which will not equal the value in the cookie. The servlet will pick up this difference and flag it as an illegal move, and an error page will be displayed. This simple mechanism makes sure the player continually moves forward and does not try to replay a previous move.

We will use the cookie for the purpose of legal protection only. All other information, such as the player's bank balance and email address, will be saved in the HTML page as form parameters that will be passed back each time the player submits a bid.

The game will be marked as over after a period of two minutes. In order for the player to be successful, he has to keep a positive balance going for two minutes, which can be very difficult. Determining the end of game will be simple. At the start of the game, the time the player began will be stored. When each new bid comes in, the servlet will check to see whether the two minutes have elapsed.

Example 20.5 shows the method that will be called when the player wants to start a new game. The method first checks to see if a valid email address has been entered; if one hasn't, the player is taken to the URL specified in the HTML parameter URL_BADLOGIN.

This could either be an error page or the beginning page so he can reinput his email address.

If the email address is valid, then the game begins. If this is the first time the servlet has been accessed by the player, then the template file for the roulette table is loaded in. The URL to this file is specified in the HTML parameter URL_TABLE. We are using the custom htmlTemplate class that has been used throughout this book.

```
public void newGame(HttpServletRequest _req, HttpServletResponse _res)
                            throws ServletException, IOException{
  String email = _req.getParameter("EMAIL");
  if ( email == null || email.indexOf("@") == -1 ){
    _res.sendRedirect( _req.getParameter("URL_BADLOGIN") );
    return;
  }


  if ( rouletteTable == null ){
    rouletteTable = new htmlTemplate( true,
                            _req.getParameter("URL_TABLE") );
  }


  roulInfo RI = new roulInfo();
  RI.form  =  "<INPUT TYPE=HIDDEN NAME=START_TIME VALUE=" +
                            System.currentTimeMillis() + ">\n" +
            "<INPUT TYPE=HIDDEN NAME=BANK_ROLL VALUE=" +RI.bank+ ">\n" +
            "<INPUT TYPE=HIDDEN NAME=EMAIL VALUE=\"" + email + "\">\n" +
            "<INPUT TYPE=HIDDEN NAME=ID VALUE=0>\n";

  //- Set Cookie
  com.nary.util.cookie.setCookie( _res, 1800, "ROULETTE",
                            ".n-ary.com", "0" );

  displayTable( _res, RI );
}
```
Example 20.5 Starting a new roulette game

Each player instance has a number of properties associated with it. To make the servlet design and development much easier, we will package this data up into a single class and pass this class around the methods. This makes for a much cleaner implementation. Example 20.6 shows the roulInfo class that the method in example 20.5 creates and fills. The parameters associated with roulInfo will be explained as we go through the examples and talk about each parameter.

An important part of the information we require includes all the fields we are going to store embedded into the HTML file, which is sent to the player's browser. This includes the time the game began, the initial score, and the player's email address.

Since we're beginning a new game, the special security tag ID is set to 0. The other half of this security mechanism is to set the cookie. This is a simple matter of setting a cookie (in this example, it's named ROULETTE). We do this through a special wrapper class called `cookie`.

Note Why use a wrapper class for something that exists in the main servlet API? At the time of this writing, the servlet API was not yet fixed on which implementation of cookie it was going to offer. By implementing a simple wrapper class, you can confidently use cookies, and when they do change, you simply have to change one method and recompile all your code. If you didn't do it this way, then as soon as the cookie API changed, you would have to make a change to all your classes that ever used a cookie.

```
class roulInfo extends Object {
  public int       bank=1000;
  public int       lastwin=0;
  public String    lastball="-";
  public String    ballspun="-";
  public String    form="";
  public String    status="";
}
```
Example 20.6   The player's information

The `displayTable(...)` method sets up the variables to be used with the `htmlTemplate` class. This solution allows us to easily display an HTML file and insert data into it without having to know the precise location of each tag.

After the cookie is set, the game is ready to be played. It's time to send out the roulette table to the player through the `displayTable(...)` method shown in example 20.7.

```
private void displayTable( HttpServletResponse _res, roulInfo RI )
                        throws ServletException, IOException{
  String key[]  = new String[5];
  String dat[]  = new String[5];

  key[0]  = "<!--BANK_ROLL-->";
  dat[0]  = RI.bank + "";

  key[1]  = "<!--LASTBALL-->";
  dat[1]  = RI.lastball + "";

  key[2]  = "<!--FORM-->";
  dat[2]  = RI.form;

  key[3]  = "<!--STATUS-->";
  dat[3]  = RI.status;

  key[4]  = "<!--LASTWIN-->";
  dat[4]  = RI.lastwin + "";
```

```
    _res.setContentType("text/html");
    PrintWriter Out = _res.getPrintWriter();
    rouletteTable.print( Out, key, dat );
    Out.flush();
}
```

Example 20.7   Displaying the roulette table

20.3.3   Generating a ball

We made the decision to generate only one ball that will be shared among all the players. We must create a background process that will create a ball every fifteen seconds.

Making a servlet serve as a placeholder for a thread is a simple task and one we have done many times in this book. In addition to the servlet class extending the `HttpServlet`, it will implement the `Runnable` interface.

Example 20.8 shows the thread creation and the `run()` method for generating the ball. We will hold a static reference to the main thread handle, and we will start it running in the `init(...)` method. The `run()` method will generate a new ball every fifteen seconds; the servlet does this by looping around, sleeping, and then creating an instance of `cBall`. Once a new instance has been created, notice the call to `notifyAll()`. This will signal all waiting clients (players) that a new ball has been generated, and they can now proceed to see if any winnings are to be collected.

```
static Thread mainThread = null;
static cBall lastBall = new cBall();

public void init(ServletConfig _Config) throws ServletException {
    mainThread   = new Thread(this);
    mainThread.start();
}

public void run(){
    for (;;){
        try{
            mainThread.sleep( ballTime );
            lastBall = new cBall();
            synchronized( mainThread ){
                mainThread.notifyAll();
            }
        }catch( Exception E ){}
    }
}
```

Example 20.8   Generating the ball with a thread

Roulette is just a simple matter of picking a number between one and thirty-six and a color. There are a number of things we have to do to make sure a true randomized ball is generated. While we generate the ball, we can map the state of it in the overall scheme of things by setting a series of flags. For example, a ball can be a number, a color, and in a certain range all at the same time. This will make the determining the winnings much easier.

Example 20.9 shows the complete class for cBall. As you can see, it is merely one constructor that f—... ...es a number between 0 and 37. In this case, we will assume 37 rep... ...t (00). The roulette table associates a color with each num... ...static string array balls.

c]

en", "Red",
ed", "Green",
en", "Red",
reen", "Red",
ed", "Green",
n", "Red",
n", "Red",
d", "Green",
n", "Red",
een", "Red",
", "Green",
n", "Red" };

.length()-2, A.length()));

```
//- Determine even or odd
if ( Ball == 37 || Ball == 0 ){
  bEven   = false;
  bOdd    = false;
}else if ( Ball%2 == 0 )
  bEven = true;
```

```
      else
        bOdd = true;

      //- Determine Range
      if ( Ball >= 1 && Ball <= 18 )
        b118 = true;

      if ( Ball >= 19 && Ball <= 36 )
        b1936 = true;

      //- Determine Colour
      if ( Colour.indexOf( "Green" ) != -1 )
        bBlack = true;
    }
}
```
Example 20.9   Randomizing a new ball

Before the method returns, various flags are set to more accurately describe the ball relative to the roulette table. This includes determining its sign, its range setting, and its color.

20.3.4   Placing a bet

So far we have seen how the game is started and how the ball is generated for each game turn. Now we have to deal with a player submitting a new bid. This involves his selecting a number of fields on the HTML roulette board, filling in the amount he wants to bet, and pressing the Submit button.

Example 20.10 shows the first step in this processing. First of all, the legality of the bid is determined by checking the value in the cookie and the value of the HTML form field ID. If they differ, then an illegal move has been made, and the player is redirected to the URL specified in URL_CHEAT.

```
String ID = com.nary.util.cookie.getCookie( _req, "ROULETTE" );
if ( ID == null || ID.equals( _req.getParameter("ID") ) == false ){
  _res.sendRedirect( _req.getParameter("URL_CHEAT") );
  return;
}

roulInfo RI = new roulInfo();
RI.bank    = Integer.parseInt( _req.getParameter("BANK_ROLL") );
RI.status  = "<BR>";
boolean bBadBet = false;
int nextBet;

try{
  nextBet = Integer.parseInt( _req.getParameter("NEXT_BET") );
}catch (Exception E){
  RI.status = "Please insert a number";
  bBadBet = true;
}
```

```
Vector bets = buildBets( _req );
```
Example 20.10   Dealing with a player's bid

Next, a `roulInfo` is created and the player's details are filled in. The score value and the value of the next bet need to be determined. Due to the complexity of the bets that can be placed via the roulette table, a list of individual bets will be created that will simplify the bid process.

Example 20.11 shows the method for building up the bids the player has placed. Each element of the `Vector` represents a single bid, each worth the amount the player filled in on the form. The HTML roulette form has each checkbox named the number it represents, which significantly reduces the complexity of the algorithm.

```
private Vector buildBets(HttpServletRequest _req ){
  Vector bets = new Vector(2);

  //- Check the numbers
  for ( int x=0; x < 37; x++ )
    if ( _req.getParameter( x+"" ) != null )
      bets.addElement( x+"" );

  if ( _req.getParameter( "00" ) != null )
    bets.addElement( "00" );

  if ( _req.getParameter( "GREEN" ) != null )
    bets.addElement( "Green" );

  if ( _req.getParameter( "RED" ) != null )
    bets.addElement( "Red" );

  if ( _req.getParameter( "ODD" ) != null )
    bets.addElement( "Odd" );

  if ( _req.getParameter( "EVEN" ) != null )
    bets.addElement( "Even" );

  if ( _req.getParameter( "1-18" ) != null )
    bets.addElement( "118" );

  if ( _req.getParameter( "19-36" ) != null )
    bets.addElement( "1936" );

  return bets;
}
```
Example 20.11   Building the bids

20.3.5   *Determining the winnings*

Up to this point we have started the roulette wheel spinning (virtually speaking) and we have the ability to take in players' bids. Now we have to determine if each player has indeed won anything—or more often than not, if he has gone bust.

This boils down to waiting for the ball to be rolled and then checking to see if the player had correctly forecast the outcome. Waiting for the ball to be generated is a simple matter of doing a `wait()` on the `mainThread` object. Remember the method shown in example 20.8, where the thread called the `notifyAll()` method after making a new ball? This is where the client waits on the ball.

Example 20.12 shows the code for checking the new ball against the player's bid. First, the player is checked to see if he has enough money in the bank to cover the bet. If not, then all bets are called off.

```
if ( bets.size()*nextBet > RI.bank || nextBet > RI.bank )
  RI.status = "You don't have enough in the bank for a bet that size";
else if ( bBadBet == false ){
  try{
    synchronized( mainThread ){
      mainThread.wait();
    }
  }catch( InterruptedException E ){}

  //- Remove bets from bank
  RI.bank -= nextBet * bets.size();

  //- Check for winnings
  if ( bets.contains( lastBall.Ball + "" ) ){
    bWin        = true;
    RI.bank     += nextBet + (35*nextBet);
    RI.lastwin  += 35*nextBet;
  }

  if ( bets.contains( "00" ) && lastBall.Ball == 37 ){
    bWin        = true;
    RI.bank     += nextBet + (35*nextBet);
    RI.lastwin  += 35*nextBet;
  }

  if ( bets.contains( "Green" ) && lastBall.Colour.equals("Green") ){
    bWin        = true;
    RI.bank     += nextBet + nextBet;
    RI.lastwin  += nextBet;
  }

  if ( bets.contains( "Red" ) && lastBall.Colour.equals("Red") ){
    bWin        = true;
    RI.bank     += nextBet + nextBet;
    RI.lastwin  += nextBet;
  }

  if ( bets.contains( "Odd" ) && lastBall.bOdd ){
    bWin        = true;
    RI.bank     += nextBet + nextBet;
    RI.lastwin  += nextBet;
  }
```

```
if ( bets.contains( "even" ) && lastBall.bEven ){
  bWin       = true;
  RI.bank    += nextBet + nextBet;
  RI.lastwin += nextBet;
}

if ( bets.contains( "118" ) && lastBall.b118 ){
  bWin       = true;
  RI.bank    += nextBet + nextBet;
  RI.lastwin += nextBet;
}

if ( bets.contains( "1936" ) && lastBall.b1936 ){
  bWin       = true;
  RI.bank    += nextBet + nextBet;
  RI.lastwin += nextBet;
}
}
```
Example 20.12   Creating the winning pot

To see if the ball satisfies any of the player's criteria, you just need to run through a series of `if` conditions and set the new bank with the new score.

20.3.6   End of game

The game is considered over if one of two things occurs: the player goes bust or two minutes have elapsed. Example 20.13 shows the code for checking to see if one of these conditions has been met.

```
long startG = Long.parseLong( _req.getParameter("START_TIME") );

if ( RI.bank <= 0 || startG+(60000*2) < System.currentTimeMillis() )
  gameOver( _req, _res, RI );
```
Example 20.13   Checking for the end of the game

20.3.7   Maintaining a high score table

The roulette servlet is purely for entertainment value. However, to give players a sense of competition, a simple High Score table will be maintained to display the top ten players' scores. Figure 20.3 shows an example of a High Score table.

An object is created for each player using the class as a template. This is demonstrated in example 20.14. This will hold the email address and the amount of money won. A list of players will be kept in a `Vector` that will be updated every time a game ends.

```
class userInfo implements java.io.Serializable {
  public String email;
  public int    money;
}
```
Example 20.14   The container class for a player

When a game ends, the servlet has to determine whether the player qualifies for the High Score table. This is easily done by having the servlet run through the table to see if

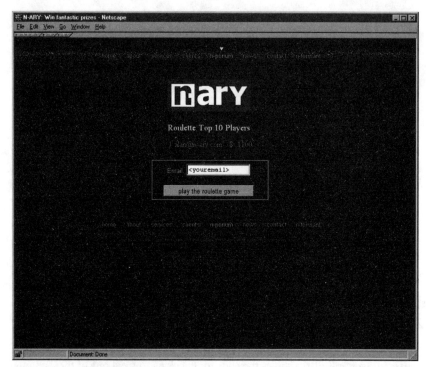

Figure 20.3   A High Score table

the player beat any of the scores. Example 20.15 shows the method for running through the table. A player can be added if the table has fewer than ten elements, or if the new money value beats an existing player.

```
boolean bAdd = false;
Enumeration E = highScores.elements();
userInfo UI;
while ( E.hasMoreElements() ){
  UI = (userInfo)E.nextElement();
  if ( RI.bank > UI.money ){
    bAdd = true;
    break;
  }
}

if ( bAdd ||  highScores.size() < 10 )
  addUser( _req.getParameter("EMAIL"), RI.bank );

_res.sendRedirect( _req.getParameter("URL_GAMEWON") );
```
Example 20.15   Checking the High Score table

If the player is lucky enough to be placed in the High Score table, then the method in example 20.16 adds him to the table. This is done by inserting the player into the correct position in the table. If more than ten players are on the table, then the method call to `setSize(…)` from the `Vector` class trims the structure down to size.

```java
private void addUser( String _Email, int _money ){
  userInfo UI = new userInfo();
  userInfo oUI;
  UI.email  = _Email;
  UI.money  = _money;
  for ( int x=0; x < highScores.size(); x++ ){
    oUI = (userInfo)highScores.elementAt(0);
    if ( UI.money >= oUI.money ){
      highScores.insertElementAt(UI,0);
      break;
    }
  }

  if ( highScores.size() == 0 )
    highScores.addElement( UI );

  if ( highScores.size() > 10 )
    highScores.setSize(10);

  saveScores();
}
```
Example 20.16   Adding a player to the High Score table

20.3.8   Complete source code

Example 20.17 shows the complete code for the roulette servlet. Notice the methods for storing and retrieving the High Score table. Because we implemented the `java.io.Seri-alizable` interface, we could easily manipulate the `Vector`.

```java
import java.io.*;
import java.util.*;
import java.text.*;
import javax.servlet.*;
import javax.servlet.http.*;
import com.nary.http.*;
import com.nary.html.*;

public class rouletteServlet extends HttpServlet implements Runnable {
  static private htmlTemplate rouletteTable = null;
  static private htmlTemplate scoreTable = null;
  static Thread mainThread = null;
  static cBall lastBall = new cBall();
  static long ballTime = 15000;
  static Vector highScores;

  public void init(ServletConfig _Config) throws ServletException {
    loadScores();
    mainThread    = new Thread(this);
    mainThread.start();
  }
```

```java
      private synchronized void loadScores(){
        try{
          FileInputStream   FS = new FileInputStream( "roulette.scores" );
          ObjectInputStream IS = new ObjectInputStream(FS);
          highScores            = (Vector)IS.readObject();
        }catch(Exception E){
          System.out.println( E );
          highScores  = new Vector();
        }
      }

      private synchronized void saveScores(){
        try{
          FileOutputStream   FS = new FileOutputStream( "roulette.scores" );
          ObjectOutputStream OS = new ObjectOutputStream(FS);
          OS.writeObject( highScores );
        }catch(Exception E){}
      }

      public void service(HttpServletRequest _req, HttpServletResponse _res)
                                    throws ServletException, IOException {
        if ( _req.getParameter( "SYS_GAMEON" ) != null )
          gameOn( _req, _res );
        else if ( _req.getParameter( "SYS_NEWGAME" ) != null )
          newGame( _req, _res );
        else if ( _req.getParameter( "SYS_DISPLAY" ) != null )
          displayScores( _req, _res );
      }

      public void run(){
        for (;;){
          try{
            mainThread.sleep( ballTime );
            lastBall = new cBall();
            synchronized( mainThread ){
              mainThread.notifyAll();
            }
          }catch( Exception E ){}
        }
      }

      public void newGame(HttpServletRequest _req, HttpServletResponse _res)
                                    throws ServletException, IOException{
        String email = _req.getParameter("EMAIL");
        if ( email == null || email.indexOf("@") == -1 ){
          _res.sendRedirect( _req.getParameter("URL_BADLOGIN") );
          return;
        }

        if ( rouletteTable == null ){
          rouletteTable = new htmlTemplate( true,
                            _req.getParameter("URL_TABLE") );
        }
```

```
    roulInfo RI = new roulInfo();
    RI.form  =  "<INPUT TYPE=HIDDEN NAME=START_TIME VALUE="
                            + System.currentTimeMillis() + ">\n" +
                "<INPUT TYPE=HIDDEN NAME=BANK_ROLL VALUE=" +
                            RI.bank + ">\n" +
                "<INPUT TYPE=HIDDEN NAME=EMAIL VALUE=\"" + email +
                            "\">\n" +
                "<INPUT TYPE=HIDDEN NAME=ID VALUE=0>\n";

    //- Set Cookie
    com.nary.util.cookie.setCookie( _res, 1800, "ROULETTE",
                            ".n-ary.com", "0" );

    displayTable( _res, RI );
}

public void gameOn(HttpServletRequest _req, HttpServletResponse _res)
                                throws ServletException, IOException{
    //- Calculate winnings
    if ( rouletteTable == null ){
      rouletteTable = new htmlTemplate( true,
                            _req.getParameter("URL_TABLE") );
    }

    //- Check to see the cookie and the ID match.
    String ID = com.nary.util.cookie.getCookie( _req, "ROULETTE" );
    if ( ID == null || ID.equals( _req.getParameter("ID") ) == false ){
      _res.sendRedirect( _req.getParameter("URL_CHEAT") );
      return;
    }

    roulInfo RI = new roulInfo();
    RI.bank    = Integer.parseInt( _req.getParameter("BANK_ROLL") );
    RI.status  = "<BR>";
    int nextBet=0;
    boolean bBadBet = false;
    boolean bWin = false;

    try{
      nextBet = Integer.parseInt( _req.getParameter("NEXT_BET") );
    }catch (Exception E){
      RI.status = "Please insert a number";
      bBadBet = true;
    }

    Vector bets = buildBets( _req );
    if ( bets.size()*nextBet > RI.bank || nextBet > RI.bank )
      RI.status = "You don't have enough in the bank for a bet that size";
    else if ( bBadBet == false ){
      try{
        synchronized( mainThread ){
          mainThread.wait();
        }
      }catch( InterruptedException E ){}
```

```
//- Remove bets from bank
   RI.bank -= nextBet * bets.size();

   //- Check for winnings
   if ( bets.contains( lastBall.Ball + "" ) ){
     bWin        = true;
     RI.bank     += nextBet + (35*nextBet);
     RI.lastwin  += 35*nextBet;
   }

   if ( bets.contains( "00" ) && lastBall.Ball == 37 ){
     bWin        = true;
     RI.bank     += nextBet + (35*nextBet);
     RI.lastwin  += 35*nextBet;
   }

   //- Check
   if ( bets.contains( "Green" ) && lastBall.Colour.equals("Green") ){
     bWin        = true;
     RI.bank     += nextBet + nextBet;
     RI.lastwin  += nextBet;
   }

   if ( bets.contains( "Red" ) && lastBall.Colour.equals("Red") ){
     bWin        = true;
     RI.bank     += nextBet + nextBet;
     RI.lastwin  += nextBet;
   }

   if ( bets.contains( "Odd" ) && lastBall.bOdd ){
     bWin        = true;
     RI.bank     += nextBet + nextBet;
     RI.lastwin  += nextBet;
   }

   if ( bets.contains( "even" ) && lastBall.bEven ){
     bWin        = true;
     RI.bank     += nextBet + nextBet;
     RI.lastwin  += nextBet;
   }

   if ( bets.contains( "118" ) && lastBall.b118 ){
     bWin        = true;
     RI.bank     += nextBet + nextBet;
     RI.lastwin  += nextBet;
   }

   if ( bets.contains( "1936" ) && lastBall.b1936 ){
     bWin        = true;
     RI.bank     += nextBet + nextBet;
     RI.lastwin  += nextBet;
   }
 }
 //- Check to see if the game is over
```

```
    long startG = Long.parseLong( _req.getParameter("START_TIME") );

    if ( RI.bank <= 0 || startG+(60000*2) < System.currentTimeMillis() )
      gameOver( _req, _res, RI );

    //- Format display for sending
    if ( bWin )
      RI.status = "Congratulations, you won!";

    if ( lastBall.Ball != 37 )
      RI.lastball = lastBall.Colour + " " + lastBall.Ball;
    else
      RI.lastball = lastBall.Colour + " 00";

    //- Set cookie
    int id = Integer.parseInt(ID) + 1;
  com.nary.util.cookie.setCookie( _res, 1800, "ROULETTE", ".n-ary.com",
id+"" );
    id = Integer.parseInt( _req.getParameter("ID") ) + 1;
    RI.form = "<INPUT TYPE=HIDDEN NAME=START_TIME VALUE="
                        +_req.getParameter("START_TIME")+">\n"+
              "<INPUT TYPE=HIDDEN NAME=BANK_ROLL VALUE=" +
                        RI.bank + ">\n" +
              "<INPUT TYPE=HIDDEN NAME=EMAIL VALUE=\"" +
                        _req.getParameter("EMAIL") + "\">\n" +
              "<INPUT TYPE=HIDDEN NAME=ID VALUE=" + id + ">\n";

    displayTable( _res, RI );
  }

  private void gameOver( HttpServletRequest _req,
                         HttpServletResponse _res, roulInfo RI )
                         throws ServletException, IOException{
    //- Game over, man!
    if ( RI.bank <= 0 )
      _res.sendRedirect( _req.getParameter("URL_GAMELOST") );
    else{
      //- Update tables and then redirect them to a good page
      boolean bAdd = false;
      Enumeration E = highScores.elements();
      userInfo UI;
      while ( E.hasMoreElements() ){
        UI = (userInfo)E.nextElement();
        if ( RI.bank > UI.money ){
          bAdd = true;
          break;
        }
      }

      if ( bAdd || highScores.size() < 10 )
        addUser( _req.getParameter("EMAIL"), RI.bank );

      _res.sendRedirect( _req.getParameter("URL_GAMEWON") );
    }
```

```
        }
    private void addUser( String _Email, int _money ){
        userInfo UI = new userInfo();
        userInfo oUI;
        UI.email   = _Email;
        UI.money   = _money;
        for ( int x=0; x < highScores.size(); x++ ){
          oUI = (userInfo)highScores.elementAt(0);
          if ( UI.money >= oUI.money ){
            highScores.insertElementAt(UI,0);
            break;
          }
        }

        if ( highScores.size() == 0 )
          highScores.addElement( UI );

        if ( highScores.size() > 10 )
          highScores.setSize(10);

        saveScores();
    }

    private void displayTable( HttpServletResponse _res, roulInfo RI )
                        throws ServletException, IOException{
        String key[]  = new String[5];
        String dat[]  = new String[5];

        key[0]  = "<!--BANK_ROLL-->";
        dat[0]  = RI.bank + "";

        key[1]  = "<!--LASTBALL-->";
        dat[1]  = RI.lastball + "";

        key[2]  = "<!--FORM-->";
        dat[2]  = RI.form;

        key[3]  = "<!--STATUS-->";
        dat[3]  = RI.status;

        key[4]  = "<!--LASTWIN-->";
        dat[4]  = RI.lastwin + "";

        _res.setContentType("text/html");
        PrintWriter Out = new PrintWriter( _res.getOutputStream() );
        rouletteTable.print( Out, key, dat );
        Out.flush();
    }

    private Vector buildBets(HttpServletRequest _req ){
        Vector bets = new Vector(2,2);

        //- Check the numbers
        for ( int x=0; x < 37; x++ )
```

```java
      if ( _req.getParameter( x+"" ) != null )
        bets.addElement( x+"" );

    if ( _req.getParameter( "00" ) != null )
      bets.addElement( "00" );

    if ( _req.getParameter( "GREEN" ) != null )
      bets.addElement( "Green" );

    if ( _req.getParameter( "RED" ) != null )
      bets.addElement( "Red" );

    if ( _req.getParameter( "ODD" ) != null )
      bets.addElement( "Odd" );

    if ( _req.getParameter( "EVEN" ) != null )
      bets.addElement( "Even" );

    if ( _req.getParameter( "1-18" ) != null )
      bets.addElement( "118" );

    if ( _req.getParameter( "19-36" ) != null )
      bets.addElement( "1936" );

    return bets;
  }

  public void displayScores(HttpServletRequest _req,
                            HttpServletResponse _res)
                      throws ServletException, IOException{
    if ( scoreTable == null )
      scoreTable = new htmlTemplate( true,
                        _req.getParameter("URL_SCORES") );

    String key[]  = new String[1];
    String dat[]  = new String[1];

    key[0]  = "<!--TABLE-->";
    dat[0]  = "";

    Enumeration E = highScores.elements();
    userInfo UI;
    int x=1;
    while ( E.hasMoreElements() ){
      UI = (userInfo)E.nextElement();
      dat[0] += "<TR><TD>" + x + "</TD>\r\n";
      dat[0] += "<TD>" + UI.email + "</TD>\r\n";
      dat[0] += "<TD> </TD><TD>$ \r\n";
      dat[0] += UI.money + "</TD>\r\n";

      x++;
    }

  _res.setContentType("text/html");
```

```
        PrintWriter Out = new PrintWriter( _res.getOutputStream() );
        scoreTable.print( Out, key, dat );
        Out.flush();
    }
}
```
Example 20.17   The complete source code for the roulette servlet

20.4   *Future extensions*

This chapter presented two fairly sophisticated online games that were implemented using a combination of servlets and HTML. The roulette servlet implemented a multiplayer game that may be extended to allow for communication between players. The servlet could be extended to provide the server for any type of card game in which the pack needs to be shared among players.

By using the threading capabilities of Java and the locking mechanisms provided by objects, such multiplayer games are relatively straightforward when compared with developing the same system in an alternative server-side language.

C H A P T E R   2 1

Banner advertising

- Understand how banners on web pages have added a new dimension to the advertising business on the Internet.
- Learn how to create a banner rotation system for a web site.

The Internet has not escaped the evil clutches of advertising executives. Someone somewhere came up with the great idea of advertising on web pages, and now the virtues of services, products, and other sites are extolled on thousands of web sites. Placing advertising banners on web pages gave advertisers much greater power in the marketplace. Instead of simply displaying colorful GIF or JPEG images on others' pages, advertisers now had the potential to steal surfers from one site to their own by encouraging users to click on the advertisements.

Because of this ability to steal surfers, the popularity of web banner advertising grew and grew. Now it's very rare to browse the web and not come across an advertisement of some sort on any type of page. This is not necessarily a bad thing—from the web administrator's point of view, if he has a popular site, then selling advertising space can be a lucrative venture. For example, at the time this book was published, the cost of advertising on Netscape's site was roughly $3,000 for one week.

To go along with the concept of selling advertising space, a number of banner exchange services have been set up. With these services, prospective advertisers place a banner on their site and for every one they display, their banner will be displayed on someone else's site for free. This type of banner program is very popular, as it offers increased traffic and awareness at no cost.

21.1   Introduction to banner advertising

Advertising on the web is done by placing a small image or line of text on a page to promote the goods or services of the advertiser. It's become the convention that most banners are of a fixed size and generally consist of some type of image. This image can be an animated GIF or a static picture. If you look at most search engines, you'll see an example of banner advertising. Figure 21.1 shows such an example on one of the big American search engines.

Advertising on the Internet is completely different from advertising in any other medium. With a magazine or television ad, the user has no interaction with the advertisement. If the advertisement is successful and the user wants more information, it is up to the user to make the move to phone, email, or write to the company in question, or find the product at a local store. Many users give up at this point, as it too much of a hassle for probably very little gain.

With advertising on the Internet, the user can click on the banner and be instantly transported to anything the advertiser wants to show the potential client. The user is now visiting another site, and is under the guidance and influence of someone else. Because of this new depth to advertising, banner promotions are growing in popularity.

Another popular form of promotion that has quickly grown fashionable is the use of banner exchange servers, as shown in figure 21.2 from the Link Exchange group (http://www.linkexchange.com/).

Instead of paying for advertising space for your web site, you can join an exchange program that displays your banner on other sites in exchange for your giving space to others. This operates on the principle of credits. For example, every time your site displays a banner, half of a credit is awarded, and for every one full credit accrued, your banner is displayed on someone else's site. This is a convenient way of increasing traffic to your site without having to purchase advertising space.

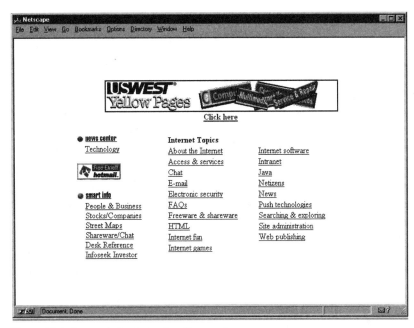

Figure 21.1 A sample banner advertisement

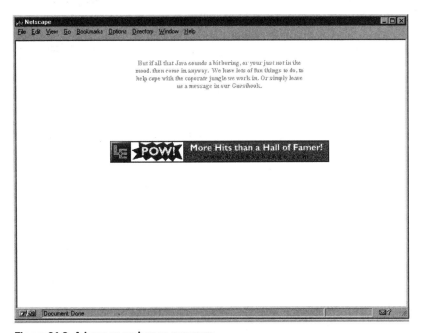

Figure 21.2 A banner exchange program

Both forms of advertising operate by placing HTML code in the source file. The code loads the banner in question. The user clicks the image that is generated and he is taken to the corresponding page. All images are fed from the server, which allows banners to be cycled on each subsequent visit so the user doesn't see the same image twice. This is the web equivalent of a rotating billboard.

The implementation of both systems relies heavily on server-side processing which, historically, has been executed using CGI scripts. The server determines which advertisement to feed the client, and it records the necessary statistics for the advertiser. These figures provide an invaluable data source to the advertiser to determine how well the advertisement is doing. For example, the advertiser can tell how many times the image has been displayed and how many times users have clicked on it.

Note Advertising on the Internet has many advantages over conventional media. For example, to gauge how well print advertisements are performing in various publications, it is not uncommon to have each advertisment have a different URL or phone number so the advertiser can see which publication or medium is generating the most response. By placing an advertisement on the Internet, the advertiser has up-to-the-minute statistics of exactly how many people have seen the advertisement, and how many people have clicked on the banner to inquire further.

This chapter will look at both forms of advertising, both banners alone and banner services. It will also show how servlets can be easily used by web administrators to provide advertising space and offer banner exchange programs. As you will discover, Java lends itself to this area of the web very well. Implementing the same procedure has been done many times using CGI; however, these solutions have proven to be very complicated and server intensive.

21.2 Real estate: selling space

The first and probably the easiest banner application to implement is the real estate version. The term "real estate" is used here as a metaphor for the way advertising space is sold. One client can consistently occupy the space, or several companies could use the space on a time-share system, where a new banner appears every time the page is refreshed.

With this version, you allocate an area on one of your web pages; when that area is accessed, it will display a different advertising banner each time the page is refreshed. A surfer will be able to click on this banner and be transported to another site somewhere on the Internet.

A number of different areas need to be addressed in order for this application to be brought to life:

1 Adding banners to and removing banners from the list of advertisers.
2 Serving the banner when the page is refreshed.
3 Maintaining and displaying banner statistics.

Each advertisement banner that is featured on the rotation list has its own set of attributes and functions. When the banner in figure 21.2, for example, is displayed in an HTML page, it must be set up so it can link to the site it's advertising and the image itself must be pulled in from somewhere. There are a couple of possible places from which this image could originate.

1. Link directly to an image on a remote site. Since the Internet is a global community, accessing one site is just as easy as accessing another, so the image the advertiser wants to use could conceivably remain on its own server. When the image is called for display, it is retrieved directly from the site that owns the banner advertisement.

2. Display the image from a local site. The advertiser submits the image they want to use. The image is then stored locally and it is served when called upon.

The main disadvantage with the first solution is that if the remote site goes down for any reason, the advertisement will become useless. Another major problem with it is the response time for the user, if the remote advertiser has a slow or busy connection to their site. With the advertisement originating from your web server for a page that resides on your web site, it is better for the actual banner image to come from your site.

One of the most useful advantages of using web-based advertising is the up-to-date statistics that are available. The advertiser can easily see how many times an image has been displayed and how many times the user has clicked on the image to jump to the advertiser's site. The ability to provide this type of information has a bearing on how the system is designed.

Table 21.1 shows data attributes associated with each banner:

Table 21.1 Banner attributes

Data	Description
siteURL	The URL of the site the user will be taken to when the image is clicked.
Image	The filename of the image that will be used as the banner.
Content-Type	The type of image, either GIF or JPEG.
Title	The title of the advertisement.
Total Display	The total number of times the advertisement has been displayed.
Total Clicks	The total number of times the advertisement has been clicked.

By packaging this data up into a class, we can build a whole system that operates around a list of these classes. The class definition shown in example 21.1 shows the data definitions, which include a number of additional counters. To give the advertiser a greater handle on their statistics, a trip-counter mechanism can be easily provided. This mechanism allows them to monitor specific periods without worrying about resetting the total counts.

```
class bannerInfo implements Serializable {
    public int     bannerID;
    public String  strImageName;
    public String  content;
    public String  strTitle;
    public String  strURL=null;

    public int     totalDisplay=0;
    public int     totalClicks=0;
    public int     lastDisplay=0;
```

```
public int  lastClick=0;
public Date  dateOfLastReset = new Date();

    //- Class method list
}
```

Example 21.1   The class definition for a banner

We will implement the second option, which will display the image from the local server. This was decided for two reasons. First, the implementation is more secure and reliable if it's kept on the same machine as the web page, and second, the first method doesn't present any interesting challenges! Not that I want to make things difficult for us for the sake of it, but the second solution really is the better solution.

Uploading the image to the site may seem like a daunting task, as it may require email attachments—or even worse, FTP procedures. The nicer solution would be for the advertiser to specify the URL of the image they wish to use and then for the servlet to collect it automatically. This is illustrated with the class method shown in example 21.2. The set-Parameters(...) method is called when the image for the banner is to be updated, such as at object creation.

The method is split into three steps. Step one involves a quick check of the URL of the image to make sure it ends with either a .gif or .jpg extension. This serves two purposes at once. First, the URL is validated; if it's not a valid extension then it's rejected. Second, the Content-Type of the image can be set when the extension is checked (you'll see how this is used later in this chapter).

Note   Notice how the servlet is being set up to handle both GIF and JPEG files. At the time of this writing, many of the sites offering advertising space and banner exchange services would only accept GIF files, with the promise to offer JPEG soon. It's a shame these sites operate using CGI scripts, as the type of image is immaterial to the operation.

The second step of the method is to create a unique name for the file in which the image will be stored. This involves taking the extension determined in step one and appending it to the filename, which is created by looking at the number of milliseconds that have elapsed since January 1970. The filename might look like this: 917889348 27475.jpg. As you can see, you're guaranteed a unique filename every time. The reason for creating a new name, as opposed to using the name of the file as stated in the URL, is to avoid conflicts with similar names. For example, ask someone to submit an advertisement—chances are he is going to call it advert.gif or something pretty generic.

```
public voidsetParameters( String _strTitle, String _strURL,
                           String _imgURL ){
    strTitle = _strTitle;
    strURL  = _strURL;

    //- Load in the GIF image
    StringTokenizer st = new StringTokenizer( _imgURL, "." );
    String fileExt;
```

```
  if ( st.countTokens() == 2 ){
    st.nextToken();
    fileExt = st.nextToken();
  }else
    return;

  if ( fileExt.compareTo( "gif" ) == 0 )
    content = "image/gif";
  else if ( fileExt.compareTo( "jpg" ) == 0 )
    content = "image/jpeg";

String strFileName= System.currentTimeMillis() + "." + fileExt;

  URL    Host;
  URLConnection      Uc;
  BufferedInputStream IS;
  BufferedOutputStream OS;

  try{
    Host= new URL( _imgURL );
    Uc  = Host.openConnection();
    IS  = new BufferedInputStream( Uc.getInputStream() );
    OS = new BufferedOutputStream( new FileOutputStream( strFileName ) );
    byte buffer[] = new byte[1024];
    int  noRead = 0;

   noRead = IS.read( buffer, 0, 1023 );
   while ( noRead != -1 ){
     OS.write( buffer, 0, noRead );
     noRead = IS.read( buffer, 0, 1023 );
   }
   OS.flush();
  } catch (Exception E ){
   return;
  }

  if ( strImageName != null )
    (new File(strImageName)).delete();

  strImageName = strFileName;
}
```

Example 21.2   Setting the parameters for a banner

The third and final step is to open up the image at the specified URL and copy it, deleting the old image if the call to this method is an update to the image. This is done by opening the URL, getting an input stream to the image, and then reading from the input stream and writing to the output stream which now represents the filename of the image on the local system.

The real estate servlet we are building will use server-side includes when delivering the banner to the HTML page and when sending out administration forms to the client for editing banner properties. This same servlet will perform many different tasks; they are all controlled by the parameters sent to it in its URL. For example, assume an alias has been set up for the servlet that results in the execution of the servlet. The administrator would add a banner using this URL:

```
/realestate.html?SYS_ADMIN=1
```

The `service(…)` method of the servlet must decode all of the different areas the servlet is to be used in and call the correct method. Checking the presence of certain control variables is an effective way to branch to the appropriate method. Example 21.3 shows how this method checks for parameters.

```
public void service( HttpServletRequest _req, HttpServletResponse _res)
                            throws ServletException, IOException{
  if ( _req.getParameter( "SYS_CLICK" ) != null )
    processClickThru( _req, _res );
  else if ( _req.getParameter( "SYS_SHOWSTATS" ) != null )
    sendOutStatsForm( _res );
  else if ( _req.getParameter( "SYS_STATSPOST" ) != null )
    processStatsForm( _req, _res  );
  else if ( _req.getParameter( "SYS_ADMIN" ) != null )
    sendOutBannerListForm( _res );
  else if ( _req.getParameter( "SYS_ADMINRESULT" ) != null )
    sendOutBannerPropForm( _req, _res );
  else if ( _req.getParameter( "SYS_IMAGE" ) != null )
    processImage( _req, _res  );
  else if ( _req.getParameter( "SYS_SINGLEBANNER" ) != null )
    processBannerPropForm( _req, _res );
  else
    bannerOutput( _res );
}
```

Example 21.3 The `service(…)` method

21.2.1 *Administration of advertisers*

In order for the servlet to display and process banners, it must first have some banners available. Again, as with many of the servlets in this book, it is best for the servlet to perform the administration tasks, as this keeps all functionality within one unit instead of having a separate servlet for different aspects.

The purpose of this servlet is to provide a rotational banner on a known page. Before this can be done, you (as the administrator) must add an advertisement to the system. As before, each banner is stored in an instance of `bannerInfo` (the class introduced in the previous section).

```
public void init(ServletConfig _servletConfig) throws ServletException {
  super.init( _servletConfig );
  loadBanners();
}

private void loadBanners(){
  try{
    FileInputStream      FS = new FileInputStream( "banner.list" );
    ObjectInputStream    IS = new ObjectInputStream(FS);
    bannerList              = (Vector)IS.readObject();
```

```
  }catch(Exception E){
    bannerList  = new Vector();
  }
}

private void saveBanners(){
  try{
    FileOutputStream     FS = new FileOutputStream( "banner.list" );
    ObjectOutputStream   OS = new ObjectOutputStream(FS);
    OS.writeObject( bannerList );
  }catch(Exception E){}
}
```

Example 21.4 The `init(…)` **method**

Example 21.4 shows the `init(…)` method for the servlet, which restores the state of the servlet upon startup. The `loadBanners()` method is a call to load in the `Vector` of `bannerInfo`. Since the `bannerInfo` is a `Serializable` object, we can easily save and retrieve the class instances.

The `Vector` data storage class will store the list of banners. This class allows us to access the banners as if they were in an array—you will discover in the *Serving the banner* section that this is exactly how we want to access them. Adding and updating the banners to the servlet is done using HTML forms.

The `sendOutBannerListForm(…)`, illustrated in example 21.5, formats the HTML form and displays a form along the lines of the one shown in figure 21.3. This is done by using the list of banners to create the form dynamically. If a banner exists in the list, it is added to the form and a checkbox is placed beside it. Checking the checkbox allows the user to edit the properties of the banner when he presses Administer.

Each banner is identified by assigning a unique ID to each one that becomes live on the system. This ID is then used to set the field names of the checkboxes, which allow the banner to be identified correctly in subsequent processing calls. Using the order in which the banner comes in the vector as the ID would render all the IDs useless—if a banner were to be deleted, the remaining banners would hold an incorrect number.

```
private void sendOutBannerListForm( HttpServletResponse _res )
                        throws IOException {
  //- Formats a new form and sends it out to the client
  _res.setContentType("text/html");
  PrintWriter Out = new PrintWriter( _res.getOutputStream() );

  Out.println( "<HTML><BODY>" );
  Out.println( "<B><I>Administer Form</I></B>" );
  Out.println( "<FORM METHOD=POST ACTION=
                        /servlet/com.nary.http.bannerServlet> <CENTER>
                        <TABLE BORDER=0>" );
  Out.println( "<INPUT TYPE=hidden NAME=SYS_ADMINRESULT VALUE=1>" );

  Enumeration E= bannerList.elements();
  bannerInfobanner;
  while ( E.hasMoreElements() ){
    banner = (bannerInfo)E.nextElement();
```

```
        Out.println( "<TR><TD ALIGN=RIGHT>" + banner.strTitle + "</TD>
                            <TD ALIGN=LEFT> <INPUT TYPE=CHECKBOX
                            NAME=\"" + banner.bannerID + "\"
                            VALUE=1> Tag banner</TD></TR>" );
    }

    Out.println( "</TABLE>");
    Out.println( "<TR><TD ALIGN=RIGHT>New Banner</TD><TD ALIGN=LEFT>
                <INPUT TYPE=CHECKBOX NAME=9999 VALUE=1></TD></TR><BR><BR>"
);
    Out.println( "<INPUT TYPE=submit VALUE=Administer> <INPUT TYPE=reset
                            VALUE=Reset>");
    Out.println( "</CENTER></FORM></BODY></HTML>" );
    Out.flush();
}
```

Example 21.5   Sending out the list of banners

Once the user has decided to either add a banner or edit an existing one, the form data is posted back to the servlet, which is then picked up and processed by the `sendOut-BannerPropForm(…)` class method, shown in example 21.6.

After posting the form shown in figure 21.3, the user expects another form to be sent from the servlet. This new form will allow him to either edit the fields or enter new fields if it's a new banner.

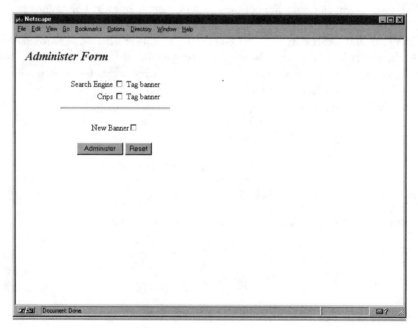

Figure 21.3 The administration form

The resulting form sent out is essentially the same as the first one, differing only in the value of its field values. Therefore, one function method can be created, `sendOutBan-`

nerForm(...), that creates the HTML form shown in figure 21.3. This function takes the
ID of the banner it is to display the attributes for and fills in the field values accordingly.
However, if the banner is a new one (signaled by an ID of 9999) all the fields are left blank,
with the ID for the banner remaining 9999 as it is inserted as a hidden field in the form.

```
private void sendOutBannerPropForm( HttpServletRequest _req,
                                    HttpServletResponse _res)
                                    throws IOException{
  _res.setContentType("text/html");
  PrintWriter Out = new PrintWriter( _res.getOutputStream() );

  //- Add new transmitter
  if ( _req.getParameter( "9999" ) != null ){
    sendOutBannerForm( _res, 9999 );
    return;
  }

  //- Edit the existing banner info
  bannerInfo banner;
  int noElements = bannerList.size();
  for( int x=0; x < noElements; x++ ) {
    banner = (bannerInfo)bannerList.elementAt( x );
    if ( _req.getParameter( banner.bannerID +"" ) != null ){
      sendOutBannerForm( _res, banner.bannerID );
      break;
    }
  }
}
```
Example 21.6   Processing the banner list form

Example 21.6 shows the method that is called as a result of the posting from the original banner list form. This form decides whether the user wants to edit or create a banner. To see if a banner is intended, simply check the status of the New Banner checkbox, which has been given the unique ID of 9999.

To see if the user intended to edit an existing banner, check the status of the banner ID checkboxes. The first one found that is checked is then prepared for editing.

Once the form shown in figure 21.4 is submitted, processing it is a rather simple task, since most of the hard work has already been done. The method shown in example 21.7 retrieves the ID of the banner this form is relating to. If it's a banner, the method creates a new instance; otherwise, it retrieves the object from the list.

Next, if the banner is flagged for deletion, it is removed from the list of other banners. If it's not flagged for deletion, the parameters for the banner are updated. This involves calling the previously discussed setParameters(...) method from the bannerInfo class, which in turn attempts to renew or create the new image file. Finally, if the banner is brand new, then a new ID must be assigned to it. This is done by incrementing the globalID integer.

```
private void processBannerPropForm( HttpServletRequest _req,
                                    HttpServletResponse _res)
                                    throws IOException (
```

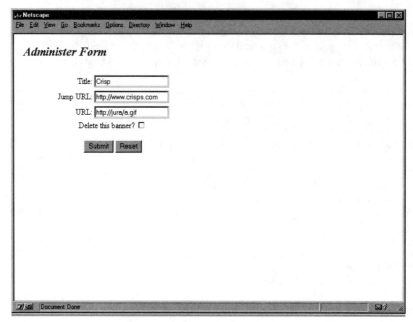

Figure 21.4 The administer form

```
 res.setContentType("text/html");
PrintWriter Out = new PrintWriter( _res.getOutputStream() );
int id = Integer.parseInt( _req.getParameter("SYS_SINGLEBANNER") );
bannerInfo banner;

if ( id == 9999 )
  banner = new bannerInfo();
else{
  banner = (bannerInfo)bannerList.elementAt( id );
  if ( _req.getParameter( "delete" ) != null ){
    int noElements = bannerList.size();
    for( int x=0; x < noElements; x++ ){
      if ( ((bannerInfo)bannerList.elementAt( x )).bannerID == id ){
        bannerList.removeElementAt( id );
        break;
      }
    }
    return;
  }
}

banner.setParameters( _req.getParameter("title"),
                      _req.getParameter("jumpurl"),
                        _req.getParameter("imageurl") );

Out.println( "<HTML><BODY>" );
if ( id == 9999 ){
```

```
    if ( banner.gifOk() ){
      globalID++;
      banner.setID( globalID );
       bannerList.addElement( banner );
    }else
      Out.println( "<B><I>Bad URL for the GIF</I></B>" );
  }

  Out.println( "<B><I>Thank you</I></B>" );
  Out.println( "</BODY></HTML>" );
  Out.flush();
  saveBanners();
}
```
Example 21.7   Processing the properties form

For this particular application area, it is probably best if only one person is allowed to add and remove banners so the site owner can make sure that all banners are suitable for the site.

21.2.2   Serving the banner

Now that all the banners have been created, along with a method for updating them, we need to look at how to actually display them. Since the application area is real estate (like our time-share example), we can simply display the banners one after another on a rotational basis. Every call to display a new banner from the servlet will take the next banner from the list and increment the global index to point to the next one. Each banner in the system will be called the same number of times.

The servlet will display the banner by inserting HTML tags in the output stream via the server-side include mechanism. Not only will the servlet insert the necessary image and the hyperlink tags, but it will also be responsible for displaying and managing the click-through process. Thus, the resulting HTML tags being inserted in the output stream may look something like this:

```
<A HREF=/realestate.html?SYS_CLICK=32>
<IMG SRC=/realestate.html?SYS_IMAGE=32></A>
```

The class method responsible for creating the inline tags is shown in example 21.8. The command line parameters SYS_CLICK and SYS_IMAGE are used, along with the ID of the banner they are referring to. This allows the servlet to correctly identify the banner when the request for the image and the click-through comes in.

```
private void bannerOutput( HttpServletResponse _res) throws IOException{
  _res.setContentType("text/html");
  PrintWriter Out = new PrintWriter( _res.getOutputStream() );

  BannerInfo banner = (bannerInfo)bannerList.elementAt( currentIndex );

  if ( banner != null ){
    Out.println( "<A HREF=/servlet/com.nary.http.
      bannerServlet?SYS_CLICK=" + banner.bannerID+">");
    Out.println( "<IMG SRC=/servlet/com.nary.http.
      bannerServlet?SYS_IMAGE" + banner.bannerID + " BORDER=0></A>" );
```

```
      banner.updateDisplayStats();
    Out.flush();
    synchronized(this){
      currentIndex++;
      if ( currentIndex == bannerList.size() )
        currentIndex = 0;
    }
  }
}
```
Example 21.8   Creating inline HTML code

Once the tags have been sent out, the banner's statistics must be updated to show that a new request has been made to display the banner. The index into the list of banners must now be updated so that a subsequent request will render the next banner in the list (or the first one if it's at the end of the list) to be displayed. Notice how the incrementation is made thread-safe to stop it from prematurely increasing past the size of the list.

The client will receive the HTML tags, and it will process them in turn. The image will be requested first, with the `processImage(…)` (example 21.9) being called to service it. This method will simply find the corresponding banner from the ID supplied with `SYS_IMAGE` parameter. The banner image will then be opened as an `InputStream`, and an `OutputStream` to the client will be created, to which the image will be copied.

Since no filenames have been exchanged with extensions, the client doesn't know what type of image file to accept. This is where Content-Type that we stored when creating the filename becomes useful. By setting the Content-Type in the output header, the client can accurately process the file as the image type indicated in the header.

Note   Even when the Content-Type was not set, the client still correctly processed the file. This happened with Netscape's browser, and I can't guarantee that it will work for all browsers. For this reason, I always recommend that you set the Content-Type header field.

```
private void processImage( HttpServletRequest _req,
                           HttpServletResponse _res) throws IOException{
  int id = Integer.parseInt( _req.getParameter( "SYS_IMAGE" ) );
  bannerInfo banner = getBanner( id );

  _res.setContentType( banner.content );

  BufferedOutputStream OS = new BufferedOutputStream(
                          _res.getOutputStream() );
  BufferedInputStreamIS = new BufferedInputStream(
                          new FileInputStream( banner.strImageName ) );
  byte buffer[]= new byte[1024];
  int noRead = 0;

  noRead = IS.read( buffer, 0, 1023 );
  while ( noRead != -1 ){
    OS.write( buffer, 0, noRead );
```

```
      noRead= IS.read( buffer, 0, 1023 );
   }
   OS.flush();
}
```
Example 21.9   Sending out the image

Once the image has been loaded, the user is presented with a nice banner on the page that is displayed. He can then click the banner if he wants more information. When he clicks the banner, it is important (from a statistical point of view) that we are told of the click. Otherwise, we would have no idea of how successful the banner is. So placing the original URL at the client side would not be the answer. Instead, the servlet must be called and the banner statistics updated, and then the client is taken to the proper link. We can do this with a simple HTTP redirect as shown in the method in example 21.10.

```
private void processClickThru( HttpServletRequest _req,
                               HttpServletResponse _res)
                          throws IOException {
   bannerInfo banner = (bannerInfo)bannerList.elementAt( currentIndex );

   if ( banner != null ){
     banner.updateClickStats();
     _res.sendRedirect( banner.strURL );
   }else
     _res.setStatus( HttpServletResponse.SC_NO_CONTENT );
}
```
Example 21.10   Providing click-through access

21.2.3   Banner statistics
One of the most important features behind advertisements on the web is the ability to get accurate statistics on the success or failure of the advertising campaign. So far, we have seen how to increment all the totals for each banner. Now we must display them. This is a simple matter of formatting an output page with each total listed in a table, as shown in figure 21.5.

Since we have the ability to reset certain subtotals, let's discuss how the reset mechanism works. We just need to provide the same sort of checkbox system that was implemented for selecting banner records from the main list. Example 21.11 shows the method used for sending out this form.

```
private void sendOutStatsForm( HttpServletResponse _res)
                          throws IOException{
   _res.setContentType("text/html");
   PrintWriter Out = new PrintWriter( _res.getOutputStream() );

   Out.println( "<HTML><BODY>" );
   Out.println( "<B>Banner Statistics</I></B>" );
   Out.println( "<FORM METHOD=POST ACTION=
                          /servlet/com.nary.http.bannerServlet>" );
   Out.println( "<CENTER><TABLE BORDER=0>" );
   Out.println( "<INPUT TYPE=hidden NAME=SYS_STATSPOST VALUE=1>" );
   Enumeration E = bannerList.elements();
   BannerInfo banner;
```

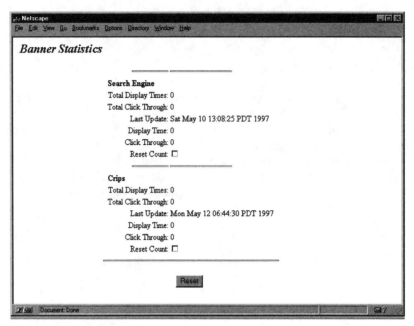

Figure 21.5 Banner statistics

```
while ( E.hasMoreElements() ){
  banner = (bannerInfo)E.nextElement();
  Out.println("<TR><TD><HR ALIGN=RIGHT WIDTH=60%></TD><TD>
              <HR ALIGN=LEFT WIDTH=60%></TD></TR>");
  Out.println( "<TR><TD ALIGH=LEFT><B>" + banner.strTitle + "</B>
              </TD></TR>");
  Out.println( "<TR><TD ALIGN=RIGHT>Total Display Times:</TD>
              <TD ALIGN=LEFT>"
              + banner.totalDisplay + "</TD></TR>" );
  Out.println( "<TR><TD ALIGN=RIGHT>Total Click Through:</TD>
          <TD ALIGN=LEFT>" + banner.totalClicks + "</TD></TR><BR>" );
  Out.println( "<TR><TD ALIGN=RIGHT>Last Update:</TD><TD ALIGN=LEFT>"
              + banner.dateOfLastReset.toString()) + "</TD></TR>" );
  Out.println( "<TR><TD ALIGN=RIGHT>Display Time:</TD><TD ALIGN=LEFT>"
              + banner.lastDisplay + "</TD></TR>" );
  Out.println( "<TR><TD ALIGN=RIGHT>Click Through:</TD><TD ALIGN=LEFT>"
              + banner.lastClick + "</TD></TR>" );
  Out.println( "<TR><TD ALIGN=RIGHT>Reset Count:</TD><TD ALIGN=LEFT>
              <INPUT TYPE=CHECKBOX NAME=" + banner.bannerID + "
                          VALUE=1></TD></TR>" );
  }

  Out.println( "</TABLE>");
  Out.println( "<INPUT TYPE=submit VALUE=Reset>");
  Out.println( "</CENTER></FORM></BODY></HTML>" );
  Out.flush();
}
```

Example 21.11 Sending the statistics form

However, the difference between implementations comes when the form is being processed. Before, when this type of form was posted, each banner was looked at to see if the user had placed a checkmark in the corresponding checkbox, thereby indicating he wanted to include the banner in the rotation. The first banner that was found was used, and the rest were ignored. With this version, all banners can potentially be reset at once.

21.2.4   Complete source code

Here is the complete source code for the banner rotation example.

```java
import java.io.*;
import java.net.*;
import java.util.*;
import javax.servlet.*;
import javax.servlet.http.*;

public class bannerServlet extends HttpServlet {

  private Vector bannerList;
  private int globalID=0, currentIndex=0;

  public void init(ServletConfig _servletConfig) throws ServletException {

super.init(_servletConfig);
    loadBanners();
  }

  public void service( HttpServletRequest _req, HttpServletResponse _res)
                          throws ServletException, IOException{
    if ( _req.getParameter( "SYS_CLICK" ) != null )
      processClickThru( _req, _res );
    else if ( _req.getParameter( "SYS_SHOWSTATS" ) != null )
      sendOutStatsForm( _res );
    else if ( _req.getParameter( "SYS_STATSPOST" ) != null )
      processStatsForm( _req, _res );
    else if ( _req.getParameter( "SYS_ADMIN" ) != null )
      sendOutBannerListForm( _res );
    else if ( _req.getParameter( "SYS_ADMINRESULT" ) != null )
      sendOutBannerPropForm( _req, _res );
    else if ( _req.getParameter( "SYS_IMAGE" ) != null )
      processImage( _req, _res  );
    else if ( _req.getParameter( "SYS_SINGLEBANNER" ) != null )
      processBannerPropForm( _req, _res );
    else
      bannerOutput( _res );
  }

  public String getServletInfo(){
    return "N-ARY: bannerServlet";
  }

  private void loadBanners(){
    try{
      FileInputStream      FS = new FileInputStream( "banner.list" );
```

```
      ObjectInputStream   IS = new ObjectInputStream(FS);
      bannerList                = (Vector)IS.readObject();
   }catch(Exception E){
      bannerList  = new Vector();
   }
}

private void saveBanners(){
  try{
     FileOutputStream    FS = new FileOutputStream( "banner.list" );
     ObjectOutputStream  OS = new ObjectOutputStream(FS);
     OS.writeObject( bannerList );
  }catch(Exception E){}
}

private bannerInfo getBanner( int _id ){
   Enumeration E = bannerList.elements();
   bannerInfo banner;

   while ( E.hasMoreElements() ){
      banner = (bannerInfo)E.nextElement();
      if ( banner.bannerID == _id )
         return banner;
   }
   return null;
}

private void processImage( HttpServletRequest _req,
                           HttpServletResponse _res) throws IOException{
  int id= Integer.parseInt( _req.getParameter( "SYS_IMAGE" ) );
  bannerInfobanner = getBanner( id );

  _res.setContentType( banner.content );

  BufferedOutputStream OS= new BufferedOutputStream(
                           _res.getOutputStream() );
  BufferedInputStream IS = new BufferedInputStream(
                           new FileInputStream( banner.strImageName ) );
  bytebuffer[]= new byte[1024];
  int noRead= 0;

  noRead= IS.read( buffer, 0, 1023 );
  while ( noRead != -1 ){
   OS.write( buffer, 0, noRead );
   noRead= IS.read( buffer, 0, 1023 );
  }

  OS.flush();
}

private void processClickThru( HttpServletRequest _req,
                 HttpServletResponse _res)
                 throws IOException {
  bannerInfobanner = (bannerInfo)bannerList.elementAt( currentIndex );
```

```
    if ( banner != null ){
      banner.updateClickStats();
      _res.sendRedirect( banner.strURL );
    }else
      _res.setStatus( HttpServletResponse.SC_NO_CONTENT );
}

  private void sendOutStatsForm( HttpServletResponse _res)
            throws IOException{
_res.setContentType("text/html");
    PrintWriter Out = new PrintWriter( _res.getOutputStream() );

  Out.println( "<HTML><BODY>" );
  Out.println( "<B>Banner Statistics</I></B>" );
  Out.println( "<FORM METHOD=POST
            ACTION=/servlet/com.nary.http.bannerServlet>" );
  Out.println( "<CENTER><TABLE BORDER=0>" );
  Out.println( "<INPUT TYPE=hidden NAME=SYS_STATSPOST VALUE=1>" );

  Enumeration E= bannerList.elements();
    bannerInfobanner;
  while ( E.hasMoreElements() ){
    banner= (bannerInfo)E.nextElement();
    Out.println( "<TR><TD><HR ALIGN=RIGHT WIDTH=60%></TD><TD>
            <HR ALIGN=LEFT WIDTH=60%></TD></TR>");
    Out.println( "<TR><TD ALIGH=LEFT><B>" + banner.strTitle + "</B>
            </TD></TR>");
    Out.println( "<TR><TD ALIGN=RIGHT>Total Display Times:</TD>
            <TD ALIGN=LEFT>" + banner.totalDisplay + "</TD></TR>" );
    Out.println( "<TR><TD ALIGN=RIGHT>Total Click Through:</TD>
            <TD ALIGN=LEFT>" + banner.totalClicks + "</TD></TR><BR>" );
    Out.println( "<TR><TD ALIGN=RIGHT>Last Update:</TD><TD ALIGN=LEFT>"
            + (banner.dateOfLastReset.toString()) + "</TD></TR>" );
    Out.println( "<TR><TD ALIGN=RIGHT>Display Time:</TD>
            <TD ALIGN=LEFT>" + banner.lastDisplay + "</TD></TR>" );
    Out.println( "<TR><TD ALIGN=RIGHT>Click Through:</TD>
            <TD ALIGN=LEFT>" + banner.lastClick + "</TD></TR>" );
      Out.println( "<TR><TD ALIGN=RIGHT>Reset Count:</TD>
       <TD ALIGN=LEFT><INPUT TYPE=CHECKBOX NAME="
            + banner.bannerID + " VALUE=1></TD></TR>" );
  }

    Out.println( "</TABLE>");
  Out.println( "<INPUT TYPE=submit VALUE=Reset>");
    Out.println( "</CENTER></FORM></BODY></HTML>" );
  Out.flush();
  }
  private void processStatsForm( HttpServletRequest _req,
            HttpServletResponse _res) throws IOException {
    _res.setContentType("text/html");
    PrintWriter Out = new PrintWriter( _res.getOutputStream() );

    //- Edit an existing banner
    Enumeration E = bannerList.elements();
```

```
       bannerInfobanner;
       while (E.hasMoreElements() ){
         banner= (bannerInfo)E.nextElement();

         if ( _req.getParameter( banner.bannerID+"" ) != null )
           banner.resetStats();
       }

    Out.println( "<HTML><BODY>" );
    Out.println( "<B><I>Thank you, Stats have been reset</I></B>" );
    Out.println( "</BODY></HTML>" );
    Out.flush();
  }


  private void sendOutBannerListForm( HttpServletResponse _res )
                     throws IOException{
    //- Formats a new form and sends it out to the client
    _res.setContentType("text/html");
    PrintWriter Out = new PrintWriter( _res.getOutputStream() );

    Out.println( "<HTML><BODY>" );
    Out.println( "<B><I>Administer Form</I></B>" );
    Out.println( "<FORM METHOD=POST
                     ACTION=/servlet/com.nary.http.bannerServlet>
                     <CENTER><TABLE BORDER=0>" );
    Out.println( "<INPUT TYPE=hidden NAME=SYS_ADMINRESULT VALUE=1>" );

    Enumeration E= bannerList.elements();
    bannerInfobanner;
    while ( E.hasMoreElements() ){
      banner= (bannerInfo)E.nextElement();
      Out.println( "<TR><TD ALIGN=RIGHT>" + banner.strTitle + "</TD>
                     <TD ALIGN=LEFT><INPUT TYPE=CHECKBOX NAME=\"" +
               banner.bannerID + "\" VALUE=1> Tag banner</TD></TR>" );
    }

    Out.println( "</TABLE>");
    Out.println( "<TR><TD ALIGN=RIGHT>New Banner</TD><TD ALIGN=LEFT>
                     <INPUT TYPE=CHECKBOX NAME=9999 VALUE=1>
                     </TD></TR><BR><BR>" );
    Out.println( "<INPUT TYPE=submit VALUE=Administer>
                     <INPUT TYPE=reset VALUE=Reset>");
    Out.println( "</CENTER></FORM></BODY></HTML>" );
    Out.flush();
  }


  private void sendOutBannerForm( HttpServletResponse _res, int _id )
                     throws IOException {
    //- Formats a new form and sends it out to the client
    _res.setContentType("text/html");
    PrintWriter Out = new PrintWriter( _res.getOutputStream() );

    //- Setup variables
    String strTitle = "";
```

```
       String strURL = "";
       String strImageURL = "";

       if ( _id != 9999 ){
          bannerInfobanner = getBanner( _id );
          strTitle= banner.strTitle;
          strURL= banner.strURL;
       }

       //- Send out the form
       Out.println( "<HTML><BODY>" );
       Out.println( "<B><I>Administer Form</I></B>" );
       Out.println( "<FORM METHOD=POST ACTION=/servlet/com.nary.http.>
                            <CENTER><TABLE BORDER=0>" );
       Out.println( "<INPUT TYPE=hidden NAME=SYS_SINGLEBANNER VALUE=" + _id
                            + ">" );

       Out.println( "<CENTER><TABLE BORDER=0>" );
       Out.println( "<TR><TD ALIGN=RIGHT>Title:</TD><TD ALIGN=LEFT>
                            <INPUT TYPE=TEXT NAME=title VALUE=\""
                            + strTitle + "\"></TD></TR>" );
       Out.println( "<TR><TD ALIGN=RIGHT>Jump URL:</TD><TD ALIGN=LEFT>
                            <INPUT TYPE=TEXT NAME=jumpurl VALUE=\""
                            + strURL + "\"></TD></TR>" );
       Out.println( "<TR><TD ALIGN=RIGHT>URL:</TD><TD ALIGN=LEFT>
                            <INPUT TYPE=TEXT NAME=imageurl VALUE=\""
                            + strImageURL + "\"></TD></TR>" );
       Out.println( "</TABLE></CENTER>");

       Out.println( "Delete this banner? <INPUT TYPE=CHECKBOX NAME=delete>"
);
       Out.println( "<BR><BR><INPUT TYPE=submit VALUE=\"Submit\">
                            <INPUT TYPE=reset VALUE=\"Reset\">");
       Out.println( "</CENTER></FORM><P></BODY></HTML>" );
       Out.flush();
    }

  private void sendOutBannerPropForm( HttpServletRequest _req,
                            HttpServletResponse _res) throws IOException{
    _res.setContentType("text/html");
       PrintWriter Out = new PrintWriter( _res.getOutputStream() );

    //- Add new transmitter
       if ( _req.getParameter( "9999" ) != null ){
       sendOutBannerForm( _res, 9999 );
       return;
    }

       //- Edit an existing banner
    bannerInfo banner;
       int noElements = bannerList.size();
    for( int x=0; x < noElements; x++ ) {
       banner= (bannerInfo)bannerList.elementAt( x );
       if ( _req.getParameter( banner.bannerID +"" ) != null ){
```

```
            sendOutBannerForm( _res, banner.bannerID );
            break;
        }
    }
}


private void bannerOutput(HttpServletResponse _res) throws IOException{
    _res.setContentType("text/html");
    PrintWriter Out = new PrintWriter( _res.getOutputStream() );

    bannerInfobanner=(bannerInfo)bannerList.elementAt( currentIndex );

    if ( banner != null ){
        Out.println( "<A HREF=/servlet/
    com.nary.http.bannerServlet?SYS_CLICK="
                            + banner.bannerID + ">" );
        Out.println( "<IMG SRC=/servlet/
    com.nary.http.bannerServlet?SYS_IMAGE" + banner.bannerID + " BORDER=0>
                        </A>" );
        banner.updateDisplayStats();
        Out.flush();

        synchronized(this){
            currentIndex++;
            if ( currentIndex == bannerList.size() )
                currentIndex = 0;
        }
    }
}


private void processBannerPropForm( HttpServletRequest _req,
                    HttpServletResponse _res) throws IOException{
    _res.setContentType("text/html");
    PrintWriter Out = new PrintWriter( _res.getOutputStream() );

    int id= Integer.parseInt( _req.getParameter("SYS_SINGLEBANNER") );
    bannerInfobanner;

    if ( id == 9999 )
        banner= new bannerInfo();
    else{
        banner= (bannerInfo)bannerList.elementAt( id );
        if ( _req.getParameter( "delete" ) != null ){
            int noElements = bannerList.size();
            for( int x=0; x < noElements; x++ ){
                if ( ((bannerInfo)bannerList.elementAt( x )).bannerID
                            == id ){
                    bannerList.removeElementAt( id );
                    break;
                }
            }
            return;
        }
    }
```

```java
    banner.setParameters( _req.getParameter("title"),
        _req.getParameter("jumpurl"), _req.getParameter("imageurl") );

    Out.println( "<HTML><BODY>" );

    if ( id == 9999 ){
      if ( banner.gifOk() ){
        globalID++;
        banner.setID( globalID );
        bannerList.addElement( banner );
      }else
        Out.println( "<B><I>Bad URL for the GIF</I></B>" );
    }

    Out.println( "<B><I>Thank you</I></B>" );
    Out.println( "</BODY></HTML>" );
    Out.flush();
    saveBanners();
  }

}


class bannerInfo implements Serializable {
  public int      bannerID;
  public StringstrImageName;
  public Stringcontent;
  public StringstrTitle;
  public StringstrURL=null;

  public inttotalDisplay=0;
  public inttotalClicks=0;
  public intlastDisplay=0;
  public intlastClick=0;
  public DatedateOfLastReset = new Date();

  public void updateDisplayStats(){
    totalDisplay++;
    lastDisplay++;
  }

  public void updateClickStats(){
    totalClicks++;
    lastClick++;
  }

  public voidsetParameters( String _strTitle, String _strURL,
        String _imgURL ){
    strTitle= _strTitle;
    strURL= _strURL;
    //- Load in the GIF image
    StringTokenizer st = new StringTokenizer( _imgURL, "." );
    String fileExt;
```

```
       if ( st.countTokens() == 2 ){
          st.nextToken();
          fileExt = st.nextToken();
       }else
          return;

       if ( fileExt.compareTo( "gif" ) == 0 )
          content = "image/gif";
       else if ( fileExt.compareTo( "jpg" ) == 0 )
          content = "image/jpeg";

       StringstrFileName= System.currentTimeMillis() + "." + fileExt;

       URL    Host;
       URLConnection      Uc;
       BufferedInputStream IS;
       BufferedOutputStreamOS;

       try{
          Host= new URL( _imgURL );
          Uc  = Host.openConnection();
          IS  = new BufferedInputStream( Uc.getInputStream() );
          OS = new BufferedOutputStream( new FileOutputStream(strFileName) );

          bytebuffer[] = new byte[1024];
          int  noRead = 0;

          noRead= IS.read( buffer, 0, 1023 );
          while ( noRead != -1 ){
             OS.write( buffer, 0, noRead );
             noRead= IS.read( buffer, 0, 1023 );
          }
          OS.flush();
       } catch (Exception E ){
         return;
       }

      if ( strImageName != null )
       (new File(strImageName)).delete();

       strImageName = strFileName;
   }

public void setID( int _ID ){
    bannerID= _ID;
}

public boolean gifOk(){
    if ( strURL == null )
       return false;
    else
       return true;
}
```

```
    public void resetStats(){
        lastDisplay= 0;
        lastClick= 0;
        dateOfLastReset = new Date();
    }
}
```
Example 21.12   The complete source code for the banner servlet

21.3 *From here*

In this chapter, we have looked at implementing banners. A number of banner server services are available on the Internet. Take some time to familiarize yourself with several of them to see which ones will benefit you the most.

CHAPTER 22

Email fortune cookies

Email is a tool of the '70s that is finding immense popularity today. Looking at the advances in other areas of communication, this basic form of communication has remained relatively untouched. Many of the email systems today, especially Internet-based email, are still enjoying the simplicity of ASCII, with binary attachments being encoded into a series of ASCII characters that are easily sent and received by many email clients all over the world.

Estimates today show that approximately ten times as many emails are sent than pieces of mail are sent through the "snail mail" channels. Like normal letters, we generally love to get email—assuming, of course, it's not junk mail. Sending email is considered to be a free process once an Internet connection has been established. This opens up the floodgates to people who are abusing the use of email.

A well-managed mailing list can yield fantastic results. A list that allows people to sign up (and, more importantly, sign off) can bring a company or organization closer to its user base.

22.1 Mailing list servlet

This section will describe the design and construction of a servlet that will manage a mailing list. A mailing list is simply a collection of email addresses that is used by companies, groups, and individuals to broadcast various announcements, share information, or mail humorous stories, for example.

The servlet in this section will manage a mailing list that allows users to automatically sign on and off. Many web sites presently collate email addresses from their mailing lists and guest books so the site owners can keep their clients up to date with new releases and product information. This method of signing users up can be an invitation for junk email, so it is important to give your members an easy means of removing themselves from the list, if they want to do so.

There are many ways for users to submit their email addresses to mailing lists. However many of these methods require the site owners to do a significant amount of administration, especially when users need to be removed from the list. Other methods require actual dedicated mailing list software. For example, one of the most popular ones is LIST-SERV from L-Soft International. This package is a complete mailing list server and it requires a special setup, using commands sent to a special email address, to configure it. Although it's a fine piece of software, it is much more than most users need.

Most mailing list moderators just want a simple, hassle-free way of collating email addresses without having to worry about answering user requests for things like signing off. The servlet presented in this chapter provides them with a very simple interface.

22.1.1 Overview

To make the signup process easy for the users, a simple one-field form will be presented to them. They will use this form to submit their email addresses so they can be added to the mailing list. A similar form will be used to remove them from the list.

Instead of complicating the whole design, let's use the same servlet for both adding and removing users. In addition, the servlet must:

- Display the complete list of email addresses already subscribed to the mailing list.
- Handle many different mailing lists.

We would be shortsighted if we designed ourselves into a corner and didn't plan to support multiple mailing lists. If we design the servlet correctly, we will only ever need one instance of the class running in the server at any one time.

Each mailing list will require a unique ID so we can correctly add users to the right list. To make things even simpler, let's remove the need for a list to be specified at startup. If the ID for a list is not found, then a new list will be created.

As you know, a mailing list is a simple list of email addresses. We need to decide on a data structure to hold this list. The first logical choice is to use the Vector class. This isn't a bad choice, but it does allow duplicated email addresses to be stored. To avoid this problem, we would have to manually search through the list each time a subscribe request came in to make sure it's not a duplicate.

A data structure that would take this duplication headache away is the Hashtable. By storing the email address as the key, we can avoid duplicates while simplifying the complexity of code.

22.1.2 Loading and saving

We want to make the servlet as hassle free as possible. This means that we have to make it immune from server starts and shutdowns. Let's assume that the mailing list is going to be very popular and have hundreds of emails. Let's also go out on a limb and assume that we will manage many of these types of lists.

Keeping the mail and the recipients in memory all the time is both wasteful and unnecessary. Why use up memory when it may be better used by another application? So let's set our servlet up so that each request to add a user to a list will load the mailing list, add the email address, and then save the mailing list back out to disk. We need routines to perform these tasks.

```
public static synchronized Hashtable loadMailListing( String _ID ){
  Hashtable ML;
    try{
    FileInputStream      FS = new FileInputStream( _ID+".mailinglist" );
    ObjectInputStream    IS = new ObjectInputStream(FS);
    ML                      = (Hashtable)IS.readObject();
  }catch(Exception E){
    ML  = new Hashtable();
  }

  return ML;
}
```
Example 22.1   Loading the mailing list

Example 22.1 shows the method used for loading the mailing list. As you can see, it uses the Object Serialization feature of the JDK. Since the java.util.Hashtable class implements the java.io.Serialization interface, we can easily save the data out to disk.

Each mailing list will be saved in its own file, using its ID and the mailinglist file extension, so we can easily find the necessary files.

If the mailing list is a new one, then the `java.io.FileInputStream` class will throw an exception stating that it can't find the file. If an exception occurs, then we assume a new list is needed and we create an empty instance of a `Hashtable`.

After the user has been added or removed, then the list can be saved back out to disk. This is a simple matter of calling the opposite methods for the object serialization classes, as shown in example 22.2.

```
public static synchronized void saveMailListing( String _ID,
                              Hashtable _MailList ){
  try{
    FileOutputStream      FS = new FileOutputStream( _ID+".mailinglist" );
    ObjectOutputStream    OS = new ObjectOutputStream(FS);
    OS.writeObject( _MailList );
  }catch(Exception E){}
}
```
Example 22.2   Saving the mailing list

22.1.3   Accepting requests

Since this servlet will deal solely with HTTP requests, we will base our new class on the `HttpServlet` class. The data being sent to the servlet will consist of only a few parameters at most: the user's email address, the mailing list ID, and the URL the user will be taken to after submitting the requested information. Therefore, instead of overriding the `service(...)` method, we will override the `doGet(...)` method. This means that the servlet will only respond to GET requests and it will ignore any POS requests.

The method shown in example 22.3 illustrates the `doGet(...)` method as it is used in the mailing list servlet. Notice how we are switching execution control depending on the parameters that are passed in.

```
public void doGet(HttpServletRequest _req, HttpServletResponse _res)
                              throws ServletException, IOException {
  if ( _req.getParameter("SYS_ADD") != null )
    addNewUser( _req, _res );
  else if ( _req.getParameter("SYS_DELETE") != null )
    deleteUser( _req, _res );
  else if ( _req.getParameter("SYS_DISPLAY") != null )
    displayUser( _req, _res );
  else
    _res.setStatus( HttpServletResponse.SC_NO_CONTENT );
}
```
Example 22.3   Processing the request

This technique gives us one servlet that will do many functions instead of lots of smaller servlets doing the same thing. By passing in an additional parameter, SYS_?????, we can check for the variable and call the corresponding method. If no control parameters are passed, then the servlet doesn't alter anything. It sends back a SC_NO_CONTENT status response in the HTTP header. The browser will then ignore this response and not move the user to another page.

The following sections will describe the processing required for control flow.

22.1.4 Adding a user

One of the main functions of the mailing list servlet is to add email addresses to a specified list. Users will be asked to fill in a simple form; this form can exist on any web page with minimal disruption. Figure 22.1 shows how the Add form might look to the user. As you can see, it is merely a text field and a Submit button. With this minimal design, the form can be integrated into most site designs without looking like it's out of place.

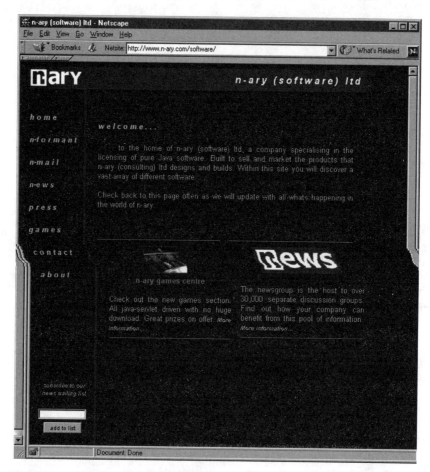

Figure 22.1 Adding a user to the mailing list

In order for us to correctly add the user, we need his email address, the ID of the mailing list, and the URL where the user will be taken to after he successfully submits his information. The HTML code for the form is shown in example 22.4.

```
<FORM ACTION="/servlet/com.nary.http.mailingList" METHOD="GET">
<INPUT TYPE="Hidden" NAME="ID" VALUE="nary">
```

```
<INPUT TYPE="Hidden" NAME="NEXT_URL" VALUE="/mailingList.html">
<INPUT TYPE="Text" NAME="EMAIL" SIZE="20">
<INPUT TYPE="Submit" NAME="SYS_ADD" VALUE="add to Mailing List">
</FORM>
```
Example 22.4   The HTML code for adding a new user

The HTML code contains all the necessary parameters, including the special `SYS_ADD` control parameter which will allow our servlet to correctly process this as an addition.

Example 22.5 shows the necessary processing for adding a user. The first thing we do is to retrieve the `Hashtable` that will house all our email addresses. It's retrieved with a call to `loadMailListing(…)` using the ID that has been passed in as an HTML parameter.

```
Hashtable MailingList = loadMailListing( _req.getParameter("ID") );
if ( MailingList != null ){
  String newUser  = _req.getParameter("EMAIL");
  if ( newUser != null && newUser.indexOf("@") != -1 ){
    newUser = newUser.toLowerCase().trim();
    if ( MailingList.containsKey( newUser ) == false ){
     MailingList.put( newUser, "" );
     saveMailListing( _req.getParameter("ID"), MailingList );
    }
  }
}
_res.sendRedirect( _req.getParameter("NEXT_URL") );
```
Example 22.5   Adding a user to the list

Before we add the email address, we'll need to do some preprocessing on it to make sure it looks like a valid email address (not that the address itself is valid), and that it doesn't have any spaces at the end or beginning. We also convert it to lowercase, as a general rule, to make it easier to spot the email address again in the future.

Let's first check to see if the email address is already in the mailing list. If the address is already in the list, then we ignore it and redirect the user to the specified URL. If it is not part of the list, we add it, using the email address as the key to the `Hashtable`. Since the `Hashtable` doesn't permit a null data value, we store an empty string value. After inserting the new element, we must write the mailing list back out to disk with a call to `save-MailListing(…)`.

22.1.5   Deleting a user

At some point, users may no longer want to be part of the mailing list. The ethical thing to do here is to remove them, but this can be quite time-consuming from an administrator's point of view. Giving users the ability to remove themselves is a big timesaver for us and it can also promote consumer confidence in a company.

The HTML form to remove an email address as illustrated in example 22.6, looks very similar to the one to add a user.

```
<FORM ACTION="/servlet/com.nary.http.mailingList" METHOD="GET">
<INPUT TYPE="Hidden" NAME="ID" VALUE="nary">
<INPUT TYPE="Hidden" NAME="NEXT_URL" VALUE="/mailingList.html">
<INPUT TYPE="Text" NAME="EMAIL" SIZE="20">
```

```
<INPUT TYPE="Submit" NAME="SYS_DELETE" VALUE="remove from Mailing List">
</FORM>
```
Example 22.6   The HTML code for deleting a user

The only differences between the Add form and the Delete form are the labels on the Submit button and the control parameters (SYS_DELETE or SYS_ADD, depending on the form being used).

The procedure to remove a user follows the same steps as for adding him to the list. Example 22.7 shows the steps to remove a user.

```
Hashtable MailingList = loadMailListing( _req.getParameter("ID") );
if ( MailingList != null ){
  String newUser  = _req.getParameter("EMAIL");
  if ( newUser != null && newUser.indexOf("@") != -1 ){
    newUser = newUser.toLowerCase().trim();
    if ( MailingList.containsKey( newUser ) ){
      MailingList.remove( newUser );
      saveMailListing( _req.getParameter("ID"), MailingList );
    }
  }
}
_res.sendRedirect( _req.getParameter("NEXT_URL") );
```
Example 22.7   Removing a user from the list

By making sure all the email addresses are stored in lowercase, with no spaces associated with them, we can easily and quickly index them. For example, if we did not transpose the characters to lowercase, then an address such as Alan@somewhere.com would not be equal to; therefore, it would not match the first occurrence and would not be removed from the list.

22.1.6 Viewing the list

Now that the servlet is happily adding and removing email addresses, we need to create a way to view all the email addresses. The chances are good that we will want to use these same email addresses elsewhere, so we need to present the list in a format that is easily manipulated or transferable to other programs. The easiest way to solve this is to list the emails as simple ASCII text, one after another in a long list.

Example 22.8 shows the method for listing the email addresses. The mailing list is loaded as usual, then we create a PrintWriter instance that will allow us to write the list to the browser. We will set the content-type to plain ASCII text.

```
Hashtable MailingList = loadMailListing( _req.getParameter("ID") );
if ( MailingList != null ){
  PrintWriter Out = _res.getWriter();
  _res.setContentType( "text/plain" );
  Out.println( "Mailing List: "+_req.getParameter("ID")+"
                           ["+MailingList.size()+ " members]" );
  Enumeration E = MailingList.keys();
  while (E.hasMoreElements())
    Out.println( (String)E.nextElement() );
```

```
    Out.flush();
}else
    _res.setStatus( HttpServletResponse.SC_NO_CONTENT );
```
Example 22.8 Displaying the list of email addresses

Writing the email addresses is a simple matter of setting up an `Enumeration` to the `Hashtable` and printing out each key one line at a time. You will then have a list of all email addresses in your browser; these addresses can then be easily be selected and copied into other applications.

The HTML code to display the email addresses is very similar to the code for adding and deleting except for the omission of the text field box. The HTML code is shown in example 22.9; you can see the use of the `SYS_DISPLAY` control parameter.

```
<FORM ACTION="/servlet/com.nary.http.mailingList" METHOD="GET">
<INPUT TYPE="Hidden" NAME="ID" VALUE="nary">
<INPUT TYPE="Submit" NAME="SYS_DISPLAY" VALUE="Display Mailing List">
</FORM>
```
Example 22.9 The HTML code for displaying the email addresses

22.1.7 Sending a mail shot

Building in the ability to send email directly from the servlet is not a major problem. After all, we have already developed classes to send email in previous chapters. For this servlet, we'll build a form that you will use to send the same email to everyone on the mailing list (figure 22.2).

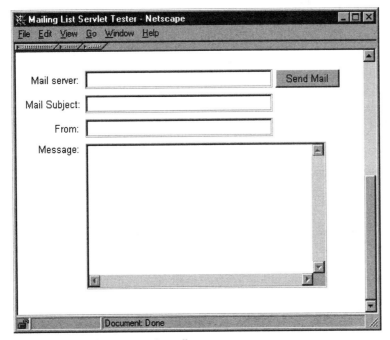

Figure 22.2 The form to send email

To correctly process this form, we will not respond to a GET, but we will respond to a POST. Using the POST method to send data ensures that we do not run into problems where the amount of data being passed exceeds the limit imposed on us (as it would if we were to use a GET directive). This time we will override the doPost(…) method.

Sending out a group email is a simple matter of loading the mailing list and sending out the same message to each address. We will send out only one email address in each message to ensure that no user can see who else is on the mailing list. Granted, this places a far greater load on the mail server, but the increased security makes it worth the extra work. Example 22.10 shows the method for performing this task.

```
Hashtable MailingList = loadMailListing( _req.getParameter("ID") );
if ( MailingList != null ){
  sendEmail  Mail = new sendEmail( _req.getParameter("MAILSERVER") );
  try{
    Vector Message = createVectorOfLines( _req.getParameter("MESSAGE") );
    String to[]    = new String[1];
    String tmp[]   = new String[0];
    Enumeration E = MailingList.keys();
    while (E.hasMoreElements()){
       to[0]  = (String)E.nextElement();
       Mail.sendMail(to, _req.getParameter("FROM"),tmp,tmp,
                          _req.getParameter("SUBJECT"), Message);
    }
    Mail.close()
  }catch(Exception E1){}
}
_res.sendRedirect( _req.getParameter("NEXT_URL") );
```
Example 22.10   Sending out a group email

You can see that the code looks very similar to the method we used to display the email addresses. The email list is gathered in much the same manner, but instead of sending it out to the client, we generate an email message. We use the same class, sendEmail, that we developed in earlier chapters for sending out mail.

Notice the method createVectorOfLines(…). This method takes the data from a TEXTAREA HTML control and converts it to a Vector of strings, where each element is a separate line. The source code for this method is shown in example 22.11.

After all the email has been sent, the connection to the mail server is closed and the user is directed to the URL passed in with the NEXT_URL parameter.

22.1.8   Complete source code

The source code in example 22.11 shows all the parts we have built as one complete piece of code. Look carefully at how it all fits together, including adding and deleting a user and generating the list.

```
package com.nary.http;

import javax.servlet.*;
import javax.servlet.http.*;
import java.io.*;
import java.util.*;
```

```
import com.nary.net.*;

public class mailingList extends HttpServlet {

  public void init(ServletConfig config) throws ServletException {
    super.init(config);
  }

  public String getServletInfo() {
    return "com.nary.http.mailingList: version 1.0";
  }

  public void doGet(HttpServletRequest _req, HttpServletResponse _res)
                             throws ServletException, IOException {
    if ( _req.getParameter("SYS_ADD") != null )
      addNewUser( _req, _res );
    else if ( _req.getParameter("SYS_DELETE") != null )
      deleteUser( _req, _res );
    else if ( _req.getParameter("SYS_DISPLAY") != null )
      displayUser( _req, _res );
    else
      _res.setStatus( HttpServletResponse.SC_NO_CONTENT );
  }

  public void doPost(HttpServletRequest _req, HttpServletResponse _res)
                             throws ServletException, IOException {
    sendMail( _req, _res );
  }

  public void addNewUser(HttpServletRequest _req,
HttpServletResponse _res)
                             throws ServletException, IOException {
    Hashtable MailingList = loadMailListing( _req.getParameter("ID") );
    if ( MailingList != null ){
      String newUser  = _req.getParameter("EMAIL");
      if ( newUser != null && newUser.indexOf("@") != -1 ){
        newUser = newUser.toLowerCase().trim();
        if ( MailingList.containsKey( newUser ) == false ){
          MailingList.put( newUser, "" );
          saveMailListing( _req.getParameter("ID"), MailingList );
        }
      }
    }
    _res.sendRedirect( _req.getParameter("NEXT_URL") );
  }

  public void deleteUser(HttpServletRequest _req,
                         HttpServletResponse _res)
                             throws ServletException, IOException {
    Hashtable MailingList = loadMailListing( _req.getParameter("ID") );
    if ( MailingList !- null ){
      String newUser  = _req.getParameter("EMAIL");
      if ( newUser != null && newUser.indexOf("@") != -1 ){
        newUser = newUser.toLowerCase().trim();
```

```
        if ( MailingList.containsKey( newUser ) ){
          MailingList.remove( newUser );
          saveMailListing( _req.getParameter("ID"), MailingList );
        }
      }
    }
    _res.sendRedirect( _req.getParameter("NEXT_URL") );
  }


  public void displayUser(HttpServletRequest _req,
                          HttpServletResponse _res)
                          throws ServletException, IOException {
    Hashtable MailingList = loadMailListing( _req.getParameter("ID") );
    if ( MailingList != null ){
      PrintWriter Out = new PrintWriter( _res.getOutputStream() );
      _res.setContentType( "text/plain" );

      Out.println( "Mailing List: " + _req.getParameter("ID")
                   + " [" + MailingList.size() + " members]" );

      Enumeration E = MailingList.keys();
      while (E.hasMoreElements())
        Out.println( (String)E.nextElement() );

      Out.flush();
    }else
      _res.setStatus( HttpServletResponse.SC_NO_CONTENT );
  }


  public synchronized void sendMail(HttpServletRequest _req,
                          HttpServletResponse _res)
                          throws ServletException, IOException {
    Hashtable MailingList = loadMailListing( _req.getParameter("ID") );
    if ( MailingList != null ){
      sendEmail  Mail = new sendEmail( _req.getParameter("MAILSERVER") );
      try{
        Vector Message  = createVectorOfLines( _req.getParameter
                          ("MESSAGE") );
        String to[]     = new String[1];
        String tmp[]    = new String[0];

        Enumeration E = MailingList.keys();
        while (E.hasMoreElements()){
          to[0]  = (String)E.nextElement();
          Mail.sendMail(to,_req.getParameter("FROM"),tmp,tmp,
                        _req.getParameter("SUBJECT"),Message);
        }
Mail.close();
      }catch(Exception E1){}
    }
    _res.sendRedirect( _req.getParameter("NEXT_URL") );
  }


  public static synchronized Hashtable loadMailListing( String _ID ){
```

```
            Hashtable ML;
    try{
      FileInputStream      FS = new FileInputStream( _ID+".mailinglist" );
      ObjectInputStream    IS = new ObjectInputStream(FS);
      ML                   = (Hashtable)IS.readObject();
    }catch(Exception E){
      ML  = new Hashtable();
    }
    return ML;
  }

  public static synchronized void saveMailListing( String _ID,
                               Hashtable _MailList ){
    try{
      FileOutputStream     FS = new FileOutputStream( _ID+".mailinglist"
);
      ObjectOutputStream   OS = new ObjectOutputStream(FS);
      OS.writeObject( _MailList );
    }catch(Exception E){}
  }

  public static Vector createVectorOfLines( String _Body ){
    Vector V = new Vector(10,5);

    try{
      BufferedReader  bodyIn = new BufferedReader(
                             new StringReader( _Body ) );
      String LineIn   = bodyIn.readLine();
      while (LineIn != null ){
        if ( LineIn.length() == 0 ) LineIn = " ";
          V.addElement( LineIn );
          LineIn   = bodyIn.readLine();
        }
        return V;
      }catch(Exception E){}
      return null;
  }
}
```

Example 22.11   The complete source code for the mailing list servlet

22.2   Fortune cookie servlet

Many of the servlets presented in this book provide a certain level of entertainment. Entertaining your web visitors is never a bad thing, since it encourages them to stay at the site longer, which increases the chances of their visiting your sections of the site. It is important to persuade people to come back to your web site—if they have a good reason to, they most probably will.

On that note, let's look at the second servlet of this chapter. This servlet builds on the mailing list servlet we just created. It offers the user the ability to receive an email a day containing various pearls of wisdom or jokes or quotes, or whatever you deem appropriate—this is often known as a fortune cookie. We will build a servlet that will need very little maintenance, and it will be very easy to use from the user's perspective.

22.2.1 Overview

This servlet is very similar to the servlet presented in the first part of this chapter. Users submit their email addresses to form a list, and that list is sent a new email once a day. So why reinvent the wheel? We'll use the same mailing list mechanism from the first servlet to act as our mailing list for this application. Since we built the first servlet with the foresight not to tie it in to any one mailing list, we can create as many different mailing lists as we want by using a unique mailing list ID for each one.

Now that we have that function of the servlet sorted out, we need to determine some attributes a fortune cookie may possess. For starters, it will need to have a unique ID. This ID will allow us to correctly refer to it in the future, and it will also allow us to support many different fortune cookies with one servlet instance. A mailing list ID also has to be associated with it; this will be the list of people that will receive the email each day.

A source for the information for the email message will be required. This is made up of a source with the cookie's text and an email template. Let's assume, for the moment, that the cookie source will be a filename; we will address this further later in this chapter. Another couple of parameters that will be associated with the file will be the delimiting string and the current position or record number in the file.

The template message text that makes up the body of the message will also be required. The actual fortune cookie will be inserted somewhere in this message body before it is sent.

We can store all this information in one easily accessible class. The class in example 22.12 will perform this task. Notice how we have implemented the `java.io.Serializable` interface so we can easily save the class instance out to disk.

```
class cookieData implements Serializable {
  public String iD="";
  public String mailID="";
  public String urlData="";
  public String delimiter="";
  public int    position=0;
  public Vector message;
}
```
Example 22.12 Fortune cookie data

Since this servlet will be called upon once a day, we will keep this information in memory and only save the data out to disk when we know something has changed. To make accessing each fortune cookie simple, we will store them in a `Hashtable` and use the IDs as the keys, with the class instance as the data.

Routines to store and retrieve this data are very straightforward, as they use the same techniques that were demonstrated in the first part of this chapter. You can see them in example 22.13.

```
private synchronized void loadCookieList(){
  try{
    FileInputStream   FS = new FileInputStream( "main.cookielist" );
    ObjectInputStream IS = new ObjectInputStream(FS);
    cookieList           = (Hashtable)IS.readObject();
  }catch(Exception E){
```

```
      System.out.println( E );
      cookieList   = new Hashtable();
   }
}

private synchronized void saveCookieList(){
   try{
      FileOutputStream    FS = new FileOutputStream( "main.cookielist" );
      ObjectOutputStream OS = new ObjectOutputStream(FS);
      OS.writeObject( cookieList );
   }catch(Exception E){}
}
```
Example 22.13   Saving and retrieving data

As with the first servlet, we will override the doGet(...) method and use a variety of
control parameters to switch the execution flow depending on the request. The following
sections will look at creating, editing, and deleting a fortune cookie. The last section will
look at how to format the database of quotes and how we send them out once a day.

Note   This saving technique is one of the major advantages of using the Object Serialization features of the Java JDK. Notice we saved only the top-level Hashtable but all
the data was saved. By saving only one class, all the referenced classes are stored with it
(assuming, of course, that each class implemented the Serializaton interface—if they
don't, they won't be saved).

22.2.2   Creating a fortune cookie

We will create a fortune cookie in exactly the same way we added a new user to a mailing
list, except this time, the user will have to fill in just a few more fields. However, we should
not really use the term "user," as this section should not be available to the general public—it should only administered by an authorized person such as an administrator.

The form shown in figure 22.3 illustrates the type of information that you need to
provide.

Once you submit this form to the servlet, we must create an instance of the data class
and save it with the rest of the fortune cookies using the method shown in example 22.14.

This method checks a list of parameters to see if any of them are null. They will be
null if the user has not filled them in. To ensure data integrity we will recheck the ones
that show as null.

```
String cookieName = _req.getParameter( "COOKIENAME" );
String mailID     = _req.getParameter( "MAILID" );
String urlData    = _req.getParameter( "URLDATA" );
String delimiter  = _req.getParameter( "DELIMITER" );
Vector Message    = mailingList.createVectorOfLines(
                          _req.getParameter( "MESSAGE" ) );
if (cookieName==null || mailID==null || urlData==null
                     || delimiter==null || Message==null ){
   _res.setStatus( HttpServletResponse.SC_NO_CONTENT );
```

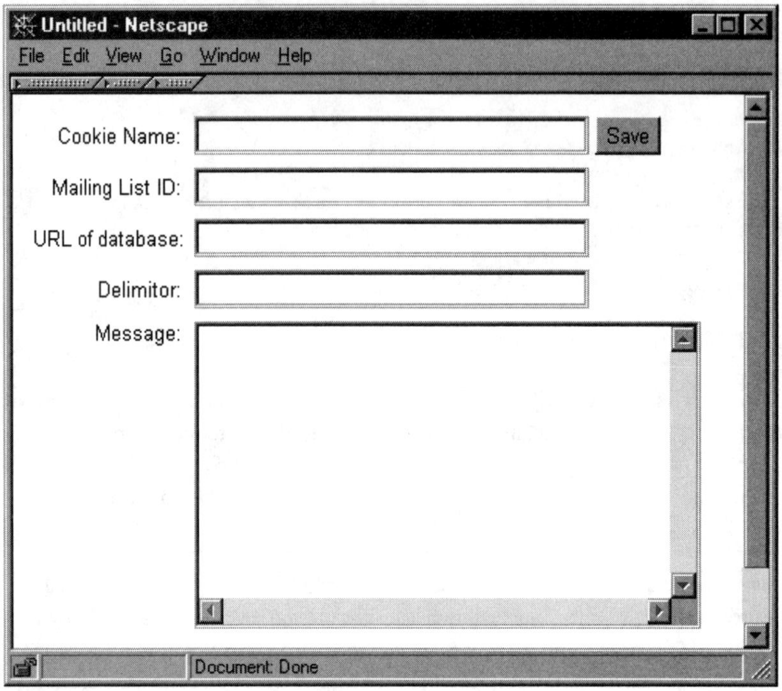

Figure 22.3 The form to create a fortune cookie

```
  return;
}

cookieData cd;
if ( cookieList.containsKey( cookieName ) )
 cd = (cookieData)cookieList.get( cookieName );
else
 cd = new cookieData();

cd.iD        = cookieName;
cd.mailID    = mailID;
cd.urlData   = urlData;
cd.delimiter = delimiter;
cd.message   = Message;
cookieList.put( cd.iD, cd );
saveCookieList();
_res.sendRedirect( _req.getParameter("NEXT_URL") );
```
Example 22.14   Creating a fortune cookie

After checking the parameters, we must look for the instance of the `cookieData`. If this is a new cookie, the main `Hashtable` will not contain the key, and therefore a new instance is created. If the key was found, then we assume this is an update and the old information is overwritten with the new.

Regardless whether it's new or updated data, the main list of cookies is saved back out to disk before the user is sent to the URL specified in the NEXT_URL parameter.

22.2.3   Editing and deleting a fortune cookie

Editing and deleting a fortune cookie will be easy. Let's assume that we don't want to keep
a list of all the fortune cookies we has registered—we would prefer to simply see them
listed, as in figure 22.4. Fortunately, having them all stored in a single `Hashtable` makes
this a rather easy task.

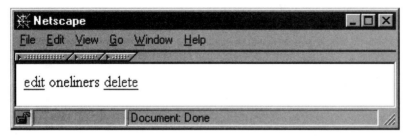

Figure 22.4 Displaying a fortune cookie

Displaying all the current features involves acting on the proper control parameter
and then sending the list as shown in the method in example 22.15.

```
PrintWriter Out = _res.getWriter();
_res.setContentType( "text/html" );
Enumeration E = cookieList.elements();
cookieData cd;
while ( E.hasMoreElements() ){
  cd  = (cookieData)E.nextElement();
  Out.println( "<A HREF=/servlet/com.nary.http.cookieServer?SYS_EDIT
                       =1&COOKIENAME="+ URLEncoder.encode( cd.iD )
                       +">edit</A> " + cd.iD +
                       " <A HREF=/servlet/com.nary.http.cookieServer
                       ?SYS_DELETE =1&COOKIENAME="+ URLEncoder.encode(
                       cd.iD )+">delete</A><BR>" );
}
Out.flush();
```
Example 22.15   Advanced fortune cookie display

This method simply creates an `Enumeration` to the `Hashtable` and creates lines of
text, one by one, linking the edit and delete functions so they're only a single click away.
This has the added advantage of allowing the servlet developer to change the way the user
edits the fortune cookie without having to make any HTML changes.

When you need to edit data for a fortune cookie, we have to format an HTML form
and send it, complete with the fields filled in from the previous data. The method shown
in example 22.16 illustrates this procedure.

```
PrintWriter Out = _res.getWriter();
_res.setContentType( "text/html" );
cookieData cd = (cookieData)cookieList.get(
                       _req.getParameter("COOKIENAME") );
```

```
Out.println( "<FORM ACTION=/servlet/com.nary.http.cookieServer
                          METHOD=GET>" );
Out.println( "<INPUT TYPE=Hidden NAME=NEXT_URL
                          VALUE=/cookieAdd.html>" );
Out.println( "<TABLE>" );
Out.println( "<TR>" );
Out.println( "<TD ALIGN=RIGHT><FONT FACE=Arial SIZE=-1>Cookie Name:
                          </FONT></TD>" );
Out.println( "<TD ALIGN=LEFT><INPUT TYPE=TEXT NAME=COOKIENAME VALUE=\""
                          + cd.iD + "\" SIZE=30> 
                          <INPUT TYPE=SUBMIT NAME=SYS_ADD VALUE=Save>
                          </TD>" );
Out.println( "</TR>" );
Out.println( "<TR>" );
Out.println( "<TD ALIGN=RIGHT><FONT FACE=Arial SIZE=-1>Mailing List ID:
                          </FONT></TD>" );
Out.println( "<TD ALIGN=LEFT><INPUT TYPE=TEXT NAME=MAILID VALUE=\""+
                          cd.mailID +"\" SIZE=30></TD>");
Out.println( "</TR>" );
Out.println( "<TR>" );
Out.println( "<TD ALIGN=RIGHT><FONT FACE=Arial SIZE=-1>URL of database:
                          </FONT></TD>" );
Out.println( "<TD ALIGN=LEFT><INPUT TYPE=TEXT NAME=URLDATA
                          VALUE=\""+cd.urlData+"\" SIZE=30></TD>");
Out.println( "</TR>" );
Out.println( "<TR>" );
Out.println( "<TD ALIGN=RIGHT><FONT FACE=Arial SIZE=-1>Delimiter:
                          </FONT></TD>" );
Out.println( "<TD ALIGN=LEFT><INPUT TYPE=TEXT NAME=DELIMITER
                          VALUE=\""+cd.delimiter+ "\" SIZE=30>
                          </TD>");
Out.println( "</TR>" );
Out.println( "<TR>" );
Out.println( "<TD ALIGN=RIGHT VALIGN=TOP><FONT FACE=Arial SIZE=-1>
                          Message:</FONT></TD>" );
Out.println( "<TD ALIGN=LEFT><TEXTAREA NAME=MESSAGE COLS=38 ROWS=10
                          WRAP=OFF>");

Enumeration E = cd.message.elements();
while ( E.hasMoreElements() )
  Out.println( (String)E.nextElement() );

Out.println( "</TEXTAREA></TD>" );
Out.println( "</TR>" );
Out.println( "</TABLE>" );
Out.println( "</FORM>" );
Out.flush();
```
Example 22.16   Generating the HTML form for editing cookie information

You can see that once the data has been found from the Hashtable, it is a simple matter to generate the HTML table that will be used to allow the user to edit the fields. When this form is submitted it calls the same code that was discussed in the last section.

Deleting the fortune cookie is much easier. We just have to locate the correct fortune cookie and remove it from the `Hashtable`, then save the new modified `Hashtable` out to disk. This is illustrated in example 22.17.

```
String cookieName = _req.getParameter( "COOKIENAME" );
if ( cookieList.containsKey( cookieName ) ){
  cookieList.remove( cookieName );
  saveCookieList();
}
_res.setStatus( HttpServletResponse.SC_NO_CONTENT );
```
Example 22.17   Deleting the fortune cookie

22.2.4   *Database format*

This servlet will be generating email on a daily basis, inserting a new piece of text each time it sends a message. This text will have to be generated from somewhere. We have a number of options open to us, including:

1   Sourcing the data from a database table.

2   Sourcing the data from a flat text file with a known delimiter.

To make it easy, we will implement the second method. Although the first option is much more efficient, it requires the additional overload of a JDBC connection, and so far, we haven't dealt with that. Forthcoming chapters will look at the whole JDBC connection concept.

You'll find data files covering all kinds of topics all over the Internet. The newsgroups are a great resource for all kinds of information, including jokes, one-liners, tips, and quotes. These data files come in a variety of different text formats. Some are delimited with a special character sequence, some are delimited with a blank line, and some have text that spans a number of lines (each line is separated by a delimiter). We want our servlet to be able to handle all types of formats.

You may have noticed but we had a field in the `cookieData` class to store a delimiter. We're now going to put that field to use. It will store the character sequence we will look for. However, not all files are stored with such a sequence, so we will define two special cases: BLANK and ONE. If the delimiter field contains these, then we know it's a different type of file.

Example 22.18 shows the method for extracting the correct record from the data file. First, the file is opened for reading by the `BufferedReader` class. This class allows us to use the convenient `readLine()` method, which returns a single line of text.

```
private String getQuotation( String _url, String _delimiter,
                             int _position ){
  String Quotation="", lineIn;
  int pos=0;
  try{
```

```
      BufferedReader inFile = new BufferedReader( new FileReader(_url) );
      while ( (lineIn = inFile.readLine()) != null ){
        if ( _delimiter.equalsIgnoreCase("ONE") ){
          if ( pos == _position )
            return lineIn;
          else
            pos++;
        }else if( _delimiter.equalsIgnoreCase("BLANK") ){
          if ( lineIn.length() == 0 )
          pos++;
if ( pos == _position+1 )
            return Quotation;
          else if ( pos == _position && lineIn.length() != 0 )
          Quotation += lineIn + "\r\n";
        }else{
          if ( lineIn.indexOf( _delimiter ) != -1 )
            pos++;
          else if ( pos == _position+1 )
            return Quotation;
          else if ( pos == _position )
            Quotation += lineIn + "\r\n";
        }
      }
    return null;
  }catch(Exception E){
    return null;
  }
}
```

Example 22.18 Retrieving the record

Once the file is open, we have to skip past the number of records that have already been read before returning the correct data. This method will vary, depending on the delimiter type. For example, for the delimiter of ONE, we simply count the number of lines and return the line represented at the _position value. The BLANK delimiter is somewhat the same, except we count the number of blank lines before returning the line.

When the delimiter is a character sequence, we have to count the number of times we see the character sequence. This is done using the indexOf(...) method, then each block of text is copied into a buffer. Once the delimiter is read again, the block of text is returned.

22.2.5 Distributing the list

At this point, let's review what we have completed so far. We have the mailing list servlet handling users subscribing to and removing themselves from the list. We have also created the interface for creating, editing, and deleting fortune cookies. We even have the method for extracting the correct record from a flat data file. So what is left? Creating the mechanism to send an email automatically once a night.

To have the servlet automatically send an email once a night, we have to set it to wait until a specific time and then trigger a method call. We therefore need to continually poll the system clock.

We can use a thread to watch for the appointed time. A servlet is simply a class that inherits the properties of the `java.servlet.Servlet` class. There is no reason why this class cannot also implement the `Runnable` class.

```
public class cookieServer extends HttpServlet implements Runnable
```

Implementing the `Runnable` class allows us to implement the `run()` method which is called when a `Thread` is brought to life, as shown in example 22.19. The first thing the method does is to calculate what time midnight is in milliseconds.

```
public void run(){
  Calendar calendar = new GregorianCalendar();
  calendar.setTime(new Date());
  calendar.set( calendar.get(Calendar.YEAR),
            calendar.get(Calendar.MONTH),
            calendar.get(Calendar.DATE), 0, 0, 0 );
  long timeToRun = calendar.getTime().getTime();

  for(;;){
    if ( System.currentTimeMillis() > timeToRun ){
      sendOutMailings();
      calendar.setTime(new Date());
      calendar.set( calendar.get(Calendar.YEAR),
            calendar.get(Calendar.MONTH), calendar.get(Calendar.DATE),
            0, 0, 0 );
      timeToRun = calendar.getTime().getTime() + (24*60*60*1000);
    }

    try{
      Thread.currentThread().sleep( 30000 );
    }catch(Exception E){}
  }
}
```

Example 22.19   The `run()` method

Then the method enters a loop that runs forever, checking to see if the current time has elapsed past midnight. This check is performed every 30 seconds. If the specified time has elapsed, then the `sendOutMailings()` method is called, which is described in section 22.1.7.

To start the thread running, we just need to place the necessary code in the `init(...)` method of the servlet, as shown in example 22.20.

```
public void init(ServletConfig config) throws ServletException {
  super.init(config);
  loadCookieList();
  new Thread(this).start();
}
```

Example 22.20   Starting the thread running

The main list of fortune cookies is loaded. Now we just need to create an instance of `Thread` with this class as a parameter to start the servlet running.

22.2.6 Formatting the email message

The final thing we need to do is to generate and format the email that will be sent to each user. The method that will do this task will be called from the `run()` method mentioned in the previous section.

But before we can send the message out, we must first generate the email body. Remember that you decided on a format for the email body when you first created the fortune cookie. This was a template in which the record would be inserted. But how would it be inserted?

Defining special fields within the template body would allow the servlet to correctly determine where the record would be inserted. For example, we use `%%COOKIE%%` and `%%COOKIEID%%` as our text holders. We search for these and replace them with the corresponding data. This is shown in example 22.21.

```
private Vector createMessage( cookieData cd ){
  String _keys[] = {"%%COOKIE%%","%%COOKIEID%%"};
  String _dat[] = new String[2];
  _dat[0]  = getQuotation( cd.urlData, cd.delimiter, cd.position );
  if ( _dat[0] == null )
    return null;

  _dat[1]  = cd.iD;
  Vector newMessage = new Vector( cd.message.size() );
  Enumeration E = cd.message.elements();
  String LineIn;
  int x,c1=0;
  while ( E.hasMoreElements() ){
    LineIn = (String)E.nextElement();
    for (x=0;x < _keys.length; x++ ){
      c1 = LineIn.indexOf(_keys[x]);
      while ( c1 != -1 ){
        try{
          LineIn  = LineIn.substring( 0, c1 ) + _dat[x] +
                              LineIn.substring( c1+_keys[x].length(),
                              LineIn.length() );
          c1 = LineIn.indexOf(_keys[x],c1+1);
        }catch(Exception E1){}
      }
    }
    newMessage.addElement( LineIn );
  }
  cd.position++;
  return ( newMessage );
}
```

Example 22.21 Inserting the data into the placeholders

This mechanism works very similar to the HTML template class we developed in chapter 8. This creates two arrays: the first set is used to search for the placeholder strings; each string is then replaced with the corresponding data and mailing list ID in the second array. We then build our new message body, looking at each line for the placeholder strings. If one is found, it is substituted.

Having built the body of the email message, we can now send out the email. This process is very similar to the method we used in the mailing list section to generate an email for each user. The source code for this method can be found in example 22.22.

22.2.7 Complete source code

Example 22.22 shows the complete source code for the fortune cookie servlet. You can see this servlet in action at http://www.n-ary.com/n-porium/.

```
package com.nary.http;

import javax.servlet.*;
import javax.servlet.http.*;
import java.io.*;
import java.util.*;
import java.net.*;
import com.nary.net.*;
public class cookieServer extends HttpServlet implements Runnable {

  private static Hashtable cookieList;
  private static String MAILHOST = "youremailserver.yourdomain.com";
  private static String MAILFROM = "mailinglist@yourdoman.com";

  public void init(ServletConfig config) throws ServletException {
    super.init(config);
    loadCookieList();
    new Thread(this).start();
  }

  public String getServletInfo() {
    return "com.nary.http.cookieServer: version 1.0";
  }

  public void doGet(HttpServletRequest _req, HttpServletResponse _res)
                           throws ServletException, IOException {
    if ( _req.getParameter("SYS_DISPLAY") != null )
      displayCookieList( _req, _res );
    else if ( _req.getParameter("SYS_ADD") != null )
      addCookie( _req, _res );
    else if ( _req.getParameter("SYS_DELETE") != null )
      delCookie( _req, _res );
    else if ( _req.getParameter("SYS_EDIT") != null )
      editCookie( _req, _res );
    else
      _res.setStatus( HttpServletResponse.SC_NO_CONTENT );
  }

  public void delCookie(HttpServletRequest _req,
                        HttpServletResponse _res)
                           throws ServletException, IOException {
    String cookieName = _req.getParameter( "COOKIENAME" );
    if ( cookieList.containsKey( cookieName ) ){
```

```
      cookieList.remove( cookieName );
      saveCookieList();
    }
    _res.setStatus( HttpServletResponse.SC_NO_CONTENT );
  }

  public void addCookie(HttpServletRequest _req,
                        HttpServletResponse _res)
                        throws ServletException, IOException {
    String cookieName = _req.getParameter( "COOKIENAME" );
    String mailID    = _req.getParameter( "MAILID" );
    String urlData   = _req.getParameter( "URLDATA" );
    String delimiter = _req.getParameter( "DELIMITER" );
    Vector Message   = mailingList.createVectorOfLines(
                        _req.getParameter( "MESSAGE" ) );
    if (cookieName==null || mailID==null || urlData==null
                        || delimiter==null || Message==null ){
      _res.setStatus( HttpServletResponse.SC_NO_CONTENT );
      return;
    }

    cookieData cd;
    if ( cookieList.containsKey( cookieName ) )
    cd = (cookieData)cookieList.get( cookieName );
    else
    cd = new cookieData();

    cd.iD         = cookieName;
    cd.mailID     = mailID;
    cd.urlData    = urlData;
    cd.delimiter  = delimiter;
    cd.message    = Message;
    cookieList.put( cd.iD, cd );
    saveCookieList();
    _res.sendRedirect( _req.getParameter("NEXT_URL") );
  }

  public void displayCookieList(HttpServletRequest _req,
                        HttpServletResponse _res)
                        throws ServletException, IOException {
    PrintWriter Out = new PrintWriter( _res.getOutputStream() );
    _res.setContentType( "text/html" );
    Enumeration E = cookieList.elements();
    cookieData cd;
    while ( E.hasMoreElements() ){
      cd = (cookieData)E.nextElement();
      Out.println( "<A HREF=/servlet/com.nary.http.cookieServer
                        ?SYS_EDIT=1&COOKIENAME="+ URLEncoder.encode(
                        cd.iD ) +">edit</A> " + cd.iD + "
                        <A HREF=/servlet/com.nary.http.cookieServer
                        ?SYS_DELETE=1&COOKIENAME="+
                  URLEncoder.encode( cd.iD )+">delete</A><BR>" );
    }
    Out.flush();
```

```
    }
private synchronized void loadCookieList(){
    try{
      FileInputStream   FS = new FileInputStream( "main.cookielist" );
      ObjectInputStream IS = new ObjectInputStream(FS);
      cookieList          = (Hashtable)IS.readObject();
    }catch(Exception E){
      System.out.println( E );
      cookieList = new Hashtable();
    }
}

  private synchronized void saveCookieList(){
    try{
      FileOutputStream   FS = new FileOutputStream( "main.cookielist" );
      ObjectOutputStream OS = new ObjectOutputStream(FS);
      OS.writeObject( cookieList );
    }catch(Exception E){}
  }
public void editCookie(HttpServletRequest _req,
                       HttpServletResponse _res)
                       throws ServletException, IOException {
    PrintWriter Out = new PrintWriter( _res.getOutputStream() );
    _res.setContentType( "text/html" );
    cookieData cd = (cookieData)cookieList.get(
                        _req.getParameter("COOKIENAME") );

    Out.println( "<FORM ACTION=/servlet/com.nary.http.cookieServer
                        METHOD=GET>" );
    Out.println( "<INPUT TYPE=Hidden NAME=NEXT_URL
                        VALUE=/cookieAdd.html>" );
    Out.println( "<TABLE>" );
    Out.println( "<TR>" );
    Out.println( "<TD ALIGN=RIGHT><FONT FACE=Arial SIZE=-1>
                        Cookie Name:</FONT></TD>" );
    Out.println( "<TD ALIGN=LEFT><INPUT TYPE=TEXT NAME=COOKIENAME
                        VALUE=\"" + cd.iD + "\" SIZE=30> 
                        <INPUT TYPE=SUBMIT NAME=SYS_ADD VALUE=Save>
                        </TD>" );
    Out.println( "</TR>" );
    Out.println( "<TR>" );
    Out.println( "<TD ALIGN=RIGHT><FONT FACE=Arial SIZE=-1
                        >Mailing List ID:</FONT></TD>" );
    Out.println( "<TD ALIGN=LEFT><INPUT TYPE=TEXT NAME=MAILID
                        VALUE=\""+ cd.mailID + "\" SIZE=30>
                        </TD>" );
    Out.println( "</TR>" );
    Out.println( "<TR>" );
    Out.println( "<TD ALIGN=RIGHT><FONT FACE=Arial SIZE=-1>
                        URL of database:</FONT></TD>" );
    Out.println( "<TD ALIGN=LEFT><INPUT TYPE=TEXT NAME=URLDATA
                        VALUE=\""+cd.urlData+"\"
                  SIZE=30></TD>" );
    Out.println( "</TR>" );
```

```
      Out.println( "<TR>" );
      Out.println( "<TD ALIGN=RIGHT><FONT FACE=Arial SIZE=-1>Delimiter:
                        </FONT></TD>" );
      Out.println( "<TD ALIGN=LEFT><INPUT TYPE=TEXT NAME=DELIMITER
                        VALUE=\""+ cd.delimiter
                  +"\" SIZE=30></TD>" );
      Out.println( "</TR>" );
      Out.println( "<TR>" );
      Out.println( "<TD ALIGN=RIGHT VALIGN=TOP><FONT FACE=Arial
                        SIZE=-1>Message:</FONT></TD>" );
      Out.println( "<TD ALIGN=LEFT><TEXTAREA NAME=MESSAGE COLS=38 ROWS=10
                        WRAP=OFF>");

    Enumeration E = cd.message.elements();
    while ( E.hasMoreElements() ){
     Out.println( (String)E.nextElement() );
    }

    Out.println( "</TEXTAREA></TD>" );
    Out.println( "</TR>" );
    Out.println( "</TABLE>" );
    Out.println( "</FORM>" );

    Out.flush();
  }


//---------------------------------------

public void run(){
   Calendar calendar = new GregorianCalendar();
   calendar.setTime(new Date());
   calendar.set( calendar.get(Calendar.YEAR),
          calendar.get(Calendar.MONTH), calendar.get(Calendar.DATE),
                        0, 0, 0 );
   long timeToRun = calendar.getTime().getTime();

   for(;;){
     if ( System.currentTimeMillis() > timeToRun ){
       sendOutMailings();
       calendar.setTime(new Date());
       calendar.set( calendar.get(Calendar.YEAR),
           calendar.get(Calendar.MONTH), calendar.get(Calendar.DATE),
                        0, 0, 0 );
       timeToRun = calendar.getTime().getTime() + (24*60*60*1000);
     }

     try{
       Thread.currentThread().sleep( 30000 );
     }catch(Exception E){}
   }
}

private void sendOutMailings(){
   //-----------------
```

```
//- Run through the list and send out the necessary emails
Enumeration E = cookieList.elements();
cookieData cd;
String to[] = new String[1];
String tmp[] = new String[0];
sendEmail  Mail = new sendEmail( MAILHOST );

while ( E.hasMoreElements() ){
  cd  = (cookieData)E.nextElement();
  Vector outMessage = createMessage( cd );
  if ( outMessage == null ){
    cd.position = 0;
    continue;
  }

  Hashtable mailList  = mailingList.loadMailListing( cd.mailID );
  if ( mailList == null )
    return;

  Enumeration E2 = mailList.keys();
  while (E2.hasMoreElements()){
    to[0]  = (String)E2.nextElement();
    Mail.sendMail( to, MAILFROM,  tmp, tmp, "n-ary Mailing List:
                   " + cd.iD, outMessage );
  }
}
saveCookieList();
Mail.close();
}

private Vector createMessage( cookieData cd ){
  String _keys[] = {"%%COOKIE%%","%%COOKIEID%%"};
  String _dat[] = new String[2];
  _dat[0]  = getQuotation( cd.urlData, cd.delimiter, cd.position );
  if ( _dat[0] == null )
    return null;

  _dat[1]  = cd.iD;

  Vector newMessage = new Vector( cd.message.size() );
  Enumeration E = cd.message.elements();
  String LineIn;
  int x,c1=0;
  while ( E.hasMoreElements() ){
    LineIn = (String)E.nextElement();
    for (x=0;x < _keys.length; x++ ){
      c1 = LineIn.indexOf(_keys[x]);
      while ( c1 != -1 ){
        try{
```

```java
            LineIn  = LineIn.substring( 0, c1 ) + _dat[x] +
                            LineIn.substring( c1+_keys[x].length(),
                            LineIn.length() );
            c1 = LineIn.indexOf(_keys[x],c1+1);
          }catch(Exception E1){}
        }
      }
      newMessage.addElement( LineIn );
    }

    cd.position++;
    return ( newMessage );
  }

  private String getQuotation( String _url, String _delimiter,
                          int _position ){
    String Quotation="", lineIn;
    int pos=0;
    try{
      BufferedReader inFile = new BufferedReader( new FileReader(_url) );
      while ( (lineIn = inFile.readLine()) != null ){
        if ( _delimiter.equalsIgnoreCase("ONE") ){
          if ( pos == _position )
            return lineIn;
          else
            pos++;
        }else if( _delimiter.equalsIgnoreCase("BLANK") ){
          if ( lineIn.length() == 0 )
            pos++;

          if ( pos == _position+1 )
            return Quotation;
          else if ( pos == _position && lineIn.length() != 0 )
            Quotation += lineIn + "\r\n";
        }else{
          if ( lineIn.indexOf( _delimiter ) != -1 )
            pos++;
          else if ( pos == _position+1 )
            return Quotation;
          else if ( pos == _position )
            Quotation += lineIn + "\r\n";
        }
      }

      //--- The mailing list has finished
      return null;
    }catch(Exception E){
      return null;
    }
  }
}
```

Example 22.22   The complete source code for the fortune cookie servlet

22.3 Future extensions

The main purpose of this chapter was to illustrate the procedure involved in creating an email mailing center. Users are allowed to sign themselves up and automatic emails are sent to them on a periodic basis. By providing such a service for their customers, the originating web site is advertised on a daily basis to very targeted audience, potentially increasing their site traffic.

The ease with which the servlet could be adapted from the first implementation to the second further demonstrated the flexibility a Java solution offers.

CHAPTER   2 3

Online shopping

- Discover what makes up an online catalog and how a servlet solution differs from a CGI or server-extension implementation.

- Learn how to implement a virtual shopping basket in which the user can add and delete items while browsing your site.

- Learn how to implement a checkout center. Once the user has browsed the online shop, he must then pay for the goods.

- See how easily two servlets can communicate with each other by sharing data through session management.

The concept of home shopping has been around for a very long time. First, there was the humble catalog. These huge paper volumes were packed full of product lines and shipped to households all over the world. The companies who sent the catalogs could only hope that customers would flip through the pages, picking out items and then ordering through the mail, or later, over the phone.

The next phase of the home shopping revolution was TV shopping. Instead of weighing down the postal service with heavy catalogs, companies purchased airtime on special TV channels to broadcast information about their products. This type of shopping should not be confused with advertising. Product manufacturers generally drive advertising efforts. In contrast, the shopping channels are run by companies which sell a variety of different manufacturers' goods. The shopping channel companies are simply resellers. Television is expensive, and selling items through the TV requires the viewer to be watching at the time the products are being previewed. Catalogs are a better advertising solution, but they're very expensive when it comes to distributing updates.

Home shopping is one area where the Internet has provided convenience for both the seller and the buyer. Implementing a web presence that supports online shopping has been conventionally done using CGI scripts and HTML cookies. This approach has not proved to be the most efficient method. But using servlets at the server side, an online shop can be implemented very efficiently and securely.

23.1 Introduction

Online shopping is probably the easiest way to shop, and in some instances, it is far more convenient than actually visiting the physical store itself. Shopping for items using a web browser has many advantages over conventional home-shopping mechanisms.

When you think about the two-inch thick catalogs sent out to potential shoppers, you have to wonder how the companies in question ever break even. The phenomenon of home shopping is here to stay. Whether or not this is socially a good thing is yet to be seen. But let's face it: looking at today's consumer's lifestyle, buying CDs and videos and books over the Internet is much faster than taking the time to go into town to shop.

Note At the time of this writing, a recent survey published the amount of money traded over the Internet on a variety of products and online services. This figure came to approximately $1.5 billion worldwide, with this amount expected to grow much larger as more people come online or have better access to the Internet.

Placing a catalog online offers many advantages to both the trader and the customer. The trader's advantages include the following:

- A 24-hour, unmanned, worldwide sales operation.
  Traders can wake up every morning and find out how much money they made overnight!
- Greater presentation possibilities for promoting goods.
  Complete product descriptions and color photographs can be very easily compiled

and displayed. Many of the current web sites selling audio CDs provide a RealAudio sample of each CD track, so the user can hear it before buying (see http://www.cd-now.com for an example of this). Book buyers can see sample chapters and read user reviews of a particular book before they make their purchases.

- Updating the catalog is much easier and cheaper.
  The second an update is made, all users will be able to see it.

- The margin of error for buying goods is significantly reduced.
  Thorough presales checks are made to make sure the user is ordering the goods he wants to order.

- Very accurate conversion rate.
  A conversion rate is a statistic commonly used by storeowners; it's the number of shoppers compared to the number of purchases.

These are the advantages for the customers:

- Confidence in the knowledge that they are ordering goods from a catalog with the most up-to-date prices, rather than from a printed catalog that begins to be dated as soon as it is published.

- Product information may be in greater detail, allowing the customer to make a more informed decision or preview certain products without the fear of having to return the item in question.

- The ability to buy items at any time of the day, any day of the week, and any week of the year.

- Delivery straight to the customer's door.

Before the advent of servlets, setting up an online shop was often a very complicated task. Conventional CGI scripts weren't really adequate for the job; fiddling around with files proved too costly in terms of server processing when trying to maintain shopping carts between client posts. The advent of HTML cookies has definitely improved the performance of the virtual shop, as it moved the responsibility of storing the shopping basket from the server to the client. But this was still far from an ideal solution.

Note An HTML cookie is a mechanism developed by Netscape to store state information at the client side between subsequent requests from the client. The server can use cookies to place customized information on the client; in a later visit, this information is presented back to the server. This saves the server from storing information about the client that may never be used again.

Many companies recognized that HTML cookies are far from ideal. So as not to miss an opportunity to make money, they developed complete solutions for traders looking to go on the Internet. While I prepared to write this chapter, I researched some of these solutions. To my surprise, I was not very impressed with the level of functionality the software solutions offered when compared with the price being charged per unit sold. Prices ranged from $200 for a system to solutions costing well in excess of $10,000. Not one of these solutions offered completely flexible options that could be tailored to fit the needs of the buyer of the software system. Some required a certain web server, others required specific scripting support, some would only work on certain databases, and some even required specific hardware to run their software. Some solutions didn't even stop their restrictions at the server side—they even had the cheek to specify the type of browser with which the virtual shop could be viewed.

Implementing a virtual shop does not need a rocket scientist, nor is it shrouded in deep mystery. The servlet-based solution presented in this chapter will not only be platform- and server-independent, but it will also remove all dependency on a browser or a backend database.

23.2 Virtual store structure

Our mission is to create from scratch an online experience that will allow a user to easily purchase items. The best way to determine our sales technique is to look at how a real shop operates and try to replicate that in the computing world. We can identify two distinct stages in a shopper's experience: he browses and chooses items, then he makes payment for the items he's selected.

The online shop can follow this exact model.

- Browsing
  The potential customer surfs a web site, viewing all prospective products and placing the ones he wants to purchase into a shopping basket.

- Paying
  Once the customer has selected all the items he wants to buy, the user must go to the checkout for payment and optional delivery instructions.

When users are browsing your site, it is important to encourage them to purchase what you are offering. This means not having them fill in long registration forms before they can do anything else. You wouldn't expect to be asked for your credit card information before entering a store, so why should you make your customers do it when they shop online?

Just as with an ordinary store, the users have baskets in which to place items. And just because they have chosen x, y, and z items doesn't mean they can't exchange them, remove one or all of them from the basket, or simply abandon the basket and make a beeline for the door.

When users go to make a purchase, more information is necessary. Only then do you ask them for their credit card information, delivery address, email address, and so on. If you place the information-gathering procedure at the checkout, users aren't instantly discouraged from using the virtual store. By the time they get to this step, most users have selected items and will proceed with the purchase.

Each of the sections, browsing and paying, has quite different processing requirements, so they will be implemented using separate servlets. One servlet will process the virtual shopping baskets and the other will process the checkout procedure. Having the servlets communicate with each other means each servlet can be kept relatively small and efficient.

The rest of this chapter describes the construction of each servlet in detail, along with the methods for sharing data between them very efficiently.

23.2.1 Catalog format

The format and layout of the virtual shop should not be in any way constrained by the implementation of the servlets. The solution should allow a system that can be tailored to any shopping web site. The web designer should be able to place as many items as he wants on a page without affecting the operation of the servlet managing the basket. Since this chapter does not focus on catalog layout, we'll assume that each product has a unique number or product code associated with it (such as the item's universal product code, or UPC). Users will be able to click a button next to each item to add that item to their baskets. This, of course, doesn't need to be a button—it can simply be a link.

As shown in figure 23.1, our very simple catalog consists of a list of items, each with its own button. When a user clicks the appropriate buttons, items are added to his basket. Since each item is identified by a unique code, the basket is merely an array of product codes that represent the items the user has chosen.

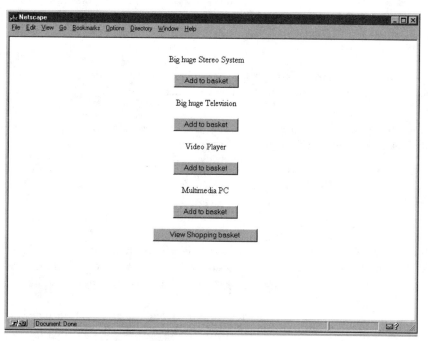

Figure 23.1 A very simple example of an online shop

Example 23.1 shows how to display product items in HTML code and place the code on the client side. As you can see in example 23.1, each form set has two items associated with it: the Submit button and one hidden field that represents the ID of the product item. By encasing each product within its own form set, the overall design of the catalog page can be kept simple.

```
Big Huge Stereo System
<FORM ACTION="/servlet/addBasket" METHOD=POST>
<INPUT TYPE=HIDDEN NAME=ITEM VALUE=12System>
<INPUT TYPE=SUBMIT NAME=ACTION VALUE="Add to basket">
</FORM>
Big Huge Television
<FORM ACTION="/servlet/addBasket" METHOD=POST>
<INPUT TYPE=HIDDEN NAME=ITEM VALUE=12TV>
<INPUT TYPE=SUBMIT NAME=ACTION VALUE="Add to basket">
</FORM>

Video Player
<FORM ACTION="/servlet/addBasket" METHOD=POST>
<INPUT TYPE=HIDDEN NAME=ITEM VALUE=32VIDEO>
<INPUT TYPE=SUBMIT NAME=ACTION VALUE="Add to basket">
</FORM>
```
Example 23.1   Loading the list of items

When each Submit button is clicked, the product information is sent to the servlet. As you will see later on in this chapter, when the servlet is accepting items for the shopping basket, it is configured to not return any new data. This allows the basket to play a passive background role, with each button click not automatically resulting in a page change.

23.3   Virtual shopping basket

Before we go deeper into the servlet construction, let's spend a little time defining a class that will hold the items as the user browses the site.

When users are browsing the various product lines and items, they must have the ability to place a particular item in their shopping basket so they can pay for it at the checkout before leaving the site. The easiest way to think about the implementation of such a mechanism is to observe how it operates in the real world.

A potential shopper goes into the store and picks up a shopping basket in which he will place items to be purchased. The virtual shop operates on exactly the same principle. The user comes to the site and starts placing items into his virtual shopping basket. The only difference is that the online shopper did not need to worry about picking up a basket; this step was automatic.

The virtual basket must be active the instant a user chooses his first item, and there mustn't be any prior requirements to log on to the system, such as answering lots of questions. The basket must:

- Keep track of the user's current items.
- Add items to the contents.
- Remove items from the contents.
- Take all the items to the checkout for processing once the user is done shopping.

The shopping basket doesn't need to be too fancy or sophisticated. Therefore, we will define a simple class that will provide this level of processing. Example 23.2 shows the class for the virtual shopping basket. You can see it is a very simple class with a very simple interface for methods to add and delete items from the basket.

```
import java.util.*;

public class virtualBasket implements java.io.Serializable {

  private Vector items = null;

  public virtualBasket(){
    items = new Vector(2);
  }

  public void addItem( String _productCode ){
    items.addElement( _productCode );
  }

  public void delItem( String _productCode ){
    items.removeElement( _productCode );
  }

  public int countItems(){
    if ( items == null )
      return 0;
    else
      return items.size();
  }

  public Vector getCodes(){
    return items;
  }
}
```

Example 23.2   The online shopping basket

We want to give the shopkeeper the ability to use existing product codes, which may come in the form of numeric or alphanumeric characters. Therefore, we just need to store a list of strings. This list will represent the items in the user's shopping basket. One of the easiest ways to store this data is through the Vector class, which will store one product item per element.

Since we are planning to use the session management aspect of the servlet API to implement this data storage, we will ask the session manager to store this object on our behalf. In order to distinguish between client requests, the server may need to store this data for later retrieval. If this is to happen successfully, then we must make sure our object is serializable.

Therefore, when the user is adding or removing items, our servlets come down to basic wrappers around this Vector class. As you will see in the next couple of sections, the servlets to control the shopping basket are very simple.

23.3.1 Adding items to the basket

In the previous section, we looked at the makeup of the class that will be used to store the item codes for products the user has selected from the web site. This section will look at what has to happen when the user clicks on a button to add an item to the shopping basket.

The first time a user selects an item, a `virtualBasket` will have to be created for them. Once this class has been created, the product code can be added to the list by simply calling the `addItem(…)` method.

We want the shopping basket implementation to be as seamless as possible. In other words, we do not want the user jumping from page to page every time he adds a product to his shopping basket. Ideally, when the user selects an item, the shopping basket should be updated with the new item.

We can achieve this effect using session management. When the user tries to add an item to the basket, the servlet must determine whether this is a new basket. This is done by asking the session manager to return the session for this particular client and then attempt to retrieve the `virtualBasket` object.

If the `virtualBasket` object is `null`, then we can assume the user needs a basket created for him. Of course, it is possible the user has turned off cookies, which would render this application somewhat useless. So let's assume that he has enabled cookies. Once the shopping basket has been created, we can call the necessary method to add the item to it.

For the first shopping session, the session manager knows nothing about the client. It has not had the opportunity to ask the client to store a cookie for it on its behalf, so we have to send an HTML page back to the client in order for the browser to correctly set the cookie. After this is done, the servlet need not return any information, only an SC_NO_CONTENT status result, which is an empty HTTP packet that tells the browser not to expect data.

Example 23.3 demonstrates this procedure. You'll see that the `service(…)` method looks to see if a product code has indeed been sent. If it has not, then the method returns by either sending back an SC_NO_CONTENT status result, or redirecting the product code to a URL parameter that was passed in.

```
import java.io.*;
import java.net.*;
import java.util.*;
import javax.servlet.*;
import javax.servlet.http.*;

public class addItemServlet extends HttpServlet{

   public void init( ServletConfig _servletConfig)
                           throws ServletException {
     super.init(_servletConfig);
   }

   public void service( HttpServletRequest _req,
HttpServletResponse _res)
                           throws ServletException, IOException{
     String productCode  = _req.getParameter("ITEM");
```

```
      if ( productCode != null ){
        HttpSession clientSession = _req.getSession( true );

        virtualBasket vBasket = (virtualBasket)clientSession.getValue
                              ("shop.basket");
        if ( vBasket == null )
          vBasket = new virtualBasket();

        vBasket.addItem( productCode );
        clientSession.putValue( "shop.basket" );

        if ( clientSession.isNew() ){
          displayThankyouPage( _res );
          return;
        }
      }

    if ( _req.getParameter("NEXT_URL") == null )
      _res.setStatus( HttpServletResponse.SC_NO_CONTENT );
    else
      _res.sendRedirect( _req.getParameter("NEXT_URL") );
  }

  private void displayThankyouPage(HttpServletResponse _res)
                              throws ServletException, IOException{
    PrintWriter Out = _res.getWriter();
    Out.println( "<HTML><BODY>" );
    Out.println( "Thank you, a new shopping basket has been created for
                              you" );
    Out.println( "</BODY></HTML>" );
    Out.flush();
  }
}
```

Example 23.3   Adding items to the shopping basket

If the user has indeed made a genuine request to add an item to the shopping basket, then the session object associated with this client is returned. Now we can attempt to retrieve the virtualBasket instance through the method call getValue(...). If this returns null, we can assume that this is the user's first visit and a basket is created.

As I've said, we need to determine whether this is a new session. We can gain this information from a call to the isNew() method, which will tell us if the session has been linked to the client. If it has not, then we need to link it; the servlet sends an HTML page back to the client's browser and hopes the client has enabled cookies.

The session manager uses cookies to match up the client connection with the objects it is storing on the client's behalf. A technique for doing this without using cookies is known as URL rewriting, where the session ID is embedded into the URL that requests the servlet. This technique requires a lot more effort from the developer.

If this is a subsequent request to add an item, the servlet will not generate the thank-you HTML page. In this instance, it looks to see if an additional NEXT_URL parameter exists; if it does, it redirects the client to the specified URL. Otherwise, an SC_NO_CONTENT is sent to the client.

23.3.2 Deleting items from the basket

The previous section discussed how the user adds items for potential purchase. But the user may change his mind and want to remove a previously held item. Fortunately, this doesn't prevent too much of a development problem.

We will provide an additional servlet that will be used to remove the particular item from the shopping basket. Example 23.4 shows this servlet. Notice how much less complicated it is compared to the one that was required to add an item. This is due to the fact that this servlet does not need to worry as much about whether the shopping basket exists. If the basket doesn't exist, then there is no point in creating a new one just to delete an item that doesn't exist. This servlet also has the benefit of not requiring a dummy HTML page to link the session with the client.

```
import java.io.*;
import java.net.*;
import java.util.*;
import javax.servlet.*;
import javax.servlet.http.*;

public class delItemServlet  extends HttpServlet{

  public void init( ServletConfig _servletConfig)
                          throws ServletException {
    super.init(_servletConfig);
  }

  public void service( HttpServletRequest _req,
                        HttpServletResponse _res)
                        throws ServletException, IOException{
    String productCode  = _req.getParameter("ITEM");
    if ( productCode != null ){
      HttpSession clientSession = _req.getSession( true );

      virtualBasket vBasket = (virtualBasket)
                        clientSession.getValue("shop.basket");
      if ( vBasket != null )
        vBasket.delItem( productCode );

      clientSession.putValue( "shop.basket" );
    }

    if ( _req.getParameter("NEXT_URL") == null )
      _res.setStatus( HttpServletResponse.SC_NO_CONTENT );
    else
      _res.sendRedirect( _req.getParameter("NEXT_URL") );
  }
}
```
Example 23.4   Deleting items from the basket

Notice how the two servlets we have developed so far are not linked to one another. They are completely independent classes because we are using the session manager to store the virtual shopping baskets and we don't need to worry about interservlet communication asking for any class instances. The ability to completely extract components from the initial implementation is one of the main benefits of using session management.

23.3.3 Removing the shopping basket

There may be a time when the user wants to remove all his items, regardless of how many items are in the basket. Providing this functionality is a simple matter of developing a small servlet that will disassociate the session from the client.

Example 23.5 shows the delBasketServlet which clears the session from the server and the client. This is achieved with a call to the method removeValue(...). This method will operate quite happily even if no previous session existed beforehand.

```
import java.io.*;
import java.net.*;
import java.util.*;
import javax.servlet.*;
import javax.servlet.http.*;

public class delBasketServlet  extends HttpServlet{

  public void init( ServletConfig _servletConfig)
                             throws ServletException {
    super.init(_servletConfig);
  }

  public void service( HttpServletRequest _req,
                          HttpServletResponse _res)
                          throws ServletException, IOException{
    HttpSession clientSession = _req.getSession( true );
    clientSession.removeValue("shop.basket");

    if ( _req.getParameter("NEXT_URL") == null )
      _res.setStatus( HttpServletResponse.SC_NO_CONTENT );
    else
      _res.sendRedirect( _req.getParameter("NEXT_URL") );
  }
}
```

Example 23.5   Deleting the entire shopping basket

Depending on the result returned from the servlet, the client cookie may not actually be deleted. But it will be harmless, as the session manager will not recognize it anymore since it was unlinked at the server side.

23.4   The checkout

After the user has been adding items (and, it is hoped, not removing too many!), he will either be ready to purchase the selected items or he will want to see the current total cost of his selected items. Either way, we need a method that will allow him to view the currently selected items.

The precise processing that is required here will be very dependent on the user's method of payment. But we will assume that another servlet will take care of that process. This servlet will deal only with displaying the items.

The servlet needs to get the basket for this particular user and display the necessary information for each item on the screen. We will use the HTML template class that has been used throughout this book to do this, but we will use it in a new way that will give the web developer even more control over the look and feel of the checkout.

Until now, we have been using the template class to replace known tags embedded in the HTML file with live data produced from the servlet. But in this instance we need to insert many rows of data, one for each product item, and we do not know the number of items when we create the HTML template. Therefore, we need to be able to repeat a known set of tags multiple times.

For example, let's assume that we are going to use an HTML table to produce a very clean product list for the items to be displayed. Each row in the table will represent a different product item. Each HTML table row has a number of HTML tags that make up the look and feel of that particular row. We need to repeat this set of tags *x* number of times into the main table.

Example 23.6 shows the basic HTML template that we will use to display the product items. Notice the tag `<!--TABLEROW-->`. This is where we want the HTML code from example 23.7 to be inserted for each product item.

```
<HTML><BODY>

<TABLE>
<!--TABLEROW-->
</TABLE>

Total Price: <!--TOTAL_PRICE-->
</BODY>
</HTML>
```
Example 23.6   The main HTML template file

Example 23.7 shows the HTML template that we will use to display the individual product items. This includes the product code, item description, and item price. Remember that the virtual shopping basket does not store all this information. It is this part that requires an interface to a product database that may contain all this data. This is beyond the scope of this chapter, but it will be addressed in the chapter covering database access with servlets.

```
<TR>
   <TD><!--PRODUCT_CODE--></TD>
   <TD><!--PRODUCT_DESCRIPTION--></TD>
   <TD><!--PRODUCT_PRICE--></TD>
</TR>
```
Example 23.7   The HTML template for the table row

In order for this servlet to do its job properly, two template file references must be passed in: one for the main file and one that describes the table row. Example 23.8 shows the servlet for displaying the checkout.

```java
import java.io.*;
import java.net.*;
import java.util.*;
import javax.servlet.*;
import javax.servlet.http.*;

public class displayCheckoutServlet   extends HttpServlet{

  public void init( ServletConfig _servletConfig)
                            throws ServletException {
    super.init(_servletConfig);
  }

  public void service( HttpServletRequest _req,
                            HttpServletResponse _res)
                            throws ServletException, IOException{
    HttpSession clientSession = _req.getSession( true );
    virtualBasket vBasket = (virtualBasket)clientSession.getValue("
                            shop.basket");
    if ( vBasket == null )
      vBasket = new virtualBasket();

    //-- Load in the template files
    htmlTemplate FB1  = new htmlTemplate( _req.getRealPath
                            (_req.getParameter("FILE1")) );
    htmlTemplate FB2  = new htmlTemplate( _req.getRealPath
                            (_req.getParameter("FILE2")) );

    PrintWriter Out = new PrintWriter( _res.getOutputStream() );
    String key[]    = new String[2];
    String dat[]    = new String[2];

    key[0]          = "<!--TABLEROW-->";
    key[1]          = "<!--TOTAL_PRICE-->";

    StringBuffer    tmp = new StringBuffer(100);
    StringWriter    psOut;
    PrintWriter     pOut;
    int             totalPrice = 0;
    String ikey[]   = new String[3];
    String idat[]   = new String[3];

    ikey[0]         = "<!--PRODUCT_CODE-->";
    ikey[1]         = "<!--PRODUCT_DESCRIPTION-->";
    ikey[2]         = "<!--PRODUCT_PRICE-->";
    Vector productLine = vBasket.getItems();
    if ( productLine != null && productLine.size() != 0 ){
      Enumeration E   = productLine.elements();
      while (E.hasMoreElements()){
```

```
        idat[0] = (String)E.nextElement();
        idat[1] = "";   //-- Description
        idat[2] = "";   //-- Price

        psOut = new StringWriter();
        pOut  = new PrintWriter( psOut );
        FB2.print( pOut, ikey, idat );
        tmp.append( psOut.toString() );
      }
      dat[0] = tmp.toString();
      dat[1] = totalPrice + "";
      FB1.print( Out, key, dat);
    }
  }
}
```

Example 23.8   Displaying the checkout

The `service(…)` method retrieves the session as normal and if a session doesn't exist, it creates one. The creation is purely to make the logic and program flow uniformly. The two template instances are created and loaded. We need to replace the instance of `<!--TABLEROW-->` with a complete body from the second template for each product item.

This is done by running around the loop of product lines and creating a buffer in memory to store the newly created template. Though the buffer is created using the template routine, the user doesn't see it, as it's hidden in the background. At the end of this loop, we simply copy this string instance into the place where the `<!--TABLEROW-->` is to appear. This is done by calling the `print(…)` method of the first template file.

This algorithm makes a simple method for displaying the product list without our having to hardcode any HTML code in the servlet. This allows you to hand over the complete system to a team of HTML developers and let them worry about the look and feel of the online store.

This servlet is not complete—it is missing the section to retrieve the necessary product information for each product. This data could be stored as the user added each item to his shopping basket, but it would be wasteful since the only time the user needs all the product information is when he gets to the checkout. To go get the list every time he adds an item may place an unnecessary load on the database.

23.5 Making payment

Adding the ability to make a payment is a straightforward task. Each time the client sends a request to the server, it includes the necessary information for the session manager to identify it. So the checkout information can be displayed at the top of the page, and a separate form that collects the user's credit card information can be displayed at the bottom. When the user posts this form to the servlet, the servlet can retrieve the shopping basket again, calculate the price to charge the user, and then proceed to process the transaction.

The session management layer has enabled us to break down the complete shopping cart system into very independent modules that can be modified without impacting the rest of the system. The session manager is doing a lot of the work for us here by managing all our data, making sure it gets saved if the server gets restarted, and managing the cookie information at the client side.

Now you can see why the shopping cart system is very easy to implement using servlets.

23.6 Future extensions

This chapter demonstrated the servlet implementation of an online shopping application. The overall design of the system was reduced to a variety of very simple servlets. The solution provided gives extensive flexibility to both the web designer and the user browsing the site.

As complete as this solution may be, a number of features could easily be added to extend it for a live system:

- Database access
  A button is associated with each catalog item so it can be included in the shopping basket. This information could be stored in a database where the catalog pages could be created dynamically rather than manually.

- Background processing
  The virtualBasket was a static class, but there is no reason why this could not have been a threaded class. While the client was browsing the site, the shopping basket servlet could have been looking up relevant products in the background. The next time the client made a request, the results could be displayed. This is the true power of session management, one that other implementations encounter a lot of difficulty in reproducing.

C H A P T E R   2 4

Servlets and JDBC

- Learn what JDBC is and how it operates.

- Discover a number of ways JDBC can be used with servlets.

- Understand how application performance can be increased through the use of a connection pool.

One of the core building blocks of any system, be it distributed, local, or virtual, is a database. At some point in the chain of processing, the ability to store and retrieve data needs to be addressed. The capacity to successfully access a database is a high priority for many projects. Add this to the current growth of the web, and the need to give some sort of front-end access to a database—the demand for database connectivity at the server side is at an all-time high.

Java has unleashed the power of databases in Java Database Connectivity (JDBC), which is its own easy-to-use database API. JDBC offers developers many advantages, such as the ability to access databases without having to worry about the underlying database.

24.1 JDBC overview

Computers were born from man's need to manipulate and store information. This information is commonly accessed from within a database environment. It would therefore be shortsighted to introduce a new language without making provisions for some sort of interface to a databank. And Java is no exception.

Many standards for accessing databases already exist in the electronic world—for example, the most popular and well-known mechanism is the Structured Query Language (more commonly referred to as SQL). The name is misleading, however, as SQL is much more than just a language for retrieving information from a database. It defines a set of commands to create, store, modify, retrieve, and manage information in a database. Providing that the SQL statements used in accessing a database conform to ANSI standards, the queries are considered to be database-independent or database-transparent. However it is not unheard of for databases to implement their own hybrid SQL extensions to give much greater efficiency, flexibility, and complexity to the query. Such statements are therefore difficult to transport to other database types.

Java developers found that they needed a framework so they could build a uniform interface over the top of a variety of database connectivity systems. Such a framework would allow developers to write a single database interface over many platforms.

This framework is known as the JDBC interface. JDBC is closely modeled on the X/open SQL Call Level Interface (CLI), which is in itself a widely accepted ANSI standard interface.

JDBC acts like a database bridge, passing SQL text strings straight to the destination database. JDBC does not parse the text string for the user; it simply acts as the bridge between the user and the database, allowing the database to parse the string. Thus, any exception errors generated originate from the database, not from the JDBC layer.

The JDBC API consists of four main classes:

- `java.sql.DriverManager`
- `java.sql.Connection`
- `java.sql.Statement`
- `java.sql.Resultset`

Since this is not a book on JDBC, we will quickly look at the four main types, then we'll move on to learn how we can best utilize them in a servlet environment.

24.1.1 DriverManager

The `java.sql.DriverManager` class is a very important one. Its main purpose is to manage the different types of JDBC database drivers. When running an application, it is the `DriverManager`'s responsibility to load all the drivers found in the system property `jdbc.drivers`.

As an example, this is where the driver for the Oracle database may be defined. This doesn't mean that a new driver cannot be explicitly stated in a program at run time without the `jdbc.drivers`. When opening a connection in code to a database it is the `Driver-Manager`'s role to choose the most appropriate driver from any of the previously loaded drivers.

24.1.2 java.sql.Connection

When a connection to the database has been established, the `java.sql.Connection` class represents a single instance of a particular session. As long as the connection remains open, SQL queries may be executed and results may be obtained. This interface can be used to retrieve information regarding the table descriptions and any other information about the database you are connected to.

By using `Connection`, a `commit` is automatic after the execution of a successful SQL statement unless `autocommit` has been explicitly disabled. In this case, a `commit` command must follow each SQL statement, or changes will not be saved. An unnatural disconnection from the database during an SQL statement will automatically result in the rollback of that query and everything else, back to the last successful `commit`.

24.1.3 java.sql.Statement

The `java.sql.Statement` interface passes to the database the SQL string that needs to be executed. It also retrieves any results from the database in the form of a `ResultSet`.

Only one `ResultSet` can be open per statement at any one point in time. For example, two `ResultSets` cannot be compared to each other if both `ResultSets` stem from the same SQL statement. If an SQL statement is reissued for any reason, the old `ResultSet` is automatically closed.

24.1.4 java.sql.ResultSet

A `java.sql.ResultSet` represents the retrieved data from a currently executed SQL statement. The data from the query is delivered in the form of a resulting table. The rows of the table are returned to the program in sequence, whereby the columns of data may be accessed.

A pointer known as a cursor holds the current retrieved record. When a `ResultSet` is returned, the cursor is positioned before the first record, and the `next` command (equivalent to the embedded SQL FETCH command) pulls back the first row. A `ResultSet` cannot go backward. In order to reread a previous retrieved row, the program must close the `ResultSet` and reissue the SQL statement. Once the last row has been retrieved the statement is considered closed; this causes the `ResultSet` to be automatically closed.

Note With JDBC v2.0, you do have the ability to move back through record sets. However this ability is dependent on the underlying JDBC driver, and as a consequence, not all of the different JDBS drivers available may support it, especially if large amounts of data have been successfully queried.

Columns can be retrieved from the current row in any order. A program may get values either using an index number for the column (starting at 1), or by explicitly stating the column name (if it's known). For portability and efficiency, columns should be retrieved in a left-to-right order and should only be read once.

24.1.5   Setting up a connection

In the previous section we quickly reviewed the JDBC API. This chapter will present a number of different methods for using this API within a servlet environment. Before we get into the mechanics of that, let's set up a test database which we can use throughout this chapter.

Since the JDK/JRE both ship with the standard JDBC-ODBC bridge, we will set up an ODBC connection (under Windows NT) which we will connect to using our servlets. Since the majority of commercial databases ship with ODBC drivers, this bridge can technically be used to connect to any database. However, be warned: the JDBC-ODBC is notorious for its instability.

Our example will use a simple Microsoft Access database, which contains a table called USER_TABLE; this table will have a number of fields for storing user details. The fields for this table will become apparent as we go through the examples.

The administration of the ODBC interface is controlled through the Windows Control Panel, and it is accessed by clicking on the icon labeled ODBC. This will bring up the dialog box shown in figure 24.1. This section lists the currently installed ODBC connections. The figure shows the existing connections. We are taking it from there and creating a connection. Select the System DSN tab, then click the Add button.

The list of currently available ODBC drivers will be presented. Highlight the Microsoft Access driver and click Next. Note that in order for you to access this driver, the Microsoft Access application will have to be installed on the local machine. If it is not, then you will not see this option.

Figure 24.2 shows the final dialog box that will be displayed. In this box, we will specify the actual settings for our database connection. The first and most important field is the Data Source Name field. This is the logical name the database will be given and it is the name we will use to refer to the database from Java. Don't put any spaces in the name.

We next need to select the database file. Click the Select button and choose the MS-Access file from the File dialog box.

That is essentially the database connection setup. However, we will be bold and add an additional username and password to the database. We do this by clicking the Advanced button and filling in the two fields.

We can now close the dialog box. If all went well with the setup, you should see the connection listed in the System DSN tab.

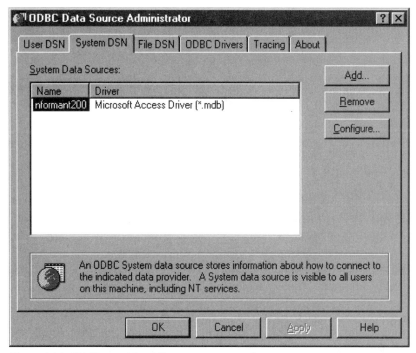

Figure 24.1 ODBC step #1: adding a new connection

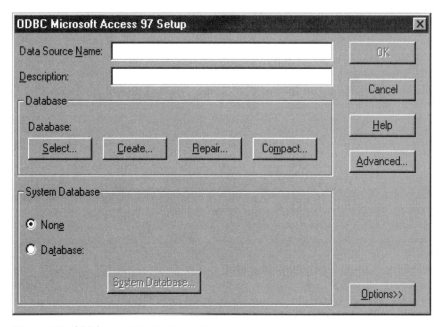

Figure 24.2 ODBC step #2: database setup

Note You'll encounter many small quirks with the ODBC bridge. For example, if you update any of the database structure, you have to open up the ODBC administration tool and click Repair. This will restore the ODBC connection again, and make sure that all subsequent JDBC requests are successful. Another annoyance with Microsoft Access is its inability to clean up after itself. If you have a database file that's 10 MB, and you delete all the records, the database will remain 10 MB in size. You can manually reduce the size by clicking the Compact button. There is no facility for doing this from within the JDBC API.

24.2 Method #1: connection per client

Now that we have our database connection all plumbed into ODBC and we have a fundamental knowledge of JDBC under our belt, let's implement our first JDBC-ready servlet.

This servlet will not do much more than display the contents of the table at the other end of the ODBC connection, but we will use this example to demonstrate a couple of different ways you can integrate JDBC with servlets.

In this example, for each client request that comes in, we will open up the connection to the database, perform a query, and then output the results back to the client.

24.2.1 Connecting to the database

Before we can run any queries on the database, we have to get a handle or reference to it. Once we have an instance of `Connection`, we can run as many queries as we want. However, we do not directly create an instance of `Connection`, but we do want to ask the `DriverManager` class to supply one for us.

The `DriverManager` will attempt to connect to the given database with the optional username and password. If it is successful, then an instance of `Connection` is returned. Example 24.1 illustrates this procedure.

```
Connection newCon = null;
try{
  Class.forName( "sun.jdbc.odbc.JdbcOdbcDriver" );
  newCon  = DriverManager.getConnection( "jdbc:odbc:nformant200",
                              "username", "password" );
}catch(Exception E){
  System.out.println( "[jdbcServlet.service():" + E + "]" );
  _res.setStatus( HttpServletResponse.SC_NO_CONTENT );
  return;
}
```
Example 24.1 Connecting to the database

Since we do not have the driver registered in the `jdbc.properties` file, we have to make sure the driver class is available to the virtual machine. We do this with a call to the `forName` method from the `Class` class. This will load and link the class name into the virtual machine. In this instance, we are looking to use the standard JDBC-ODBC driver that ships with the JDK. This driver is controlled by the class `sun.jdbc.odbc.JdbcOdb-cDriver`.

Next, we have to call the method `getConnection(...)` from the `DriverManager` class. We pass in a database URL as the first parameter. This is the location of the database we are attempting to connect to. The format of this URL is

```
jdbc:<subprotocol>:<subname>
```

In our example, the *subprotocol* is ODBC, with the *subname* being the name we called the database in the Control Panel, as described earlier.

If all goes well, a newly created `Connection` will be returned. But things don't always go as planned—for example, the wrong *subname* could be supplied. Be careful to get the case correct; some drivers are fussy. Another common problem is when the connection refuses to connect. Check to see that no one else has a session open to it. Most databases have a limit to the number of concurrent connections that can be open at any one time (this includes shutting down the file in MS-Access if it is open).

24.2.2   Running the query

Now that we've successfully opened the connection to the database, the database is now ready for querying. Since this is such a generic example, let's run a query that will return the complete table data: every column and every row. We will print this data back out to the client with a row per line.

Using the JDBC API we don't need to know the name of the columns beforehand (nor the data type, for that matter). We can ask the assistance of a helper class. You'll learn later.

The SQL query in our instance will be:

```
SELECT * FROM USER_TABLE
```

It will begin with a creation of a `Statement` class. We make a call to the `Connection` class with the `createStatement()` method, which will return a new instance of `Statement`. From here we can execute the SQL statement above with a call to `executeQuery(...)`.

This method will return a `ResultSet` instance, which represents the new result table. Only one `ResultSet` can be active per statement.

Example 24.2 shows the code used to execute the query. Since this example has asked for all the columns back, we get a handle to the `ResultSetMetaData` class from the `ResultSet` class. This class handles all the information that describes the data that was returned. In our example, we are only interested in the number of columns that were returned. But this class gives access to all the data types of each column and the column name, if it's available.

Running through each row of the result table is done using the `next()` method. This method moves the table cursor on one row. Unless you are using a full JDBC version 2 driver, you will not be able to return to a previous row. If you need to, you will have to rerun the query.

```
Statement Statmt;
```

```
ResultSet Res;
PrintWriter Out = new PrintWriter( _res.getOutputStream() );

try{
  Statmt = newCon.createStatement();
  Res   = Statmt.executeQuery( "SELECT * FROM USER_TABLE" );

  ResultSetMetaData RM = Res.getMetaData();
  while (Res.next()){
    String columnString = "";
    for ( int x=0; x < RM.getColumnCount(); x++ ){
      columnString += Res.getString(x+1) + " ";
    }

    Out.println( columnString );
  }

  Res.close();
  Statmt.close();
  newCon.close();
}catch(SQLException E){
  System.out.println( "[jdbcServlet.service():" + E + "]" );
  _res.setStatus( HttpServletResponse.SC_NO_CONTENT );
  return;
}
```
Example 24.2   Running the query

This servlet does nothing fancy except return all the data, one row at a time per line. This is done by building up a temporary string of the column data by making a call to retrieve the data in each column of the result table. The `getString(…)` method returns the column data in the given column index in the form of `String`. The `ResultSet` method provides a `getXXX(…)` method for each of the data types available.

Once the query is complete, the result set, the statement, and the connection are closed. It is important to close them down in the correct order, or an `SQLException` will be thrown.

24.2.3   *Complete source code*

Example 24.3 shows the complete `jdbcServlet` that houses the JDBC example shown above.

```
import java.io.*;
import java.sql.*;
import javax.servlet.*;
import javax.servlet.http.*;

public class jdbcServlet extends HttpServlet {

  public void service( HttpServletRequest _req, HttpServletResponse _res)
                             throws ServletException, IOException{

    Connection newCon = null;
    try{
```

```
        Class.forName( "sun.jdbc.odbc.JdbcOdbcDriver" );
        newCon  = DriverManager.getConnection( "jdbc:odbc:nformant200",
                            "username", "password" );
    }catch(Exception E){
      System.out.println( "[jdbcServlet.service():" + E + "]" );
      _res.setStatus( HttpServletResponse.SC_NO_CONTENT );
      return;
    }

    Statement Statmt;
    ResultSet Res;
    PrintWriter Out = new PrintWriter( _res.getOutputStream() );

    try{
      Statmt = newCon.createStatement();
      Res    = Statmt.executeQuery( "SELECT * FROM USER_TABLE" );

      ResultSetMetaData RM = Res.getMetaData();

      while (Res.next()){
        String columnString = "";

        for ( int x=0; x < RM.getColumnCount(); x++ ){
          columnString += Res.getString(x+1) + " ";
        }

        Out.println( columnString );
      }

      Res.close();
      Statmt.close();
      newCon.close();
    }catch(SQLException E){
      System.out.println( "[jdbcServlet.service():" + E + "]" );
      _res.setStatus( HttpServletResponse.SC_NO_CONTENT );
      return;
    }

    Out.flush();
  }
}
```

Example 24.3   The complete `jdbcServlet` **source code**

24.2.4   *Performance*

From a technical point of view, the servlet in this example is perfect. It opens up a connection to a database, runs a query, displays the results, and closes the connection down again. It's a textbook example, one might even say.

However, from a practical point of view, it is useless and you would not use it in a real world example. Why, you ask?

For every client request that comes in, a database connection is created. This is not a major problem if only one person at a time comes to your web site. However, this isn't the case. We have to assume that many people will be accessing the servlet at once. Therefore, we could potentially use up all the concurrent slots on a database engine.

The servlet is also very inefficient. The JDBC API tells us we can happily reuse the `Connection` class, with no need to open and close it all the time. Ironically, making the connection to the database can be one of the most time-consuming operations performed. But this servlet does it for every client request.

One potential way around this problem is to have the `Connection` class be static, starting off live as a `null`. When the first client request comes in, it can create the database connection, and each subsequent connection can then reuse that connection. However, you still have to safeguard against multiple hits; implementing the `SingleThreadModel` interface from the servlet API can easily resolve this issue.

Although it's technically correct, the `SingleThreadModel` is still very restrictive. First, only one client thread can run through the `service(…)` method at any one time. Second, what if we develop another servlet to operate from the same database? Do we have to create another connection to the database?

For these reasons, the implementation in the next section is a much better, cleaner solution.

24.3 Method #2: connection pool

This section will demonstrate the design and implementation of a class that will be used to manage all the connections for the database.

24.3.1 Overview

We want to be able to open up a pool of connections. Every time a class needs to run a query, it will ask for a connection from the pool. If one is available, the connection is temporarily lent to the class on the condition that it is returned after it's used. If one isn't available, then the class can wait for one to become available.

One of things we don't want to have to do is to carry around a reference to the connection pool. This would make it awkward, as we would have to make sure all classes had a reference to it. Fortunately, with Java we don't have to worry about this.

We will design a class, `dbBroker`, that will handle all the connections. It will also be responsible for the distribution of the actual connections. In order not to have to carry an instance to this class around with us, we will make all the public methods static, with the class itself holding the reference to an instance of itself.

Example 24.4 shows how to set up this class. Before a method retrieves a connection from the pool, it first must make a call to `dbBroker.getInstance()`. This is a call to verify that an instance has been created and is ready to serve.

```
public class dbBroker {

  private static dbBroker Broker = null;

  public synchronized static void getInstance(){
    if ( Broker == null )
      Broker = new dbBroker();
```

```
    }
  }
```
Example 24.4   Setting up the connection pool

To make sure this class isn't created outside of this connection class, we will make the constructor private. The next section will look at what happens in this constructor.

24.3.2   Managing new connections

The connection pool will manage the connections to the database. This includes monitoring the connections as they are requested, maintained, and closed by other classes. To make things a little easier, we will define a wrapper class for each Connection and these classes will be used to store all the necessary information associated with the "hire" of the connection.

The class, dbConnection (example 24.5), shows all the methods and data for each Connection. In addition to the Connection object, a flag to indicate its current status will be kept. This flag will be set when a class is using the Connection, using the setActive() method.

In multiuser systems, it can often be difficult to estimate the number of concurrent connections that are actually needed. To make this an easier decision, we will keep a little statistical information on each Connection, including the number of times the Connection has been used, the average time for each use, and the maximum time a connection has been kept out for. The dbConnection handles all this information through the use of the setActive() and setInActive() methods.

```
class dbConnection extends Object {
  public Connection Con;
  public boolean     bActive;
  public long        timeTaken;
  public long        averageTime;
  public long        maxTime;
  public int         hitRate;

  public dbConnection( Connection _Con ){
    Con      = _Con;
    bActive = false;
    timeTaken    = 0;
    averageTime = 0;
    hitRate      = -1;
    maxTime      = -1;
  }

  public void setInActive(){
    bActive = false;
    long t = System.currentTimeMillis() - timeTaken;
    if ( t < 120000 )
      averageTime += t;

    timeTaken    = 0;
    if ( t > maxTime )
      maxTime = t;
  }
```

```
public void setActive(){
  bActive = true;
  timeTaken   = System.currentTimeMillis();
  hitRate++;
}

public long getAverage(){
  if ( hitRate == 0 ) return 0;
  return averageTime/(long)hitRate;
}

public String toString(){
  return "[Hit: " + hitRate + "] [Avg.: " + getAverage() + "]
          [Use: " + bActive + "] [Max: " + maxTime + "]";
}
}
```

Example 24.5 The wrapper class for a connection

When a class makes a call to dbBroker.getInstance(), the constructor shown in example 24.6 is run. This constructor will create the number of necessary connections and make them available for use.

One of the criteria for the connection pool was to remain generic, and not to have any specific detail about the opening of the database distributed all over the system. Therefore, this class will open up a special file that will describe the complete connection parameters. We can therefore control all the parameters through a simple text file, and access these parameters with the java.util.Properties class.

```
private dbBroker(){
  Properties INI = new Properties();
  try{
    INI.load( new FileInputStream("dbbroker.ini") );
    dbDriver  = INI.getProperty( "driver" );
    dbName    = INI.getProperty( "database" );
    dbUser    = INI.getProperty( "username" );
    dbPassword= INI.getProperty( "password" );
    noCon     = Integer.parseInt(INI.getProperty("connections"));
  } catch (Exception E){
    System.out.println( "[dbBroker:" + E + "]" );
    System.out.println( "[dbBroker: Please ensure you have the following
                                fields: " );
    System.out.println( "[dbBroker: driver=" );
    System.out.println( "[dbBroker: database=" );
    System.out.println( "[dbBroker: username=" );
    System.out.println( "[dbBroker: password=" );
    System.out.println( "[dbBroker: connections=" );
    System.out.println( "[dbBroker: in a file named dbbroker.ini]" );
  }

  dbList  = new Vector();

  //-- Attempt to open the database connections
  Connection Con;
```

```
for ( int x=0; x < noCon; x++ ){
  Con = openConnection();
  if ( Con != null )
    dbList.addElement( new dbConnection(Con) );
}
}
```
Example 24.6   Creating the instance of dbBroker

The database driver, database name, username, and password will be stored in the dbBroker class. This will allow us to reopen any connections if necessary without the need to reload the file. Another parameter that is read in is the number of connections the pool manager will manage.

Each connection will be stored in a list using the Vector class. Knowing the number of connections to be created makes filling up this list a trivial matter. For each connection, a call to the method in example 24.7 is made and the openConnection() method attempts to create a new Connection instance. If it's successful, then a instance of dbConnection is created and inserted into the list.

```
private Connection openConnection(){
  Connection newCon = null;
  try{
    Class.forName( dbDriver );
    newCon  = DriverManager.getConnection( dbName, dbUser, dbPassword );
  }catch(Exception E){
    System.out.println( "[dbBroker.openConnection():" + E + "]" );
    newCon = null;
  }
  System.out.println( "[dbBroker.openConnection(): Success " );
  return newCon;
}
```
Example 24.7   Opening the connection to the database

You can see that the method for creating the Connection instance is no different from the method we used in the servlet in the first section.

24.3.3   Controlling connections

We will allow classes access to the connection pool through two methods: pop() and push(...). The pop() method will look through the list of connections for a connection that is not in use. If one is found, then it is flagged as active and the Connection is returned.

If one is not available, then this suggests that all the connections are presently being used. If this is the case, then the method call will be suspended until one does become available. We can do this with a call to wait(). When the method returns, we will reattempt to get a free connection. The method shown in example 24.8 illustrates this process.

```
public static Connection pop(){
  synchronized( Broker ){
    dbConnection dbCon;
    for (;;){
      dbCon = Broker.getFreeConnection();
```

```
        if ( dbCon != null )
          break;

        if ( dbCon == null && Broker.dbList.size() != 0 ){
          try{
            Broker.wait();
          }catch(Exception E){}
        }
      }

      if ( Broker.dbList.size() == 0 ){
        System.out.println( "[dbBroker.pop: No free connections" );
        return null;
      }else{
        dbCon.setActive();
        return dbCon.Con;
      }
    }
  }
}
```

Example 24.8 Getting a connection

The method call `getFreeConnection()`, which can be seen in the complete source code later in this section, simply runs through the `Vector` of `dbConnections` looking for an inactive connection.

Once a class has finished using the connection, it is returned with a call to the `push(...)` method (example 24.9). The method looks for the corresponding wrapper class that holds this connection. Once the wrapper class is found, the connection is cleaned up with a call to `commit()` and `clearWarnings()`. This guarantees that no errors or warnings roll over to the next use.

If something goes wrong with this cleanup procedure, an `Exception` will be thrown. In this instance, the `Connection` is closed and a reattempt to open it is made. After the `Connection` has been placed back into the list as inactive, a call to `notifyAll()` notifies any waiting classes that are waiting on a free class.

```
public static void push( Connection _Con ){
  if ( Broker == null || _Con == null ) return;

  synchronized (Broker){
    //-- Need to check the validity of the connection
    dbConnection dbCon = Broker.getConnection( _Con );
    if ( dbCon == null )  return;

    //-- Check the status of the connection
    try{
      dbCon.Con.commit();
      dbCon.Con.clearWarnings();
    }catch(Exception E){
      Broker.closeConnection( dbCon.Con );
    }

    if ( Broker.isClosed(dbCon.Con) ){
      dbCon.Con  = Broker.openConnection();
```

```
       if ( dbCon.Con == null ){
         System.out.println( "[dbBroker.push: Failed to reopen a dead
                               connection]" );
         Broker.dbList.removeElement( dbCon );
         return;
       }
     }else{
       dbCon.setInActive();
     }
     Broker.notifyAll();
   }
}
```

Example 24.9   Releasing the connection

24.3.4   Verifying connections

It would be useful to print out all the statistical information that is being held every so often. To do this, we can set the dbBroker class as a threaded class and have it print out the statistics of each dbConnection class once every period.

The method shown in example 24.10 sleeps for thirty minutes before printing out a status report detailing the average use time, maximum time of the connection, and the number of times the connection has been accessed.

```
public void run(){
  int debugCount=0;
  for (;;){
    debugCount++;
    if ( debugCount%30 == 0 ){
      Enumeration E = dbList.elements();
      dbConnection dbCon;
      while (E.hasMoreElements()){
        dbCon = (dbConnection)E.nextElement();
        System.out.println( "[dbBroker.run(): " + dbCon.toString() );
      }
    }

    try{
      Thread.currentThread().sleep( 60000 );
    }catch(Exception E1){}
  }
}
```

Example 24.10   Checking the connections

24.3.5   Using the pool manager

Now that we've created the pool manager, we can use it. We will use the same example we used before and replace the service(…) method with a much improved version.

The complete database creation section has been replaced with a simple call to dbBroker.getInstance() and then dbBroker.pop(). As shown in example 24.11, the dbBroker class will do all the necessary loading and connecting to the database, and return a clean Connection instance.

```java
public void service( HttpServletRequest _req, HttpServletResponse _res)
                            throws ServletException, IOException{
  dbBroker.getInstance();
  Connection newCon = dbBroker.pop();
  Statement Statmt;
  ResultSet Res;
  PrintWriter Out = new PrintWriter( _res.getOutputStream() );

  try{
    Statmt = newCon.createStatement();
    Res    = Statmt.executeQuery( "SELECT * FROM USER_TABLE" );

    ResultSetMetaData RM = Res.getMetaData();

    while (Res.next()){
      String columnString = "";

      for ( int x=0; x < RM.getColumnCount(); x++ ){
        columnString += Res.getString(x+1) + " ";
      }

      Out.println( columnString );
    }

    Res.close();
    Statmt.close();
    dbBroker.push( newCon );
  }catch(SQLException E){
    System.out.println( "[jdbcServlet.service():" + E + "]" );
    _res.setStatus( HttpServletResponse.SC_NO_CONTENT );
    return;
  }

  Out.flush();
}
```

Example 24.11 Setting up the connection pool

After we have finished using the connection, we return it back to the pool manager with a call to dbBroker.push(...). As you can see, there is no need to hold a separate instance to dbBroker, as all the methods are accessed through static calls.

24.3.6 Complete source code
Example 24.12 shows the complete source code for the dbBroker connection pool manager.

```java
import java.sql.*;
import java.util.*;
import java.io.*;

public class dbBroker extends Thread {

  private static dbBroker Broker = null;
```

```
private String  dbDriver,dbName,dbUser,dbPassword;
private int noCon;
private Vector  dbList;

private dbBroker(){
  Properties INI = new Properties();
  try{
    INI.load( new FileInputStream("dbbroker.ini") );
    dbDriver  = INI.getProperty( "driver" );
    dbName    = INI.getProperty( "database" );
    dbUser    = INI.getProperty( "username" );
    dbPassword= INI.getProperty( "password" );
    noCon     = Integer.parseInt(INI.getProperty("connections"));
  } catch (Exception E){
    System.out.println( "[dbBroker:" + E + "]" );
    System.out.println( "[dbBroker: Please ensure you have the
                         following fields: " );
    System.out.println( "[dbBroker: driver=" );
    System.out.println( "[dbBroker: database=" );
    System.out.println( "[dbBroker: username=" );
    System.out.println( "[dbBroker: password=" );
    System.out.println( "[dbBroker: connections=" );
    System.out.println( "[dbBroker: in a file named dbbroker.ini]" );
  }

  dbList  = new Vector();

  //-- Attempt to open the database connections
  Connection Con;
  for ( int x=0; x < noCon; x++ ){
    Con = openConnection();
    if ( Con != null )
      dbList.addElement( new dbConnection(Con) );
  }

  new Thread(this).start();
  System.out.println("[dbBroker: " + dbList.size() + " connections
                       opened]" );
}

public void run(){
  int debugCount=0;
  for (;;){
    debugCount++;
    if ( debugCount%30 == 0 ){
      Enumeration E = dbList.elements();
      dbConnection dbCon;
      while (E.hasMoreElements()){
        dbCon = (dbConnection)E.nextElement();
        System.out.println( "[dbBroker.run(): " + dbCon.toString() );
      }
    }

    try{
```

```
          Thread.currentThread().sleep( 60000 );
      }catch(Exception E1){}
  }
}

public synchronized static void getInstance(){
   if ( Broker == null )
     Broker = new dbBroker();
}

public static Connection pop(){

   synchronized( Broker ){
     dbConnection dbCon;
     for (;;){
       dbCon = Broker.getFreeConnection();
       if ( dbCon != null )
         break;

       if ( dbCon == null && Broker.dbList.size() != 0 ){
         try{
            Broker.wait();
         }catch(Exception E){}
       }
     }

     if ( Broker.dbList.size() == 0 ){
       System.out.println( "[dbBroker.pop: No free connections" );
       return null;
     }else{
       dbCon.setActive();
       return dbCon.Con;
     }
   }
}

public static void shutdown(){
   if ( Broker == null ) return;

   Enumeration E = Broker.dbList.elements();
   dbConnection dbCon;
   while (E.hasMoreElements()){
     dbCon = (dbConnection)E.nextElement();
     Broker.closeConnection( dbCon.Con );
   }
}

public static void push( Connection _Con ){
   if ( Broker == null || _Con == null ) return;

   synchronized (Broker){
     //-- Need to check the validity of the connection
     dbConnection dbCon = Broker.getConnection( _Con );
     if ( dbCon == null )  return;
```

```
      //-- Check the status of the connection
      try{
        dbCon.Con.commit();
        dbCon.Con.clearWarnings();
      }catch(Exception E){
        Broker.closeConnection( dbCon.Con );
      }

      if ( Broker.isClosed(dbCon.Con) ){
        dbCon.Con  = Broker.openConnection();
        if ( dbCon.Con == null ){
          System.out.println( "[dbBroker.push: Failed to reopen a dead
                             connection]" );
          Broker.dbList.removeElement( dbCon );
          return;
        }
      }else{
        dbCon.setInActive();
      }
      Broker.notifyAll();
    }
  }

  private Connection openConnection(){

    Connection newCon = null;
    try{
      Class.forName( dbDriver );
      newCon  = DriverManager.getConnection(
                             dbName, dbUser, dbPassword );
    }catch(Exception E){
      System.out.println( "[dbBroker.openConnection():" + E + "]" );
      newCon = null;
    }

    System.out.println( "[dbBroker.openConnection(): Success " );
    return newCon;
  }

  private void closeConnection( Connection _Con ){
    try{
      _Con.close();
    }catch(Exception E){}
  }

  private boolean isClosed( Connection _Con ){
    try{
      return _Con.isClosed();
    }catch(Exception E){
      return true;
    }
  }
  private synchronized dbConnection getConnection( Connection _Con ){
    Enumeration E = dbList.elements();
```

```
      dbConnection dbCon;
      while (E.hasMoreElements()){
        dbCon = (dbConnection)E.nextElement();
        if ( dbCon.Con   == _Con )
          return dbCon;
      }
      return null;
    }


  private synchronized dbConnection getFreeConnection(){
    Enumeration E = dbList.elements();
    dbConnection dbCon;
    while (E.hasMoreElements()){
      dbCon = (dbConnection)E.nextElement();
      if ( dbCon.bActive == false )
        return dbCon;
    }
    return null;
  }
}
```

Example 24.12   The complete `dbBroker` class source code

24.3.7   *Performance*

One of the biggest performance improvements over and above the first process is the way this servlet shares database connections. By having one class manage all the connections, we can guarantee a level of connection performance to the database. For example, if 100 clients suddenly come in to the servlet all at once, the database will not get hit with 100 requests for connections.

Since the pool manager is implemented as a static class, we don't need to worry about holding a reference to it or needing to pass it around to all the necessary classes that require a database connection. The pool manager is automatically keeping statistics on your database use. This means you can make a more informed decision on the precise requirements and number of connections that are required to be open at any one time.

24.4   *Future extensions*

This chapter presented you with an alternative to the highly inefficient method of database handling. A servlet is not like a normal application where you have a degree of control over the usage patterns. A servlet is called into action when a client makes a request; therefore, the traditional way of handling database connections has to be rethought.

Although it is already highly efficient, the `dbBroker` could be extended to include the ability to handle multiple pools. This would allow connections to different databases to be handled and manipulated at once. This is an essential feature for applications that require a distributed database layer.

C H A P T E R   2 5

Internet chats

One of the guiding principles of the Internet is this: people must be able to share information easily. Not many people know that the first application to make people sit up and take serious notice of the Internet was electronic mail. This was the first piece of software that allowed people from different parts of the world to communicate with each other at a very low cost. Although email was revolutionary at that time, things have advanced since then. Internet developers have now gone beyond simple email capabilities, and chat-based systems are now very popular. A chat system enables people to communicate with each other in real time, sending small lines of text that the recipient can instantly reply to. This is different from email communication where the recipient has to read a message in his In Box before replying to it; the time between receiving and replying to messages can vary. Chat systems also allow online conferences to take place.

One of the more popular forms of Internet chat is Internet Relay Chat (IRC). To use this chat system you must have an IRC client installed on your machine. Because of this requirement, web-based chat systems have become increasingly popular over IRC-based chat systems.

In this chapter we will present both an HTML-based chat system and an applet-based system. This chapter will demonstrate one of the methods used to make an applet communicate with a servlet.

25.1 Chat introduction

Chat systems allow users from all over the world to talk interactively with each other through text-based conversions. At the moment, many types of chat systems exist, but one of the most popular systems is the IRC service. This system offers many different areas or rooms in which people can meet and talk with other people worldwide. If a person wants to use the IRC system, an IRC client has to be installed on his computer. This system enables him to connect to the server and exchange messages. One of the most popular IRC clients for the WinTel platform is mIRC.

In order for a user to use such a chat system, he must abandon his web browser and use a custom piece of software which is a little inflexible for many systems that have strict usage policies. As a consequence, not everybody knows IRC even exists. It's one of the Internet's best kept secrets!

To overcome the need for additional software at the client side, web-based chat systems were developed. The first ones used CGI and HTML. With this type of chat system, the user had to update the web page every so often to see if any new messages had been posted via an HTML form. Web designers offered simple chat systems on their web sites to bring in additional traffic. As you will see later, CGI could not keep up with the demand that chat systems placed on the server. As a result, Java-based chat systems were introduced.

The alternative to continually creating HTML forms is for an applet to run automatically at the client side; the applet updates the client when new messages arrive. An applet provides a much cleaner and more efficient solution to the HTML-based system.

By providing an applet-based chat service, you can offer online support and conferencing services to your users. Currently, the business community tends to underutilize this technology, dismissing it as a novelty or something only used for chatting with friends. But talking to people from other countries through an Internet chat system is far cheaper than the equivalent phone call, and it has the extra advantage of being able to store complete conversations in a simple text file.

Note The reason why the business community has been slow to catch on to the great functionality that Internet chat systems have to offer is anyone's guess. I recently read a book about building intranets in which the author claimed that chat systems were of no use to international business. This type of ignorance and shortsightedness has no place in today's ever-changing work environment, where more and more people are relying on remote communications with each other. Chat systems can save a company an enormous amount of money if they're used properly. Consider a very famous quote from a memo found at Western Union in 1876:

"This 'telephone' has too many shortcomings to be seriously considered as a means of communication. The device is inherently of no value to us."

Consider this a warning to those who don't believe.

This chapter implements both an HTML-based chat system and a Java applet-based chat system. By carefully designing the servlet at the server side, the same servlet can service both an applet and an HTML client solution. This allows people using the HTML version to chat with those using the Java applet version, thus providing them with the best of both worlds. The differences between the two systems lie in how the client interacts with the chat server. For example the applet-based chat displays new text instantly, but the HTML-based chat has to wait until the next polling interval.

We'll first develop an HTML-only chat servlet. If we carefully change a couple of methods, the servlet will be able to serve Java clients equally as well.

25.1.1   HTML chat

HTTP is not a broadcast protocol; it is stateless. Once the client has read the HTML source, no more data is sent. So, at face value, HTTP doesn't seem to be the most logical choice to front-end a chat system. However, the newer version of HTML has push/pull capabilities, meaning the client can be set up to automatically request any resource on the Internet that is addressable via a URL. This is done through the META tags in the page's header field.

```
<META HTTP-EQUIV=REFRESH CONTENT="30;URL=index.html">
```

Therefore, a web-based chat could operate by having the servlet update a single HTML file with the new message posted from a conversation participant. The HTML-based chat system simplifies the process to a single HTML form that accepts a user's contribution and then appends it to the main chat page (figure 25.1).

The web page in figure 25.1 is constructed in two parts. The first part is the HTML form that takes in the user's message and name. The second part is a list of the most recent messages posted to the group. This list grows as the number of posts on the topic increases.

Since you are using a servlet to provide this solution, and since servlets allow you to do a lot more than conventional CGI solutions, you can make a decision right away that

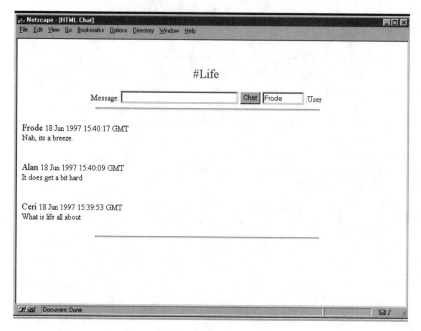

Figure 25.1 An example of an HTML-based chat client

will improve efficiency. Instead of the servlet appending the chat dialogue to an HTML file every time, the HTML chat file can be created dynamically on demand every time the client requests it. This will reduce the overhead of opening and writing to a file on every post. The URL to the HTML chat form will not link to a static file on the web server, but to a servlet alias that will dynamically generate it on demand.

These are the requirements for the HTML chat servlet:

1 Collate new postings to the conversation.

2 Provide more than one topic of conversation. The same servlet can provide the support for many different topics.

3 Provide the page to the client for the conversation in question.

For the sake of the servlet implementation, each topic of conversation will take place in a different room. This will allow users to have conversations with groups of people more easily, as opposed to everyone on the chat system listening to the same conversation.

25.1.2 Message format

If the page for the conversation is to be created for each client request, the servlet has to keep a certain number of messages. For this implementation, assume that the last ten messages are kept. Additionally, two other fields must be kept: the name of the user that posted the message and the date the message was received. Packaging this data into a class makes handling each message very easy, as shown in example 25.1.

```
class cChatMessage extends Object {
  public String Message;
  public String User;
  public Date    Posted;

  public cChatMessage( String _Message, String _User ){
    Message = _Message;
    User    = _User;
    Posted  = new Date();
  }
}
```
Example 25.1   The class definition for the message

When the message is created, it is time-stamped with the current date and time; this allows us to easily track the age of each message.

25.1.3   Adding a new message

The servlet will hold a list of rooms and each room will hold the last ten messages. When a new post is made to the conversation, another cChatMessage instance must be created and inserted into the correct data structure. Each room will be addressed by its name, and the hash table data structure will be used. One method to accomplish this storage would be to create an array of ten items in which to store the messages. However, this is not the best solution; using the Vector structure is a much better way to go. The data structure stores objects in an array-type structure, with items one after another and accessible using an index number. This way we can store the messages in history order, with the newest message at the head of the list.

```
private void addMessage( String _Room, String _User, String _Mess ){
  Vector RoomMessages;

  //- Create the room if it doesn't already exist
  if ( RoomPool.containsKey( _Room ) == false ){
    synchronized( RoomPool ){
      RoomMessages = new Vector();
      RoomPool.put( _Room, RoomMessages );
    }
  }else
    RoomMessages = (Vector)RoomPool.get( _Room );

  synchronized( RoomMessages ){
    RoomMessages.insertElementAt( new cChatMessage( _Mess, _User ) ,0 );
      if ( RoomMessages.size() > 10 )
        RoomMessages.setSize( 10 );
  }
}
```
Example 25.2   Accepting a new message

Example 25.2 shows the method for accepting new messages to the system. The list of rooms is stored in the hash table referenced by the RoomPool variable. Three parameters are required for every update: the room in which the conversation took place, the message the user posted, and the name of the user who posted the message. The Vector structure for the specified room is retrieved. If the room exists, the vector is successfully returned. However, if no room of that name exists, then a room is created. Since this is a multithreaded servlet, we must take care not to corrupt the hash table holding the list of rooms. The hash table data can be corrupted if more than one thread attempts to create a room.

Once the correct room has been chosen, a new instance of cChatMessage is created and inserted at the head (or start) of the vector. This is done so the most recent postings can be found easily by searching from the start of the list. As with the creation of a new room, the insertion of a new message is made thread-safe. It is more likely that threads will be inserted at the same time than the idea of two rooms being created at the same time.

To guarantee that there are only ever ten items in the list, when the list is larger than ten items, it is truncated and the older items are dropped off.

25.1.4 Updating the page

A new page is sent out every time the client posts a new message, or when the client side asks for a refresh using the META tag mechanism. Creating the page for the client is a three-step process.

First, the HTML header information is sent out to the client with the special META tag so that the client may update automatically. An alias is set up so that the /chat.html URL will invoke the servlet. Setting up an alias is web server-specific, but refer to chapter 3, *Java web server*, for information on creating an alias using JWS. Along with the URL, two additional parameters are included: the room and the username.

```
http://<yourhost>/chat.html?room=Coffee&user=Ceri
```

Next, the HTML form is formatted and sent out. The form is kept at the top of the page, so the user doesn't have to scroll the page down every time a refresh occurs. The message field of the form is made blank, as you would expect, but the user field is already filled in with the name of the user from that particular client. This saves users from having to type in their names all the time. To make sure the username is maintained through the refresh phase, it is passed in as one of the parameters. Example 25.3 shows the method for sending the HTML form to the client.

```java
private void sendUpdate( String _Room, String _User,
                         HttpServletResponse _res ) throws IOException{
  Vector RoomMessages = (Vector)RoomPool.get( _Room );
  if ( _User == null )
    _User = "";

  _res.setContentType("text/html");
  PrintWriter Out = new PrintWriter( _res.getOutputStream() );

  Out.println( "<HTML><HEAD><TITLE>HTML Chat</TITLE>" );
  Out.println( "<META HTTP-EQUIV=REFRESH CONTENT=\"30;URL=
                        /chat.html?room=" + _Room + "&user="
                        + _User + "\"></HEAD>" );
  Out.println( "<BODY TEXT=#000000 BGCOLOR=#FFFFFF LINK=#0000EE
                        VLINK=#551A8B ALINK=#FF0000><BR>" );
  Out.println( "<CENTER><BR><FONT COLOR=#0000FF SIZE=+2>");
  Out.println( "#" + _Room + "</FONT>" );
  Out.println( "<BR><FORM METHOD=POST ACTION=/chat.html>" );
```

```
Out.println( "Message: <INPUT TYPE=TEXT NAME=message VALUE=\"\"
                        SIZE=32>");
Out.println( "<INPUT TYPE=SUBMIT VALUE=Chat>");
Out.println( "<INPUT TYPE=TEXT NAME=user VALUE=\"" + _User + "\"
                        SIZE=10> :User" );
Out.println( "<INPUT TYPE=HIDDEN NAME=room VALUE=" + _Room + ">
                        </CENTER>" );
Out.println( "<HR ALIGN=CENTER WIDTH=60%>" );
cChatMessage UD;
int size;

if ( RoomMessages == null )
  size = 0;
else if ( RoomMessages.size() < 10 )
  size = RoomMessages.size();
else
  size = 10;

for ( int x=0; x < size; x++ ){
  UD = (cChatMessage)RoomMessages.elementAt( x );
  Out.println( "<BR><P><FONT COLOR=#0000FF SIZE=+1>" + UD.User +
                        "</FONT> "
                        + UD.Posted.toGMTString() );
  Out.println( "<BR>" + UD.Message + "</P>" );
}

Out.println( "<HR ALIGN=CENTER WIDTH=60%></BODY></HTML>" );
Out.flush();
}
```
Example 25.3   Updating the page for the client

All that remains to be sent out is the last batch of messages that came in. In this
instance, you are sending out the last ten messages, with the most recent one at the top of
the page. Running through the first ten elements of the list is a simple matter of setting up
a for loop. If you set the end of index to be either ten or the number of items in the list
(whichever is the smallest), the number of actual messages kept can be increased without
upsetting the output routine. One reason this is useful is that the user can choose how
many messages he wants displayed at any one time.

25.1.5   Complete source code

Example 25.4 shows the complete source code for the chat_html servlet. This servlet is
based on the HttpServlet class, overriding both the init(...) and the service(...) methods. The service(...) method only has one real function in the servlet, and that is to
determine whether the client request is for a refresh or if it's adding a new message to the
conversation. Either way, a fresh page is sent out to the client.

```
import java.util.*;
import java.io.*;
import javax.servlet.*;
import javax.servlet.http.*;

public class chat_html extends HttpServlet {
```

```java
private HashtableRoomPool;

public void init(ServletConfig _config) throws ServletException{
  super.init(_config);
  RoomPool = new Hashtable();
}

public void service( HttpServletRequest _req, HttpServletResponse _res)
                    throws ServletException, IOException{
  String Room= _req.getParameter( "room" );
  String User = _req.getParameter( "user" );
  String Mess = _req.getParameter( "message" );

  if ( Room == null ){
    _res.setStatus( HttpServletResponse.SC_NO_CONTENT );
    return;
  }

  if ( (User != null && Mess != null) &&
      (User.length() != 0 && Mess.length() != 0 ))
    addMessage( Room, User, Mess );

  sendUpdate( Room, User, _res );
}

private void sendUpdate(String _Room,String _User,
                        HttpServletResponse _res) throws IOException{
  Vector RoomMessages = (Vector)RoomPool.get( _Room );
  if ( _User == null )
    _User = "";

  _res.setContentType("text/html");
  PrintWriter Out = new PrintWriter( _res.getOutputStream() );

  Out.println( "<HTML><HEAD><TITLE>HTML Chat</TITLE>" );
  Out.println( "<META HTTP-EQUIV=REFRESH CONTENT=\"30;URL=
                    /chat.html?room=" + _Room + "&user="
                    + _User + "\"></HEAD>" );
  Out.println( "<BODY><BR>" );
  Out.println( "<CENTER><BR><FONT COLOR=#0000FF SIZE=+2>");
  Out.println( "#" + _Room + "</FONT>" );
  Out.println( "<BR><FORM METHOD=POST ACTION=/chat.html>" );
  Out.println( "Message: <INPUT TYPE=TEXT NAME=message VALUE=\"\"
                    SIZE=32>");
  Out.println( "<INPUT TYPE=SUBMIT VALUE=Chat>");
  Out.println( "<INPUT TYPE=TEXT NAME=user VALUE=\"" + _User + "\"
                    SIZE=10> :User" );
  Out.println( "<INPUT TYPE=HIDDEN NAME=room VALUE=" + _Room + ">
                    </CENTER>" );
  Out.println( "<HR ALIGN=CENTER WIDTH=60%>" );
  cChatMessage UD;
  int size;
```

```
      if ( RoomMessages == null )
        size = 0;
      else if ( RoomMessages.size() < 10 )
        size = RoomMessages.size();
      else
        size = 10;

      for ( int x=0; x < size; x++ ){
        UD = (cChatMessage)RoomMessages.elementAt( x );
        Out.println( "<BR><P><FONT COLOR=#0000FF SIZE=+1>" + UD.User +
                            "</FONT> " + UD.Posted.toGMTString() );
        Out.println( "<BR>" + UD.Message + "</P>" );
      }

      Out.println( "<HR ALIGN=CENTER WIDTH=60%></BODY></HTML>" );
      Out.flush();
  }

  private void addMessage( String _Room, String _User, String _Mess ){
      Vector RoomMessages;

      //- Create the room if it doesn't already exist
      if ( RoomPool.containsKey( _Room ) == false ){
        synchronized( RoomPool ){
          RoomMessages = new Vector();
          RoomPool.put( _Room, RoomMessages );
        }
      }else
        RoomMessages = (Vector)RoomPool.get( _Room );

      synchronized( RoomMessages ){
        RoomMessages.insertElementAt( new cChatMessage( _Mess, _User ) ,0
);
        if ( RoomMessages.size() > 10 )
          RoomMessages.setSize( 10 );
      }
  }
}
```

Example 25.4   The complete source code for the HTML chat servlet

Notice how much functionality exists in this relatively small servlet. Not only is it providing a complete HTML-based chat system, but it's also able to support multiple conversations at once. The next section details the Java applet version of the chat system, but instead of creating yet another chat system, the servlet we just created will be modified slightly to support applets, in addition to its current capabilities. Users will then be able to talk to each other using a variety of different mechanisms.

25.2   Applet-based chat

A Java applet provides the user with a much nicer and friendlier interface to a chat server. An applet runs on the client's browser and it can provide a much more sophisticated front end. The HTML version, though functional, can take up too much room in a page, leaving no space for additional site information.

Current Java chat clients connect to the server using TCP sockets. A connection to the server is made via a socket session and communication then begins. This is the most efficient way of transferring data back and forth to the applet. Additionally, since the applet is talking with the host from which it came, there is no security violation.

Not every one can use this technique, however. If a client is surfing behind a company firewall, such foreign protocols will not be allowed through. Generally, only HTTP packets, and sometimes FTP packets, are allowed through. This is one of the downfalls of an applet chat client—the inability to communicate through firewalls. This potential problem has been accounted for by the servlet accepting both HTTP and the custom data packets.

This section will demonstrate two different methods for a Java applet to talk to the server. The first method will use the HTTP protocol and the second version will use socket streams. Instead of creating two different applets to communicate with two different servlets, one client version will be developed along with one servlet version.

25.2.1 Applet-based version

Any communication method used to connect to the server shouldn't make an impact on the user interface. Users don't care how they are connected; they just care that they are connected, that they have a place to enter their name and their message, and that they can view messages coming back from the server. A basic applet is shown in figure 25.2.

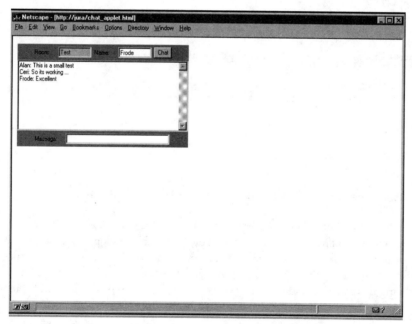

Figure 25.2 The chat applet used to connect to the chat servlet

An applet is a plug in or module that is placed somewhere on an HTML page. The applet shown consists of three different areas. The top section contains the room and username information. The middle section is the main message panel where the incoming messages will be displayed. The bottom section allows the user to submit a new message.

If you are familiar with Java applet construction and the Abstract Window Toolkit (AWT) package, you may wish to skim through the next section, then go directly to the server-side section, which details the communication method.

Chat applet construction   Creating an applet is similar to creating a servlet. With servlets, the interface servlet is used as the base class for all servlets; with applets, the `Applet` class from the `java.Applet` package is used as the basis of all applets.

The `Applet` class definition, shown in example 25.5, defines the skeleton for the chat applet.

```
import java.applet.*;

public class chat_applet extends Applet implements Runnable {
  public void init(){
    //- Do something
  }

  public void run(){
    //- Do something
  }
}
```
Example 25.5   Loading the distribution list

The `chat_applet` class is based on the `Applet` class, and this example implements the `Runnable` interface. This basically means the applet will run in a separate thread. As with a servlet, the `init()` method is called at program startup, and it contains all the initialization code. The user interface will be set up here. To implement the user interface shown in figure 25.2, a number of interface objects are employed, as shown in example 25.6.

```
TextField Name;
TextField Room;
TextField Message;
TextArea  MessageArea;
Button    ChatButton;
```
Example 25.6   Variable declaration

In addition to these control objects, a number of labels exist. When laying out controls in a Java applet, the labels are not placed using pixel coordinates. Instead, they are laid out in relation to each other. This allows the applet to look the same, no matter what platform it is run on. Describing the layout is done through special classes known as layout managers, in which each control is described using its relative position to other controls.

Note As part of the standard library, Java provides the very powerful AWT. The AWT contains all of the classes used to create user interfaces and graphical output. As you can imagine, this package is very rarely used in servlets, although you saw an example in chapter 14 of where a servlet can use it. The AWT is a very big area of Java, and many books cover only this topic.

Many different layout managers are included in the AWT package, and each has its own specific application area. Layout managers can be mixed, providing the developer with great flexibility for producing platform-independent applets. The chat client applet uses the simplest layout managers: `BorderLayout` and `FlowLayout`.

Example 25.7 shows the complete `init()` method, minus all of the connection-specific calls. The first thing the method does is create the control instances. Once they're created, it changes certain attributes of the control instances. For example, to make this applet stand out, the background is set to bright red. However, all the text-input boxes therefore inherit the color from the panel below, and they also become bright red. Changing the background color of the control can be done using the same `setBackground(...)` method call.

The user shouldn't be able to change the room or enter text in the main message panel, but he can insert text into the new message box. Setting these attributes is done using a single method call to the controls `setEditable(...)`. For the two text controls in question, the inputs are disabled (with the text control for the room being set to a light gray) to illustrate the fact that the user can't modify them.

```
public void init(){
  LabeltempLabel;
  Name  = new TextField( 8 );
  Room  = new TextField( getParameter("room"), 8 );
  Message= new TextField( 32 );
  MessageArea= new TextArea();
  ChatButton= new Button( "Chat" );

  setBackground( Color.red );
  Name.setBackground( Color.white );
  Room.setBackground( Color.lightGray );
  Message.setBackground( Color.white );
  MessageArea.setBackground( Color.white );
  MessageArea.setEditable( false );
  Room.setEditable( false );

  //- Lay out these controls in an order pleasing to the eye
  setLayout( new BorderLayout() );

  Panel top = new Panel();
  top.add( new Label( "Room:" ) );
  top.add( Room );
  top.add( new Label( "Name:" ) );
  top.add( Name );
```

```
    top.add( ChatButton );
    add( "North", top );

    Panel bottom = new Panel();
    bottom.add( new Label( "Message:" ) );
    bottom.add( Message );
    add( "South", bottom );
    add( "Center", MessageArea );

    show();
    t = new Thread( this );
    t.start();
}
```
Example 25.7 The `init()` method

After you create and set up the controls, they need to be placed somewhere on the screen. In Java, a window is described as a panel. A panel can be made up of other panels and controls, and these panels then can be laid out in relation to each other. This applet uses the `BorderLayout` manager class. This class divides the panel up into five areas, as shown in figure 25.3.

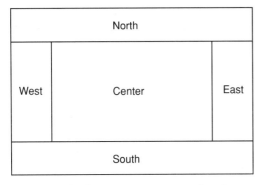

Figure 25.3 Laying out components using the `BorderLayout` **manager class**

Panels, or controls, can be placed in the areas around the outside, with the remaining space being occupied by the center area. The chat applet has five controls that require placement in the upper area: two labels, two text areas, and one button. Since you know these controls will always be placed together, they are placed into a panel of their own, which is itself placed in the top area of the window. Once this panel is created and the controls are placed using the `FlowLayout` manager, the panel is added to the upper panel using this method call:

```
add("North", top);
```

The bottom area of the screen is constructed in much the same way, with the controls laid out in a panel, and the panel added to the bottom area of the window. Once you have placed the majority of your controls, you want the main message area to take up the remaining area on the window. This is done by placing the `TextArea` control in the center section using the following method:

```
add("South", MessageArea);
```

Once you have placed all the controls in the correct areas, a call to the method `show(...)` will make them active.

Now that the controls are all placed, you need some way to be alerted whenever users click the Chat button, or when they press the Return/Enter key after entering a new message. Every interface control sends out events. An event is sent whenever one of the following occurs:

- Users click the control with the mouse.
- Users move the mouse over a control.
- Users click or release a key.
- A control has gained or lost the input focus.
- A control is going to be updated.

Note The room the user will be chatting in will be controlled through parameters passed in to the applet from the HTML code. As with servlets, an applet can have a number of parameters associated with it, and it is defined in much the same way as parameters for server-side-include servlets.

```
<APPLET CODE=chat_applet.class HEIGHT=300 WIDTH=400>
<PARAM NAME="room" VALUE="Life">
</APPLET>
```

If you control the room in this manner, the user can't create his own rooms. This control allows the web designer to create separate chat rooms for different areas of the site and to control all of them through the HTML tags.

When an event does occur, a special `Event` object is created that describes the event; this object is sent to the control's parent panel. To catch an `Event`, declare the `handle Event(...)` method in the parent panel, as shown in example 25.8.

```
public boolean handleEvent(Event _E){

  if ((_E.target == Message && _E.key == 10)||
      (_E.target == ChatButton && _E.id == Event.ACTION_EVENT)){
    //- Either the Return key was pressed or the Chat button was clicked
    return true;
  }
  return super.handleEvent(_E);
}
```
Example 25.8 The `handleEvent(...)` method

For this application, pressing the Return key and clicking a button will be the only events caught. Everything else may be processed normally. Checking for the specific events is simple; check the parameters of the `Event` class passed into the method. Since a number of controls can be generating events independently, you can determine the origin of the event from the target variable of the `Event` class. This holds a reference to the control, which can be tested against the reference created inside the `init()` method of the applet.

After you set up event processing, the basic shell of the applet is completed. This class may be compiled and run in any Java-enabled browser. Though it currently doesn't do much in the way of chatting, it does look pretty.

Note The `Event` mechanism is very powerful, and it operates along the same lines as the messaging system found in the Microsoft Windows API. Each panel has its own event manager, and when an event from a control is generated, it is passed up the line of panels until a handler is found. In this example, the event from the button click would have been passed to the panel that was used to form the top cluster of controls. No handler was found, so it was passed up to the next panel. It is important to pass the event on up the system, if it is not required at that particular level. You do this by calling the base method:

```
super.handleEvent( _E );
```

This ensures that other areas of the system correctly receive the event.

25.2.2   HTTP-based version

Certain clients won't be able to connect to a chat server using the more efficient socket method, so instead of leaving them out in the cold, we will use an alternative method to connect them. Certain clients can't connect because firewalls don't pass data from unknown socket ports, as this is seen as a security risk. Generally, firewalls will allow HTTP or web traffic to pass through without problem. To get around this limitation, the applet will talk to the chat server using the HTTP protocol.

Having the applet do a POST to the servlet, and then reading the response back from the server, will get through the firewall. You know this is possible because if it weren't, the applet couldn't have been accessed in the first place.

Client-side version   The applet will operate in much the same way as the HTML client. Every thirty seconds, the applet will make a request to the servlet for an update of its message list. With the HTML client, every time the page was reloaded the last ten messages were displayed, but this would not work for the applet. If the applet were to display the last ten messages every time the page was reloaded, the following options would have to be considered:

- The message window only displays the last ten messages.
- The applet parses the HTML file, extracting the latest messages.

Neither of these solutions is ideal. What we need is a hybrid of the two. The applet version should offer a much better interface to the chat server than the normal HTML form; therefore, having the message window display only the last ten messages isn't really a step forward. Right now, the servlet sends out too much data in the fact that the messages are sent out in a single block.

When the applet makes a GET request to the servlet, the servlet must send back only the messages the applet has not yet displayed, and they must be in a very simple text format with each message occupying a single line. That way, the applet doesn't have to worry about parsing the incoming file; it only has to worry about displaying it.

You can limit the messages by assigning a unique ID to each message. This ID will keep increasing as new messages are added. Therefore, when the applet makes a request, it can send the ID of the last message it displayed. The servlet then can send out all the messages between that ID and the current message ID.

The code shown in example 25.9 implements the routine to send a new message to the server. Gathering all the data to be sent is a simple matter of calling the getText() method for each text control. This data, along with the last message ID, is packaged up as parameters and sent to the server as part of the URL. For example, user "Ceri" in the room "Life" with a message of "Hello" would result in this URL:

```
http://<server>/chat.html?applet=1&room=Life&message=Ceri##Hello
```

This would cause the servlet to be invoked, with the parameters applet, room, and message being available to it.

Note When packaging up the data, notice how the message parameter was first encoded using the URLEncoder.encode(...) method. Certain characters are not allowed in a URL, and they must be encoded prior to sending the data. For example, a space is not allowed in the middle of a URL. The URLEncoder.encode(...) method takes a string as input, encodes it to the proper MIME standard, and returns the resulting string.

Notice how the sendMessage(...) method is constructed in such a way that it can be used for updating the message display, even if a user hasn't posted a new message. By looking at the incoming parameter and checking for null lengths, the URL that is constructed is either the new message URL or simply an updated URL. The processing from that point on is exactly the same as before.

```
private void sendMessage(String nMess){
   String nUser = Name.getText();
   String nRoom = Room.getText();
   String outURL;

   if (nUser.length()!=0 && nRoom.length()!= 0 && nMess.length()!= 0)
      outURL = "chat.html?applet=" + lastID + "&room=" + nRoom
               + "&message=" + URLEncoder.encode(nUser + "##" + nMess);
   else
      outURL = "chat.html?applet=" + lastID + "&room=" + nRoom;

   try{
      URL host = new URL("http://www.n-ary.com/" + outURL);
      DataInputStream In = new DataInputStream(new
                           BufferedInputStream(host.openStream()));
      readLine(In);
```

```
  }catch(Exception E){
    System.out.println(E);
  }
}
```

Example 25.9 The first version of `sendMessage(...)`

Once the connection to the servlet has been made, an input stream is created to the output from the server, which allows the text to be read line by line. Example 25.10 shows the method for reading the output from the server.

```
private void readLine(DataInputStream In) throws IOException {
  String Line;
  StringTokenizer st;
  while ((Line=In.readLine()) != null){
    st = new StringTokenizer(Line, "##");

    if (sPort == null)
      lastID = Integer.parseInt(st.nextToken());

    MessageArea.setText(MessageArea.getText() + st.nextToken()+ ": " +
                         st.nextToken() + "\n");
  }
}
```

Example 25.10 Displaying the lines from the server

Each line that comes back is formatted into three parts, each separated using the ## delimiter. The parts are the message ID, the username, and the message text. Since the messages will be sent back in the order in which they were posted, it is safe to set the las-tID to the last message ID on each loop iteration. This will allow for easy retrieval of messages from that point on. Setting the message window to the new message text is a simple matter of using the setText() method, remembering to append to the existing data—otherwise, the message window will display only the last message that was sent.

The applet, as with the HTML form version, must periodically poll the server for new messages. The same thirty-second timeout period will be used for the applet. To poll the server, the applet is set up as a threaded class. Overriding the run() method (shown in example 25.11) creates a place to continually poll the server.

```
public void run(){
  for (;;){
    try{
      t.sleep( 30000 );
    }catch( Exception E ){}

    if ( bUpdate == false )
      sendMessage( "" );
  }
}
```

Example 25.11 Updating the message display

By creating a for loop that loops forever, we can set up a polling mechanism to request messages every 30 seconds by calling the sleep method inside the loop. Notice the simple locking mechanism around the call to the `sendMessage()` method. Requesting an update from the server while the applet was posting a new message would definitely cause some interesting results. When the applet is performing a post, it sets the `bUpdate` flag to `true`. After it's completed, it sets the flag back to `false`, thereby allowing the poll method to update.

Server-side version   Adding the functionality to handle the applet's request is not that big of a job. First, the client request has to be distinguished from either an applet or an HTML form. Since the applet will be sending the applet parameter, and the HTML version will not, you can use this to switch control. Inserting the following code into the start of the `service(…)` method will do the trick.

```
String applet = _req.getParameter("applet");
if (applet != null)
  appletRequest(_req, _res);
```

Adding in a new message to the message list is done in exactly the same way as in the previous example, as shown in example 25.12. The only exception is that when a message is created it is assigned a unique ID. This is done in the constructor of the `cChatMessage` class. Retrieving the parameters for the message is a combination of both parameter gathering and parsing, using `##` as the delimiter.

```
String message = _req.getParameter("message");
String Room    = _req.getParameter("room");

if ( message != null ){
  StringTokenizer st = new StringTokenizer( message, "##");
  String User = st.nextToken();
  String Mess = st.nextToken();

  if ( (User != null && Mess != null) && (User.length() != 0 &&
                              Mess.length() != 0))
    addMessage( Room, User, Mess );
}
```
Example 25.12   Adding a new message from the applet

Once the message has been added to the list of messages in the room, the output to the applet must be constructed, as shown in example 25.13. As with the HTML version, a handle to the message list is retrieved by first getting a reference to the room. The content-type is set to plain text, since you don't want any additional coding to be performed on the output stream. The applet is expecting all of the messages that it hasn't yet received, and this is controlled through a simple ID system.

By running through the list, starting at the bottom and working up to the top, each message ID can be checked. If it's greater than the applet ID, it will be formatted and sent out.

```
if (RoomPool.containsKey(Room)){
  cRoom  Rm    = (cRoom)RoomPool.get(Room);
  Vector vList = Rm.getMessagePool();
  cChatMessage cMess;
```

```
_res.setContentType("text/plain");
PrintWriter Out = new PrintWriter(_res.getOutputStream());

int id = Integer.parseInt(_req.getParameter("applet"));

for (int x=vList.size()-1; x >= 0; x--){
  cMess = (cChatMessage)vList.elementAt(x);
  if (cMess.id > id)
    Out.println(cMess.id +"##"+ cMess.User +"##"+ cMess.Message);
}

Out.flush();
}
```
Example 25.13   Loading the list of messages to be displayed

In the previous version of the servlet, the message queue was set to hold ten messages. Since applets have the ability to display more than the last ten messages, increasing this to fifty makes more sense, but the HTML version will still only display the last ten.

At this point, you have a chat servlet that will support both an HTML client and an applet client. The applet client operates through the HTTP protocol in much the same way as the HTML client.

25.2.3   Socket-based version

Although it's very functional and usable, the HTTP version doesn't quite measure up in performance and speed issues; the user only gets a fresh list of messages every thirty seconds. A more advanced and efficient system is to have the client and server communicate with each other over TCP sockets. A socket-based connection allows the server to send an update to the applet the instant a new message is received, thus eliminating the thirty-second waiting period for new messages.

For this application, the chat server will listen for incoming connections on port 5432.

Client-side version   From the applet side of the equation, opening the connection to the server is a matter of creating another Socket class instance and specifying the host name and the port to connect to, as shown in example 25.14. If the connection to the server fails, an exception is thrown. The creation could fail for many reasons: the host may be down, the server where the connection is sent is not running, or the security manager disallows a connection to that particular host.

By using this feature of the Socket class, you can place all the socket creation inside one method and have it return the Socket instance or null depending on its success. One of the great features of sockets under Java is the ease with which data can be transferred over them. Once a socket has been opened, an input and output stream can be retrieved, and they can then be used to create any of the standard stream classes.

```
private Socket connectToServer(int _PortID){
  //- Attempts to open a connection
  try{
    Socket s = new Socket("<yourhost>", _PortID);
```

```
    Out = new PrintStream(s.getOutputStream());
    In  = new DataInputStream(s.getInputStream());

    return s;
  }catch( Exception E ){
    return null;
  }
}
```

Example 25.14   Opening the connection to the server

The previous applet version used the `DataInputStream` for reading data from the server. By creating a reference to the same class, you can reuse all the reading routines developed earlier. By creating the `connectToServer(...)` method, shown in example 25.14, you can call this at applet startup, and if it returns `null`, the applet will use the HTTP method for communicating with the server. Otherwise, it will use the more efficient socket channel.

Sending out data will be done the same way as before, except that when inside the `sendMessage(...)` method, the state of the socket class will be checked. If it's not `null`, the code shown in example 25.15 will be executed.

```
if (sPort != null){
  if (nMess.length() != 0)
    Out.println(nRoom + "##" + nUser + "##" + nMess);

  return;
}
```

Example 25.15   Sending a message

Notice how `sendMessage(...)` returns as soon as the message has been posted to the server—it doesn't wait for a reply because the data is read by another part of the program. Use the `readLine()` method from the `DataInputStream` to read the data from a socket. Inside the `run()` method of the applet, you can check the socket reference to determine which communication method is being used. If the socket method is being used, you can set up a reading method using the already developed `readLine(...)` method, as shown in example 25.16.

Note The `readLine()` method from the `DataInputStream` class will block until data is available at the socket. Blocking is where the method will not return until sufficient data has arrived that will satisfy the condition of the method. This is a very powerful way of reading sockets, and by creating a small loop, it's also very effective.

```
if (sPort != null){
  try{
    readLine(In);
  }catch(IOException E){
    return;
```

```
    }
}
```
Example 25.16   Reading text from the server

At this stage, you have an applet that will attempt a connection to the chat server, and if that fails, it will resort to the HTTP method. Adding the functionality for both connection methods did not double the size of the applet, but it gave you double the features.

Server-side version   Adding the functionality to accept socket connections isn't that complicated, but it does require careful design. When an applet makes a socket connection, the servlet's `service(...)` method will not be called. A separate thread will handle all of the communications. The servlet is acting merely as a data pool for the thread, sharing the rooms and messages. When a new applet connects, the main server thread will accept the connection and then spawn a new thread to handle the communication between the applet and the server, thus freeing up the server to accept additional client connections. Figure 25.4 demonstrates this interaction.

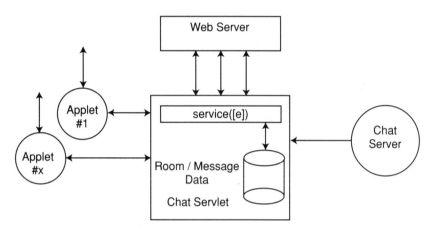

Figure 25.4 The chat server overview

When the servlet first starts, it creates and starts the execution of a thread that will listen for incoming requests at a specific port address. When a connection is received, a method from the servlet class is called, along with the socket reference, to let the servlet decide what it wants to do with the new client connection. The thread then returns to its post to listen for subsequent client connections. The class implementation in example 25.17 shows the `cChatServer` class. This class is started and created in the `init()` method of the servlet:

```
new cChatServer( this, 5432 );
```

In the constructor of this class, a new thread is created and started, which results in the `run()` method being called.

```
class cChatServer implements Runnable{
```

```
   Thread t;
   int     Port;
   chat_all Parent;

   public cChatServer(chat_all _Parent, int _Port){
     Port = _Port;
     Parent= _Parent;
     t     = new Thread(this);
     t.start();
   }

   public void run(){
     try{
       ServerSocket ChatServer = new ServerSocket(Port);
       for(;;){
         Socket NewIncoming = ChatServer.accept();
         Parent.acceptNewApplet(NewIncoming);
       }
     }catch( Exception e ){}
   }
}
```

Example 25.17   The chat server thread

The `run()` method creates a server socket. This is a special socket that sits and listens for connections on the specified port.

Next, a call to `accept()` will block execution until a new connection is accepted, returning a new socket instance when one is called.

Note   Anyone who has coded socket applications on various platforms will recognize the interface to the socket level and appreciate the ease with which Java delivers this technology. Building Winsock applications for the Microsoft Windows platform isn't this easy!

This thread sits and executes quite happily, listening and accepting new connections. When a new connection is made, the method from the servlet class (shown in example 25.18) is called. This creates a class instance that looks after the applet session, the `cAppletSession` class.

```
public void acceptNewApplet(Socket _sPort){
  cAppletSession aS = new cAppletSession(this, _sPort);
  AppletPool.put(_sPort, aS);
  aS.start();
}
```

Example 25.18   The servlet class accepting a new connection

Each room will hold a list of references to `cAppletSession` instances; this will then move the responsibility of the applet updates to the `cRoom` class, where most of the work is performed anyway. When an applet session is first created, the room it will belong to is not known; therefore, a separate temporary list has to be held to store all of the unassigned applets. As soon as the first message comes in, the applet will be assigned to the specific room.

When a connection is accepted, a new thread needs to be created to handle the communication. This class will have two main responsibilities: sending data out to the client and receiving data from the client. As with the socket connection routines used in the applet, the same procedure applies. An input and output stream is created, and if they are successful, the class runs in a loop, looking for lines of text. Conversely, sending data is a simple matter of packaging the data up and passing it on to the output stream. Example 25.19 shows the class that is used to communicate with the client.

```
class cAppletSession extends Thread{

  public Integer sPort;
  public Socket iPort;
  PrintStream Out = null;
  public String lastRoom = null;
  static chat_all Parent=null;

  public cAppletSession(chat_all _Parent, Socket _iPort){
    sPort      = new Integer(_iPort.getPort());
    iPort      = _iPort;
    Parent= _Parent;
  }

  public void run(){
    DataInputStream In;

    try{
      In = new DataInputStream(iPort.getInputStream());
      Out= new PrintStream(iPort.getOutputStream());
    }catch(Exception E){
      return;
    }

    try{
      String LineIn;
      while ((LineIn=In.readLine())!=null)
        Parent.appletSocketNewMessage(LineIn, this);

      iPort.close();
    }catch(Exception E){}

    Parent.killApplet(this);
  }

  public void sendMessage(String _User, String _Message){
    try{
      Out.println(_User + "##" + _Message);
    }catch(Exception E){
      Parent.killApplet(this);
    }
  }
}
```

Example 25.19   The cAppletSession class

When a message has come in from the client, it is passed to the function shown in example 25.20. This function takes the line it received and decodes it to retrieve the room, username, and message information. The room instance for this applet session is retrieved, and then the message is sent to the room as normal. If the room doesn't exist, then one is created. This is controlled through the getRoom(...) method, which you can see in part of example 25.23.

```
public void appletSocketNewMessage(String _LineIn, cAppletSession _aS){
  StringTokenizer st = new StringTokenizer(_LineIn, "##");

  String Room = st.nextToken();
  String User = st.nextToken();
  String Mess = st.nextToken();

  if (Room == null || Room.length() == 0)
    return;

  if (_aS.lastRoom == null)
    AppletPool.remove(_aS.sPort);

  cRoom rm = getRoom(Room, _aS);
  rm.addMessage(Mess, User);
}
```
Example 25.20   Accepting a new message

The cRoom class has to be modified to take account of the new communication medium. Earlier, a new message was simply added to the start of the list and then returned, but now it must send an update out to all the applet sessions. Each room holds a list of cAppletSession references. These are the current applets that are connected and talking in the room.

The maintenance of this list is done through the two class methods shown in example 25.21: addapplet(...) and removeApplet(...). Using the hash table data structure and the socket port number as the index, each applet session can be checked and referenced easily.

```
Hashtable AppletPool;
public void addApplet(cAppletSession _aS){
  if (AppletPool.containsKey(_aS.sPort) == false)
    AppletPool.put(_aS.sPort, _aS);
}

public void removeApplet(cAppletSession _aS){
  if (AppletPool.containsKey(_aS.sPort))
    AppletPool.remove(_aS.sPort);
}
```
Example 25.21 Maintaining the applet sessions

As before, a new message instance is created and added to the top of the list, thus keeping the regime where the most up-to-date message is at the front of the list. Notice how the message list has been increased from ten items to fifty. This was done to provide greater flexibility to the applet sessions without bogging the HTML clients down with too much data.

After the message has been added in, the connected applets have to be updated with the new message, no matter what its source is. Updating the applets is done by running through the hash table of applet sessions, calling the method sendMessage(...) (example 25.22) for each one.

```
public synchronized void addMessage( String _Mess, String _User ){
  idPool++;
  MessagePool.insertElementAt(new cChatMessage(_Mess, _User,idPool) ,0 );
  if ( MessagePool.size() > 50 )
    MessagePool.setSize( 50 );

  //- Send out to the applets
  Enumeration E = AppletPool.elements();
  while ( E.hasMoreElements() )
    ((cAppletSession)E.nextElement()).sendMessage( _User, _Mess );
}
```
Example 25.22 Sending a new message to the room

25.2.4   Complete source code

Example 25.23 shows the complete source code for the final version of the servlet that handles all the applet communications. You will notice a few subtle differences between this version and the one presented for the pure HTML client version—namely, methods have been added to maintain applet connections and bridge the gap between the three different connection methods.

```
import java.util.*;
import java.io.*;
import java.net.*;
import javax.servlet.*;
import javax.servlet.http.*;

public class chat_all extends HttpServlet{
  private Hashtable      RoomPool;
  private Hashtable      AppletPool;

  public void init(ServletConfig _config) throws ServletException {
    super.init(_config);
    RoomPool   = new Hashtable();
    AppletPool = new Hashtable();

    new cChatServer(this, 5432);
  }

  public void service(HttpServletRequest _req,HttpServletResponse _res)
                         throws ServletException, IOException{
    String applet     = _req.getParameter("applet");
    if (applet != null)
      appletRequest(_req, _res);
    else{
      String Room     = _req.getParameter("room");
      String User = _req.getParameter("user");
      String Mess = _req.getParameter("message");
```

```
  if (Room == null){
        _res.setStatus(HttpServletResponse.SC_NO_CONTENT);
        return;
      }

      if ((User != null && Mess != null) && (User.length() != 0 &&
                          Mess.length() != 0))
        addMessage(Room, User, Mess);

      sendUpdate(Room, User, _res);
    }
  }

  public void acceptNewApplet(Socket _sPort){
    cAppletSession aS = new cAppletSession(this, _sPort);
    AppletPool.put(_sPort, aS);
    aS.start();
  }

  public synchronized void killApplet(cAppletSession _aS){
    if (_aS.lastRoom == null)
      AppletPool.remove(_aS.sPort);
    else
      ((cRoom)RoomPool.get(_aS.lastRoom)).removeApplet(_aS);
  }

  public void appletSocketNewMessage(String _LineIn, cAppletSession _aS){
    StringTokenizer st = new StringTokenizer(_LineIn, "##");

    String Room     = st.nextToken();
    String User = st.nextToken();
    String Mess = st.nextToken();

    if (Room == null || Room.length() == 0)
      return;

    if (_aS.lastRoom == null)
      AppletPool.remove(_aS.sPort);

    cRoom rm = getRoom(Room, _aS);
    rm.addMessage(Mess, User);
  }

  private cRoom getRoom(String _Room, cAppletSession _aS) {
    cRoom rm;

    if (_Room.equals(_aS.lastRoom) == false){
      if (_aS.lastRoom == null || RoomPool.containsKey(_aS.lastRoom)) {
        if (_aS.lastRoom != null)
          ((cRoom)RoomPool.get(_aS.lastRoom)).removeApplet(_aS);
      }

      if (RoomPool.containsKey(_Room)){
        rm = (cRoom)RoomPool.get(_Room);
```

CHAPTER 25 INTERNET CHATS

```
        rm.addApplet(_aS);
      }else{
        rm = new cRoom();
        RoomPool.put(_Room, rm);
        rm.addApplet(_aS);
      }
      _aS.lastRoom = _Room;
    }
    else
      rm = (cRoom)RoomPool.get(_Room);

    return rm;
  }

  private void appletRequest(HttpServletRequest _req,
                             HttpServletResponse _res)
                             throws IOException{
    int id = Integer.parseInt(_req.getParameter("applet"));
    String message  = _req.getParameter("message");
    String Room             = _req.getParameter("room");

    if (message != null){
      StringTokenizer st = new StringTokenizer(message, "##");
      String User = st.nextToken();
      String Mess = st.nextToken();

      if ((User != null && Mess != null) && (User.length() != 0 &&
                          Mess.length() != 0))
        addMessage(Room, User, Mess);
    }

    //- Send out the message
    if (RoomPool.containsKey(Room)){
      cRoom      Rm = (cRoom)RoomPool.get(Room);
      Vector     vList = Rm.getMessagePool();
      cChatMessage cMess;
      _res.setContentType("text/plain");
      PrintWriter Out = new PrintWriter(_res.getOutputStream());

      for (int x=vList.size()-1; x >= 0; x--) {
        cMess = (cChatMessage)vList.elementAt(x);
        if (cMess.id > id)
          Out.println(cMess.id +"##"+ cMess.User+"##"+ cMess.Message);
      }
      Out.flush();
    }
  }

  private void sendUpdate(String _Room, String _User,
                          HttpServletResponse _res) throws IOException{
    cRoom      Room = (cRoom)RoomPool.get(_Room);
    if (_User == null)
      _User = "";
```

```
        _res.setContentType("text/html");
        PrintWriter Out = new PrintWriter(_res.getOutputStream());

        Out.println("<HTML><HEAD><TITLE>HTML Chat</TITLE>");
        Out.println("<META HTTP-EQUIV=REFRESH CONTENT=\"30;
                             URL=/chat.html?room=" + _Room + "&user="
+ _User + "\"></HEAD>");
        Out.println("<BODY><BR>");
        Out.println("<CENTER><BR><FONT COLOR=#0000FF SIZE=+2>");
        Out.println("#" + _Room + "</FONT>");
        Out.println("<BR><FORM METHOD=POST ACTION=/chat.html>");
        Out.println("Message: <INPUT TYPE=TEXT NAME=message VALUE=\"\"
                             SIZE=32>");
        Out.println("<INPUT TYPE=SUBMIT VALUE=Chat>");
        Out.println("<INPUT TYPE=TEXT NAME=user VALUE=\"" + _User + "\"
                             SIZE=10> :User");
        Out.println("<INPUT TYPE=HIDDEN NAME=room VALUE=" + _Room + ">
                             </CENTER>");
        Out.println("<HR ALIGN=CENTER WIDTH=60%>");
        cChatMessage UD;
        Vector RoomMessages=null;
        int size;

        if (Room != null)
          RoomMessages = Room.getMessagePool();

        if (Room == null || RoomMessages == null)
          size = 0;
        else if (RoomMessages.size() < 10)
          size = RoomMessages.size();
        else
          size = 10;

        for (int x=0; x < size; x++){
          UD = (cChatMessage)RoomMessages.elementAt(x);
          Out.println("<BR><P><FONT COLOR=#0000FF SIZE=+1>"
                     + UD.User + "</FONT> " + UD.Posted.toGMTString());
          Out.println("<BR>" + UD.Message + "</P>");
        }

        Out.println("<HR ALIGN=CENTER WIDTH=60%></BODY></HTML>");
        Out.flush();
    }

    private void addMessage(String _Room, String _User, String _Mess){
      cRoom Room;

      //- Create the room if it doesn't already exist
      if (RoomPool.containsKey(_Room) == false) {
        synchronized(RoomPool) {
          Room = new cRoom();
          RoomPool.put(_Room, Room);
        }
      }else
```

```
    Room = (cRoom)RoomPool.get(_Room);

  synchronized(Room){
    Room.addMessage(_Mess, _User);
  }
 }
}
```

Example 25.23   The complete source code for the servlet that handles all the applet communications

25.3   *Performance*

This last servlet has given site administrators a great tool for providing chat capabilities on their web sites. Not only can they offer live chats, but they can also offer users two different front ends, regardless of whether the user is behind a firewall. The site administrator can be confident that any visitors to his site will be able to chat. But which method is the more efficient?

It doesn't take too much thought to figure out that the applet connecting through the socket to the chat server will be the more efficient. The following information will prove why this is so.

For a test condition, assume there are twenty users, each chatting for ten minutes, each submitting a new message every thirty seconds. The users would have to be chatting very quickly to achieve this level of use, but for the sake of argument, let's assume this is possible. Now let's calculate the bandwidth requirements for each method.

The HTML client version and the applet using the HTTP protocol use exactly the same transfer mechanism, with the applet using slightly less bandwidth, since it doesn't require the complete message list to be posted with every update.

Each page sent to the browser is approximately 1.8K in size, and it is transferred in its entirety. Therefore, twenty users submitting a message twice every minute will equate to

```
1.8K x 2 x 20 = 72K per minute  (1.2K per second)
```

with forty server hits per minute.

25.3.1   *Applet #1: HTML version*

Each transfer from the server results in only the size of the message being sent. Assuming that a message is 100 bytes in length, this is quite a big message, so it's a good starting point for our calculation.

Since there are twenty people all posting two messages every minute in our example, this means each applet will be updated with ten new messages every thirty seconds, or twenty messages every minute, which equates to

```
100 x 2 x 20 = 4K per minute (~0.06K per second)
```

with forty server hits per minute.

25.3.2   Applet #2: socket version

As with the previous applet, the message size for each servlet will be assumed to be 100 bytes in length. And, as before, twenty people posting two messages a minute equates to the same transfer rates:

```
100 x 2 x 20 = 4K per minute (~0.06K per second)
```

but with zero hits on the web server.

25.3.3   Performance summary

Table 25.1 summarizes the information of the three preceding methods.

Table 25.1 Performance summary

HTML	Client	Applet#1	Applet#2
Web server hits	40	40	0
Number of web pages	40	0	0
Outgoing bytes	72K	4K	4K

As we expected, the socket-based method is the most efficient way of communicating with the chat server, with the applet version using HTTP data coming in a close second.

25.4   Future extensions

This chapter presented a very flexible implementation of a web-based chat server which gives the user two different ways to talk online, including a "hack" for firewall restrictions. The servlet to provide all of this functionality was very straightforward, with Java doing most of the work for you.

The applet is a much nicer interface to the HTML form. A number of improvements could be made to the applet:

- Object serialization
  Instead of using simple text messages, the applet could use the special class for storing messages and send the class back and forth using object serialization.

- Room selection
  The room in which the applet is talking is fixed through HTML. Providing a list of rooms, and having the user choose one by selecting it from a drop-down list, would allow greater mobility.

- Color selection
  Users could choose their own color scheme using a simple color palate.

The chat server itself could have a number of extensions added to it:

- User information
  At the moment, the user information is not stored at all, as this data can be changed at will. An implementation that allows the user to enter in his or her email address, and find other email addresses, would bring into line a more sophisticated IRC.

- IRC hook-in
  At the moment, the chat server talks in its own small world. Though this is useful, it may be advantageous to provide a live link into certain IRC channels; this link would allow chat users from your system to talk to the IRC community.

C H A P T E R   2 6

Servlets and RMI

- Learn the basics of Remote Method Invocation and how it gives you the ability to design and implement distributed systems without many of the headaches associated with them.

- Discover how a servlet can act as an RMI server.

Many powerful programming tools are available to Java developers. Looking back just ten years ago, many developers only heard about the features within the core API in university classes, and the features were not really used in practical applications. But now, a feature like multithreading has become very easy to use, and it's difficult to develop an application without having at least one thread doing some routine task.

Another great leap forward relates to the ease with which communications are used. Socket-based communications are no longer a mystery, as Java used them to introduce the notion of object serialization. This is the process by which objects can be represented as a single stream of bytes, making it easy to save or pass the objects to another application.

Along with the models to develop sophisticated multithreaded applications and the ability to move objects among different applications, Java has now introduced the developer community to another advanced feature: the ability to run methods on a remote host. This is called true distributed computing.

This chapter takes a look at the whole Remote Method Invocation (RMI) aspect of Java and how it can be used within the servlet environment.

26.1 RMI overview

RMI allows an object to live and run on a remote machine. The object is controlled remotely by calling methods, in exactly the same way methods would be called by the local application. This is a very powerful facility as it removes all processing loads from the local processor and places them on another. It also allows for true multiprocessing across networks. For example, you could build a distributed system that could off-load all intensive database queries to a dedicated database machine, thus freeing up the resources on the local machine to do other tasks.

RMI uses the underlying object serialization techniques to safely pass objects back and forth, so any object that implements the object serialization interface can be easily used in an RMI environment.

Before we look at how the servlet world can take advantage of RMI, let's look at building a simple application that requests a remote machine to compute information.

26.1.1 Creating the remote object

In order for an object to run remotely, we have to create it with a number of special additions. Here's a very trivial example to illustrate the whole RMI procedure. The pull to implement the traditional "Hello World" is very strong; resisting temptation, we will implement something slightly different.

Let's build an application that will perform a simple query and return the result as an object. We will create a simple database wrapper class that will be used as our stepping stone into the database.

One of the major advantages of this type of example is that it allows all the database logic to reside on one machine so we don't have to worry about installing the necessary JDBC drivers on the local machine.

First, we'll create an object that will represent the result from our query. In this example, we want to return a record for a given student's name. We will create a class that handles all the functionality, as shown in example 26.1. This class will perform the actual database query itself, keeping all the intelligence within the class. As you can see, we're using a very simple student record; only the name, age, and email address are stored. When the class is first created, it makes a query to a database to fill in the necessary records.

```
public class cStudent implements java.io.Serializable {

    public String name;
    public int     age;
    public String email;

    public cStudent(){}

    public cStudent( String _name ){
      //-- Query the database for
      //-- this student record
    }
}
```

Example 26.1   The wrapper class for the student information

Since this is a chapter on RMI and not JDBC, there's no point in detailing the actual database code in this chapter. For more details, refer to the chapter on servlets and JDBC.

Notice that the class shown in example 26.1 is implementing the Serializable interface from the object serialization section. We are doing it this way as we plan for this class to be passed back to the client from the remote machine. RMI passes objects around using the object serialization techniques that have been demonstrated throughout this book.

This is not the class that will be called remotely; it is merely used to pass back the result. We need to now define a class that will actually be run by the remote host. We will call this class rmiDatabaseRunner, and figure 26.1 shows how it fits into our example.

The rmiDatabaseRunner class will be live on the remote computer and methods will be called from the local machine. The actual object instance resides on the remote computer, not the local one. Therefore, instead of creating a new object on the local machine, we call one of the RMI methods to retrieve an instance to an object that will be created on the remote machine.

Let's think for a moment about the overall system. In order for us to compile our local application, we need the class files for rmiDatabaseRunner. Getting the class file would prove a bit clunky and restrictive. The whole idea of distributed processing is to keep all the intelligence in one place. What if the class for the remote were updated? Would that mean all the RMI clients would need to be recompiled to take into account the new change?

Another potential downside to getting the class files is security. Using distributed processing, you can hide or abstract all the processing away from the local machine. Requiring

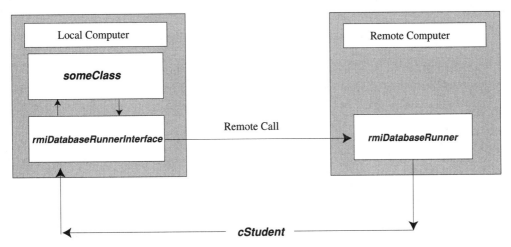

Figure 26.1 RMI schematic

the class files to reside on the local machine would decrease the abstraction model with the potential for the client to discover the secrets of the server processing.

Fortunately, the designers of the RMI API predicted this potential shortcoming and placed the necessary hooks to avoid it.

Instead of publishing the complete class for each client that has the ability to create and run a class remotely, only the interface is released; this interface details the methods that can be run remotely. Example 26.2 shows the interface file for our new class that will be created and run remotely.

```
public interface rmiDatabaseRunnerInterface extends java.rmi.Remote {
  public cStudent getStudent( String _name )
                              throws java.rmi.RemoteException;
}
```

Example 26.2   The remote interface for rmiDatabaseRunner

As you can see, we are making only one method available remotely—the getStudent(…) method that will return an instance of cStudent upon its completion.

As you can imagine, due to the very nature of what we're trying to accomplish here, there's a great potential for things to go wrong. Think about what is going on, and then think about it running over a dial-up connection over a slow, old modem. Many things could go wrong, including the remote server running the class crashing, losing power, getting rebooted, or experiencing anything that would stop it from running the current task.

For this reason, the calling class must have some way of detecting such problem areas. This is accomplished by insisting on each remote method throwing the java.rmi.RemoteException exception if something goes wrong, including anything from network failure to machine dropouts.

In order for the class to be perfect for remote positioning it has to extend the `java.rmi.Remote` class, which ensures the necessary hooks are available to the RMI layer to handle this class.

At this point, we have created the class that will be used to return the student record and we have defined the interface the remote class will implement. Now we have to define the actual class that will implement this interface. Example 26.3 shows the code for the new `rmiDatabaseRunner` class.

```
import java.rmi.*;
import java.rmi.server.*;

public class rmiDatabaseRunner extends UnicastRemoteObject
                            implements rmiDatabaseRunnerInterface {

  public rmiDatabaseRunner() throws java.rmi.RemoteException {

    super();
    //- Open up any database
    //- connections that may be required
  }

  public cStudent getStudent( String _name )
                            throws java.rmi.RemoteException {
    return new cStudent( _name );
  }
}
```

Example 26.3 The implementation of the `rmiDatabaseRunner` interface

In this example, we have implemented the method we defined in the interface shown in example 26.2. This class, in addition to implementing the interface, extends the `UnicastRemoteObject` from the `java.rmi.server` package. It also provides the support for the object to exist remotely, and makes sure that all references are maintained across machines. All RMI classes must extend this class if they are to be run remotely. If they do not, then the class has to accept all responsibility for handling the communications. For this reason, the `super()` method is called in the constructor of this class to make sure the `UnicastRemoteObject` can initialize properly.

Example 26.3 shows the code that will actually run on the remote machine; it will not be anywhere near the local or calling machine. When the `getStudent(…)` method is called, an instance of `cStudent` is created, which in itself results in a database query. This new object is then returned to the calling machine.

26.1.2 Making the remote object available

Now that we've created the class that will be created and run remotely, we have to make it available for requests from remote machines. To do this, we have to create a server for it that will listen for requests to a particular instance.

In this example, we will implement a `main(...)` method that will allow the class to run on its own, without the aid of another. As we will discover later, this is not the way we will implement it for use with a servlet.

A number of steps are required to successfully set up an object so it's ready for requests. The first step is to install a security manager. We will use the default security manager `RMISecurityManager`. It allows the object to perform most operations. We set the security manager by making the following call:

```
System.setSecurityManager( new RMISecurityManager() );
```

We must next create an instance of the object that will be used to service requests. Calling the following method will do this task:

```
rmiDatabaseRunner DR = new rmiDatabaseRunner();
```

As soon as this class is created, it begins to listen for requests on port 1099. Listening for requests is due to the underlying call to `super()` in the constructor, which in turn allows the `UnicastRemoteObject` to initialize properly.

Finally, we must give the object some easy way of being called. Setting this up is very much like setting up a servlet alias.

```
Naming.rebind("//<yourhost>/databaseRunner", DR );
```

This creates a mapping for that particular class instance for a given name. The remote client will use this unique name to connect. This procedure will be shown in the following section. Putting all our work so far together yields the `main(...)` method shown in example 26.4.

```
public static void main(String[] args) {
  try{
    System.setSecurityManager( new RMISecurityManager() );
    rmiDatabaseRunner rmiDatabaseRunner = new rmiDatabaseRunner();
    Naming.rebind("//<yourhost>/databaseRunner", DR );
  }catch(Exception E){
    System.out.println("Oops: " + E );
  }
}
```

Example 26.4   The new `main(...)` **method**

Compilation + run time   The last section dealt with the physical Java code that is used to create an RMI object which can be called remotely. However, a number of steps need to be taken in order to make this object come alive.

After compiling the class as normal, we need to create the necessary stub files that will be used by both the RMI server and any client that wishes to use the class. You've probably seen these files in your <jdk_root>/bin directory and wondered what they are. Well, wonder no more.

An additional postcompiler needs to be run on the class that implements your custom interface. This is achieved by using the `rmic <classname>` utility, which operates very much like the main Java compiler.

Running the postcompiler will result in two files being produced:

```
<yourclassname>_Skel.class
<yourclassname>_Stub.class
```

After it has run, we need to start up the RMI registry server. This provides the client with a simple name resolution service which translates a name to an actual object instance. Before running this program you need to make sure the two files produced using the `rmic` compiler are in the `classpath`. Run the registry using

```
start rmiregistry
```

This needs to run before any client can connect to the object. After it is running, you can safely start up the main server for the object we want to share.

```
java rmiDatabaseRunner
```

After this process has finished, the object is now available for remote connections to use it.

26.1.3 Calling the remote object

In the previous section we created all the necessary pieces for the remote side of the RMI equation. In this section, we will look at the steps required to actually call the remote object.

In order for us to run a method in the remote object, we must first get a reference to it. This is done with a call to the `lookup(...)` method from the `java.rmi.Naming` class. This takes in a URL (minus the protocol) to the remote object and attempts to make a connection to the server and retrieve a reference.

If that process is successful, the class can be called as if it were locally sourced as opposed to running on a remote machine. If anything goes wrong (such as the host can't be located due to a network error) then a `RemoteException` is thrown to reflect the problem.

Example 26.5 shows the client program used to connect and run a method remotely. The client is only allowed the run methods that were declared in the interface from which the class is implemented.

```
import java.rmi.*;
import java.rmi.server.*;

public class rmiClient {

  public static void main(String[] args) {
    try{
```

```
        rmiDatabaseRunner DR = (rmiDatabaseRunner)Naming.lookup
                              ("//<yourserver>/databaseRunner");
        cStudent studentRecord = DR.getStudent("ceri");
    }catch(Exception E){
        System.out.println("oops: " + E );
    }
  }
}
```

Example 26.5   Using the remote object

When compiling this class, we have to make sure the necessary stub and skeleton files are in the class path. Failure to locate these files will result in the object not being able to run methods remotely.

26.2   Servlets and RMI

The first part of this chapter discussed the basics of Remote Method Invocation. We built a simple RMI server and then connected to it using an application. The whole premise behind RMI is to give developers the ability to design and implement distributed systems without worrying about the actual logistics of moving objects around or the headache of calling methods remotely.

RMI can be used very easily with servlets. When it is, it provides a rich interface to all clients. By implementing an RMI interface, you are giving both HTML clients and Java clients the ability to use the code within a servlet.

To demonstrate this ability, we will design a servlet that will service either an HTTP or an RMI request. This servlet could be used in a search engine scenario, for example. Consider advertising your search intelligence with both an HTML and an RMI interface. You could then license your back-end software and charge clients that use the RMI interface instead of the HTML front-end. Imagine that InfoSeek started offering an RMI interface to the main database. Think how many Java clients would start using this new feature.

This is but one example of the way RMI and servlet-based technology can be used. More conventional uses may not be so commercial.

26.2.1   The servlet as an RMI server

To make our implementation easier, we will allow only one method call to be made remotely and we will use our example that was shown in the beginning of this chapter.

Remember that a servlet is just a class. There is no reason why it can't implement this interface in addition to any of the servlet specific classes, as shown in example 26.6.

```
public class rmiServlet extends UnicastRemoteObject,HttpServlet
                        implements rmiDatabaseRunnerInterface
```
Example 26.6   Defining the servlet

As usual, we have to provide a constructor for our RMI object; we normally don't do this with servlets. But this doesn't present a problem, as you'll see in example 26.7. The remote method that is going to be called is also shown.

```
public rmiServlet(){
  //- Open up any database
  //- connections that may be required
  super();
}

public cStudent getStudent( String _name )
                        throws java.rmi.RemoteException {
  return new cStudent( _name );
}
```
Example 26.7 Inserting the necessary RMI methods

In our application that was discussed at the beginning of this chapter, we created a class instance and bound it to the name server. We don't need to worry too much about creating an instance (since we know the server will do this for us), but we still need to bind it to the name server. The best place for this is in the call to the init(...) method, since we know it's only called once for every new instance. This is shown in example 26.8.

```
public void init(ServletConfig _config) throws ServletException {
  super(_config);
  try{
    System.setSecurityManager( new servletRMISecurityManager() );
    Naming.rebind("//<yourhost>/databaseRunner", this );
  }catch(Exception E){
    System.out.println("Oops: " + E );
  }
}
```
Example 26.8 The new init(...) method

We now have to define the security manager; in this instance, we will create our own (it will be detailed in the next section). Next, we need to bind the servlet/RMI to the logical name of databaseRunner, which will be used to retrieve an object instance to it.

Example 26.9 shows the complete servlet. Notice how easy it is to add RMI capability. This servlet is now ready for use by either a web browser or a Java class. The dual usage has the advantage of sharing resources and logically grouping like servers together.

```
import java.rmi.*;
import java.rmi.server.*;
import javax.servlet.*;
import javax.servlet.http.*;

public class rmiServlet extends UnicastRemoteObject,HttpServlet
                    implements rmiDatabaseRunnerInterface {

  public rmiServlet(){
    //- Open up any database
    //- connections that may be required
    super();
  }
```

```
public cStudent getStudent( String _name )
                            throws java.rmi.RemoteException {
    return new cStudent( _name );
}

public void service( ServletRequest _req, ServletResponse _res)
                            throws IOException{
    //- Handle HTTP requests
}

public void init(ServletConfig _config) throws ServletException {
    super(_config);
    try{
        System.setSecurityManager( new servletRMISecurityManager() );
        Naming.rebind("//<yourhost>/databaseRunner", this );
    }catch(Exception E){
        System.out.println("Oops: " + E );
    }
}
}
```

Example 26.9   The complete servlet source code

By coupling the power of RMI with servlets, you can create a complete application server to provide the stepping stone for any type of client to access the resources running in your server environment.

Alternative security manager   Running in a servlet environment may entail hosting third-party servlets. To do this, you need to have some control over what the RMI object will be allowed to perform. For example, you may not want the class to write or listen for socket requests. You can easily stop this by creating a new security manager; this is done by extending the RMISecurityManager, as shown in example 26.10.

```
import java.io.*;

public class servletRMISecurityManager
                            extends java.rmi.RMISecurityManager {

    public synchronized void checkWrite(FileDescriptor fd){
        throw new SecurityException();
    }

    public synchronized void checkAccept(String host, int port){
        throw new SecurityException();
    }
}
```

Example 26.10   Alternative security manager

The RMISecurityManager defines a whole host of methods that check the permissions of given operations. If an operation is to be disallowed, then an exception is thrown. We can easily override the standard methods and call the exceptions immediately. This is a very simple way to restrict the use of potential rogue RMI objects.

26.3 Summary

This chapter introduced the concept of distributed computing and showed how Java has brought distributive power to the doorstep of the developer through the use of RMI. Distributed computing allows objects to exist on other virtual machines while maintaining the ability for remote objects to call methods from them.

Adding this power to servlets creates a very powerful tool, which increases the servlet's productivity. By allowing the servlet to take on the role of an RMI object, a whole application server can be developed using servlet technology.

C H A P T E R 2 7

Servlet-to-servlet communication

CHAPTER CONCEPTS

- Discover how servlets communicate with each other using common base classes.
- Learn how servlets share data resources and reuse objects as they work together.

Java has brought great advances in programming within easy reach of all developers. Powerful constructs such as multithreading and advance communication are now relatively easy for you to utilize in your programs. Java has also initiated a very strong sense of object orientation. The ability to reuse code and not reinvent the wheel each time you program is a great improvement over alternative programming languages.

In order for you to reap the benefits of reusable code, the language must support mechanisms by which you can build reusable objects and plug them together. Java has these mechanisms—the servlet API is no stranger to object reuse. This chapter will outline the different methods in which servlets can share data with one another. This communication promotes the concept of solving a problem only once and then applying that solution to many different areas.

As this chapter will illustrate, you, as a servlet developer, have a lot of choices for how you can best reuse your servlet classes.

27.1 Common base class

A servlet is run in response to a client connection. It is designed to be lightweight and to process the client request as quickly as possible, thus freeing the server up so it can immediately process the next request that comes in. A servlet should never try to do everything itself. In a large system it is better to produce many smaller servlets, as opposed to a small number of large servlets. The longer a servlet spends servicing a request, the fewer the clients the servlet can process in a given time.

If smaller servlets are to be built, the ability to share information between the servlets is paramount, instead of the one-servlet-solution-fits-all approach.

One of the easiest ways for a servlet to share information (this works for classes as well), is to share common objects through inheritance—where the servlets are extended from a class other than HttpServlet or GenericServlet. To illustrate this concept, consider the example shown in figure 27.1.

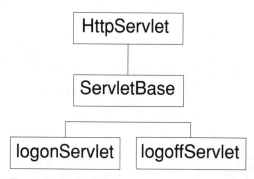

Figure 27.1 Inheritance

Suppose we had two servlets in our system: one to log a user onto our system and the other one to log him off. Let's assume that the reason we want a user to logon and logoff again is to enable us to connect to a specific database. Now, let us assume that the server will share various methods, such as a simple check to see if the user is already logged on.

We can develop methods for this simple check and place a copy of them in each servlet. However, since it's a database connection, let's also assume that we will be sharing database connections between the servlets.

Many different methods are available to facilitate method sharing and data pooling. For this section, we will use the simplest method.

Instead of each servlet extending the `HttpServlet`, each will extend the capabilities of `ServletBase`, which is a custom class we will build. This class will itself extend the `HttpServlet` class, but it will also add other methods to allow the servlets to intelligently handle the database connections.

Example 27.1 shows the basic skeleton implementation for the `ServletBase` class. You'll notice that it looks very similar to a normal servlet, except it doesn't override the `service(...)` method or any of the `doXXX(...)` methods. It does, however, override the `init(...)` method. In our example, it needs to open up a connection to the database; this connection will be shared through the `static Connection` variable. This will be performed when the servlet first initializes.

However, please note a very important fact. The `init(...)` method will be called multiple times if multiple servlets inherit this class, because each particular servlet needs to be initialized and needs to go through the complete servlet life cycle. Since we don't want to have additional database connections open, we'll check to see if the connection has been opened, and if so, we'll skip that section of the method.

```
public class ServletBase extends HttpServlet{
  static Connection databaseConnection = null;

  public void init(ServletConfig _config) throws ServletException{
    super.init(_config);
    if ( databaseConnection == null )
      //- Open up the database connection
  }

  protected boolean isLoggedOn( String _username ){
    return true;
  }

  protected boolean logUserOn( String _username ){
    return true;
  }
}
```

Example 27.1   The basic implementation for the `ServletBase` class

The two additional methods, `isLoggedOn(...)` and `logUserOn(...)`, are support functions that are accessible by all servlets that extend this class.

So now that we have developed the new base class, let's look at how we can use it. Example 27.2 shows the `logonServlet` class that will log a user onto the system. This class, instead of extending the `HttpServlet` class, extends the `ServletBase` class. Notice that the `logonServlet` class does not override the `init(...)` method because the base class is taking care of this for us.

```
public class logonServlet extends ServletBase{
  public void service(HttpServletRequest _req, HttpServletResponse _res)
                           throws ServletException{
    if ( isLoggedOn( _req.getParameter("USERNAME") ) ){
      //- Display a message indicating they are already logged on
    }else{
      logUserOn( _req.getParameter("USERNAME") );
    }
  }
}
```

Example 27.2   Using the new `ServletBase` **class**

The 2.1 version of the servlet API doesn't require the `init(…)` method to be overridden like the previous versions insisted it should be, so it may be left out without any adverse effects.

The `logonServlet` can now call methods from the underlying base class without having to wrestle with any object references. This allows the `logonServlet` class to easily share common methods and data without keeping a reference to a collection class.

This ability to share is not hard, and it's not new. It is used throughout Java to create groups of logical units, and it can be easily be used in the world of servlets, where the need to share data is even more important.

27.1.1   Sharing data

If the previous method seems a little clunky and too much of a hassle, the 2.1 version of the servlet API introduces a way to share objects among servlets. It operates along the same lines as the session management functionality, but it is completely done on the server side.

With session management, you associated an object with a given client session. The session manager attempted to return the same object to you each time that particular client made a request. This was done using cookies or URL rewriting. Objects were stored using a unique string to reference them.

Servlets can now benefit from this technology through the `ServletContext` interface. Each servlet runs within some sort of environment, which describes various parameters associated with the main servlet environment, such as the document root and any mappings that may exist. This is known as the `ServletContext`. A servlet belongs to only one `ServletContext` method and the server's web administrator controls the method.

For example, a server running virtual hosts would have a different `ServletContext` for each virtual host. This has the advantage of logically grouping servlets while maintaining different security models for each type.

The `ServletContext` can store objects on behalf of servlets running within its context. Some methods allow a servlet to add and remove objects and to determine which objects are stored. These objects can be retrieved and modified by other servlets running within the context.

Let's now look at how we could share a database connection among servlets using the `ServletContext` mechanisms. Example 27.3 shows a simple example where we create a database connection from some method and ask the `ServletContext` to store it for us under the name `"database.connection"` using the `setAttribute(…)` method.

```
public class logonServlet extends HttpServlet{
  public void service(HttpServletRequest _req, HttpServletResponse _res)
                                 throws ServletException{
    ServletContext thisContext = getServletContext();

    //-- Assume some method creates a new connection class
    Connection newConnection = createConnection();

    thisContext.setAttribute( "database.connection", newConnection );

    //-- Return some output to the client
  }
}
```

Example 27.3   Storing an object

Retrieving the database connection again is just as easy as setting it. Example 27.4 shows another servlet, running within the same context, which attempts to retrieve the object back.

```
public class logoffServlet extends HttpServlet{
  public void service(HttpServletRequest _req, HttpServletResponse _res)
                                 throws ServletException{
    ServletContext thisContext = getServletContext();

    //-- Assume some method creates a new connection class
    Connection newConnection = thisContext.getAttribute(
                               "database.connection");
    if ( newConnection == null )
      //- Database has not been opened yet


    //-- Return some output to the client
  }
}
```

Example 27.4   Retrieving an object

If the object has not been stored, the getAttribute(...) method will return null. As you can see, the whole storage and retrieval system operates very much like the cookie system—so this can be thought of as server-side cookies!

Example 27.5 illustrates another useful method from the ServletContext interface. The ability to discover which objects are in existence is a very handy feature; for example, it enables you to discover whether any initialization has been performed. The getAttribute-Names() method returns an Enumeration to the list of stored objects, which can then be returned using the getAttribute() method.

```
public class allServlet extends HttpServlet{
  public void service(HttpServletRequest _req, HttpServletResponse _res)
                                 throws ServletException{
    ServletContext thisContext = getServletContext();

    //-- Assume some method creates a new connection class
    Enumeration E = thisContext.getAttributeNames();
```

```
        while ( E.hasMoreElements() ){
          String name = (String)E.nextElement();
          System.out.println( "Object: " + name );
        }
    }
}
```

Example 27.5   Looking at all the objects

We have now seen methods for storing and retrieving data. One additional method allows you to remove a given object from the `ServletContext`. This method, `removeAttribute(…)`, ensures that the `ServletContext` no longer holds a reference to the object.

So the ability to share data among servlets running within the same context is straightforward enough. But what if the servlet isn't running within the same context? What if a servlet running on another machine or another virtual host has data that the current servlet needs? Have no fear; help is at hand.

The 2.1 servlet API introduces a new interface that allows servlets to get an external reference to a context. This is done through an overloaded version of `getServletContext(…)` which takes in the URL of the servlet you wish to retrieve the context for. An example of this call is shown in example 27.6.

```
public class otherServlet extends HttpServlet{
  public void service(HttpServletRequest _req, HttpServletResponse _res)
                       throws ServletException{
    ServletContext otherContext = getServletContext
                         ("http://<otherdomain>/servlet/allServlet");

    //-- Assume some method creates a new connection class
    Enumeration E = otherContext.getAttributeNames();
    while ( E.hasMoreElements() ){
      String name = (String)E.nextElement();
      System.out.println( "Object: " + name );
    }
  }
}
```

Example 27.6   Retrieving remote contexts

Assuming the remote host allows this kind of information to be returned, the `ServletContext` will be returned. However if it does not, then the method will return `null`. Calling this method will not invoke the servlet running in the other context, nor will it interpret any processing that that remote servlet may be doing at that point.

Using this new mechanism from the 2.1 servlet API, you can easily share objects with other developers, including other contexts.

27.1.2   Servlets working together

In the previous section, we looked at a number of ways to share objects between servlets. In most instances these methods are used to share common data resources such as database connections. Sharing objects allows the server to operate more efficiently. Now, thanks to the new addition to the 2.1 API, servlets can work together in yet another way.

In past releases of the API, a technique known as servlet chaining was possible. In servlet chaining, the output of one servlet fed the input to another. The second servlet, or the next one in the chain, could perform additional processing before sending the result out to the client. Although this was useful, it was a bit clunky to operate. To begin with, the chaining mechanism had to be set up by the web administrator, and it could not be performed dynamically. Also, the servlet had no control over whether it should be in a chain. From the developer's point of view, no API control was possible.

The new 2.1 API has made this feature much more accessible. You have the ability to insert the contents of one servlet within the output of another, and you can pass a request on to another servlet for processing.

The following sections will show you how you can use these features in your servlets.

27.1.3 Forwarding a request

You may find a time when it's better to pass a request on to another servlet for processing. For example, consider a servlet that acts as a front-end processor for a search engine. Depending on the result of the query, different servlets could be used to generate the actual output. The first servlet would take in all the search parameters, run the query, and pass the results on to a specific servlet for output. The advantage over the conventional servlet-chaining model is that the servlet can decide at run time which output servlet will be used, as opposed to relying on a web administrator to set up the mapping. This is particularly useful in an ISP environment where the developer has to rely on a third party to get this right.

To handle this scenario and the one in the next section, a new interface was developed. The RequestDispatcher interface is the glue that controls the flow between servlets and output streams such as HTTP clients, files, or even Java Server Pages (JSP).

Before you can send control to another servlet, you must first get the necessary RequestDispatcher for that particular servlet. This is controlled through the method call getRequestDispatcher(…) from the ServletContext interface. You specify the Uniform Resource Interface (URI) to the servlet, and assuming the call doesn't fail because of security violations, the necessary RequestDispatcher reference is returned.

From here, you can make a call to the forward(…) method, which passes on the request to the servlet represented by the RequestDispatcher. Let's look at an example of this in action.

Example 27.7 shows a typical use of this mechanism. Assume that the forwardServlet shown takes in a search query from the user. It first retrieves an instance to the context it is running within. Using this reference, a call to retrieve the RequestDispatcher for the xyzServlet is performed. It will be used to generate our output.

```
public class forwardServlet extends HttpServlet{
  public void service(HttpServletRequest _req, HttpServletResponse _res)
                        throws ServletException{
    ServletContext xt = getServletContext();
    RequestDispatcher xyzServlet = xt.getRequestDispatcher
                        ("http://<domain>/servlet/xyzServlet");

    //- Do any preliminary processing
    _req.setAttribute( "database.results", new Results() );
```

```
xyzServlet.forward( _req, _res );
  }
}
```
Example 27.7   Forwarding a request

Before we pass on the request for processing, we run the query. The next servlet will be used to process the results for this query, so we need some mechanism to pass the results to the next servlet.

As demonstrated in the previous section, sharing objects between servlets is not that big a problem; we simply ask the `ServletContext` to store the data for us. But this is not satisfactory, as the objects being shared take no account of the client request. Storing the results this way would be very dangerous since only one copy of the results would exist per `ServletContext`, as opposed to one copy per client request.

You could use session management to get around this problem, but since the data hasn't actually made it back to the client, it's not an ideal solution.

Thanks to the `ServletRequest` object, help is available. There are methods that allow servlets to ask that the `ServletRequest` object store objects for them on its behalf, ensuring that the object remains intact for the duration of the client session. The first servlet can then pass data to the second servlet without worrying about multiple client sessions.

As you'll see in example 27.8, the method for storing data is exactly the same as was demonstrated for storing objects using the `ServletContext`. The equivalent `getAttribute(…)` methods exist to allow the servlet to retrieve the objects again.

When you are forwarding a request to another servlet for processing, the first servlet is not permitted to do anything to the output, including setting any HTTP status fields. As soon as the first servlet makes an attempt to retrieve an output stream, then the call to `forward(…)` will fail. The calling servlet is permitted to continue running after the call, but it must not make any attempt to communicate back to the original client.

27.1.4   Inserting a request

The previous section looked at when the complete request is passed on to another servlet for processing. Although this procedure is very useful, it is restrictive—only one servlet can produce the final output. There are times where it would be nice if servlets could cooperatively work together to create the output. For example, you could have one servlet conduct or control the flow, calling other servlets to insert content as and when needed.

Fortunately the 2.1 API supports this usage. The previous section introduced the `forward(…)` method from the `RequestDispatcher` interface. To insert content into the current output stream, the `insert(…)` method is available from the same interface. This method operates in exactly the same way as `forward(…)` in that it accepts a `ServletRequest` and `ServletResponse` as parameters.

Only this time, the called servlet is not meant to set any headers. If it does (any cookie settings, for example), then it is not guaranteed to be successful. As before, data can be passed to the servlet using the `ServletRequest` interface that was shown in the previous section.

Example 27.8 shows an example of the `insert(…)` method. As before, it retrieves a reference to the `RequestDispatcher` of the servlet we wish to use. We create some output from the original servlet and then call the secondary servlet ten times, so it can insert its output to the original client request.

```
public class insertServlet extends HttpServlet{
  public void service(HttpServletRequest _req, HttpServletResponse _res)
                              throws ServletException{
    ServletContext xt = getServletContext();
    RequestDispatcher xyzServlet = xt.getRequestDispatcher
                              ("http://<domain>/servlet/xyzServlet");

    PrintWriter Out = _res.getWriter();
    Out.println( "This is from the insertServlet " );
    for(int x=0; x < 10; x++ )
      xyzServlet.insert( _req, _res );

    Out.println( "This is the end of the print servlet " );
  }
}
```
Example 27.8   Inserting content

There is no limit to the number of times or number of servlets you can ask to insert output on behalf of others. Using this technique, you have the ability to create sophisticated servlet systems that can all work closely together, thus reducing the total number of servlets that the server must develop and handle.

27.2 Summary

This chapter introduced the features that are available to you for sharing data between servlets. This functionality, as well as the ability to have servlets share the responsibility of processing the client request by collaborating on the output generation, was a major step forward in servlet ideology.

APPENDIX A

CHAPTER CONCEPTS

- This appendix contains the complete 2.1 servlet API. The API ships in two packages: `javax.servlet` and `javax.servlet.http`. Each package and its classes are listed in alphabetical order.

A.3 javax.servlet

A.3.1 javax.servlet.GenericServlet

```
public abstract class GenericServlet implements Servlet, ServletConfig,
                              java.io.Serializable {
  public void destroy()
  public String getInitParameter(String name)
  public Enumeration getInitParameterNames()
  public ServletConfig getServletConfig()
  public ServletContext getServletContext()
  public String getServletInfo()
  public void init(ServletConfig config) throws ServletException
  public void init() throws ServletException
  public void log(String msg)
  public void log(String message, Throwable t)
  public abstract void service(ServletRequest req, ServletResponse res)
                              throws ServletException,IOException
}
```
Example 1

This class is used as the base class for the majority of all servlets, with developers overriding the service method to process client requests.

```
import javax.servlet.*;
import java.io.*;

public class userServlet extends GenericServlet {
  public void service( ServletRequest _req, ServletResponse _res)
                    throws ServletException, IOException{
    _res.setContentType("text/plain");
    PrintWriter Out = _res.getWriter();
    Out.println( "Hello World!" );
    Out.flush();
  }
}
```
Example 2

```
javax.servlet.GenericServlet.destroy().
```

Syntax: `public void destroy()`

Description: The `init(...)` method is the first method to be called in a
               servlet's lifetime; the `destroy()` method is the last method
               called. It is called just before the servlet is unloaded from
               memory.

```
public void destroy(){
  System.out.println("This servlet has left the building!");
}
```
Example 3

If the servlet requires its internal data structure to be saved to disk so it may be loaded at a later date, I suggest that you don't rely on the `destroy()` method being called. For example, if the server crashes or gets restarted, this method will not be accessed.

`javax.servlet.GenericServlet.getInitParameter(String _name)`

Syntax:	`public String getInitParameter(String name)`
Parameters:	`String` – The name of the startup parameter.
Returns:	`String` – The value of the specified startup parameter.
Description:	When the servlet starts up, a number of initialization parameters may be passed to it. These parameters are specified using the `key/value` paired mechanism.

```
String Name = getInitParameter("count_hit");
```
Example 4

`javax.servlet.GenericServlet.getInitParameterNames()`

Syntax:	`public Enumeration getInitParameterNames()`
Returns:	`Enumeration` to the list of parameter names.
Description:	When retrieving parameters from the servlet at start-up, the exact syntax or variable names might not be known. This method returns an enumeration to the list of the parameters that are present at servlet startup.

```
Enumeration E;
String key, value;
E = getInitParameterNames();
while ( E.hasMoreElements() ){
      key = (String)E.nextElement();
      value = getInitParameter( key );
      System.out.println( "Key: " + key + " Value: " + value );
}
```
Example 5

`javax.servlet.GenericServlet.getServletConfig()`

Syntax:	`public ServletConfig getServletConfig()`
Returns:	`ServletConfig` – Object reference to the servlet's startup data.
Description:	This method gets a reference to the object containing all the startup information. This method allows processing of the initialization data to be done outside of the `init()` method.

```
ServletConfig Sc;
Sc = getServletConfig();
String value = Sc.getInitParameter( "count" );
counter = Integer.parseInt( value );
```
Example 6

```
javax.servlet.GenericServlet.getServletContext()
```

Syntax:	`public ServletContext getServletContext()`
Returns:	`ServletContext` – Object reference to the servlet's running environment.
Description:	This method is used to return a reference to the object that holds the environment information about the server the servlet is running in.

```
ServletContext Sc;
Sc = getServletContext();
System.out.println( "Version of Server: " +
Sc.getMajorVersion()
                              + "." +
Sc.getMinorVersion() );
```
Example 7

```
javax.servlet.GenericServlet.getServletInfo()
```

Syntax:	`public String getServletInfo()`
Returns:	`String` – Descriptive text about the servlet, such as the author, version, and copyright date.
Description:	This method is intended to be a placeholder for the developer. When this method is called, it will return the author, version and copyright date of the servlet.

```
public String getServletInfo(){
  return "Another fine example of servlet engineering: 2.1";
}
```
Example 8

```
javax.servlet.GenericServlet.init(ServletConfig c)
```

Syntax:	`public void init(ServletConfig c)`
Parameters:	`ServletConfig` – Servlet startup information.
Throws:	`ServletException`
Description:	When the servlet is loaded, this method is called first. If your servlet requires any initialization, this method is usually overloaded.

```
public void init(ServletConfig c) throws ServletException{
  super.init(c);
        String value = _config.getInitParameter( "count" );
      counter = Integer.parseInt( value );
}
```
Example 9

If you intend to override this method, remember to call the `init(…)` method of the underlying method. This ensures that all necessary initialization is performed correctly.

```
javax.servlet.GenericServlet.init()
```

Syntax:	`public void init()`
Throws:	`ServletException`
Description:	When the servlet is loaded, this method is called first. If your servlet requires any initialization, this method is usually overloaded.

```
public void init() throws ServletException{
       String value = _config.getInitParameter( "count" );
     counter = Integer.parseInt( value );
}
```
Example 10

If you intend to override this method, you do not need to call the underlying `init()` method. The servlet engine takes care of this for you.

```
javax.servlet.GenericServlet.log(String msg)
```

Syntax:	`public void log(String msg)`
Parameters:	`String` – The string that is to be stored.
Description:	This method logs the given message to the server's log file. Since many different sources could be writing to the log file, the method adds the servlet class name to the front of the text so each entry can be easily identified.

```
log("This is a test to see what is written");
```
Example 11

```
javax.servlet.GenericServlet.log(String msg, Throwable t)
```

Syntax:	`public void log(String msg, Throwable t)`
Parameters:	`String` – The string that is to be stored.
	`Throwable` – The string that is to be stored.
Description:	This method logs the given message to the server's log file. Since many different sources could be writing to the log file, the method adds the servlet class name to the front of the text, to allow each entry to be easily identified.

```
try{
  //-- Something might go wrong
}catch(ServletException E){
  log("This is a test to see what is written", E);
}
```
Example 12

```
javax.servlet.GenericServlet.service(ServletRequest req,
                    ServletResponse res)
```

Syntax:	`public abstract void service(ServletRequest req,`
	`Servlet Response res)`
Parameters:	`ServletRequest` - Reference to the client input.
	`ServletResponse` - Reference to the client output.
Throws:	`ServletException, IOException`
Description:	The service method is called for every successful client connection that requires processing. When subclassing from this class, an implementation for this method body has to be provided.

```
public void service( ServletRequest _req, ServletResponse _res)
        throws ServletException, IOException{
 _res.setContentType("text/plain");
 PrintWriter Out = _res.getWriter();
 Out.println( "Hello World!" );
 Out.flush();
}
```
Example 13

Since servlets run in a multithreaded environment, this method is not thread-safe. If the service method is to modify shared data, it can be made thread-safe by use of standard thread mechanisms such as `synchronized`.

A.3.2   javax.servlet.RequestDispatcher

```
public interface RequestDispatcher {
  public void forward(ServletRequest request, ServletResponse response)
                  throws ServletException, IOException;
  public void include(ServletRequest request, ServletResponse response)
                  throws ServletException, IOException;

}
```
Example 14

The `RequestDispatcher` interface is implemented by the servlet engine. It is used to pass control to another servlet for processing.

```
javax.servlet.RequestDispatcher.forward(ServletRequest req,
                        ServletResponse res)
```

Syntax:	`public abstract void forward(ServletRequest req,`
	`ServletResponse res)`
Parameters:	`ServletRequest` - Reference to the client input.
	`ServletResponse` - Reference to the client output.
Throws:	`ServletException, IOException`
Description:	The `forward(...)` method is used to pass the complete client request to another servlet for processing.

```
ServletContext xt = getServletContext();
RequestDispatcher xyzServlet = xt.getRequestDispatcher
                        ("http://<domain>/servlet/xyzServlet");
```

```
xyzServlet.forward( _req, _res );
```
Example 15

The calling servlet is not permitted to do anything that would affect the output to the client; otherwise, the forward(...) method call will fail.

```
javax.servlet.RequestDispatcher.include(ServletRequest req,
                        ServletResponse res)
```

Syntax: `public abstract void include(ServletRequest req,`
                 `ServletResponse res)`

Parameters: `ServletRequest` - Reference to the client input.

                 `ServletResponse` - Reference to the client output.

Throws: `ServletException, IOException`

Description: The `include(...)` method is used to insert output from
                 another servlet into the output of the calling servlet.

```
ServletContext xt = getServletContext();
RequestDispatcher xyzServlet = xt.getRequestDispatcher
                        ("http://<domain>/servlet/xyzServlet");

PrintWriter Out = _res.getWriter();
Out.println( "This is from the insertServlet " );
for(int x=0; x < 10; x++ )
  xyzServlet.insert( _req, _res );

Out.println( "This is the end of the print servlet " );
```
Example 16

The servlet called cannot set any HTTP headers in the output stream.

A.3.3   javax.servlet.Servlet
```
public interface Servlet {
  public void init(ServletConfig config) throws ServletException;
  public ServletConfig getServletConfig();
  public void service(ServletRequest req, ServletResponse res)
                        throws ServletException, IOException;
  public String getServletInfo();
  public void destroy();
}
```
Example 17

The servlet interface is the base for all servlets. This interface is used to create Gener-icServlet, from which HttpServlet and all other servlets are based.

```
javax.servlet.Servlet.init(...)
```

Syntax: `public abstract void init( ServletConfig _config )`

Parameters: `ServletConfig` - Object reference to the servlet's configuration
                 data.

Description: This is the first method that is called when the servlet initially loads. A reference to the servlet's startup data, such as any initial parameters that are passed in, is available.

`javax.servlet.Servlet.getServletConfig()`

Syntax: `public ServletConfig getServletConfig();`

Returns: `ServletConfig` – A reference to the interface that holds all the startup data.

Description: This method is used to get a reference to the object containing all the startup information. This method allows processing of the initialization data to be accessed outside of the `init(...)` method.

`javax.servlet.Servlet.service(...)`

Syntax: `public void service(ServletRequest req, Servlet Response res)`

Throws: `ServletException, IOException`

Parameters: `ServletRequest` - Reference to the client input.

                 `ServletResponse` - Reference to the client output.

Description: The service is called for every client connection that has been successfully made. To aid in processing the client request, a reference to both the client's input and output is presented.

`javax.servlet.Servlet.getServletInfo()`

Syntax: `public String getServletInfo()`

Returns: `String` – Information about the servlet.

Description: This method is intended to be a placeholder for the developer. When it's called, it will return the author, version, and copyright date of the servlet.

`javax.servlet.Servlet.destroy()`

Syntax: `public void destroy()`

Description: The `init(...)` method is the first method to be called in a servlet's lifetime; the `destroy()` method is the last method called, just before the servlet is unloaded from memory.

A.3.4   javax.servlet.ServletConfig

```
public interface ServletConfig {
  public abstract ServletContext getServletContext();
  public abstract String getInitParameter( String _name );
  public abstract Enumeration getInitParameterNames();
}
```
Example 18

The `ServletConfig` interface is used by the server for passing data to the servlet about its operating environment and any startup parameters that may have been passed to the server.

`javax.servlet.ServletConfig.getServletContext()`

Syntax:	`public ServletContext getServletContext()`
Returns:	`ServletContext` – Object reference to the servlet's running environment.
Description:	This method is used to return a reference to the object that holds the environment information about the server that the servlet is running in.

```
ServletContext Sc;
Sc = getServletContext();
System.out.println( "Version of Server: " + Sc.getMajorVersion()
                                  + "." + Sc.getMinorVersion() );
```
Example 19

`javax.servlet.ServletConfig.getInitParameter(String name)`

Syntax:	`public String getInitParameter(String name)`
Parameters:	`String` – The name of the startup parameter.
Returns:	`String` – The value of the specified startup parameter.
Description:	When the servlet starts up, a number of initialization parameters may be passed to it. These parameters are specified using the `key/value` paired mechanism.

```
String Name = getInitParameter("count_hit");
```
Example 20

`javax.servlet.ServletConfig.getInitParameterNames()`

Syntax:	`public Enumeration getInitParameterNames()`
Returns:	`Enumeration` to the list of parameter names.
Description:	When retrieving parameters from the servlet at startup, the exact syntax or variable names are sometimes not known. This method returns an enumeration to the list of the parameters that are present at servlet startup.

```
Enumeration E;
String key, value;
E = getInitParameterNames();
while ( E.hasMoreElements() ){
      key = (String)E.nextElement();
      value = getInitParameter( key );
```

```
                  System.out.println( "Key: " + key + " Value: " + value );
}
```
Example 21

A.3.5   javax.servlet.ServletContext

```
public interface ServletContext {
  public Object getAttribute( String _name );
  public Enumeration getAttributeNames();
  public ServletContext getContext(String uri);
  public int getMajorVersion();
  public int getMinorVersion();
  public String getMimeType( String _file );
  public String getRealPath( String _path );
  public URL getResource(String uri);
  public InputStream getResourceAsStream(String uri);
  public RequestDispatcher getRequestDispatcher(String uri);
  public String getServerInfo();
  public void log( String _msg );
  public void log( String _msg, Throwable t );
  public void setAttribute( String name, Object O );
  public void removeAttribute(String name);
}
```
Example 22

The server will pass environmental information to the servlet regarding the system it is running using this interface.

`javax.servlet.ServletContext.getAttribute(String name)`

Syntax:	`public Object getAttribute(String name)`
Parameters:	`String` – The name of the parameter.
Returns:	`Object` – The object of the parameter.
Description:	To make sharing data between servlets easier, you can ask the `ServletContext` to store data for you on its behalf. A unique string references the data. This method retrieves a previously stored object.

```
myData = (MYDATA)getServletContext().getAttribute("mydata.value");
```
Example 23

`javax.servlet.ServletContext.getAttributeNames()`

Syntax:	`public Enumeration getAttributeNames()`
Returns:	`Enumeration` to a list of attribute names.
Description:	To make sharing data between servlets easier, you can ask the `ServletContext` to store data for you on its behalf. A unique string references data. This method returns an enumeration back to all the object names currently being held.

```
Enumeration E = getServletContext().getAttributeNames();
```

```
while (E.hasMoreElements())
   System.out.println("Attribute: " + (String)E.nextElement() );
```
Example 24

`javax.servlet.ServletContext.getContext(String uri)`

Syntax:	`public ServletContext getContext(String uri)`
Parameters:	`String` – URI to the servlet.
Returns:	`ServletContext` for the servlet.
Description:	This method returns the `ServletContext` for the given servlet.

```
ServletContext SC = getServletContext().getContext
                           ("/servlet/anotherServlet");
```
Example 25

If the `ServletContext` cannot be located or is denied for security reasons, `null` is returned.

`javax.servlet.ServletContext.getMajorVersion()`

Syntax:	`public Object getMajorVersion()`
Returns:	`int` – The version number.
Description:	This method returns the major version number of the servlet API. It would return 2 for this API.

```
System.out.println("Major Version: " +
                        getServletContext().getMajorVersion() );
```
Example 26

`javax.servlet.ServletContext.getMinorVersion()`

Syntax:	`public Object getMinorVersion()`
Returns:	`int` – The version number.
Description:	This method returns the major version number of the servlet API. It would return 1 for this API.

```
System.out.println("Minor Version: "
                        + getServletContext().getMinorVersion() );
```
Example 27

`javax.servlet.ServletContext.getMimeType(String _file)`

Syntax:	`public String getMimeType(String file)`
Parameters:	`String` – URI to a file.
Returns:	String of the MIME type.
Description:	This method is used to determine the MIME type of any given file. If the file type cannot be determined, this method returns `null`.

```
String mimeType = getServletContext().getMimeType( "/logo.gif" );
//- Returns 'image/gif'
```
Example 28

The MIME type is determined by the settings of the servlet engine.

`javax.servlet.ServletContext.getRealPath(String _path)`

Syntax:	`public String getRealPath(String file)`
Parameters:	`String` – The URL to a file.
Returns:	String of the full system path name.
Description:	This method takes the virtual path parameter and applies the alias rules that exist in the server to return the real path.

```
String realpath = getServletContext().getRealPath(
                         "http://www.n-ary.com" );
```
Example 29

This method may only be used for translations on the server the servlet is running. If for some reason the translation from virtual to real cannot be executed, `null` is returned.

`javax.servlet.ServletContext.getResource(String uri)`

Syntax:	`public URL getResource(String uri)`
Parameters	`String` – The path name to a file/servlet.
Returns:	The URL of the resource.
Description:	This method reads the file and uses the servlet engine to create a URL to that file.

```
URL urlDir = getServletContext().getResource( "/examples/file.html" );
```
Example 30

This method is used to have a servlet gain access to any file on the system, regardless of the location of the file.

`javax.servlet.ServletContext.getResourceAsStream(String uri)`

Syntax:	`public URL getResourceAsStream(String uri)`
Parameters:	`String` – The path name to a file/servlet.
Returns:	The `InputStream` to the resource.
Description:	This method reads the file and uses the servlet engine to create an `InputStream` to that file.

```
InputStream urlIn = getServletContext().getResourceAsStream
                                        ( "/examples/file.html" );
```
Example 31

```
javax.servlet.ServletContext.getRequestDispatcher(String uri)
```

Syntax: public requestDispatcher getRequestDispatcher
                (String uri)

Parameters: uri – To the servlet or JSP page.

Returns: The RequestDispatcher for the servlet.

Description: This method returns a RequestDispatcher to the specified
                servlet. This allows the servlet to be used for forwarding
                and including client requests.

```
ServletContext xt = getServletContext();
RequestDispatcher xyzServlet = xt.getRequestDispatcher
                        ("http://<domain>/servlet/xyzServlet");

xyzServlet.forward( _req, _res );
```
Example 32

```
javax.servlet.ServletContext.getServerInfo()
```

Syntax: public String getServerInfo()

Returns: String – Information about the servlet engine.

Description: This method returns version numbers and information
                about the underlying servlet engine.

```
ServletContext xt = getServletContext();
System.out.println("Servlet Engine:" + xt.getServerInfo() );
```
Example 33

```
javax.servlet.ServletContext.log(String msg)
```

Syntax: public void log(String msg)

Parameters: String – The String that is to be stored.

Description: This method logs the given message to the server's log file
                for this context. Since many different sources could be
                writing to the log file, the method adds the servlet class
                name to the front of the text to allow each entry to be easily
                identified.

```
getServletContext().log("This is a test to see what is written");
```
Example 34

```
javax.servlet.ServletContext.log(String msg, Throwable t)
```

Syntax: public void log(String msg, Throwable t)

Parameters: String – The String that is to be stored.

Throwable: The String that is to be stored.

Description:	This method logs the given message to the server's log file for this context. Since many different sources could be writing to the log file, the method adds the servlet class name to the front of the text to allow each entry to be easily identified.

```
try{
  //-- Something might go wrong
}catch(ServletException E){
 getServletContext().log("This is a test to see what is written", E);
}
```
Example 35

`javax.servlet.ServletContext.setAttribute(String name, Object O)`

Syntax:	`public void setAttribute(String name, Object O)`
Parameters:	`String` – The name of the parameter.
Parameters:	`Object` – The object that you wish to store.
Description:	To make sharing data between servlets easier, you can ask the `ServletContext` to store data for you on its behalf. A unique string references data.

```
getServletContext().setAttribute( "mydata.value", new MYDATA() );
```
Example 36

`javax.servlet.ServletContext.removeAttribute(String name)`

Syntax:	`public void removeAttribute(String name)`
Parameters:	`String` – The name of the parameter.
Description:	To make sharing data between servlets easier, you can ask the `ServletContext` to store data for you on its behalf. A unique string references data. This method removes the object from the `ServletContext`.

```
getServletContext().removeAttribute( "mydata.value" );
```
Example 37

A.3.6   javax.servlet.ServletException

```
public class ServletException extends Exception {
  public ServletException();
  public ServletException( String _msg );
  public ServletException( String _msg, Throwable cause );
  public ServletException( Throwable cause );
  public Throwable getRootCause();
}
```
Example 38

This exception is used to indicate that a problem has occurred while processing a method from the servlet API.

```
javax.servlet.ServletException.ServletException()
```

Syntax:	`public ServletException()`
Description:	This exception can be created and thrown to illustrate that an error has occurred somewhere in the servlet.

```
throw new ServletException( "It's all gone pear shaped!" );
```
Example 39

```
javax.servlet.ServletException.getRootCause()
```

Syntax:	`public Throwable getRootCause()`
Description:	This exception class can be used to catch nested exceptions. For this reason, this method returns the original cause, if it's available.

```
try{
  //--- ARGH!
}catch(ServletException E){
  throw new Exception( E.getRootCause() );
}
```
Example 40

A.3.7   javax.servlet.ServletInputStream

```
public abstract class ServletInputStream extends InputStream {
  public int readLine(byte _b[], int _off, int _len) throws IOException;
}
```
Example 41

This class adds extra functionality for reading data from the client to the `Input-Stream`.

```
javax.servlet.ServletInputStream.readLine(byte _b[], int _off, int _len)
```

Syntax:	`public int readLine(byte b[], int off, int len)`
Parameters:	`byte`—Reference to the client input.
	`int` offset – The start position where the calling program starts reading.
	`int` length—The length of the data to be read.
Returns:	`int`—The number of bytes read.
Throws:	`IOException`
Description:	This method is used for reading data from the client. It reads bytes into the given array starting at the given index and continuing until the number of bytes specified have been read or a "\n" is received.

```
public void service( ServletRequest _req, ServletResponse _res)
                      throws ServletException, IOException{
      ServletInputStream IS = _req.getInputStream();
      byte buffer[] = new byte[ 1024 ];
      int noRead;
```

```
        noRead = IS.read( buffer, 0, 1024 );
}
```
Example 42

If the "\n" is encountered before the number of bytes has been read, the method returns the number of bytes actually read, including the "\n" itself.

A.3.8 javax.servlet.ServletOutputStream

```
public class ServletOutputStream extends OutputStream {
  public ServletOutputStream();

  public void print( String _s ) throws IOException;
  public void print( boolean _b ) throws IOException;
  public void print( char _c ) throws IOException;
  public void print( int _i ) throws IOException;
  public void print( long _l ) throws IOException;
  public void print( float _f ) throws IOException;
  public void print( double _d ) throws IOException;

  public void println() throws IOException;
  public void println( String _s ) throws IOException;
  public void println( boolean _b ) throws IOException;
  public void println( char _c ) throws IOException;
  public void println( int _i ) throws IOException;
  public void println( long _l ) throws IOException;
  public void println( float _f ) throws IOException;
  public void println( double _d ) throws IOException;
}
```

Example 43

This class allows you to send data to the client. Closing or flushing this class will send all the data to the client.

```
javax.servlet.ServletOutputStream.print()
```

Syntax:	public void print(...)
Parameters:	Any standard data type.
Description:	This method takes the given parameter and writes it to the output device, without a carriage return.

```
public void service( ServletRequest _req, ServletResponse _res)
                              throws ServletException, IOException {
  ServletOutputStream OS = _res.getOutputStream();
  OS.print( "String Example" );
  OS.print( true );
  OS.print( 'a' );
  OS.print( 12 );
  OS.print( 765312332 );
  OS.print( 1.2 );
  OS.print( 54.23423412312 );
}
```
Example 44

```
javax.servlet.ServletOutputStream.println(…)
```

Syntax: `public void println(…)`

Parameters: Any standard data type.

Description: This method takes the given parameter and writes it to the
                     output device, with a carriage return and line feed.

```
public void service( ServletRequest _req, ServletResponse _res)
                               throws ServletException, IOException {
  ServletOutputStream OS = _res.getOutputStream();
  OS.println( "String Example" );
  OS.println( true );
  OS.println( 'a' );
  OS.println( 12 );
  OS.println( 765312332 );
  OS.println( 1.2 );
  OS.println( 54.23423412312 );
}
```
Example 45

A.3.9   javax.servlet.ServletRequest

```
public interface ServletRequest {
  public Object getAttribute( String name );
  public Enumeration getAttributeNames();
  public String getCharacterEncoding();
  public int getContentLength();
  public String getContentType();
  public ServletInputStream getInputStream() throws IOException;
  public String getParameter( String name );
  public Enumeration getParameterNames();
  public String[] getParameterValues(String name);
  public String getProtocol();
  public BufferedReader getReader() throws IOException;
  public String getRemoteAddr();
  public String getRemoteHost();
  public String getScheme();
  public String getServerName();
  public int getServerPort();
  public void setAttribute(String name, Object O);
}
```
Example 46

This interface is used to gather information from the client for every request that is
made to the service method.

```
javax.servlet.ServletRequest.getAttribute(String name)
```

Syntax: `public Object getAttribute(String name)`

Parameters: `String` – The name of the parameter.

Returns: `Object` – The object of the parameter.

| Description: | To make sharing data between servlets easier, you can ask the `ServletRequest` to store data for you on its behalf. A unique string references data. This method retrieves a previously stored object. |

```
myData = (MYDATA)_req.getAttribute("mydata.value");
```
Example 47

Use this method to pass data between servlets when forwarding or including a request.

`javax.servlet.ServletRequest.getAttributeNames()`

Syntax:	`public Enumeration getAttributeNames()`
Returns:	`Enumeration` – To a list of attribute names.
Description:	To make sharing data between servlets easier, you can ask the `ServletRequest` to store data for you on its behalf. A unique string references data. This method returns an enumeration back to all the object names currently being held.

```
Enumeration E = _req.getAttributeNames();
while (E.hasMoreElements())
  System.out.println("Attribute: " + (String)E.nextElement() );
```
Example 48

Use this method to pass data between servlets when forwarding or including a request.

`javax.servlet.ServletRequest.getCharacterEncoding()`

Syntax:	`public String getCharacterEncoding()`
Returns:	`String` – A character set.
Description:	This method returns the character set (if known) for encoding the input body of the request.

```
System.out.println( _req.getCharacterEncoding() );
```
Example 49

`javax.servlet.ServletRequest.getContentLength()`

Syntax:	`public String getContentLength ()`
Returns:	`int` – The length of the input request.
Description:	This method returns the length (if known) of the input request.

```
System.out.println( _req. getContentLength () );
```
Example 50

```
javax.servlet.ServletRequest.getContentType()
```

Syntax:	`public String getContentType ()`
Returns:	`String` – The MIME type.
Description:	This method returns the MIME type (if known) of the input request.

```
System.out.println( _req. getContentType () );
```
Example 51

```
javax.servlet.ServletRequest.getInputStream()
```

Syntax:	`public InputStream getInputStream()`
Returns:	The `InputStream` to the request.
Throws:	`IOException`
Description:	This method returns an `InputStream` to the client request. If a `BufferedReader` has already been created, an exception will be thrown.

```
public void service( ServletRequest _req, ServletResponse _res)
                    throws ServletException, IOException{
    ServletInputStream IS = _req.getInputStream();
    byte buffer[] = new byte[ 1024 ];
    int noRead;
    noRead = IS.read( buffer, 0, 1024 );
}
```
Example 52

```
javax.servlet.ServletRequest.getParameter(String name)
```

Syntax:	`public String getParameter (String name)`
Parameter:	`String` – The name of the parameter.
Returns:	`String` – The value of the parameter
Description:	This method returns the HTML parameter that was passed in (either through the query string or part of a post), with the given name. If it is not found, a `null` is thrown.

```
System.out.println( _req.getParameter("EMAIL") );
```
Example 53

This method is case-sensitive when referring to HTML parameters.

```
javax.servlet.ServletRequest.getParameterNames()
```

Syntax:	`public String getParameterNames()`
Returns:	The `Enumeration` to the parameters.
Description:	This method returns an `Enumeration` to the list of parameters that was passed in to the servlet from the client.

```
Enumeration E = _req.getParameterNames();
while( E.hasMoreElements() )

    System.out.println( "Parameter: " + (String)E.nextElement() );
```
Example 54

`javax.servlet.ServletRequest.getParameterValues(String name)`

Syntax:	public String[] getParameterValues(String name)
Parameter:	String – The name of parameter.
Returns:	String– An array of all the parameters.
Description:	This method returns all the values associated with a given parameter value. In HTML, it is legal to have more than one variable with the same name but with different values.

```
String [] result = _req.getParameterValues("CHECKBOX");
for(int x=0; x < result.length; x++ )
    System.out.println( "Value: " + result[x] );
```
Example 55

If the parameter does not exist, `null` is returned.

`javax.servlet.ServletRequest.getProtocol()`

Syntax:	public String getProtocol ()
Returns:	String – The HTTP protocol type.
Description:	This method returns the HTTP protocol version.

```
System.out.println( _req. getProtocol () );
```
Example 56

`javax.servlet.ServletRequest.getReader()`

Syntax:	public BufferedReader getReader ()
Returns:	The InputStream to the request.
Throws:	IOException
Description:	This method returns a BufferedReader to the client request. If an InputStream has already been created, an exception will be thrown.

```
public void service( ServletRequest _req, ServletResponse _res)
                        throws ServletException, IOException{
        BufferedReader IS = _req.getReader();
}
```
Example 57

`javax.servlet.ServletRequest.getRemoteAddr()`

Syntax:	public String getRemoteAddr ()
Returns:	String – IP address.

Description: This method returns the IP address of the client making the request.

```
System.out.println( _req. getRemoteAddr () );
```
Example 58

`javax.servlet.ServletRequest.getRemoteHost()`

Syntax: `public String getRemoteHost ()`
Returns: `String` – Qualified name.
Description: This method returns the full qualified name of the client making the request. If the full name is not available, the IP address is returned.

```
System.out.println( _req. getRemoteHost () );
```
Example 59

`javax.servlet.ServletRequest.getScheme()`

Syntax: `public String getScheme ()`
Returns: `String` – Scheme.
Description: This method returns the scheme that was used to send this request. For example: HTTP.

```
System.out.println( _req. getScheme () );
```
Example 60

`javax.servlet.ServletRequest.getServerPort()`

Syntax: `public String getServerPort ()`
Returns: `int` – Socket number.
Description: This method returns the port number on which the client request was received.

```
System.out.println( _req. getServerPort() );
```
Example 61

`javax.servlet.ServletRequest.setAttribute(String name, Object O)`

Syntax: `public void setAttribute(String name, Object O)`
Parameters: `String` – The name of the parameter.
Parameters: `Object` – The object that you want to store.
Description: To make sharing data between servlets easier, you can ask the `ServletRequest` to store data for you on its behalf. A unique string references data.

```
_req.setAttribute( "mydata.value", new MYDATA() );
```
Example 62

Use this method to pass data between servlets when forwarding or including a request.

A.3.10 *javax.servlet.ServletResponse*

```
public interface ServletResponse {
  public getCharacterEncoding();
  public ServletOutputStream getOutputStream() throws IOException;
  public PrintWriter getWriter() throws IOException;
  public void setContentLength( int _len );
  public void setContentType( String _type );
}
```

Example 63

This interface is used for presenting the servlet-generated data to the client from the servlet class.

```
javax.servlet.ServletResponse.getCharacterEncoding()
```

Syntax:	`public String getCharacterEncoding()`
Returns:	`String` – Character set.
Description:	This method returns the character set (if known) for encoding the output body of the request.

```
System.out.println( _res.getCharacterEncoding() );
```
Example 64

```
javax.servlet.ServletResponse.getOutputStream()
```

Syntax:	`public OutputStream getOutputStream()`
Returns:	The `OutputStream` to the request.
Throws:	`IOException`
Description:	This method returns an `OutputStream` to the client request. If a `PrintWriter` has already been created, an exception will be thrown.

```
public void service( ServletRequest _req, ServletResponse _res)
                        throws ServletException, IOException{
  PrintWriter Out = new PrintWriter( _res.getOutStream() );
  Out.println(" HELLO WORLD " );
}
```
Example 65

```
javax.servlet.ServletResponse.getWriter()
```

Syntax:	`public OutputStream getOutputStream()`
Returns:	A `PrintWriter` to the request.
Throws:	`IOException, UnsupportedEncodingException`

Description: This method returns a `PrintWriter` to the client request. If an `OutputStream` has already been created, an exception will be thrown.

```
public void service( ServletRequest _req, ServletResponse _res)
                         throws ServletException, IOException{
  PrintWriter Out = _res.getWriter();
  Out.println(" HELLO WORLD " );
}
```
Example 66

```
javax.servlet.ServletResponse.setContentLength(int len)
```

Syntax: `public String setContentLength(int length)`
Parameters: `int` length – Data length.
Description: This method sets the content length of the response to the client.

```
_res.setContentLength( 1024 )
```
Example 67

```
javax.servlet.ServletResponse.setContentType(String type)
```

Syntax: `public void setContentLength(int length)`
Parameters: `int` length – Data length.
Description: This method sets the content MIME type of the response to the client.

```
_res.setContentType( "text/html" )
```
Example 68

A.3.11 javax.servlet.SingleThreadModel
Syntax: `public interface SingleThreadModel`
Description: This interface, when implemented, ensures that no more than one thread is running in the service method at once. This is particularly useful if you don't want to worry about your variables becoming corrupted due to multiple requests.

```
public class trustmeServlet extends HttpServlet
                         implements SingleThreadModel{
  //-- service method as per normal servlet
}
```
Example 69

A.3.12 javax.servlet.UnavailableException
```
public class UnavailableException extends ServletException{
  public UnavailableException(Servlet servlet, String message);
```

```
public UnavailableException(int seconds, Servlet servlet,
                            String message);
public Servlet getServlet();
public int getUnavailableSeconds();
public boolean isPermanent();


}
```
Example 70

This exception is used if the servlet is presently not ready to process client requests. This could be due a database connection that is not yet initialized or some other intensive processing that has not been completed. The servlet engine can queue the client request for x number of seconds before it attempts to process again.

```
javax.servlet.UnavailableException.UnavailableException(Servlet Serv,
                            String msg)
```

Syntax:	`public UnavailableException(Servlet Serv,` `String msg)`
Parameters:	`Servlet Serv` – The reference to the servlet. `String msg` – The message to display about the exception.
Description:	This exception can be created and thrown to illustrate that the servlet will be permanently unavailable.

```
throw new UnavailableException ( this, "Its all gone pear shaped!" );
```
Example 71

```
javax.servlet.UnavailableException.UnavailableException(int sec,
                            Servlet Serv, String msg)
```

Syntax:	`public UnavailableException(Servlet Serv,` `String msg)`
Parameters:	`int Sec` – The number of seconds for which the servlet will be unavailable. `Servlet Serv` – The reference to the servlet. `String msg` – The message to display about the exception.
Description:	This exception can be created and thrown to illustrate that the servlet will be temporarily unavailable.

```
throw new UnavailableException ( 10, this, "Its all gone pear shaped,
                            back in 10 seconds" );
```
Example 72

```
javax.servlet.UnavailableException.getServlet()
```

Syntax:	`public Servlet getServlet() Returns` `Servlet Serv - The reference to` the servlet.
Description:	This method is used by the servlet engine to determine which servlet threw the exception.

```
javax.servlet.UnavailableException.getUnavailableSeconds()
```

Syntax: `public int getUnavailableSeconds ()`

Returns   int – The number of seconds.

Description: This method is used by the servlet engine to determine the number of seconds the servlet expects to be unavailable.

```
javax.servlet.UnavailableException.isPermanent()
```

Syntax: `public boolean isPermanent ()`

Returns   boolean – `true` or `false`.

Description: This method is used by the servlet engine to determine if the servlet is going to be unavailable for the duration of the server session.

A.4   *javax.servlet.http*

This package, which is part of the servlet API, is specifically designed for servlets communicating with the client via the HTTP protocol.

A.4.1   *javax.servlet.http.Cookie*

```
public class Cookie implements Cloneable{
  public Cookie(String name, String value);
  public String getComment();
  public String getDomain();
  public int getMaxAge();
  public String getName();
  public String getPath();
  public boolean getSecure();
  public String getValue();
  public int getVersion();
  public void setComment(String comment);
  public void setDomain(String domain);
  public void setMaxAge(int expiry);
  public void setPath(String uri);
  public void setSecure(boolean flag);
  public void setValue(String value);
  public void setVersion(int v);
}
```
Example 73

This class implements the HTTP cookie as it was introduced by Netscape Communications and defined in RFC2109.

```
javax.servlet.http.Cookie.Cookie(String name, String value)
```

Syntax: `public Cookie(String name, String value)`

Parameters: `String name` – The name of the cookie.

                    `String msg` – The value.

Description:	This constructor creates a new cookie with the specified name and value. When the cookie is set in the stream, any previous cookie with the same name is overwritten.

```
Cookie newCookie = new Cookie("name","ceri");
Res.addCookie( newCookie );
```
Example 74

`javax.servlet.http.Cookie.getComment()`

Syntax:	`public String getComment()`
Returns:	`String` – The comment of the cookie.
Description:	This method returns the comment field associated with the cookie, or `null` if one is not present.

```
Cookie newCookie = new Cookie("name","ceri");
newCookie.setComment("a wonderful cookie");
Res.addCookie( newCookie );
System.out.println( newCookie.getComment() );
```
Example 75

`javax.servlet.http.Cookie.getDomain()`

Syntax:	`public String getDomain()`
Returns:	`String` – The domain of the cookie.
Description:	This method returns the domain for which this cookie is active, or `null` if one is not present.

```
Cookie newCookie = new Cookie("name","ceri");
newCookie.setDomain(".n-ary.com");
Res.addCookie( newCookie );
System.out.println( newCookie.getDomain() );
```
Example 76

`javax.servlet.http.Cookie.getMaxAge()`

Syntax:	`public int getMaxAge()`
Returns:	`int` – The age of the cookie.
Description:	This method returns the number of seconds for which this cookie will be active, or –1 if no time has been specified.

```
Cookie newCookie = new Cookie("name","ceri");
newCookie.setMaxAge( 100000 );
Res.addCookie( newCookie );
System.out.println( newCookie.getMaxAge() );
```
Example 77

`javax.servlet.http.Cookie.getName()`

Syntax:	`public String getName()`
Returns:	`String` – The name of the cookie.

Description: This method returns the name of the cookie.

```
Cookie newCookie = new Cookie("name","ceri");
Res.addCookie( newCookie );
System.out.println( newCookie.getName() );
```
Example 78

`javax.servlet.http.Cookie.getPath()`

Syntax: `public String getPath()`

Returns: `String` – The path for the cookie.

Description: This method returns the path information for which this cookie will be sent, or `null` if the cookie is not present.

```
Cookie newCookie = new Cookie("name","ceri");
newCookie.setPath( "/" );
Res.addCookie( newCookie );
System.out.println( newCookie.getPath() );
```
Example 79

`javax.servlet.http.Cookie.getSecure()`

Syntax: `public boolean getSecure ()`

Returns: `boolean`

Description: This method returns `true` if the cookie is only to be sent when it is secure (`https`).

```
Cookie newCookie = new Cookie("name","ceri");
Res.addCookie( newCookie );
System.out.println( newCookie.getSecure() );
```
Example 80

`javax.servlet.http.Cookie.getValue()`

Syntax: `public String getValue()`

Returns: `String` – The value for the cookie.

Description: This method returns the value of the cookie.

```
Cookie newCookie = new Cookie("name","ceri");
Res.addCookie( newCookie );
System.out.println( newCookie.getValue() );
```
Example 81

`javax.servlet.http.Cookie.getVersion()Syntax:public int getVersion()`

Syntax: `public int getVersion()`

Returns: `int` – The version of the cookie.

Description: This method returns the version number of the cookie. If the version value is `0`, then this method complies with the original Netscape specification, where `1` implies compliance with RFC2109.

```
Cookie newCookie = new Cookie("name","ceri");
Res.addCookie( newCookie );
System.out.println( newCookie.getVersion() );
```
Example 82

`javax.servlet.http.Cookie.setComment(String comment)`

Syntax:	`public void setComment(String comment)`
Parameters:	`String` – The comment of the cookie.
Description:	This method sets the comment field for the cookie. Only version 1 cookies support this feature.

```
Cookie newCookie = new Cookie("name","ceri");
newCookie.setComment("a wonderful cookie");
Res.addCookie( newCookie );
System.out.println( newCookie.getComment() );
```
Example 83

`javax.servlet.http.Cookie.setDomain(String domain)`

Syntax:	`public void setDomain(String domain)`
Parameters:	`String` – The domain of the cookie.
Description:	This method sets the domain to which this cookie will be sent. The following example will send the cookie for all hosts which contain ".n-ary.com," assuming that the servlet that is running the code is within the domain itself.

```
Cookie newCookie = new Cookie("name","ceri");
newCookie.setDomain(".n-ary.com");
Res.addCookie( newCookie );
System.out.println( newCookie.getDomain() );
```
Example 84

`javax.servlet.http.Cookie.setMaxAge(int expiry)`

Syntax:	`public void setMaxAge(int expiry)`
Parameters:	`int` – The age of the cookie in seconds.
Description:	This method sets the length of time the client system will keep the cookie. A value of 0 will delete the cookie at the client. If the value is less than 0, the cookie only lives for as long as the client browser remains open.

```
Cookie newCookie = new Cookie("name","ceri");
newCookie.setMaxAge( 100000 );
Res.addCookie( newCookie );
System.out.println( newCookie.getMaxAge() );
```
Example 85

`javax.servlet.http.Cookie.setPath(String uri)`

Syntax:	`public void setPath(String uri)`
Parameters:	`String` – The path for the cookie.
Description:	This method sets the path information which this client will be sent. The following example only sends the client when the user is accessing any directory (or subdirectory) of [/examples].

```
Cookie newCookie = new Cookie("name","ceri");
newCookie.setPath( "/examples/" );
Res.addCookie( newCookie );
System.out.println( newCookie.getPath() );
```
Example 86

`javax.servlet.http.Cookie.setSecure(boolean flag)`

Syntax:	`public getSecure (boolean flag)`
Parameters:	`boolean`
Description:	This method determines whether the cookie should be sent when the user is using a secure protocol.

```
Cookie newCookie = new Cookie("name","ceri");
newCookie.setSecure( true );
Res.addCookie( newCookie );
System.out.println( newCookie.getSecure() );
```
Example 87

`javax.servlet.http.Cookie.setValue(String value)`

Syntax:	`public void getValue(String value)`
Parameters:	`String` – The value for the cookie.
Description:	This method sets the data value for the cookie. The value should not contain any white space, brackets, parentheses, equals signs, commas, double quotes, slashes, question marks, colons, semicolons, or the @ character.

```
Cookie newCookie = new Cookie("name","ceri");
newCookie.setValue("another_value");
Res.addCookie( newCookie );
System.out.println( newCookie.getValue() );
```
Example 88

`javax.servlet.http.Cookie.setVersion(int v)`

Syntax:	`public void setVersion(int v)`
Parameters:	`int` – The version of the cookie.
Description:	This method sets the version number of the cookie. A value of 0 signifies compliance with the original Netscape specification; a value of 1 implies compliance with RFC2109.

```
Cookie newCookie = new Cookie("name","ceri");
newCookie.setVersion(0);
Res.addCookie( newCookie );
System.out.println( newCookie.getVersion() );
```
Example 89

A.4.2   *javax.servlet.http.HttpServlet*

```
public class HttpServlet extends GenericServlet implements Serializable{
  protected void doDelete(HttpServletRequest req,HttpServletResponse res)
                         throws ServletException,IOException;
  protected void doGet(HttpServletRequest req,HttpServletResponse res)
                         throws ServletException,IOException;
  protected void doHead(HttpServletRequest req,HttpServletResponse res)
                         throws ServletException,IOException;
  protected void doOptions(HttpServletRequest req,HttpServletResponse
                         res) throws ServletException,IOException;
  protected void doPost(HttpServletRequest req,HttpServletResponse res)
                         throws ServletException,IOException;
  protected void doPut(HttpServletRequest req,HttpServletResponse res)
                         throws ServletException,IOException;
  protected void doTrace(HttpServletRequest req,HttpServletResponse res)
                         throws ServletException,IOException;
  protected void service(HttpServletRequest req,HttpServletResponse res)
                         throws ServletException,IOException;
  protected long getLastModified(HttpServletRequest req);
}
```
Example 90

This class should be used for HTTP-based servlets.

```
javax.servlet.http.HttpServlet.doDelete(HttpServletRequest req,
                         HttpServiceResponse res)
```

Syntax:	`protected void doDelete(HttpServletRequest req, HttpServletResponse res)`
Parameters:	`HttpServletRequest` - Reference to the client input.
	`HttpServletResponse` - Reference to the client output.
Throws:	`ServletException, IOException`
Description:	The `doDelete()` method is called for every client connection that is made using the HTTP DELETE operation. When subclassing from this class, an implementation for this method body has to be provided. If this method is not over ridden, the servlet will respond with an HTTP BAD_REQUEST status.

```
javax.servlet.http.HttpServlet.doGet(HttpServletRequest req,
                          HttpServiceResponse res)
```

Syntax: `protected void doGet(HttpServletRequest req,`
                  `HttpServletResponse res)`

Parameters: `HttpServletRequest` - Reference to the client input.

                  `HttpServletResponse` - Reference to the client output.

Throws: `ServletException, IOException`

Description: The `doGet` method is called for every client connection that
                  is made using the HTTP GET operation. When subclassing
                  from this class, an implementation for this method body
                  has to be provided. If it is overridden, then by default, pro
                  cessing for the HTTP HEAD operation is implemented. If
                  this method is not overridden, the servlet will respond with
                  an HTTP BAD_REQUEST status.

```
javax.servlet.http.HttpServlet.doHead(HttpServletRequest req,
                          HttpServiceResponse res)
```

Syntax: `protected void doHead(HttpServletRequest req,`
                  `HttpServletResponse res)`

Parameters: `HttpServletRequest` - Reference to the client input.

                  `HttpServletResponse` - Reference to the client output.

Throws: `ServletException, IOException`

Description: The `doHead` method is called for every client connection
                  that is made using the HTTP HEAD operation. When subclassing
from this class, an implementation for this method body has to be provided. It is not necessary to override this method, as the default implementation provides a body.

```
javax.servlet.http.HttpServlet.doOptions(HttpServletRequest req,
                          HttpServiceResponse res)
```

Syntax: `protected void doOption(HttpServletRequest req, Http`
                  `ServletResponse res)`

Parameters: `HttpServletRequest` - Reference to the client input.

                  `HttpServletResponse` - Reference to the client output.

Throws: `ServletException, IOException`

Description: The `doOption` method is called for every client connection
                  that is made using the HTTP OPTIONS operation. It is not
                  necessary to override this method, as the default implemen-
                  tation provides functionality.

```
javax.servlet.http.HttpServlet.doPost(HttpServletRequest req,
                    HttpServiceResponse res)
```

Syntax:	`protected void doPost(HttpServletRequest req,` `HttpServletResponse res)`
Parameters:	`HttpServletRequest` - Reference to the client input. `HttpServletResponse` - Reference to the client output.
Throws:	`ServletException, IOException`
Description:	The `doPost` method is called for every client connection that is made using the HTTP POST operation. If this method is not overridden, the servlet will respond with an HTTP BAD_REQUEST status.

```
javax.servlet.http.HttpServlet.doPut(HttpServletRequest req,
                    HttpServiceResponse res)
```

Syntax:	`protected void doPut(HttpServletRequest req,` `HttpServletResponse res)`
Parameters:	`HttpServletRequest` - Reference to the client input. `HttpServletResponse` - Reference to the client output.
Throws:	`ServletException, IOException`
Description:	The `doPut` method is called for every client connection that is made using the HTTP PUT operation. If this method is not over-ridden, the servlet will respond with an HTTP BAD_REQUEST status.

```
javax.servlet.http.HttpServlet.doTrace(HttpServletRequest req,
                    HttpServiceResponse res)
```

Syntax:	`protected void doTrace (HttpServletRequest req,` `HttpServletResponse res)`
Parameters:	`HttpServletRequest` - Reference to the client input. `HttpServletResponse` -Reference to the client output.
Throws:	`ServletException, IOException`
Description:	The `doTrace` method is called for every client connection that is made using the HTTP TRACE operation.

```
javax.servlet.http.HttpServlet.service(HttpServletRequest req,
                    HttpServiceResponse res)
```

Syntax:	`protected void service(HttpServletRequest req,` `HttpServlet Response res)`
Parameters:	`HttpServletRequest` - Reference to the client input. `HttpServletResponse` - Reference to the client output.
Throws:	`ServletException, IOException`
Description:	The service method is called for every client connection that has been successfully been made and that requires pro-

cessing. When subclassing from this class, an implementation for this method body has to be provided.

```
public void service( HttpServletRequest _req, HttpServletResponse _res)
        throws ServletException, IOException{
  _res.setContentType("text/plain");
  PrintWriter Out = _res.getWriter();
  Out.println( "Hello World!" );
  Out.flush();
}
```
Example 91

Since servlets run in a multithreaded environment, this method is not thread-safe. If the service method is to modify shared data, it can be made thread-safe by use of standard thread mechanisms such as synchronized.

javax.servlet.http.HttpServlet.getLastModified(HttpServletRequest req)

Syntax:	protected long getLastModified(HttpServletRequest req);
Parameters:	HttpServletRequest - Reference to the client input.
Returns:	long – The date of the last modification.
Description:	This method should be overridden so the servlet may accu rately determine when the content was last modified.

```
public long getLastModified ( HttpServletRequest _req) {
      return System.currentTimeMillis();
}
```
Example 92

A.4.3   javax.servlet.http.HttpServletRequest

```
public interface HttpServletRequest extends ServletRequest {
  public String getAuthType();
  public Cookie[] getCookies();
  public long getDateHeader( String _name );
  public String getHeader( String _name );
  public Enumeration getHeaderNames();
  public int getIntHeader( String _name );
  public String getMethod();
  public String getPathInfo();
  public String getPathTranslated();
  public String getQueryString();
  public String getRemoteUser();
  public String getRequestedSessionId();
  public String getRequestURI();
  public String getServletPath();
  public HttpSession getSession();
  public HttpSession getSession(boolean create);
  public boolean isRequestedSessionIdValid();
  public boolean isRequestedSessionIdFromCookie();
```

```
public boolean isRequestedSessionIdFromURL();
}
```
Example 93

This interface is used for receiving HTTP-type information from the client. To access HTTP-specific information from the `GenericServlet` interface, simply cast the `ServletRequest` to `HttpServletRequest`.

`javax.servlet.http.HttpServletRequest.getAuthType()`

Syntax:	`public String getAuthType();`
Returns:	`String` – The authentication method.
Description:	This method returns the authentication method used by the client.

```
System.out.println( res.getAuthType() );
```
Example 94

`javax.servlet.http.HttpServletRequest.getCookies()`

Syntax:	`public Cookie[] getCookies();`
Returns:	`Cookies`– An array of cookies.
Description:	Returns all the cookies that were present when the client made the request. Returns an empty array if no cookie was present.

```
Cookie list[] = res.getCookies() );
```
Example 95

`javax.servlet.http.HttpServletRequest.getDateHeader(String name)`

Syntax:	`public long getHeader(String name);`
Parameters:	`String` – The header name.
Returns:	`long` – The header value.
Description:	Returns the header value associated with the header name. Not all servers support this feature.

```
System.out.println( res.getHeader("Agent") );
```
Example 96

`javax.servlet.http.HttpServletRequest.getHeader(String name)`

Syntax:	`public String getHeader(String name);`
Parameters:	`String` – The header name.
Returns:	`String` – The header value.
Description:	Returns the header value associated with the header name. Not all servers support this feature.

```
System.out.println( res.getHeader("Agent") );
```
Example 97

`javax.servlet.http.HttpServletRequest.getIntHeader(String name)`

Syntax:	`public int getHeader(String name);`
Parameters:	`String` – The header name.
Returns:	`int` – The header value.
Description:	Returns the header value associated with the header name. Not all servers support this feature.

```
System.out.println( res.getHeader("Agent") );
```
Example 98

`javax.servlet.http.HttpServletRequest.getMethod()`

Syntax:	`public String getMethod();`
Returns:	`String` – The HTTP method.
Description:	This method returns the HTTP method that was used to send this request.

```
System.out.println( res.getMethod() );
```
Example 99

This would include `POST`, `GET`, `TRACE`, `PUT`, `HEAD`, `DELETE`, etc.

`javax.servlet.http.HttpServletRequest.getPathInfo()`

Syntax:	`public String getPathInfo();`
Returns:	`String` – The path information.
Description:	This method returns the optional path information that may exist just after the servlet and just before the query string.

```
System.out.println( res.getPathInfo() );
```
Example 100

`javax.servlet.http.HttpServletRequest.getPathTranslated()`

Syntax:	`public String getPathTranslated();`
Returns:	`String` – The path information.
Description:	This method returns the translated path information.

```
System.out.println( res.getPathTranslated() );
```
Example 101

`javax.servlet.http.HttpServletRequest.getQueryString()`

Syntax:	`public String getQueryString();`
Returns:	`String` – The query string.

Description: When the user requests information from the server, an
                   optional query string can be added to the end of the
                   address, in the form of key/value pairs. For example,
                   the method would return

```
System.out.println( res.getQueryString() );
```
Example 102

This method returns null if no query string is present.

```
javax.servlet.http.HttpServletRequest.getRemoteUser()
```

Syntax: public String getRemoteUser();
Returns: String – Remote user.
Description: When the client makes a request, it is sometimes common
                   for the username to be posted with the request.

```
System.out.println( res.getRemoteUser() );
```
Example 103

If no username is present, null is returned.

```
javax.servlet.http.HttpServletRequest.getRequestedSessionId()
```

Syntax: public String getRequestedSessionId();
Returns: String – The session ID.
Description: This returns the session ID associated with this request.

```
System.out.println( res. getRequestedSessionId() );
```
Example 104

If no username is present, null is returned.

```
javax.servlet.http.HttpServletRequest.getRequestURI()
```

Syntax: public String getRequestURI();
Returns: String – The request URI.
Description: When the client makes a request to the server, it is in the
                   form of a URL. This method returns the URI used by the
                   client to make the request.

```
System.out.println( res.getRequestURI() );
```
Example 105

```
javax.servlet.http.HttpServletRequest.getServletPath()
```

Syntax: public String getServletPath();
Returns: String – The servlet path information.

Description: This method returns the part of the URI that represents the path of the servlet being run.

```
System.out.println( res.getServletPath() );
```
Example 106

```
javax.servlet.http.HttpServletRequest.getSession()
```

Syntax: `public HttpSession getSession();`
Returns: `HttpSession` – The session reference.
Description: This method returns the session reference to this client. If no session exists, a new session is created.

```
HttpSession currentSession = res.getSession();
```
Example 107

```
javax.servlet.http.HttpServletRequest.getSession(boolean create)
```

Syntax: `public HttpSession getSession(boolean create);`
Parameters: `boolean` – Create session.
Returns: `HttpSession` – The session reference.
Description: This method returns the session reference to this client. If no session exists and the value of `false` is passed in, no new session is created. If this is the case, a `null` is returned if no session is present.

```
HttpSession currentSession = res.getSession(false);
```
Example 108

```
javax.servlet.http.HttpServletRequest.isRequestedSessionIdValid()
```

Syntax: `public boolean isRequestedSessionIdValid();`
Returns: `boolean`
Description: This method checks to see if a session exists for this client request.

```
if ( res.isRequestedSessionIdValid() )
  HttpSession currentSession = res.getSession();
```
Example 109

```
javax.servlet.http.HttpServletRequest.isRequestedSessionIdFromCookie()
```

Syntax: `public boolean isRequestedSessionIdFromCookie();`
Returns: `boolean`
Description: This method checks to see if a session is supported using the cookie mechanism.

```
if ( res.isRequestedSessionIdFromCookie() )
  System.out.println("This session is using cookies");
```
Example 110

```
javax.servlet.http.HttpServletRequest.isRequestedSessionIdFromURL()
```

Syntax:	public boolean isRequestedSessionIdFromURL();
Returns:	boolean
Description:	This method checks to see if a session is supported using the URL rewriting mechanism.

```
if ( res.isRequestedSessionIdFromURL() )
  System.out.println("This session is using URL rewriting");
```
Example 111

A.5   *javax.servlet.http.HttpServletResponse*

```
public interface HttpServletResponse extends ServletResponse {
  public void addCookie(Cookie cookie);
  public boolean containsHeader(String name);
  public String encodeRedirectURL(String url);
  public String encodeURL(String url);
  public void setStatus( int _sc );
  public void sendError( int _sc ) throws IOException;
  public void sendError( int _sc, String msg )throws IOException;
  public void sendRedirect( String _location ) throws IOException;
  public void setDateHeader( String _name, long _date );
  public void setIntHeader( String _name, int _value );
  public void setHeader( String _name, String _value );

  public static final int SC_CONTINUE = 100;
  public static final int SC_SWITCHING_PROTOCOLS = 101;
  public static final int SC_OK = 200;
  public static final int SC_CREATED = 201;
  public static final int SC_ACCEPTED = 202;
  public static final int SC_NON_AUTHORITATIVE_INFORMATION = 203;
  public static final int SC_NO_CONTENT = 204;
  public static final int SC_RESET_CONTENT = 205;
  public static final int SC_PARTIAL_CONTENT = 206;
  public static final int SC_MULTIPLE_CHOICES = 300;
  public static final int SC_MOVED_PERMANENTLY = 301;
  public static final int SC_MOVED_TEMPORARILY = 302;
  public static final int SC_SEE_OTHER = 303;
  public static final int SC_NOT_MODIFIED = 304;
  public static final int SC_USE_PROXY = 305;
  public static final int SC_BAD_REQUEST = 400;
  public static final int SC_UNAUTHORIZED = 401;
  public static final int SC_PAYMENT_REQUIRED = 402;
  public static final int SC_FORBIDDEN = 403;
  public static final int SC_NOT_FOUND = 404;
  public static final int SC_METHOD_NOT_ALLOWED = 405;
  public static final int SC_NOT_ACCEPTABLE = 406;
  public static final int SC_PROXY_AUTHENTICATION_REQUIRED = 407;
```

```
    public static final int SC_REQUEST_TIMEOUT = 408;
    public static final int SC_CONFLICT = 409;
    public static final int SC_GONE = 410;
    public static final int SC_LENGTH_REQUIRED = 411;
    public static final int SC_PRECONDITION_FAILED = 412;
    public static final int SC_REQUEST_ENTITY_TOO_LARGE = 413;
    public static final int SC_REQUEST_URI_TOO_LONG = 414;
    public static final int SC_UNSUPPORTED_MEDIA_TYPE = 415;
    public static final int SC_INTERNAL_SERVER_ERROR = 500;
    public static final int SC_NOT_IMPLEMENTED = 501;
    public static final int SC_BAD_GATEWAY = 502;
    public static final int SC_SERVICE_UNAVAILABLE = 503;
    public static final int SC_GATEWAY_TIMEOUT = 504;
    public static final int SC_HTTP_VERSION_NOT_SUPPORTED = 505;
}
```

Example 112

This interface is used for transmitting HTTP-type information to the client. To access HTTP-specific information from the `GenericServlet` interface, simply cast the `ServletResponse` to `HttpServletResponse`.

`javax.servlet.http.HttpServletResponse.addCookie(Cookie cookie)`

Syntax:	`public void addCookie (Cookie cookie)`
Parameters:	`Cookie` – The cookie.
Description:	This method sets the specified cookie to the response of the client. This method can be used multiple times to set different cookies.

```
Cookie newCookie = new Cookie("name","ceri");
newCookie.setPath( "/examples/" );
Res.addCookie( newCookie );
System.out.println( newCookie.getPath() );
```
Example 113

`javax.servlet.http.HttpServletResponse.containsHeader(String name)`

Syntax:	`public boolean containsHeader(String name)`
Parameters:	`String` – The header name.
Returns:	`boolean`
Description:	This method checks to see if the given header attribute has been set.

```
if ( Res.containsHeader("Agent") )
  System.out.println("Its set!");
```
Example 114

`javax.servlet.http.HttpServletResponse.encodeRedirectURL(String url)`

Syntax:	`public String encodeRedirectURL (String name)`
Parameters:	`String` – The URL.

Returns:	`String` – The encode URL.
Description:	This method encodes the URL, making it ready for a subsequent request to `sendRedirect(...)`. This method is here for convenience.

```
String URL = Res.encodeRedirectURL("/examples/test");
```
Example 115

`javax.servlet.http.HttpServletResponse.encodeURL(String url)`

Syntax:	`public String encodeURL (String name)`
Parameters:	`String` – The URL.
Returns:	`String` – The encode URL.
Description:	This method encodes the URL, making it ready for a subsequent request to `sendRedirect(...)`. This method encodes any session ID that may be present if the servlet engine is using URL rewriting to maintain sessions.

```
String URL = Res.encodeURL("/examples/test");
```
Example 116

`javax.servlet.http.HttpServletResponse.setStatus(int sc)`

Syntax:	`public String setStatus(int sc)`
Parameters:	`int` – The status code.
Description:	This method sets the status response of the outgoing HTTP header.

```
Res.setStatus(HttpServletResponse.SC_OK);
```
Example 117

`javax.servlet.http.HttpServletResponse.setError(int sc)`

Syntax:	`public String setError(int sc)`
Parameters:	`int` – The status code.
Description:	This method sets the error response of the outgoing HTTP header.

```
Res.setError (HttpServletResponse.SC_FORBIDDEN);
```
Example 118

`javax.servlet.http.HttpServletResponse.setError(int sc, String msg)`

Syntax:	`public String setError(int sc)`
Parameters:	`int` – The status code.
	`String` – The error message.
Description:	This method sets the error response of the outgoing HTTP header, with ar. optional error message.

```
Res.setError (HttpServletResponse.SC_FORBIDDEN, "Oops");
```
Example 119

```
javax.servlet.http.HttpServletResponse.sendRedirect(String url)
```

Syntax:	`public String sendRedirect(String url)`
Parameters:	`String` – The URL to redirect.
Description:	This method sets the header `SC_MOVED_TEMPORARILY` and redirects the client to the specified URL. Note that a full URL is recommended to ensure proper operation.

```
Res.sendRedirect("http://www.n-ary.com/");
```
Example 120

```
javax.servlet.http.HttpServletResponse.setDateHeader
                        (String name, long date)
```

Syntax:	535 `public void setDateHeader (String name, long date)`
Parameters:	`String` – The name to set.
	`long` – The date to set.
Description:	This method is used to set a field in the header of the out going response to the client.

```
Res.setDateHeader("Agent",System.currentTimeMillis() );
```
Example 121

```
javax.servlet.http.HttpServletResponse.setIntHeader(String name,
                        int value)
```

Syntax:	`public void setDateHeader (String name, int value)`
Parameters:	`String` – The name to set.
	`int` – The date to set.
Description:	This method is used to set a field in the header of the out going response to the client.

```
Res.setDateHeader("Agent", 12 );
```
Example 122

```
javax.servlet.http.HttpServletResponse.setHeader(String name,
                        String value)
```

Syntax:	`public void setDateHeader (String name, String value)`
Parameters:	`String` – The name to set.
	`String` – The date to set.
Description:	This method is used to set a field in the header of the out going response to the client.

```
Res.setDateHeader("Agent", "xyz" );
```
Example 123

A.5.1 *javax.servlet.http.HttpSession*

```
public interface HttpSession {
  public long getCreationTime();
  public String getId();
  public long getLastAccessedTime();
  public int getMaxInactiveInterval();
  public Object getValue(String name);
  public String[] getValueNames();
  public void invalidate();
  public boolean isNew();
  public void putValue(String name, Object value);
  public void removeValue(String name);
  public int setMaxInactiveInterval(int interval);
}
```
Example 124

The HttpSession is a mechanism that allows a persistent association over multiple requests from the same client.

```
javax.servlet.http.HttpSession.getCreationTime()
```

Syntax:	public long getCreationTime();
Returns:	long – The session creation date.
Description:	This method returns the date the session was created as milliseconds.

```
HttpSession currentSession = res.getSession();
System.out.println( currentSession.getCreationTime() );
```
Example 125

```
javax.servlet.http.HttpSession.getId()
```

Syntax:	public String getId();
Returns:	String – The session ID.
Description:	This method returns the session identifier that is being used to represent this particular session.

```
HttpSession currentSession = res.getSession();
System.out.println( currentSession.getId() );
```
Example 126

```
javax.servlet.http.HttpSession.getLastAccessedTime()
```

Syntax:	public long getLastAccessedTime();
Returns:	long – The session access time.
Description:	This method returns the time when the client last sent this session. If the session is new, -1 is returned.

```
HttpSession currentSession = res.getSession();
System.out.println( currentSession.getLastAccessedTime() );
```
Example 127

`javax.servlet.http.HttpSession.getMaxInactiveInterval()`

Syntax:	`public int getMaxInactiveInterval();`
Returns:	`int` – The active time.
Description:	This method returns the number of seconds the session can stay alive without a client request before the servlet engine removes the method.

```
HttpSession currentSession = res.getSession();
System.out.println( currentSession.getMaxInactiveInterval() );
```
Example 128

`javax.servlet.http.HttpSession.getValue(String name)`

Syntax:	`public Object getValue(String name);`
Parameters:	`String` – The name of the object.
Returns:	`Object` – A reference to the data.
Description:	This method returns the object for the given name. If the object does not exist, the method returns `null`.

```
HttpSession currentSession = res.getSession();
MYDATA mydata = (MYDATA)currentSession.getValue("mydata");
```
Example 129

`javax.servlet.http.HttpSession.getValueNames()`

Syntax:	`public Object getValueNames();`
Returns:	`String`- An array pointer to all data objects.
Description:	This method returns an array to the list of all the object names held by this session.

```
HttpSession currentSession = res.getSession();
String[] list = currentSession.getValueNames();
for(x=0;x<list.length;x++)
   System.out.println("Name: " + list[x] );
```
Example 130

`javax.servlet.http.HttpSession.invalidate()`

Syntax:	`public void invalidate ();`
Description:	This method invalidates the current session. All data held is removed.

```
HttpSession currentSession = res.getSession();
CurrentSession.invalidate();
```
Example 131

```
javax.servlet.http.HttpSession.isNew()
```

Syntax:	`public boolean isNew();`
Returns:	`boolean`
Description:	This method returns `true` if this session is new. If it is new, the client, at this point, doesn't know anything about it.

```
HttpSession currentSession = res.getSession();
if( currentSession.isNew() )
  System.out.println("Brand new!");
```
Example 132

```
javax.servlet.http.HttpSession.putValue(String name, Object value)
```

Syntax:	`public void putValue (String name, Object value);`
Parameters:	`String` – The name of the object.
	`Object`
Description:	This method puts the specified object into the session for storage. If the object is serializable, it will be stored between server restarts.

```
HttpSession currentSession = res.getSession();
currentSession.putValue( "mydata", new MYDATA() );
```
Example 133

```
javax.servlet.http.HttpSession.removeValue(String name)
```

Syntax:	`public void removeValue(String name);`
Parameters:	`String` – The name of the object.
Description:	This method removes the specified object from the session.

```
HttpSession currentSession = res.getSession();
currentSession.removeValue( "mydata" );
```
Example 134

```
javax.servlet.http.HttpSession.setMaxInactiveInterval(int interval)
```

Syntax:	`public void setMaxInactiveInterval(int interval);`
Parameters:	`int` – The active time.
Description:	This method sets the number of seconds the session can stay alive without the client request before the servlet engine removes the session data.

```
HttpSession currentSession = res.getSession();
currentSession.setMaxInactiveInterval( 18000 );
```
Example 135

A.6   *javax.servlet.http.HttpSession BindingEvent*

```
public class HttpSessionBindingEvent extends EventObject{
   public HttpSessionBindingEvent(HttpSession session, String name);
   public String getName();
   public HttpSession getSession();
}
```
Example 136

This object is sent to convey information about the session.

`javax.servlet.http.HttpSessionBindingEvent.getName()`

Syntax: `public void getName()`

Returns: `String` – The session name.

Description: This method returns the session name.

```
public class mydata implements HttpSessionBindingListener{
   String someData;

   public void valueBound(HttpSessionBindingEvent event){
      System.out.println("I am being stored in a session");
      System.out.println( event.getName() );
   }
}
```
Example 137

`javax.servlet.http.HttpSessionBindingEvent.getSession()`

Syntax: `public void getName()`

Returns: `HttpSession` – The session.

Description: This method returns the session.

```
public class mydata implements HttpSessionBindingListener {
   String someData;

   public void valueBound(HttpSessionBindingEvent event){
      System.out.println("I am being stored in a session");
      HttpSession thisSession = event.getSession();
   }
}
```
Example 138

A.6.1   *javax.servlet.http.HttpSessionBindingListener*

```
public interface HttpSessionBindingListener{
   public void valueBound(HttpSessionBindingEvent event);
   public void valueUnbound(HttpSessionBindingEvent event);
}
```
Example 139

Objects that are going to be stored in the session can implement this interface so they can be notified of a change in data.

```
javax.servlet.http.HttpSessionBindingEvent.valueBound
                            (HttpSessionBindingEvent E)
```

Syntax: `public void valueBound(HttpSessionBindingEvent E);`

Parameters: `HttpSessionBindingEvent E` – Event.

Description: This method is called when the session accepts this object into storage.

```
public class mydata implements HttpSessionBindingListener {
  String someData;

  public void valueBound(HttpSessionBindingEvent event){
    System.out.println("I am being stored in a session");
  }
}
```
Example 140

```
javax.servlet.http.HttpSessionBindingEvent.valueUnbound
                            (HttpSessionBindingEvent E)
```

Syntax: `public void valueUnbound(HttpSessionBindingEvent E);`

Parameters: `HttpSessionBindingEvent E` – Event.

Description: This method is called when the session removes this object from storage.

```
public class mydata implements HttpSessionBindingListener {
  String someData;

  public void valueUnbound(HttpSessionBindingEvent event){
    System.out.println("I am being removed from a session");
  }
}
```
Example 141

A.6.2   *javax.servlet.http.HttpUtils*

```
public class HttpUtils {
  public static StringBuffer getRequestURL(HttpServletRequest request);
  public static Hashtable parsePostData(int len,  ServletInputstream in);
  public static Hashtable parseQueryString(String s);
}
```
Example 142

This class is a small group of utilities that provide extra processing for some HTTP servlets.

```
javax.servlet.http.HttpUtils.getRequestURL(HttpServletRequest request)
```

Syntax:	`public static Object getRequestURL (HttpServlet` `Request name);`
Parameters:	`HttpServletRequest` – The client request.
Returns:	StringBuffer
Description:	This method reconstructs the URL being used by the client to invoke this servlet. It does not include any query string information that may have been present. A `StringBuffer` is returned so the servlet may add information.

```
StringBuffer SB = HttpUtils.getRequestURL( req );
```
Example 143

```
javax.servlet.http.HttpUtils.parsePostData(int len,
                        ServletInputstream in)
```

Syntax:	`public static Hashtable parsePostData(int len,` `ServletInputStream in);`
Parameters:	`int len` – The length of the data. `ServletInputstream` – Reference to the input stream from the client.
Returns:	`HashTable` – Reference to the `key/value` data pairs.
Description:	This method constructs a `Hashtable` of `key/value` pairs from an `inputstream`. It is useful for posts of the MIME type [`application/x-www-form-urlencoded`], which occurs when uploading a file, for example.

```
javax.servlet.http.HttpUtils.parseQueryString(String s)
```

Syntax:	`public static Hashtable parsePostData(String _S);`
Parameters:	`String` – The query string.
Returns:	`HashTable` – Reference to the `key/value` data pairs.
Description:	This method constructs a `Hashtable` of `key/value` pairs from a string.

A P P E N D I X   B

CHAPTER CONCEPTS

- The majority of user data from the client is retrieved from environment variables within CGI scripts. This appendix gives the equivalent servlet method for each CGI variable.

CGI variable	Servlet equivalent
AUTH_TYPE	String HttpServletRequest.getAuthType()
CONTENT_LENGTH	String ServletRequest.getContentLength()
CONTENT_TYPE	String ServletRequest.getContentType()
REMOTE_ADDR	String ServletRequest.getRemoteAddr()
REMOTE_HOST	String ServletRequest.getRemoteHost()
SCRIPT_NAME	String HttpServletRequest.getServletPath()
PATH_INFO	String HttpServletRequest.getPathInfo()
PATH_TRANSLATED	String HttpServletRequest.getPathTranslated()
QUERY_STRING	String HttpServletRequest.getQueryString()
SERVER_PROTOCOL	String ServletRequest.getProtocol()
SERVER_PORT	int ServletRequest.getServerPort()
SERVER_NAME	String ServletRequest.getServerName()
SERVER_SOFTWARE	String ServletContext.getServerInfo()
REQUEST_METHOD	String HttpServletRequest.getMethod()
REMOTE_USER	String HttpServletRequest.getRemoteUser()
XXXX	Object ServletRequest.getAttribute(String _name)

For all other fields, use the `Object ServletRequest.getAttribute( String _name )`. For example, to retrieve the browser the client is using, use the following line of code:

```
String Browser = (String) ServletRequest.getAttribute( "User-Agent" )
```

A P P E N D I X   C

- This appendix lists Java sites and resources.

C.7 Main Java sites

- JavaSoft (http://www.javasoft.com)
  The mother of all Java sites. You'll find all the new Java technologies here, along with lots of documentation.

- Java Web Server (http://jserv.javasoft.com)
  Specific information on the servlet API and the server API.

- Sun Microsystems (http://www.sun.com)
  Lots of information about Java network computers.

- N-ARY (http://www.n-ary.com)
  Information on all aspects of Java, especially servlets and JDBC.

- Servlet Workshop (http://www.servletworkshop.com)
  Site dedicated to all aspects of servlets.

- Java Centre (http://www.java.co.uk)
  Information specific to the United Kingdom, covering Java news, contacts, applets, and exhibitions.

- Blackdown (http://www.blackdown.org)
  The premier site for ports of Java to Linux. Includes the JWS1.1 port.

C.8 Java source banks

- JARS (http://www.jars.com)
  The Java Applet Rating Service (JARS) provides one of the best depositories for good quality Java applets. Each applet is reviewed by a panel of international judges.

- Developer (http://www.developer.com)
  One of the original places to get Java applets/beans and ActiveX controls.

- Servlet Source (http://www.servletsource.com)
  One of the original places to get Java servlets.

- Java Repository (http://java.wiwi.uni-frankfurt.de)
  German-based site that houses an excellent collection of Java applets.

- The Java Consortium (http://www.javaconsortium.com)
  A great-looking site that houses many Java applets.

- ACME Laboratories (http://www.acme.com)
  This site has some excellent free classes that make programming Java a little bit easier.

C.9 Online Java magazines

- JavaWorld (http://www.javaworld.com)
  One of the best online Java magazines out there. If you can only subscribe to one magazine, make this the one.

- Java Developers Journal (http://www.javadevelopersjournal.com)
  The web-based version of the popular publication of the same name. This site has a number of interesting articles and applets.
- Servlet Central (http://www.servletcentral.com)
  A magazine devoted to all things servlet.

C.10 Java jobs

- Team Java (http://www.teamjava.com)
  If you need a Java programmer, this is the place to visit. It's an excellent site full of useful contacts and other sites.

C.11 Other useful sites and resources

- Liquid Organization (http://www.liquid.org)
  Discover how a user interface should have the information float as opposed to having it sink.
- Symantec (http://www.symantec.com)
  One of the best sites for the most popular Java IDE in use today.
- Mailing list: workshop@servletworkshop.com
  This is one of the best lists on which to get all your servlet-based questions answered.
- Newsgroups: comp.lang.java.programmer, comp.lang.java.api.

index

connection pool manager 434
connectToServer(…) 458
CONTENT 295
CONTENT_LENGTH 94
CONTENT_TYPE 94
Content-Type 125, 229
Cookie 316
cookie 200, 313, 314, 315, 333, 335, 405, 484
cookies operate 313
core processing 328
createStatement() 425
cStudent 474
custom htmlTemplate 334

D

data 443
database 303
database.connection 484
databaseRunner 478
DataInputStream 458
DataOutputStream 82, 168
dbBroker 428, 434, 438
dbBroker class 431, 433
dbBroker.getInstance() 428, 430, 433
dbBroker.pop() 433
dbBroker.push(…) 434
dbConnection 429, 431, 432, 433
debugger 77
delBasketServlet 414
Deutsch, L. Peter 13
displayTable(…) 335
distributed computing 480
doDelete(…) 29
doGet(…) 29, 123, 142, 246
doHead(…) 29
Domain 315
doOptions(…) 29
doPost(…) 29, 123, 131, 142, 246
doPut(…) 29
doTrace(…) 29
doXXX(…) 483
DriverManager 421, 424, 425
dynamically 487

E

Eiffel 10, 11
encasing 408
ENCTYPE 123
Enumeration 249, 485
Event 452, 453
Exact search 288
Exception 77, 432
executeQuery(…) 425

F

FastCGI 95
FETCH 421
File 250, 251
FileInputStream 114, 304
FilenameFilter 251
FileOutputStream 126
firewall 467, 468
FirstPerson 10
flagged 431
FlowLayout 451
for(…) 328
form set 408
forName 424
forward(…) 487, 488
forwardServlet 487
Frame 227
Free Agent 175
front-end processor 487
FTP 17, 167

G

GATEWAY_INTERFACE 94
generic 430
GenericServlet 26, 28, 32, 107, 144, 200, 225, 482
GET 18, 95, 141, 146, 149, 246, 454
get() 110
getAttribute() 485
getAttribute(…) 485, 488
getAttributeNames() 485
getConnection(…) 425
getContentLength() 27

getContentType() 27, 127
getDomain 317
getFile(…) 138
getFreeConnection() 432
getInitParameter(…) 24, 204
getInitParameterName() 24
getMaxAge 316
getName 316
getNextParameter() 127, 131
getOutputStream() 28
getParameter(…) 110, 145, 151, 204
getParameterValues(…) 146
getPath 317
getRealPath(…) 25, 132, 304
getRemoteAddr() 108
getRemoteHost() 27
getRequestDispatcher(…) 487
getRoom(…) 462
getSecure 317
getServletConfig() 24
getServletContext() 24
getServletContext(…) 486
getServletInfo() 24
getString(…) 426
getStudent(…) 473, 474
getValue(…) 412
.gif 8
GIF 92, 104, 224, 226
Gosling, James 9
Graphics 226
gzip 132

H

handleEvent(…) 452
hash table 443, 444
hash table data structure 443
Hashtable 110
headers 488
hire 429
HTML 6, 210, 214
htmlTemplate 329, 335
HTTP 2, 19, 312, 448
HTTP cookies 312
Http ServletResponse 123

HTTP status fields 488
HTTP/1.0 145
HTTP_ACCEPT 94
HTTP_USER_AGENT 94
HttpServlet 123, 133, 144, 200, 299, 336, 482, 483
HttpServlet class 445
HttpServletRequest 31, 145, 304, 322
HttpSession 322, 323
HttpSessionBindingListener 324

I

IDE 77
image/jpeg 124
implements rmiDatabaseRunnerInterface 478
incremental 333
indexOf(…) 128, 136, 294
InfoSeek 286, 287
init() 114, 450, 453, 459
init(…) 24, 26, 29, 107, 144, 201, 204, 214, 336, 445, 478, 483, 484
initialization 485
InputStream 126
insert(…) 488
interface 486
Internet Relay Chat (IRC) 440
IP address 106
IRC 440
IRC service 440
isDirectory() 250
isLoggedOn(…) 483
isNew() 412
ISP 487

J

Java applet 313
Java Server API 5, 14
java.Applet 449
java.io 250
java.io.Serializable 322, 343
java.lang.Class 19
java.lang.Object 78
java.net 167
java.rmi 476

OS/2 97
output routine 445
own form 408

P

parser 254
Path 315
PATH_INFO 94
PATH_TRANSLATED 94
Perl 95, 161
placeholder 336
plug in 228, 332
polling interval 441
pool 428
pool manager 431, 433, 434, 438
pop() 431
port 1099 475
POST 95, 141, 142, 146, 149, 185, 246, 453
postcompiler 476
Precedence search 288
print(...) 136, 417
print(...) method 164
println(...) 83
PrintStream 148
PrintWriter.println(...) 29
Project Oak 10
push(...) 431, 432

Q

QUERY_STRING 94

R

random() 205
RandomAccessFile 114, 304
range setting 338
readLine() 127, 128, 168, 208, 458
readLine(...) 127, 458
relative link 247
REMOTE_ADDR 94
REMOTE_HOST 94
REMOTE_USER 94
RemoteException 476
removeApplet(...) 462

removeAttribute(...) 486
req.getCookies() 317
REQUEST_METHOD 94
RequestDispatcher 487, 488
ResultSet 421, 425
ResultSet method provides a
        getXXX(...) 426
ResultSetMetaData 425
ResultSets 421
rmic compiler are in the classpath 476
rmiDatabaseRunner 472
RMISecurityManager 475, 479
RoomPool 443
roulette 331
roulInfo 334, 339
run() 336, 455, 459, 460
Runnable 336, 449

S

SC_NO_CONTENT 411, 412
SCRIPT_NAME 94
search engine 286. 487
Secure 315
SecurityException 251
SecurityManager 21
SELECT * FROM USER_TABLE 425
sendmail 96
sendMessage(...) 454, 458, 463
sendRedirect(...) 122, 149, 165, 216
Serializable 472
SERVER_NAME 94
SERVER_PORT 94
SERVER_PROTOCOL 94
SERVER_SOFTWARE 94
service(...) 26, 29, 30, 107, 114, 123, 142,
        150, 202, 205, 217, 246, 303, 306,
        323, 411, 417, 428, 433, 445, 456,
        459, 483
servlet alias 475
servlet chaining 486
ServletBase 483
servlet-chaining 487
ServletContext 24, 484, 485, 486, 487, 488
ServletExec 61